SAGE was founded in 1965 by Sara Miller McCune to support the dissemination of usable knowledge by publishing innovative and high-quality research and teaching content. Today, we publish over 900 journals, including those of more than 400 learned societies, more than 800 new books per year, and a growing range of library products including archives, data, case studies, reports, and video. SAGE remains majority-owned by our founder, and after Sara's lifetime will become owned by a charitable trust that secures our continued independence.

Los Angeles | London | New Delhi | Singapore | Washington DC | Melbourne

Advance Praise

This volume is a superb celebration of the fiftieth anniversary of *Contributions to Indian Sociology*, the leading journal in its field, which includes an excellent collection of essays on many different topics by a diverse group of anthropologists and sociologists from both India and the rest of the world. For novice students and experienced researchers alike, this volume will be an invaluable exploration of contemporary Indian society and culture, as well as an insight into how they are being critically studied today.

C. J. Fuller,
Professor Emeritus, Department of Anthropology,
London School of Economics, London, UK

A wonderful book ... *Critical Themes in Indian Sociology* is imaginative, knowledgeable, contemporary and, importantly, easy to read. Many chapters focus on traditional objects of enquiry: village; caste; marriage, family and kinship; religion; culture, nation, the rural and urban *but* from a present day perspective. They bring in new data and themes, even as they engage with old debates of 'usefulness', concepts and methods in a 'global' academia where the 'locals' continue to matter.

Maitrayee Chaudhuri,
Professor,CSSS, Jawaharlal Nehru University, New Delhi

This volume is a fitting tribute to an extraordinary journal and in the range of its contributions shows the same commitment to variety, conceptual sophistication and empirical anchoring, which has made *Contributions* a mirror of the best in Indian sociology and anthropology.

Arjun Appadurai,
Goddard Professor in Media,
Culture and Communication, New York University

CRITICAL
THEMES
in
INDIAN
SOCIOLOGY

CRITICAL THEMES
in
INDIAN
SOCIOLOGY

Edited by
SANJAY SRIVASTAVA
YASMEEN ARIF
JANAKI ABRAHAM

SAGE

Los Angeles | London | New Delhi
Singapore | Washington DC | Melbourne

First published in 2019 by

SAGE Publications India Pvt Ltd
B1/I-1 Mohan Cooperative Industrial Area
Mathura Road, New Delhi 110 044, India
www.sagepub.in

SAGE Publications Inc
2455 Teller Road
Thousand Oaks, California 91320, USA

SAGE Publications Ltd
1 Oliver's Yard, 55 City Road
London EC1Y 1SP, United Kingdom

SAGE Publications Asia-Pacific Pte Ltd
18 Cross Street #10-10/11/12
China Square Central
Singapore 048423

Published by Vivek Mehra for SAGE Publications India Pvt Ltd, typeset in 10/12.5 pts ITC Stone Serif by Zaza Eunice, Hosur, Tamil Nadu, India and printed at Chaman Enterprises, New Delhi.

Library of Congress Cataloging-in-Publication Data

Names: Srivastava, Sanjay, editor. | Arif, Yasmeen, editor. |
 Abraham, Janaki.
Title: Critical themes in Indian sociology/edited by Sanjay Srivastava,
 Yasmeen Arif, Janaki Abraham.
Description: New Delhi, India: SAGE Publications India, 2019. | Includes
 bibliographical references and index.
Identifiers: LCCN 2018048558 | ISBN 9789352807956 (hbk: alk. paper) |
 ISBN 9789352807963 (epub 2.0) | ISBN 9789352807970 (ebook)
Subjects: LCSH: Sociology–India.
Classification: LCC HM477.I4 C75 2019 | DDC 301.0954–dc23 LC record available at https://lccn.loc.gov/2018048558

ISBN: 978-93-528-0795-6 (HB)

SAGE Team: Rajesh Dey, Guneet Kaur Gulati, Syeda Aina Rahat Ali and Ritu Chopra

For Triloki Nath Madan and Patricia Uberoi,
past editors and steadfast friends of
Contributions to Indian Sociology

Thank you for choosing a SAGE product!
If you have any comment, observation or feedback,
I would like to personally hear from you.

Please write to me at **contactceo@sagepub.in**

Vivek Mehra, Managing Director and CEO, SAGE India.

Contents

Introduction*

The journal *Contributions to Indian Sociology* (*CIS*) was founded by Louis Dumont and David Pocock in 1957 but ceased publication in 1966. In 1967, at the initiative of T.N. Madan, a new series recommenced publication, this time from New Delhi. The year 2016 was the 50th year of the new series. It is this occasion that we commemorate in the present volume. Historically, the journal has had a very wide remit—in terms of readers, writers and topics—and the task of reflecting this aspect in a volume such as this was a complex one. Initially, we had planned on two volumes. However, given the disparate nature of the contributions we had in mind—to pay proper heed to what *CIS* has stood for—it became extremely difficult to imagine how we might organise the articles in order that there might be two 'thematically coherent' volumes. We finally decided to proceed with just one volume that takes up key concerns within Indian-related sociology. We believe that the final product is a genuine tribute to the life history of the journal and testimony to the generosity it attracts among sociologists around the world. We would, ideally, have liked the present volume to be out in 2016 itself. However, a project of this magnitude—coordinating a large number of contributors based in different parts of the world—has its own mind. We seek the readers' indulgence and hope that they will agree that the adage 'good things take time' finds adequate reflection in the pages of the current volume.

*The editors wish to thank Bikram Sharma, Editorial Associate, *Contributions to Indian Sociology*, for his invaluable assistance in preparing the book for publication.

There is much to celebrate in the 50 years of the journal. *CIS* has been an important space for sociological scholarship on India and for debate and dialogue among sociologists and social anthropologists globally. It has been the site of rich ethnographic and empirical work and conceptual formulations. As mentioned earlier, the themes that the journal has covered have been vast and range from caste, Hinduism and kinship in the early years of the journal to those of suicide, urban trans-formations and violence more recently. The section 'For a Sociology of India', which started as an article in the first avatar of the journal and then continued as a space for debate, has provided a vibrant context for articulations of very diverse views on the sociology of India. As Brazilian anthropologist Mariza Peirano (1991: 322) wrote in an article published under the same title,

> This debate must be included in the history of anthropology as an exemplary case of a different kind of discussion. Perhaps no other debate has lasted, as this one has for more than thirty years; perhaps no other recorded discussion has involved anthropologists of so many nationalities (including French, English, Indian, German, Norwegian, Swiss and New Zealander) offering diverse theoretical perspectives; and perhaps no other debate has emphasised as this one the concep-tion of anthropology as a possibility of translation and communica-tion among different cultures....

In commemorating 50 years, our intention was not to 'review' the journal through these decades but to bring together the writings of a number of scholars on the diverse themes that have been critical to scholarship in sociology and social anthropology. When the editors of this volume approached authors from India and around the world about possible contributions that would commemorate *CIS*'s 50th anniversary, the response was both immediate and enthusiastic. This volume is the result of the goodwill the journal enjoys among scholars of widely varying interests, as well as those at different stages in their careers.

Our brief to contributors was quite straightforward: we were not seeking intellectual or institutional histories of Indian sociology. These already have a valuable presence in recent academic publishing (see, e.g., Patel 2016; Sundar et al. 2000; Uberoi et al. 2007), including its practice (Chaudhuri 2003). We intended the volume to be an accessible introduction to a range of themes in the sociology of India during the 20th and 21st centuries. This, however, is by no means an exhaustive list, nor has it sought to be that. Instead, the discussions in different chapters point to changes in both sociological debates and concepts, methods and themes.

We have sought to keep the chapters relatively brief, as well as requested contributors to keep their pieces largely free of jargon, in order that students and a wider readership might feel more inclined to pick up the volume. Our argument is quite simple: human welfare cannot be advanced without an understanding of different forms of power and the social complexities that lie in the way of redistributing resources in a highly unequal society and that the discipline of sociology is fundamental to illuminating this context. Furthermore, what we mean to suggest is that a sociological sensibility is able to interrogate the idea of 'usefulness' itself and that in order to do this, we should suspend judgement on what is 'useful' as a sociological project. In this way, we strongly champion a non-instrumental view of the sociological project. This is, perhaps, a key difference in how sociology was imagined in the decades that immediately followed independence from colonial rule—with 'nation-building' as a significant sociological goal—and contemporary way of thinking about the discipline. We do not, however, wish to suggest that a significant strand of the post-independence scholarship characterised scholarly proclivities among all of India's early sociologists.

The other aspect of a changed sociological sensibility concerns the emphatic *qualitative* turn in Indian sociology, an aspect that significantly distinguishes it from both early sociology in India and contemporary sociological trends in North America. Powerful voices in early Indian sociology sought to interpret the discipline as physical science manqué (Ghosh 2014). To take up another point that is also of specific relevance to India, in a post-colonial society, a discipline that so significantly relies upon the English language cannot but also reflect the differing forms of cultural capital that make for knowledge formations (see, e.g., Rege 2011). Finally, in this context, a great deal of 'Indian sociology' continues to be characterised by scientism—the tendency to 'prove' the validity of a knowledge claim through quantification. It appears to us that no intellectual history of the discipline in India would be incomplete without a consideration of the politics of language and that of scientism. Perhaps these are two defining characteristics of the history of social sciences and humanities in the post-colonial world.

Travelling Concepts

We hope that through the essays in the present volume, some part of the journey that Indian sociology has made over the past five decades will come to life. One dramatic shift in Indian sociology or a sociology of India as evident in the pages of *CIS* over the years is the idea of the unity of Indian social life. When we consider the multiplicity of influences upon human life, it is difficult to speak of a Patidar way of life or a Kashmiri Pandit way of life. This is not to say that Patidars and Kashmiri Pandits may not speak of their life ways in these terms, rather that sociologists are warier of accepting such terms without critical scrutiny of the politics and histories of self-identification. Not only this, in these 50 years we can no longer assume the stability of entities or concepts such as the village or caste or religious community (an argument well made in Jodhka's and Waghmore's chapters on the village and caste, respectively). Indeed, that staple of Indian sociology—the rural and its concomitant, agricultural practices—may no longer be, as Krishnamurthy points out in her contribution, what it was. Through an analytical lens that takes us from the ambiguous positioning of the grain heap, a *locus classicus* of the famously studied Jajmani system, central to Indian sociology, Krishnamurthy gives us another reading that translates the grain heap into the starting point of a conceptual path that leads to economic agents, material cultures and cultural meanings of economic activity.

Not only caste, referred to as a gatekeeping concept for Indian sociology (see Appadurai 1986b; Das 2003), has changed very significantly as an institution over this period but so has the manner in which it is understood. In particular, the conceptualisation of caste has changed dramatically, as have the methods employed to study 'caste-ness', most importantly as it relates to autobiographical writing and literature in different Indian languages. The numerous sharp critiques that followed the publication in English of Louis Dumont's *Homo Hierarchicus*, including a special issue of *CIS* dedicated to a discussion of the book (1971), are indicative of the strength of debate and discussion on caste, and critical to the understanding of caste subsequently carried forward. Dumont has been critiqued for presenting a Brahmanical view of caste which, in turn, was linked to his argument that people who suffered in this system of hierarchy consented to their treatment (see, e.g., Das 1995; Madan 1971; Mencher 1975). Further, as Waghmore's and Michelutti's chapters tell us, contrary to the prediction that caste would disappear over time, it remains a significant institution in everyday life and has taken on new meanings in the efflorescence of contemporary political mobilisations. Waghmore presents the idea of civility as a means of examining changes in caste, especially in relation to citizenship, justice and equality concerns which were not central to the early work on caste. Another significant change is also in taking seriously the writings of B.R. Ambedkar, whose works brought power and discrimination centre stage to the study of caste and caste practices (for critiques of the marginalisation of Ambedkar's writing, see Kannabiran 2009; Rege 2013).

The centrality of caste in Indian sociological literature has not, however, completely overwritten engagements with class. Indeed, in Milton Singer's study of social change in Tamil Nadu, caste and class were brought together within the analytical framework of 'modernisation' (Singer 1972). The connection between caste and class has more recently been explored—also, coincidentally, for South India—by Fuller and Narasimhan's (2014) study of Tamil Brahmins. One of the most fruitful engagements with class in India has been through the sociology of education. In addition to the 'reproduction' approach (Bourdieu and Passeron 1977), studies have paid close attention to the complexities of the local situation within which schooling in India is embedded. It is this landscape that forms the focus of attention in Meenakshi Thapan's chapter in the volume. Thapan's contribution shows us how colonial and post-colonial contexts of schooling in India have produced a terrain that fulfils neither the goal of providing genuinely humanistic education nor that of fully equipping the majority of students for the instrumental ends of securing gainful employment.

Moving on to another significant theme within Indian sociology, while the volume does *not* have a dedicated chapter on kinship—a subject that has been an important theme in *CIS*—several essays address key issues in the study of kinship: for example, Perveez Mody elaborates on the concept of intimacy and briefly looks at its relation with scholarship on kinship and marriage; Shalini Grover discusses divorce, a subject on which there is little scholarship; in talking about aging in India, Sarah Lamb draws from her long periods of fieldwork in West Bengal to discuss aging, familial care and residence; Renu Addlakha, in her exhaustive discussion of disability studies in India, points to the literature on disability and familial care; Rajni Palriwala looks at shifts in the study of gender as expressed in a few journals including *CIS*; and Srimati Basu discusses the intertwined nature of law, property and familial relationships. Further, Paul Boyce and Rohit Dasgupta discuss law and the illegitimacies of certain intimacies. Most of these chapters also look at the interface between the state, kin and community, a theme that has been important to kinship studies.

Various contributions to this collection also powerfully demonstrate sociology's capacity to explicitly engage with topics whose traces lie in a great deal of sociological writings about Indian society while not necessarily emerging as foci in their own right. What is important, we would like to emphasise, is the manner in which lineages of the present are sought to be located within longstanding sociological concerns. It is in the vein that Sara Dickey's chapter on cinema-viewing practices and Raka Ray's contribution on 'middle class-ness' can be located within broader socio-economic processes such as enduring concern with class and caste identities. Alpa Shah writes on contemporary 'tribal' identities and Perveez Mody explores the meaning of intimacies, with both authors making important connections between the present and topics that have animated sociological concern for a very long time, namely, hierarchies and the quest for equality. In a similar vein, Joseph Alter on cultures of masculinities and Paul Boyce and Rohit Dasgupta in their jointly written chapter point to caste, ethnicity and gender that, in different ways, structure meanings of alternative sexualities in the present. As well, Amita Baviskar's chapter shows us how food is a critical site through which caste and class differences are asserted.

Gender, sexuality and food—the topics addressed by Palriwala and Alter, Boyce and Dasgupta, and Baviskar, respectively—have, of course, been areas that have interested sociologists of India for quite some time. Hence, Leela Dube explicitly utilised gender as a political framework to explore relations of power among women and men in different contexts (see, e.g., Dube 1988, 2001; see also Vatuk 2001). Similarly, scholars have dealt with sexuality in myriad ways, including contexts of marriage (Fruzzetti 1982; Uberoi 1995), women's 'erotic imagination' (Raheja and Gold 1994) and middle-class women and sexuality (Puri 1999). And food is, of course, in many ways a 'staple' of a variety of approaches to Indian life: studies of who eats with whom and how this defines social location in religious and hierarchical worlds are so numerous as to hardly need mention. What is different about approaches to gender, as presented by Alter, is the foregrounding of an aspect that has largely lain silent in studies of women's position in Indian society. The processes of masculinity, hinted at in Dube (1988), are now fully taken up as topics in their own right, informed by feminist theory and attentive to the ethnographic method as a way of capturing gendered reality. The odd anthropological study that addressed the issue (e.g., Carstairs 1958) has given way to sustained attention to the topic, seeking to flesh out 'gender' as a relationship.

Further, while sexuality has been a point of discussion within the sociology of India, it is primarily—if not exclusively—the social dimensions of the *heterosexual* context that have been explored. More recent sociological writings—such as those represented by Boyce and Dasgupta here—have sought to destabilise the heteronormative moorings of academic work through focusing on non-heterosexual contexts, arguing that apart from intrinsic worth, the topic also allows us to reconfigure ideas of family, kinship, power and intimacies. This is a crucial shift that is of significance to kinship studies in general.

The reconfiguration of sociological knowledge as far as diet is concerned relates to the kinds of avenues Baviskar urges us to explore beyond the well-covered areas of its role in systems of religious and caste identity. Public dining, the travels of 'Indian' food beyond national boundaries, newer kinds of food items that index 'cosmopolitan' habits and the contexts of the *lack* of food for certain sections of the population are important ways in which the new focus on the topic allows us to familiar areas of sociological concern.

New Directions

An area of research that not only widens the sociological oeuvre but could also be seen as instituting an entirely new domain of study consists of the recent focus on consumerism. 'Consumerism' differs from 'consumption' in as much as the former concerns the wider domain of the relationship with mass-produced goods that now play such a significant part in the making of modern identities. Changes in economic and social spheres in India have led to deeper entanglements between people and commodities that enjoin us to more rigorously explore the 'social life of things' (Appadurai 1986b; see also Brosius 2010; Mathur 2014). Van Wessel's contribution tracks this relatively new horizon of research through focusing on both consumption as a context of self-making—or aspirations—as well as the problem of overconsumption and the consequences of this for the natural environment within and through which social life unfolds. Van Wessel proposes to address the twin issues of consumerism and its consequences through the notion of 'sustainable consumption'. This, she suggests, is an important manner in which sociological research and 'social relevance' might come together.

To think about the widened fields of sociological research is to also reflect upon the changing nature of the discipline itself and to free ourselves from the burden of marking out immoveable disciplinary boundaries and methodologies. In recent times, sociology's relationship with history, political science, media studies, sexuality and queer studies, feminism, and cultural and human geography, among others, has produced scholarship that has both immeasurably broadened the discipline's horizons and reconfigured our ability to grasp social complexity. What has remained 'sociological' about sociology in India, however, is the attention to method which consists in the rigorous combination of fieldwork and theoretical analyses. It is for this reason that, for example, sociological studies of social media, sexual cultures, the state, organ transplants, the media and their audiences, bureaucracies, and advertising agencies—relatively new areas of research—can still be located within disciplinary boundaries, and this even though they continuously push and expand these boundaries.

As mentioned earlier, the move towards interdisciplinarity has had a salutary effect on the sociology of India. Moreover, a move towards looking beyond the academy for the production of knowledge has also characterised the last few decades in particular. One change has been that the spread of literacy brought with it a greater engagement with producing knowledge about one's own community. The idea of the 'native anthropologist' has globally been a point of discussion as more and more people outside the academy, and informally, took to studying *themselves* through writing tracts about the origin of the caste, constructing genealogical charts of their families using the latest software available on the Internet and writing family and community histories. Sociology and social anthropology have been internally enlivened to the intersubjectivity of anthropologists and informants even if our representations of these are always partial (see, e.g., Trawick 1992). A range of different writing strategies and collaborations (see, e.g., Alter 1999; Gold and Gujjar 2002) have sought to address issues of power in sociological/anthropological projects. Given the colonial origins of the discipline, this has been of particular concern. Simultaneously, methodological shifts and shifts in the subjects of study have brought dramatic changes in the nature of fieldwork and fieldwork sites. There is no doubt that the influence of social movements and student movements have brought significant changes within sociology and how it is taught in schools and universities. This is seen, for example, in the field of disability studies (as argued by Renu Addlakha), gender and sexuality studies (as suggested by Rajni Palriwala) and for scholarship on caste (Waghmore). A greater emphasis on inequality, citizenship and justice has led to interesting writings and reflections on pedagogic practices and exclusions in centres of higher education (see, e.g., Deshpande and Zacharias 2013). Guru (2002) has pointed to how caste inflects the politics of knowledge production within academia. Events on Indian university campuses point to continued discrimination of Dalits in institutions of higher education, and these too have pointed to the need to debate and discuss marginalisations and discrimination of all kinds in public fora, and reflect on pedagogic practices and aspects of the production of knowledge that perpetuate this discrimination.

Interdisciplinarity has played a significant role in leading sociologists to explore areas that were largely regarded as best left to 'specialists'. One of these is medicine and health. In her contribution on the topic, V. Sujatha suggests that there has been an opening out of existing analytical parameters to include social questions of power, experience, legitimacy, state politics and policies—colonial or otherwise—and, importantly, the archive as well as the contemporary material. The resulting narrative is nuanced and far more capable of including considerations of integrative practices that display a richness in both epistemology and research protocols in approaches towards understanding medicinal practices in India. The idea that a very specific kind of expert knowledge is required to comprehend 'technical' topics is also problematised by Rita Brara's deliberations on environment and climate change. She speaks of the manner in which sociology has had wrest ground from the physical sciences to speak of the environment in a manner that positions it as part of a *social* context. The ways in which physical environments 'encounter... the life world', as Brara puts it, constitute the making of a sociology of the environment.

A widening of analytical parameters is also obvious in Copeman and Quack's contribution on contemporary religiosities. They trace the lively debate over the suitability of the term 'secularism' in Indian circumstances and proceed towards an understanding of contemporary religiosities through linking the realm of the religious to a variety of others, such as class aspirations and consumerism, in order to suggest that religiosity both draws upon and nurtures the so-called secular domains. Tulasi Srinivas' piece on new religious movements (NRMs) sits well along that by Copeman and Quack. She suggests that NRMs are embroiled in the processes of the present and, notwithstanding their resemblance to 'ancient' forms, they are most usefully understood as spiritual 'products' made out of materials of modernity. 'Spiritual capitalism' is an apt term Srinivas deploys to describe this situation. In India, as we know, a dark side of religion is religious violence. Ronie Parciack's take on religious violence brings together the usually separated binaries of nation state/community, religion/secular and metaphysical/political. She offers an ethnographic take on informal media like printed and audiovisual texts from the conflict-ridden city of Ayodhya to speak of these fusions and frictions, thereby widening the ways in which we think of the topic.

If religion has been significant in engendering a national imaginary, a concept that is frequently conflated with it, 'the folk', has also been a significant fuel for this imagination. Roma Chatterji's discussion on how the notion of the folk supported and articulated a national imaginary traverses multiple forms of dance, drama and pictorial art. This leads to a nuanced assembling of artistic practices whether they are sourced in the mythical, the religious, the indigenous or the western. It should be obvious that the state looms large in discussion of all kinds of cultural practices, including religion and ideas of folk-ness. It is only recently, however, that the state itself has become an object of socio-logical and anthropological enquiry. Touching on some of the most prominent writings on the Indian state from historians, political sci-entists to sociologists, Thomas Blom Hansen narrates a comprehensive take on the idioms used to understand the Indian state—for instance, the legacies of colonialism, the imaginaries of the post-colonial or the practices of government that amplify the question of caste politics or the dysfunctionalities of corruption.

Lawrence Cohen's essay offers a specific rendition of state-ness through a reading of Aadhaar, India's recent and massive biometric identity project. Reading through ethnographic vignettes that lay out an innovative array of contexts that he compiles and calls an archive, Cohen sets out the parameters of the future trajectories of an anthro-pology of identity in India. The idea of technology as modernity is also explored in the contribution by Nicholas Nisbett and Aditi Bhonagiri on Internet cultures. They suggest that Internet cultures have not necessarily been the radical technological break that has ushered in political or social transformation, as it might have been expected or promised.

Technology is also a site of identity politics and Carol Upadhya's essay reflects an approach that teases out the possible interfaces between India's 'new economy' and its work practices. Work related to infor-mation technology and communication, Upadhya suggests, profiles a match with middle-class aspirations linked to individual motivation, merit and achievement. The essay could be read productively along with Raka Ray's contribution on middle class-ness. Themes of labour and work in a broader context are taken up in Geert De Neve's essay on how labour issues have developed in Indian sociology, drawing from a more classical location in rural or agrarian contexts to the cur-rent horizon of urban labour seen in sectors related to information technology, service industries and special economic zones (SEZs). Along with technology, the city is a key site for many of the processes and relations outlined earlier. Indeed, the urban lends a very specific inflection to social life itself. Smriti Srinivas suggests, however, that the urban focus in Indian sociology has been slow in developing and, in many ways, is still finding its feet. She argues persuasively for the necessary recognition of the centrality of the urban in the locational nuances of the region.

Reflections

A reading together of these essays could suggest some of the cross-currents and intersectionalities that touch upon both the descriptive and the analytic interventions. The essays that engage with the themes of labour, work and class—De Neve, Upadhya and Ray—sensitise us to the enduring concerns of exploitative labour as much as revealing the newer profiles and locations under which labour and work find definition and form. The problems of legal regimes or work cultures, for instance, show the pathways that these issues can follow. From Upadhya, we can trace a link to Nisbett and Bhonagiri's essay on Internet cultures, where both suggest the forms of social formations—whether as work profiles or as a mediated form of sociality—that present themselves for sociological and anthropological mapping in a technologising milieu. The movement of technology into large-scale governmental projects suggests a powerful development in Indian statecraft, as Cohen outlines. In these and other concerns appearing in almost all of the essays, we also note the ways in which localised Indian contexts of reference connect with global sociologically framed issues and concerns of research.

The state as a sociological category per se traces its own evolution in Blom Hansen's essay and at the same time remains entrenched in the many and often fraught intersections with work, law (Basu), governmentality, religion and political violence in India—just to mention a few vectors. The point worth noting is that the state, in its national imaginings or its governmentalities, remains a constant in issues ostensibly far apart as Chatterji's folk aesthetics, Krishnamurthy's agricultural markets, Jodhka's village society, Cohen's Aadhaar identification techniques, Parciack's religious violence or Sujatha's medicinal research and practices. These kinds of movement of a sociological category or conceptual motif across terrains suggest the importance of identifying analytical constructs that provide access to emerging and innovative sociological concerns—and in that process aid the process of formulating research problems. In addition to the 'state', that kind of movement appears also to animate a social anthropological staple such as 'religion' in a set of essays—Srinivas', Parciack's and Copeman/Quack's, for instance—to etch out a sense of the present that informs 'religion' in India as much as it expands the concept to encompass reflections upon epistemologies of violence, questions of belief, practice or even 'spiritual capitalism', social movements, gender questions and more.

All in all, the gradual building up of thickness in a given area—like that of agrarian structure into agricultural markets and relationships between education, technology and class—shows the richness with which research objects evolve and find form and texture in ethnographic locations as much as in conceptual framings. The relative lack of thickness, so to speak, in the urban question (as Smriti Srinivas points out) calls for, on the one hand, an etching of a sociological map of connecting empirical motifs and parameters, like that evident in the current work on gender, sexualities, intimacies, violence, media and religion. On the other hand, it asks that we develop a methodological tendency to connect with other disciplines such as history, geography, law and philosophy. Perhaps, the quest that remains unsaid but finds expression in these essays is the importance of paying detailed attention to the crafting of a research object that can and will draw from the meaning-making potential of conceptualisations that could be excavated from the human sciences at large. This is common in much of sociology/social anthropology, but perhaps less explicit in sociology in India.

We take the liberty of making a few tentative suggestions as to what could spur on sociology in and of India. When Appadurai (1986b) talked of caste as a 'gatekeeping' concept that predominates Indian social anthropology and sociology about three decades ago (just as 'honour and shame' did for Mediterranean, for instance), he suggested a crucial epistemological point about how paradigmatic concerns can dominate the sensing of the sociological. However, our intent in this volume has not been to revisit these paradigms in order to overturn them or show their diminishing relevance, but rather to suggest a fundamental point. That is, we hope these essays have traced the ways in which dominant paradigms have retained their traction and gained density in emerging empirical locations, concerns and issues. These intents have not meant a comprehensive tracing of these articulations until the time of publication but more a representation of the diversity of issues and concerns that inform the academic content of social anthropology/sociology in and of India. As we received and read through the richly nuanced essays from the contributors, it was very clear that, among other things, this volume could be an important pedagogic reference as well at various levels of university education. The much too brief outline of the essays in this introduction cannot signal the potential of how the volume might be engaged with in a classroom.

In that spirit, we would like to mention a few concerns that add to the pedagogic potential. A gap that remains to be suitably framed and filled is the question of method and epistemology. We referred earlier to the 'qualitative turn' that sociology in India has been privileging which might suggest the 'peripheral' or 'provincial' turn that sociology had taken in post-colonial locations when translating 'American' sociology. To that, we add further nuance by underlining the point that the conventional split between social anthropology and sociology has been understood as between qualitative and quantitative, whereby, on the one hand, northern (or metropolitan) locations have conventionally employed quantitative methods to study their own societies. On the other hand, ethnographic work was meant as a more classical anthropological approach, which was applied in the study of 'other', often 'far away', societies. However, as with the human sciences at large, the ethnographic method has become a mode with which to access and represent research in much of metropolitan sociology and elsewhere. Social anthropology in India has largely been a combination of both qualitative and quantitative methods in the sense that these are the perspectives that sociologists or social anthropologists (both terms used interchangeably now) are trained in and the way that local syllabi are constituted.

We repeat these concerns here to flag a concern that may need reflection: Is there a need to frame and articulate methodological and epistemological concerns in Indian social anthropology? Could these reflections frame a contribution to the wider notions of sociological/social anthropological research in ways that illuminate the negotiations that are universal and disciplinary at large but particular and locational as well? To illustrate, in urban studies, the critique of universal theory has been in the shape of perspectives that speak as 'theory from the south'—thus, in urban studies, proposing 'slum as theory' becomes a way of negotiating the lacunae perceived in global theory. An epistemological frame peculiar to local context makes an appearance. We wonder, just as gatekeeping concepts provided theoretical parameters with which to negotiate a region and its specificities, is it necessary to articulate these negotiations as theoretical constructs for the discipline at large and not limited to the region as such? At the same time, how can we incorporate the possible range of variation within the Indian subcontinent—not just in approach but in syllabi as well? While such critiques and their importance continue to be debated, the issues raised in the essays in this volume not just point to the importance of recognising these concerns but also push towards posing another crucial question—that of comparative ethnographic work. This has not been a visible trend within social anthropology in India (see Arif 2015, 2016). While funding and several other concerns of accessibility of non-India field-sited from India have been the chief deterrents to such endeavours, the area studies paradigm has been the limited framing that seems to continue to guide and shape social anthropology from and in India. In many ways, this is a reflection of the discipline in post-colonial contexts in various locations of Asia, Africa and Latin America—but the lack is far more pronounced in social anthropological practices in India than in those other locations. From that perspective, the worlding of Indian sociology or social anthropology remains an unfinished, or perhaps an uninitiated, discussion. However, some reflection on that possibility has been the recent opening up of a 'World Anthropology' section in the *American Anthropologist* which has recently carried essays on the question (Arif 2016; Das and Randheria 2014).

Somewhat connected to the issues of connecting Indian sociology to wider comparative horizons is another question in the human sciences: that of disciplinary coherence as well as multidisciplinarity and its pedagogical, epistemological concerns. For instance, how do syllabi in Indian sociology find their focus or emphasis? How is the discipline imagined in pedagogical practice? What 'foundations' continue to influence the shaping of syllabi and what have been the critical influences that have made significant changes? Questions like these will continue to be a part of collective moments like this volume. In many ways, a small but significant concern is what questions does an 'intra' disciplinary conversation in and of India bring to the fore, some part of which, we hope, this volume has expressed.

These essays, we hope, will be accessible to a readership beyond academic circles as we believe in the fundamental significance of the social sciences—beyond the discipline of economics—in understanding the past and present of Indian society in particular and human life in general. This collection is particularly important, we feel, in light of what appears to be contemporary downgrading of the social sciences which are seen as not particularly useful to the task of economic 'progress' and material or social welfare. Ironically, though, the downgrading is accompanied by an intense political struggle over the kind of social science that is most 'relevant' for our time. And, though the latter story cannot be fully narrated here, a collection such as this, at least implicitly, points to the themes and styles that professional sociologists deem valuable.

We end with a note of thanks to our invited authors. As mentioned earlier, authors were given a fairly simple brief, that is, exploring social complexity in an accessible manner. Each has interpreted our request with varying interweavings of the personal, the conceptual and the disciplinary. Given that each topic under discussion demands the difficult exercise of fitting within limited space a wide range of debates and discussions as well as a narrative over time, the essays have managed to cover vast horizons as well as insight. Finally, each provides valuable bibliographies that are often found only under extensive reviews and that is another important contribution to the pedagogic and archival potential of this volume.

References

Alter, Joseph. 1999. *Knowing Dil Das: Stories of a Himalayan Hunter*. Philadelphia, PA: University of Pennsylvania Press.

Appadurai, Arjun. 1986a. *The Social Life of Things: Commodities in Cultural Perspective*. Cambridge: Cambridge University Press.

———. 1986b. 'Theory in Anthropology: Center and Periphery'. *Comparative Studies in Society and History* 28 (2): 356–61.

Arif, Yasmeen. 2015. 'The Audacity of Method'. *Economic & Political Weekly* 50 (1): 53–61.

———. 2016. 'Anthropologizing the World and Worlding the Anthropologist'. *American Anthropologist* 118 (4): 848–51.

Bourdieu, Pierre and J.-C. Passeron. 1977. *Reproduction in Education, Society and Culture*. Translated by R. Nice. London: SAGE.

Brosius, Christiane. 2010. *India's Middle Class: New Forms of Urban Leisure, Prosperity and Consumption*. Delhi: Routledge.

Carstairs, G. Morris. 1958. *The Twice-born: A Study of a Community of High-caste Hindus*. Bloomington, IN: Indiana University Press.

Chaudhuri, Maitrayee, ed. 2003. *The Practice of Sociology*. New Delhi: Orient Longman.

Das, Veena. 1995. 'The Anthropological Discourse on India: Reason and Its Other'. In *Critical Events: An Anthropological Perspective on Contemporary India*, edited by Veena Das, 25–54. New Delhi: Oxford University Press.

———, ed. 2003. *The Oxford India Companion to Sociology and Social Anthropology*. New Delhi: Oxford University Press.

Das, Veena and Shalini Randheria. 2014. 'Democratic Strivings, Social Sciences and Public Debates: The Case of India'. *American Anthropologist* 116 (1): 160–65.

Deshpande, Satish and Usha Zacharias, eds. 2013. *Beyond Inclusion: The Practice of Equal Access in Indian Higher Education*. London, New York and New Delhi: Routledge.

Dube, Leela. 1988. 'Hindu Girls in Patrilineal India: On the Construction of Gender'. *Economic & Political Weekly* 23 (18): WS11–WS19.

———. 2001. *Anthropological Explorations in Gender: Intersecting Fields*. New Delhi: SAGE.

Fruzzetti, L. 1993 (1982). *The Gift of a Virgin: Women, Marriage Ritual and Kinship in Bengali Society* (new Introduction). New Delhi: Oxford University Press.

Fuller, C.J. and Haripriya Narasimhan. 2014. *Tamil Brahmans: The Making of a Middle-class Caste*. Chicago: University of Chicago Press.

Ghosh, Anjan. 2014. 'Ramakrishna Mukherjee in Conversation with Anjan Ghosh'. *Sociological Bulletin* 63 (1): 113–40.

Gold, Ann Grodzins and Bhoju Ram Gujjar. 2002. *In the Time of Trees and Sorrows: Nature, Power and Memory in Rajasthan*. Durham, NC: Duke University Press.

Guru, Gopal. 2002. 'How Egalitarian Are the Social Sciences in India?' *Economic and Political Weekly* 37 (50): 5003–09.

Kannabiran, Kalpana. 2009. 'Sociology of Caste and the Crooked Mirror: Recovering B R Ambedkar's Legacy'. *Economic & Political Weekly* 44 (4): 35–39.

Madan, T.N. 1971. 'On the Nature of Caste in India—A Review Symposium on Louis Dumont's *Homo Hierarchicus*: Introduction'. *Contributions to Indian Sociology* 5 (1): 1–13.

Mathur, Nita, ed. 2014. *Consumer Culture, Modernity and Identity*. New Delhi: SAGE.

Mencher, Joan P. 1975. 'The Caste System Upside Down or the Not So Mysterious East?' *Current Anthropology* 15 (4): 469–94.

Patel, Sujata, ed. 2016. *Doing Sociology in India: Genealogies, Locations, and Practices*. New Delhi: Oxford University Press.

Peirano, Mariza G.S. 1991. 'For a Sociology of India: Some Comments from Brazil'. *Contributions to Indian Sociology* 25 (2): 321–27.

Puri, Jyoti. 1999. *Woman, Body, Desire in Post-colonial India*. London and New York, NY: Routledge.

Raheja, Gloria Goodwin and Ann Grodzins Gold. 1994. *Listen to the Heron's Words: Reimagining Gender and Kinship in North India*. Berkeley, CA: University of California Press.

Rege, Sharmila. 2010. 'Education as *Trutiya Ratna*: Towards Phule–Ambedkarite Feminist Pedagogical Practice'. *Economic & Political Weekly* 45 (44–45): 88–98.

———. 2011. 'Youth Cultures: Tracing the Process of "Defamiliarising the Familiar"'. In *Defamiliarising the Familiar: Youth Cultures. WS 08, Batch of 2011*. Pune: Krantijyoti Savitribai Phule Women's Studies Centre, University of Pune.

———. 2013. *Against the Madness of Manu: B.R. Ambedkar's Writings on Brahmanical Patriarchy*. New Delhi: Navayana.

Singer, Milton. 1972. *When a Great Tradition Modernizes: An Anthropological Approach to Indian Civilization*. New York, NY: Praeger.

Sundar, Nandini, Satish Deshpande and Patricia Uberoi. 2000. 'Indian Anthropology and Sociology: Towards a History'. *Economic & Political Weekly* 35 (24): 1998–2002.

Trawick, Margaret. 1992. *Notes on Love in a Tamil Family*. Berkeley: University of California Press.

Uberoi, Patricia. 1995. 'When Is a Marriage Not a Marriage? Sex, Sacrament and Contract in Hindu Marriage'. *Contributions to Indian Sociology* (N.S.) 29 (1–2): 319–45.

Uberoi, Patricia, Nandini Sundar and Satish Deshpande. 2007. *Anthropology in the East: Founders of Indian Sociology and Anthropology*. New Delhi: Permanent Black.

Vatuk, Sylvia. 2001. '"Where Will She Go? What Will She Do?" Paternalism Toward Women in the Administration of Muslim Personal Law in Contemporary India'. In *Religion and Personal Law in Secular India: A Call to Judgment*, edited by G.J. Larson, 226–38. Bloomington, IN: Indiana University Press.

The State as an Ethnographic Object

Thomas Blom Hansen

'What is a state if it is not a sovereign?' asked Clifford Geertz in 2004 in one of his very last articles. An older 'island and mountain anthropology' had been ill-equipped to understand the rough and tumble of birth of new nations and states across the Global South in the 20th century, Geertz admitted. Anthropologists, from the marginal locations they studied, had accepted the dominant fiction projected by all would-be nation states as 'leviathan machines': the fiction that the state comprehensively ruled a territory and a population by means of modern and rational forms of unitary governance (Geertz 2004). The power of the colonial and post-colonial states had mostly been fictional and ineffective, often violent and ruthless, enabling dominant elites to consolidate their power. Geertz suggested that anthropologists were uniquely equipped to investigate and understand the ensuing 'confusion'—his term for the complicated, historical layers of authority, power, attachments and loyalty that today constitute states and politics in most of the world. Here, Geertz usefully summed up the rationale for the new, ethnographically embedded way of studying and conceptualising phenomena that the discipline for so long had considered outside its purview: the projection of state power through public rituals, violence and symbols; the extension and reproduction of governance and regulation of a vast range of domains—from foreign investments to setting up a local health clinic, or imposing environmental safety standards in a mining region; and the upholding of the state's core attribute—the monopoly of violence—through policing, prison systems, border controls and a security apparatus.

This new 'anthropology of the state' began in the 1990s and has since then become one of the liveliest areas within the discipline, supplanting an older, moribund 'political anthropology' that had focused mainly on so-called traditional modes of power, kingship and authority (Spencer 1997).

But how did a concept like 'the state' that for generations was seen as exterior to the anthropological enterprise become an object of abiding ethnographic concern? What new insights and analytical frames did this enable? Accounting for this requires a global perspective, but modern and colonial India plays a seminal part in it, as a space of theorisation as well as a historical and ethnographic terrain where 'the state' at one and the same time was highly visible, ubiquitous and yet strangely alienated from 'society'.

Let me begin on a semantic note. In English, the term 'state' (derived from the Latin term *status*/rank/prestige and French term *etat*) is mainly used in a more formal sense for a sovereign entity and polity as a whole. 'Reasons of state' are considerations that concern the very security and stability of a polity and the realm. The term 'government', by contrast, denotes in everyday speech the administration of people and territory and is derived from medieval French (*gouvernement*) like many other related terms related to law, property and rule that were introduced in Britain after the Norman conquest. As is well known, it is the term 'government' rather than 'the state' that is used in everyday speech to refer to public policies, budget allocations and public property administered by the government on behalf of the state. This standard semantic slippage between 'government' and 'state' is at the heart of well-known conservative political arguments that demand severe cuts in government expenditure and the public sector while advocating a strengthening of all the central institutions of the state—army, security, police, foreign policy, etc. In other words, opposing the government while loving the state.

This distinction between 'the state' (as in a sovereign realm) and government (as in the apparatus of administration) corresponds quite well with the distinction in modern Hindi between *raj/raja* and *sarkar*, and their respective denotations. As I shall argue below, the tension between the notion of a more-or-less legitimate political community or rule (raj) and the administration of authority over people and territory

(sarkar) is actually more consequential and has deeper historical reso-
nances in South Asia than in many other parts of the world. The depth
of this tension, I will argue, may well account for why analysing and
theorising 'the state' as an object in South Asia turned out to be a vein
so rich in narrative force, moral imagination and social contestation.

From State Theory to Governmentality

Until the early 1990s, deploying words like state power or 'the state'
as analytical terms would immediately identify a writer as a Marxist.
New debates on the nature of the modern state had been at the heart
of Western European Marxism ever since the translation of the Italian
Marxist Antonio Gramsci's *Prison Notebooks* into French and English
in the late 1960s (Gramsci 1971). Louis Althusser's work on 'Ideology
and Ideological State Apparatuses' (1971) was directly influenced
by Gramsci and so was Nicos Poulantzas' (1973) very influential
formulation about the 'relative autonomy of the state'. The legend-
ary 'Poulantzas–Miliband debate' of the early 1970s[1] concerned the
relationship between class power and the state. Miliband argued that
modern capitalist states were invariably dominated by bourgeois interests, while Poulantzas pointed out that 'the state' should be thought
of as a broad ensemble of historically evolved institutions, ideologies
and practices that had internal contradictions and constituted and
had grown to become a source of power and domination that could
not be reduced to simple class power. The terms of this debate were
French and German (etat/staat), and influential theorists like Bob Jessop
retained the term 'state' as the analytical term that encompassed both
daily public administration and the core institutions of the sovereign
realm like military and police (Jessop 1990). Yet the chief problem in
this debate remained the boundaries and definition of the state as a
concept and an identifiable sociological entity.

To the empirically inclined historian and sociologist, 'state theory'
appeared abstract and formulaic, more beholden to Marx's and
Gramsci's texts than to any observable reality. The two most influential
formulations that subsequently informed the ethnographic approach
to the state were both critics of Marxist state theory. In his widely cited
article 'Some Notes on the Difficulty of Studying the State', historical

[1] For a clear and informed overview, see Bob Jessop's summary: https://
bobjessop.org/2014/01/14/dialogue-of-the-deaf-some-reflections-on-the-pou-
lantzas-miliband-debate/ (accessed on 24 June 2017).

sociologist Philip Abrams reversed the standard Marxist formula when he suggested that 'the state is not the reality which stands behind the mask of political practice. It is itself the mask which prevents our seeing political practice as it is' (Abrams 1977: 82).

Abrams argued that the 'idea of the state' as an expression of 'res publica, a public reification' (ibid.) was a historical project of legitimisation and construction that political and social elites engaged in across the world. Rather than studying the functions of the state, as Marxists were wont to do in order to show its efficacy, Abrams called for a study of how the state announces its own presence as a 'state idea', and how the institutions and presence of this 'idea' have become naturalised and embedded in different societies.

The other, and more influential, criticism of the implied belief among Marxists in the state as a natural function of class power came from Michel Foucault. In *Discipline and Punish*, he called for a 'cutting off the king's head in political theory' by which he meant abandoning the notion of the state as a reified unity (Foucault 1969). Foucault argued that the very form of public authority had changed from an older exterior relationship between subjects and the sovereign to a modern interior relationship between diverse practices of government, not all of which emanated from the state in a legal–formal sense, and the multiple subject positions this dispersion produced. This perspective on government was later elaborated into studies of the 'mentalities of government' in a range of fields from institutions to knowledge formations and later the 'technologies of the self' (Foucault 1994). In Timothy Mitchell's influential formulation, the modern state was an abstraction arising from multiple, dispersed but ever more intense forms of (self)government and (self)disciplining (Mitchell 1991). This 'state effect' transformed the relationship between power and authority, and produced modernity by imposing an altogether new epistemic regime of knowing and acting on self and society, which in turn produced modern subjects, distanced from their traditional past (Mitchell 1988). A modern society was, in other words, a governmentalised society. Or in Kaviraj's formulation, the exercise of sovereignty became increasingly an 'internal affair' as states became predominantly engaged in transforming the arrangements of social power within their own societies than fighting and conquering external enemies (Kaviraj 2012: 5).

These theoretical interventions enabled a move away from seeing the state as a reified reality standing behind most phenomena and relationships (as in Althusser), and instead see 'the state' as an idea projected through symbolic and institutional practices, as well as a form of imaginary reality arising from dispersed, uneven, incoherent and often violent attempts to impose public order, governance and intelligibility upon a recalcitrant reality. The state exists as an ongoing project of projection, coercion and persuasion, or 'languages of stateness' that encompasses both the state as more permanent, symbolic realm and the daily realities of ongoing administration (Hansen and Stepputat 2001).

However, the tension between the two sides of the state—embodying the polity as such versus the everyday exercise of public authority and government—was not always clarified by scholars, because it so rarely was clear-cut in practical politics or in governmental practices. Many anthropologists became comfortable with a somewhat simplified Foucauldian view of the state as a dispersed landscape of administrative and epistemic techniques imposed upon vernacular life-worlds. Meanwhile, the more ideational and symbolic imaginings of state power, authority and sovereignty as 'real abstractions' attracted less attention despite the fact that the discrepancy between such abstractions and the flaws of practical government constitutes the central force field of modern politics across the world. In short, as the anthropology of the state developed, the attention to politics and the dynamics of democracy gradually slid out of view.

The Indian State Between Dominance and Hegemony

At one level, the scholarly debates on the nature of the state in India follow the general theoretical schema outlined above from Marxism over Gramsci to Foucault. However, it was far from a one-way traffic. The historical specificity of the Indian subcontinent became, I will argue, an important global staging ground for the contemporary conceptualisations of the modern state.

Up to the 1960s, scholars and intellectuals, whether liberal adherents to modernisation theory or Marxists, generally subscribed to a teleological view of the modern colonial state as a historical midwife of modernity, capitalism and later national sovereignty embodied in the post-colonial Nehruvian state.

The general consensus was that the emergence of the colonial state marked an epochal, epistemic shift in how both raj and sarkar were presented to Indian subjects, along with the transformative power unleashed by capital and modern administrative technologies.[2] The key debates concerned the character of this state: deformed by the specificity of its dominance by 'comprador classes' (Alavi 1972); or weakened by the unresolved tensions between the industrial bourgeoisie, the dominant agrarian elite and other elite factions (Bardhan 1984); and dominated, if not wholly captured, by powerful regional caste-and-class formations (Frankel and Rao 1989).

However, alongside this broad tendency, historians as different as Chris Bayly, Ranajit Guha and Bernard Cohn were questioning how deeply the colonial state had actually managed to penetrate and rule Indian society. In his early work, Bayly had shown the immense spatial fluidity and social dynamism of the 18th-century North India where the company state only slowly emerged as a significant player, often relying on inadequate and unreliable information (Bayly 1983, 1996). Unconvinced that the details of colonial administration always made a categorical difference to colonial subjects, Bayly suggested that across India, various proto-nationalities—*rashtra* (nation), *qaum* (community/people)—predated colonial rule and should be thought of as deep moral templates of what was, and is, considered legitimate forms of sovereignty/raj (Bayly 1998).

In Ranajit Guha's magnum opus *Elementary Aspects of Peasant Insurgency in Colonial India*, the idea of a deep historical continuity in perceptions of authority and injustice among the poor and subaltern majority in the subcontinent received its most systematic treatment from a distinctly Gramscian and Hegelian perspective. For Guha, the moral notion of a rightful and just insurgency is written into subaltern consciousness and has changed very little in the past centuries. Referring to popular resistance to the excesses of the Emergency in 1977, he concludes, 'So long as landlord authority continues to function as a significant element of the ruling culture (…) all mass struggles will tend to model themselves on the unfinished projects of Titu, Kanhu, Birsa and Meghar Singh' (Guha 1983: 336). Guha later extended this analytical frame of a deep epistemic, if not ontological gulf, between elite and subaltern framings of authority and justice to apply to the colonial state and the colonised as a whole. In his well-known essay 'Dominance Without Hegemony and Its Historiography', Guha describes two competing idioms: one British, liberal and universalist

---

[2] *Producing India* is the most recent and most sophisticated restatement of this point of view informed by the Henri Lefebvre's spatial history of capital (Goswami 2004).

and the other described as 'pre-colonial/Indian and semi feudal'. The British universe of 'order, improvement, obedience and rightful dissent' is fundamentally incompatible with the Indian schema of 'danda, dharma, bhakti and dharmic protest' and as a result, the colonial state remained completely 'exterior' to broader social life in India; it does not really penetrate the moral life of most communities (Guha 1989). The result was a form of perpetual despotism, 'domination without hegemony'. The target of this essay was what Guha described as standard nationalist history writing in India that de facto embraced the colonial historiography by conflating the triumphalist history of the colonial state with the history of India as such, leaving out very different vernacular histories, and the experience of colonialism by the vast subaltern majority.

Bernard Cohn's detailed studies of the Benares region, rich in biographical detail, local terminology and telling vignettes, depicted the Company officials not as mere precursors of what was to become a more fully evolved administrative machine by the early 20th century but as individuals struggling to interpret and divine the world they found themselves in, often failing and alienating local allies because of epistemic misunderstandings and conflicts (Cohn 1987). His famous essay on the creation of the Imperial Durbar in 1877 on the same spot where British officers had desecrated the Mughal palace in Delhi in 1858 summed up Cohn's view of the colonial state as epistemologically alien, often clumsy but also introducing durable changes in how statecraft and authority were conceptualised (Cohn 1983). Cohn's historical studies of colonial institutions and discourses (much of it Foucauldian *avant la lettre*)—law, community, political representation, objective measurement and sociology—demonstrated that colonial institutions had deep effects insofar as they became new resources and arenas for contestation among groups and communities whose sense of their own histories predated British conquest by many centuries. For Cohn, in short, the colonial state introduced new forms of *sarkari* (governmental) practices, but it was far from obvious to him to what extent deeper registers of legitimate rule, raj, had changed.

Cohn credited Gandhi and the nationalist movement with inventing a broadly nativist register of conduct that rejected Western dress, technology and food, which in turn reconfigured older ritual/symbolic languages into the performative idioms of mass politics that came to define political life in modern India—the *padyatra*, the public fast, the *dharna*, etc. (Cohn 1987: 678–79). Unlike their pre-colonial roots, these rituals all depended on and projected *janata*/the people as a new source of political legitimacy, raj and utopia, the heart of the modern rashtra/nation, the 'inner domain' whose virtues remained unsullied by the alien and the 'outer' domain of the (foreign) sarkar (Chatterjee 1993). As importantly to our story here, this nationalist imagination introduced a powerful genre of moral 'anti-politics' into India's public culture, by which I mean a style of critique of governmental practices, corruption and mismanagement, a politics that posits itself as standing outside electoral politics and outside 'the system' as such, representing the purity of 'the people' (Chakrabarty 2007). This genre of anti-politics reified the state as 'external' to society and has been important across the political spectrum, not least inside in the contemporary Hindu nationalist movement (Hansen 1999).

The notion of the modern state as exterior and alien to popular cultural epistemic schemas continued as a deep, if not always explicit, theme in many of the contributions to the Subaltern Studies volumes throughout the 1980s and 1990s. It was an analytical matrix that seemed to fit the late colonial moment of intensified and more scientific governance particularly well. However, this matrix turned out to be less helpful in understanding the character, functions and popular perceptions of the post-colonial state as it expanded and became an integral part of social and economic life across the country in the decades after independence.

The State as a Moral and Political Object

In his widely cited book on India's five decades of independence, Sunil Khilnani (1998: 41) asserted that the post-colonial state had managed to constitute itself as 'the core of Indian society', a material and symbolic fact of life of most Indians. While perhaps overstating his case, Khilnani was surely right in pointing out that five decades of semi-planned License Raj and an ever more vigorous democratic and electoral politics had meant that sarkari institutions—schools, block development offices, state transport buses and jobs/careers in the burgeoning public sector—were part and parcel of the social imagination of the vast majority of Indians. However, the rhetorical commitment to development, justice and social improvement by the political elites was almost invariably belied by the incompetence and poorly resourced realities of the local sarkar. The state had become ubiquitous, but it was conspicuously weak, often captured by local elites and interest to a point where it almost ceased to exist, leaving a veteran scholar of North Indian politics to suggest that Uttar Pradesh had descended into 'a Hobbesian state of disorder' (Brass 1997: 60). Anthropologists such as Bailey (1963) and Robinson (1988) and social scientists such as Brass (1987), Kohli (1991) and Harriss-White (2003) had described how electoral politics enabled local caste elites to capture public state resources. It had been somewhat less noticed that the same electoral and democratic processes had deepened significantly and had made ideas of a more just and inclusive popular national community (rashtra) based on 'the people' (lok/janata) into political common sense among very broad sections of the population. However, it did not happen in the language of unitary republican citizenship but mediated by categories of language, caste and religious community. Across India, in the 1980s, massive lower-caste movements rose to political prominence on demands for expanded affirmative action, or reservations, in education and public service. Their rallying cry was not 'traditional' caste identities but rather the bureaucratic category of 'OBCs (Other Backward Classes)', a residual census category encompassing many impoverished communities across the country, now appropriated as an emotionally meaningful identity to millions of people.

This indicated two things: (a) that the promise of being included in the wider polity could override many shortcomings of actual governmental function (Jaffrelot 2002) and (b) that bureaucratic categories, and the resources and functions of the state, were now deeply embedded in the social and cultural imagination of ordinary Indians. The state was no longer alien but a vernacular cultural fact.

If the Nehruvian state and its institutions had tried to embody and signify the nation and the new polity in the decades after independence, by the late 1980s, it was popular democracy and the rough and tumble of electoral politics that now condensed and expressed political imagination and social aspirations.

Not surprisingly, misgivings about the routinisation of corruption became a point of articulation of affective claims on the state by new emergent social groups, by the older elites who felt they were losing control and indeed by a range of perceptive anthropologists. Akhil Gupta's seminal article 'Blurred Boundaries: The Discourse of Corruption, the Culture of Politics and the Imagined State' (Gupta 1995) used an ethnographic account of bribe giving in the village of Alipur in Uttar Pradesh to unpack popular perceptions of the state. This decisive intervention demonstrated that 'the state' indeed could be made into an ethnographic object in two ways: first, as the practical relationship between local villagers and townspeople and equally local bureaucrats and officers; second, that the larger 'translocal' apparatus of the state was equally alive in the 'imagination' of villagers, or what Gupta calls 'the discursive construction of the state'—something Gupta's informants associate with national-level figures they learn about through various media (Gupta 2012: 100–07). In a powerful article some years later, Jonathan Parry suggested that bribes and corruption are widely condemned in India because many Indians had to some extent 'internalized the universalistic and impersonal values associated with modern bureaucracy' (Parry 2000: 29). He also suggested that it is the expanding centrality of the state in the life of most Indians that makes the experience of corruption such a generalised sentiment. This centrality made condemnation of corruption one of the few moral causes that most Indians could agree on.

Both Gupta and Parry insisted on the term 'the state' to denote both the local and corrupt incarnation of the state, and its imagined, perhaps more 'universalistic', ideal form. This duality between the local and the imagined could be more richly conceptualised as a split between sarkar and a more encompassing notion of the polity as such. I had earlier proposed to understand the perceptions of the state as always/ already split into a 'profane' and a 'sublime' dimension, one imperfect and corrupt, the other a more durable ideal form relatively impervious to real-life imperfections of sarkari practice (Hansen 2000). Although the term 'sublime' was read, gratuitously, by some colleagues as a moral endorsement of the state as such (see, for instance, Das 2006), it is obvious that social scientists of India and South Asia do need to have a differentiated analytical vocabulary to properly appreciate 'the state' as a complex ethnographic object, an object that not only can be seen as a dispersed set of bureaucratic operations but also exists as an ideational construct, an 'idea' of a shared polity, articulated in local and vernacular forms (see, e.g., Bate 2009; Benei 2008; Burghart 1990; Mitchell 2010; Osella and Osella 2000).

Most of the literature on the state in India and South Asia in the past decade have taken a predominantly Foucauldian approach to studies of governmental practices and the post-liberalisation state in South Asia (e.g., Ghertner 2015; Hull 2012; Legg 2007; Sivaramakrishnan and Gupta 2011). This body of work has either avoided the question of the polity as an 'idea' altogether or assumed that such ideational constructs are embedded within the larger colonial and post-colonial modernist state project. Even Gupta (2012) in his synthetic work *Red Tape: Bureaucracy, Structural Violence and Poverty in India* elects to view the state almost entirely through the prism of bureaucratic function, the work of writing and the structural violence embedded in the very functioning of the state apparatus. There are notable exceptions, such as

Corbridge and Harris (2003), that take a broader, historically informed view of how the forces of democracy have reshaped the functions and significations of the Indian state. But on the whole, most of what became understood as the 'anthropology of the state' concerns itself with the routine operations of government at many levels of Indian society.

This reorientation of the study of the state has happened at a time when the role of state as sarkar in its classical post-colonial incarnation was under pressure from, firstly, the demands made by a burgeoning private sector and, secondly, the pressures from a vigorous popular democracy. Since the early 1990s, sections of the business community, international monetary institutions and critics of endemic corruption have advocated a 'rolling back' of state regulation in many fields, and to decentralise policies and responsibilities away from Delhi towards the states. However, the Indian state is not shrinking; its reach is stronger and deeper than before (think of NREGA or the Aadhaar biometrical registration scheme), while its repressive powers are stronger and more threatening to both minorities and dissenting groups than ever before (think of the Unlawful Activities Act of 2004, or the continuing impunity of the Army and other security agencies in Northeast India and Kashmir). The main reason for this continued expansion of the state is that Indian society still remains relatively less 'governmental-ised'—that is, less effectively regulated by law, taxation and formal government—than other developing economies and societies. Most laws in India are never fully implemented, vast proportions of public funds are misappropriated and, at the local level, both the administration of justice and everyday regulation are captured and change hands between powerful social and political forces. As a result of this systemic dysfunction, the scramble for development across contemporary India is driven by ambitions to show administrative ('sarkari') prowess and tangible results such as modern infrastructure and buildings.

Such processes of development and state expansion are not merely effects of an inevitable unfolding of the governmentalisation of modern life as a Foucauldian perspective would assume. It is, rather, the out-come of fierce political competition for resources, domination and control. The state is not merely a remote sarkar, or a set of bureaucratic functions; it is more than ever before an immensely valuable political prize, an apparatus that can be mobilised and dominated at various levels to install new symbols of political power, to enforce, or not enforce, countless laws and regulations (Michelutti 2008). This struggle can be so intense and partisan that it hollows out sarkari institutions and impedes the very functioning of the state, as Witsoe has argued with regard to Bihar (Witsoe 2013). This 'politicisation' of the state, the bureaucracy and the judiciary demonstrates Kaviraj's (2012) conclusion that in modern societies, the exercise of sovereignty is largely an 'internal affair'. The struggle over the control of the state is about access to material resources, about the aspiration to monopolise violence and about epistemic control. But it is as much a struggle over how to shape the very symbols of sovereign power, the means of domination, and the ideological framing of the polity itself, the rashtra and the raj. The scholarship on the Maoist insurrection in different parts of India has shown convincingly that what animates militancy is the promise of a different kind of polity rather than details of sarkari regulation (Kunnath 2012; Shah 2010). Banerjee's (2014) study of why ordinary Indians vote shows with startling clarity that for the poorer communities, voting is an exercise in hope, self-assertion and self-respect in the face of a sarkar that constantly fails and ignores them. Again, the promise of inclusion into the polity is stronger than the encounters with the sarkar.

A Stranger No More: The State as a Cultural Category?

In the past decades, multiple studies of the immensely dynamic world of democratic politics, cultural politics and popular mobilisations of all kinds (only some of which are referenced here) have made South Asia one of the prime global foci for a new anthropology of politics. Meanwhile, the anthropology of the state, especially in its Foucauldian variant, has been carving its own niche, analysing policies, planning, development schemes, technical rationalities and the impact of 'neoliberalism' (a term that sits awkwardly with the contemporary Indian state). The result has been a stronger and more embedded understanding of how the Indian state actually governs, or as often governs through inaction. Yet this body of work has gradually been removed from the rough and tumble of democratic politics, questions of law, rights (*haq*), and the enormous force of ideology, nationalism and morality in social life. In short, it has been removed from many of the issues that the early ethnographic accounts of state practices promised to bring together (see, e.g., Fuller and Benei 2000). The effect of separating the analysis of government and bureaucracy from questions of law, sovereignty and morality has been an unfortunate perpetuation of the older framing of the state in India and South Asia as epistemically alien, reifying and somewhat incommensurable with local categories. As I have suggested, this mode of analysis is decidedly unhelpful in understanding what drives the huge emotional and political investment in turning the state into a symbolic expression of the nation and the polity, be that in the Nehruvian era (Roy 2007) or in the contemporary BJP/RSS version of the Hindu *rashtra* (nation). It is also relatively unhelpful in understanding the affective investment in the Constitution and the principle of law, and legal reasoning, by many of the marginalised lower-caste, Dalit and tribal movements across India (see De 2014).

As I see it, the challenge for any ethnographic analysis of the state in the future is to be able to hold together in one single frame the actual functioning of sarkari institutions (repressive and non-repressive) with a simultaneous attention to how political forces and popular demands constantly shape 'the state'—that strange but potent compound of practical administration and perpetual promises of encompassment and recognition of all elements of a polity. Studies of how state practices and resources are embedded within local and vernacular universes of politics have proven much more fecund and promising than the now well-worn assumptions about the state being an 'external', alien epistemic force. Let me mention a few recent examples:

In a recent book called the *The Demands of Recognition*, Townsend Middleton (2015) investigates how local political forces in the tea district of Darjeeling shifted their strategy from demanding autonomy and some self-determination for what they hoped to be a new 'Gorkhaland' to instead become recognised as a tribal community, a process that implies a set of constitutionally guaranteed rights, reservation schemes and more control over land. This process included regular visits by a large number of government enumerators and official state anthropologists to observe and rate the performance of Gorkha rituals as properly tribal. Middleton shows how an analysis of governmentality can be joined with a deep ethnographic analysis of the enactment of claims and rituals of sovereignty and cultural autonomy. He also shows that the promise of inclusion into the modern Indian republic is very powerful indeed, but that this desire for inclusion as citizens is articulated through the state's official ethno-cultural categories. Many of these categories began their career in the colonial state, but today they are wholly appropriated by local political and social forces, and given meaningful political and affective life through a process of democratic politics.

Beatrice Jaurequi's (2016) new work on policing in the populous state of Uttar Pradesh in North India shows that even this repressive branch of the state is not 'external' in any meaningful sense but actually the very opposite. The chief challenge of the police force is to maintain autonomy and authority in a complex political system that constantly entangles police officers in local disputes and power games, and in a context where sovereignty is fragmented and multiple and where the state possesses no monopoly of violence, and merely represents the greater potential of violence and manpower.

Brighupati Singh's recent work also reintroduces classical themes of sovereignty and utopian and sacral polities in an intriguing analysis of life, erotics and striving in a tribal community in Rajasthan (Singh 2015).

Finally, Lucia Michelutti's ongoing work on kinship and politics depicts vernacular cosmologies of power among lower-caste Yadav politicians and caste movements (once itinerant pastoral and trading communities) that have effectively subsumed and appropriated bureaucratic resources of affirmative action and symbols of state power. These communities have reinvented themselves as a modern political community by mastering the game of competitive electoral politics, control over state resources and re-purposing an older historical narrative of honour, strength and divinity, associated with Krishna, the protector of cows and, of course, cow herders.

CODA

As I have indicated above, we can understand the emergence of 'the state' as an ethnographic object in India as a peculiar epistemic journey from colonial 'externality' to a ubiquitous, inefficient and often violent and contested presence in the life of most communities and individuals in modern India. It is this peculiar omnipresence of the state in a society that is less 'governmentalised' than most, and more governed by other forms of authority generated by forces of caste, religious community and electoral politics, that has allowed social scientists to 'see' and analyse the bureaucratic and sarkari dimensions of 'the state' more clearly than in many other societies. Yet the challenge remains to develop frames of analysis that can comprehend the state not merely as external, violent and/or morally tainted but also as a machine, and a horizon, that promises inclusion, justice and care. To return to my starting point, the political community always has two bodies, two dimensions: one of concrete administration, sarkar, and another vague but morally eternal and powerful (raj or rashtra). Even the most banal sarkari institution, however flawed, only retains a measure of force and importance because it stands in for something much larger behind it. Reversely, the larger polity and political authority requires concrete manifestation, force and acts of generosity to be credible and believable. In the constant tension, failure, non-identity and striving for approximation between these two bodies lie the force and promise of politics itself. That must be the starting point for any ethnography of the state.

References

Abrams, P. 1977. 'Some Notes on the Difficulty of Studying the State'. *Journal of Historical Sociology* 1 (1): 58–89.

Alavi, Hamza. 1972. 'The State in Postcolonial Societies: Pakistan and Bangladesh'. *New Left Review* I74 (July–August): 59–81.

Althusser, Louis. 1971. *Lenin and Philosophy and Other Essays*. London: New Left Books.

Bailey, F.G. 1963. *Politics and Social Change: Orissa in 1959*. Berkeley, CA: University of California Press.

Banerjee, M. 2014. *Why India Votes*. London: Routledge.

Bardhan, P. 1984. *The Political Economy of Development in India*. Oxford: Blackwell Publishers.

Bate, B. 2009. *Tamil Oratory and the Dravidian Aesthetic: Democratic Practice in South India*. New York, NY: Columbia University Press.

Bayly, C.A. 1983. *Rulers, Townsmen and Bazaars: North Indian Society in the Age of British Expansion, 1770–1870*. Cambridge: Cambridge University Press.

———. 1996. *Empire and Information: Intelligence Gathering and Social Communication in India, 1780–1870*. Cambridge: Cambridge University Press.

———. 1998. *The Origin of Nationality in South Asia: Patriotism and Ethical Government in the Making of Modern India*. Cambridge: Cambridge University Press.

Benei, V. 2008. *Schooling Passions: Nation, History and Language in Western India*. Stanford, CA: Stanford University Press.

Brass, P. 1987. *Caste, Faction and Party in Indian Politics: Election Studies*. Delhi: Chanakya Publishers.

———. 1997. *The Theft of an Idol: Text and Context in the Representation of Collective Violence*. Princeton, NJ: Princeton University Press.

Burghart, R. 1990. *The Conditions of Listening: Essays on Religion, History and Politics in South Asia*. New Delhi: Oxford University Press.

Chakrabarty, Dipesh. 2007. '"In the Name of Politics": Democracy and the Power of the Multitude in India'. *Public Culture* 19 (1): 35–58.

Chatterjee, P. 1993. *The Nation and Its Fragments: Colonial and Postcolonial Histories*. New Delhi: Oxford University Press.

Cohn, Bernard. 1983. 'Representing Authority in Victorian India'. In *The Invention of Tradition*, edited by E. Hobsbawm and T. Ranger, 165–210. Cambridge: Cambridge University Press.

———. 1987. *An Anthropologist among the Historians*. New Delhi: Oxford University Press.

Corbridge, S. and J. Harris. 2003. *Reinventing India: Liberalization, Hindu Nationalism and Popular Democracy*. Cambridge: Polity Press.

Das, Veena. 2006. *Life and Words: Violence and the Descent into the Ordinary*. Berkeley, CA: University of California Press.

De, Rohit. 2014. 'Rebellion, Dacoity and Equality: The Emergence of the Constitutional Field in Postcolonial India'. *Comparative Studies of South Asia, Africa and the Middle East* 34 (2): 260–78.

Forbess, Alice and Lucia Michelutti. 2013. 'From the Mouth of God: Divine Kinship and Popular Democratic Politics'. *Focaal: Journal of Global and Historical Anthropology* 2013 (67): 3–18.

Foucault, Michel. 1969. *Discipline and Punish*. London: Tavistock.

———. 1994. 'Technologies of the Self'. In *Ethics: Subjectivity and Truth*, edited by Paul Rabinow, 223–52. London: Allen Press.

Frankel, F. and S. Rao, eds. 1989. *Dominance and State Power in Modern India*. Vols 1 and 2. New Delhi: Oxford University Press.

Fuller, C.J. and V. Benei, eds. 2000. *The Everyday State and Society in Modern India*. New Delhi: Social Science Press.

Geertz, C. 2004. 'What Is a State if It Is Not a Sovereign? Reflections on Politics in Complicated Places'. *Current Anthropology* 45 (5): 577–85.

Ghertner, A. 2015. *Rule by Aesthetics: World Class City Making in Delhi*. New York, NY: Oxford University Press.

Goswami, Manu. 2004. *Producing India: From Colonial Economy to National Space*. Chicago, IL: University of Chicago Press.

Gramsci, Antonio. 1971. *Selections from the Prison Notebooks*. London: Lawrence and Wishart.

Guha, Ranajit. 1983. *Elementary Aspects of Peasant Insurgency in Colonial India*. New Delhi: Oxford University Press.

———. 1989. 'Dominance Without Hegemony and Its Historiography'. In *Subaltern Studies VI*, edited by Ranajit Guha. New Delhi: Oxford University Press.

Gupta, Akhil. 1995. 'Blurred Boundaries: The Discourse of Corruption, the Culture of Politics and the Imagined State'. *American Ethnologist* 22 (2): 375–402.

Gupta, A. 2012. *Red Tape: Bureaucracy, Structural Violence and Poverty in India*. Durham, NC: Duke University Press.

Hansen, T.B. 1999. *The Saffron Wave: Democracy and Hindu Nationalism in Modern India*. Princeton, NJ: Princeton University Press.

———. 2000. 'Governance and Myths of State in Mumbai'. In *The Everyday State and Society in Modern India*, edited by C.J. Fuller and V. Benei, 31–67. New Delhi: Social Science Press.

Hansen, T.B. and F. Stepputat, eds. 2001. *States of Imagination: Ethnographic Explorations of the Postcolonial State*. Durham, NC: Duke University Press.

Harriss-White, B. 2003. *India Working: Essays on Society and Economy*. Cambridge: Cambridge University Press.

Hull, M. 2012. *Government of Paper: The Materiality of Government in Urban Pakistan*. Berkeley, CA: University of California Press.

Jaffrelot, C. 2002. *India's Silent Revolution*. New York, NY: Columbia University Press.

Jaurequi, B. 2016. *Provisional Authority: Police, Order and Security in India*. Chicago, IL: University of Chicago Press.

Jessop, Bob. 1990. *State Theory: Putting the Capitalist State in Its Place*. Cambridge: Polity Press.

Kaviraj, S. 2012. *Trajectories of the Indian State*. Delhi and Hyderabad: Orient BlackSwan.

Khilnani, Sunil. 1998. *The Idea of India*. Harmondsworth: Penguin.

Kohli, Atul. 1991. *Democracy and Discontent: India's Growing Crisis of Governability*. Princeton, NJ: Princeton University Press.

Kunnath, George. 2012. *Rebels from the Mud Houses: Dalits and the Making of the Maoist Revolution in Bihar*. Delhi: Social Science Press.

Legg, Stephen. 2007. *Spaces of Colonialism: Delhi's Urban Governmentalities*. London: Blackwell Publishers.

Michelutti, L. 2008. *The Vernacularisation of Democracy: Politics, Caste and Religion in India*. Delhi and London: Routledge.

Middleton, T. 2015. *The Demands of Recognition: State Anthropology and Ethno Politics in Darjeeling*. Stanford, CA: Stanford University Press.

Mitchell, Lisa. 2010. *Language, Emotion and Politics in South India: The Making of a Mother Tongue*. Bloomington, IN: Indiana University Press.

Mitchell, T. 1988. *Colonising Egypt*. Cambridge: Cambridge University Press.

———. 1991. 'The Limits of the State: Beyond Statist Approaches and Critics'. *American Political Science Review* 85 (1): 77–96.

Osella, F. and C. Osella. 2000. 'The Return of King Mahabali: The Politics of Morality in Kerala'. In *The Everyday State and Society in Modern India*, edited by C.J. Fuller and V. Benei, 137–62. New Delhi: Social Science Press.

Parry, J. 2000. 'The Crisis of Corruption and the "Idea of India": A Worm's Eye View'. In *The Morals of Legitimacy*, edited by I. Pardo, 27–56. Oxford: Berghahn Books.

Poulantzas, Nicos. 1973. *Political Power and Social Classes*. London: New Left Books.

Robinson, M. 1988. *Local Politics: The Law of the Fishes—Development Through Political Change in Medak District, Andhra Pradesh*. New Delhi: Oxford University Press.

Roy, Srirupa. 2007. *Beyond Belief: India and the Politics of Postcolonial Nationalism*. Durham, NC: Duke University Press.

Shah, Alpa. 2010. *In the Shadows of the State: Indigenous Politics, Environmentalism and Insurgency in Jharkhand, India.* Durham, NC: Duke University Press.

Spencer, J. 1997. 'Post-colonialism and the Political Imagination'. *The Journal of the Royal Anthropological Institute* 3 (1): 1–19.

Singh, B. 2015. Poverty and the Quest for Life: Spiritual and Material Striving in Rural India. Chicago, IL: University of Chicago Press.

Sivaramakrishnan, S. and A. Gupta, eds. 2011. The State in India after Liberalization: Interdisciplinary Perspectives. London: Routledge.

Witsoe, Jeffrey. 2013. Democracy against Development: Lower-caste Politics and Political Modernity in Postcolonial India. Chicago, IL: University of Chicago Press.

2

The Folk and the Making of an Indian Aesthetic

Roma Chatterji

FIGURE 2.1

'This is me and my *parchhayi* (shadow), my *antaratma* (inner self)', said Kalabai Shyam, pointing to a black and white picture of a woman's face in profile, her unbound hair veiling a tiny silhouette of the same face, also in profile, facing in the same direction as the larger face that was covered with dots in Kalabai's signature style (Figure 2.1). I was drawn to this picture because it seemed so different from the fantastic beasts and enchanted nature-scapes that are the common subjects of Gond paintings.[1] As a portrait, Kalabai's depiction of herself seemed to trouble the conventional division between folk or tribal and high art, unlike the former which is supposed to be abstract—presenting iconic images that transcend human time and space (Swaminathan 1987)—and the latter where portraiture is associated with true likeness 'with a recognizable image of a known face' (Jariwala 2010: 11). 'People are scared of their shadows, but they should not be. That is why I have drawn it with my face', Kalabai continued prodded by my questions about the subject of her drawing.

I was not sure what to make of Kalabai's comments at the time—her figurative use of 'shadow' to talk about the 'inner self'—but later when I started reading on aesthetics, specifically on ideas of mirroring as they occur in Indian images, I came across an article on the subject by the Abhinavagupta scholar David Peter Lawrence that seemed to provide a way to understand her 'self-portrait'. In an article on Abhinavagupta's use of the analogy of reflection, Lawrence (2005: 583) says that some schools of Indian philosophy make a distinction between self as witness and bodily self 'as reflected in the eyes of others, a mirror or a plate of water'. But reflection is also said to be constitutive of iconography that enables access to the divine through the process of mirroring.[2] But why should one be scared of the shadow as an image of the inner self? It was the multidisciplinary work of Hans Belting (2011) that gave me the answer—the presence of the image often denotes an absence so that portraiture in many cultures is associated with death. In the light of this discussion, Kalabai's self-portrait was an act of great courage.

I start with a discussion of Kalabai's self-portrait, a one-off experiment which has not been repeated in her oeuvre or in other paintings in the Gond style which tend to express values that modern urban publics recognise as representative of folk art, that is, they use a pictorial vocabulary

[1] Commonly described as an 'Adivasi' art form, Gond art evolved in the interface between members of the Pardhan Gond community, the traditional bards among the Gonds and Bharat Bhawan, a cultural institution set up in Bhopal by the government of Madhya Pradesh under the stewardship of the artist Jagdish Swaminathan in the 1980s. The Pardhan Gonds, a bardic community well known for their elaborate oral epics, are not known to be a traditional community of painters, though their repertoire of images is clearly inspired by their vibrant mythological universe. In a sense, Gond art is a new, hybrid, folk art form, shaped both by its interaction with metropolitan art worlds and by a mode of learning and production that is craft-based in that new artists learn by copying the work of a master to whom they are apprenticed (Chatterji 2012). I make no distinction between folk and tribal or Adivasi art in this essay.

[2] Abhinavagupta was a 10th-century philosopher who is best known for his philosophical commentaries on the *Natyashastra* and *Dhwanyaloka*.

that is collective, based on myth and are largely unreflexive having being passed down over generations through modes of artisanal learning, precisely to draw attention to the larger political purpose that folklore has served to articulate an alternative Indian aesthetic. Thus, in this chapter, I do not offer a review of the discipline of folkloristics and the way it is practised in India. Instead, I examine the category of folk and the ways in which it is imbricated in certain kinds of discourses about national culture and the reverberations that it has in art practices today. My perspective is shaped by the writings of the early folklorists whose work reflect distinctive regional traditions of scholarship that cannot be generalised to a pan-Indian perspective. The advantage of this orientation is that it allows me to include writings in the vernacular along with mainstream English texts. I tend to focus on Bengali writers, though I have included other important Indian scholars to be able to make a more inclusive argument.

What Is Folk Culture?

Even though the term 'folk' in India did not carry the connotations of an essentialised *volksgeist* (folk spirit) that the German word suggests, it did contribute to the development of a distinctive orientation to the ideology of nationalism. Perhaps it is misleading to speak of ideology in the singular in a country as diverse as India. There have been diverse cultural movements that have contributed to the discourse of Indian nationalism, and it is impossible to describe them all within the scope of one chapter. Instead, my focus will be on a few distinctive voices whose contributions to the discourse on culture are still of considerable significance. Most scholarly reviews of folklore's contribution to projects of nationalism in Europe have tended to focus on its role in legitimising dominant ideas about national identity serving as a hinge between myth and history—ideas that are considered passé today (Fischer 2009; Kirshenblatt-Gimblett 1998). In some parts of India, however, folklore came to articulate an oppositional stance to the culture of the mainstream—to sanskritic culture—and thereby offered hope for India's future and for the reconstitution of its national heritage along more equitable and democratic lines. Thus, Durga Bhagwat (1958) makes a case for the co-presence of India's diverse folk traditions as transformations of ancient literary cultures which must have evolved through the absorption of folk elements. While the same could be said for other countries as well, she says that the Indian case is unique because it is only here that Vedic, non-Vedic and aboriginal cultural streams coexist as living traditions in contradistinction to most other countries whose classical traditions have become extinct. She takes the national motto 'Unity in Diversity' as a premise for research in regional folk cultures and asks that it be demonstrated empirically shorn of its ideological trappings. At the time when Bhagwat was writing her major works, the project of building a culture for the 'imagined community' of the nation was considered to be a responsibility shared by scholars, politicians and administrators alike. However, national culture was not conceived in some synthetic, supranational fashion but as one enabling 'deep horizontal comradeship' across diverse people (Anderson 1983: 16). In contemporary times, this way of conceptualising folklore still finds echoes in cultural fields such as literature and dance and has been repositioned to think about artistic creativity in new and exciting ways. Such repositionings necessarily involve some kind of translation—between languages, disciplines and cultures. It is precisely this kind of cultural translation that inspired the Indologist Ananda Coomaraswamy (1877–1947) to reflect on the meaning of terms such as 'folk' and 'popular' or 'high' and 'cultivated' (Coomaraswamy 1956). In an attempt to find an equivalence for the high art/low art binary in India, he found that their Sanskrit equivalents entailed a redistribution of values between the terms. Thus, *marga* which means 'high', 'spiritual' or 'universal' is opposed to *desi* or 'local' which also designates popular entertainment. According to this distinction, the folk arts, he felt, must be included in the category of marga because they deal with mythological subjects, while sophisticated forms such as the miniature paintings produced in the Mughal courts in medieval India are desi because their subjects are largely secular. For Coomaraswamy, 'marga' and 'desi' do not designate the art and culture of the elite and peasants but refer instead to different modes of orientation. Mythological subjects transcend the topicality of everyday life and, when presented aesthetically, must be universalised (*samanya*) so that the spectators of artworks must detach themselves from the scenes depicted to be able to appreciate their aesthetic qualities (Gnoli 1956). Indeed, Kalabai's self-portrait seems to conform to Coomaraswamy's thesis as it transcends historical time, imaging an idea rather than representing empirical reality.

Folklore's temporality—the disjunction between the contemporary and the contemporaneous—and questions about its relevance as a university-level discipline in the face of a mutating subject matter have led to its dispersal across a range of humanist disciplines which may take up one or more aspects of what was once conceived of as the subject of folkloristics (Kirshenblatt-Gimblett 1998). Delhi University, for instance, does not have a separate folklore department, but subfields such as 'oral literature', 'intangible heritage' and 'folkways and performance' are taught in the departments of literature, history, anthropology, sociology and geography, respectively. Yet the very disjunction that folklore is thought to represent—being *in* the present but not *of* it, as Barbara Kirshenblatt-Gimblett (1998) says—has been used effectively by a host of creative practitioners to reconstitute their artistic practices. I will briefly mention some of the experiments in art, dance, drama and literature that have self-consciously used folkloric ideas, but first a brief account of the historical background of folklore activism is in order. Much of the discussion focuses on Bengal as one of the early regions to experience British colonialism and consequently folkloric activity. Unlike other regions such as Tamil Nadu which also experienced colonial rule very early on, Bengal did not have a distinctive classical heritage that could be used to articulate its cultural heritage, and it was in folk culture that Bengali nationalists sought inspiration for their political beliefs (Blackburn 2003). Two writers who have been particularly influential in bringing ideas of Bengali folk culture to the mainstream are Gurusaday Dutt (1882–1941), a colonial administrator who was exposed to Bengal's grass-roots culture while serving in several rural districts, and Dinesh Chandra Sen (1866–1939) who helped set up the department of Bangla literature in Calcutta University.

Dutt (1990) believed that folk culture *was* the national culture of Bengal—a fact sometimes forgotten by Bengali intellectuals who were influenced by the kind of rational humanism represented by the Bengal Renaissance. It existed in a relationship of unbroken continuity with pre-Aryan Indian civilisation but was also able to absorb the best of what the Aryans had to offer when they came to Bengal. It was able to synthesise both civilisational streams. However, it was only able to express its true significance in certain phases of Bengal's political history. That is when it was freed from the domination of pan-Indian imperial powers, namely the Guptas, Palas and Senas that held sway until about the 12th century. He made a distinction between the 'patroned' or aristocratic and courtly marga (way) and '*sahaja*' marga—the simple and popular way represented by the rural people–village artists whose artistic activity was absorbed into the activities of everyday life.

An interesting feature of the folklore discourse in Bengal is the way in which culture is thought to be a product of self-conscious choice. Folk culture is presented as one among several different forms of cultural orientation and folk artists are thought to shape their work according to the tastes of their audience. Thus, when talking of the art of the Chitrakar, a community of bards who displayed painted scrolls to illustrate the stories that they sung, Dutt says that they reserved the more abstract, spiritual style for their own people in the villages and used the more 'realistic' style when they had to cater to the sophisticated urban elite (Chatterji 2012; Dutt 1990).

Jamini Roy (1887–1972), the artist, made this point even more explicitly. Roy was trained at the Government School of Art in Calcutta and learned to paint in the European style. His contact with nationalist ideas expounded by scholars such as Dutt led him to search for a purely indigenous style and thus to the Chitrakars of his native district, Bankura. Impressed by the sophisticated forms of abstraction that was part of the visual vocabulary of the folk arts in India, he was moved to compare them with the ancient rock arts of Europe that had also inspired the Primitivists' interrogation of art practices in the West.[3] However, he thought that unlike the artists who were responsible for pre-historic cave paintings, the Bengali Chitrakars made a conscious choice in the matter of style. This was because they worked in an environment where they were exposed to more technically mature schools of art. Their work was embedded in a mythic universe which gave shape to their artistic consciousness. He believed that it was only in cultures that had vibrant mythic traditions that art forms could produce abstractions that achieved symbolic significance. He said that without myths, abstractions were nothing but geometrical forms and were not part of the lived experience of creative art. Without myth, art could no longer be considered as part of the lived experience of a community but instead became a matter of individual subjectivity as had happened in Europe after the Reformation when Christianity lost its mythic moorings (Dey and Irwin 1944).[4]

Dinesh Chandra Sen (1986) also thought that Bengali folklore, especially folk literature, could become a source of national revival—a mirror reflecting a future national culture for an India freed from colonial rule. His interest in vernacular literature evolved in the context of colonial rule that assumed that Bangla literature was a modern phenomenon, shaped by Western ideas. Inspired by Rabindranath Tagore, the doyen of Indian culture, he set out to demonstrate that Bengal had a literature that was autonomous, free from the influence of religion and myth, and therefore worthy of study in its own terms by embarking on a project of documenting folk literature (Sen 1986). In 1923, Sen published the first volume of his collection of epic songs from East Bengal called

[3] Unlike Primitivism in avant-garde Western art which while celebrating the formal properties of so-called 'primitive art' still ascribed to it negative qualities on naiveté and lack of technical sophistication, Indian scholars and artists were also interested in the production practices of actual artists and the revival of craft techniques (Mitter 2007; Morphy and Perkins 2006).

[4] Coomaraswamy (1956: 139), by contrast, believed that village people were unconscious bearers of folk memory and that folklore was 'a sort of ark that, in which the wisdom of a former age is carried over (tiryate) the period of dissolution…'. This wisdom is not necessarily understood by the people but forms part of their living tradition.

Mymensingher Gitika (The Ballads of Mymensingh; Sen 1923). It was received with great enthusiasm both for the verbal artistry of the songs and their humanist sensibility that seemed to be free from any religious coloration. Sen attributed this to the location of Mymensingh, a region that was marginal to the political centre of Bengal and thus sheltered from the civilisational influences of Brahminical Hinduism and British colonialism. He felt that the down-to-earth sensibility, individualism and, above all, secular spirit expressed by the protagonists of these songs were markedly different from the classical Bengali literature that was predominantly religious in character. The communities to which the poets belonged, according to Sen, were syncretic in nature, with a mix of Hindu and Islamic influences, but revealed, above all, a folk spiritually that pre-dated the advent of these two religions in Bengal.[5]

Unlike Coomaraswamy, who did not make a distinction between the folk and the aristocratic in the sphere of religion and who was largely concerned with Hinduism, the Bengali folklorists discussed here used the idea of folk syncretism—an amalgam of Hindu and Muslim beliefs and practices—to carve out a distinctive space for Bengali culture within the larger scheme of Indian national culture. Whatever the differences between them, however, they all turned to a particular vision of the folk to articulate a particular nationalist aesthetic and an alternate source of civilisational history that could carry India forward towards independence and *swaraj* (independence or self-rule). It is precisely this idea—that the folk can serve as a repository for indigenous values—that has inspired creative use of the term in more recent times. It is also worth noting that Sen and other Bengali folklorists who valourised a folk ethos that transcended institutionalised religion were very different from scholars and reformers in Maharashtra such as M.G. Ranade or G.S. Ghurye, for instance, who sought to indigenise values such as rationality and liberalism by locating them within Hindu shastric texts (Shaikh 2015).[6] In the next section, I turn to some of the critical experiments in fields such as dance, literature, drama and painting that

---

[5] The ballads were sung chiefly by Muslims and low-caste Hindus (Sen 1988). The Chitrakars, a community that inspired many of Dutt's ideas about folk spirituality, are also largely Muslim, though their traditional narrative repertoire cuts across the mythological universes of both Islam and Hinduism (Chatterji 2012).

[6] Lest we think that this may signal a regional distinction between Bengal and Maharashtra, it is worth noting that the Maharashtrian scholar Ramchandra Chintaman Dhere (2011) discusses the important folk deity Vitthal who was already being glorified as one who could silence the vedas, the smritis and the puranas in the songs of the Bhakti saints in medieval Maharashtra.

have used the folk idiom to both critique and provide alternate sources of history and culture.

Inscribing the 'Folk' in the Arts

In Gurusaday Dutt's formulation, the 'folk' and 'classical' operate as binaries signifying alternative repertoires of practice and orientation. Writing at a time when the 'classical' dances of India were being codified and 'integrated into a nationalist genealogy' in the 1930s, he thought that the folk dances could provide a source for 'national self-expression' as opposed to decadent forms such as nautch as kathak was then called (Dalmia 2006: 158). Mahua Mukherjee (2004), a dancer trained in the bharatanatyam style, though more famous for her attempts to trace the roots of and codify a classical dance form for Bengal, has sought inspiration from Dutt's writings (Dutt 1954) on dance to try and use folk dance forms such as *chho* and *raibeshe* for a reconstituted classical dance to which she has given the name *goudiyo nritya* after the kingdom of Gaudya in West Bengal. She follows Dutt in thinking that Bengal's 'folk' dances expressed its vitalist ethos but departs from him in blurring the distinction between the folk and the classical. In an argument that seems to resemble that of Coomaraswamy, she finds the traces of an ancient classical dance form in the contemporary folk dances of Bengal. Thus, folk culture becomes the repository for Bengal's cultural heritage forgotten by a newly urbanised elite that was fascinated by all things 'Western'—be it Hindustani music and kathak dance that came to Calcutta from Awadh with its former ruler Wajid Ali Shah exiled to Bengal by the British or European literature and drama–literary forms brought in by the British themselves.

The turn to folk culture to source indigenous values is prominent in the field of drama as well, especially in the 1970s and 1980s when there were concentrated efforts to re-energise urban theatre by using the performative potential of folk forms to escape the naturalistic conventions of the proscenium stage. Although experimental use of such forms was not new as the Indian People's Theatre Association had been advocating their use to spread political messages to the masses since its inception in the 1940s, it was through the mediation of Brechtian theatrical techniques that folk forms made their entrance on the urban stage. Important dramatists such as Habib Tanvir (1923–2009), Vijay Tendulkar (1928–2008) and Girish Karnad (b. 1938) used some forms of folk theatre such as *nautanki* and *nacha* to address contemporary sociopolitical issues. Brecht's use of fables and a loose epic structure with performative devices such as masks, chorus and frontal address to break out of the naturalistic tendency of verisimilitude could be used to address traditional aesthetic notions such as *sadharikarna* or generalisation, whereby actors were supposed not to identify too closely with the overall personalities of the characters they were enacting but use their roles to convey an idealised depiction that allowed for the transcendence of topical time and space and enabled a universalistic humanist critique that was not confined to a restrictive view of history (Dalmia 2006).

If folk forms were deployed to create an indigenous idiom for Indian theatre and debunk the naturalistic conventions as tired Western imports, literary experiments with the novel by Bengali authors such as Mahasweta Devi (1926–2016) seemed to be doing the opposite by providing a naturalistic frame to interpret medieval narratives in Bangla such as the *Chandimangal Kavya* authored by Mukundaram Chakrabarti. *Vyad Kanda* or *The Book of the Hunter*, a novel written by Mahasweta Devi (2002), is a fictional re-inscription of the epic poem eulogising the goddess Chandi. Mahasweta Devi is one of India's foremost novelists whose powerful fiction brings together Adivasi or tribal history with that of colonial and post-colonial subalterns. She emphasises the role of story, rumour, myth and legend to articulate the unwritten histories of India's early inhabitants (Spivak 2002). The *Chandimangal* consists of a series of stories about the different incarnations of the great goddess. The sequential order in which the stories are presented reveals the gradual expansion of goddess worship as she acquires converts first among the wild animals, then among forest dwelling tribal communities and finally in the wider society with converts from high Hindu castes (S. Sen 1975). The historically accurate description of the different communities that were settled in Kalketu's kingdom, the life-like sketches of the protagonists and the human voices of the animal supplicants, supposedly a political allegory on the social effects of the Mughal invasion of Bengal (D.C. Sen 1986), were some of the features that attracted Devi to Mukundaram's text. She seeks inspiration from the detailed description of the social environment of the human protagonists[7] in Mukundaram's work to use myths to create fictionalised histories to empower subaltern groups.

If traces of a pre-Western realism can be found in Mukundaram's detailed descriptions of the forest environment and tribal communities of medieval Bengal by Mahasweta Devi in her creative search for literary expression, it was the opposite value of transcendence that the painter Jagdish Swaminathan saw in tribal and folk art. It is fitting that I end my chapter with a discussion of Swaminathan's thoughts on what he called 'numen', the reflection on the sacred in Gond art, an example

---

[7] This is precisely the definition of naturalism in literature (Dalmia 2006).

of which was mentioned in the introduction. What Swaminathan saw in Gond art that inspired his own work was the way in which these folk artists were able to use pure colour to transcend gross materialism and express a divine presence based on their profound understanding of their mythological universe. Rather than thinking of colour as an attribute of objects that occupied pictorial space, they thought of colour as organising the pictorial field, creating an alternate conceptual landscape in which a few archetypal figures could be used to express a humanistic spirituality that transcended historical time. Interestingly, Swaminathan's reflections on mythic time might well have been influenced by his reading of the anthropologist Claude Levi-Strauss as it may have been by currents in avant-garde Western art.[8] The work of Levi-Strauss allowed him to think of Gond art, located in the primordial time of myth, with his own humanist vision and to think of them as contemporaries, occupying a time that was continuous and synchronic in which both kinds of art were structural transformations of each other (cf. Levi-Strauss 1964). In the light of this discussion, Kalabai's self-portrait no longer seems an aberration within the larger Gond tradition. Instead, we can think of it as located within a spacious present in which it coexists with Swaminathan's work. But are there models that Kalabai may have sourced for such a novel depiction? At the time when Kalabai painted her self-portrait, she also drew powerful images of the river Narmada in anthropomorphic form—a face, mouth open to disgorge a stream of water, hair awry, much like the depiction in the portrait. As I have already mentioned, these paintings were radical departures from Kalabai's conventional repertoire. These paintings occurred at a time when Kalabai was staying at the Crafts Museum in Delhi and had the opportunity to interact with folk artists from other parts of India, more specifically Chitrakars, who are famous for depicting scenes of natural disasters in anthropomorphic form. The Chitrakar images are part of a larger story that represents natural disasters as signs of the divine play (*lila*) of the goddess. The face disgorging water then is not only an anthropomorphic depiction of the river in spate but also the face of the goddess who bears witness to her own lila, reminding recalcitrant devotees of her presence (Chatterji 2014). In a thoughtful introduction to a work on masked rituals in India, David Shulman (2006) says that what you see stares back at you. The eye does not merely look outward at an external world but also inward and sees itself. The self is mirrored in the eye and becomes visible, revealed from within so that the act of seeing

[8] Alfred Gell (2013) shows how the idea of duree or temporal continuity in which change can be thought of as a kind of structural transformation rather than historical discontinuity may be an important intellectual current in the modernists epoche reflected not just in art but in philosophy and anthropology as well.

becomes a way of inhabiting the self. Shulman's story is sourced from the *Chandayoga Upanishad*, part of India's ancient textual tradition, a tradition to which Kalabai has no direct access. Yet her painting, a face surrounded by a halo of hair through which its miniature replica can be glimpsed, captures the suggestion of the multiple surfaces through which the self may come to view itself, the act of painting understood to be a way of drawing the self out on to a surface.[9] As Coomaraswamy and others suggest, the narrative repertoires of bardic and artisinal communities may well be repositories for philosophical ideas that are accessed not only through stories but also in other repertoires of folk practice. From this perspective, the 'folk' suggests not so much an imbrication with the local but an orientation that is open to other regions of thought and expression, stretching back into the past and looking forward towards a future that is only dimly perceived in the reflecting surfaces of its diverse expressions.

References

Anderson, Benedict. 1983. *Imagined Communities: Reflections on the Origin and Spread of Nationalism*. London: Verso Books.

Belting, Hans. 2011. *An Anthropology of the Image: Picture, Medium, Body*. Princeton, NJ: Princeton University Press.

Bhagwat, Durga. 1958. *An Outline of Indian Folklore*. Mumbai: Popular Book Depot.

Blackburn, Stuart. 2003. *Print, Folklore and Nationalism in Colonial South India*. Delhi: Permanent Black.

Chatterji, Roma. 2012. *Speaking with Pictures: Folk Art and the Narrative Imagination in India*. Delhi: Routledge.

———. 2014. 'Event, Image, Affect: The Tsunami in the Folk Art of Bengal'. In *Suffering, Art, and Aesthetics*, edited by Ratiba Hadj-Mussa and Michael Nijhawan, 75–98. New York, NY: Palgrave Macmillan.

Coomaraswamy, A.K. 1956. 'The Nature of Folklore and Popular Art'. In *Christian and Oriental Philosophy of Art*, edited by A.K. Coomaraswamy, 130–43. New York, NY: Dover.

Dalmia, Vasudha. 2006. *Poetics, Plays and Performances: The Politics of Modern Indian Theatre*. New Delhi: Oxford University Press.

Devi, Mahasweta. 2002. *The Book of the Hunter* (translated from Bangla by Sagaree and Mandira Sengupta). Kolkata: Seagull Books.

Dey, Bishnu and John Irwin. 1944. *Jamini Roy*. Calcutta: Indian Society of Oriental Art.

[9] I am grateful to Anirudha Raghavan for drawing my attention to this text.

Dhere, Ramchandra Chintaman. 2011. *The Rise of a Folk God: Vitthal of Pandharpur*. Translated by Anne Feldhaus. New York, NY: Oxford University Press.

Dutt, Gurusaday. 1954. *The Folk Dances of Bengal*. Edited by Ashok Mitra. Calcutta: Birendra Sahay Dutt.

———. 1990. *Folk Arts and Crafts of Bengal: The Collected Papers*. Calcutta: Seagull Books.

Fischer, Michael M.J. 2009. *Anthropological Futures*. Durham, NC: Duke University Press.

Gell, Alfred. 2013. 'The Network of Standard Stoppages'. In *Distributed Objects: Meaning and Mattering after Alfred Gell*, edited by Lian Chua and Mark Elliot, 88–113. New York, NY: Berghan.

Gnoli, R., trans. 1956 (1985). *The Aesthetic Experience According to Abhinavagupta*. Varanasi: Chowkhamba Sanskrit Series.

Jariwala, Kapil. 2010. 'Introduction'. In *The Indian Portrait*, edited by Rosemary Crill and Kapil Jariwala, 11–17. Ahmadabad: Mapin.

Kirshenblatt-Gimblett, Barbara. 1998. 'Folklore's Crisis'. *Journal of American Folklore* 111 (441): 281–327.

Lawrence, D.P. 2005. 'Remarks on Abhinavagupta's use of the Analogy of Reflection'. *Journal of Indian Philosophy* 33: 583–599.

Levi-Strauss, Claude. 1964. *Totemism*. Translated by Rodney Needham. London: Merlin Press.

Mitter, Partha. 2007. *The Triumph of Modernism: India's Artists and the Avant-Garde 1922–1947*. New Delhi: Oxford University Press.

Morphy, Howard and Morgan Perkins. 2006. *The Anthropology of Art: A Reader*. Oxford: Blackwell Publishers.

Mukherjee, Mahua. 2004. *Gaudiyo Nritya*. Calcutta: The Asiatic Society of Bengal.

Sen, Dinesh Chandra. 1923. *Mymensingher Gitika* (The Ballads of Mymensingh). Calcutta: University of Calcutta Press.

———. 1986. *History of Bengali Language and Literature* (lectures delivered at Calcutta University in 1909). Delhi: Gyan Publishing House.

Sen, Sukumar, ed. 1975. *Kavikankan Mukundaram's Chandimangal*. Delhi: Sahitya Akademi.

Shaikh, Juned. 2015. 'Imagining Caste: Photography, the Housing Question and the Making of Sociology in Colonial Bombay, 1900–1930'. In *The Visual Turn*, edited by Sandra Freitag, 94–117. Oxon: Routledge.

Shulman, David. 2006. 'Introduction'. In *Masked Ritual and Performance in India: Dance, Healing and Performance*, edited by David Shulman and Deborah Thyagarajan, 1–16. Ann Arbor, MI: University of Michigan Press.

Spivak, Gayatri Chakravarty. 2002. '"Telling History": Gayatri Chakravarty Spival Interviews Mahasweta Devi'. In *Chotti Munda and His Arrow*, edited by Mahasweta Devi and translated by Gayatri Chakravarty Spivak, ix–xxviii. Kolkata: Seagull Books.

Swaminathan, J. 1987. *The Perceiving Fingers: Catalogue of Roopankar Collection of Folk and Adivasi Art*. Bhopal: Bharat Bhavan.

3

Religious Violence
A Sociological Perspective

Ronie Parciack

For Asma Agbarieh-Zahalka

Violence and the Question of Religious Settings

The multitude of interpretations and debates on 'religious violence' are enigmatic and concomitantly saturated with blind spots. The concept of religious violence has been dealt with by a variety of methods and approached from a whole spectrum of theological, philosophical and doctrinal perspectives. It covers a large discursive span beginning with the issue of theodicy[1] but simultaneously, in a way subverting the premises encompassed by theodicy, sets in motion a secularised, human, sociological perspective that denies any metaphysical setting and deciphers it as an imagined backdrop that can be employed to ignite violence between human societies. The question of authority—foundationalism, in Derridean terms—mediates and validates these acts.

---

[1] Wendy Doniger-O'Flaherty (1976) opens her book *The Origins of Evil in Hindu Mythology* with the question of theodicy. Drawing on C.S. Louis and John Hick, she addresses the collision between the notions of omnipotence and 'goodness' ascribed to the divine authority and the presence of evil (Doniger, i).

By 'the question of authority', I refer to the key asset of religious systems: an ultimate, singular and stable source of authority that endows all layers of reality, whether metaphysical or empirical, with significance and validation. It is noteworthy that such theorisation has been made within monotheistic–transcendental frameworks[2] that are anchored (on orthodox planes) in a single unequivocal authority (god) which is trans-spatial and trans-temporal, and binds both individual subjects and the social fabric. The ultimate, indisputable singularity of this authority was deciphered in the modern era as the ultimate source of violence. Following Søren Kierkegaard (2006 [1843]), Immanuel Kant (1991: 43), Emmanuel Levinas (1971: 4) and Jacques Derrida (1967: 228), the contemporary philosopher Hent de Vries reads transcendental violence as a paradigmatic precondition for any form of violence, whether empirical, historic, psychological or physical. Violence is both a transcendental ideal and an empirical reality (De Vries 2012 [2002]: 41–42).

The transcendental/monotheistic setting is considered prone to violence because of its non-sharable singularity. In the empirical–social plane, monotheistic traditions stress the exclusiveness of god's chosen people, which creates a structured hierarchy of supremacism and a symbolic division separating god's people from all others, and more broadly differentiates the pure from the impure. Furthermore, a violent ritualism embedded in the trope of 'cutting a covenant' between God and the chosen community forms the nexus between violence, the sole authority and the subordinated community and subject (Drake 2013; Schwartz 1997: X, 5–6, 10, 75; Timmer 2013; Trisk 2011). Violence is thus embedded in the philosophical and metaphysical premises of religious systems, whether overt or covert. As Kant argued, the origin of supreme power 'is not discoverable by the people who are subject to it' (quoted in Trainor 2006: 769).

The mistaken corollary to monotheistic/transcendental cultures is that polytheistic systems such as the ones prevalent in contemporary India and throughout South Asian history exude tolerance and non-violence because there are a multitude of gods (i.e., sources of authority) and a deep-rooted ontological decentralisation. However, it would be wrong in any case to ascribe violence to the structure of religious systems: despite the unequivocal structure (at least on orthodox planes) of monotheistic systems, it is impossible to continuously link violence

---

[2] I prefer this term over 'Abrahamic religions', as it stresses the metaphysical premises of the monotheist religions and their aspiration for a singular locus of authority—and not their shared origin.

to its single source of authority. Moreover, polytheistic systems are not the polar opposite of monotheism; rather, the religious, theological, mythical and epistemic foundations of South Asian religious traditions reveal some significant similarities to non-polytheistic traditions as regards the issue of violence.

Which South Asian symbolic and religious assets could serve as a backdrop for inherent violence? One example is what David Shulman (1986) termed the 'cosmological structure' in the early vedas which bases creation on sacrifice (such as in Ṛg-Veda 10: 90). Violence is thus ingrained in vedic metaphysics. The violent course of human history also resonates in additional Brahminic notions such as the natural course of *saṃsāric* existence associated with the *Upaniṣadic* tradition, and the cyclic perception of deterioration and enhanced destructiveness of *Yugas* associated with *purāṇic* traditions.[3] The acknowledgement of the inevitability of violence underlies epic literature (e.g., the ultimate wars in the Mahābhārata and Vālmiki's Rāmāyaṇa) as well as the models of Kṣatriyas in classical Brahminism. Examples include Rāma and his archetypic war against Rāvaṇa,[4] or Arjuna standing in the liminal space of Kurukṣetra/Dharmakṣetra doubting whether violent acts are *dharmic* (and in this sense, religious) and whether the outcomes of violence should lead to refraining from war.[5] Kṛṣṇa's preaching in the Bhagavad-Gītā constitutes a comprehensive paradigm for religiously validated violence, which is seen as a comprehensive protection of the world orders. Violence, in this context, involves a metaphysical cognisance (of the world, of the self), as well as actions adhering to the cosmic order and a devotional frame oriented towards the ultimate, trans-empirical end (Bhagavad-Gītā 2: 34, in Theodor 2010: 85).

Violent acts are thus deciphered as part of a dharmic life, a foundational element that religions signify through cosmic and metaphysical and social devices. In modern times, violent acts have been validated and legitimated in the Indian Hindu-nationalist discourse and the

[3] In this sense, the cyclic perception of time may parallel the fall from Paradise in transcendental religions (Doniger 1976: 17).

[4] According to common understanding, Rāma stands for non-violence due to the fact that he does not fight Bharata to restore his position and heir. But see Pollock's differentiation between Rāma's 'brothers' and demonised 'Others' (Pollock 1993: 282–83).

[5] Notably, it is important to relate to a common distinction regarding the source of evil. Doniger argues that Christianity has always distinguished 'natural evil' from 'moral evil', whereas within Brahminic backdrop both are perceived as aspects of the same phenomenon (Doniger 1976: 6).

ways the South Asian ancient community was imagined as a modern nation.[6] The power ascribed to violent acts to preserve the world order should not be underestimated. However, modern sociology takes a perspective based on humanist and secularised thought that excludes the notion of a transcendental authority from signifying systems and stresses the role of human societies and their contemporary power hubs to account for violence.

Towards the Politic: The Modern State and the Sources of Institutional Violence

The issue of violence is closely linked to questions of power. The mutual dependence of power and violence makes violence a twin to the political. Power hubs structuring and dominating the social world thus form the primary institutions channelling violence in human societies. The prime institution in the contemporary global world—the nation state— is therefore the main agent in the institutionalisation of violence in modern societies. Violence by the nation state is commonly considered secular, since nationalism is believed to be rooted in the collapse of religious systems, and thus empirical power interests are generally deciphered as detached from any transcendental framework and mainly as a means to achieve stability of both pre-modern and modern political frames (like the ruler in Machiavelli's *The Prince*). However, the modern nation state is not only signified through empirical frames despite the modern aspiration to detach religion from the state (van der Veer and Lehmann 1999: 3). Rather, state power symbolically links the political to the metaphysical.

Religious aspects can be embedded in state power in several ways: (a) through an essentialist quality embedded in the idea of the nation, (b) through the stance of the sovereign ruler and (c) through the authority to legislate and thus to form the social world. The essentialist premise of nationalism sees the nation as an essence that is above the temporal; thus, nationalism forms the metaphysical web in the global structure. All nations differ from all others and thus the nations can be hierarchised along 'internal' and 'external' lines and, as influenced by idealism and German romanticism, by purity and impurity (Fichte 1968; White 2005). In the Indian context, the Brahminic conceptualisation of alterity as the impure *mleccha* (people outside the

---

[6] See G.B. Tilak's famous use of the Bhagavad-Gītā as an authorisation of violence (Sharma 2002: 209).

Aryan-Sanskritic culture) also echoes this ritualistic/religious dimension within the allegedly 'secular' idea of the nation.

As regards the status of authority, Derrida placed the (earthly) ruler and god on the same level with regard to their most extreme gestures. He compared miracles (god's doing) to a state of emergency (the ruler's doing). Both dominate and delineate daily life and extend beyond it. Both manifest and embody the highest power and authority, and thus violence, that links the empirical with the metaphysical. Despite Rousseau's ideal of civil religion and the aspiration to fulfil it through the establishment of civil society and democratic mechanisms within the modern nation state, the modern nation state is the mirror of the religious in the sense that it functions as an all-signifying principle, lays the groundwork for a dogmatic life and frames the individual subject as well as the social space. 'No doubt', as Trainor (2006: 770) puts it,

> The foundation of the authority of law and government is 'mystical' in the sense that the term definitely connotes a 'deep' quest into the true meaning or essence of our subjectivity (as individuals and as participants in the general will or in the life of civil society as a collective subject) and of our own self.

In contrast to the image of modern democracy as the product of the Enlightenment, and as the incorporation of a set of liberal values in the fabric of modern social worlds, all state frameworks draw on their total, all-signifying potency ascribed primarily to religious systems ('traditional religion', as van der Veer and Lehmann 1999 called it to differentiate it from the framework of the modern state). Sovereign, all-signifying political authority taps religious dimensions as well as violence. This may conflict with van der Veer's earlier claim that the model of religious nationalism (referring to India and Israel) is exceptional,[7] and prompts a more nuanced reading of nationalism/citizenry discourses.[8]

Religious Nationalism: The Indian Case

The nation state of modern India emphasises a citizenry/nationalist discourse in which Indian nationhood is derived from Brahminic

---

[7] Among the new religious nation states are Iran, Sudan, Afghanistan, Algiers, India and Israel (Baber 2000: 62).

[8] Shani (2010) lists a number of citizenry discourses among which citizens may fluctuate: liberal, republican, ethno-national and, finally, the 'non-statist'.

components. The core of the Hindu-nationalist ethos is the Hindutva ideology (as termed by V.D. Savarkar 1923)[9] that defines Indian territory as a sacred geography seen as a divine incarnation (Goddess Bhārat Mātā—Mother India) and endows Hinduism with a supremacist authority to underscore India's social and symbolic capital (Bhatt 2001: 94–99). This discourse crystallised in pre-sovereign British India and culminated in the 1947 partition, which Ishtiaq Ahmed (2002: 10) considered to be the source of a prevalent 'pathological politics', namely communal dynamics based on violence, rigid demarcations, exclusion and subordination that shaped sovereign India's international relationships (particularly vis-à-vis Pakistan) as well as domestic politics, and especially affected groups identified by religious categories (an 'objectification of communities' in the terminology of Thomas Blom Hansen 1999: 65). The modern Indian nation state can be broadly seen as an ethnic democracy with a Hindu majority that hostilely positions itself (with ample assistance from institutions such as the RSS, VHP, Shiv Sena and others) against all 'Others', first and foremost of which are Muslim communities, Christians, Sikhs and others. Hinduism, as Vinay Lal (2009: 8–9) argued, has undergone a process of 'masculinisation' or as Sikata Banerjee (2012) termed it 'muscularisation' defined as strength, that is, violence.

Hindutva is not the sole citizenry discourse in India;[10] however, it became dominant with the powerful rise of the Hindu right as of the 1980s, with peaks such as the *Rāmjanmabhūmi* campaign, the demolition of Babri Masjid in 1992, the Gujarat riots in 2002–03, the Batla House encounter (2008), and endless cases of communal violence that have further kindled mutual aggression. These communal tensions were acerbated in debates over concrete capital (the issue of affirmative acts and quotas), symbolic capital (questions over political participation) and in the aftermath of the serial terror attacks on major Indian cities (Mumbai in 2003, 2006, 2008 and 2011; New Delhi in 2008; Varanasi in 2006 and 2010; Jaipur in 2008; and Ahmedabad in 2008) and symbolic emblems, including an attack on the Indian Parliament in 2001. The assumed or actual involvement of Islamic terrorists or terrorists

[9] Indian nationalism is not a monolith, and Hindutva is not the sole discourse; modern India is constitutionally defined as a secular democracy; socialist ethos prompted especially during the Nehruvian decades.

[10] Indian democracy is considered as a flexible mechanism offering multiple notions of citizenship among which citizens may fluctuate: Shani (2010) lists four: liberal, republican, ethno-national (Hindutva) and the discourse of the non-statist.

allegedly supported by the Islamic state of Pakistan further contributed to communal hostility and enhanced Islamophobic images in mainstream media (Anand 2005).

Communal violence has thus become synonymous with religious violence. But is this correct? Talal Asad (1993: 116) resents the tendency to separate religion and sociopolitical power, and argues that it is the product of the Western/modern binary division between 'spirit' and 'matter'. Simply stated, this is the way religions function in the social space. However, modern social space tends towards a strict categorisation and an institutional, formal setting. Therefore, religious violence in contemporary India has been mainly studied on 'concrete', sociopolitical planes or symbolic spheres (representational mechanisms and mainstream mass media) with regard to formal Hindu–Muslim relationships. Most studies have tended not to recognise states of ambiguity, multiple belongings or a refusal to adhere to formal identity categorisation that may offer a more nuanced reading of religious–political planes. The multiplicity of religious world(s) in the Indian here and now thus encounters epistemological blind spots.[11]

But the adherence to strict identity categorisation is misleading, and no less deceptive is the nexus between institutionalised politics and mainstream mass media. Mainstream media, whether controlled directly by political mechanisms such as censorship and state broadcasting authorities (Farmer 2009) or indirectly through market forces, tends to emphasise dominant, hegemonic ideologies. The important studies on communal representations through hegemonic state apparati—mainly state television (Rajagopal 2001) and mainstream cinema—and those devoted to relatively marginal industries such as the cassette culture (Manuel 1993) and the video revolution (Brosius 2005)[12] exemplify the strong ties between mainstream mass media, market forces, social elites and institutionalised politics. Yet other voices have scarcely been heard.

The third millennium marked the advent of new, accessible, low-cost digital media technologies that paved the way for a radical transformation in the agency and participation of minority, underprivileged and

[11] Notably, some cases of multiplicity of denominators have also served for the re-establishment of single significance—see Jaffrelot's (2011: 58) notion of 'strategic syncretism' or the debate made by Shail Mayaram (2012) about violence and syncretism.

[12] I consider it 'mainstream' as Brosius' (2005) work helped understand the links between the rise of Jain Studios and that of the BJP.

underrepresented groups in the Indian mediascape. Through new and low-cost and non-regulated media, counter hegemonic stances can be voiced in the open, and new studies may address these planes and cure the 'epistemological blindness' these informal arenas suffer from. The future of research, as I see it, does not lie in the formal impact of the state through hegemonic state apparati but rather in contending arenas and frames and primarily at the vernacular level of the sociopolitical order (as defined by Michelutti 2008: 1) on the provincial (Gold 2015) and non-scriptural (Hasnain 2008) and on peripheral discourses and informal media channels.

Stated succinctly, these arenas can (a) contribute to the awareness of a radicalisation of violent trends and demands that the formal discourse does not allow, (b) provide testimonies of shared or liminal spaces that the formal state discourse is unaware of, but they can serve to prompt narratives resisting the binary and 'pathological politics' and (c) contribute to a rewriting of religious histories, including the discourse of religious nationalism from 'Hindu', 'Muslim' or shared perspectives.

Towards a Non-state Sociology

The example below provides a brief example of informal media and the way they can voice highly powerful trends regarding religious violence in India and specifically in the disputed locus of Ayodhyā. The importance of Ayodhyā derives from the stance of the Rāmāyaṇa as an establishing ethos underpinning Hindu nationalism and its sharp communal denominations: this is the kingdom from which Rāma was expelled and to which he returned to set up his utopian rule of Rāma Rājya—an authoritative paradigm of ideal rule. Ayodhyā is not only a symbolic utopian arena, but since the 1992 demolition of the Babri Masjid, it also denotes a traumatic site that governments officially work to pacify. The tendency to divorce potential clashes in this site from state power institutions echoes clearly in the Indian here and now: in late December 2015, the *Indian Express* reported that VHP leaders together with Rāma *bhakts* from Gujarat and Rajasthan transported 35 tons of pink sandstone to herald the projected reconstruction of Rāma's temple in Ayodhyā's *Rāmjanambhūmi* (birthplace of Rāma).[13] The activists denied they had any support from the central BJP-led government.

---

[13] http://indianexpress.com/article/cities/lucknow/ayodhya-supply-of-stones-will-put-pressure-on-centre-to-build-ram-temple/ (accessed on 11 February 2016).

Yet informal discourse can not only shed light on the specific discourses that counter state official stances but also challenge the authority and power of the state, its institutions and symbolic capital.

New Media in Ayodhyā: The Informal Discourse on Divine Presence and Human Violence

I visited Ayodhyā and collected the primary sources for this study in local bazaars in late 2012. More than 20 years after the demolition of Babri Masjid, Ayodhyā is a pilgrimage destination mainly for Hindus who climb the congested alleys leading from the main road to the birthplace of Rāma (Rāmjanmabhūmi), where the fallen Babri Masjid stood. Rāmjanmabhūmi is now a secluded military zone, surrounded by barbed wire fences and armed guards. Like other pilgrimage sites, local bazaars are institutionalised around the site and sell goods targeted at pilgrims, including versions of the Rāmāyaṇa, wooden Rām sandals, candies to ritually mark the accomplishment of their pilgrimage, ritual musical instruments (cymbals) and piles of Hanumān's weapons (gadā) in deep saffron. Above all, video compact discs (VCDs) and thin printed booklets are on sale in many stalls that become more conspicuous and louder as the visitors climb up the 700 m to the top of the hill.

These printed and audiovisual texts are all the product of recent developments in the field of digital media and the considerable drop in prices of print and audiovisual production. This has led to new products, new participants and actors who take stances that cannot be expressed in mainstream media, and currently stake an unprecedented claim on the Indian mediascape. These texts function as new oral traditions or new purāṇas that take on the media's classical social role in forming new communities through the ideologies they convey. These ideologies may, at times, stress extremist positions. My case study consists of a tract entitled *Shree Rāmjanambhūmi ka Raktranjit Itihās* (Swami Pundit Srīrām Gopāl Pāndey 'shārad' n.d.)[14] and several VCDs. The VCDs are not only sold but also screened on public monitors placed above the stalls that repeatedly show the mosque's demolition. VCD songs praising Rām, depicting the demolition within devotional *karseva* (sacred service) frames, promising that the temple will still be

---

[14] The publication house is described as Sāhitya Ratna Prakāshak ('the treasures of literature'), Pundit Dvārika Prasād Śivgovind Pustakalay (the library of Pundit Dvārika Prasād Śivgovind), Kotwali ke sāmne (opposite the central police station), Śrī Ayodhyā ji (Ayodhyā).

rebuilt, are played loudly. The VCDs constitute the pilgrims as well as the spectators as *karsevaks* involved in the demolition and ensuring the future construction of Rām's temple. The utopian design of the temple, often displayed in the Hindu right's hubs and representation arenas, is superimposed on the figures of pilgrims in the VCDs (*Ramji ka Mandir, Ram Sub Bol Ayodhya main*, both produced by Ambey) and on the sacred landscapes of Ayodhyā.

Through these sights and sounds, the pilgrims become participants in a ritualistic repetition of an establishing and uniting event that becomes a sort of *Rām-Līlā*, re-enacting the demolition publicly through informal, underregulated media. Again, the informal component is crucial here, as officially the state denounced the demolition and condemned it. Notably, the state does not exist in the discourse shaped by this informal media; nor does the 2010 Allahabad High Court verdict or any other state agency or act.

Re-narrating the History of the Lost and Found

Modern/academic historiographic discourse is filled with doubt concerning the Ayodhyā temple/mosque dispute. 'Sacred Centres', as van der Veer (1994: 11) argued, 'are alleged to transcend history, it is clear that over the course of religious history, they are "invented"—"found", as well as "refound" and also "lost"'. Van der Veer claims that the Rāmjanmabhūmi controversy goes back to the time of the British rule (2), but the *Shree Rāmjanmabhūmi ka Raktranjit Itihās* booklet provides new knowledge in the form of a detailed historiography of the place as a distinct arena in which riots occurred long before Babur's time (the booklet mentions Huns, Buddhists and Shakas but states that they never dared touch Rāma's birthplace [10]). After Babur came to the throne, Rāmjanmabhūmi became the centre of clashes between Hindu and Muslim communities, placed mostly (but not always) along the binary Rāma-Rāvaṇa dividing line. *Shree Rāmjanmabhūmi ka Raktranjit Itihās* counts 77 attacks on the mosque, dating from Babur's times onwards: 4 during Babur's rule, 20 under Akbar's, 30 under Aurangzeb's and so on, although in the 1990s, only one karseva attack was conducted (30, 36–51).

The tract constitutes the past through a Hindu-nationalist prism, though detached from the agency and authority of the state. The mosque's demolition is guided by divine authority and is performed and commanded directly by Rāma (4, 60). Through partial, incoherent but detailed information grounded in both empirical and trans-empirical, historical and 'a-historical' layers, a convoluted, enigmatic discourse is formed to single out Rāmjanmabhūmi's enemies—Muslims, as well as contemporary and past rules. Both the past and present tenses enliven Rāmjanmabhūmi as a prolonged ritual of sacred war against formal sociopolitical institutions: past rulers during Babur's time prevented Hindus living outside Ayodhyā to enter it (19), while the contemporary state (i.e., the Central government, local legislative assemblies, the judicial system and the police) is defined as hostile Others acting arbitrarily to prevent bhakts from accessing the holy site (66, 67) and is generally described as forces that are uninterested and ignorant of the importance of Rāmjanmabhūmi (65).

Although it encourages highly hostile stands towards the state and its institutions, in its fragmented and convoluted way, the booklet also constitutes an aperture for restructuring the relationships between local religious communities. Despite structuring the self as Hindu, and the overt hostility towards Islamic rulers and emblems (see the description of the mosque as devoid of minarets [53, 62]), the booklet seems to prompt a discourse of shared spaces. It recounts that the mosque Babur wanted to build could not be erected because the walls collapsed on one another (13) until it became a shared space renamed as pure place (*pāk-sthān*) of Sītā (14, 54). Notably, it is not described as a space that should only be for 'Hindus'. 'The bloody history never wanes', the text concludes on page 45, 'and there is no hope for it to ever cool down—all due to the fact that the English built a wall separating the Hindu *Rāmjanmabhūmi* and the Muslim *Babri Masjid*'. While advancing non-state stances mainly directed at an extremist and violent pole, the informal media also consist of ambiguous ways and traverse the binary boundaries.

References

Ahmed, Ishtiaq. 2002. 'The 1947 Partition of India: A Paradigm for Pathological Politics in India and Pakistan'. *Asian Ethnicity* 3 (1): 9–28.

Anand, Dibyesh. 2005. 'Violence of Security: Hindu Nationalism and the Politics of Representing "the Muslim" as a Danger'. *The Round Table* 94 (379): 203–15.

Asad, Talal. 1993. *Genealogies of Religion: Discipline and Reasons of Power in Christianity and Islam*. Baltimore, MD: Johns Hopkins University Press.

Baber, Zaheer. 2000. 'Religious Nationalism, Violence and the Hindutva Movement in India'. *Dialectical Anthropology* 25 (1): 61–76.

Banerjee, Sikata. 2012. *Muscular Hinduism: Gender, Violence and Empire in Indian and Ireland, 1914–2004*. New York, NY and London: New York University Press.

Bhatt, Chettan. 2001. *Hindu Nationalism: Origins, Ideologies and Modern Myths*. Oxford and New York, NY: Berg Publishers.

Brosius, Christian. 2005. *Empowering Visions: The Politics of Representation in Hindu Nationalism*. London: Anthem Press.

De Vries, Hent. 2012 (2002). *Religion and Violence: Derrida and the Theologico-Political*. Tel Aviv: Resling (Hebrew).

Derrida, Jacques, 1967. *L'Écriture et la Différence* [*Writing and Difference*]. Paris: Éditions du Seuil.

Doniger-O'Flaherty, Wendy. 1976. *The Origins of Evil in Hindu Mythology*. Berkeley, CA: University of California Press.

Drake, H.A. 2013. 'Monotheism and Violence'. *Journal of Late Antiquity* 6 (2): 251–63.

Farmer, Victoria. 2009. 'Nation, State and Democracy in India: Media Regulation and Government Monopoly'. Paper presented at the International Communication Association preconference on India and Communication Studies, Chicago, IL, 19–20 May.

Fichte, Johann Gottlieb. 1968. *Addresses to the German Nation*. New York, NY: Harper & Row.

Gold, Daniel. 2015. *Provincial Hinduism: Religion and Community in Gwalior City*. New York, NY and London: Oxford University Press.

Hansen, Thomas Blom. 1999. *The Saffron Wave: Democracy and Hindu Nationalism in Modern India*. Princeton, NJ: Princeton University Press.

Hasnain, Nadeem, ed. 2008. *Beyond Textual Islam*. New Delhi: Serials Publications.

Jaffrelot, Christophe. 2011. *Religion, Caste and Politics in India*. New York, NY: Columbia University Press.

Kant, Immanuel. 1991. *Kant's Political Writings*. Cambridge: Cambridge University Press.

Kierkegaard, Søren. 2006 (1843). *Fear and Trembling*. Cambridge: Cambridge University Press.

Lal, Vinay, ed. 2009. *Political Hinduism: The Religious Imagination in the Public Sphere*. New Delhi: Oxford University Press.

Levinas, Emmanuel. 1971. *Totalité et Infini–Essai sur L'Extériorité*. Dordrecht: Kluwer Academic Publishing.

Manuel, Peter. 1993. *Cassette Culture: Popular Music and Technology in North India*. Chicago, IL: The University of Chicago Press.

Mayaram, Shail. 2012. 'Syncretism'. In *Encyclopedia of Global Religion*, edited by Roof Wade Clark and Juergensmeyer Mark, 1251–53. Thousand Oaks, CA: SAGE.

Michelutti, Lucia. 2008. *The Vernacularisation of Democracy: Politics, Caste and Religion in India*. New Delhi: Routledge.

Pāndey, Swami Pundit Srīrām Gopāl, 'sharad'. n.d. *Shree Rāmjanmabhūmi ka Raktranjit Itihās* (The Bloody History of Shree Rāmjanmabhūmi). Ayodhyā: Sāhitya Ratna Prakāshak.

Pollock, Sheldon. 1993. 'Ramayana and Political Imagination in India'. *Journal of Asian Studies* 52 (2): 261–97.

Rajagopal, Arvind. 2001. *Politics after Television: Hindu Nationalism and the Reshaping of the Public in India*. Cambridge: Cambridge University Press.

Savarkar, Vinayak Damodar. 1923. *Hindutva: Who Is a Hindu?* Bombay: Veer Savarkar Prakashan.

Schwartz, Regina. 1997. *The Curse of Cain: The Violent Legacy of Monotheism*. Chicago, IL and London: University of Chicago Press.

Shani, Ornit. 2010. 'Conceptions of Citizenship in India and the "Muslim Question"'. *Modern Asian Studies* 44 (1): 145–73.

Sharma, Arvind. 2002. *Modern Hindu Thought: The Essential Texts*. Oxford and New York, NY: Oxford University Press.

Shulman, David. 1986. *Chapters in Indian Poetry*. Tel Aviv: Broadcast University Press (Hebrew).

Theodor, Itamar. 2010. *Exploring the Bhagavad Gita: Philosophy, Structure and Meaning*. Surrey: Ashgate.

Timmer, Daniel. 2013. 'Is Monotheism Particularly Prone to Violence? A Historical Critique'. *Journal of Religion and Society* 15: 1–15.

Trainor, Brian T. 2006. 'The State as the Mystical Foundation of Authority'. *Philosophy and Social Criticism* 32 (6): 767–79.

Trisk, Janet. 2011. 'The Violence of Monotheism'. *Journal of Theology for South Africa* 140: 73–90.

Van der Veer, Peter. 1994. *Religious Nationalism: Hindus and Muslims in India*. Berkeley, CA: University of California Press.

Van der Veer, Peter and Hartmut Lehmann, eds. 1999. *Nations and Religion: Perspectives on Europe and Asia*. Princeton, NJ: Princeton University Press.

White, Richard. 2005. 'Herder: On the Ethics of Nationalism'. *Humanitas* 18 (1 and 2): 166–81.

4

Contemporary Religiosities

Jacob Copeman and Johannes Quack

Introduction

Warmest congratulations to *CIS* (new series) on its 50th volume! It would be difficult to overstate the distinguished contribution of the journal to not only South Asian studies but also the social sciences and humanities more broadly. *CIS* has facilitated and intensified discussions of many seminal arguments and controversial topics in South Asian studies, one of the most famous being that which went under the heading 'For a sociology of India', as part of which the appropriate approach to 'religion' in South Asia is crucial. We do not seek to provide here a full and fair review but rather one that is perforce partial and selective in the extreme and which seeks to give a sense of 'where we have got to and where we are going' in the study of contemporary religiosities and the specific role of *CIS* therein. Since both authors conduct ethnographic research in India, and given space constraints, this article will train its sights there.

In certain of its earlier articles, a problematic (implicit) equation was drawn between India and Hinduism.[1] This equation connected to academic debates concerning whether or not there is a single system

[1] Probably due to this bias, a special number was devoted to Muslim communities in South Asia in 1972.

or common feature that unites Indian, or Hindu, society. Moreover, for a long time, 'religion' was assumed to be at the core of Hindu India, feeding into descriptions by Max Weber (1963: 369–70) and others of India as the quintessential land of religion. Additionally, Hindu religiosity was primarily represented on the basis of reified textual and Brahminic sources and associated with caste, kinship and ritual, the most influential contribution arguably being Louis Dumont's *Homo Hierarchicus* (1980). This is the basis of the problematic equation of India with Hindu, and Hindu with a ubiquitous and pervasive caste and hierarchy-based religiosity.

We consider this genealogy to be important and misleading simultaneously, a variation of an ambivalence to which we return throughout this chapter. The contemporary study of religion and society in India cannot be understood without taking into account the influence of this genealogy, exemplified best by the French anthropologist Dumont and his critics (see Madan 1971). Those who must be mentioned here include the first editor of *CIS*, T.N. Madan (2011), who has reflected on Dumont's role and on the roles of Radhakamal Mukerjee, D.P. Mukerji and M.N. Srinivas[2] with respect to Indian anthropology and sociology in general, and *CIS* in particular. A further important figure is the American anthropologist McKim Marriott (1989) and his proposal for an 'ethnosociology' established in counter-distinction to Dumont's all-encompassing structural opposition between (religious/ritual) purity and impurity. For Marriott, this opposition is only one element of a much larger transactional system of 'coded substances', especially with respect to bodily fluids and food (see below and Khare 1998).[3]

Marriott's attempt to understand 'India through Hindu categories' may be understood not only as a continuation of the older *CIS* debate, 'For a Sociology of India', but also as a prelude to later discussions such as Dipesh Chakrabarty's (2000: 16) observation that in his and

---

[2] Such lists of influential forebears are necessarily partial. C.N. Venugopal (2004: 12), for example, listed the following 'Indian writers' who have contributed to the making of the sociology of religion in India: J.H. Hutton, C.V.F. Haimendorf, A.K. Coomaraswamy, B.K. Sarkar, G.S. Ghurye, N.K. Bose, Louis Dumont, Iravaty Karve and T.N. Madan.

[3] Marriott's contribution was in turn critically discussed in *CIS* (1990, vol. 24, issue 2), on which Marriott commented in *CIS* (1991, vol. 25, issue 2). But even if his overall approach was largely rejected, his influence should not be underestimated. Marriott's notion of the 'dividual', for example, had its own career in scholarship on India and beyond, for example, being taken up in the much-celebrated book *The Gender of the Gift* by Marilyn Strathern (1988).

in other postcolonial approaches, 'European thought is at once both indispensable and inadequate'. Debates concerning the deconstruction and reconstruction of an 'Indian sociology' also display an ambivalence, highlighting distinct traditions and the underlying asymmetries in their recognition, on the one hand, and attempts to move beyond the question of the 'Indianness' of academic approaches, which entails an 'India vs the West' lens and the marginalisation of non-Hindu communities, on the other hand.

A related ambivalence can be stated with respect to the importance of studying matters of hierarchy and caste, which were of the greatest importance in the work of both Dumont and Marriott. It comes as no surprise that it is very frequently around these totemic themes that discussions of 'religion' have centred within the last 50 volumes of *CIS*. We have already mentioned the problematic equation of India with Hinduism, and Hinduism with religiosity and caste. These equations have been criticised from various angles. Appadurai (1986) questioned how certain regions of the world are studied through particular tropes with, for instance, research on Africa focusing on 'tribes', and that on India on religion and caste. Also notable within this line of thinking is Inden's (2001) critique, in *Imagining India*, of what he sees as the essentialisation and reduction of India to the themes of religion and Hinduism, with caste at its centre and all of this inherent to the 'Indian mind'.

Moreover, in the wake of Foucault and Said and other post-colonial approaches, the notorious argument for the 'Western construction' of Hinduism, introduced and implemented in India by way of British colonial bureaucratic processes, was formulated.[4] None of the related interventions went uncontested (see, e.g., Bloch, Keppens, and Hegde 2010; Fitzgerald 1996; Lorenzen 2006; and on Inden's *Imagining India*, see in particular the scathing review by Knopf 1992). And although at first blush these are yesterday's debates, they are necessarily kept in mind by the complex, ongoing and often fierce identity politics attached to them—debates that are not restricted to narrow academic circles. Most prominently, intellectuals influenced by the ideology of Hindutva refute arguments about the apparent Western 'invention' of Hinduism. Ever since the 19th century, Hindu intellectuals and sections

---

[4] Initially the term 'Hindu', so the argument goes, was used by colonial rulers as a residual term, under which they categorised most people living on the subcontinent who were neither Christian nor Muslim. Almost none of these 'Hindus' would have classified themselves as such, and some would still not do so.

of the Hindu elite have attempted to establish Hinduism as a 'world religion' and to invalidate religious and cultural differences between groups constituted by them under the label 'Hinduism' in order to position this unified block against others—mainly against Muslims (see Hansen 1996). These political groups stage religion through large public processions (*yatras*) and use every opportunity to accuse their opponents of favouring non-Hindu minorities and therefore of being 'pseudo-secular' (anti-Hindu). At least some Hindu majoritarians[5] thereby attempt to construct Hinduism as a unified religious system followed by a majority of Indians.

According to its Constitution, however, India is a secular nation that upholds the right of citizens to freely worship and propagate any or no religion or faith. Scholarly and public debates address the question of whether 'secularism' is as indispensable and inadequate as the concept of 'religion' seems to be. Certainly, there are ongoing discussions among Indian intellectuals about what kind of 'secularism' would be appropriate for India, if any, and whether religious and non-religious cultural practices are readily distinguishable at all. Some scholars—especially Ashis Nandy (2004) and T.N. Madan (2004: 302)—argue that South Asia's major religious traditions are 'constitutive of society' and therefore that any attempts to delineate a distinct secular sphere along the lines of European societies are highly problematic. Others argue that there is a specific form of Indian secularism based on pre-colonial and colonial distinctions between religious and non-religious social spheres that could serve as a model for other parts of the world (Bhargava 2004: 6). A third group of scholars embrace the secularism imported to India and criticise Nandy and Madan for implicitly siding with the Hindu right (see, e.g., Baber 2006; Nanda 2003).

Turning below to more recent developments in approaches to contemporary religiosities, we will see how some of the ambivalences introduced in this section are reproduced anew, or 'recombined', in them. On the one hand, then, the concerns of classical studies are still very present in the sociology and anthropology of religion in India. There are manifold continuities or spectres of classical works that haunt contemporary projects. On the other hand, contemporary studies have opened new avenues for approaching these concerns and conceptualising them in new ways. Specifically, and in reference to certain strands in our own

---

[5] Members of this body do not necessarily align themselves with the Hindu right—see, for instance, Roberts' (2016: Chapter 4) discussion of M.K. Gandhi's positioning of Dalits as Hindus.

work that connect with them, we call attention to recent approaches to religion that centre on the themes of (a) the maintenance and dissolution of religious boundaries, (b) non-religion/indifference and (c) (bi)instrumentalism.

Some Recent Research and Concerns[6]

Religious Boundaries

As we noted above, classical works tended to equate India and Hinduism. Contemporary studies of religious frontiers, especially works of ethnography that engage with all their complexities, complicate such an equation. Although study of the drawing and questioning of religious boundaries is not new (see, e.g., Oberoi 1994), we want to highlight here how recent work has allowed us to move beyond communal politics and the solidifying of oppositional identities, important though these processes are, and encounter different dimensions of inter-religious life. We identify three key emphases here: those of non-communalism, scalar religiosities and (inter)religious naming. Religion at the frontier is itself ambivalent—it is a site not only of contraries and troubled trafficking of desires and concepts (Das 2012) but also of everyday co-habitation. Analysis of it is, too: matters of caste, hierarchy and ritual remain not only indispensible to our understandings but also misleading when considered only on their own terms and not in relation to larger burdens of belonging and ways in which they might feature in aspirations towards an idea of the (religious) self as otherwise than one is.

Non-communalism: Many would argue that religion in South Asia has become an inherently politicised phenomenon (Riaz 2010), and that transformations in belief and ritual practice are implicated in the emergence of new, aspirational middle and upper middle classes (see, e.g., Brosius 2010). In this context, a problem in the correlation between identity and class is the question of how religion factors into a new kind of Indian modernity. Although there are many different dimensions to this, much has been written on Hindu nationalism as the defining feature of such a modernity. But, while undoubtedly significant, the sensibilities of religiously inclined middle-class Indians are not in some simple way reducible to Hindu rightist views. The distribution of such views and activism is uneven and ambiguous and other identities and

---

[6] We reiterate that this is inevitably coloured by our own preoccupations and concerns and not intended to be exhaustive.

allegiances may overshadow or move them out of the picture, as Gold (2015) makes clear in his work on what it means to live a religious life in 21st-century provincial India (Gwalior). Indeed, the Hindu right organisers we meet in his study are figures of melancholy, who struggle to make their mark. Following from Gold's work, we make the simple, but in fact quite far-reaching, point that Hindu nationalism is both a vital phenomenon and not always a salient one.

Moreover, some of the most significant recent work on communalism has focused as much on its rarity in particular places as on its painful manifestations. Parry and Struempell (2008), for instance, investigate why it occurs in some places and not—or less so—in others, while Roberts (2016), in his ethnography on belonging and conversion to Pentecostalism among Dalit slum residents in Chennai, shows how the diverse religious makeup of families in the slum means that Hindus and Christians cannot subsist there as separate communities, thereby forestalling the sorts of communal conflicts found elsewhere.[7]

Scalar religiosities: Here we proceed from Das' insight that 'religious pluralism is the normal condition in which religious subjectivities are formed'—the analyst's task is to 'track how religious diversity occurs at different scales of social life' (2014: 82). Indeed, recent studies of South Asian religious lives have demonstrated the scalar nature of affiliations, the nature of which might cause the analyst to rescale her own understanding of boundaries. To return to Roberts' (2016) work: set in a time and place of anti-conversion politics and laws, and *against* common sense discourse that sees conversion as relationally damaging and founded on material inducements, we see how on one level religious boundaries are not challenged by these conversions at all. This is because there is an inclusive 'logic of slum religion' that operates according to the relative power of different deities. While basically all gods are recognised as genuine, only some of them are actively worshipped. This selection is often not stable; people routinely abandoned some gods they had heretofore been worshipping and switched allegiance to others across 'scholastic' divides of religious traditions (ibid.: 177–78). The point is whether or not a particular deity is willing and able to address their problems. If unable, their abandonment is perfectly routine. Slum dwellers do not see themselves as choosing between competing systems (Hinduism and Christianity)—they can be

---

[7] Roberts' book joins recent works by Mosse (2012), Henn (2014) and others in forming part of a nascent South Asian focus in the anthropology of Christianity.

described as displaying a 'pragmatic' rather than a 'scholastic religiosity' (Quack 2013).[8] 'Diversity' thus operates under the larger sign of slum religion; and so to return to the problematic of the nature of religious boundaries, at one level there are none, and on another—as we have seen—intra-family religious pluralism acts as a bulwark to communal conflict.

The point is that the lived shifting scales of social life, according to which the convictions and practices of people with respect to religious boundaries can differ in different situations and at different 'levels', need to be mirrored in the scales of analysis. As the classical studies on caste and ritual alluded to above make clear, religious boundaries are often understood to be incontrovertible when it comes to life cycle rituals—inter-religious marriages, for example, are a contentious matter in most of South Asia, and death rituals almost always take place according to the procedures of one's own religious community. Religious boundaries lead people's actions quite differently, however, if we compare formalised rituals with other 'scales' of social life—for instance, the search for healing and succour (see Quack 2017a). Based on research in a Sufi shrine, Bellamy (2011) also employs a scalar analytical shift in arguing for the necessity of reconsidering debates about the nature of religion itself in contemporary India. Her point is that while Muslim saints' shrines differ in various ways across the subcontinent, they have one thing in common in all being places where individuals of all religious backgrounds search for help. For Bellamy, pilgrims of all religious, caste and class backgrounds recognise such shrines as being of the same fundamental type; she therefore suggests that

> Dargāh culture is properly understood as a (religious) culture in and of itself, rather than a culture that draws its forms of authority and practice from Hinduism, Islam, or a syncretic combination of the two. Rather than 'Hindu' or 'Muslim', Indian dargāh culture is South Asian. (Bellamy 2011: 6)

Paying attention to the scalar dimensions of diversity, we suggest, allows us to see religious boundaries in a different way.

---

[8] But while Roberts emphasises what is often called 'pragmatic' religion, this does not mean that for slum dwellers religion is amoral. On the contrary, it is very much about morality and moral reform. (This is important because pragmatic religion is frequently counter-posed to religion understood as a moral phenomenon.)

(Inter)religious naming: Returning to Gold's (2015) work on provincial Hinduism, an interesting sub-theme in it is the semiotic instability of personal names—both of deities and of humans—which sometimes come into view as icons of composite religiosity, as with the name of Shri Pir Saheb Raje Vali, which contains both Islamic and Hindu elements, whose *dargah* in Gwalior is attended by Muslims and Hindus. But at other times and places, the saint's name may become synonymous with exclusive religion: the 'same' saint is known elsewhere by the Hindu name 'Baba Chaitanya Nath', since according to some of his Hindu followers, he was 'really' a Hindu Nath yogi who had disguised himself as a Muslim (Gold 2015: 155; cf. Lee 2015). We also meet male Muslim Ram Lila performers who play female roles in the epic who take on Brahminic names and identities while on tour due to the special reverence Ram Lila actors receive from devotees even when offstage: 'Irfan could play a convincing Sita on stage and a convincing Sanjay on the street' (ibid.: 121–22). Although such slippages result from devotion to craft rather than some kind of soaring ethical statement, it is a devotion that appears to eclipse any pressure exerted by those who would police religious borders, demonstrating hopeful habitation of, or a kind of lived compatibilism between, other religious identities.

Indeed, we suggest here that ethnography and theory of naming practices has emerged as a promising way of opening up other aspects of religious boundaries. For instance, several essays in a recent edited volume on names in South Asia (Copeman and Das 2015) suggest that though the strong association between name and caste or religion is the product of diverse procedures by which group boundaries have been solidified by both their interactions with the state and various kinds of reform movements, caste associations and other mechanisms for removing any ambiguity with regard to the straightforward identification of name with the social group, the semiotic instability, or excess, of the name can allow for different paths. For instance, we may find the intentional production of categorical uncertainty through experimental juxtaposition of different religious elements (Copeman 2015), or simple acts of naming as critique of communal enmity in hate-filled post-partition India and Pakistan (Bruce 2015; cf. Banerjee 2008).

Non-religion/Indifference

If a focus on religious boundaries can complicate the equation found in classical works between India and Hinduism, study of non-religion also allows us to think about religion in India in different terms and thereby loosen the other equation we discussed above—between India and religion. We suggest here that to pay attention to non-religion and religious indifference is once more to both acknowledge and question the importance of religion in India.

Secularism and detachment from forces of religion are of course longstanding concerns in the sociology and anthropology of South Asia. But in the existing scholarship on this region, as elsewhere, secularism is frequently invoked as an abstract intellectual doctrine or in terms of its legal–constitutional status. If anthropology is philosophy with the people left in (Ingold 1992), secularism in India has mostly been analysed with the people left out. This has, however, recently begun to change, with an increasing number of studies seeking to move beyond intellectualised debates in order to access the lived, practical dimensions of secularism. It is worth noting that the studies we gloss here form part of a growing discussion of non-religion globally that seeks to take its manifestations seriously in ethnographic terms (see, e.g., Blanes and Oustinova-Stjepanovic 2015).

In our own work, we have focused our attention on the organised criticism of religion (Copeman and Quack 2015; Copeman and Reddy 2012; Quack 2012a, 2012b), delineating the particularities of rational-ism and non-religion as a way of life. This work has entailed a kind of balancing act between acknowledging the pervasiveness of religion and the prevailing importance of caste without corroborating the frequently unchallenged assumption that all Indians are 'notoriously religious' and only to be understood as *homines hierarchici*. Study of rationalism in the activist mode—for example, its often-mediatised anti-superstition and miracle exposure campaigns (Quack 2012a) and its promotion of body donation as means of enacting materialism and social reform (Copeman and Quack 2015)—has formed the primary subject matter of this research. Yet, if this research goes some way towards redressing the balance, there lies the danger of opposing religion to some unified other in binary terms. We, therefore, suggest an alternative way forward here by highlighting approaches to religion that are more ambivalent, graded and indeterminate.

Based on a combination of ethnographic and biographical approaches, we engaged with people not located at the centre of a reli-gious field, for example, who generally ignore or reject religious beliefs and practices associated with their religious communities (see Quack 2017b). 'Religious indifference' is understood here to be a gradual, tem-poral, situational stance that involves least possible engagement with mainstream religious concerns. In order to illustrate such a stance, we briefly introduce Prakash whose case we view as exemplary in showing how, in situations of seemingly pervasive religion, indifference can be expressed by choosing a way of least possible engagement.[9]

Prakash was born in 1994 and has a brother who is two years younger than him. His parents came from Uttar Pradesh to Delhi, where his father studied at a prestigious college, later becoming a professor at another college as famous as the first. While Prakash says that he neither believes nor practises anything associated with Hindu religion(s), he is ambivalent with respect to the label 'Hindu', accepting it due to his family background: 'My family members are Hindu so I am a Hindu, I was born as a Hindu so that's it'. The family is classified as belonging to the 'Other Backward Class' (OBC) category, but in this particular case, we are dealing with an affluent upper-middle-class family residing in a well-off neighbourhood of New Delhi.

Whenever we asked which personal experiences connected to religion come to his mind when looking back on his life, Prakash answered that he has no idea how to relate his life to something religious. Moreover, the social and political roles of religion in India are not an issue for him. Only when asked directly his opinion on religion does he give an answer—that religion may be both 'good and bad in a way'. But he would immediately add that he 'never really thought much about that'. Such statements clearly show little personal engagement; his answers to such questions generally are ad hoc attempts to deal with a topic not of major concern to him.

We could provide further ethnographic and biographical evidence of his indifference to the religious concerns of his social environment. We want to focus here, however, on those few incidences where Prakash was simply unable to avoid engagement with religious matters. Probably not surprisingly, these occasions were intimately connected with topics highlighted by some of the classical studies of religion in India that we mentioned in the first part of this essay, namely the interrelated topics of food and ritual. First, Prakash narrated a situation when he and some acquaintances, for whom he was working as a cinematographer, stopped to have beef biryani in Old Delhi. Having never eaten cow or buffalo meat in his life, he declined the food because something 'kept mocking, nagging me in the head that I shouldn't. These little things. My grandmother would mind, these things just kept nagging me in the head'. The second case is related to religious rituals, which Prakash considers to be 'stupid and pointless'. His main example here is how

[9] We met with Prakash in August 2013 and September 2016 in New Delhi. For further background on him and the respective study, see Quack (2017b).

after the death of his grandfather two things occurred: pundits had to be paid for elaborate rituals and he and his brother were supposed to shave their heads. Prakash's brother did not want to do this, and his refusal resulted in heated arguments with the grandmother. Prakash did shave his head, although he considered it unnecessary. He thought that his brother made too much of an issue out of it, whereas 'I didn't mind, so I did it'. The difference between the contentious position of his brother and his own more or less indifferent line of least engagement was thereby underlined.

The indifferent stance generally displayed by Prakash is founded upon an underlying attitude of disinterestedness. The question of whether he gets his head shaved or not is not an important one for him—he neither cares to actively promote nor condemns such practices. Rather, he chooses the way of least engagement. While Prakash's brother takes a confrontational anti-religious position, Prakash manoeuvres between both the religiosity of the family members and the pronounced non-religiosity of his brother. Despite these challenges from different sides, Prakash tries to remain 'neutral' and detached from any one single-defined standpoint. Only where this is unavoidable, for example, with respect to rituals and food, does Prakash sometimes find himself in situations where a full detachment is impossible.

Due to his family's accumulated economic and cultural capital, Prakash is able to 'afford' to ignore family-organised religious issues to some degree just as he could 'afford' to not know his caste background until he was 16 years old. In many other scenarios, indifference to religion (and caste) is more difficult to uphold. In pursuing this line of enquiry, then, we must be careful to acknowledge how social position may affect one's ability to remain detached from matters of caste and religious behaviour and belonging. With this preliminary sketch, we hope to have shown a possible way of circumventing the reductive religion vs secular binary. The worm's eye view of the ethnographer allows him or her to approach contemporary religiosities 'from behind', that is, through the eyes of people who consider themselves not religious and who question its all-encompassing pervasiveness, thereby bringing to light different kinds of ambivalences.

Bi-instrumentalism

In a noteworthy *CIS* contribution from 2006, A.M. Shah drew attention to 'a significant recent change' in the domain of sects and Hindu social structure, namely

The involvement of sects in modern, secular, developmental activities: setting up hospitals, schools, colleges, universities and homes for senior citizens, and organising relief work after earthquakes, fires and floods. These activities bring not only the leaders and the laity but also the sect as a whole and the state into closer relationship. They also seem to give a new meaning to religion. (Shah 2006: 244)

Although not as novel as Shah suggests (see, e.g., Watt 2005), it would be true to say that there has been an intensification and transformation of religious service schemes, and also that this 'give[s] a new meaning to religion' to some degree. As one would expect, on the coattails of this intensification has been a renewed scholarly interest in this area. The intensification and diversification of social service engagements that we speak of here hold beyond the Hindu 'sects' discussed by Shah (e.g., on Islam, see Rehman and Lund-Thomsen 2014; on Jainism, see Laidlaw 2007). However, we focus below on those undertaken by guru-led organisations, some of which we might identify as Hindu, others as possessing both 'Sikh' and 'Hindu' characteristics.

To invoke the category of 'religion' as subject and agent in these processes—as both instrumentaliser and instrumentalised—is again at once both indispensable and inadequate. It is inadequate because speaking of religion as a kind of resource, potentially available for varied developmental, state, reformist and other social projects, seems to presuppose a certain understanding of religion (its distinction from politics or culture), and a secular–religious divide that is not unproblematic (Asad 2003). Yet the category remains indispensable. Freitag (1996) has shown how politics and religion were conceptually and ideationally separated from one another via a number of legal and bureaucratic processes of colonial rule. This is not to say that 'religion' remained discretely sectioned off from other domains of social life, but that the theory that it should be was and continues to be current. In light of this, we think that it is possible to speak of instrumental uses of religion without falling into the trap identified by Asad and while keeping in mind the fact that operationalisations of 'religion' are consequent on prior deeds of purification that constitute this mode of operationalisation as the act of bringing separated categories into a particular kind of relation. Moreover, we want to emphasise that the process is one of bi-instrumentalism, or 'double capture', since both entities take on qualities of the other while maintaining independent identities—it is not always clear who is using whom. Plenty has been written about instrumentalisation of 'religion' for political ends, far less on other modes of instrumentalisation of religion and less still on bi-instrumentalism—but this is changing.

Those who instrumentalise 'religion' are far less interested in its articulation than its 'operationalisation'—in its tool-like ability to be put to use to achieve particular ends (Kelty 2004: 548, 555). Instrumentalisation will almost always result in the religion in question being treated as singular, unambiguous and 'generified' (cf. the discussion above on the construction of a unified religious system).[10] We would go so far as to suggest that objectified and applied versions of 'religion' are one of the most significant ways in which religion is conceptualised and enacted in present-day India. At the same time, the institutions and authorities that singularise religious traditions in order to operationalise them do not count either on their own potential to be transformed or indeed made tool-like, via the encounter.

Guru organisations' social service activities, which sometimes substitute for forms of welfare provision formerly associated with the state,[11] are consequent on the harnessing of a relationship of radical asymmetry (*guru seva*, service of the guru) for welfare or development ends. But the transfer at stake is not just that of formerly state operations to non-state actors but also conversely and just as much of logics associated with the domain of *bhakti* to that of governance/development/projects of social reform. An 'authoritarian' aspect of devotional relationships is thus repurposed in order to produce humanitarian or developmental effects—as we briefly show below through a case study of the Sant Nirankaris.[12]

Central here is the idea of the guru as an inclusive singularity (Copeman and Ikegame 2012)—a kind of magnified person who

[10] See, for instance, Copeman (2006) on deployment of simplified Hindu ascetic tropes as a means of promoting body and organ donation.

[11] This can take the form of a kind of outsourcing: for instance, after the 2004 Asian Tsunami, the Indian government assigned the Sant Nirankaris one of the Andaman Islands to administer aid to, and when in 2007 the rate of farmer suicides in Maharashtra could finally be ignored no longer, 'instead of attending to the problems of indebtedness and low infrastructural facilities under which cotton farmers in Vidharbha labour, the ministers [advocated] breathing lessons by Sri Ravishankar and religious discourses by other assorted swamis' (Gupta 2009: 81).

[12] The Sant Nirankari movement forms part of an inclusive reformist tradition that crosses formal Hindu–non-Hindu 'community' boundaries. Along with other likeminded reformist movements, the Sant Nirankaris are connected with and draw inspiration from the *sant* tradition of North India: a loose family of nonsectarian saints, often from lower-caste backgrounds who criticised elaborate upper-caste rituals and practices of idol worship.

'contains' a devotee constituency mobilizable not only for electoral but also developmental purposes. For instance, the recruitment of voluntary blood donors in the country is conducted according to just such a model of mobilisation (Copeman 2009). As the head of the government body, the National AIDS Control Organization (NACO) told us: 'Religion is one of the important factors in India that we must tap for voluntary blood donors'. This reflects the prevalent view among proponents of social change in India—articulated more than a century ago by Swami Vivekananda—that they must pursue their projects through active engagement with its religion. Blood donor recruiters treat gurus' devotees as part of the guru's own expanded personhood, a shortcut method of acquiring blood; the recruitment of one (the guru) constitutes the mass recruitment of his many followers.

Certainly, guru organisations are a resource for NACO and other bodies such as the Red Cross—the Sant Nirankaris account for much as 20 per cent of Delhi's voluntarily donated blood. What ethnography reveals, however, is how gurus and their devotees themselves instrumentalise NACO and others in employing blood donation to define themselves and their internal struggles in becoming new kinds of subjects: (a) Economically disadvantaged devotees who find it difficult to financially contribute to the organisation adopt blood donation enthusiastically because it makes accessible an area of Nirankari collective life (giving) to those to whom it had until that point been problematic. (b) The anonymous conditions of voluntary donation map onto, become coextensive with and a technology to achieve the central theological tenet of universal brotherhood (*sarvbhaumik bhratritva*). (c) Pandya (2016 [2015]) rightly points out that the harnessing of guru organisations as practitioners of government/development may be morally fraught, contentious and go wrong—the demands of bhakti may not accord with those of government and state agencies. In the case of the Nirankaris, we see this not only in the often agitated state of devotees when they are found unfit for blood donation—being declined, say, due to low haemoglobin may be experienced as equivalent to being declared unfit to serve the guru—but also when guru organisations' propensity for one-time mass super-charity events, which we see in the Dera Sacha Sauda devotional order's serial world record accomplishments, falls foul of hospitals' requirement of a smooth and consistent blood supply. Bi-instrumentalism thus acknowledges not only the processes by which 'religion' may be mobilised as a tool-like resource but also that such mobilisations may be marked by instability and disjunctions, and that it is not always clear who is using whom.

Conclusion

We argued that studying 'contemporary religiosities' in India is in many respects an ambivalent undertaking, suggesting that the very use of the concept of religion in India is both 'indispensable and inadequate' at the same time, just as it is the case with respect to its 'Others': the secular, secularism and non-religion. Similarly, the focus on caste, hierarchy, ritual, etc. in the sociology and anthropology of religion in India seems both inevitable and misleading, threatening to represent India through a reified textual, colonial and Brahminic understanding of Hinduism. We argued that classical studies are without doubt crucial points of reference that still influence contemporary work on religion. However, this rich body of work has also been complemented by new perspectives and approaches, as we tried to demonstrate with respect to three themes: religious boundaries, non-religion and indifference, and bi-instrumentalism. These themes question the problematic equation of India with religion and particularly with Hinduism as well as the association between Hinduism and a ubiquitous caste and hierarchy-based religiosity, without ignoring important insights from classic studies which argue for the pervasiveness of religion in general and caste in particular. In all these cases, we hold that declaring something as indispensable and important as well as inadequate and misleading is not problematic as such, but rather a fruitful chance to further reflect about the factors behind such ambivalences.

References

Appadurai, Arjun. 1986. 'Theory in Anthropology: Center and Periphery'. *Comparative Studies in Society and History* 28 (2): 356–361.

Asad, Talal. 2003. *Formations of the Secular: Christianity, Islam, Modernity.* Cultural Memory in the Present series. Stanford, CA: Stanford University Press.

Baber, Zaheer. 2006. *Secularism, Communalism and the Intellectuals.* Gurgaon: Three Essays Collective.

Banerjee, Mukulika. 2008. 'Introduction'. In *Muslim Portraits: Everyday Lives in India,* edited by Mukulika Banerjee. xii-xv. Delhi: Yoda Press.

Bellamy, Carla. 2011. *The Powerful Ephemeral: Everyday Healing in an Ambiguously Islamic Place.* Berkeley, CA: University of California Press.

Bhargava, Rajeev. 2004. *Secularism and Its Critics.* New Delhi: Oxford University Press.

Blanes, Ruy Llera, and Galina Oustinova-Stjepanovic. 2015. 'Introduction: Godless People, Doubt, Atheism.' *Social Analysis* 59 (2): 1–19.

Bloch, Esther, Marianne Keppens, and Rajaram Hegde, eds. 2010. *Rethinking Religion in India: The Colonial Construction of Hinduism*. London and New York, NY: Routledge.

Brosius, Christiane. 2010. *India's Middle Class: New Forms of Urban Leisure, Consumption and Prosperity*. New Delhi: Routledge.

Bruce, Gregory M. 2015. 'Names and the Critique of History in Urdu Literature: From Manto's "Yazid" to Zaigham's "Shakuntala"'. *South Asia Multidisciplinary Academic Journal* (12): 2–19.

Chakrabarty, Dipresh. 2000. *Provincializing Europe: Postcolonial Thought and Historical Difference*. Princeton, NJ: Princeton University Press.

Copeman, Jacob. 2006. 'Cadaver Donation as Ascetic Practice in India'. *Social Analysis* 50 (1): 103–26.

———. 2009. *Veins of Devotion: Blood Donation and Religious Experience in North India*. New Brunswick, NJ: Rutgers University Press.

———. 2015. 'Secularism's Names: Commitment to Confusion and the Pedagogy of the Name'. *South Asia Multidisciplinary Academic Journal* (12): 2–22.

Copeman, Jacob, and Veena Das, eds. 2015. 'On Names in South Asia: Iteration, (Im)propriety and Dissimulation'. *South Asia Multidisciplinary Academic Journal* (12): 2–21.

Copeman, Jacob, and Aya Ikegame. 2012. 'Guru logics'. *HAU: Journal of Ethnographic Theory* 2 (1): 289–336.

Copeman, Jacob, and Johannes Quack. 2015. '"Godless People" and Dead Bodies: Materiality and the Morality of Atheist Materialism'. *Social Analysis* 59 (2): 20–61.

Copeman, Jacob, and Deepa S. Reddy. 2012. 'The Didactic Death: Publicity, Instruction and Body Donation'. *HAU: Journal of Ethnographic Theory* 2 (2): 59–83.

Das, Veena. 2012. 'The Dreamed Guru: The Entangled Lives of the Amil and the Anthropologist'. In *The Guru in South Asia*, edited by Jacob Copeman and Aya Ikegame, 133–55. London: Routledge.

———. 2014. 'Cohabiting an Interreligious Milieu: Reflections on Religious Diversity'. In *A Companion to the Anthropology of Religion*, edited by Janice Boddy and Michael Lambek, 69–84. Malden, MA: Wiley-Blackwell.

Dumont, Louis. 1980. *Homo Hierarchicus: The Caste System and Its Implications*. Revised ed. Chicago, IL: University of Chicago Press.

Fitzgerald, Timothy. 1996. 'From Structure to Substance: Ambedkar, Dumont and Orientalism'. *Contributions to Indian Sociology* 30 (2): 273–88.

Freitag, Sandria. 1996. 'Contesting in Public: Colonial Legacies and Contemporary Communalism'. In *Making India Hindu: Religion, Community, and the Politics of Democracy in India*, edited By David Ludden, 211–34. Delhi: Oxford University Press.

Gold, Daniel. 2015. *Provincial Hinduism: Religion and Community in Gwalior City*. Oxford: Oxford University Press.

Gupta, Dipankar. 2009. *The Caged Phoenix: Can India Fly?* New Delhi: Viking.

Hansen, Thomas Blom. 1996. 'The Vernacularisation of Hindutva: The BJP and Shiv Sena in Rural Maharashtra'. *Contributions to Indian Sociology* 30 (2): 177–214.

Henn, Alexander. 2014. *Hindu–Catholic Encounter in Goa: Religion, Colonialism, Modernity*, Bloomington, IN: University of Indiana Press.

Inden, Ronald. 2001. *Imagining India*. Bloomington, IN: Indiana University Press.

Ingold, Tim. 1992. 'Editorial'. *Man*, n.s., 27 (4): 693–96.

Kelty, Christopher M. 2004. 'Punt to Culture'. *Anthropological Quarterly* 77 (3): 547–58.

Khare, R.S. 1998. 'The Issue of "Right to Food" Among the Hindus: Notes and Comments'. *Contributions to Indian Sociology* 32 (2): 253–78.

Knopf, David. 1992. 'Review of *Imagining India* by Ronald Inden'. *Journal of the American Oriental Society* 112 (4): 674–77.

Laidlaw, James. 2007. 'The Intension and Extension of Well-being: Transformation in Diaspora Jain Understandings of Non-violence'. In *Culture and Well-being: Anthropological Approaches to Freedom and Political Ethics*, edited by Alberto Corsín Jiménez, 156–79. London: Pluto.

Lee, Joel. 2015. 'Jagdish, Son of Ahmad: Dalit Religion and Nominative Politics in Lucknow'. *South Asia Multidisciplinary Academic Journal* (11): 2–15.

Lorenzen, David N. 2006. *Who Invented Hinduism: Essays on Religion in History, New Perspectives on Indian Pasts*. New Delhi: Yoda Press.

Madan, Triloki Nath. 1971. 'On the Nature of Caste in India: A Review Symposium on Louis Dumont's Homo Hierarchicus'. *Contributions to Indian Sociology* 5 (1): 1–81.

———. 2004. 'Secularism in Its Place'. In *Secularism and Its Critics*, edited by Rajeev Bhargava, 297–320. New Delhi: Oxford University Press.

———. 2011. *Sociological Traditions: Methods and Perspectives in the Sociology of India*. New Delhi: SAGE.

Marriot, McKim. 1989. 'Constructing an Indian Ethnosociology'. *Contributions to Indian Sociology* 23 (1): 1–39.

———. 1991. 'On "Constructing an Indian Ethnosociology"'. *Contributions to Indian Sociology* 25 (2): 295–308.

Mosse, David. 2012. *The Saint in the Banyan Tree: Christianity and Caste Society in India*. Berkeley, CA: University of California Press.

Nanda, Meera. 2003. *Prophets Facing Backward: Postmodern Critiques of Science and Hindu Nationalism in India*. New Brunswick, NJ: Rutgers University Press.

Nandy, Ashis. 2004. 'The Politics of Secularism and the Recovery of Religious Tolerance'. In *Secularism and Its Critics*, edited by Rajeev Bhargava, 321–44. New Delhi: Oxford University Press.

Pandya, Samta P. 2016. 'Governmentality and Guru-led Movements in India: Some Arguments from the Field'. *European Journal of Social Theory* 19 (1): 74–93.

Parry, Jonathan, and Christian Struempell. 2008. 'On the Desecration of Nehru's "Temples": Bhilai and Rourkela Compared'. *Economic & Political Weekly* 39 (19): 47–57.

Quack, Johannes. 2012a. *Disenchanting India: Organized Rationalism and Criticism of Religion in India*. New York, NY: Oxford University Press.

———. 2012b. 'Organized Atheism in India: An Overview'. *Journal of Contemporary Religion* 27 (1): 67–85.

———. 2013. '"What Do I Know?" Scholastic Fallacies and Pragmatic Religiosity in Mental Health Seeking Behaviour in India'. *Mental Health, Religion & Culture* 16 (4): 403–18.

———. 2017a. 'Leading and Misleading Religious Boundaries: Lessons from (Mental) Health Seeking Practices in India'. In *Mental Health at the Intersection of Religion & Psychiatry*, edited by Helene Basu, Roland Littlewood, and Arne Steinforth. Berlin and London: LIT Verlag.

———. 2017b. 'Bio- and Ethnographic Approaches to Indifference, Detachment, and Disengagement in the Study of Religion'. In *Religious Indifference: New Perspectives from Studies on Secularization and Nonreligion*, edited by Johannes Quack and Cora Schuh. Berlin and New York, NY: Springer.

Rehmana, Uzma, and Peter Lund-Thomsen. 2014. 'Social Support at a Sufi Lodge in Punjab, Pakistan'. *Contemporary South Asia* 22 (4): 377–88.

Riaz, Ali. 2010. *Religion and Politics in South Asia*. Oxon and New York, NY: Routledge.

Roberts, Nathaniel. 2016. *To Be Cared For: The Power of Conversion and Foreignness of Belonging in an Indian Slum*. Berkeley, CA: University of California Press.

Shah, Arvind M. 2006. 'Sects and Hindu Social Structure.' *Contributions to Indian Sociology* 40 (2): 209–48.

Strathern, Marilyn. 1988. *The Gender of the Gift: Problems with Women and Problems with Society in Melanesia*. London: University of California Press.

Venugopal, C.N. 2004 'Foreword'. In *Sociology of Religion in India*, edited by Rowena Robinson, 12–13. New Delhi: SAGE.

Watt, Carey Anthony. 2005. *Serving the Nation: Cultures of Service, Association, and Citizenship*. Delhi: Oxford University Press.

Weber, Max. 1963. *Hinduismus und Buddhismus*. 2 vols. Tuübingen: Mohr.

5

Artful Living
New Religious Movements in and of South Asia

Tulasi Srinivas

Introduction

Religious innovation is a much ignored topic of scholarly study. So much so that scholarly interest in new religious movements (known as NRMs), where innovation is originary, only emerged in the late 1980s in the West following the belated recognition of a systemic and systematic wave of religious innovation post Second World War (Lewis 2003; Wyon 1962). The young seekers of the post-Vietnam 1960s era were attempting to look beyond the modern West for spiritual answers towards the mystical and folk traditions of the East such as Buddhism, and to historical and feminist traditions that had long been suppressed such as Wiccanism (Woodhead and Heelas 2000). The ensuing development of popular and populist religious and spiritual traditions, largely hybrid and yet deeply personal, took hold in the popular imagination, and as they spawned newer and more artful forms of religious engagement, they became defined in their entirety as NRMs (Hammer and Rothstein 2012; Woodhead et al. 2009). The definition itself implied a distance and difference from the supposed dogmatic and traditional viewpoint of religious studies, the dominant Judeo-Christian paradigm (Hexham et al. 2004).

Gordon Melton (2004: 73–75), a religious studies scholar, defines NRMs based on this historicisation of scholarly interest as 'primary religious groups/movements that operate apart from the dominant religious culture in which they are located usually taken to be the Christian West'. The antiseptic naming of the phenomenon is purposeful, seen as a counterpoint to the more potent, pejorative and political usage of the words 'cults' or 'sects' (Dawson 1998; Lewis and Melton 1992; Melton 1978; Melton in Lewis 2002: 17–23). From the Western perspective, NRMs can encompass both Neo-pagan worship and spiritualist movements that often imply a resistance to the dominant religious traditions of the West (Bryant and Ekstrand 2004). But in South Asia, NRMs are neither a new phenomenon nor particularly stringently 'religious'. In a country like India, where religious faith is a dynamic conditioning factor for the vast majority of people, NRMs have taken a variety of forms: the biomedical moral such as Reiki healing or crystal therapy, the spatial moral such as the popularity of vastu shastra combined with feng shui and the Swaminarayan Sanstha, the medical existential such as Baba Ramdev's yogic meditation and Buddhist mindfulness techniques, the existential educational such as the Art of Living seminars and many more (Carrette and King 2005; Oliver 2012).

For our purposes, here I will extend the definition of an NRM beyond the viewpoint of the West and its dominant Judeo-Christian traditions to a more contemporary multi-perspectival understanding. I suggest that any blended or singular sacred and spiritual form, process or structure, emergent at the margins of the major 'world religions', often incorporating elements from several of the world religions, folk religions, spiritualist and naturalist forms of worship and divinity, and having sufficient adherents to be seen as a religious alternative, can be classified as an NRM (Hunt 2010). NRMs are perceived (by others and by themselves) to be alternatives to the mainstream world religions in their normative forms (Lewis 2003), providing an enormous scope for reinterpretation in order not only to legitimise the aspiration of various sections of the population but also to justify changes in the existing order of social and sacred relationships.

NRMs are characterised by a number of shared traits. These religions are, by definition, 'new'; they offer innovative religious responses to the conditions of the modern world, despite the fact that most NRMs represent themselves as rooted in ancient traditions. These movements are often highly eclectic, pluralistic and syncretistic; they freely combine doctrines and practices from diverse sources within their belief systems (Barker 1982: 1–20). NRMs take on the task of answering age-old questions in new and fertile ways, or so their adherents believe (Clarke 2006: 2–5). The rise of NRMs is sometimes thought to meet the emotional and spiritual needs of those suffering from the destructive impact of colonialism, modernisation and globalisation in a familiar world (Juergensmeyer 2006). NRMs have arisen to address specific needs that many people cannot satisfy through more traditional religious organisations or through modern secularism such as feelings of loss, anomie, moral decay, fear of uncertain times, the anxiety of precari-ous living conditions and religious violence (Chryssides and Wilkins 2006). Movements, by their inherent definition, imply a populist and democratic charter, but NRMs are usually founded by a charismatic and sometimes highly authoritarian leader who is thought to have extraor-dinary powers or insights and sometimes even worthy of worship as a saint, god or demigod (Versluis 2014; Williamson 2010). Some NRMs are apocalyptic or millenarian, revisionist movements, an assemblage of religious and spiritual ideologies that are often led by a charismatic head (Gold 1998). NRMs include self-help religious groups such as Scientology or Rajneeshism (Urban 2016) with visions of a violent end to all life, personal salvation and a rebirth into a 'New Age' (Woodhead and Heelas 2000: 1–30).

Every historical enquiry has its saturation point, beyond which a new enquiry is simply an old enquiry repackaged, and on that principle, it seems that we have yet to reach the peak of studies of NRM in and of South Asia, not only because of the proliferation, innovation and depth of NRM in this part of the world but also because each enquiry into South Asian NRMs yields new insights into the entirety of the NRM phenomenon as a whole. NRMs in South Asia are invariably associated with Hinduism, as a place of innovation within the Hindu tradition, though in fact many are forming bridges between Hinduism and Sufi Islam such as the Sai Baba movement (S. Srinivas 2008; T. Srinivas 2010) or Hinduism and Sikhism such as Dera Sacha Sauda (Copeman 2009). But NRMs in South Asia vary as they are associated with one phenom-enon more than any other: guruship (Copeman and Ikegame 2012).

Guruship in South Asia

Early studies of NRM did not distinguish them from sectarian movements within Hinduism. Raymond Brady Williams' study of Swaminarayan Sanstha was, in hindsight, the study of an emergent NRM but was seen at the time as a study of sectarian Hinduism. Only several decades later was it thought to be a study of an NRM (Kim, 2010, 2012a, 2012b). Similarly, Babb's (1986) unique comparative study of three Hindu NRMs—the Sathya Sai movement, the Radha Soami and the Brahma Kumaris—that centred around the relationship between charismatic individuals and their emergent devotional followings was originally seen as a study of sectarian diversity within Hinduism. Only in retrospect were the three sects seen as NRMs in the making by later scholars (S. Srinivas 2008; T. Srinivas 2010).

The category of Hindu NRMs is useful to distinguish between modern Hinduism and so-called 'big-tradition' Hinduism, but NRMs have imprecise boundaries extending both historically and thematically. Scholars tend to include some groups that have claimed they are not Hindu (Arya Samaj, Ramakrishna Mission) or not religious (Transcendental Meditation). In fact, the discourse shows an automatic and unreflexive conflation of the category of NRMs with modern guru movements: the creations of charismatic individuals who create new doctrine and new rituals. But one can and should interrogate the classification of guru movements as a 'new' religious movement in the South Asian context for the guru–shishya parampara has been a central structural component of Hindu transmission and tradition. Arguably, classifying guru movements as 'new' supports Richard King's (1999) argument of the inherent Orientalism of the discipline of religious studies. Further, whether guru movements can, in fact, be classified as a 'movement' is questionable, given their hierarchical structure and leadership, has been raised by a number of scholars (Gold 1982).

The study of NRMs in South Asia implicitly raises important problems. On the one hand, sectarians explicitly see themselves as unique, different and in disagreement with each other. On the other hand, by classifying them as a category joined by certain commonalities, scholars suggest that they share a hidden consensus and a more basic agreement (Babb 1986: 4). Images and practices appear as matters of consensus to outsiders precisely because they differ from their own plausibility infrastructures. What NRMs expect their adherents to consent to and what is the act of consenting are very blurred. Many NRMs like the Sathya Sai movement do not demand any kind of moment of conversion yet they demand loyalty from followers (T. Srinivas 2010: 100–20).

But the question of belief also separated insiders and outsiders to the movement, those who converted into the movements seen as devotees, and outsiders often seen as hostile. This separation is mirrored by early scholars of the guru movements who felt an obligation to mention and dissect their positionality with regard to the gurus (Babb 1986). The question of the devotee is marked and is a second problem in the study of guru movements. Although devotees constantly talk about themselves as individuals, they do not talk about selfhood. Much in the Hindu tradition says that I-ness (*ahamta*) and mine-ness (*mamta*) are the problems to be eliminated, that the self is an act of extreme ego and so guru movements uncomfortably straddle this philosophical divide. But such problems are minor quibbles in a rich field of study (Kakar 1991).

As a conversation topic, guruship can elicit all sorts of reactions in South Asia: incredulity, fascination, humour, dread, ridicule and indignation, and a full gamut of the metaphysical (Babb 1986; T. Srinivas 2010), psychological (Kakar 1982; Lindholm 2002) and ethnographic explorations (Narayan 1989). For public intellectuals worried about a resurgence of superstition, guruship has been explicable in terms of everything from the failure of modern secularism to superstitious attempts at assuaging economic anxieties and social uncertainties, to right-wing Hindutva schemes for excusing lack of education and awareness (Dasgupta 2006; Jaffrelot and van der Veer 2008).

In fact, then the variegated and dynamic literature demonstrates that NRMs largely refer to gurus and their followers in the context of their multiple roles in South Asian society and culture. Gurus, also known as *Baba, Bhagawan Fakir, Sant* and godman locate themselves in the intersection between god and man evidence to their devotees of their uncontainability across domains, their access to magical powers (often attributed to superhuman or divine birth), their healing skills and their superhuman ability to read minds. These plural forms of guruship draw attention not only to the guru's mimetic proficiency but also to the complex role of the guru in the religious and cultural imagination (Copeman and Ikegame 2012).

Constructing and Deconstructing the Guru

In the early epoch of scholarly study, NRMs were largely thought to be offshoots of traditional Hinduism and gurus were thought to be charismatic leaders of established sectarian branches. Indeed, it was not until the late 1990s when studies of Shirdi Sai Baba, Sathya Sai Baba and other NRMs that developed purely as guru movements in independent India that gurus were seen as creative, revolutionary figures who shaped new forms of syncretic religion in and beyond the subcontinent (Forsthoefel and Humes 2005; Urban 2016; Warrier 2005; Williamson 2010).

And yet though by the end of the 1990s we had several scholarly and devotional tracts about many gurus and their movements, local, national and international to explore, something mysterious remained, and that mystery as always in the lives of the gurus and their followers is how they did what they did and why. It is this mystery of faith that most studies of guruship attempt to deconstruct. Studies of guru movements at this time explored the systems of signification that establish and build the guru's authenticity—lineage, deportment, charisma and hagiography—as well as the necessary attributes of the devotee—attitude, surrender, obedience and devotion. Devotees craft elaborate hagiographies of mysterious births and divine ordination. Gurus interact with devotees regularly through daily *darshan* or sacred viewing, religious talks and lectures—live and recorded—magical acts of prestidigitation, and radio, television and webcasts emphasising their sacredness.

Christopher Jaffrelot notes in his article in *The Caravan*[1] magazine about the contemporary guru Baba Ramdev, provocatively titled 'Swami without Sampradaya', that these godmen–gurus are heirs to an old legacy that harks back not to Vivekananda and the spiritually enlightened Hindu master but to Swami Chinmayananda, one of the cofounders of the VHP along with former RSS member S.S. Apte in 1964. Jaffrelot states, 'Since then, dozens of saffron-clad sadhus have epitomised the same characteristics—belonging not to a traditional sampradaya (system of spiritual knowledge), but often serving instead as self-initiated "spiritual masters"'. The ancient educational and knowledge-sharing structure, the guru–shishya parampara, is transformed in modern Hinduism to an authoritarian head and his/her global following of acolytes often numbered in the millions for the better known gurus such as Sri Sathya Sai Baba and Sri Sri Ravi Shankar. As Max Weber, the sociologist noted of charismatic individuals, the guru is, for his believers (and most, though not all, gurus are male) head of a religious order with its own belief systems, a charismatic, often divinely magical leader. By the mid-1990s, the study of guru movements was well established.

Interestingly, Jaffrelot has argued that modern guruship is not contiguous with its ideological forbear. The guru–shishya parampara has changed profoundly in the modern secular moment.

They do not retain the individualised and interactive guru–shishya modus operandi of teaching spiritual knowledge, but communicate their message almost in adlike sound bites from TV studios, and group

[1] http://www.caravanmagazine.in/perspectives/ramdev-swami-without-sampradaya (accessed on 14 June 2016).

yoga sessions. The aesthetics of new religious movements are unambiguous ... large ashrams, gun running, tax evasions gold thrones, status and power, private jets, hidden bank accounts and vast sums of money. (Jaffrelot 2011: 23)

Jaffrelot's expression of the novelty of the guru as a modern religious figure. Modern gurus are significantly lightning rods of social conflict. Jaffrelot's assessment of the modern guruscape as conflict-ridden underscores what Gene Thursby (2011: 6–29) has defined acrostically as the PEST problem: the Power of the gurus and how it is imagined, the Economic structure of guru-led movements, the Sexual scandals around gurus and, finally, the nature of the gurus' Teachings and their ambiguities. This is a useful metric to examine what Copeman and Ikegame (2012) call 'guru logics' of 20th- and 21st-century guru movements.

Guru Power and Logics

Guru movements are products of and responses to modernity, globalisation, pluralism and the scientific worldview (Clarke 2006; Dasgupta 2006). The historicisation and concordant legitimacy of a new religious movement is a boundary that is rigorously policed by followers. Part of the study of guru movements has been to understand their provenance to include them as modern Hinduism. Scholars have argued that the persistence and longevity of gurus in a subcontinental religion (by which I mean both Islam and Hinduism and the hybridisation that occurs between them, and between them and folk religions) is evidence of a resistance to if, not failure of the secularisation paradigm. Gurus were seen as revolutionary, recasting Hinduism's worst evils such as patriarchy or caste, or as salvific to renew and rejuvenate Hinduism's fading present by turning to tradition. For example, Rajneesh advocated a free-love programme encouraging his devotees to free themselves of the constrictions of convention in terms of sexuality appealing to 'modern' Indians, but others like Swami Pramukh of the Swaminarayan movement were seen less as charismatic leaders and more as bearers of a tradition that harkened back to renew Hinduism's roots. Accordingly, the study of gurus and their movements splits into a study of gurus who are local, who reside in South Asia, who then achieve a global following through the work of devotion or *seva* to make individual gurus known globally such as Sri Sri Ravi Shankar and his Art of Living Foundation located in Bengaluru.

By the 1990s, some of the more successful of these guru movements had developed a global armature exporting their theologies, building a global infrastructure to support it. I term these international gurus 'hyper gurus'. Hyper gurus like Sathya Sai Baba began to build a global coalition of devotees, expanding their national links further and further. The globalisation of the guru was a key to their ability to attract a global devotional base largely from the West but also from other parts of the world (T. Srinivas 2010), part of what Copeman and Ikegame (2012: 1–10) refer to as the guru's 'uncontainability', his/her expansive possibility. Joanne Punzo Waghorne has a fascinating and timely study of contemporary 'global gurus', her term for these international hyper gurus, in the complex multi-religious and national landscape of Singapore, that speak to the question of the geographical and cultural 'uncontainability' of guruship in general (Waghorne, in Penkower and Pintchman 2014).

I have argued elsewhere that hyper gurus like Sathya Sai Baba create a 'grammar of diversity' that enables a cultural translation model which encourages the expansion (T. Srinivas 2010). The hyper guru attracts and crosses sectarian boundaries and even religious boundaries through a universalistic message of unity and salvation through service. Additionally, some gurus may travel internationally leaving their ashrams in South Asia to spread their gospel, though this is rare.

Guru Economies, Erotics and Governmentalities

The ideal guru in the Weberian ideal type was celibate, exorcised of all desire, but modern gurus are a far cry from that image. Rather, if contemporary news stories are to be believed, their desire for power, wealth and sex is rivalled only by their hunger for attention. A guru who shot to prominence in the 2000s with his daily televised early morning yoga routines, Baba Ramdev, started a medical company called Patanjali Ayurved in 1997. The company had smashed all expected records for profit, garnering $1 billion of sales in 2016.[2] It is poised, or so the economic analysts at newspapers suggest, to overtake the storied pharmaceutical giant, Colgate-Palmolive.[3] Baba Ramdev argues that his success is evidence of his divinity. In a second illustration, after the death of Sathya Sai Baba, when his bedchamber was unlocked, 300 kg

---

[2] http://economictimes.indiatimes.com/industry/cons-products/fmcg/patanjali-on-track-to-hit-1-billion-sales-in-fy17/articleshow/51422878.cms (accessed on 12 June 2016).
[3] Ibid.

of silver, 100 kg of gold and millions of rupees were found.[4] Such excess suggests that spiritual capitalism is successful, and that guru economies are about the creation of empires of wealth. Rumours abound of guru's tax-evasion schemes as religious and charitable trusts that many gurus have secret Swiss Bank accounts, that they corral valuable land and that they are wealthy beyond belief.

Gurus and their followers have always been the subject of probing newsworthy stories about belief and tradition; in the past decade, not only have guru movements proliferated but also the scandalous headlines about gurus in and of India abound. The most widely talked about sexual scandal involved Swami Nityananda and his sex photos and sex video with a young actress named Ranjitha in his ashram.[5] The news media followed the story as Nityananda was accused of rape, fled the police and was finally caught and given a 30-year sentence.[6] The expectation of gurus and of NRMs in general is a containment of the gurus' sexuality a celibacy in keeping with the ideal type in Hinduism of the celibate sannyasin (mendicant or holy man). The sexual exploits of these gurus are therefore seen as all the more shocking. Sathya Sai Baba, as I noted in my work, was accused of homosexual pedophilia, though he was never convicted in a court of law (T. Srinivas 2010). Guru Rajneesh, known in his later life as Osho, capitalised upon the 'shock factor' the seeming paradox of speaking of gurus and sexual mores in one breath, advocating and enacting his free love seminars and casing scandal in other fashion forever, separating the celibate mendicant from the modern figure of the guru (Urban 2016). In many cases, guru movements police the bodies of devotees stringently for sexual and dietary misdemeanours, while the body of the guru is seen as divine and holy, and therefore beyond containment. The boundary of insider–outsider is so strong that to the group establishes itself as a substitute for the family and other conventional social groupings. This often leads to the devotee abandoning the 'outside world' leaving him or her open to sexual and other forms of exploitation.

Gurus use their power for political as well as financial gain. In a BBC interview on the popularity of gurus, sociologist Shiv Visvanathan stated that proximity to a guru legitimises a politician and adds to

---

[4] http://timesofindia.indiatimes.com/india/More-gold-found-in-Sai-Babas-room/articleshow/9290417.cms (accessed on 14 June 2016).

[5] http://indiatoday.intoday.in/story/swami-nithyananda-arrest-the-story-of-why-he-is-in-trouble/1/200560.html (accessed on 14 June 2016).

[6] Ibid.

his/her power.[7] India's most powerful prime minister, the late Indira Gandhi, would often turn to her yoga guru Dhirendra Brahmachari for advice. The political and governmental functions of guru-ship is 'guru governmentality'—not just another agency of devolved governance in an era of economic liberalisation, but the retooling of the radical asymmetry of the guru–devotee relationship in order to produce 'humanitarian' or 'developmental' effects. From the devotees' point of view this can hardly be glossed as 'secular' but is ascribed to the guru's ability to bring together the community of followers for philanthropic effort (Copeman and Ikegame 2012: 1–20). Swapan Dasgupta (2005) claims that the real energy of contemporary Hinduism lies in these 'living saints' far more accessible than purohits or pontiffs. Dasgupta's claim suggests that we see the guru as a religious showman who can soothe the febrility of middle-class Indians (Kakar 1982). With their enormous landholdings, ashrams, bank accounts and 24/7 television appearances, the modern gurus are the CEOs of a brand of spirituality crafted to suit the modern spiritualist sensibility (Singleton and Goldberg 2013).

The modern bourgeois Hindu devotee of a guru largely seems to choose to ignore the guru's wrongdoing, and this wilful ignorance has sparked a passionate debate about the nature of belief and 'superstition' in modern India (Srinivas 2017) while further empowering the guru. While gurus have always had political benefactors, in the past five years, gurus have actively politicised their movements, cleverly indicting politicians as corrupt and indifferent to the plight of ordinary people. Baba Ramdev made his television yoga platform a space to indict all politicians, though notably those of the Congress party, joining Arvind Kejriwal in a populist uprising that built upon Anna Hazare's anti-corruption movement to create the national Aam Aadmi Party (ordinary man) that won the Delhi legislative election in 2013. The guru movements have also become more politically active, championing political and populist causes. For example, Sri Sri Ravishankar's Art of Living Foundation appears to support a verdant and green message with 'river conservation' and 'green footprints' as part of their e-message.[8] Unfortunately, however, this well-intentioned message often gets lost in the political reality of everyday. In a recent 'World Culture' festival underwritten by the Art of Living Foundation on the banks of the river

[7] http://www.bbc.com/news/world-asia-india-30110374 (accessed on 14 June 2016).
[8] http://www.artofliving.org/sites/www.artofliving.org/files/wysiwyg_imageupload/The%20Art%20of%20Living's%20Environmental%20Initiatives.pdf (accessed on 14 June 2016).

Yamuna, the National Green Tribunal, an environmental watchdog group, logged massive pollution levels in the river due to the massive construction project for the festival.[9]

The Rise of the Female Guru

While most of the work on guruship focuses on male gurus, beginning with Maya Warrier's delightfully thought-provoking work on Ma Amtritanandamayi or 'the hugging amma', studying the female guru in contrast to the abundance of male gurus became a serious endeavour. The unique consideration of the rise of the female guru gave rise to an exciting revisiting of the guru paradigm in toto: interrogating accepted tropes of saintliness and interaction (Khandelwal 2005), sanyas and celibacy (DeNapoli 2014) and hierarchy and godhood (Gold 1982) that had been inflected by the assumption of masculinity. In Warrier's (2005: 2) analysis of Ma Amritanandamayi's global guruship, her unique darshan style which involved hugging each and every person she met underscores her central question of how modernity and modern selfhood come to be negotiated in a guru's fold, a timely reflection on modern Hinduism. Indeed, the entire discourse around the guru as woman has upended established categories of guruship (Pechilis 2004). Where previous considerations of guruship had focused largely on magical acts and superstition, the development of a devotional base and sexual scandals, the conversation around female guruship introduced the spectrum of female sexuality and emotive expression from nun-like sadhus (DeNapoli 2014) to the hugging indulgences of the global Mata (Lucia 2014).

Future Scholarship: The Afterlife of Gurus and Beyond

In the past few years, scholarship on guru movements has centred around the death of prominent gurus and the 'afterlife' of their movements. Orianne Aymard alerts us to the death of the guru and the worship of the guru in a postmortem 'cult'. She proposes a new vision of holiness by revealing a posthumous way of venerating female gurus (Aymard 2014). Tracing the afterlife of guru's icons and relics from graveyards to shrines, Aymard argues that the Ma Anandamayi movement, became more successful after her death through the expansion

---

[9] http://indiatoday.intoday.in/education/story/art-of-living-festival-destroying-yamuna-floodplain/1/616497.html (accessed on 14 June 2016).

of her 'mobile' charisma through sacred objects and relics (T. Srinivas 2010). Karline Mclain (2016), in her study of the afterlife of the Muslim Fakir Shirdi Sai Baba, a century after his death, interrogates his growing posthumous popularity among Hindus by examining the global pilgrimage to the shrine town of Shirdi in Maharashtra, India. Here, NRMs underline the newness of the old and the place of memory in the new.

In sum, then, the scholarship on NRMs in South Asia has indicated a robust and growing field that not only fills out the margins of what we think of as religion but also, in the process, redefines the perspective of its definition. It suggests that what we think of, in the sidelines of our vision as scholars may in fact be entire world awaiting discovery.

References

Babb, Lawrence A. 1986. *Redemptive Encounters: Three Modern Styles in the Hindu Tradition*. Comparative Studies in Religion and Society. Berkeley, CA: University of California Press.

Barker, Eileen. 1982. *New Religious Movements: A Perspective for Understanding Society—Studies in Religion and Society*. New York, NY: Edwin Mellen Press.

———. 1999. 'New Religious Movements: Their Incidence and Significance'. In *New Religious Movements: Challenge and Response*, edited by Bryan Wilson and Jamie Cresswell, 15–31. London, Routledge.

Bromley, David G. 2004. 'Whither New Religions Studies? Defining and Shaping a New Area of Study'. *Nova Religio: The Journal of Alternative and Emergent Religions* 8 (2): 83–97.

Bryant, Edwin F. and Maria Ekstrand. 2004. *The Hare Krishna Movement: The Postcharismatic Fate of a Religious Transplant*. New York, NY: Columbia University Press.

Carrette, Jeremy and Richard King. 2004. *Selling Spirituality: The Silent Takeover of Religion*. London: Routledge Press.

Chryssides, George D. and Margaret Z. Wilkins. 2006. *A Reader in New Religious Movements*. London and New York, NY: Continuum.

Clarke, Peter B. 2006. *New Religions in Global Perspective: A Study of Religious Change in the Modern World*. London and New York, NY: Routledge.

Copeman, Jacob. 2009. *Veins of Devotion: Blood Donation and Religious Devotion in North India*. New Brunswick, NJ: Rutgers University Press.

Copeman, Jacob and Aya Ikegame. 2012. *The Guru in South Asia*. Edinburgh South Asia Studies. London: Routledge.

Dasgupta, Swapan. 2005. 'Evangelical Hindutva'. *Seminar* 545 (January).

———. 2006. 'Gods in the Sacred Marketplace: Hindu Nationalism and the Return of the Aura in the Public Sphere'. In *Religion, Media and the Public Sphere*, edited by B. Meyer and A. Moore, 251–72. Bloomington, IN: Indiana University Press.

Dawson, Lorne L. 1998. *Comprehending Cults: The Sociology of New Religious Movements*. Toronto and New York, NY: Oxford University Press.

DeNapoli, Antoinette. 2014. *Real Sadhus Sing to God: Gender, Asceticism and Vernacular Religion in Rajasthan*. New York, NY and Oxford: Oxford University Press.

Forsthoefel, Thomas A. and Cynthia Ann Humes. 2005. *Gurus in America*. SUNY Series in Hindu Studies. Albany, NY: State University of New York Press.

Gold, Daniel. 1982. 'The Lord as Guru in North Indian Religion Hindi Sant Tradition and Universals of Religious Perception'. PhD Dissertation. University of Chicago.

———. 1988. *Comprehending the Guru: Toward a Grammar of Religious Perception*. American Academy of Religion Academy Series. Atlanta, GA: Scholars Press.

Hammer, Olav and Mikael Rothstein. 2012. *The Cambridge Companion to New Religious Movements*. Cambridge Companions to Religion. Cambridge and New York, NY: Cambridge University Press.

Hexham, Irving, Stephen Rost and John Morehead. 2004. *Encountering New Religious Movements: A Holistic Evangelical Approach*. Grand Rapids, MI: Kregel Academic & Professional.

Hunt, Stephen. 2010. *New Religions and Spiritualities: The Library of Essays on Sexuality and Religion*. Farnham and Burlington, VT: Ashgate.

Jaffrelot, Christopher. 2011. *Religion, Caste and Politics in India*. Oxford, New York and New Delhi: Oxford University Press.

Jaffrelot, Christophe and Peter van der Veer. 2008. *Patterns of Middle Class Consumption in India and China*. Los Angeles, CA: SAGE.

Juergensmeyer, Mark. 2006. *The Oxford Handbook of Global Religions*. Oxford and New York, NY: Oxford University Press.

Kakar, Sudhir. 1982. *Shamans, Mystics, and Doctors: A Psychological Inquiry into India and Its Healing Traditions*. 1st ed. New York, NY: Knopf.

———. 1991. *The Analyst and the Mystic: Psychoanalytic Reflections on Religion and Mysticism*. New Delhi: Viking Press.

Kim, H. 2010. 'The Swaminarayan Movement and Religious Subjectivity'. In *The Idea of Gujarat: History, Ethnography and Text*, edited by E. Simpson and A. Kapadia, 207–28. New Delhi: Orient Blackswan.

———. 2012a. 'A Fine Balance: Adaptation and Accommodation in the Swaminarayan Sanstha'. In *Gujarati Communities Across the Globe: Memory, Identity and Continuity*, edited by S. Mawani and A. Mukadam, 141–56. Stoke-on-Trent, United Kingdom: Trentham Books.

———. 2012b. 'The BAPS Swaminarayan Temple Organisation and Its Publics'. In *Public Hinduisms*, edited by J. Zavos, P. Kanungo, D. Reddy, et al., 417–39. New Delhi: SAGE.

King, Richard. 1999. *Orientalism and Religion: Postcolonial Theory, India and 'the Mystic East'*. London and New York, NY: Routledge.

Lewis, I.M. 2003. *Ecstatic Religion: A Study of Shamanism and Spirit Possession*. 3rd ed. London and New York, NY: Routledge.

Lewis, James R. and J. Gordon Melton. 1992. *Perspectives on the New Age.* SUNY Series in Religious Studies. Albany, NY: State University of New York Press.

Lindholm, Charles. 2002. 'Culture, Charisma, and Consciousness: The Case of the Rajneeshee'. *Ethos* 30 (4): 357–75.

Lucia, Amanda J. 2014. *Reflections of Amma: Devotees in a Global Embrace.* Berkeley, CA: University of California Press.

Melton, J. Gordon. 1978. *The Encyclopedia of American Religions.* Wilmington, NC and Detroit, MI: McGrath Publishing and Gale Research, Thomson Gale.

———. 2004. 'Toward a Definition of "New Religion"'. *Nova Religio: The Journal of Alternative and Emergent Religions* 8 (1): 73–87.

Narayan, Kirin. 1989. *Storytellers, Saints, and Scoundrels: Folk Narrative in Hindu Religious Teaching.* Publication of the American Folklore Society, New Series. Philadelphia, PA: University of Pennsylvania Press.

Oliver, Paul. 2012. *New Religious Movements: A Guide for the Perplexed.* Continuum Guides for the Perplexed. London and New York, NY: Continuum.

Pechilis, Karen. 2004. *The Graceful Guru: Hindu Female Gurus in India and the United States.* New York, NY: Oxford University Press.

Penkower, Lisa and Tracy Pintchman. 2014. *Hindu Ritual at the Margins: Innovations, Transformations, Reconsiderations.* Columbia, SC: University of South Carolina Press.

Singleton, Mark and Ellen Goldberg. 2013. *Gurus of Modern Yoga.* Oxford and New York, NY: Oxford University Press.

Srinivas, Smriti. 2008. *In the Presence of Sai Baba: Body, City, and Memory in a Global Religious Movement.* Numen Book Series: Studies in the History of Religions. Leiden and Boston, MA: Brill.

Srinivas, T. 2017. 'Doubtful Illusions: Magic, Wonder and the Politics of Virtue in the Sathya Sai Movement'. *Journal of African and Asian Studies* 52 (4): 1–31.

Srinivas, Tulasi. 2010. *Winged Faith: Rethinking Globalization and Religious Pluralism Through the Sathya Sai Movement.* New York, NY: Columbia University Press.

Thursby, Gene. 2011. 'The Study of Hindu New Religious Movements'. *Nova Religio: The Journal of Alternative and Emergent Religions* 15 (2): 6–19.

Urban, Hugh B. 2016. *Zorba the Buddha: Sex, Spirituality, and Capitalism in the Global Osho Movement.* Berkeley, CA: University of California Press.

Versluis, Arthur. 2014. *American Gurus: From American Transcendentalism to New Age Religion.* Oxford, New York and New Delhi: Oxford University Press.

Waghorne, Joanne Punzo. 2014. 'From Diaspora to (Global) Civil Society: Global Gurus and the Processes of De-ritualization and De-ethnization in Singapore'. In *Hindu Ritual at the Margins: Innovations, Transformations, Reconsiderations*, edited by Lisa Penkower and Tracy Pintchman, 186–207. Columbia, SC: University of South Carolina Press.

Warrier, Maya. 2005. *Hindu Selves in a Modern World: Guru Faith in the Mata Amritanandamayi Mission.* London and New York, NY: Routledge Curzon.

Williamson, Lola. 2010. *Transcendent in America: Hindu-inspired Meditation Movements in America.* The New and Alternative Religions Series. New York, NY: New York University Press.

Woodhead, Linda and Paul Heelas. 2000. *Religion in Modern Times: An Interpretive Anthology.* Oxford and Malden, MA: Blackwell Publishers.

Woodhead, Linda, Hiroko Kawanami and Christopher H. Partridge. 2009. *Religions in the Modern World: Traditions and Transformations.* 2nd ed. London and New York, NY: Routledge.

Wyon, Olive. 1962. *Living Springs: New Religious Movements in Western Europe.* Philadelphia, PA: Westminster Press.

6

Villages and Villagers in Contemporary India

Surinder S. Jodhka

At the time of India's independence, when sociologists/social anthropologists and other social scientists were beginning to initiate some form of independent research on Indian society, there was near unanimity among academics and the political class that India lived in its villages spread across diverse regions of the subcontinent. According to this common-sense view, even when people in different regions of the country spoke different languages, ate different kinds of food, held different religious beliefs and had varied kinship practices, they were presumed to have many similarities that united them all: namely being embedded in institutions such as the caste system, the village community and the joint family. The popular slogan 'unity in diversity' was not simply about mobilising communal harmony between Hindus and Muslims but was also an important way of imagining India's nationhood. It was a claim and a statement of timeless continuity of the idea of India, which not only made Indians a political people, a nation, but also a society and culture (a civilisation!) with an underlying unity and commonality of values, belief systems and institutional arrangements, even when its diversities were hard to ignore.

Those who studied Indian society—professional sociologists/social anthropologists—had to uncover those underlying arrangements and the diverse forms in which they presented themselves empirically. The village in India was not simply a demographic category, a matter of administrative classification, but also the critical site where the empirics of Indian society and culture could be observed and studied. It was thus also a useful methodological category, a convenient entry point into the ground realities of the vast lands that had come to be organised in the framework of a nation state (see Srinivas 1955).

Those from the other social science disciplines, economists or political scientists, also recognised the centrality of these institutions even when they did not become the primary focus of their research and engagement. They saw their own roles as agents of change. The Indian village and its caste system represented India's past tradition(s) that needed to be changed through economic development and political democracy. To become modern, Indians had to move out of the village and its agrarian economy to towns and cities. Economists and political scientists looked to sociologists and social anthropologists to enlighten them about the complexities of traditional social life (Beteille 1980; Jodhka 1998).

Although at the time of its independence from colonial rule in 1947, a large majority of India's population indeed lived in its more than half a million villages, the number of those who lived in urban settlements was also not insignificant. India already had a total of 1,827 urban conglomerations in 1901, accommodating nearly 10 per cent of its total population. The colonial rulers founded and developed some of these cities such as Calcutta and Bombay, but their proportion was very small. Most of them had been part of Indian social life since much before colonial rule was established in the region. In other words, despite the predominance of political and anthropological common sense of the times that presented native India as a land of 'village republics', the 'urban' was also an important reality in the pre-colonial history of the region.

Besides the presence of relatively big cities such as Agra, Banaras and Hyderabad, the region in the pre-colonial period also had an urban imagination reflected in the presence of a well-developed artisan industry, urban architecture and religious centres. The state power, local craft and pilgrimage, all had an urban orientation. As is now well known, the so-called Indian village was never an isolated and autonomous entity. Quite like in most other parts of the world, the rural in the South Asian region existed and reproduced itself in relation to the local state power, market networks and cultural/religious flows.

An obvious implication of the dominance of a village and caste-centric view of Indian society has been that until very recently, students of rural India did not look at the Indian village or its reproduction through its relationship with urban realities. Similarly, researching on India through its urban life had to wait for quite some time to become a subject of interest among the students of Indian society.

This chapter is not a story of the social transformation of India from a tradition-bound rural to a social and economic life organised around the modern city, an unfolding of the evolutionary process of urbanisation, nor is it a narrative of a dearth or deficiency of it. I attempt a brief overview of some patterns of change experienced in a variety of forms across the subcontinent. Despite the continued diversity of the rural experience, I would like to argue that the models of national development implemented by the Indian state in post-independence period have brought about some interesting changes across regions of the subcontinent. I focus specifically on (a) the dynamics of rural–urban demographics, (b) the processes of rural development and changes in the agrarian economy and (c) the processes of democratisation with specific reference to the changing dynamics of caste and power in the Indian village and beyond.

Demographics: Rural and Urban

Even though 'rural' and 'urban' are often used as innocuous demographic categories, they are also viewed as two types of societies. The rural is almost always imagined as being small in size, with simple forms of social organisation, primarily agrarian, and tradition bound. In contrast, the urban is complex, large in size, primarily industrial and a market-driven modern formation. In this view, the two types of settlements represent different stages in social and economic evolution of human societies. In the evolutionary journey of modernisation, the rural gives way to the urban to which people living in rural areas move, leaving behind the agrarian life and switching to a range of non-farm occupations.

With the process of development and modernisation actively unfolding in the developing countries of the South, urbanisation is seen as an obvious indicator of positive social change. As they become modern with time, all countries of the Third World are also expected to become urban. Over the past century or so, the proportions of urban populations have indeed been growing almost everywhere. Countries like India, China or Brazil today have some of the largest urban conglomerations.

By 1951, India already had more than 17.29 per cent of its total population (nearly 62 million people) living in 2,853 urban settlements (Datta 2006: 4–6). The proportion of the urban population grew by nearly three times over the past century, from 10.29 per cent in 1911 to 18.24 per cent by 1971, and further to 31.16 per cent in 2011. This would seem even more dramatic when we look at the absolute numbers. Urban population of India grew from around 26 million in 1901 to 109 million in 1971, and further to 377 million in 2011. While some of it is indeed a consequence of internal growth of urban populations, a large proportion of the increase is a result of the processes of urbanisation, migrations from rural to urban areas and transformation of rural settlements into urban centres.

However, the demographic story of India is not all that simple. While the proportion of rural population has indeed been declining over the years, though rather slowly, and many of its villagers have over the years and over generations moved to cities, the absolute number of those living in rural settlements has also not declined. On the contrary, rural populations in absolute terms have also been growing quite consistently, from 212.5 million in 1901 to 480 million in 1971, and to 742 million in 2001. According to the 2011 Census, India had 833 million people living in rural settlements. The size of the rural population in 2011 was nearly four times of what it was in 1901.

The story is equally complicated when we come to the dynamics of settlements. Following the logic of urbanisation, in India too, over the years, many erstwhile rural settlements have been subsumed by the ever-growing cities. A good number of them have also been designated as 'urban' by the administrative system. This is evident from the fact that in the decade from 2001 to 2011, the number of urban centres in India went up from 5,161 to 7,935, largely because of the conversion of rural settlements into urban centres. However, during the same period, the number of rural settlements has been growing consistently. Their numbers grew from 567,000 in 1901 to 638,588 in 2001, and further to 640,867 in 2011.

The demographic dynamics of rural India is made even more complex by diversities across regions and settlements. The nature of social life and size of settlements vary significantly, depending upon regional ecologies. Sometime back, Bernard Cohn (2000: 142–43) identified three kinds of rural settlements: First, the nucleated pattern, the typical village of the anthropologist's imagination. They are multi-caste with houses and streets close to each other. They are typical of the plains of northern/northwest India and in some parts of the south of India.

Second, the hamleted villages. These villages usually have a central settlement with 'several hamlets, and satellite settlements scattered over the fields of the village'. These are 'more typical of middle and lower Ganges and parts of Tamil Nadu and Andhra' (ibid.: 142). Third, the dispersed category where there is no 'obvious village, because homesteads are dispersed, generally on or near the fields owned or worked on by the agriculturists. This form of settlements is found in wide range of regions, from the Kerala coast to the hill regions of the northern and central highlands' (ibid.: 142–43).

Besides the obvious ecological and economic diversities, these differences also have a demographic side to them. Despite its centrality in India's political and policy imagination, demographically, the village is a residual category. All those settlements that do not qualify to be urban are rural. In terms of population, the size of a rural settlement could vary from 50 or 100 persons to a highly dense settlement of 30,000 persons and even more. This is also reflected in the demographic spread of the rural population. For example, even though the Indian Census lists more than 600,000 settlements as rural, more than half of the total rural population (over 54%) lives in roughly 3 per cent of relatively bigger size villages numbering 18,768, which had population of over 2,000 each in the year 2001. Nearly 220,000 rural settlements had less than 500 people (see IDFC 2013: 4). The Indian village is thus a fluid category with diversity of size and social composition. Despite many social and economic changes, the rural demographics remain diverse and tend to defy any logic of evolutionary change. Even when urban is expanding, the rural is not disappearing or even declining in the Indian case.

Dynamics of Rural Development

The nationalist leadership had a diversity of views on the value of village life and its possible futures. The patriarch of the Indian nationalist movement, Gandhi, advocated for a revival of the presumed traditional Indian village. It was only through such a recovery of the lost Indian village that the hangover of the colonial past could be shed and the country could move on to the path of true *swaraj* (independence or self-rule). Even though he recognised the presence of caste and untouchability, and also landlessness, as facts of rural life, he visualised, almost romanticised, the Indian village to be a community based on notions of interdependence, self-sufficiency and simple living. While he recognised the need of reforming the village, he did not want it to be transformed and modernised through the use of Western technology (Jodhka 2002).

While the Gandhian perspective has remained influential and has inspired some of the policies initiated by the independent Indian state, it could not become the dominant view in the mainstream development thinking on rural India during the post-independence period. Nehru, India's first prime minister, and to an extent Ambedkar, the chairperson of the Drafting Committee of the Indian Constitution, shaped much of the mainstream thinking on the Indian village. Nehru's view of the village was also very close to the conceptions of social and economic change in the Western theories of economic development and modernisation popular with economists and sociologists of the time. The Indian village, in this view, was a site of backwardness and poverty, and much of this was because of the prevailing institutional arrangements (land relations), values and belief systems (tradition bound, caste) and the primitiveness of technology (in its agrarian economy). Thus, the future of the village lay in its modernisation through introduction of modern technology, change in land relations and inculcation of rational values through education.

Even though the primary focus of Nehruvian economic planning was development of industrial infrastructure, the rural population could not be ignored. They made for a large majority of the Indian people, who had all become voters and citizens in independent India. Their mobilisations during the nationalist movement had raised hopes for a better life and the new ruling elite had to respond to fulfil those aspirations. The dominant models of economic growth also visualised an intrinsic relationship between the growth of the rural sector and urban industry.

The Indian state initiated a large number of programmes and policies to start the process of rural development. These included the famous community development programmes (CDPs), the land reform legislations, incentivising rural cooperatives, etc. They were to lay the ground for economic growth in rural areas through changing the local-level institutional frames of economic life that were viewed as inhibiting economic growth. These initial measures produced mixed results. Even though they were often criticised for their conceptual flaws and poor implementation, they did produce some positive effects, albeit with significant regional variations, and not always along intended lines. For example, even the limited success of land reform legislations helped in changing agrarian relations in some states as well as created conditions for later economic changes. Similarly, despite all its drawbacks, rural cooperatives did benefit from official patronage wherever the local-level leadership could mobilise itself (see Dhanagare 1984; Dube 1958; Herring 1977; Jodhka 2003; Joshi 1976).

Over the years, the focus of the state's approach to rural development shifted to technology-oriented incentives for agricultural growth and on poverty alleviation. The introduction of Green Revolution technology in some select pockets during the late 1960s was a clear indication of a shift from relational or institutional approach to a productivity-oriented approach to agrarian change. While the new technology helped in accelerating growth of rural economy, its benefits did not 'trickle down' to the landless and the poor. Growing concern with poverty among the global development community during the 1970s translated into the introduction of beneficiary-oriented programmes for those with very low incomes and ever insecure employment in the form of the Integrated Rural Development Programme (IRDP), or more recently, the National Rural Employment Guarantee Scheme (NREGS, which became MGNREGA after it was passed as an Act by the Indian Parliament in 2005 and was named after Mahatma Gandhi).

Along with these major initiatives, the Government of India keeps working with a variety of schemes focused on the welfare and empowerment of sections of rural people: women, Scheduled Castes and Scheduled Tribes. Most of these programmes are executed through local-level administrative and political structures. Besides facilitating the working of national-level programmes, state governments also work with their own agenda of rural development. Beginning with the 1990s, the involvement of civil society organisation, the NGOs, has also been growing in rural development activities. Some of these organisations work with their own money, which they mobilise from a variety of sources, including from international development agencies, while some are also funded directly by agencies of the Indian government.

Development and Social Change

These initiatives from the above, coupled with the larger processes at work, have transformed almost every aspect of rural life: social, economic and political. However, the experience and nature of change varies significantly across regions of the county. Given the already differentiated nature of rural society in India on caste and community lines, coupled with significantly differentiated land ownership patterns, the experience of change has also been quite varied within each region.

Much has been researched and written about the changes in the agrarian economy and the social relations around land. Even the limited success of the land reform legislation helped in weakening the zamindari system (absentee landlordism). Similarly, the success of Green Revolution technology, even though confined to a few pockets, ushered in a new energy and excitement in popular and policy discourses on the Indian agriculture during the 1970s. Even when critiques pointed to its limited spread and possible social and ecological 'side effects', it produced a sense of pride in the Indian development community and among the newly emergent rural elite.

Interestingly, deliberations on Indian agriculture in development circles until the mid-1960s were hopelessly negative and centred mostly on subjects like the technological backwardness of Indian agriculture and the social conservativeness of the peasantry. One of the representative conceptualisations of this mainstream discourse on Indian agriculture during the 1950s could be found in the early writings of Daniel Thorner. The backwardness of Indian agriculture, he argued, could be attributed to the historically evolved structure of social and power relations in the countryside, which were unique to India, which produced a 'build-in depressor' (Thorner 1956: 12).

The growing use of high-yielding varieties of seeds, chemical fertilisers, pesticides and new machines raised the productivity of land severalfold and nearly solved India's national problem of food scarcity in a rather short time. The success of the Green Revolution brought the discourse on Indian agriculture out of the 'limbo of cow dung economics' and 'dismissive contempt' with which development professionals saw it (Byres 1972: 100). As the agrarian economy began to show some dynamism, new types of questions began to be raised and debated. Scholars started collecting empirical data on various aspects of the changes taking place on the ground. Although everyone did not turn into its admirer, or become a 'green revolutionary', the fact that something hitherto unknown was happening in these pockets where new agrarian technology had been introduced was widely recognised (see Jodhka 2016).

From the simple concerns of elementary economics, such as who benefited from the new technology and who did not, to complex questions of social and cultural change in the Indian countryside, all were examined empirically and debated with passion in the pages of journals like *Economic & Political Weekly* (EPW) and the *Journal of Peasant Studies* (JPS). The famous 'mode of production debate' among economists and anthropologists of Marxist persuasion on the nature of emerging social relations of production in Indian agriculture was a direct outcome of this growing new interest of social science scholars in the changing rural scenario in the wake of the Green Revolution (see Thorner 1982).

The face of the Indian countryside in Green Revolution pockets started changing very rapidly. In terms of social groups, the most visible beneficiaries of this change were the substantial landowners from the locally dominant caste groups who had traditionally been landowners and cultivators. The locally dominant castes consolidated their position in the regional power structure and acquired a new sense of confidence. The rise of dominant caste farmers in the 1970s also set in motion a phase of populist politics at the regional and national levels. The newly emerged agrarian elite did not speak only for 'his' own caste or class but also on behalf of the entire village. His identification with the village was not just political or that of a representative of a section of the village, but he also saw himself to be the natural spokesperson of the village.

However, this excitement about Green Revolution and modernisation of Indian agriculture did not last for too long. By the mid-1980s, the Indian countryside began to show a new kind of restiveness. Interestingly, this restiveness was pronounced particularly in pockets that had experienced the Green Revolution. The surplus-producing farmers began to mobilise themselves into unions, demanding subsidies on farm inputs and higher prices for their produce. Market economy, they argued, was inherently against the farm sector and favoured the urban industry and middle-class consumers. Given the unequal power relations between the town and countryside, they argued, the agricultural sector suffered from unequal terms of trade, the evidence of which could be seen in the growth of indebtedness among the cultivating/farming classes.

Farmers mobilised themselves in different parts of India quite successfully for over a decade. Although the movements had a local character in terms of leadership and strategies of mobilisation, they coordinated their activities across regions. In a sense, they were quite successful in getting their agenda accepted at the level of national politics. The farmers' movements of the 1980s also signalled the rise of a new social category of rural people who had prospered with Green Revolution, were connected closely to the market economy and saw their fate being conditioned by the market but who also aspired to go beyond the village. The agrarian economy could not satisfy their aspirations for social and cultural mobility. They began to move out of the village, from their local seats of power to legislative assemblies in the state capitals. The surplus they generated from agriculture went into education, urban trade and other non-agricultural activities (Balagopal 1987: 1545; Omvedt 1992; Rutten 1995; Upadhya 1988).

The adoption of Green Revolution technology effectively translated into more intensive agriculture and a shift to new and multiple crops. This required much greater involvement of labour, which attracted a large inflow of seasonal migrant workers from relatively depressed pockets of the neighbouring states. For example, Punjab and Haryana began to receive a large volume of migrant labour from Bihar and eastern Uttar Pradesh. Thus, new technology also began transforming social relations in those regions. The decades of the 1970s and 1980s saw a gradual loosening of caste ties almost everywhere in the subcontinent (Karanth 1996). Dominance of the dominant castes or that of the big landowners could no longer be taken for granted (Krishna 2003; Mendelsohn 1993). The traditional ties of dependence, the *jajmani* structures of caste and systems of prolonged labour attachments (bondage) began to disintegrate everywhere. The new technology prompted formalisation of production relations in the Green Revolution pockets (Bhalla 1976; Jodhka 1994) and growing outmigration from the less-developed regions provided escape from semi-feudal dominations in regions where the new technology did not reach until much later (Rodgers and Rodgers 2011; Rodgers et al. 2016).

Rural Power and Democratisation

As is evident from the above discussion, despite its many pitfalls and lacunae, by the 1970s, the state policies of rural social and economic change had begun to transform India's countryside in quite a fundamental way. While the economic change unleashed by new technologies and demographic processes of migration significantly enhanced the pace of integration of the rural economy with that of the regional and national economies, the new state also worked towards integration of rural landscapes into the democratic political processes of the nation. A variety of official programmes targeted for rural development and poverty alleviation also enhanced the bureaucratic reach of the nation state into the everyday life of the village.

The initial decades after independence saw benefits of much of the development initiatives from above going to the already influential and powerful. In most cases, the dominant groups and families of the village were also able to capture the local-level democratic institutions (Dube 1958; Herring 1977; Moore 1966; Thorner 1964). However, as integration of the village with the larger political and economic order grew, the logic of politics at the local level also began to change. Rise of the plebian in the Indian democracy (Jaffrelot and Kumar 2009) also had an effect on the local power structure. A new type of local-level leader, the *naya neta*, who was primarily a political entrepreneur, emerged to challenge the authority of the traditional patriarch. Although caste and economic power continued to matter, the primary source of influence of these political entrepreneurs was drawn from their ability to assist their fellow villagers with a range of services and networks; from helping with getting a ration card made, to submitting an application for a development scheme, to connecting with political leaders in the state capital (see Jodhka 2014; Krishna 2003; Manor 2012), there were a whole range of spheres in which they acquired a position of indispensability.

Emergent Ruralities

Shifts in the country's economic orientation during the early years of the 1990s, coupled with the unfolding of other processes popularly described as globalisation, changed the imaginings of rural India quite significantly. Even when the demographic weight of the rural continues to be large and politically significant, and agriculture still formally 'employs' nearly half of its working people, the village rarely figures in the 'post-liberal' narratives of emerging India. The dominant view of the globalising India today is constructed in its metropolitan centres by the rising urban middle classes.

This decline of the village is not only in the imagination of emerging India, but the relative weight of rural economy, particularly in agriculture, has also seen a rather rapid decline. Besides providing employment to a large majority of working Indians, returns from the agricultural sector also made up more than half of India's national income. By the middle of the second decade of the 21st century, its share was down to a mere 13 per cent or 14 per cent of the national GDP. Agriculture is no longer even the major contributor to rural incomes with non-farm economic engagements, both locally and from outside, contributing a major chunk to this. Many of the rural households that are formally enumerated as being employed in agriculture are in reality 'pluri-active' (Lindberg 2005), where some members of the family also work outside agriculture.

With growing marginalisation of the rural and decline of agriculture, social science research interest on rural and agrarian economy also declined during the 1990s. Unfortunately, it is only when incidents of farmers' suicides began to be reported with greater frequency from different regions of the country that agriculture returned to academic and political platforms. Rural India, in this new narrative, appears as a site of gloom and depression where real incomes are declining and farmers are perpetually distressed.

Besides this 'narrative of crises', the post-1990s India also framed the Indian rural in a 'narrative of integration'. Invoked broadly in a positive tenor, the advocates of this narrative point to the manifold expansion of rural infrastructure, roads and communication networks and the rise of the rural consumer. All these changes have brought the village closer to the town, and the rural residents, at least a section of them, are increasingly adapting to an urban way of life. The rising aspiration, growing desire for education and disenchantment with agriculture among the younger generation of farming families have all worked towards creating an outward orientation (Djurfeldt et al. 2008; Himanshu and Stern 2016; Jodhka 2014). Some have gone to the extent suggesting that the 'rural' as a category needed to be revised, and it ought to be seen as some kind of low-order urban or 'rurban' (Gupta 2015). Perhaps the most important agency of change in this context has been the spread of education to rural hinterlands. Becoming educated is to become qualified to move out of the village (Kumar 2014).

While there is an element of truth in both the narratives on the contemporary rural, they share many problematic assumptions on the nature of emergent Indian ruralities, despite many apparent differences. Perhaps the most obvious of these is an imagining of its decline, positively or negatively. Further, they also work with the notion of the Indian rural as a singular category framed in the populist binary of the rural–urban. This binary has its origins in the classical modernisation frames of understanding social transformations in the developing world.

However, the realities of rural in India have always been very diverse, horizontally (or regionally) as well as vertically (in terms of caste–class divisions), and it continues to be so even today. As I have discussed above, the nature of rural social formations has varied quite significantly across regions of India. These diversities have been shaped by plural histories of different regions, their ecological diversities or even the sizes and shapes of settlements.

The divisions on caste and class lines continue to matter and shape the nature of change being experienced on the ground. Even when the relational structures change, prejudice of the dominant caste groups against the ex-untouchables communities survives and sharpens, which often manifests itself in different forms of violence and denial of democratic entitlements (Jodhka 2015; Jodhka and Louis 2003; Martin 2015; Picherit 2015). These narratives of the rural tend to undermine the continued significance of caste in rural life. The 'agrarian crisis' narrative, for example, tends to present every rural resident as a cultivating farmer, while in reality, nearly half of the rural households, generally those from Dalit and lower OBC communities, have always been landless in most regions of the country. They do not see themselves as peasants/farmers. Thanks to growing mechanisation and declining size of landholdings, employment opportunities that agriculture generates have been coming down. Thus, many among the landless can no longer find employment in agriculture. Some of them do not like the farm work. They prefer to, or have to, float around in search of viable employment. The trajectory of these footloose villagers has been very different from that of those from the farming communities from the dominant castes, who continue to be the sole signifiers of the rural in these narratives.

The experience of change varies very significantly across regions and communities. The nature of rural–urban integration and the value of categories like 'rurban' also varies significantly depending on the region and its trajectories of change. Even when the economic integration of rural settlements is high in a given region, the nature of change may not imply any substantive urbanisation of the rural. For example, the increased circular migrations of labour from the depressed pockets of regions like Bihar though transforms the local-level caste–class relations, yet rural landscapes remain quite 'backward' and peripheral in the larger economy. The substantive nature of disadvantages and deprivations has not seen much change.

However, this is not to understate the magnitude of change the rural and the agrarian social orders have seen in the subcontinent over the past half century or so. Even the categories of rural and agrarian, which have often been used interchangeably by social scientists, policymakers and popular media, are becoming increasingly differentiated. As I have tried to show in this chapter, the notion of 'agrarian' no longer encompasses the 'rural'—socially, economically and politically. Thus, a decoupling of the rural from the agrarian will perhaps be a useful move for future research and policy/political engagements on what continues to be two-thirds of India.

References

Balagopal, K. 1987. 'An Ideology of the Provincial Propertied Class'. *Economic & Political Weekly* 21 (36–37): 2177–78.

Beteille, A. 1980. 'The Indian Village: Past and Present'. In *Peasants in History: Essays in Honour of Daniel Thorner*, edited by E.J. Hobsbaum, W. Kule, A. Mitra, K. N. Raj and I. Sach, 107–20. New Delhi: Oxford University Press.

Bhalla, S. 1976. 'New Relations of Production in Haryana Agriculture'. *Economic & Political Weekly* 11 (13): A23–A30.

Byres, T.J. 1972. 'The Dialectics of India's Green Revolution'. *South Asian Review* 5 (2): 99–106.

———. 2000. *India: The Social Anthropology of a Civilization*. Delhi: Oxford University Press.

Datta, Paranati. 2006. 'Urbanisation in India', 1–16. Available at: http://www.infostat.sk/vdc/epc2006/papers/epc2006s60134.pdf (accessed on 25 March 2016).

Dhanagare, D.N. 1984. 'Agrarian Reforms and Rural Development in India: Some Observations'. *Research in Social Movements, Conflict and Change* 7 (1): 177–201.

Djurfeldt, G., V. Athreya, N. Jayakumar, S. Lindberg, A. Rajagopal and R. Vidyasagar. 2008. 'Agrarian Change and Social Mobility in Tamil Nadu'. *Economic & Political Weekly* 43 (45): 50–61.

Dube, S.C. 1958. *India's Changing Villages: Human Factors in Community Development*. Ithaca, NY: Cornell University Press.

Gupta, Dipankar. 2015. 'The Importance of Being "Rurban" Tracking Changes in a Traditional Setting.' *Economic and Political Weekly* L (24): 37–43.

Herring, R.J. 1977. 'Land Tenure and Credit-capital Tenure in Contemporary India'. In *Land Tenure and Peasants in South Asia*, edited by R.E. Frynkenberg, 120–58. New Delhi: Manohar Publishers.

Himanshu and Nicholas Stern. 2016. 'Six Decades in a North Indian Village'. In *The Changing Village in India*, edited by Himanshu, Praveen Jha and Gerry Rodgers, 87–118. New Delhi: Oxford University Press.

IDFC. 2013. *India Rural Development Report*. IDFC Rural Development Network. New Delhi: Orient BlackSwan.

Jaffrelot, C. Sanjay Kumar, ed. 2009. 'Rise of the Plebeians'. In *The Changing Face of Indian Legislative Assemblies*. New Delhi: Routledge.

Jodhka, S.S. 1994. 'Agrarian Changes and Attached Labour: Emerging Patterns in Haryana Agriculture'. *Economic & Political Weekly* 29 (39): A102–106.

———. 1998. 'From "Book-View" to "Field-View": Social Anthropological: Constructions of the Indian Village'. *Oxford Development Studies* 26 (3): 311–32.

———. 2002. 'Nation and Village: Images of Rural India in Gandhi, Nehru and Ambedkar'. *Economic & Political Weekly* 37 (19): 3343–53.

Jodhka, S.S. 2003. 'Agrarian Structures and their Transformations'. In *Oxford India Companion to Sociology and Social Anthropology*. Vol. II. Edited by Veena Das, 1213–43. New Delhi: Oxford University Press.

———. 2014. 'Emergent Ruralities: Revisiting Village Life and Agrarian Change in Haryana'. *Economic & Political Weekly* 49 (26–28): 5–17.

———. 2015. *Caste in Contemporary India*. New Delhi: Routledge.

———. 2016. 'A Forgotten "Revolution": Revisiting Rural Life and Agrarian Change in Haryana'. In *The Changing Village in India*, edited by Himanshu, Praveen Jha and Gerry Rodgers, 155–93. New Delhi: Oxford University Press.

Jodhka, S.S. and Prakash Louis. 2003. 'Caste Tensions in Punjab: Talhan and Beyond'. *Economic & Political Weekly* 38 (28): 2923–26.

Joshi, P.C. 1976. *Land Reforms in India: Trends and Perspectives*. New Delhi: Allied Publishers.

Karanth, G.K. 1996. 'Caste in Contemporary Rural India'. In *Caste: Its Twentieth Century Avatar*, edited by M.N. Srinivas, 87–109. Delhi: Penguin.

Krishna, Anirudh. 2003. 'What Is Happening to Caste? A View from Some North Indian Villages'. *The Journal of Asian Studies* 62 (4): 1171–93.

Kumar, Krishna. 2014. 'Rurality, Modernity and Education'. *Economic & Political Weekly* 49 (31): 38–43.

Lindberg, Steffan. 2005. 'Whom and What to Fight? Notes and Queries on Indian Farmers Collective Action under Liberalisation and Globalisation'. Unpublished seminar paper. Punjab University, Patiala.

Manor, James. 2012. 'Accommodation and Conflict'. *Seminar* 633 (May): 14–18.

Martin, Nicolas. 2015. 'Rural Elites and the Limits of Scheduled Caste Assertiveness in Rural Malwa, Punjab'. *Economic & Political Weekly* 50 (52): 37–44.

Mendelsohn, O. 1993. 'The Transformation of Authority in Rural India', *Modern Asian Studies*, 27 (4): 805–42.

Moore, B., Jr. 1966. *Social Origins of Dictatorship and Democracy*. Middlesex: Penguin.

Omvedt, Gail. 1992. 'Capitalist Agriculture and Rural Classes in India'. In *Class, State and Development in India*, edited by B. Berberogly. New Delhi: SAGE.

Picherit, David. 2015. 'Dalit Mobilisation and Faction Politics in Rural Andhra Pradesh: Everyday Life of a Dalit NGO and Agricultural Labour Union'. *Economic & Political Weekly* 50 (52): 74–82.

Rodgers, G., Sunil K. Mishra and Alakh N. Sharma. 2016. 'Four Decades of Village Studies and Surveys in Bihar'. In *The Changing Village in India*, edited by Himanshu, Praveen Jha and Gerry Rodgers, 119–54. New Delhi: Oxford University Press.

Rodgers, G. and J. Rodgers. 2011. 'Inclusive Development? Migration, Governance and Social Change in Rural Bihar'. *Economic & Political Weekly* 46 (23): 43–50.

Rutten, M.A.F. 1995. *Farms and Factories: Social Profile of Large Farmers and Rural Industrialists in West India*. New Delhi: Oxford University Press.

Srinivas, M.N. 1955. 'Village Studies and Their Significance'. In *Rural Profiles* (Vol. 1), edited by D.N. Majumdar, 95–100. Lucknow: Ethnographic and Folk Culture Society.

Thorner, A. 1982. 'Semi-feudalism or Capitalism? Contemporary Debate on Classes and Modes of Production in India'. *Economic & Political Weekly* 17 (49–51): 993–99, 2061–86.

Thorner, D. 1956. *The Agrarian Prospects of India*. Delhi: University Press.

———. 1964. *Agricultural Co-operatives in India*. Bombay: Asia Publishers.

Upadhya, Carol B. 1988. 'The Farmer–Capitalists of Coastal Andhra Pradesh'. *Economic & Political Weekly* 23 (27 and 28): 1376–82, 1433–42.

7

Fields, Markets and Agricultural Commodities

Mekhala Krishnamurthy

Reconceiving the Grain Heap

In the literature on the economic anthropology of India, the post-harvest grain heap has given rise to a veritable mountain of ethnographic material. Generations of anthropologists have visited and revisited the threshing floor to observe and record the division of the grain heap among different members of the village community, 'the locus classicus' of a moneyless, redistributive transactional order widely known as the *jajmani* system (Vasavi 1998: 43). In numerous accounts, village exchange between high-caste landowning patrons and their service-providing clients was noted to have always been made through payments in kind and based entirely within a 'non-market economy regulated by customary rights and privileges and intrinsically bound up with caste relationships' (Harriss 2005: 527). For quite some time now, this view of village economy and society has also been thoroughly questioned, not only by field analyses of village-based grain transactions that differ significantly from the jajmani system (Vasavi 1998) but also in trenchant critique that has argued that the jajmani system did not constitute a system at all, and was really the construction of a highly successful 'anthropological fiction' (Fuller 1989: 34). In an important essay entitled 'Misconceiving the Grain Heap', Fuller (1989) contrasted the pre-ponderance of anthropological writings on the traditional, unchanging non-monetary rural economy with extensive historical evidence on the role of markets, monetary exchange and cash revenue systems across diverse regions of agrarian India. In doing so, Fuller hoped that his critical deconstruction of the jajmani system and its 'bucolic symbol' might help 'to clear the path to more productive analysis of forms of exchange in Indian society, including those which centre on the grain heap, as well as to better comparative understanding of money and the market' (ibid.: 45, 58).

Unfortunately, sociologists and social anthropologists of India have been far less interested in following the grain out from the fields and the threshing floors than one might have expected. As other reviews of the discipline have noted before, the remarkable lack of ethnographic engagement with agricultural markets (and in fact with markets more generally) in India has been a serious omission (Fuller 1989; Harriss 2005; Vidal 2003). Indeed, one could say that anthropologists, who might have once been all 'too readily beguiled' by the grain heap (Fuller 1989: 34), have not really allowed themselves to be beguiled nearly enough. For, as an excursion into a market yard will quickly reveal, grain heaps are constantly in the making and usually conceal as much as they reveal.

This is certainly true of the heaps of soya bean and wheat in Harda Mandi in Madhya Pradesh (MP). In this particular market, open auctions are conducted directly from covered platforms, where a small number of bullock carts and a much larger number of tractor trolleys filled with produce from the surrounding villages are lined up by farmers for sale. As the auction proceeds, heaps of grain and oilseeds build up over the course of the day in a rectangular compound that one enters immediately after crossing the auction sheds. Traders' shops and godowns line the yard and two electronic weighbridges and numerous manual weighing scales dot and define the area, where produce is weighed, deposited, mixed, bagged, stitched, dragged, stacked and stored or dispatched according to the day's plans for different buyers. This is also the site where commodities are physically transferred from the ownership of the producer to the custody of the procurer through a series of tasks performed by labourers, paid for in part by the two main parties on either side of the heap. Farmers must cover the costs of the offloading and weighing of their lot, but from the point at which the weight has been determined and the produce deposited outside the trader's shop, all the remaining labour and supervision costs are to be borne by the buyer. Much is at stake here at this site of transfer, technique, vigilance, manipulation, exploitation and resistance. And yet none of this is easily apparent except to those routinely involved in the making and managing of grain heaps from day-to-day and across marketing seasons.

Take, for example, a common mandi practice called the *paala* or the mixing of soya bean. Here, all the soya bean bought from numerous farmers by a particular trader is first deposited in a single heap and then, a group of women labourers physically mix the produce by shifting it from one heap to another, using rectangular tin scoops, their multiple, simultaneous actions mixing the material more evenly as it gathers in the new heap. This manual process is an attempt to 'make the ratio' (ratio *banana*), which in the case of soya bean involves three parameters of fair average quality (FAQ): moisture content, damaged seeds and foreign material. For commission agents, maintaining the ratio is vital because if you fail to deliver on the specifications, the plant receiving the consignment will make deductions on your fixed commission. In practice, agents and traders buy different lots of soya bean, below, around and above FAQ in the auction. The challenge is to mix these different lots in such a way that it will pass the quality check at the plant at the price set for the day, minimising deductions and maximising margins.

For soya bean processors, practices like the paala are a 'major headache', demanding constant scrutiny and enforcement of conditions in their relationship with mandi commission agents. This mixing, they also feel, disincentivises farmers to take steps to clean their produce before bringing it into the market. Unsurprisingly, mandi traders hold a different position. In a context where produce is of highly variable quality, grown and harvested under the diverse conditions and constraints of small-holder cultivation, they argue, this ability to take different lots of seed—moist and dry, bold and shrivelled—and to turn them into one large lot, to make them into one ratio (*ek jaise banana*), is not malpractice but the 'skill' and 'mastery' of mandi trade. As a senior trader put it, 'When you do the *paala*, you are working with what you have, what is already there. You are making the most of the different qualities of *maal* (produce, material) that comes into the market'. In his view, this is the difference between 'accommodation' and 'adulteration', and the reason that the mandi can produce a buyer and a price for virtually every quality, from spotless seed to little more than mud.

Here, on the market floor, then, it is not the division of the grain heap but its mixing that one has to pay attention to, and, with it, to critical dilemmas around questions of quality and the 'moral economy of grades and standards' in market life (Busch 2000). Similarly, there is a great deal that can be gleaned about the structure, organisation and dynamics of the commodity system from the character, composition and distribution of grain heaps across marketing seasons, or by tracing significant shifts in local market power to whether the weight comes before the heap or the heap before the weight in routine marketing procedure, or further, in following the micro movements from the heap to the stack—and in the process unpacking changing labour practices and politics in the mandi yard. In each instance, the grain heap thus reconceived is an invitation to analyse complex and changing relations of commodity exchange and market practice, and an entry point into a rich and insightful collection of works that may help us think afresh some of the key themes and questions in the economic sociology and anthropology of India.

Institutional Complexity and Intermediaries

Commodity markets are not only a part of an agrarian structure, but they also bring to it significant institutional diversity and complexity, and generate dense networks of interconnection and exchange with the non-agrarian economy. This complexity is best articulated by the field economist Barbara Harriss-White, who stands out among scholars for the length, depth and range of her engagement with Indian agricultural markets across different contexts. Agricultural markets, her work shows, need to be robustly conceptualised as much more than a thin 'layer of buying and selling', restricted to transactions between producers and wholesalers. They are 'systems of circulation' through which commodities move, not only by means of market exchange but also through other transactional forms and relations.

> Loan repayments, payments to labour, and rental contracts (all of which may involve payments in kind) are just as much a part of the system of circulation as buying and selling, processing, transport and storage. The last three activities, however, transform the commodity in form, space, and time. These activities link the circulation of a commodity with the circulation of money, and with the exploitation of labour and land…. Market-making institutions are draped all over this system and the repercussions of change in institutions of circulation are felt in institutions of production. (Harriss-White 2008: 24–25)

Add to this the diversity of non-market relationships on which markets depend and the multiple and contradictory roles of the regulatory state, and you have highly intricate and dynamic agro-commercial complexes that demand empirical specification while ensuring that even merely adequate description is difficult to accomplish.

These systems are characterised by complexity in activity and contractual diversity. 'Trading firms may buy, sell, broker, store, transport, process, produce, finance production, and finance trade. There are two to the 9th possible combinations of these nine activities and there are other activities'. Similarly, parties involved in agricultural markets also engage in a wide variety of contractual forms, 'from spot contracts through advance, and/or futures agreements, attached, repeated or relational forms, to internal transfers'. Contracts not only affect rights of control over tangible commodities but also reference the 'intangible social attributes and obligations that are frequently entangled in the contract'. And they are not restricted to commodity exchange alone since commodities once purchased may also be used in tribute, gift and redistribution. Finally, contracts may be written but are frequently verbal, adhere to formal or legal rules or follow customary norms, and involve a plurality of institutions for dispute resolution (ibid.: 26–27).

Intermediaries exist throughout systems of agricultural production, exchange and circulation, and simplistic views of intermediaries as distortionary figures in agricultural commodity markets are well off the mark. Rather, as Denis Vidal (2000: 128) shows, in complex wholesale markets for grain (and equally for other kinds of agricultural produce), 'it is the presence of intermediaries and the different functions they assume that defines and characterises the market'. Take the case of Naya Bazaar in the old city in Delhi, one of the most important grain markets in North India and a major centre for grain export outside the country. 'Most of the grain which passes through Delhi', Vidal notes, 'is neither produced nor processed nor consumed in Delhi itself' (ibid.: 133). Here, commission agents, acting on behalf of distant trading parties, are crucial to the making of transactions, but the nature of commercial arrangements 'blurs practically any distinction between the main parties of a transaction (the "real" buyers and the "real" sellers) and the intermediaries'. For instance, it makes little sense to

> Consider a trader who has paid 80 percent of a load of grain which is stocked in a godown belonging to him and who has the charge of selling it on behalf of his client as a simple intermediary. Similarly, if he buys some grain with his own money for a client who has given precise indications of the quality and quantity of grain he wants, and if he takes only a fixed commission on the price, will he be considered a trader or a commission agent? (ibid.: 136)

In such cases, commission agents not only bear the risk of carrying the costs until settlement in systems where delayed payments are a fairly frequent occurrence, but they are also constantly on the lookout, at every stage of the process, for opportunities to extend their margins. Such distinctions, then, not only appear rather immaterial in the thick of transactions, but also tend to be analytically unproductive. Instead, a deeper engagement with the institutional complexity of commodity markets, along the lines outlined above, can open up new ways of thinking about systems of exchange and circulation, the diversity of contractual relations and their conduct, and the concentration and dispersal of control, risk and profit among multiple market actors, some of whom play overlapping and even contradictory roles as 'conglomerate' capitalists in agro-commercial circuits (Harriss-White 2008: 22; Krishnamurthy 2014). At the same time, market actors themselves draw important distinctions, on and off the books and in their own ethical calculations, about these different roles, the market identities and reputational status they convey, the question of self-respect, and the taste of the profit and loss they might bring in (Gold 2009; Krishnamurthy 2013).

Commodities and Quidity

In India, as elswhere, agricultural markets are fundamentally commodity-specific in terms of their institutional forms and marketing practices. Harriss-White uses the term 'quidity' to describe the 'essence or particularity' of commodities, referencing both their physical characteristics and material content, as well as their social and cultural meanings and moral qualities. Physical quidity (such as divisibility or perishability) significantly determines the economic, social, spatial and seasonal/temporal organisation of production and trade, 'but quidity is often a mix of the physical and the social so that things determine markets in unpredictable ways' (Harriss-White 2003: 208). Moreover, commodities are continuously being transformed in transfer and movement (including during periods of holding or storage), while by-products are constantly commodified and have their own circuitry and sites of exchange and distribution. In the rice cluster in Arni, Tamil Nadu, for example, husk is now a commodity itself and is used both to make holy pastes and as a base for silicon chips; rice bran is traded as an intermediate good in the solvent extraction industry and is used as cattle feed for local milk production; broken rice is fed to cattle and to some humans, while de-oiled bran cake is an export commodity, dispatched as cattle feed to the EU (Harriss-White 2016: 120).

Places—of origin and destination—have always been vital to commodity character and are also vitalised and re-made by processes of commodification and market exchange. In colonial India, Satish Deshpande (2003: 59) suggests, 'commodities appear to have functioned as mnemonic devices, aids for imagining the nation in its geographical spread and specificity'. If, in general, such associations between particular places and the things they produce are thought to have significantly weakened, if not been erased by the regimes of late capitalism and the conditions of relentless commodification, recent work on global agri-food systems point to the powerful and often paradoxical reinscriptions of territory and locality that are taking place in different parts of India and the world. We see this vividly, for example, in controversial attempts by an American company to patent basmati rice (Vidal 2005), in the social construction of a geographical indication (GI) for Goan *feni* (Rangnekar 2011) and in movements for fair trade, GI and Gorkhaland as they variously attempt to reinvent the Darjeeling tea plantation (Besky 2014). These works explore contending visions of what justice in the market might mean and the ways in which 'intellectual legal distinctions' (ibid.: 21) like GI connote and confer property rights and juridical protection over particular commodities and the 'geographic appellations' by which they come to be known (Rangnekar 2011: 2046). In the process, 'different coalitions of interest coalesce in the making and remaking of place' through acts of specification that recognise and reify certain elements within dynamic cultural repertoires of production while erasing others. As Dwijen Rangnekar (2011: 2054) shows in the case of the registration of a GI for *caju feni*, 'the specifications reveal paradoxes between the celebration of place and its transformation through a global legal vehicle'. Ironically, while GIs have been described as conventions of place, 'authored by producers' and mobilised in movements of localisation and resistance (ibid.: 2057), the commodities themselves are often only prized for their distant appeal and evoke ambivalent responses by those who grow them such as the plantation workers who find Darjeeling tea to be far too expensive and too bland for their taste (Besky 2014) or the Himachali apple farmers who expressed contempt for the exotically named produce growing on their plots, 'which they refused to consider as real fruit' (Vidal 2005: 55).

The Social and the Technical

The relationships between commodities and places are steeped in regional histories, political economies and agroecologies. Here, an older and quite pioneering series of works on the comparative sociology of agricultural cooperatives helps reveal the social, technical and political complexity—and contingency—involved in the successes and failures of large-scale institutional experiments in collective marketing in different contexts (Attwood and Baviskar 1987; Baviskar and Attwood 1984). First, commodity characteristics again prove critical. In this case, the high degree of perishability and the large economies of scale from bulk processing were integral to the viability of dairy and sugar cooperatives in Gujarat and Maharashtra. Second, in both cases, historical conditions and the regional dynamics of agricultural production played key roles. Kheda district in Gujarat was known for its high levels of dairy production well before the first cooperatives were established, and the cooperative sugar factories that came up in western Maharashtra did so after a series of economic and political innovations along an 'irrigation frontier'. Third, in highly differentiated agrarian systems, cooperatives were able to forge and sustain a unique alignment of interests among large and small growers, resolving tricky technical and institutional challenges like the perennial 'cane-supply problem' facing sugar factories. And fourth, such 'pragmatic alliance making' was aided by the agrarian social structure; in Maharashtra, for instance, there was the presence of a common, loosely defined intermediate caste of small and large cultivators, the Marathas (Attwood and Baviskar 1987: A-47). But, both the Marathas and the Patidars in Gujarat realised the importance of including other castes in the effective running of the cooperatives while leveraging their political connections to protect the co-ops and using their controlling interests in the cooperatives to consolidate regional political power (Baviskar and Attwood 1984: 105).

Despite subsequent reversals in performance and rampant corruption in Maharashtra's sugar cooperatives, that experience is still a stark contrast to what we learn about the conditions of sugarcane marketing in Uttar Pradesh (UP) through the historical archive (Amin 1984), economic and social geography (Jeffrey 2002) and intra-regional analysis of eastern and western UP (Damodaran and Singh 2007). In UP, state-run district cane societies act as intermediaries between farmers and sugar mills, and are charged with controlling the supply of sugarcane to specific units during the season. This is done by fixing a quota of how much sugarcane a farmer can supply in any given year and through the distribution of supply slips or *parchis*. In places like Meerut, this system gave rise to competition among rich Jat farmers, who used all kinds of influence to try to raise their quotas and get their hands on parchis. Cane Society officials responded by promoting a 'shadow market in supply slips' and demanding bribes for their timely release, while weighment clerks extracted hefty illegal rents as 'on-the-top' incomes (Jeffrey 2002: 32). In the meanwhile, poor farmers often found their quotas dwindle inexplicably and their supply slips disappear; as one such farmer dejectedly remarked, the slips must have just gone off and 'wandered on the road' (ibid.: 34).

The power of the parchi in sugarcane marketing in UP resonates with the 'cutting' of slips in favour of well-connected farmers, who drew on the strength of their 'settings' with local market functionaries to bypass the long queues in the blistering heat of a major state-run wheat procurement season in Harda Mandi in MP, even as district administrators and mandi functionaries responded with novel strategies, including an SMS-based registration system in an effort to address this and other particular problems in the field (Krishnamurthy 2012). More generally, these circulating slips of paper draw attention to the remarkable vitality of the various materials, 'market devices' and measures used at every stage of the marketing process—in auctions, sampling, grading, weighment, payment, bagging, storage, transport, etc. (Callon et al. 2007). Mundane, intimate, contested and politically charged, a market ethnographer will be made constantly aware of these active, ethical elements in the agricultural market and its pulsating logistical life.

Composites and Futures

Among all the aspects of agricultural commodity markets, price is the most prominent and elusive, the most material and abstract. It is also the most politically sensitive; price movements index political stability and volatility, nowhere more powerfully than in the case of the commodity prices of staple foods. As E.P. Thompson (1971) demonstrated in his seminal work on the food riot and the price of bread in the markets of 18th-century England, 'the questioning of simple equations between things and their prices is a sure sign of fundamental unrest' (Guyer 2009: 204). These questions arise even as people seem to be more acutely and openly aware than ever before that all prices are 'composites' and 'fictions—literally the results of narratives of creation, addition and subtraction' (ibid.). In India, agricultural costs and prices for producers, and retail prices of food for consumers, are integral to the everyday lives and popular understandings of the state and/of the market, both at the local level and in its more distantly powerful forms. Here, price—in hard numbers and loaded acronyms—appears and disappears from view in the compositional journeys and processes of realisation in numerous instances: in minimum support prices (MSPs) for farmers, in the public distribution system (PDS) for poor citizens, in the consumer price index (CPI) and public reactions to food inflation, in rounds of negotiation at the WTO, in fertiliser subsidies, in mandi fees, in tax exemptions to 'agriculturalists', in post-harvest bonuses and loan waivers, in crop insurance schemes, and the recent addition of a Krishi Kalyan (farmer welfare) Cess on retail invoices, in debates around foreign direct investment (FDI), in the proposed legislation on the Goods and Services Tax (GST), in current proposals for a common National Agricultural Market (NAM), and in various other unfolding developments. All of this calls for much closer and much more creative ethnographic attention.

In keeping with global interest in the subject, one critical area that has received some significant scholarly attention is the futures market and the play of speculation in agricultural commodities. In recent times, this interest has been sparked by a government order in 2003, authorising derivatives trading in the form of futures contracts, lifting an over 50-year-old ban on their use in Indian agricultural commodity markets. But contemporary futures trading through national electronic platforms are part of a much longer history involving the development of regional exchanges for particular commodities and the preoccupation of regulators with the 'indigenous'(especially Marwari) predilection for speculation and its economic and social effects (Birla 2009; Dantwala 1937; Timberg 1978). Focusing on a period of rapid financialisation between 1925 and 1947, the historian Ritu Birla (2015: 393, 402) details 'a shift in the governing of vernacular speculation from policing to administrative procedure in formal exchanges', from the criminalisation of gambling to a focus on the intentionality of the futures contract, to the legal and governmental embrace of financial speculation, validating what remains a 'play with uncertainty as risk management'. In the early 21st century, old and new anxieties animate the ambiguous relationship between the mandi and the *dabba*, literally 'the box', the mandi's word for the electronic commodity exchanges, the virtual futures trading platforms embodied in the computer, its screen constantly blinking with blue and red buy–sell numbers (Kumar 2010; Krishnamurthy 2013). Muddying old regulatory distinctions, the dabba is viewed by local Marwari traders in MP as nothing less than '*sarkari*-approved *satta*' (state-sanctioned gambling) that fries the small fish in the market pond, provoking critical debate in grain and oilseed mandis around questions of dominance and self-control, derivatives and the politics of detachment, temporal manipulation and its margins, and about the correct order of things, especially the fundamental relationship between the physical and the virtual in governing market life (Krishnamurthy 2013). Elsewhere, over cups of tea, Kolkata's guild-like community of brokers and the productive and communicative infrastructures of the trade have presented multiple obstacles to the financialisation of tea, generating a hybrid system of brokerage, 'with digital technologies wedged awkwardly into the old outcry model' (Besky 2016: 24).

Finally, however, across agricultural markets and rural hinterlands, speculation is not only about the exchange of commodities at a price point in the future but also about the exchange of possible futures themselves, especially for the many farmers and labourers negotiating complex movements and livelihoods in an increasingly diverse, volatile and precarious agrarian present (Cross 2014; Levien 2013; Sarkar 2015). This movement is, of course, inextricably bound to the prices and futures of land, its changing classification, division, diversion, acquisi-tion, use and development. Historically, regional variations in the dis-tribution and investment of the gains from the agricultural surplus, as well as in patterns of distress-driven diversification within rural regions and from villages to towns and cities, have been vital to the remarkably varied dynamics of Indian industrialisation and urbanisation (Baker 1984; Bayly 1983; Cadène and Vidal 1997; Chari 2004; Damodaran 2008; Harriss-White 2016; Jeffrey 2010; Lerche 2014; Ludden 1999). These vital interlinkages and their emergent effects only seem to be getting more energetic, complicated and unpredictable, demanding a new critical imagination and sustained fieldwork within and across the rural, urban and agrarian: fertile grounds for future sociological and anthropological work.

References

Amin, Shahid. 1984. *Sugarcane and Sugar in Gorakhpur*. New Delhi: Oxford University Press.

Attwood, D.W. and B.S. Baviskar. 1987. 'Why Do Some Co-operatives Work but Not Others: A Comparative Analysis of Sugar Co-operatives in India'. *Economic & Political Weekly* 22 (26): A38–A49, A51–A56.

Baker, Christoper. 1984. *An Indian Rural Economy, 1880–1955: The Tamilnad Countryside*. New Delhi: Oxford University Press.

Baviskar, B.S. and D.W. Attwood. 1984. 'Rural Co-operatives in India: A Comparative Analysis of Their Economic Survival and Social Impact'. *Contributions to Indian Sociology* 18 (1): 85–107.

Bayly, C.A. 1983. *Rulers, Townsmen and Bazaars: North Indian Society in the Age of British Expansion, 1770–1870*. Cambridge: Cambridge University Press.

Besky, Sarah. 2014. *Darjeeling Distinction: Labor and Justice on Fair-trade Tea Plantations in India*. Berkeley, CA: University of California Press.

———. 2016. 'The Future of Price: Communicative Infrastructures and the Financialization of Indian Tea'. *Cultural Anthropology* 31 (1): 4–29.

Birla, Ritu. 2009. *Stages of Capital: Law, Culture, and Market Governance in Late Colonial India*. Durham, NC and London: Duke University Press.

———. 2015. 'Speculation Illicit and Complicit: Contract, Uncertainty, and Governmentality'. *Comparative Studies of South Asia, Africa and the Middle East* 35 (3): 392–407.

Busch, Lawrence. 2000. 'The Moral Economy of Grades and Standards'. *Journal of Rural Studies* 16 (3): 273–83.

Cadène, Phillipe and Denis Vidal, eds. 1997. *Webs of Trade: Dynamics of Business Communities in Western India*. New Delhi: Manohar Publishers.

Callon, Michel, Yuval Millo and Fabian Muniesa, eds. 2007. *Market Devices*. Malden, MA and Oxford: Blackwell Publishers.

Chari, Sharad. 2004. *Fraternal Capital: Peasant-workers, Self-made Men and Globalization in Provincial India*. Delhi: Permanent Black and Orient Longman.

Cross, Jamie. 2014. *Dream Zones: Anticipating Capitalism and Development in India*. London: Pluto Press.

Damodaran, Harish. 2008. *India's New Capitalists: Caste, Business and Industry in a Modern Nation*. Ranikhet: Permanent Black.

Damodaran, Harish and Harvir Singh. 2007. 'Sugar Industry in Uttar Pradesh: Rise, Decline and Revival'. *Economic and Political Weekly* 42 (4): 3952–57.

Dantwala, M.L. 1937. *Marketing of Raw Cotton in India*. Calcutta: Longmans, Green and Co.

Deshpande, Satish. 2003. *Contemporary India: A Sociological View*. New Delhi: Penguin India.

Fuller, C.J. 1989. 'Misconceiving the Grain Heap: A Critique of the Concept of the Indian Jajmani System'. In *Money and the Morality of Exchange*, edited by Maurice Bloch and Jonathan Parry, 33–63. Cambridge: Cambridge University Press.

Gold, Ann Grodzins. 2009. 'Tasteless Profits and Vexed Moralities: Assessments of the Present in Rural Rajasthan'. *Journal of the Royal Anthropological Institute* 15 (2): 365–85.

Guyer, Jane. 2009. 'Composites, Fictions, and Risk: Toward an Ethnography of Price'. In *Market and Society: The Great Transformation Today*, edited by Chris Hann and Keith Hart, 203–20. Cambridge: Cambridge University Press.

Harriss, John. 2005. 'South Asia'. In *A Handbook of Economic Anthropology*, edited by James Carrier, 526–36. Cheltenham: Edward Elgar Publishing.

Harriss-White, Barbara. 2003. *India Working: Essays on Society and Economy*. Cambridge: Cambridge University Press.

———. 2008. *Rural Commercial Capital: Agricultural Markets in West Bengal*. Oxford: Oxford University Press.

———. 2016. 'Local Capitalism and the Development of the Rice Economy 1973–2010'. In *Middle India and Urban–Rural Development: Four Decades of Change*, edited by Barbara Harriss-White, 97–130. New Delhi: Springer India.

Jeffrey, Craig. 2002. 'Caste, Class and Clientalism: A Political Economy of Everyday Corruption in Rural North India'. *Economic Geography* 78 (1): 21–41.

———. 2010. *Timepass: Youth, Class, and the Politics of Waiting in India*. Stanford, CA: Stanford University Press.

Krishnamurthy, Mekhala. 2012. 'States of Wheat: The Changing Dynamics of Public Procurement in Madhya Pradesh'. *Economic & Political Weekly* 47 (52): 72–83.

———. 2013. 'Margins and Mindsets: Enterprise, Opportunity and Exclusion in a Market Town in Madhya Pradesh'. In *Enterprise Culture in Neoliberal India: Studies in Youth, Class, Work and Media*, edited by Nandini Gooptu, 207–21. London: Routledge.

———. 2014. 'First Transaction, Multiple Perspectives: The Changing Terms of Commodity Exchange in a Regulated Agricultural Market in Madhya Pradesh'. In *Indian Capitalism in Development*, edited by Judith Heyer and Barbara Harriss-White, 85–101. London: Routledge.

Kumar, Richa. 2010. 'Mandi Traders and the *Dabba*: Online Commodity Futures Markets in India'. *Economic & Political Weekly* 45 (31): 63–70.

Lerche, Jens. 2014. 'Regional Patterns of Agrarian Accumulation in India'. In *Indian Capitalism in Development*, edited by Judith Heyer and Barbara Harriss-White, 47–65. London: Routledge.

Levien, Michael. 2013. 'The Politics of Dispossession: Theorizing India's "Land Wars"'. *Politics & Society* 41 (3): 351–94.

Ludden, David. 1999. *An Agrarian History of South Asia*. Cambridge: Cambridge University Press.

Rangnekar, Dwijen. 2011. 'Remaking Place: The Social Construction of a Geographical Indication for *Feni*'. *Environment and Planning A: Economy and Space* 43 (9): 2043–59.

Sarkar, Swagato. 2015. 'Beyond Dispossession: The Politics of Commodification of Land under Speculative Conditions'. *Comparative Studies of South Asia, Africa and the Middle East* 35 (3): 438–50.

Thompson, E.P. 1971. 'The Moral Economy of the English Crowd in the Eighteenth Century'. *Past & Present* 50 (1): 76–136.

Timberg, Thomas A. 1978. *The Marwaris: From Traders to Industrialists*. New Delhi: Vikas Publishing House.

Vasavi, A.R. 1998. 'Provisioning Transactions and the Reproduction of Agrarian Social Orders'. *Contributions to Indian Sociology* 32 (1): 43–65.

Vidal, Denis. 2000. 'Markets and Intermediaries: An Enquiry about the Principles of Market Economy in the Grain Market of Delhi'. In *Delhi: Urban Space and Human Destinies*, edited by Veronique Dupont, Emma Tarlo and Denis Vidal, 125–39. New Delhi: Manohar Publishers.

———. 2003. 'Markets'. In *Oxford India Companion to Sociology and Social Anthropology*. Vol. II, edited by Veena Das, 1123–35. New Delhi: Oxford University Press.

———. 2005. 'In Search of "Basmatisthan": Agro-nationalism and Globalization'. In *Globalizing India: Perspectives from Below*, edited by Jackie Assayag and Chris Fuller, 47–64. London: Anthem Press.

8

The Nation, De-duplicated

Lawrence Cohen

Cards on the Table

There is this table at a coffee house in Delhi where a talkative group of retired men, some former journalists, sit in the afternoons. On occasion, I join them to get advice on new projects.

It was the summer of 2012. Like many, I was beginning to think about India's much publicised national biometric identity, branded Aadhaar, Hindi for 'foundation'. I had just made a photostat copy of a friend's Aadhaar card. I frequently had conversations with strangers and friends about Aadhaar cards that had or had not arrived in the post. One of the men at the table watched me writing notes on the photostat: this led to a question on what I was doing with a duplicate of an Aadhaar card, and then to a conversation on what the new cards promised, or threatened.

The others weighed in on the topic of Aadhaar and other 'I-cards', government IDs. Things grew animated.[1] The first man complained that he had been registered for Aadhaar, putting his fingerprints and

---

[1] My description of speech and scene here and throughout is based on immediate notes rewritten and expanded usually about 1–2 hours after a conversation.

eyes to the machine to have their form captured as data, but had not received his card. As if to show me that he was a proper subject of an I-card world, he began removing identification papers from his wallet. Here was his driver's licence, voter ID card and PAN card, displaying the permanent account number required of taxpayers. Another man pushed aside his cup and followed suit. Soon the coffee house table was littered with multiple instances of ID, most laminated, a few nakedly paper.

This scene, not atypical in expressing the affective and proliferative charge of the I-card at this moment, is offered to set up the dominant pedagogy of Aadhaar by the extraordinary bureaucracy created to capture the biometrics of all residents of India. I mean extraordinary literally: The Unique Identification Authority of India (hereafter UIDAI or the Authority) was not set up with 'statutory' authority, under the rule of law, and the commitment of its engineer designers to make Aadhaar a ubiquitous platform for more and more future technologies of government and commerce was framed under the logic of the engineering problem, rather than the political constitution. Preceded by other massive projects like the Delhi Metro subway that were similarly constituted as public–private partnerships (PPPs) with an eye to efficiency exceptional to ordinary bureaucratic procedure and chain of command, UIDAI was for its first half decade of operation unique even among the other large PPPs in the degree of its working outside of law.

By a 'pedagogy' of Aadhaar, I refer to an instructive message offered by personnel at many levels of UIDAI's operation, from its founder and initial director Nandan Nilekani to contracted workers capturing the biometrics of the nation's residents and coordinating the identification the Authority grants and distributes. This message: 'Aadhaar is not a card but only a number'. Nilekani has made the point across a range of the media through which he has constituted a vigorous publicity of national biometrics. I have heard the same message offered where Aadhaar is being inserted into scenes of distribution, delimiting access to subsidised foodstuffs, scholarships, pensions, workfare wages, licences for housing and mobility, and more generally credit and cash economies. Aadhaar is becoming important, and increasingly necessary, for sustaining life and care. We might follow the Authority—for whom Aadhaar is not a statutory apparatus of citizenship but is offered as something like a gift to all 'residents' of the nation—in terming that life synonymous with this emergent form a matter of Residence. And this Residence is a matter not of Card but of Number. It seems to me that Aadhaar might be treated as though a new language has inserted itself into the world: I hint at the possible contours of such a language here through the use of capitalisation.

What this language is capturing exceeds the temporal frame of this essay. I wrote it before the 2016 demonetisation and the linking of Aadhaar to more and more capacities of the state and market appeared to realise a far grander dematerialisation: not only was there a national pedagogy of 'no-Card' but also of 'no-Money', the latter supplemented by claims that such dematerialisation would hit at the privilege of elites and the machinations of Pakistan. Here, I focus on the earlier and ongoing pedagogy of no-Card. This pedagogy is enunciated in scenes that bear some formal similarity to the one in the coffee house, where cards, present and absent, are laid on the table. Thus, when I was doing an interview in 2012 with transgender clients of a Mumbai AIDS support NGO who had participated in an Aadhaar Camp, a debate emerged over how varied I-cards (Aadhaar, PAN, voter ID, ration cards) differently helped or hindered the particular gendering needed to negotiate public transit, court cases, male kin and other situations. A social worker who had helped set up the Camp and had been trained in the proper understanding of Aadhaar got impatient at the lengthy discussion of multiple 'cards'. 'Friends', she said, closing down the discussion, 'you must understand that Aadhaar is only a Number. It is not a Card'.

The message—not Card, only Number—is central to Aadhaar's formative rationale, or in the engineering language of its designers, to its Concept. Concept work is ubiquitous to engineering design (Hubka and Eder 1988) and the clarification and 'proof' of a concept organise relations to the client (here, the Government of India). This Concept offers a new analysis for the nation as a problem space: an account of the nation's unrealised place in history, given the scale and persistence of its human margin. The Concept is explicitly designed to rethink what an earlier technocracy would have labelled underdevelopment. The new technocracy—and the Concept is explicitly generational, with what we might call an Oedipal feel—draws less on the 20th-century cybernetic figure for collective assemblages, 'system', than on the distinctive if closely related totality of the Database. The problem for governance is best conceived not as underdevelopment, where development is a metric differentiating social systems, but as an inevitable and entropic deformation of all Databases termed Duplication.

What is Duplication? If one terms the unit of the Database the Record, the challenge for new Data entered is whether these are to be associated with an existing Record (and if so, which) or constitutive of another, novel Record. If, say, Mr Dumont subscribes to *Contributions to Indian Sociology*, and then renews his subscription using a slightly different name, perhaps adding Louis, will the latter event be linked to the existing record or will a second, duplicate Dumont be added? Periodically, databases need to be De-duplicated to ensure that each Record refers to a Unique entity, one that we may or may not, given the legacy of the aforementioned Dumont, wish to call the individual.

For the engineers behind Aadhaar, India is beset by Duplicates. For reasons of length—economics of 'paper' journals—I do not turn to important recent thinking on generics, pirates or branding, a constitutive limit of the argument set out here. But it is worth attending to Duplicates as set out by the Concept: I move between interviews and conversations with contracted UIDAI engineers in Bengaluru and Delhi and in California's Silicon Valley, sites where Aadhaar is being variously deployed, and the vigorous publicity of the Concept across two national governments in turn.

Duplicates are constituted within the publicity of Aadhaar along an axis with two poles. We might term the first pole 'duplication-from-above', such as the familiar spectre of a powerful 'nexus' or 'racket' diverting the commonweal to itself by 'duplicating' the records of legitimate needy beneficiaries within the Database of a government welfare programme and claiming benefits in the name of these Duplicate or 'Ghost' beneficiaries. (A Ghost is any name that cannot properly be attached to a living being: it need not be the name of a once-living person.) Duplication-from-above may presume access to the Database and the power to seed it with duplicate Records. It is the logic of a fodder scam or medical school admissions racket. We might term the other pole 'duplication-from-below', implying non-elite actors that may not have access to the Database but that attempt to mobilise Duplicate or Ghost ID instruments—such as false documents—to gain access to welfare distributions or other services or to introduce a new Record into the Database and thus as a single person or household to be able to make claims via more than one Record. Duplication-from-below makes life possible if it can engender the flow of payments, subsidies, goods, credit or more generally what is understood as Service, critical for the urban migrant without easy access to legitimate ID (Srivastava 2012). All this Duplication produces Leakage and the presumptive inefficiency noted by neoliberal analysis.

The new technocracy takes as its premise that India is a Database. Duplicates proliferate in Databases: one does not need moralising critique. The challenge is technical: to de-duplicate India. If Duplication has two poles, one must address De-duplication accordingly. One must secure the database from duplication-from-above. Such security will involve more than the logic of the boundary. It will involve reimagining the Record, freeing it as I will argue below from both biography and territory. And one must limit the ability of claimants of Record, persons if you like, to proliferate ID instruments and to Duplicate themselves.

A key means to trouble the proliferation of Duplicates is what one might term the devaluation, or more accurately the transposition, of the material. Devaluation and transposition operate in several ways. The way I discuss here is the refusal of paper identity in the iterated pedagogic claim that Aadhaar is 'not a card'. If duplication-from-below is enabled by a massive economy of 'false' documents, the document itself is demoted from being a material extension of an identity to merely a sign of it, in this case the sign only of a threshold (register-ing for Aadhaar) and its effect (legitimate association with a number bound to one's fleshly form, that is to one's Biometrics). It is as if the mandarins of UIDAI are insisting on a Saussurean dichotomy between signifier (only a card) and signified (you), as opposed to the possibil-ity of an alternate material-semiotic ideology (Keane 2003; Mahmood 2009) in which both (Card and you) are bound up in a non-arbitrary and indivisible manner. But the move by UIDAI should not be con-ceived as a standard operation of modernisation, that is, a refusal of the non-arbitrary as magical or backward, for in an act of transposition, the flesh replaces the card as the indivisible and non-arbitrary (Unique) index and icon of you.

'The Card That Everyone Has Been Talking About': Fragments Towards an Archive

Given official insistence on Aadhaar being 'not a card', not subject that is to Duplication, how then to think with its affective and proliferative 'card-ness'? Here I offer a modest experiment, setting down 13 texts in order of publication, each taken from the mainstream English or Hindi press, and gesturing towards what we might term the 'thing' of Aadhaar, what it is, across a range of media intimate with official vernacular. The experiment reprises everyday literate practice in the face of new media and disaggregated propaganda circuits, and suggests that such 'reprise' be taken seriously as method in the human sciences. The texts I have chosen exemplify one or more of four genres, by no means a sufficient catalogue of Aadhaar's publicity: (a) extensions of official pedagogy and reports (not always correct) of currently proper or forthcoming ways to get, replace or use Aadhaar; (b) reports of failure (numbers and/or cards not issued, confusingly issued or issued to spurious, that is Duplicate, entities); (c) critique of or resistance to governance through Aadhaar;

and (d) crime beat and police reporting in which Aadhaar increasingly figures as evidence.

Several of the items allude to a conflicted and shifting relation between the Authority and a different state entity 'also' collecting biometric data at the national scale, the National Population Registry or NPR: this relation will be discussed below.

1. April 2010: 'New Delhi: The 16-digit unique identification number to be assigned to each individual by the Unique Identification Authority of India (UIDAI) will now come under the new name "AADHAR" and will also bear a logo.... [Both] were made public at a meeting chaired by UIDAI chairman Nandan Nilekani, who said these two symbols were necessary to make the scheme and the number recognisable and communicate the spirit and essence of the mandate to the people and win their confidence. The unique number will be the "AADHAR" or foundation through which the citizen can claim his/her rights and entitlements when assured of equal opportunities, as symbolised by the logo, which has the halo of the Sun on the imprint of a thumb'.[2]

    Commentary: Note the distinction, expressed by Nilekani, between the gifts of Number, which offers persons Identity, and of its Symbols—Name and Logo—which offer persons confidence in the new Authority. Symbolic form, visually and in language, is needed in order to achieve a Mandate among 'the people'. But Number stands apart: If not for the need to mobilise affect (confidence), the random number of a person's Aadhaar can be understood to be beyond any signification except the 'unique' index to an individual. Nilekani gestures to the core of the Concept: that De-duplication demands an entity 'outside' of language and all representation save the index to unique biotic form. But 'politics' requires the affective consolidation of Mandate, through Symbol. At the origin, then, language and form intrude, of necessity, as the brand, the 'merely symbolic'. Finally, note the string length: Aadhaar as 16 digits. A month later, a UIDAI 'white paper' will suggest a length of 12 digits as more amenable to memorisation (Kanakia et al. 2010).

---

[2] K. Balchand, 'UID Number Gets Brand Name, Logo', *The Hindu* (National), 26 April 2010.

2. April 2010: 'Aadhaar, or the 12-digit unique identification (UID) number that will identify the 1.2 billion residents of the country, will have an additional four digits that will be hidden from the common man. "[The] ... provision of extra four digits ... would be a post-fix for this 12-digit number for pin-based identification. So, UID will become a 16-digit number for our use and the database ...," [said] Ram Sewak Sharma, Director General and Mission Director of ... UIDAI. These four digits, which the authority terms a "virtual number," will change as and when the resident changes his pin number or residence'.[3]

Commentary: This article appears after Aadhaar's public branding and a month before the white paper is published with its 12-digit mnemonic. The rationale of secret numbers tied to place (here a resident's address) offered by Sharma, a bureaucrat with a growing public reputation for probity, stands at odds with the Concept and with almost all official publicity before and since. The idea that UIDAI would reserve four digits to encode a registrant's spatial location over time (part of what I am terming the biographical) runs strongly against a *techne* and 'ethos' that framed Aadhaar as that which can stand for nothing but the Uniqueness of the Resident. One important strand of anti-Aadhaar critique takes the form of conspiracy theory, a form that sharply differentiates public pronouncements from the private intentions of Nilekani, his inner circle and his supporters in the government. UIDAI cultivates the appearance of transparency: the design of 'hidden' numbers represents an anomaly. I will term it a 'Duplicate' to the dominant Concept of the engineers. Whether it points to an earlier and abandoned Concept, to a mistake on Sharma's or the reporter's part, or indeed to a commitment to a hidden archive kept from the 'common man' and that sustains accusation of the Authority's duplicity, we might acknowledge that a Concept has a tendency to proliferate Duplicates of itself. There is from the outset of the project a vertiginous feel to its publicity, a sense that the massive, possibly realist and probably sublime effort to de-duplicate India is beset by its own internal duplication. 'Sublime' gestures towards Thomas Hansen's (1999) argument for the anti-political governance of the development state echoed in Sharma's statement that UIDAI will best function to the extent it keeps certain information uncommon. Finally, of note is that this partial and hidden 4-digit string is 'virtual' unlike

[3] Kirtika Suneja, '16-digit Aadhaar to Have Four Hidden Numbers', *Business Standard* (New Delhi), 28 April 2010.

the 12-digit Aadhaar. Here, at least the anomaly is consistent with the Concept in that the public and knowable, memorable Number is the ground of the real.

3. September 2010: '782474317884. With this number, Ranjana has become the first Indian to get the UID (Unique Identification). Prime Minister Manmohan Singh and United Progressive Alliance [UPA] Chairperson Sonia Gandhi launched the Aadhaar project on Wednesday and presented UIDs to ten people here…. Dr Singh … said, "UID will help the hundreds of people in India, whose pride was hurt for so many years because of the lack of an identity. This will be their source of recognition from now on…. Nandurbar [Ranjana's village] was chosen because this is a symbol that this scheme will first benefit the tribals and the needy people in this country," he said. The village which barely had a road till this function, has no school and the water tank is newly built and painted…. [Another villager] Jalubai Thackarey is well aware of all this. Even though elated that she got to meet Sonia Mai, she says she needs a pukka house. "She didn't say, but I know she will give us houses. Only this card cannot do anything"'.[4]

Commentary: A resident who embodies the 'common' in being poor, female, rural and tribal is the first person to receive Aadhaar. Her village is 'explicitly' a Symbol. This article mobilises a hermeneutic of suspicion as the familiar scene of leaders arriving to eradicate poverty reenacts the pathos of the political promise as it tends towards the Symbolic. In another article, Ranjana is quoted as saying that Sonia, the Congress party president and senior member of the Gandhi–Nehru dynasty, was 'her Aadhaar', that is, her foundation.[5] Ranjana sets Sonia, the patron upon whom village Residents must rely in this moment of promise or pathos, against her Card if she is to move beyond the Symbolic. The distinction between Number and Card is less relevant than that between the trace of a promise (Card) and its realisation (Sonia). This opposition is reanimated during the 2014 elections, before the UPA is voted out of power and replaced by the National Democratic Alliance (NDA) under Narendra Modi, who criticises the Aadhaar project throughout the campaign. Ranjana is revisited ('"We have no money. No jobs. Just a card," she

<hr />

[4] Amruta Byatnal, 'Tembhli Becomes First Aadhar [sic] Village in India', *The Hindu* (National), 29 September 2010.
[5] Press Trust of India, 'Sonia Is My "Aadhaar," Says First UID Recipient', *The Times of India*, 29 September 2010.

says, "How will I eke out a living with a card?" ... Ranjana is tired ... and refuses to pose with her Aadhaar card.... But, her photograph with the prime minister and the Congress president [is] hung right up there with photographs of Hindu deities').[6] In this electoral repetition, Sonia's realness is still separate from that of the Card (and Number), but it is called into question by its equation to that of the divine: a matter either of confusion in which Ranjana errs in deifying Sonia or of iconoclasm in which the gods more generally cannot be counted on in these times.

4. February 2011: 'The number will not be in the form of a card. Instead, residents will receive a letter from the UIDAI giving them their UID number and the information registered against it. The letter will have a tear away portion that can double up as a card for reference'.[7]

Commentary: By 2011, the publicity of Aadhaar shifts from a reliance on the Common Resident in the third person (Ranjana, for example) to hailing the Resident directly. This Internet article appears early in a period (2011–13) when I am beginning to have conversations with elite and middle-class friends in which they essay a parallel shift from a third-person relation (getting Aadhaar for one's domestic servants or other employees, and increasingly for one's elderly parents and other relations) to a first-person relation (getting Aadhaar for oneself and for others) to the Authority.

Here, Residents get 'a letter' *addressed* to them, confirming the gift of Number in the wake of biometric collection. Under the Concept, no such letter is needed: the gift and promise of Aadhaar should be borne on one's fingertips. But to address failures and affects of non-receipt (recall the men in the coffee house) and to amplify the Mandate, letters must circulate and a secondary level of reference, not Number and Flesh indexing one another but Letter on the one hand and Name and Address on the other, is needed, what the Authority terms 'demographic information': location and biography. The letter has a 'tear-away' portion (but instead of the cavalier relation implied by 'tearing', elsewhere in official pedagogy you are instructed to 'cut') which can 'double up' as a Card. Here, albeit in the perhaps inexpert hands of a reporter, we encounter the

---

[6] Pravin Nair, 'First Aadhaar Card Owner Struggles for a Living', *Hindustan Times*, 20 April 2014.

[7] Harshada Karnik, 'A Guide to Understanding UID Number', *Live Mint*, 21 February 2011.

secondary reference of Card as the Duplicate to the primary reference of Number, as explicit an account of the ontological stakes for UIDAI as one finds. Despite the purity of the Concept, in which Aadhaar stands against the fall into Duplication, the pragmatics with the shift to the Resident in the second person involve the need for 'reference' and thus doubling up. But mark the 'cut': that studied action which dangerously releases the Card as a floating signifier, a Duplicate, as but a visceral or animal necessity, a 'tear'.

5. June 2012: 'Coriander and an apple, as per the Unique Identification Authority of India (UIDAI), are residents of India as they have been given an Aadhaar number ... an Aadhaar card with the number 4991 1866 5246 was issued in the name of Mr Kothimeer (coriander), son of Mr Palavu (pulao), resident of Mamidikaya Vuru (raw mango village) of Jambuladinne in Anantapur district of Andhra Pradesh'.[8]

Commentary: Nilekani is relatively successful in creating his Mandate for Aadhaar in urban India. In 25 interviews I did between 2012 and 2015 in Delhi (with employees and customers in a cooking gas distribution agency), Varanasi (with residents in Nagwa slum, where I have worked since 1988) and Mumbai (among transgender, kothi, men who have sex with men (MSM) and gay clients of the NGO mentioned above), Aadhaar is generally referred to in the future tense, as something that would or could guarantee identity in a way ordinary identification papers did not, and as something that might better guarantee access to state and commercial services in a more timely, less corrupt and more respectful way. Specific and repeated accounts of failure—of the Aadhaar card not arriving in the promised window of time, most commonly of Aadhaar not yet being useful in cutting corruption—seldom diminish this expectation. I want to place the considerable space given by regional and national media to failures of De-duplication—here, a coriander plant receiving an Aadhaar number—in the context of such anticipatory force.

For critics with whom I have spoken, such risible failures exemplify the fundamental error of the Concept: that effective Government by De-Duplication is possible. For project engineers with whom I have spoken, such failures offer the challenge of improving procedures. Inside the Concept, Hanuman and the coriander plant do not have Aadhaar cards as there is no such thing as a Card. What has erred is a system of secondary reference requiring

[8] Manan Kumar, 'Coriander S/o Pulao, Aadhaar No 499118665246', *DNA*, 28 June 2012.

biography, proving the Concept in that the very need for language endangers the purity of Number.

My sense here is that these news items might work other than as signs of either the failure or the imperfect realisation of the Concept. They may stage a mode of laughter encompassing both failure and promise, through the ascension of the non-human—here a plant, elsewhere domestic animals or famously the deity Hanuman—to Residency. Again, the divine intrudes into the Concept at precisely the limit to its utopian reference (depending on pure Number), as it collapses into secondary or Duplicate reference, the Symbol, the Name. Hanuman and coriander matter because of their physicality in and with their Cards, a visual or experiential supplement that cannot be dispensed with, much as the publicity of Aadhaar, which amplifies its presumptive Mandate, depends on circulated images of Residents with Cards, tokens of the gift and promise of the new Foundation (Figure 8.1). The intrusion of that which troubles the pure numeracy of the Resident—whether the great Lord Hanuman or the humble coriander plant—suggests that Aadhaar's Mandate, its claim on the political, is not separable from the propensity to proliferate, the will to Duplicate.

6. October 2012: 'Existing PAN holders can also add information of their AADHAAR number … while applying for a new PAN card…. All the NPR [National Population Register] cards will also have Aadhaar numbers, and thus PAN, NPR and Aadhaar would be linked with each-other in the ultimate run…. The government had earlier this year devised an integrated approach to end the conflict between UIDAI and NPR…. The chip-based Multipurpose National Identity Card issued by the NPR will capture 15 details of every individual.

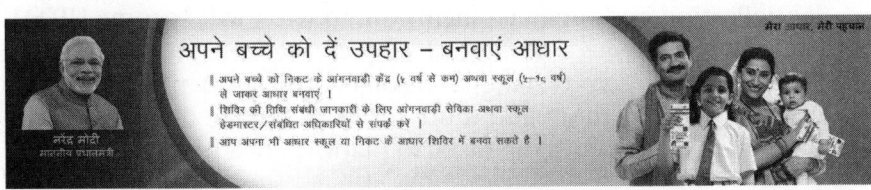

FIGURE 8.1 *Masthead of Aadhaar web portal on 19 September 2016, inaugurating 'Phase 2' of the Project with the imperative 'Give your children the gift of having Aadhaar made', and the familiar quartet of state family planning pedagogy (duplication under firm control), each child holding an uncut Aadhaar receipt, legible as Card.*

So, the stage is set for a coordinated functioning of the three critical individual identification modes—PAN, NPR and Aadhaar. All the three together will be a potent tool for any government agency to do profiling of any individual'.[9]

Commentary: This article, in the *Business Standard*, vitiates the dominant publicity of Aadhaar, to wit that the Number only 'federates' the varied information 'silos' of India but does not 'converge' or 'aggregate' them, and that the Authority can only perform a single act, that is, to affirm or deny that 'you are you', activating pure identity stripped of biography. Here, in contrast, if the Concept is not the master but must share a security 'ecosystem' (Rajadhyaksha 2013) with instrumentalities in parallel with it, then 'any government agency' has immense power to 'profile' each 'individual'. At stake is the relation of Aadhaar to other parallel massive Databases.

To understand this relation, one might return to the 1980s and 1990s and the emergence of Data as the ground of security under two interwoven imperatives: 'territorial' (tracking migrant and terrorist) and 'financial' (tracking welfare recipient, debtor or worker in proprietary Databases). By the first decade of the 2000s, one can trace two parallel clusters of security at the Cabinet level, one aligned with the Defence Ministry and the second with the Finance Ministry and Planning Commission. The former cluster is organised around the problem of regional surveillance along the Border with Pakistan and the Indian Ocean. The problem scales up to the need to differentiate 'citizens' from infiltrators across the nation, and the mechanism of scaling up is the existing infrastructure and norms of the National Census, an archive of 'residents'. What emerges is the National Population Register, or NPR. Parallel to this process is the scaling up of a range of Databases organised around labour credentialisation and financial inclusion, to what will become UIDAI. The latter, to create a numerical subject free from the duplicating tendency of biography, takes as its object the Resident, but with its growing scale, as more and more forms of service distribution are linked to it, it becomes the de facto platform of a new 'citizenship'.

From 2010 to 2014, the conflict between NPR and Aadhaar has sharpened and plays out at the Cabinet level of the UPA government. How is security to be hierarchised? The struggle is one between opposed values. Aadhaar is organised to minimise

---

[9] Santosh Tiwari, 'PAN, AADHAAR, NPR: Govt. Looks at Grand Alliance', *Business Standard* (New Delhi), 9 October 2012.

biographical data fields and to deterritorialise its subject. One of the designing engineers in Silicon Valley, near my university, tells me, 'We didn't even want to attach the number to a name or a photo'. The Concept was Number attached to Unique biometrics. 'Nothing else'. The challenge for NPR comes to seem the opposite: not deterritorialisation but hyperterritorialisation—to attach as many data fields as are manageable to the new identity. NPR is not organised around a pedagogy of its immateriality but draws as in this excerpt upon the figure of the chip-based Smart Card. To borrow a figure from Dumont, struggle plays out as a contest for encompassment, with something like a revolving hierarchy to take Charles Malamoud's (1982) figure. At times, Aadhaar is placed under the NPR; at times, Nilekani and the Authority appear to be able to constitute the master identity. In this article, not only NPR and Aadhaar are in play but also the PAN card, and the hierarchy of encompassment is left unspecified but with the edge going to NPR through the material device of the chip.

7. May 2013: 'Some cards have ended up with pictures of an empty chair, a tree or a dog.... Asked about the cases ... UIDAI deputy director general Ashok Dalwai said no system was foolproof.... "To avoid such errors, we have in place another team to go through the printed Aadhaar cards, to check for manual duplication"'.[10]

Commentary: In the face of a mounting publicity of De-duplication failure, UIDAI officials here turn to the Card as a 'supplement', in some Derridean sense. Conceptually, the Card is nothing, an absence, a secondary reference, and yet given the persistence of the Duplicate haunting the Concept, it becomes the presence needed to catch errant flora, fauna or divinities. Ashok Dalwai like Ram Sewak Sharma is a senior bureaucrat with a reputation for probity. As with the earlier anomaly, the IAS officer is charged with speech that departs from the Concept: more generally, standard administration becomes supplement to the Authority.

8. March 2015: '[The] Chief Election Commissioner [noted that]: "...the Aadhaar numbers will be linked to the elector's photo identity card. And then India will be the only country in the world where there will be complete biometric of voters ... not a single fraud or duplicate"'.[11]

[10] Times News Network, 'Dogs, Trees, and Chairs Have Aadhaar Cards', *The Times of India*, 31 May 2013.
[11] Arshad Ali, 'Will Link Aadhaar Number to Voter ID Cards to Ensure No Duplicacy: CEC H.S. Brahma', *The Indian Express* (Kolkata), 22 March 2015.

Commentary: Modi and the NDA win powerfully in 2014. Despite persistent criticism of UIDAI by the NDA during the election, the government quickly embraces it. Although some critics extract schadenfreude from the NDA needing to turn back to UPA social welfare programmes despite its election rhetoric, Modi only augments his authority and charisma through Aadhaar. The Aadhaar-enabled Modi persona emerges as managerial and panoptic. A high-level IAS officer passes on a joke to me at a Silicon Valley party of an NDA politician at the airport off to America on a junket, when he receives a phone call from Modi, using Aadhaar to track his whereabouts and question his attire. I heard many such jokes, of a piece with a new informal publicity of Aadhaar as a means for the PM to keep tabs on bureaucrats and ministers and ensure they appear at the office. The contest between deterritorialising Aadhaar and hyperterritorialising NPR seems to end. If there is an encompassment, it is as if the persona of the sovereign leader encompasses both, via a security apparatus that simultaneously allows the UIDAI engineers to exercise their original Concept and capture the full spectrum of the state's welfare while extending the state's demand to know.

In this article, the Voter Identification Card is to be encompassed. I did an interview in 2013 with a former Chief Election Commissioner who tells me he had been excited by UIDAI's Concept and offered Nilekani the immense database the Election Commission had assembled. But Nilekani, the Commissioner says ruefully, turned him down. The engineers I interviewed that year tell me that the goal was to create a nation-as-database (Cohen 2016) of unprecedented, De-duplicated quality, not piggybacking on an existing state apparatus seen to be mired in vested interests and their duplication-from-above. But now, as the new government works to give Aadhaar the statutory backing it has always lacked, UIDAI appears to be enfolding all the other cards into its Number, becoming the One Platform, as it were, to rule them all.

9. May 2016: '[Interview with Aruna Sharma, Secretary of DeitY, Department of Electronics and Information Technology]: "We have laid down cables in 80,000 panchayats. There are some issues in making them operative. They are cracking it.... Aadhaar is a tool to ensure that money ... is reaching to the right person. The giver of money has every right to know that you are the right person. So the government can always ask you to give your Aadhaar number." [Q: What will be the mechanism to update the database?] "There are

only six corrections which happen. Births [1] and deaths [2] are two which will be done by the Registrar General. Then there is marriage: a girl goes out of a family [3] and joins another family [4]. Then a family moves out completely [5] or a family splits [6]"'.[12]

Commentary: The formally secular UPA government establishes DeitY, the Department of Electronics and Information Technology, in 2012, under the Ministry of Communications, the upstretched Y marking the acronym's distinction from divinity and yet like some hierophany or jyotirlinga embodying what Rudolf Otto might have termed its *tremendum*. When Secretary Sharma offers these comments, DeitY has not yet been elevated to an independent ministry (MeitY), but is already becoming the site, as opposed to the earlier warring contenders of Defence and Finance under the UPA, for locating the 'complete biometric' of security under NDA. Here, I call attention to three features of Sharma's wide-ranging comments.

a. Panchayat digitisation is lagging, limiting the state promise (and threat) of Aadhaar under MeitY universalising welfare distribution as direct cash transfer, and the lag is not underplayed but rendered explicit within an engineering discourse of problems framed and solved (we are cracking it).

b. The government as the 'distributor' (Ferguson 2015) of welfare or as it is officially termed Service, the emergent condition of biological citizenship (Petryna 2002) under neoliberalism and the failure of wage labour to capture the future (Sanyal 2007), is here framed as a patron or, if we play the game of the sociology of India, as sovereign donor. Playing off Raheja's (1988) classic typology of donation, this kind of gift produces a cosmos with the sovereign at its centre. Here, however, the political subject is not secured as him or herself: the 'giver of money has every right to know that you are the right person'; that is, the sovereign to constitute itself as the centre of a cosmos of rule must continually De-duplicate its Residents. This insistence not only on a pragmatic engineering of distribution but also on the 'right identity' is a critical feature of an emergent form, the 'nation-as-database' grounded in a figure of 'the government as a sovereign giver with a "right to know"'.

[12] Pratap Vikram Singh, 'Using Data to Improve Social Welfare Schemes', *Governance Now* (New Delhi), 9 May 2016.

c. Although the Authority has consistently attempted to limit the ability of the biographical to deform and duplicate its Number, at this moment, Sharma offers a scheme of six corrections that mediate between deterritorialisation and hyperterritorialisation by limiting the subsequent intrusion of biography into the management of the database to 'sex'. And these six profoundly overdetermine the biometric subject as gendered, as in thrall to virilocal patriarchy, and, at the risk of the wrong word, as heterosexual. Once again as with R.S. Sharma and Ashok Dalwai, a bureaucrat is put in the position of mediating Aadhaar in the world and in a way that must betray the radical Concept and locate it not only in individual biography but within the whole matrix of normative kinship.

10. June 2015: 'Printing of plastic Aadhaar cards for residents will gain momentum with common service centres commissioned by Tamil Nadu Arasu Cable TV Corporation (TACTV) all set to start operations at zonal offices of Chennai Corporation soon.... "The paper quality of Aadhaar card is not good. Residents are waiting for printers to be commissioned at Zonal offices to get their Aadhaar plastic identity card," said Tamil Selvan, a Chennai Corporation councilor in Ambattur zone.... [O]fficials claimed ... residents with Aadhaar number will be able to walk in and print a plastic card. They will have to pay ₹30 for a plastic Aadhaar card in case they have received the [paper] card already'.[13]

Commentary: Despite the Concept's persistent devaluation of the material, here the desire for plastic and the fragility of paper lead a regional PPP towards a possible betrayal of the Authority via an apparent fallacy of misplaced concreteness. The concrete carries its own limit in the matter of available printers. Around this time (2014–16), an increasing number of reports describe scams in which a proliferating set of fakes were being used, in some cases involving 'real' Aadhaar Numbers being inserted into a range of 'fake' Cards. Plastic Aadhaar is offered to stabilise the De-duplicating apparatus at a moment when the authenticity of the thing is called into increased question: again, De-duplication requires an (impossible) supplement.

11. November 2015: '"Please do pay the banks the commissions they need to make it [DBT, Direct Benefit Transfer] profitable," the

[13] Aloysius Xavier Lopez, 'Print Your Plastic Aadhaar Card in City Offices Soon', *The Hindu* (Chennai), 14 June 2015.

[Reserve Bank of India] Governor said, adding that India is on the verge of a "paper-less, cash-less, presence-less economy"' (Sharad Raghavan 2015).

Commentary: One notes the juxtaposition between the enthralling possibility of a 'presence-less economy', in which presence itself is revealed as the engine of duplication (reminiscent of Advaita and Buddhist debate), and the worry that unless private banks receive actual commissions on the coming government of service distribution, this enthralling possibility will collapse. The value and future of negation require money: the nexus of private finance and the state must be preserved. Again, monetary payment to private financial institutions appears to supplement the imagined future biopolitics keeping populations alive through an ever more 'presence-less' apparatus of life extension through service distribution. Crudely, one might argue that Aadhaar's rationale, the leakage of duplication, has been transmuted into Commission. A range of impossible entities (impossible in a truly de-duplicated and presence-less world)—the Card, ennobled in plastic; the Commission, maintaining the private as all transactions become Service; the Biography, routinised through normative kinship; and the Leader, incorporating the Number within his panoptic reach—stand between the sovereignty of the Concept and its failure.

12. July 2016: 'Afzaz ... afflicted with diphtheria, died.... Mohammed Niyas, Senior Resident at the hospital ... [wrote on Facebook] "I cursed all the vaccine hate-mongers in Kerala ... the anti-vaccine mafia in our State".... T.P. Abdullakoya Madhani, president of the Kerala Nadvathul Mujahideen, an organisation that propagates Islamic beliefs, debunks ... vaccination being a Western conspiracy to make Muslims infertile.... "Anything the government does is viewed with suspicion. When Aadhaar was introduced, many said it was an attempt at profiling. But now almost every Muslim household in the State has Aadhaar cards"'.[14]

Commentary: The article, condemning minority conspiracy theory, offers an official Muslim acknowledgement of the prevalence of deep suspicion and the need for its refusal to evade cruel death, with acceptance of the 'Aadhaar card' offering a hopeful narrative. Aadhaar with its undecidable 'signature of the state' (Das 2003) carries threat yet here dampens the appeal of the presumptively irrational, normalising the minority. As with the presence of

[14] G.R. Rajeev, 'The Fallacies of the Faithful', *The Hindu*, 9 July 2016.

the coriander plant, what is achieved in such accounts may be more than or other to a normalisation, as the Card physically comes to lodge itself in the intimate space of the household.

13. September 2016: 'A shirt, an Aadhaar card and the torso of a 31-year-old man who had been reported missing earlier last month were found nearly a kilometre away from his Vikhroli residence on Tuesday.... "His body was in a bad condition and the dogs may have played havoc with it," said [an] officer'.[15]

Commentary: I have begun to notice mention of Aadhaar cards in police reporting of crime scenes. The card appears to function narratively in one of at least two ways. (a) Duplicate Aadhaar cards are displayed in a way analogous to contraband like gold bars or sachets of illegal drugs, part of the recognisable matter of criminal proliferation. (b) Aadhaar becomes a new means, within the publicity of forensics, of identifying the corpse. In both the cases noted here, it is the Card that serves the purpose and not the biometric, the fingerprint leading to Number. The point is not that Aadhaar biometrics are not and will not be used for forensic investigation or police surveillance. Nor is it as the case of the decomposed torso above that the friability of fleshly traces limits the utility of a biometric identity, though the latter has been a serious concern among both Aadhaar's critics and its engineers with a far greater number of persons whose fingerprints have abraded from time, accident and labour, and who fail to demonstrate identity to receive service, credit and wage payments.

The point is rather that in tabloid scenes of matter gone awry— of bodies torn apart and rotting, of persons found radically out of moral compass, in kinship and gender, in hotel rooms or waste spaces—the Aadhaar card becomes a familiar presence, no less than in the homely spaces of normative kin and residence. New or stock photographs that accompany the first of these sub-genres, of Aadhaar as contraband, often show the mass of duplicate cards as a rotting, festering thing. Massed paper files in visual or verbal rendition have long signified the state's encapsulation, secretion, inequitable rationalization, and radical devaluation of life, identity, expectation, and appeal. Piles of files suggest landscapes of death and willed forgetting and abandonment.

[15] Mohamed Thaver, 'Mumbai Police Find "Remains" of Man Missing Since August 13', *The Indian Express*, 4 September 2016.

Conclusion

The Concept dreams of the eradication of paper. But paper, in the case of the Aadhaar card, takes on a miasmatic life. Far from sterile, it is productive of myriad denatured forms. On the one hand, the Card becomes the necessary supplement to the Concept, and its proliferation cannot easily be stopped. Aadhaar's official publicity itself must repeatedly insert the Card within the immediate demands of a hack to fix the most recent bug in the unfolding of the ever expansive (and to critics aptly terrifying) Concept. In the world of the Concept, in short, the transformation of paper to electronic data is a kind of eugenic or tropical medicine that would stem the dangerous fecundity of duplication. But duplication is built in.

Aadhaar's life has a second register. It is not simply the Duplicate that engenders the fear of mass and miasma. India, to be de-duplicated, must be conceived as a Database. Nation-as-database is distinct from nation-as-population. Even if we recognise that the historical emergence of the figure of population relies upon instruments of accountancy, Data increasingly taken as value becomes not just the apparatus for knowing, governing or destroying population life but also a kind of life in and of itself. Databases do not just allow the state's governing of population life or the nation's passionate attachment to itself as population organism. Databases as sodalities of Data live and die in themselves. Data are awakened to productive life; alternately, Data rot. Imagine UIDAI's Database of all Residents if the NDA government had not secured its statutory force and the courts had effectively shut it down. The will to animate such archives, the claim that the life of the nation depends on the life of its Data, may extend or transform our sense of a politics organised around the death or life of population.

'Dark data' indexes all information that ever more extensive apparatuses of sensors and digital memory hold but do not yet exploit. The figure is bound up to the manifest destiny of extraction capitalism. The Authority would will India into the great Database, to life and light, the jewel in the network, from an arguably ever more hegemonic perception of its Duplicated darkness.

References

Cohen, Lawrence. 2016. 'Duplicate, Leak, Deity'. *Limn* (6). Available at: http://limn.it/duplicate-leak-deity/ (accessed on 23 May 2018).

Das, Veena. 2003. 'The Signature of the State: The Paradox of Illegibility'. In *Anthropology in the Margins of the State*, edited by Veena Das and Deborah Poole, 225–52. Santa Fe, NM: School of American Research Press.

Ferguson, James. 2015. *Give a Man a Fish: Reflections on the New Politics of Distribution*. Durham, NC: Duke University Press.

Hansen, Thomas Blom. 1999. *The Saffron Wave: Democracy and Hindu Nationalism in Modern India*. Princeton, NJ: Princeton University Press.

Hubka, Vladimir and W. Ernst Eder. 1988. *Theory of Technical Systems: A Total Concept Theory for Engineering Design*. Berlin: Springer-Verlag.

Kanakia, Hemant, Srikanth Nadhamuni and Sanjay Sarma. 2010. 'A UID Numbering Scheme'. White Paper (May). Delhi: Unique Identification Authority of India.

Keane, Webb. 2003. 'Semiotics and the Social Analysis of Material Things'. *Language & Communication* 23: 409–25.

Mahmood, Saba. 2009. 'Religious Reason and Secular Affect: An Incommensurable Divide?' *Critical Inquiry* 35: 836–62.

Malamoud, Charles. 1982. 'On the Rhetoric and Semantics of Purusartha'. In *Way of Life: King, Householder, Renouncer*, edited by T.N. Madan, 33–54. Delhi: Motilal Banarsidass.

Petryna, Adriana. 2002. *Life Exposed: Biological Citizens after Chernobyl*. Princeton, NJ: Princeton University Press.

Raheja, Gloria Goodwin. 1988. *The Poison in the Gift: Ritual, Prestation, and the Dominant Caste in a North Indian Village*. Chicago, IL: University of Chicago Press.

Rajadhyaksha, Ashish. 2013. 'Digital Delivery of Services: The Indian Landscape'. In *Aadhaar: The Digital Ecosystem*, edited by Ashish Rajadhyaksha, xi–l. Bengaluru: Centre for the Study of Culture and Society.

Sanyal, Kalyan. 2007. *Rethinking Capitalist Development: Primitive Accumulation, Governmentality and Post-colonial Capitalism*. New Delhi: Routledge.

Sharad Raghavan, T.C.A. 2015. 'Finance Minister and RBI Governor Bat for Aadhaar'. *Hindu*, 7 November 2015. https://www.thehindu.com/business/Economy/finance-minister-and-rbi-governor-pat-for-aadhaar/article7851698.ece (accessed on 25 August 2018).

Srivastava, Sanjay. 2012. 'Duplicity, Intimacy, Community: An Ethnography of ID Cards, Permits and Other Fake Documents in Delhi'. *Thesis Eleven* 113 (1): 78–93.

9

Internet Cultures

Nicholas Nisbett and Aditi Bhonagiri

Introduction: Internet Cultures vs Internet-mediated Cultures

The focus of this essay is on some of the major themes emerging from the last decade or so of research on Internet cultures in India. But rather than a trawl through this literature, the themes were selected by the authors because whilst conveying nuanced sociological and ethnographic considerations of the Indian experience, they also speak to wider scholarly debates with global relevance that have tried to map the sociocultural impacts of the Internet since its conception (Hine 2000; Miller and Slater 2000). The particularity of Indian experience acts as a counterpoint to some of the more naïve and earlier sociologies of the Internet which championed the transformative and emancipatory possibilities of the Internet as a virtual space drawing on fluid identities, geographies and wider possibilities (Cairncross 1997; Greig 2002; Stone 1991; Turkle 1995). But these studies also form part of an emerging literature considering Internet cultures in a multitude of geographical settings, and the tensions evolving in such spaces in the interaction between the local and global, the embodied and the symbolic or the human and non-human (Whitehead and Wesch 2012). A common theme throughout the papers examined here is that Internet cultures exist not as separate and virtual cultural spaces, but as spaces that both mediate and multiply social relations rooted in wider ontologies. 'Internet-mediated cultures' may be a better way of capturing the way in which the Internet is enabling social and cultural forms for the vast majority of Indian users.

Spaces of Freedom?

Much of the work on Internet cultures in India has, perhaps unsurprisingly, considered the role of the Internet in predominantly 'youth' cultures. Here, Internet-based social spaces have been assumed to offer participants a set of spaces away from everyday regulation and control, a range of 'free zones' for the pursuit of 'wild and everyday activities' (Rangaswamy and Arora 2015: 2) and spaces for the pursuit of pleasure and illicit youth behaviour (Chakraborty 2012; Doron 2012; Ganesh 2010; Rangaswamy and Arora 2015). The Internet has also taken on a role as a space for constructing, expressing and experimenting with self-identity, internalising national identities such as 'Indianness' (Doron 2012)[1] and as a space for articulating aspiration (N. Kumar 2014; Pathak-Shelat and DeShano 2014). For its participants, it has appeared to offer a space for lower income but literate youth to realise ambitions associated with the modernity of technology and the knowledge or 'network society' (Castells 2000; Nisbett 2009; Pathak-Shelat and DeShano 2014).

A closer perusal of the same literature leads to questions, however, of the novelty and uniqueness of these online spaces and the extent to which they allow real rupture with past social structures. To be sure, they do offer new opportunities, particularly for young people, to contest and subvert social norms. This includes, for example, subverting gendered space and rigid parental structures, particularly when experimenting with new forms of dating and courtship both online and offline (Doron 2012; Nisbett 2006; Pathak-Shelat and DeShano 2014). But online spaces can work equally to reinforce such structures and/or create new forms of gendered spaces. In the case of cyber-matchmaking, for example, Agrawal describes how information and communication technologies (ICTs) have helped reinforce old institutions such as the 'arranged marriage' in the face of globalisation (Agrawal 2015), whilst Doron similarly describes how the dimensions of freedom allowed by young women's cell phone usage in North India are curtailed by the practical and moral demands of prevailing social relations and institutions (Doron 2012). Doron's study is a remedy to any wider hype surrounding the growth in Internet use and social media granted by rapidly growing cell phone ownership and cell phone-based social media

[1] S. Chakrabarti, 'Young India, New Hunger for Identity', *The Hindu*, 29 August 2015.

and chat. Cell phone access among low-income families in Varanasi is severely restricted and controlled according to a woman's status in the family. Young women entering the patrilocal family as new wives are very unlikely to have access to their own phone—instead, they are reliant on restricted and controlled access to a family phone that is likely to be an older generation model without Internet access (ibid.).

Granted, there are numerous examples of where the Internet and ICTs more widely have created new possibilities for sociality by dint of both their ethereality and multiplicity. Ganesh, for example, explains how ICTs enable an arena where sexuality is actively constituted and reconstituted in multiple ways by men who have sex with men (MSM) in Mumbai (Ganesh 2010). Her research describes how ethereal and multiple interactions are used in different contexts in the constitution of *Kothi* identity and in the pursuit of relationships and pleasure (which include: '[g]etting aroused at bus-stops, hook-ups on trains, finding love and sex through numbers written on toilet walls, the missed calling, text-relationships, [blue film] sharing and accessing porn on-the-go'; Ganesh 2010: 36). Rangaswamy and Arora (2015) and Nisbett (2006, 2009) have described how participants in online chatting in, respectively, urban slums in Chennai and Hyderabad, and lower-middle-class parts of Bengaluru, aimed to progressively blur the distinctions between online and offline relationships. In both cases, online fora were used as a 'romantic gateway' (Rangaswamy and Arora 2015: 13) to otherwise impractical or improbable relationships with the opposite sex, including those from higher social classes. Chakraborty (2012), by way of contrast, describes how among young Muslim women living in Kolkata's urban slums, the Internet is considered as a safe space because it 'reduces the physical risks of courtship in a community which disapproves of public interaction between unmarried men and women' (Chakrabarti 2015: 198). However, she questions the extent to which such online relationships remain completely risk free. Here, once again, bringing the relationship into 'real life' remains an option for the women to test that relationships are not some untrustworthy version of 'timepass' (here, a casual tryst; Chakraborty 2012).

Continuities of Communication

Rather than be caught up in the new epochalism which marked the first generation of Internet sociology (Stone 1991; Turkle 1995), a number of these same authors writing on India are also keen to stress the continuities, rather than the ruptures, with older technologies of literacy and communication. Young people have always been adept at adapting new technologies to help overcome the bounds placed on their sexuality and courtship. For example, in Ahearn's study, protagonists are presented with a new world of possibilities enabled by their own literacy and adoption of the technology of writing and exchange of letters (Ahearn 2001). Both Doron (2012) and Nisbett (2009) refer to this study of love-letter writing in rural Nepal to draw the similarities between Internet and mobile phone-based communication and older 'technologies of the self' (Foucault, cited in Doron 2012: 415–20) in generating conscious subjectivities which can both draw on and disrupt immediate moral worlds (ibid.). Thus, whilst new forms of courtship and elopement ensue, there are considerable downsides for those who pursue the greatest rupture with existing social practices of courtship and marriage and who lose, as a result, the security and backing of family and community (Doron 2012: 419).

Likewise, comparisons have been made between the new social spaces available to young people online and those available offline as a way of questioning whether online social spaces offer something considerably new. Here, scholars have drawn attention to the broad literature on youth space and place which has long considered the articulation of youth identity in new social spaces represented by coffee shops, bars or those older spaces such as 'street corners' that, as Jeffrey (2010: 465) notes, provided spaces where young men hung out together engaging in 'timepass' or being 'useless' but were able to create 'youthful solidarities… across caste and caste boundaries' and, thus, 'positive social identities' (Miller and Slater 2000; Nisbett 2007; Whyte 1993). So representing simply the most recent evolution of technologies of the self, literacy or youth social space—the Internet and the cultures that it enables—need to be considered as an extension of existing social phenomena, rather than a radical departure.

The same considerations extend to the role of the body and embodiment in online communications. Whereas once the Internet was seen to enable the proliferation of online worlds inhabited by virtual identities divorced of their bodily constraints (Stone 1991; Turkle 1995), in many of the works considered here, online cultures and the communications spawned therein 'do' lead back to the bodies attached to the communications. And more often than not, these bodies have physical and geographical identities which structure their communication online.[2] It has been described already how many participants in

[2] Although not covered in the works cited here, we might note how 'selfie' culture is leading to a new negotiation of shared bodily images among Internet and social media users.

online communications are engaged in a continual struggle to revert communications back to their embodied and place-bound lives (Nisbett 2006; Pathak-Shelat and DeShano 2014; Rangaswamy and Arora 2015). As Pathak-Shelat and DeShano write of Gujarati small towns and rural areas: 'Indian youth of small towns and rural places still live in collective social structures that shape their orientations. New media are at the periphery of their lives, as these youth have strong interpersonal connections that are rooted in geographic proximity and active school experiences' (Pathak-Shelat and DeShano 2014: 985).

Internet Cultures as Symbolic Capital

Rather than positing such reversion to offline reality as being a 'failure' of forays into online fora, research on such contexts has repeatedly stressed the everyday utility of the symbolic currency gained from online activity and computer literacy (Nisbett 2013; Pathak-Shelat and DeShano 2014; Rangaswamy and Arora 2015). Here, the novelty of the technology, the promise of connectedness to global modernity and advanced capitalism, and the claims of meritocratic social mobility which attach to technology use and ICT-based employment conspire to create an aspirational youth culture shaped around the meritocratic claims of the network or knowledge society. The reality, however, is somewhat displaced from the aspirational rhetoric. Families share in such aspirations, whether in the purchase of a computer (Pathak-Shelat and DeShano 2014) or in repeated investments in educational capital via short backstreet training courses (Chakraborty 2012; Nisbett 2013). For the young Muslim women in Kolkata's urban slums studied by Chakraborty, computer education is seen as part of the training to be a '"good Muslim girl" as a wife and a mother' (Chakraborty 2012: 205) and to represent acceptable capital within the marriage market, rather than necessarily leading to work outside the home. For the lower-middle-class men encountered by Nisbett in a similar backstreet computer training environment, repeated attempts at gaining yet further capital through more and more types of computer languages and different types of certification did not lead to the coveted software jobs expected (Nisbett 2013). But in both situations—and others encountered in other parts of rural and urban India (Pathak-Shelat and DeShano 2014; Rangaswamy and Arora 2015)—there is real symbolic capital attached to 'knowing computers' which transcends any purely instrumental gain in the perceived rewards of a software or other 'modern' job. This might include the positive appraisal of parents, peers or potential suitors. In Chakraborty's (2012) example, there is additional utility to the young women themselves in that they suddenly find themselves skilled with the technological wherewithal to take part in illicit Internet chat.

Such findings have led a number of authors to re-examine the instrumentalist assumptions behind many approaches to Internet use which stem from development discourses first encountered around the turn of the millennium and still dominant in the form of 'ICT for development' (ICT4D or ICTD; Mazzarella 2010; Rangaswamy and Cutrell 2012). Such discourses have been criticised for pre-judging acceptable use of technology as particular socio-economic outcomes in development contexts and thus 'looking only at a narrow slice of the full range of human experience of the people who use the technologies' (Rangaswamy and Cutrell 2012). Alternative approaches, then, advocate considering the wider potentials of Internet use studied, ethnographically, in situ, to capture 'the emergent potentials of a system of mediation' (Mazzarella 2010: 798) which lie somewhere between Internet hype and its associated repudiation. Mazzarella describes how, a decade on from peak ICT4D hyperbole, the discourse 'has not so much imploded as become normalised' (Mazzarella 2010: 799). But it is the understanding gained of the 'deflated' and everyday realities of normalised IT use—the NGO project hijacked by young men for porn browsing (Mazzarella 2010: 794) or the computer literacy skills hijacked by young women for chatting (Chakraborty 2012)—which is the necessary precursor to drawing any wider conclusions about the socio-economic impact of Internet use. At the very least, this requires an acknowledgement that such impacts have stepped outside the narrow confines of the assumed and original benefits of ICT4D. The danger, otherwise, is that '[a]dopting a narrow development lens can miss the actual engagements and ingenious strategies marginal populations use to integrate technologies into their daily lives' (Rangaswamy and Cutrell 2012: 62).

Political Cultures of the Internet

Mazzarella has described the tensions in the ways in which ICT4D discourses in India brought together a number of different ideological and rhetorical objectives, from neoliberalism and individual entrepreneurialism, to nationalism and regionalism, to wider movements around social activism and transparency (Mazzarella 2010: 797). This demonstrates how the assumptions surrounding ICT as a development paradigm were already highly politicised.

It is no surprise that much of the energy that has been funnelled in to ICT4D projects has been directed towards its political potential.

Assumptions about the Internet as an emancipatory space for identity and bodily politics were also carried through to assumptions about its potential for political activism. Several recent papers have considered the range of political discourse and activism online and point to a number of political cultures which are now mediated by the Internet which can be classed as both emancipatory and reactionary. That is to say that political cultures on the Internet mirror the broad spectrum of political activities which exist without the mediation of the Internet—assumptions that online activism would offer an outlet for primarily socially liberal or left politics seem, in retrospect, quite naïve.

Of course, this is not to downplay the accomplishments of the types of online activism which have pursued progressive politics—which is documented by, for example, Chattopadhyay, in the case of the feminist campaign following Hindutva inspired attacks on party-going women in Mangalore (Chattopadhyay 2011) and papers examining the spaces offered for Dalit activism and presence online (de Kruijf 2015; Kumar and Subramani 2014). But these are necessarily juxtaposed against the globalised networks of Hindu chauvinism documented by Therwath (2012). Similar sentiments among young-middle-class and elite Hindus in more national contexts are examined by Mohan (2015) or numerous media reports of the proliferation of extreme-right and misogynist Internet 'trolls'.[3]

Interesting across these and other examinations of Internet-based politics (see also S. Kumar 2015; Lodhia 2014; Punathambekar 2015) is the role that the Internet can play in constructing national identities and subjectivities. In Therwarth's (2012) study of 'Cyber-Hindutva', this is an important part of the process of imagined communities once described by Benedict Anderson where nationalist imaginaries are in juxtaposition with the realities of global and migratory lives. Here, 'skype-shakhas' and 'E-shakhas' have been launched as branches of the RSS catering to the Hindutva diaspora; and a wider network of pro-Hindutva news sites and portals function to root and anchor a diasporic community who find themselves in mainly North American and British settings. Therwarth cites Latour in describing how an understanding of web-based nationalism turns on its head the usual assumption of online=virtual and offline=material/real: 'The Web re-materializes

[3] S. Bhushan, 'The Power of Social Media: Emboldened Right-wing Trolls Who Are Attempting an Internet Purge', *The Caravan*, 28 September 2015. Available at: http://www.caravanmagazine.in/vantage/power-social-media-emboldened-right-wing-trolls (accessed on 24 May 2018).

things that were virtual: one can follow now, affiliations, exchanges of arguments, one can render traceable things that were not, and thus to ask oneself the question of what it means to have a political position, to take a position' (Latour 2010, cited in Therwath 2015). This is consistent also with the findings of those studies which have considered the role of the Internet in more emancipatory projects in support of minorities (Chattopadhyay 2011; de Kruijf 2015; Kumar and Subramani 2014), where, for example, '[n]ew media serves as a surrogate social-political space where gradual legitimisation and the solidification of the politics of belonging occur prior to the deployment of the movement in real-politik' (Chattopadhyay 2011: 65). Importantly, for Chattopadhyay, 'The "successful" transition from an entirely online communication to offline communication and the corresponding transition from token protest, resistance, and support to tangible material confrontations are necessary to tread outside the elusive sphere of clicktivism' (Chattopadhyay 2011: 65).

Conclusions

Notwithstanding Latour's remarks, Chattopadhyay's conclusion here mirrors those earlier findings with regard to online youth courtship and underlines the need felt by Internet users to materialise relationships and identities formed via the mediation of ICTs. This leads to the wider conclusion (previewed at the beginning of this chapter) that Internet cultures exist rarely in isolation from the broader sweep of human relations which collectively constitute any number of human cultures and societies.

These sociological and anthropological accounts of the everyday emergent cultural forms mediated by the Internet are important because of their contribution to deep-seated ontological questions regarding bodily and symbolic communication. Cutting through the hype on the relationship between the embodied (or real) and the symbolic (or virtual), the Internet sociologist Zeynep Tufecki (2012: 34) has written,

The proliferation of digital technologies has made us no more post-human than the invention of writing or the creation of those breathtaking Palaeolithic cave paintings at Chauvet... we are no less human than the first time an ancestor picked up a stick to extend an arm. On the other hand, this extension, like all the others, is surely not without consequence.

Documenting these consequences as experienced by Indian Internet users contributes to this wider understanding of the Internet as a further extension of the simultaneously symbolic and bodily possibilities made possible by human invention.

References

Agrawal, A. 2015. 'Cyber-matchmaking Among Indians: Re-arranging Marriage and Doing "Kin Work"'. *South Asian Popular Culture* 13 (1): 15–30.

Ahearn, L.M. 2001. *Invitations to Love: Literacy, Love Letters and Social Change in Nepal*. Ann Arbor, MI: University of Michigan Press.

Cairncross, F. 1997. *The Death of Distance: How the Communications Revolution Will Change Our Lives*. London: Orion Business Books.

Castells, M. 2000. *The Rise of the Network Society*. 2nd ed. Oxford: Blackwell Publishers.

Chakraborty, K. 2012. 'Virtual Mate-seeking in the Urban Slums of Kolkata, India'. *South Asian Popular Culture* 10 (2): 197–216.

Chattopadhyay, S. 2011. 'Online Activism for a Heterogeneous Time: The Pink Chaddi Campaign and the Social Media in India'. *Proteus* 27 (1): 63–68.

De Kruijf, J. 2015. 'The Dalit I Define: Social Media and Individualized Activism in Subaltern Spheres'. *Pacific Asia Journal of the Association for Information Systems* 7 (4): 11–24.

Doron, A. 2012. 'Mobile Persons: Cell Phones, Gender and the Self in North India'. *The Asia Pacific Journal of Anthropology* 13 (5): 414–33.

Ganesh, I.M. 2010. '"Mobile Love Videos Make Me Feel Healthy": Rethinking ICTs for Development'. *IDS Working Papers* 2010 (352): 1–43.

Greig, J.M. 2002. 'The End of Geography? Globalization, Communications, and Culture in the International System'. *Journal of Conflict Resolution* 46 (2): 225–43.

Hine, C. 2000. *Virtual Ethnography*. London: SAGE.

Jeffrey, C. 2010. 'Timepass: Youth, Class, and Time Among Unemployed Young Men in India'. *American Ethnologist* 37 (3): 465–81.

Kumar, C. Suresh and R. Subramani. 2014. 'Internet as an Alternative Media for Dalits in India: Prospects and Challenges'. *IOSR Journal of Humanities and Social Science (IOSR–JHSS)* 19 (2): 125–29.

Kumar, N. 2014. 'Facebook for Self-empowerment? A Study of Facebook Adoption in Urban India'. *New Media & Society* 16 (7): 1122–37.

Kumar, S. 2015. 'Contagious Memes, Viral Videos and Subversive Parody: The Grammar of Contention on the Indian Web'. *International Communication Gazette* 77 (3): 232–47.

Latour, B. 2010. 'Avoir ou ne pas avoir de réseau' ['That's the Question']. In *Débordements: Mélanges offerts à Michel Callon* edited by Akrich M et al., 257–68. Paris: Presses de l'Ecole des Mines.

Lodhia, S. 2014. '"Stop Importing Weapons of Family Destruction!" Cyberdiscourses, Patriarchal Anxieties, and the Men's Backlash Movement in India'. *Violence Against Women* 20 (8): 905–36.

Mazzarella, W. 2010. 'Beautiful Balloon: The Digital Divide and the Charisma of New Media in India'. *American Ethnologist* 37 (4): 783–804.

Miller, D. and D. Slater. 2000. *The Internet: An Ethnographic Approach.* Oxford: Berg.

Mohan, S. 2015. 'Locating the "Internet Hindu" Political Speech and Performance in Indian Cyberspace'. *Television & New Media* 16 (4): 339–45.

Nisbett, N. 2006. 'The Internet, Cybercafés and the New Social Spaces of Bangalorean Youth'. In *Locating the Field: Space, Place and Context in Anthropology*, edited by S. Coleman and P. Collins, 129–47. London: Berg.

———. 2007. 'Friendship, Consumption, Morality: Practicing Identity, Negotiating Hierarchy in Middle Class Bangalore'. *Journal of the Royal Anthropological Institute* 13 (4): 935–50.

———. 2009. *Growing Up in the Knowledge Society: Living the IT Dream in Bangalore.* New Delhi: Routledge.

———. 2013. 'Youth and the Practice of IT Enterprise: Narratives of the Knowledge Society and the Creation of New Subjectivities Amongst Bangalore's IT Aspirants'. In *Enterprise Culture in Neoliberal India: Studies in Youth, Class, Work and Media*, edited by N. Gooptu, 175–89. Oxford: Routledge.

Pathak-Shelat, M. and C. DeShano. 2014. 'Digital Youth Cultures in Small Town and Rural Gujarat, India'. *New Media & Society* 16 (6): 983–1001.

Punathambekar, A. 2015. 'Satire, Elections, and Democratic Politics in Digital India'. *Television & New Media* 16 (4): 394–400.

Rangaswamy, N. and P. Arora. 2015. 'The Mobile Internet in the Wild and Every Day: Digital Leisure in the Slums of Urban India'. *International Journal of Cultural Studies* 19 (6): 611–26.

Rangaswamy, N. and E. Cutrell. 2012. 'Anthropology, Development and ICTs: Slums, Youth and the Mobile Internet in Urban India'. *Information Technologies and International Development* 9 (2 Special Issue): 51–63

Stone, A.R. 1991. 'Will the Real Body Please Stand up? Boundary Stories About Virtual Cultures'. In *Cyberspace: First Steps*, edited by M. Benedikt, 81–118. Cambridge, MA: MIT Press.

Therwath, I. 2012. 'Cyber-Hindutva: Hindu Nationalism, the Diaspora and the Web'. *Social Science Information* 51 (4): 551–77.

Tufekci, Z. 2012. 'We Were Always Human'. In *Human No More: Digital Subjectivities, Unhuman Subjects and the End of Anthropology*, edited by N.L. Whitehead and M. Wesch, 33–47. Boulder, CO: University of Colorado Press.

Turkle, S. 1995. *Life on the Screen: Identity in the Age of the Internet*. New York, NY and London: Simon & Schuster.

Whitehead, N.L. and M. Wesch. 2012. *Human No More: Digital Subjectivities, Unhuman Subjects and the End of Anthropology*. Boulder, CO: University of Colorado Press.

Whyte, W.F. 1993. *Street Corner Society: The Social Structure of an Italian Slum*. 4th ed. Chicago, IL and London: University of Chicago Press.

10

Schooling and Culture

Bringing Schools into Sociology

Meenakshi Thapan

Sociology in India has enriched our understanding of institutions and processes in different contexts and spheres of social life. In all these aspects, education has somehow remained marginal to the interests of sociologists and is even now considered a banal and uninspiring area of study. This is partly a result of departments of sociology in universities that shape disciplinary frames through emphasising the study of more compelling and 'relevant' themes for research in contemporary India. Sociology of India, for example, largely focuses on caste and gender issues; economic sociology focuses on aspects of the economy in the context of the state or particular economies in different parts of India or elsewhere; sociological theories focus largely on theories emanating from Western traditions that we have learnt to interweave and incorporate into our own perspectives so that we do not really have a unique sociological framework/s that we can truly call our 'own'. Nowhere do we find education central to the discussion, debate and research in mainstream sociology departments around the country.[1] Departments of education have some sociologists who work in the area but even they are few and far between. The struggle, therefore, has been to bring

[1] See Chanana (2011), who has traced a survey of the sociological analyses of schools in India and the methods used to study them.

the sociology of education, with a focus on the sociology of schooling, into mainstream sociology, as an exciting and innovative research area.

Education is the pulse of a nation that is encapsulated betwixt tradition and modernity, besieged by voices that cling to the past, throttle dissent and agency and, simultaneously, seek to take India into the 21st century. This is the dilemma of education in present times, and it is this swiftly changing and vastly ambivalent landscape that makes education such a rich and fascinating area of study. To use a cliché, it is in the schools that the destiny of a nation resides, and this is nowhere truer than in this country where we are struggling to still cut our umbilical cord with the vestiges of colonialism as well as define new ways of being ourselves in a rapidly changing and evolving global framework. It is in this sense that, as sociologists, we seek to understand the institutional structures, pedagogic encounters and social interaction that animate schools from being mere structures into cultures, products of human imagination and intervention in often vastly opposing and differentiating ways.

Schools as Institutions and as Processes

Schools in India inhabit hugely divergent spaces, both territorially and ideologically. The vast majority of schools are government-run across the country with a mandate to educate every child. However, as is well known, the pedagogy, infrastructure and facilities that are provided are often abysmal and default on several counts. Children enter school but do not often complete schooling due to a slew of factors, including seeking early employment in the informal sector, familial restrictions especially for girls, exclusion of Dalits and other marginalised children, as well as the fact that what goes on in schools does not appeal to children.[2] It is by and large of not much interest or relevance to their lives and is often far removed from their imagination. In addition, most teachers overemphasise textbook-based learning through rote memorisation and are unable to bring to life the different subjects being taught in the classroom.

According to the Global Education Monitoring (GEM) report (UNESCO), India is 50 years behind in implementing its own goals

[2] For an understanding of these factors and their consequences, see, for example, Nambissan (2011), Balagopalan (2014) and Majumdar and Mooij (2011). See Velaskar (2015) for an insightful analysis of inherent inequalities in the educational system and the reproduction of educational disadvantage in India.

for universal education. India will probably realise universal primary education by 2050, universal lower education by 2060 and universal secondary education in 2085 (UNESCO 2016). The UNESCO report further concludes that over 60 million children in India receive little or no formal education and that there are 11.1 million children who are out of school in the lower secondary level, the highest figure in the world. A further 2.9 million children do not even attend primary school (ibid.). This indicates very clearly that, even after almost 70 years of independence, India is still struggling with the implementation of its education policies, notably by the Education Commission (1964–68)[3] and others that followed. The more recent Right to Education (RTE) Act (2009) has sought to rectify this lacuna in school education by seeking to provide free and compulsory quality schooling to all children.[4] The UNESCO report is, however, a damning indictment of the state of education in this country and speaks volumes for the lack of official commitment to address a basic right, that of education, and the sheer absence of will to implement goals. Mired in officialdom and bureaucracy, India's schooling system that impacts not only the lives of children but of teachers as well is creaking and failing, and unless urgent steps for redressal are taken, with passion and commitment, a likely collapse is imminent.[5]

We may argue that the school is a significant physical and intellectual space within which knowledge is disseminated and received. The school, however, is not merely a building where information and technical skills are imparted, some social skills inculcated, examinations conducted, students assessed and eventually certified. It is also that moral and symbolic space where socialisation takes place, where identities are constructed and differentiated on the basis of gender, caste,

---

[3] See Naik (1997: 9 ff.) for a detailed outline of the policy and its recommendations.

[4] The implementation of this Act has not necessarily had the desired effects and there have been criticisms. See, for example, Shah and Agarwal (2010) and Bose (2014).

[5] At the same time, it is important to consider the view, raised by Balagopalan, that those children who are 'out of school' have now been moved from the category of 'child labour' to the 'promised domain of "free and compulsory education"' (2014: 4). Balagopalan argues that a non-Western view about education for all, or one that seeks to usher India onto a global socio-economic stage, must be considered for societies who are experiencing a 'post-colonial modernity' and where children may require a different kind of education. In a study marked by rich ethnography and finely tuned analysis, Balagopalan draws our attention to marginal children, street children, all those who constitute 'child labour' in a postcolony and urges us to cease from seeing them as 'undesirable lives' that need transforming.

class, race and ethnicity, among others, where young minds follow socially constructed and established paths of learning, memorising as well as challenging the given limits of knowledge and, importantly, where peer cultures are formed, exist and tend to shape everything that takes place in school. Peer cultures also define students' relations with the world outside school. Social networks, career aspirations, 'individual' goals, 'personal' ambitions and behavioural modes are all influenced by these peer cultures which are heterogeneous and amorphous in nature, changing with time, interests and age cohorts.

In general, schools may be understood as institutions based on certain organisational principles derived from the structures they inhabit, embedded in an official educational discourse and constrained by the very frameworks that define them as spaces of learning. All schools have a charter, whether this is articulated or left opaque, and the charter may or may not resonate with official definitions of schooling or with the pedagogic processes in a school. Schools such as those run by religious trusts have well-defined frameworks that state their intentions and goals very clearly, as do schools run by private trusts of varying kinds.[6]

[6] For example, a random search reveals that among other institutions, a madrasa in South Delhi describes itself and its goals as such:

A well known Madrasa named Madrasa TALEEM-Ul-QURAN established in March 1992, in the premises of Masjid Haji Langa. In its vicinity, there are two of the most prestigious institutions for higher learning viz. J.N.U. and I.I.T. There are also a number of private and government schools in this area. However, within the close location of the Masjid in Delhi and its neighboring states, are living a large number of poor Muslim families with little or no means to afford education to their children. The organizers feel the need to create a framework of basic religious education in which due importance would be given to the learning of the QURAN, the SHARIAT (Islamic Law) and other aspects of Islam, it is well known for teaching Tajweed. With this learning the child could then be introduced to formal school subjects in keeping with present day requirements. We have strived to achieve our goal of combining the highest ethical values of Islam with modern requirements which stress the knowledge of Computer, Science and technology etc. (http://www.hajilangatrust. org/, accessed on 4 May 2016)

The organisation not only asserts its religious identity but also seeks to establish its secular character through its emphasis on 'modern' education, science, technology and so on. Through their charter, the school seeks to express itself to both a traditional clientele who may send their children to school for conventional knowledge derived from the scriptures and market itself to those who seek a more contemporary educational framework for their wards.

Similarly, government schools have well-stated aims about their intent and purpose, clearly stated on the website of the relevant department of education. Private schools have their own agenda which they seek to highlight on public platforms as well. For example, the Muni International School, a 'budget' (low-income) private school located in West Delhi, advertises itself as a 'truly democratic school' where 'each student is given equal opportunity to learn, express, lead, share and contribute in all matters of learning, management and innovation'.[7] There is an effort to appeal to a clientele that values quality education as well as a 'democratic' spirit and is willing to consider this alternative, non-competitive outlook in an unpretentious location.

By contrast, the elite Doon School located in a lush green landscape in Dehradun is a much sought-after school with parents registering their boys as soon as they are born. It does not hesitate to advertise itself as 'one of India's finest schools, with a strong intellectual heartbeat, an unequivocal commitment to social service, a curriculum that develops leadership and alumni network with a global reputation'.[8] This school has the confidence, which no doubt comes with power and privilege, to identify itself as one of the best schools in India with complete lack of humility or restraint. It is also in the educational marketplace to sell what it values the most: a particular idea of 'modern' masculinity and social accomplishment.[9] Clearly, ideas and practice are closely intermeshed and do not always resonate with religious identities alone.

Similarly, Saamar International Public School in Bengaluru advertises that 'Saamar students are a blend of modern education with Islamic values' (http://www.saamar.org, accessed on 7 May 2016). The school website further adds that in an increasingly changing world, where 'profit oriented consumerism, or, materialism, is gaining ground and where ethics and values are fast diminishing, the School aims to balance the two so that ethics and values remain steadfast' (http://www.saamar.org/info.html, accessed on 7 May 2016). A co-educational school, this institution caters to an urban middle-class population. The Convent of Jesus and Mary (CJM) in New Delhi does not explicitly state its religious underpinnings, although it is apparent in the name: 'We try to inculcate the virtues of the heart, mind, body and soul to engender an overall development of personality. The academic curriculum is supplemented by physical training, value education, co-curricular activities and vocational training'. (www.cjmdelhi.com/HolisticEducation.aspx, accessed on 9 September 2016).

[7] For more details, see www.muniinternationalschool.org (accessed on 8 September 2016).

[8] www.doonschool.com (accessed on 8 September 2016).

[9] See Srivastava (2015) for an analysis of the Doon School in the context of culture and 'modernity'. See also Srivastava (1998).

Benei (2009) focuses on the relationship between 'ideas' and schooling in the context of developing an emotional and visceral bonding to 'the nation' and thereby building a form of 'banal nationalism' among young children. This is another form of the inculcation of school ideals among young children. Focusing on schools in western Maharashtra, Benei locates her argument in a framework that celebrates the '*emotional and embodied* production of the political' (ibid.: 5). Schools in India, especially those with political affiliations of some kind, tend to instil their ideological commitments into the curriculum in an often rigid and deterministic manner, as the work of Sarkar (1996), Sundar (2005) and others so clearly tell us. At the same time, if the anthropologist observes the school in its routine and in children's and parents' constructions of the same, we can see that school goals often diverge from those of the main stakeholders. Peggy Froerer's work (2007) on the Saraswati Shishu Mandir Primary School in Chhattisgarh seeks to uncover this significant dimension of school life where aspirations do not coincide and this speaks for the agency of children in articulating their aspirations and those of their parents.

To some extent, schools are not only influenced by their charter but also tend to function more or less according to the norms and guidelines of the school boards to which they are affiliated. The ideological statements and charters, therefore, remain statements of the ideals that schools perhaps aspire to without really seeking to fulfil them in any meaningful or lasting way. This, however, points to an important conclusion that schools are largely utilitarian institutions where state-directed educational goals are fulfilled in somewhat exacting and unimaginative ways.

Schools nonetheless do not exist merely as institutions, as the people in them, who animate them, and give them life, as it were, constitute them. It is in this sense that we might understand schools in a non-institutional framework, as 'processes', that endure over time. Processes are continuous and express themselves through relationships formed around ideas, texts, people and nature. These also constitute learning spaces through which the culture of the school emerges and endures over time. Such processes provide a particular quality to the school which we may understand as ethos, culture or the particular ambience that enriches any school and gives it life. This ethos is built, for example, by the relationship between ideas and their practice in an institutional setting, how these are sought to be understood and executed by a multiplicity of participants, what pedagogic processes and methods they use, relationships among and between themselves, and several other processes that prevail within schools. Such processes, dominated also by the relationships of participants, including parents and the community, to nature and the environment, build and shape the culture of any school. At the same time, there is great variety in school cultures as there is diversity in cultures of schooling. The great array of schools in India points to diverse cultures: even within the government-run schools, there is a range of schools that create cultures that lend an ethos to them that is unique in the same way as are the cultures of religious trust schools, or alternative schools.[10]

Culture as Value in Schools

A significant part of this space of culture that is significant to schooling processes, and indeed to the life of the institution as such, is that of value, which is that ineffable core of an institution that rests on both the structures it inhabits and the processes that give it meaning. In other words, both the formal organisational aspects of schooling and its culture rest on the core principle of value. We may understand this value as that essence which embodies the core principles of the school as well as the processes through which the school is actually engaged in the transaction of both its practical aspects and the values or ethics it seeks to communicate.

Values, as ethical modes of conduct, are central to school life. In a sense, this view of the school embodies a certain preoccupation with the moulding of young minds into 'good' citizens with 'good' values emanating from Islam, Christianity or Hinduism, as the case may be. At the same time, such a view does not exclude those schools that do not prescribe to an overt religious perspective or framework. There could also be a concern with inculcating a 'modern' education, a 'secular' worldview, a 'holistic' education and other such categories that seek to promote education in a non-traditional or conservative framework.[11]

[10] For thick descriptions and analyses of school cultures, see, for example, Benei (2009), Gogoi (2014), Deka (2014), Bhandari (2014), Matthan et al. (2014), Gupta (2015), Dore (2014) and Thapan (2006 [1991]).

[11] Srijan School, for example, in Delhi advertises itself as a school committed to a holistic development of the child: 'Progressive and secular in its philosophy, The Srijan School, follows a child-oriented approach, looking upon each child as an individual and providing an educational programme which stresses the importance of the total development of the child—head, heart and hand' (http://thesrijanschool.com/philisophy.php#home, accessed on 8 May 2016).

Seeking to understand the culture as value in schools, we may begin with the colonialist paradigm that emphasised an English education, celebrated mental over manual labour and attempted to build 'tradition' as the English saw it. The colonialist view was carried forward by the nationalists who, as Seth (2008) succinctly puts it, bestowed the 'gift' of a particular kind of education on to an India seeking freedom and 'modernity'. Western education, however, failed to transform India as it took on a utilitarian hue with the nationalists: 'it was being compartmentalised or quarantined, put into that slot of "that which enables one to get ahead in life", instead of refashioning the understanding of what constitutes the good life' (Seth 2008: 31).

This resulted in an educational ethos where cramming, rote learning and submission to authority became the norm, and education became the means to an end to get ahead, gain a promotion and succeed at any cost. In this process, education lost its soul, as it were, and became embedded in the quagmire of petty hopes and ambitions without paying attention to the enduring qualities, skills and knowledge that education may provide, apart from the possibilities of enriching a critical outlook and a global perspective.

M.K. Gandhi was the first to seek to break from such a perspective with his scheme of Basic National Education in 1937 which suggested free and compulsory education for all children between 7 and 14 years of age in the vernacular language of the region in which the school was to be located. In 1909, Gandhi (1997 [1909]) had sought to reject Western civilisation as a moral force. He believed that civilisation itself was a moral enterprise and any civilisation that emphasised the politics of power and the economics of self-interest, as did Western civilisation, deserved to be discarded. Education was the primary source for the development of morality, and 'character education' became a value that education must impart. This meant bringing our 'senses under subjection' and putting our 'ethics on a firm foundation' (Gandhi 1997 [1909]). Although Gandhi was critical of religious education per se, he believed that it is still possible to teach an ethics that is grounded in

The Rishi Valley School run by the Krishnamurti Foundation, India, states its intention:

> To awaken the intelligence and the generosity of spirit in students so that they are able to meet an increasingly complex world without losing their humanity. The cultivation of a global outlook, a love of nature and a concern for mankind are all part of our educational aims. (www.rishivalley.org/school/aims.htm, accessed on 9 September 2016)

religion in a non-fundamentalist fashion. His mistrust of 'modern' education, essentially a form of education that included teaching through irrelevant textbooks and a meaningless curriculum, provided the basis for his scheme for a new form of education for modern India. The development of 'moral and mental faculties' is part of this education, and it is with the nurturance of both these equally important capabilities, he believed, that it would be possible to produce good citizens. Gandhi was convinced by the triumph of 'goodness', a core value, over the evil forces that tend to be part of social relations. Basic Education, with its emphasis on right values, love for the earth, crafts through manual labour, languages and indigenous culture, as well as academic training, was to provide the bedrock for this goodness.[12]

The search for 'goodness' and for the good society has been the concern of several other educators. In the work of the radical teacher J. Krishnamurti, we find a considered emphasis on the development of the 'good' society for the renewal of human life in its entirety. Krishnamurti considered 'right' education an essential corollary to the growth of the good society. At the heart of Krishnamurti's work was an essential understanding that society can only change if there is a transformation in an individual's consciousness, and this can come about through 'right' education. 'Living' in itself, for Krishnamurti, with his emphasis on 'daily' existence, in all its psychological perplexity and complexity, was far more important than grappling with an obscure search for 'truth' or the 'meaning of life' that was disconnected from everyday reality. 'Goodness' for Krishnamurti did not, therefore, emerge from a search or striving for transformation but from understanding and 'right' actions. Krishnamurti's emphasis on 'goodness' as the foundation of a new society underlies his plea for a society devoid of any kinds of contradictions or dichotomies. A society without 'national economic divisions' underscores his obvious concern for the ending of economic and social inequalities. However, Krishnamurti emphasised that none of this can come about without an inner renewal or change

[12] See Kumar (1997) for a review of Gandhi's endeavours in education. Gandhi's efforts in the field of education did not meet with great success due to the rapid efforts to industrialise and modernise India, to keep up with Western advancements in science and technology. See Didyala (2010) for a report on the failure of Gandhian schools in Gujarat. A recent news item informs us that the school where Gandhi studied in Rajkot is being converted to Gandhi Smriti Museum and the school administration has been asked to vacate the school immediately (DeshGujarat, 3 September 2016, http://deshgujarat.com/2016/09/03/mahatma-gandhis-school-in-rajkot-to-be-converted-into-museum; accessed on 8 September 2016).

and education is, therefore, the foundation on which the good society will build itself.[13]

The emphasis on cognitive learning and academic achievement has resulted in schooling cultures that underscore a competitive environment, skewed teaching and learning patterns, and a lack of attention to the emotional contexts of learning.[14] It has been well known for some time now that reason and emotion go together in the growth of a child and need to be developed together. As Immordino-Yang and Damasio (2007: 3) tell us,

> Recent advances in the neuroscience of emotions are highlighting connections between cognitive and emotional functions that have the potential to revolutionize our understanding of learning in the context of schools. In particular, connections between decision making, social functioning, and moral reasoning hold new promise for breakthroughs in understanding the role of emotion in decision making, the relationship between learning and emotion, how culture shapes learning, and ultimately the development of morality and human ethics.

The ability to realise a child's 'goodness' does not rest on young children alone, with some help from an educator, as Rousseau (1977) had us believe. Significantly, it rests on the ability of schools and teachers to provide an ethos, a culture, wherein cognition and emotion are both equally valued and nurtured so as to enable the development of a morality that is not steeped in religious diktats, nationalism or petty virtue but rests on a sense of the 'moral worth' of individuals. The state, therefore, needs to go beyond the idea of providing 'free and compulsory education for all' and focus on the quality of schooling not merely in terms of its academic content, transaction and evaluation patterns alone. The focus on developing a critical consciousness is also not enough.[15] School cultures must enable the development of

---

[13] See Krishnamurti (2011). The Krishnamurti Foundation (India) runs five residential schools in different parts of India and also publishes an annual *Journal of the Krishnamurti Schools.*

[14] In addition, parents' 'aspirational regimes' (Sancho 2013) for the 'success' of their children are resulting in the rapid growth of coaching institutions and an environment of 'shadow education' that tends to, in turn, influence pedagogy inside schools.

[15] The works of Friere (1974, 1977), McLaren (1995, 1998) and Giroux (1983, 2011) have focused on this aspect of learning and made a significant contribution to pedagogy in different contexts.

a secular morality that engenders empathy, consideration and human-ism. Durkheim (1961 [1938]: 217) was simultaneously committed to an understanding of the psychological bases of the child that took into account 'altruism' as an equal partner to 'selfishness'. He sought to instil the importance of the view that even within our egotism, there is always 'something other than ourselves' (1961 [1938]: 224). In this duality, there is the possibility for making the child truly social and ready for collective life through the discipline and rigour (albeit with-out punishment) of the school environment and the curriculum. This points to the significance of the school's role in promoting ideas and values that may be absorbed and appreciated by the intrinsic goodness in the child. Such a view that emphasises the importance of schools as socialising agents in society also points to the urgency with which we need to foreground the study of schools in contemporary sociology.

References

Balagopalan, Sarada. 2014. *Inhabiting 'Childhood': Children, Labour and Schooling in Postcolonial India*. London: Palgrave Macmillan.

Benei, Veronique. 2009. *Schooling India: Hindus, Muslims and the Forging of Citizens*. New Delhi: Permanent Black.

Bhandari, Parul. 2014. 'In Quest of Identity: Student Culture in a Religious Minority Institution'. In *Ethnographies of Schooling in Contemporary India*, edited by Meenakshi Thapan, 182–224. New Delhi and London: SAGE.

Bose, Noyonika. 2014. 'The Wrongs in the Right to Education'. Available at: https://kafila.org/2014/08/30/the-wrongs-in-the-right-to-education-noynonika-bose/ (accessed on 8 September 2016).

Chanana, Karuna. 2011. 'The Sociologies of the School'. In *Schooling, Stratification and Inclusion: Some Reflections on the Sociology of Education in India*, edited by Yogendra Singh, 34–80. Delhi: NCERT (The National Council of Educational Research and Training).

Deka, Maitrayee. 2014. 'Schooling and the Production of Student Culture: Principles and Practice'. In *Ethnographies of Schooling in Contemporary India*, edited by Meenakshi Thapan, 66–103. New Delhi and London: SAGE.

Didyala, Amrita. 2010. 'Gandhian Schools Hit by Lack of Funds, Teachers; May Face Closure'. *The Indian Express*. February 9, 2010. https://indianexpress.com/article/cities/gandhian-schools-hit-by-lack-of-funds-teachers-may-face-closure-2/ (accessed on 25 August 2018).

Dore, Bhavya. 2014. 'Living in the Bubble: Rishi Valley School and the Sense of Community'. In *Ethnographies of Schooling in Contemporary India*, edited by Meenakshi Thapan, 271–332. New Delhi and London: SAGE.

Durkheim, Emile. 1961 (1938). *Moral Education: A Study of the Theory and Application of the Sociology of Education*. New York, NY: The Free Press.

Friere, Paulo. 1974. *Education for Critical Consciousness*. London: Bloomsbury Publishing.

———. 1977. *Pedagogy of the Oppressed*. Harmondsworth: Penguin Books.

Froerer, Peggy. 2007. 'Disciplining the Saffron Way. Moral Education and the Hindu Rashtra'. *Modern Asian Studies* 41 (5): 1033–71.

Gandhi, M.K. 1997 (1909). *Hind Swaraj and Other Writings*. Cambridge: Columbia University Press and Foundation Books.

Giroux, Henry. 1983. *Theory and Resistance in Education*. South Hadley, MA: Bergin and Garvey.

———. 2011. *On Critical Pedagogy*. New York, NY: Bloomsbury Publishing.

Gogoi, Anannya. 2014. 'Kiranjyoti Vidyalay: A Sociological Narrative of a Government School'. In *Ethnographies of Schooling in Contemporary India*, edited by Meenakshi Thapan, 104–53. New Delhi and London: SAGE.

Gupta, Latika. 2015. *Education, Poverty and Gender: Schooling Muslim Girls in India*. New Delhi: Routledge, Taylor and Francis.

Immordino-Yang, Mary Helen and Antonio Damasio. 2007. 'We Feel, Therefore We Learn: The Relevance of Affective and Social Neuroscience to Education'. *Mind Brain and Education* 1 (1): 3–10.

Krishnamurti, J. 2011. *Why Are We Being Educated?* Chennai: Krishnamurti Foundation India.

Kumar, Krishna. 1997. 'Mohandas Karamchand Gandhi (1869–1948)'. In *Thinkers on Education*. Vol. 2, edited by Zaghloul Morsy, 507–15. Delhi: UNESCO Publishing, and Oxford and IBH Publishing.

Majumdar, Manabi and Jos Mooij. 2011. *Education and Inequality in India. A Classroom View*. London and New York: Routledge, Taylor and Francis.

Matthan, Tanya, Chandana Anusha and Meenakshi Thapan. 2014. 'Being Muslim, Becoming Citizens: A Muslim Girls' School in Post-riot Ahmedabad'. In *Ethnographies of Schooling in Contemporary* India, edited by Meenakshi Thapan, 224–70. New Delhi and London: SAGE.

McLaren, Peter. 1995. *Critical Pedagogy and Predatory Culture*. London: Routledge.

———. 1998. *Life in Schools: An Introduction to Critical Pedagogy in the Foundations of Education*. Reading, MA: Addison Wesley Longman Inc.

Naik, J.P. 1997. *The Education Commission and After*. Delhi: APH Publishing Corporation.

Nambissan, Geetha B. 2011. 'Education of Tribal Children in India: Sociological Perspectives'. In *Schooling, Stratification and Inclusion: Some Reflections on the Sociology of Education in India*, edited by Yogendra Singh, 177–93. Delhi: NCERT (The National Council of Educational Research and Training).

Rousseau, Jean-Jacques. 1977. *Emile*. Translated by Barbara Foxley. London: Everyman's Library, and J.M. Dent and Sons.

Sancho, David. 2013. 'Aspirational Regimes: Parental Educational Practice and the New Indian Youth Discourse'. In *Enterprise Culture in Neoliberal*

India: Studies on Youth, Class, Work and Media, edited by Nandini Gooptu. London and New York, NY: Routledge, Taylor and Francis.

Sarkar, Tanika. 1996. 'Educating the Children of the Hindu Rashtra: Notes on RSS Schools'. In *Religion, Religiosity and Communalism*, edited by P. Bidwai, H. Mukhia and A. Vanaik. New Delhi: Manohar Publishers.

Seth, Sanjay. 2008. *Subject Lessons: The Western Education of Colonial India*. New Delhi: Oxford University Press.

Shah, Parth J. and Shreya Agarwal. 2010. 'Right to Education Act: A Critique'. Available at: www.rightoteducation.in/right-education-act-critique (accessed on 8 September 2016).

Srivastava, Sanjay. 1998. *Constructing Post-colonial India: National Character and the Doon School*. London and New York, NY: Routledge.

———. 2015. 'Schooling, Culture and Modernity'. In *Education and Society: Themes, Perspectives, Practices* (Oxford in India Readings in Sociology and Social Anthropology), edited by Meenakshi Thapan, 118–50. Delhi: Oxford University Press.

Sundar, Nandini. 2005. 'Teaching to Hate: The Hindu Right's Pedagogical Program'. In *Revolution and Pedagogy*, edited by Tom Ewing, 195–218. New York: Palgrave Macmillan.

Thapan, Meenakshi. 1991/2006. *Life at School. An Ethnographic Study*. New Delhi: Oxford University Press.

UNESCO. 2016. *Education for People and Planet: Creating Sustainable Futures for All*. Global Educational Monitoring Report. UNESCO. Available at: en.unesco.org/gem-report (accessed on 24 May 2018).

Velaskar, Padma. 2015. 'Educational Stratification, Dominant Ideology, and the Reproduction of Educational Disadvantage in India'. In *Education and Society: Themes, Perspectives, Practices* (Oxford in India Readings in Sociology and Social Anthropology), edited by Meenakshi Thapan, 428–48. New Delhi: Oxford University Press.

11

Cultures of Work in India's 'New Economy'

Carol Upadhya

Introduction

Sociologists have mapped some of the myriad social and cultural changes that have occurred in India following the economic reforms of the 1990s, from the expansion and transformation of the middle class and the globalisation of cities to the new media landscape and growing consumer culture. But other developments of the post-liberalisation era have been relatively understudied, especially changing patterns of work and employment. With the dismantling of public-sector industries, increased private capital investment and the expansion of the service sector, a range of new organisations, occupations and forms of work have appeared, from highly paid employment in software engineering or financial services to less skilled and low-paid jobs in security, house-keeping, retail, transport and the like.

Although these shifts have profound implications for the liveli-hoods and social security of workers across social classes, and have opened up new possibilities for social mobility, sociological research on these developments has been very uneven. Most scholarly atten-tion has been given to the 'new economy' jobs that emerged with the growth of outsourcing, especially in back office and software services, which have provided lucrative employment for several million edu-cated youth. Within this sector, call centres have attracted the most sociological interest, perhaps because they most visibly represent the effects of economic globalisation in India. In line with the contours of the current literature on cultures of work in post-liberalisation India, this essay focuses mainly on work and workers in the offshore 'knowledge industries'.

'New' Work

In Indian sociology, questions of work and occupation have generally been addressed through the lens of social structures such as caste, class, gender or household, rather than from the perspective of labour or the workplace. Although sociologists have produced significant studies of labour in modern industries and the informal economy in India (De Neve 2005; Parry 2013; Parry et al. 1999), and more recently of precarious work in export-oriented factories and special economic zones (Chari 2004; Cross 2009, 2010), large sections of India's industrial, commercial and corporate landscapes have hardly been explored. Moreover, studies of formal sector labour or organisational culture in India rarely speak to international debates in the sociology of labour or anthropology of work, nor do they usually draw comparative insights from other contexts. But as India has become more tightly linked into transnational networks of production, finance and services, the new forms of work, organisation and management that have emerged have important parallels elsewhere (e.g., Freeman 2000). Across the world, the transition to post-industrialism and globalisation have reshaped workplace cultures and routines and altered the social meanings of labour—changes that in India are reflected particularly in the 'new economy' workplaces of the information technology (IT) and IT-enabled services (ITES) sector.

One of the most important social consequences of economic restructuring in India has been the expansion and transformation of the middle class. Sociologists have examined the social and cultural implications of rising incomes, changing social aspirations and new consumption practices (Baviskar and Ray 2011; Jaffrelot and van der Veer 2008; Srivastava 2007); attendant spatial and cultural transformations especially in the metro cities (Brosius 2010; Srivastava 2014); and the role of the media and transnational mobility in the refashioning of middle class and urban cultures (Mankekar 1999, 2015; Uberoi 2006; Udupa 2015), among other themes. Within this literature, however, there is surprisingly little discussion of the restructuring of the urban economy and occupational structure that have underwritten these social and cultural shifts. Fernandes (2006), in her path-breaking study of the 'new middle class', first pointed to the growing dependence of upwardly mobile sections of the middle class on private sector employment, and the concomitant marginalisation of white-collar government employees, in the post-liberalisation scenario (also see Ganguly-Scrase and Scrase 2009).

In cities such as Bengaluru, Chennai and Pune, urban growth and transformation and the expansion of the service sector have been closely linked to rising incomes within the 'new middle class' segment composed mainly of IT industry employees. Sociologists have explored the connections between the rise of the IT–ITES sector and class restructuring, particularly its implications for the middle class (Fuller and Narasimhan 2007, 2014; Radhakrishnan 2011a; Upadhya 2011). Several studies highlight the significance of the 'IT dream' (Nisbett 2009) in shaping the aspirations of lower-middle-class urban youth and their mobility strategies (Mankekar 2010; Upadhya 2016a). There is some evidence that IT professionals are drawn mainly from the old middle class (Remesh 2004; Rothboeck et al. 2001; Upadhya 2016b), but several scholars have attempted to map more precisely the socio-economic coordinates of India's army of offshore IT workers to assess whether these new industries have facilitated social mobility for non-middle-class groups (Krishna 2014; Krishna and Brihmadesam 2006).

The business process outsourcing (BPO) and call centre industries seem to have more social diversity compared to the IT industry, suggesting that these jobs have indeed provided a route to upward mobility for some educated youth. However, it is the spectacle of young people working on night shifts and mimicking American or British accents to serve foreign customers that drew the most attention from sociologists. Call centres also received considerable media coverage in the early days, leading to the circulation of images of their employees as dissolute, westernised youth and feeding into popular middle-class ideas about the dangers of globalisation. Accordingly, an important focus of scholarly research has been the gender implications of these new kinds of jobs, especially for women's autonomy and agency in the context of strong middle-class moral codes governing family relations and sexuality (Basi 2009; Patel 2010). Radhakrishnan (2011b) argues that the figure of the woman IT professional, who combines professional success with an approved model of Indian femininity, has become iconic of the 'new India', in contrast to the woman call centre agent whose 'free' lifestyle and sexualised body encapsulate the threat to Indian middle-class values that is posed by globalisation.

Changing Work: Individuation and the New Middle Class

While much of the sociological research on India's offshore economy concerns the interconnections between work and the wider social world, several studies focus more directly on the changing nature of labour, employment and organisational practices in the IT and BPO industries, and on workers' experiences in these workplaces (Upadhya and Vasavi 2008)—questions that are difficult to research in multiple ways (Upadhya 2008). The cultures of work and management that have been instituted in these corporate settings recall older theoretical questions about work, power, agency, subjectivity and identity that were highlighted in classic sociological studies of industrial labour (Burawoy 1979; Willis 1977). But the emerging work culture in India's 'new economy' closely resembles the regime of individualised and 'flexible' employment documented by sociologists studying post-industrial work in the advanced economies (Beck 2000; Sennett 2006). Lack of job security but relatively high salaries are central features of India's private sector today, in contrast to public sector jobs which provided the 'old middle class' with economic security but relatively low incomes.

This shift in the nature of employment has been legitimised by a neoliberal ethic of individualised achievement which has become hegemonic within the new middle class, as educated professionals are drawn into a competitive job market framed by the tropes of 'merit' and entrepreneurialism (Gooptu 2013a). The growing individualisation and flexibilisation of work, employee identities and career strategies (Beck and Beck-Gernsheim 2002; Upadhya 2016b: Chapter 3) are reinforced by 'new workplace' organisational practices such as performance-linked compensation and promotion systems. 'New Age' management ideology has replaced earlier direct modes of organisational control, and the labour process is now controlled through 'subjective' techniques such as the promulgation of a strong corporate culture and teamwork (Kunda 1992; Ray and Sayer 1999). Reflecting these global developments in management ideology, a globally circulating set of 'soft' organisational practices (Heelas 2002) has been adopted by IT and ITES organisations in India, as well as (in varying degrees) by service industries such as retail and hospitality (Gooptu 2009). These organisational practices aim to create 'self-driven', autonomous workers (Thrift 1997), transforming the employment relationship from an economic contract into one in which managements aim to refashion the very selves of workers. The ideal of the entrepreneurial worker reflects a conception of the self as a 'bundle of skills', in which workers must constantly upgrade and market their skills if they are to succeed in the competitive world of work (Gershon 2014). The neoliberal model of the self (Rose 1998) circulates within the corporate sector and the middle class in India, disseminated not only through management practices but also via various spiritual movements and self-actualisation organisations (Gooptu 2013b; Rudnyckyj 2010; Upadhya 2013). A key organisational practice that is deployed to refashion worker subjectivities is 'soft skills' training. Both IT and BPO companies in India prioritise these training practices, which suggests that workers in these industries are expected to reshape themselves according to the authorised corporate model. In training sessions, employees are taught to become 'professional', 'customer-oriented', self-managing, 'good team players' and so on—attributes of a globally appropriate worker (Upadhya 2016b: Chapter 5).

A parallel, and apparently contradictory, development in the management of 'immaterial labour' (Hardt and Negri 2005) is the digitalisation of the labour process. Under the 'rule of code' (Aneesh 2006), many tasks are now performed through the use of computers and information systems, which directly or indirectly structure and control the labour process. The most discussed example of what Aneesh (2006) terms 'algocratic governance' is the automated regulation of call flows and measurement of productivity in call centres, creating an 'electronic panopticon' (Bain and Taylor 2000) in which workers have little control over their own labour or time. Similar systems operate in software services organisations as well, where the work of software engineers is closely monitored, outputs are precisely measured and performance constantly assessed by managers and clients (including from offshore locations) through IT systems and detailed quantitative 'quality control' methods (Aneesh 2001, 2009; Ilavarasan 2008; Upadhya 2009, 2016b: Chapter 3). Conversely, while studies of call centres and BPOs have highlighted the routinised, technology-mediated nature of work and the 'neo-Taylorist' modes of organisational control (Huws 2003; Mirchandani 2004; Nadeem 2011; Taylor and Bain 2005), these organisations also deploy subjective management techniques such as creating a 'fun' or college-like workplace atmosphere and representing the job as 'empowering' (Remesh 2008; Vasavi 2008). The combination of such New Age practices with rationalised labour processes and IT-enabled management systems creates a powerful system of control over these 'knowledge workforces' (Gill and Pratt 2008).

A third trend in management practice is a 'cultural labour process' (Hakken 1999) in which communication, collaboration and knowledge-sharing are considered key to productivity and profit.

Although work in these new workplaces is individualised, several scholars have pointed out that the 'immaterial labour process' depends not only on controlling mental labour of workers and capturing their 'knowledge' but also on the production and management of social relations (Böhm and Land 2012). In this context, communication and language become commodified as labour (Heller 2010; Shankar and Cavanaugh 2012). 'Language work' ranges from the highly scripted protocols of customer interactions in call centres to the more autonomous (yet regulated) communications that IT professionals are expected to perform with colleagues and clients (Urciuoli and LaDousa 2013).

Studies of call centres have focused on the inculcation of practices of 'impersonation' (Mankekar 2010), mimesis or 'authenticity work' (Mirchandani 2012a), as employees are trained in conversational English, accent modulation and customer interaction skills. Indian call centres (and their customers) no longer expect workers to imitate American or British accents and instead teach them to speak in what is framed as a 'neutral accent'. This policy aims to facilitate 'global' forms of communication by 'neutralising' or erasing cultural differences within transnational workspaces (Aneesh 2015). The software outsourcing industry similarly emphasises soft skills training, particularly in 'communication skills', which are seen as essential to the smooth functioning of cross-border projects. But in contrast to call centres, IT organisations focus on more subtle dimensions of communication such as 'assertiveness training' and negotiation and teamworking skills. In addition, communication skills are usually supplemented with lessons in 'cultural sensitivity' to facilitate communication within cross-border virtual teams and with foreign clients, where cultural differences are thought to lead to misunderstanding (Mayer-Ahuja 2014). Cross-cultural training practices purvey reified notions of cultural identity in a process of 'cultural streamlining' that transforms 'Indian culture' into 'appropriate difference' (Radhakrishnan 2011b). Cultural training is also designed to teach Indian software engineers how to adapt themselves to the global corporate workplace by imbibing accepted communication and interactional styles (Upadhya 2016b: Chapter 5).

Another focus of sociological studies of IT–ITES workspaces has been the despatialisation and disembodiment of work, as software engineers and call centre workers perform most of their work virtually (Aneesh 2006, 2012). However, scholars have noted that offshore labour is also deeply embodied (Mirchandani 2015; Mukherjee 2008), as IT and ITES workers spend long hours tethered to their workstations. Call centre workers often experience temporal and social displacement and health problems due to working on night shifts, as offshore companies generate value through 'time arbitrage' (Nadeem 2009). The work performed by transnational customer service workers is embodied in other ways as well, as it involves communicative work and emotional labour (Hochschild 1983) that has profound implications for their identities, subjectivities and life-worlds. Customer service agents are trained in 'emotion work' (framed as 'communication skills'), that is, how to handle difficult customers who often subject them to racialised and sexualised abuse (Mirchandani 2012b)—encounters that reinforce gendered racial hierarchies across national borders (Vora 2015). Mankekar and Gupta (2016) build on Hardt's (1999) concept of 'affective labour' to analyse the peculiar mix of social, emotional, embodied and IT-mediated labour that is typical of call centres, and how it creates a range of 'intimate' social relations that entangle the selves and bodies of employees in the production process and production of value itself.

Most studies of India's offshore economy have focused on organisations and workers within India, highlighting the phenomenon of 'virtual migration' (Aneesh 2006), as work is carried out through ICT systems that link workers, team members and customers located across the world. A relatively neglected dimension of IT work is the actual physical mobility (temporary and circular, or long-term migration) of Indian software engineers, and the disorientation, alienation and instability that many experience while working abroad (Amrute 2010). Indian IT workers often face racism and 'cultural branding' as 'cheap Indians', stereotyping that inflects their sense of self as they renegotiate their identities in new contexts (Amrute 2014, 2016; Upadhya 2016b: Chapter 6). Given that transnational mobility is central to the Indian IT industry, it is striking that studies of Indian IT professionals rarely draw on insights from transnational or diaspora studies, which have extensively theorised such experiences (e.g., Ong 1999; Vora 2013). Conversely, the local embedding of IT professionals, and the ways in which older social structures have shaped the production of the IT workforce, is an understudied question.

Conclusion

As this discussion suggests, an understanding of the changing nature of labour and forms of power in India's new economy workplaces would benefit from widening our gaze to develop a comparative perspective. The rise of the IT–ITES industry in India is in many ways an outcome of the restructuring of production under late capitalism and expanding globalisation (Castells 1996; Harvey 1989). Yet sociologists must also remain sensitive to local social contexts and economic histories if we are to understand how new modes of work and value production emerge from complex interactions on the ground, as circulating capital encounters existing social and cultural formations. For instance, mapping the 'bodyshopping' system through which many Indian IT workers went abroad to work in the early years of the industry, Xiang (2007) found that access to engineering education, computer training and employment opportunities were deeply embedded in regionally rooted networks of caste and kinship. This insight, which I built on in a recent study of engineering colleges in Coastal Andhra (Upadhya 2016a), is striking, given that the IT industry claims to operate purely on the basis of 'merit' (Upadhya 2007). The cultures of work and modalities of production and organisation that characterise an industry which has become an emblem of India's new modernity remain in many ways entangled in older structures of sociality and accumulation.

Thus, a substantial body of sociological work has painted an insightful picture of work, workers and workspaces in India's offshore 'knowledge industries', exploring the broader social ramifications of these new occupations. But there remains great scope for research on the bewildering array of service sector jobs and modes of employment that have emerged in major cities and smaller towns across India following liberalisation—from the ubiquitous pizza and Flipkart delivery 'boys' who can be seen zipping around city roads on their motorcycles, to the uniformed security guards that man the gates of every commercial and residential complex, the young men and women who sell consumer goods in glitzy malls and brand name stores, and the new occupational category of 'self-employed' Uber drivers. Countless young people have moved from small towns and rural areas to larger cities to search for (often low-paid and insecure) employment in new industries such as hospitality, housekeeping and retail, yet we know little about these service economy workers, their conditions or experiences of work, the pathways of employment migration, or the consequences of this occupational restructuring for the reproduction or destabilisation of existing social inequalities, cultural identities and modes of value production. This is a major gap in our knowledge that sociologists should address in the future.

References

Amrute, Sareeta. 2010. 'Living and Praying in the Code: The Flexibility and Discipline of Indian IT Workers in a Global Economy'. *Anthropology Quarterly* 83 (3): 519–50.

Amrute, Sareeta. 2014. 'Proprietary Freedom in an IT Office: How Indian IT Workers Negotiate Code and Cultural Branding'. *Social Anthropology* 22 (1): 101–17.

———. 2016. *Encoding Race, Encoding Class: Indian IT Workers in Berlin*. Durham, NC: Duke University Press.

Aneesh, A. 2001. 'Skill Saturation: Rationalization and Post-industrial Work'. *Theory and Society* 30 (3): 363–96.

———. 2006. *Virtual Migration: The Programming of Globalization*. Durham, NC: Duke University Press.

———. 2009. 'Global Labor: Algocratic Modes of Organization'. *Sociological Theory* 27 (4): 347–70.

———. 2012. 'Negotiating Globalization: Men and Women in India's Call Centers'. *Journal of Social Issues* 68 (3): 514–33.

———. 2015. *Neutral Accent: How Language, Labor, and Life Become Global*. Durham, NC: Duke University Press.

Bain, Peter and Phil Taylor. 2000. 'Entrapped by the "Electronic Panopticon"? Worker Resistance in the Call Centre'. *New Technology, Work and Employment* 15 (1): 2–18.

Basi, J.K. Tina. 2009. *Women, Identity and India's Call Centre Industry*. London: Routledge.

Baviskar, Amita and Raka Ray, eds. 2011. *Elite and Everyman: The Cultural Politics of the Indian Middle Classes*. New Delhi: Routledge.

Beck, Ulrich. 2000. *The Brave New World of Work*. Cambridge: Polity Press.

Beck, Ulrich and Elisabeth Beck-Gernsheim. 2002. *Individualization: Institutionalized Individualism and Its Social and Political Consequences*. London: SAGE.

Böhm, Steffen and Chris Land. 2012. 'The New "Hidden Abode": Reflections on Value and Labour in the New Economy'. *The Sociological Review* 60 (2): 217–40.

Brosius, Christiane. 2010. *India's Middle Class: New Forms of Urban Leisure, Consumption and Prosperity*. New Delhi: Routledge.

Burawoy, Michael. 1979. *Manufacturing Consent: Changes in the Labour Process Under Capitalism*. Chicago, IL: University of Chicago Press.

Castells, Manuel. 1996. *The Information Age: Economy, Society and Culture*. Vol. I, *The Rise of the Network Society*. Oxford: Blackwell Publishers.

Chari, Sharad. 2004. *Fraternal Capital: Peasant-Workers, Self-made Men, and Globalization in Provincial India*. Delhi: Permanent Black.

Cross, Jamie. 2009. 'From Dreams to Discontent: Educated Young Men and the Politics of Work at a Special Economic Zone in Andhra Pradesh'. *Contributions to Indian Sociology*, n.s., 43 (3): 351–79.

———. 2010. 'Neoliberalism as Unexceptional: Economic Zones and the Everyday Precariousness of Working Life in South India'. *Critique of Anthropology* 30 (4): 355–73.

De Neve, Geert. 2005. *The Everyday Politics of Labour: Working Lives in India's Informal Economy*. New Delhi: Social Science Press.

Fernandes, Leela. 2006. *India's New Middle Class: Democratic Politics in an Era of Economic Reform*. Minneapolis, MN: University of Minnesota Press.

Freeman, Carla. 2000. *High Tech and High Heels in the Global Economy: Women, Work and Pink-Collar Identities in the Caribbean*. Durham, NC: Duke University Press.

Fuller, Christopher J. and Haripriya Narasimhan. 2007. 'Information Technology Professionals and the New-rich Middle Class in Chennai (Madras)'. *Modern Asian Studies* 41 (1): 121–50.

———. 2014. *Tamil Brahmans: The Making of a Middle-class Caste*. Chicago, IL: University of Chicago Press.

Ganguly-Scrase, Ruchira and Timothy J. Scrase. 2009. *Globalization and the Middle Classes in India: The Social and Cultural Impact of Neoliberal Reforms*. London: Routledge.

Gershon, Ilana. 2014. 'Selling Your Self in the United States'. *PoLAR: Political and Legal Anthropology Review* 37 (2): 281–95.

Gill, Rosalind and Andy Pratt. 2008. 'In the Social Factory? Immaterial Labour, Precariousness and Cultural Work'. *Theory, Culture & Society* 25 (7–8): 1–30.

Gooptu, Nandini. 2009. 'Neoliberal Subjectivity, Enterprise Culture and New Workplaces: Organised Retail and Shopping Malls in India'. *Economic & Political Weekly* 44 (22): 45–54.

———, ed. 2013a. *Enterprise Culture in Neoliberal India: Studies in Youth, Class, Work and Media*. London: Routledge.

———. 2013b. 'New Spiritualism and the Micro-politics of Self-making in India's Enterprise Culture'. In *Enterprise Culture in Neoliberal India: Studies in Youth, Class, Work and Media*, edited by Nandini Gooptu, 73–89. London: Routledge.

Hakken, David. 1999. *Cyborgs@cyberspace? An Ethnographer Looks to the Future*. New York, NY: Routledge.

Hardt, Michael. 1999. 'Affective Labor'. *Boundary 2* 26 (2): 89–100.

Hardt, Michael and Antonio Negri. 2005. *Multitude: War and Democracy in the Age of Empire*. New York, NY: Penguin.

Harvey, David. 1989. *The Condition of Postmodernity: An Enquiry into the Origins of Cultural Change*. Oxford: Basil Blackwell.

Heelas, Paul. 2002. 'Work Ethics, Soft Capitalism and the "Turn to Life"'. In *Cultural Economy*, edited by Paul du Gay and Michael Pryke, 78–96. London: SAGE.

Heller, Monica. 2010. 'The Commodification of Language'. *Annual Review of Anthropology* 39: 101–14.

Hochschild, Arlie Russell. 1983. *The Managed Heart: Commercialization of Human Feeling*. Berkeley, CA: University of California Press.

Huws, Ursula. 2003. *The Making of a Cybertariat*. New York, NY: Monthly Review Press.

Ilavarasan, P. Vigneswara. 2008. 'Software Work in India: A Labour Process View'. In *In an Outpost of the Global Economy: Work and Workers in*

India's Information Technology Industry, edited by Carol Upadhya and A.R. Vasavi, 162–89. New Delhi: Routledge.

Jaffrelot, Christophe and Peter van der Veer, eds. 2008. *Patterns of Middle Class Consumption in India and China*. New Delhi: SAGE.

Krishna, Anirudh. 2014. 'Examining the Structure of Opportunity and Social Mobility in India: Who Becomes an Engineer?' *Development and Change* 45 (1): 1–28.

Krishna, Anirudh and Vijay Brihmadesam. 2006. 'What Does It Take to Become a Software Professional?' *Economic & Political Weekly* 41 (30): 3307–14.

Kunda, Gideon. 1992. *Engineering Culture: Control and Commitment in a High-tech Corporation*. Philadelphia, PA: Temple University Press.

Mankekar, Purnima. 1999. *Screening Culture, Viewing Politics: An Ethnography of Television, Womanhood and Nation in Postcolonial India*. Durham, NC: Duke University Press.

———. 2010. 'Becoming Entrepreneurial Subjects: Neoliberalism and Media'. In *The State in India After Liberalization: Interdisciplinary Perspectives*, edited by Akhil Gupta and K. Sivaramakrishnan, 213–31. London: Routledge.

———. 2015. *Unsettling India: Affect, Temporality, Transnationality*. Durham, NC: Duke University Press.

Mankekar, Purnima and Akhil Gupta. 2016. 'Intimate Encounters: Affective Labor in Call Centers'. *Positions* 24 (1): 17–43.

Mayer-Ahuja, Nicole. 2014. *'Everywhere Is Becoming the Same'? Regulating IT-work Between India and Germany*. Translated by Parnal Chirmuley and Petra Besemann. New Delhi: Social Science Press.

Mirchandani, Kiran. 2004. 'Practices of Global Capital: Gaps, Cracks, and Ironies in Transnational Call Centres in India'. *Global Networks* 4 (4): 355–73.

———. 2012a. *Phone Clones: Authenticity Work in the Transnational Service Economy*. Ithaca, NY: ILR Press.

———. 2012b. 'Learning Racial Hierarchies: Communication Skills Training in Transnational Customer Service Work'. *Journal of Workplace Learning* 24 (5): 338–50.

———. 2015. 'Flesh in Voice: The No-touch Embodiment of Transnational Customer Service Workers'. *Organization* 22 (6): 909–23.

Mukherjee, Sanjukta. 2008. 'Producing the Knowledge Professional: Gendered Geographies of Alienation in India's New High-tech Workplace'. In *In an Outpost of the Global Economy: Work and Workers in India's Information Technology Industry*, edited by Carol Upadhya and A.R. Vasavi, 50–75. New Delhi: Routledge.

Nadeem, Shehzad. 2009. 'The Uses and Abuses of Time: Globalization and Time Arbitrage in India's Outsourcing Industries'. *Global Networks* 9 (1): 20–40.

———. 2011. *Dead Ringers: How Outsourcing Is Changing the Way Indians Understand Themselves*. Princeton, NJ: Princeton University Press.

Nisbett, Nicholas. 2009. *Growing Up in the Knowledge Society: Living the IT Dream in Bangalore*. New Delhi: Routledge.

Ong, Aihwa. 1999. *Flexible Citizenship: The Cultural Logics of Transnationality*. Durham, NC: Duke University Press.

Parry, Jonathan P. 2013. 'Company and Contract Labour in a Central Indian Steel Plant'. *Economy and Society* 42 (3): 348–74.

Parry, Jonathan P., Jan Breman and Karin Kapadia, eds. 1999. *The Worlds of Indian Industrial Labour*. New Delhi: SAGE.

Patel, Reena. 2010. *Working the Night Shift: Women in India's Call Center Industry*. Stanford, CA: Stanford University Press.

Radhakrishnan, Smitha. 2011a. 'Gender, the IT Revolution and the Making of a Middle-class India'. In *Elite and Everyman: The Cultural Politics of the Indian Middle Classes*, edited by Amita Baviskar and Raka Ray, 193–219. New Delhi: Routledge.

———. 2011b. *Appropriately Indian: Gender and Culture in a New Transnational Class*. Durham, NC: Duke University Press.

Ray, Larry and Andrew Sayer, eds. 1999. *Culture and Economy After the Cultural Turn*. London: SAGE.

Remesh, Babu P. 2004. 'Labour in Business Process Outsourcing: A Case Study of Call Centre Agents'. NLI Research Studies Series No. 051/2004. Noida: V.V. Giri National Labour Institute.

———. 2008. 'Work Organisation, Control and "Empowerment": Managing the Contradictions of Call Centre Work'. In *In an Outpost of the Global Economy: Work and Workers in India's Information Technology Industry*, edited by Carol Upadhya and A.R. Vasavi, 235–62. New Delhi: Routledge.

Rose, Nikolas. 1998. *Inventing Our Selves: Psychology, Power and Personhood*. Cambridge: Cambridge University Press.

Rothboeck, Sandra, M. Vijaybaskar and Vasudevan Gayathri. 2001. *Labour in the New Economy: The Case of the Indian Software Labour Market*. New Delhi: International Labour Organization.

Rudnyckyj, Daromir. 2010. *Spiritual Economies: Islam, Globalization, and the Afterlife of Development*. Ithaca, NY: Cornell University Press.

Sennett, Richard. 2006. *The Culture of the New Capitalism*. Hyderabad: Orient Longman.

Shankar, Shalini and Jillian R. Cavanaugh. 2012. 'Language and Materiality in Global Capitalism'. *Annual Review of Anthropology* 41: 355–69.

Srivastava, Sanjay. 2007. *Passionate Modernity: Sexuality, Class, and Consumption in India*. New Delhi: Routledge.

———. 2014. *Entangled Urbanism: Slum, Gated Community and Shopping Mall in Delhi and Gurgaon*. New Delhi: Oxford University Press.

Taylor, Phil and Peter Bain. 2005. '"India Calling to the Far Away Towns": The Call Centre Labour Process and Globalization'. *Work, Employment and Society* 19 (2): 261–82.

Thrift, Nigel. 1997. 'The Rise of Soft Capitalism'. *Cultural Values* 1 (1): 29–57.

Uberoi, Patricia. 2006. *Freedom and Destiny: Gender, Family, and Popular Culture in India*. New Delhi: Oxford University Press.

Udupa, Sahana. 2015. *Making News in Global India*: Media, Publics, Politics. Cambridge: Cambridge University Press.

Upadhya, Carol. 2007. 'Employment, Exclusion and "Merit" in the Indian IT Industry'. *Economic & Political Weekly* 42 (20): 1863–68.

———. 2008. 'Ethnographies of the Global Information Economy: Research Strategies and Methods'. *Economic & Political Weekly* 43 (17): 64–72.

———. 2009. 'Controlling Offshore Knowledge Workers: Power and Agency in India's Software Industry'. *New Technology, Work and Employment* 24 (1): 2–18.

———. 2011. 'Software and the "New" Middle Class in the "New India"'. In *Elite and Everyman: The Cultural Politics of the Indian Middle Classes*, edited by Amita Baviskar and Raka Ray, 167–92. New Delhi: Routledge.

———. 2013. 'Shrink-wrapped Souls: Managing the Self in India's New Economy'. In *Enterprise Culture in Neoliberal India: Studies in Youth, Class, Work and Media*, edited by Nandini Gooptu, 93–108. London: Routledge.

———. 2016a. 'Engineering Equality? Education and Im/mobility in Coastal Andhra Pradesh, India'. *Contemporary South Asia* 24 (3): 242–56.

———. 2016b. *Reengineering India: Work, Capital, and Class in an Offshore Economy*. New Delhi: Oxford University Press.

Upadhya, Carol and A.R. Vasavi, eds. 2008. *In an Outpost of the Global Economy: Work and Workers in India's Information Technology Industry*. New Delhi: Routledge.

Urciuoli, Bonnie and Chaise LaDousa. 2013. 'Language Management/ Labor'. *Annual Review of Anthropology* 42: 175–90.

Vasavi, A.R. 2008. '"Serviced from India": The Making of India's Global Youth Workforce'. In *In an Outpost of the Global Economy: Work and Workers in India's Information Technology Industry*, edited by Carol Upadhya and A.R. Vasavi, 211–34. New Delhi: Routledge.

Vora, Kalindi. 2015. *Life Support: Biocapital and the New History of Outsourced Labor*. Minneapolis, MN and London: University of Minnesota Press.

Vora, Neha. 2013. *Impossible Citizens: Dubai's Indian Diaspora*. Durham, NC: Duke University Press.

Willis, Paul. 1977. *Learning to Labor: How Working Class Kids Get Working Class Jobs*. New York, NY: Columbia University Press.

Xiang Biao. 2007. *Global 'Body Shopping': An Indian Labour System in the Information Technology Industry*. Princeton, NJ: Princeton University Press.

12

The Sociology of Labour in India

Geert De Neve

Labouring in 'Village' India

While it is now a challenge to review the expansive sociology of labour in India, it was not until the 1970s that labour became an explicit theme of study for anthropologists and sociologists of the subcontinent—with some notable exceptions such as the hugely influential early work of scholars like Breman (1985, 1993, 1994, 1996) and Holmström (1976). Until then, the study of labour was largely subsumed within broader studies of agrarian relations and village economies, and broadly focused on two types of relationships.

The first was the study of the '*jajmani* system', which for long offered an almost hegemonic image of village labour relations. The jajmani system was conceived of as a 'traditional' division of labour between dominant agrarian castes and a range of specialised castes that served the former in exchange for various customary payments by the *jajman* (patron), either in kind or in cash (Fuller 1989; Kolenda 1963). The labour involved in such relationships was conceptualised as the delivery of 'services' and 'duties' strictly regulated by hereditary occupations. While Dumont (1970: 108) considered these as part of wider caste-based reciprocal relationships, his perspective was later criticised not only for projecting an orientalist view of a closed 'village India' removed from money and markets but also for ignoring the power imbalances shaping the interdependencies. Indeed, jajmani relations played a pivotal role in the maintenance and reproduction of the economic power of dominant, landed castes, who used the purity–pollution axis to secure long-term subservience from the labouring classes (Mencher 1974). The debate about the nature of jajmani relationships was fixated on the structural and functionalist dimensions of the institution, leaving little space for an exploration of how such relationships were actually enacted and reproduced, let along lived and experienced.

A second preoccupation with labour focused on the interactions between landowning castes and those huge swathes of the rural population outside the world of jajmani reciprocity: the predominantly landless agricultural labourers whose relationship with landowners was fraught with exploitation and patronage, and marked with either casual employment or permanent attachment (Breman 1985, 1993, 1994). Breman's study (1993) of landless labourers in South Gujarat presents one of the most comprehensive pictures of how exploitation worked to keep low-caste and tribal communities at the bottom of the heap. Patronage provided the minimal subsistence required to reproduce a rural labour force whose toil was essential to agrarian production. Bonded labour made up the underbelly of patron–client relationships and was pervasive in agriculture until only a couple of decades ago (Brass 1990; Carswell and De Neve 2013a). Generations of farm servants were permanently tied to landowners, paid in kind (later cash) and effectively prevented from freely selling their labour in the market. Brass (1990: 37) contends that 'worker attachment is a form of unfreedom, the object of which is to discipline…, control and cheapen labour-power by preventing or curtailing both its commodification and the growth of a specifically proletarian consciousness'. Unfree labour was often coercive and exploitative, and located at the centre of the class struggle between dominant landowners and agricultural labour. Capitalism in India, as indeed elsewhere, is clearly not incompatible with unfreedom—it actively thrives on it and produces it.

Particularly central to Breman's oeuvre are his accounts of the changing nature of agrarian labour relations in the post-independence era. The rapid casualisation of rural labour in the latter decades of the 20th century not only removed much of the patronage that once provided basic security to landless labourers but also gave rise to a footloose proletariat hunting and gathering for waged work (Breman 1994, 1996). Increased labour mobility and access to new forms of off-farm work were accompanied by two new processes of labour recruitment, both of which transformed—but rarely alleviated—the exploitation that rural labour had been subjected to. On the one hand, the gradual expansion of the non-agrarian economy led to an intensification of labour circulation, with landless labourers now scanning rural and urban areas in search for work. This set a trend towards the deployment of labour on a casual basis and towards a decline in job security as cheaper and more flexible migrant labour came to displace local workforces (Mosse et al. 2002; Rogaly 1996; Rogaly and Rafique 2003). On the other hand, while bonded labour had, by and large, disappeared from agriculture by the end of the 20th century, it re-emerged across non-farm sectors, including brick kilns, powerlooms, stone quarries, gem-cutting workshops and construction sites (Breman et al. 2009; De Neve 1999; Kapadia 1995a; Picherit 2009; Srivastava 2009). It was Breman who aptly coined the term 'neo-bondage' to capture the novel ways in which labour mobility continues to be curtailed to the benefit of employers (Breman 1996). Bondage is now based on debt (usually through loans against wages), takes the form of a less personalised and more contractual employment relationship, is time-bound rather than permanent, and tends to be mediated by a jobber or contractor who recruits and manages migrant workforces (see also Breman and Guérin 2009). The high incidence of debt bondage outside agriculture and involving predominantly migrant labour points to the nature of contemporary capitalist accumulation in India, which continues to thrive on unfreedom, soaring levels of indebtedness and the vulnerability of marginalised social groups at the lowest levels of society.

Whilst the harshest forms of bondage continue to undermine any expression of labour agency, ethnographic accounts also revealed that labourers have their own ways of challenging and resisting employers' attempts to immobilise them. Active strategies of repaying debts and shifting factories as well as subtle tactics of foot-dragging, indiscipline and even escape often successfully undermine employers' desperate search for a stable and permanent workforce (De Neve 1999; Kapadia 1995a). The binding of labour can paradoxically undermine employers' power to discipline their workforce as the latter cannot be easily dismissed in case of poor performance. As a result, employers and labour contractors are often wary of binding labour for longer periods of time, and instead prefer temporary immobilisation over permanent attachment. Rural labour processes clearly need to be understood in relation to the vagaries of neoliberal capital, which itself thrives on a range of labour-deployment strategies that include bonded labour at one end, temporarily tied and contract labour in the middle, and casual or flexible labour at the other end (Guérin 2013).

Agrarian labour in India has undergone two further transformations more recently. The first is the increased use of contract labour, in which teams of male or female workers take on contracts for a specific agricultural task and move between rural employers (Carswell 2013; Kapadia 1995b). While this frees employers from any long-term commitments to workers, it leaves the latter with a much more precarious employment situation and forms part of the broader process of casualisation that marks much of India's informal economy today. The second is the feminisation of agricultural work. In a review of rural India, Harriss-White and Janakarajan (2004: 172) conclude that 'women have come to dominate the labour input into agriculture and [now] provide over half of all farm labour, largely as casual wage labourers'. This feminisation of agricultural labour, in which women often perform back-breaking work for low pay and on casual contracts, has been observed across a range of recent case studies (Carswell 2016; Garikipati 2008; Guérin et al. 2014) and reflects a gendered pattern of opportunity in which men avail of the mobility and flexibility required to access off-farm work, while women's options often remain limited to what is available within the village economy. However, the recent roll-out of various social welfare schemes, and of MGNREGA in particular, is offering rural women alternative sources of income while producing more encouraging effects such as a rise in female agricultural wages and a strengthening of women's bargaining power vis-à-vis rural employers (Carswell and De Neve 2013b, 2014; Pankaj and Tankha 2010).

From Field to Factory: Mapping Changing Landscapes of Labour

Rural and agrarian labour, however, form only a part of the study of labour in India today. As labour came to town and factory, so did the sociology of its processes and transformations. With the study of industrial labour, sociological research was given a new impulse, and fields of investigation that had long been neglected began to attract scholarly interest. The recruitment and deployment of labour in factories and industrial workshops, the mediating role of jobbers and labour contractors, the practices of subcontracting and outsourcing, the role of the state in regulating and protecting labour, and the transformation of social structures and identities in industrial environments, all received unprecedented attention.

A first map of industrial labour was sketched by Holmström in 1976. Epitomised by the image of the 'citadel' of security and relative prosperity, he depicted a dual economy, and hence a dual society, marked by a sharp boundary separating those inside the citadel of secure organised sector employment—the 'aristocracy of labour'—from those outside who live in a world of insecurity and informality, desperately trying to climb the walls (Holmström 1976: 137). Later, however, Holmström corrected this image as too simple and suggested:

> The organized/unorganized boundary is not a wall but a steep slope. Indian society is like a mountain, with the very rich at the top, lush Alpine pastures where skilled workers in the biggest modern industries graze, a gradual slope down through smaller firms where pay and conditions are worse and the legal security of employment means less, a steep slope around the area where the Factories Act ceases to apply..., a plateau where custom and the market give poorly paid unorganized sector workers some minimal security, then a long slope through casual migrant labour and petty services to destitution. (1984: 319)

In this picture, there is no single path 'up' but rather countless trajectories of upward and downward mobility across a range of jobs, firms and industries. A key point of debate concerns whether the majority of the labouring poor can access the better-paid and more rewarding jobs on the higher slopes.

In Breman's view, few are able to do so. Offering his own map, he argues that 'the landscape of labour has the appearance of a vast plain broken by many larger and smaller hills' (Breman 1996: 225). The hills are zones of work where the top jobs resemble formal sector employment, while the vast plain is where the massive underclass is found who lack the assets and equipment necessary to undertake the uphill march. Those who do try to climb up encounter all sorts of obstacles, while the majority are forced 'to stay at the bottom and have no choice but to go out hunting and gathering a wage' (Breman 1996: 225). A key feature of this labour landscape that became accentuated in the post-liberalisation era is that 'employers in every branch of economic business encircle themselves with a fairly small core of permanent workers through whom a reserve of casual workers can be drawn in and dismissed, in accordance with the need of the moment' (ibid.). It is such processes of casualisation and informalisation that produce the 'flexible' labour required by the capitalist production regimes of post-liberalisation India.

This distinction between permanent secure employment and casual work is one which Parry has picked up more recently in his research on the state-run steel plant in Bhilai. He contends that while the sociology of India has long considered the distinction between manual and non-manual labour the defining feature of what separates the 'working' from the 'middle' classes, the distinction between *naukri* (secure employment) and *kam* (insecure wage labour) forms, in fact, 'a sharper and more socially salient marker of class boundaries' (Parry 2013a: 349). While the Bhilai Steel Plant had around 65,000 employees on its direct payroll in the late 1980s, this regular labour force has been reduced by half and replaced by much cheaper and irregularly employed contract workers over the last 25 years. Apart from illustrating the drastic informalisation of work among what was once the aristocracy of labour, Parry's ethnography also reveals how the two kinds of workforce— regular and contract labour—have come to form distinct social classes, in terms of both the material rewards and security of their employment 'and' the lifestyles, consumption patterns and aspirations that mark their social worlds (Parry 2013b). Not only has the gap between these two labour forces widened with the liberalisation of the economy, but the boundary between them has also become increasingly impenetrable. To put it in Holmström's language, the citadel itself has shrunk and any hope of climbing its walls has largely evaporated in the post-liberalisation era. Even where it once existed, secure employment is rapidly being replaced with temporary, contract-based and casual work that offers little hope of mobility or security in the long run.

A particularly insightful analysis of the changing position of labour in contemporary India is offered by Sanyal and Bhattacharyya (2009) and Bhattacharyya and Sanyal (2011), who examine the new locations of labour in relation to the nature of capitalist development. They highlight intensifying processes of 'dispossession without proletarianisation or exploitation' (2009: 3), which lead to the exclusion of labour from the accumulation economy. This new 'surplus' labour force consists of 'dispossessed producers whose traditional livelihoods were destroyed but who were not absorbed in the modern sector' (ibid.: 36). Crucially, excluded or surplus labourers do not constitute a reserve army of labour waiting to be employed, but a population that is altogether 'surplus' to the needs of the capitalist economy and hence no longer contributes to capitalist accumulation (see Li 2010). This excluded labour force, they argue, is relegated to the informal economy, parts of which are linked to the circuits of capital via subcontracting and outsourcing and parts of which constitute a space 'outside' capitalist accumulation altogether. Sanyal and Bhattacharyya (2009: 37) suggest that such an 'understanding of the informal economy places it right at the heart of capitalist development and yet outside the circuit of capital—an outside that is expanded along with and in proportion to capitalist accumulation'.

Self-employment and petty commodity production, alongside the direst forms of casual employment, mark this 'outside' or 'need' economy, where economic activity aims at meeting subsistence needs. While the extent of this labour force's disconnection from capitalist production can be debated, it is certainly fair to state that increasing populations remain excluded 'from the more dynamic sectors of the economy and engage in activities of such low productivity as barely to allow for survival' (Corbridge et al. 2013: 99).

Class, Consciousness and Collective Action

Apart from theorising the ways in which capitalism actively produces excluded labour forces, Sanyal and Bhattacharyya's analysis also revives old conversations about the nature of class formation, consciousness and collective action among India's labouring classes. A now extensive revisionist historiography has critiqued earlier essentialist and teleological explanations of class formation on the subcontinent. For quite some time, India's incomplete industrial transformation was understood in essentialist terms: primordial loyalties, rural attachments, caste- and community-based identities, and a religious worldview were taken as the 'cultural essences' that prevented industrial capitalism from emerging in its universal (read Western) form and that suppressed class consciousness. Chakrabarty (1989: 89), for example, commented that the Calcutta's jute mill workers related to the factory and its machinery through a 'rural' (read 'primitive') outlook and that they had 'not yet' acquired the industrial mind which long-term familiarity with industrial work is supposed to breed. Peasants coming to town would always remain peasants, irrespective of how they were integrated in capitalism production processes. It was suggested that the formation of an Indian working class would remain incomplete and fragmented because of persistent 'pre-industrial' or 'peasant' identities. Such an understanding of class formation, however, was rooted in a strikingly narrow understanding of class as a homogeneous, static and inherent feature of capitalist production.

The sociology of Indian labour is greatly indebted to the work of the historian Chandavarkar whose monumental work on the origins of industrial capitalism and the nature of labour politics in late colonial India brought politics back into the study of class. Rather than assuming the static identity and consciousness of novice urban labour forces in India, Chandavarkar pointed to the unavoidably fragmented nature of class formation, the diversity of overlapping and intersecting working-class sections, and the gradual—and often temporary—shifts in workers' consciousness. Importantly, he emphasised that workers' politics can only be explained 'in terms of the playing out of diverse sets of power relations rather than simply as an effect of their relationship to the means of production' (Chandavarkar 1998: 9). In doing this, Chandavarkar considered the workplace 'and' the urban neighbourhood as the pivotal sites where class consciousness, collective solidarities and social identities are being produced, negotiated and challenged (Chandavarkar 1994: 1–11, 1998: 8–10). This revisionist historiography informed subsequent ethnographic studies in a number of ways. First, historians showed that class is never the only identity that informs one's consciousness and actions. Gooptu (2001: 5) argued for an examination of 'the interaction and overlap of diverse forms of political action and social identities of the poor based on class, labour, caste, religion or nation', without giving any of these a priori relevance. Sociologists and anthropologists subsequently developed this approach by zooming in on relations 'in' production, on shop floor interactions and on neighbourhood networks to reveal how labour politics always emerge within specific historical, cultural and spatial contexts (De Neve 2005).

Second, class identities are themselves constituted—and fragmented—by the modalities of caste, kinship and gender, among others. In a fascinating study of women and labour in late colonial Bengal, Sen (1999: 100) critiqued the view that the 'male experience of class is thought to stand for class experience as a whole' and examined not only how women experienced being 'working class' differently from their male co-workers but also how the 'working class' was fragmented along spatial and gender lines. Sen argued that skill, in particular, was a social construct; it was never 'an objective economic fact, it was an ideological category imposed on certain kinds of work by virtue of gender and the power of the workers who performed these tasks' (ibid.: 105). In a study of Calcutta's jute mill workers, Fernandes (1997) further deconstructed the perspective that sees the working class as a monolithic entity, by showing how the 'working class' is itself constructed through the politics of gender and community. Differences of gender and community create factions within the 'working class' that not only prevent the consolidation of a single working-class consciousness but also protect the interests of particular sections of the labour force such as male workers or workers from specific regional or religious backgrounds (ibid.: 27–88). Indeed, working classes are always historically and socially produced through the shifting and overlapping constructions of gender, religion and community, and it is in the intersectionality of these diverse categories that multiple, yet partial, expressions of class consciousness emerge.

A powerful ethnographic illustration of the highly gendered and fractured nature of the 'working class' is found in Kapadia's study of the gem-cutting industry in Tamil Nadu, which revealed that labour relations are not always or primarily mediated by class; they may as much be mediated by caste, gender or other social identities. In the gem-cutting workshops, women's relationship with their employers were wholly mediated by their husbands, who received a joint wage, negotiated cash advances and interacted with the workshop owner on behalf of both of them. Kapadia (1999: 340) concluded that women formed an altogether different working class from men, and one which enjoyed considerably fewer freedoms: 'while men were the acknowledged bonded labourers [of employers], women workers were the unacknowledged bonded workers of men'. Such novel perspectives encouraged a more comprehensive understanding of worker identities as made up of caste, gender, kinship and religion, as well as class, and promoted a more open-ended and less teleological analysis of labour politics.

Finally, historians and other scholars of labour have pointed to the shifting nature and meaning of caste in contexts of industrial employment. While caste identities and powerful patron–client relationships with employers and contractors can constitute a divisive force on the shop floor and hinder the rise of a wider class consciousness (Picherit 2009), at times, as Breman (1996: 257) has shown among migrant workers in town, 'caste consciousness can undergo scale enlargement in such a way that it approaches class consciousness: recognizing members of other sub-castes as fellow sufferers and feeling solidarity with them'. It can rarely be known a priori what sorts of solidarities caste or religion will produce or prevent. Chandavarkar (1994: 401) rightly argued that rather than to explore divisions, tensions and rivalries within industrial workforces, it might be more productive to ask why and how workers, who are often deeply divided by opposed interests and fragmented labour markets, manage to come together at all, and around what specific issues they manage to mobilise resistance.

Sanyal and Bhattacharyya raise novel questions about the changing nature of working-class mobilisation in the post-liberalisation era. With the decline of traditional trade union representation and the exclusion of working populations from the circuits of capitalist production, novel forms of associational power are emerging that are more community based and follow new tactics of mobilisation (RoyChowdhury 2003; Sanyal and Bhattacharyya 2009: 41–42). The 'dispossessed fight back through silent encroachment on property' (Sanyal and Bhattacharyya 2009: 42) or by resisting dispossession and eviction from urban land that sustains their livelihood (Raman 2015). Such mobilisations reshape capital–labour relations: rather than focusing on the exploitation of wage labour, their primary aim is to protect access to the basic sources of subsistence that keep the excluded alive. It is in this struggle that new alliances and forms of activism emerge, and that labour politics begin to take an altogether new shape in the struggle against capital.

In *India Working*, Harriss-White made the fundamental point that while much work in India falls outside the purview and regulation of the state, this does mean that such work is not regulated at all. Rather, informal or unorganised work is regulated by the social structures and institutions of accumulation, which include caste, gender, religion and space, as well as the social fragmentation of labour markets (Harriss-White 2003: 241). Importantly, recent processes of liberalisation are 'not dissolving this matrix of social institutions but reconfiguring them slowly, unevenly and in a great diversity of ways' (Harriss-White and Gooptu 2001: 90). While caste and gender have been well researched, Vera-Sanso's important study of the labouring poor in Chennai has highlighted a much neglected yet vital social dimension of accumulation: age. Vera-Sanso's findings reveal that the aging poor—and older women in particular—continue to make substantial, yet under-recognised and under-valued contributions to family, national and global economies until well into old age. Older women not only work until much later in life than commonly assumed, but they 'are often self-supporting, support husbands and subsidise the incomes of younger relatives' (Vera-Sanso 2012: 324), and their activities are critical to the functioning of the urban economy such as through domestic work and street vending. Yet, at the same time, older women not only suffer cumulative disadvantages in the labour market, but globalisation and liberalisation policies are also further undermining their livelihoods (ibid.: 325). Indeed, urban labour market restructuring, downward wage pressures, the rise of international retailers and urban beautification projects increasingly squeeze them out of their already marginal urban niches and threaten their earning abilities. Such transformations seriously challenge their livelihoods and those of the families they support at the bottom of urban society. Clearly, even in the absence or failure of direct state regulation, the social institutions of accumulation regulate workers' lives and, in the era of liberalisation, they further squeeze the opportunities of already marginalised workforces—often female, low-caste and ageing—while excluding others (Sanyal and Bhattacharyya 2009; Vera-Sanso 2012).

New Sites of Labour: SEZs, IT and the Service Economy

Over the last decade or so, sociologists and anthropologists of labour in India have turned their attention to novel labour forces and newly emerging issues. Labour in special export zones (SEZs) and industrial enclaves, employees in the thriving IT and software industry, and the fast-growing service sector workers who sustain India's expanding consumer culture have become new subjects of ethnographic research. While studies ask 'what's new?' about such forms of employment, the answers point to remarkable continuities and consistencies with the fate of labour in the 'old' economy of agrarian production and industrial manufacturing. Cross (2010: 355), for example, explored the 'structural continuities and dynamic interconnections' between working lives inside the Visakhapatnam SEZ in Andhra Pradesh and the world of informal work outside of it. Both in Worldwide Diamond located inside the SEZ and in the informal economy surrounding the zone, terms and conditions of work were broadly similar, working lives were marked by precarious and insecure livelihoods, and political subjectivities lacked the inalienable rights and entitlements that guarantee formal citizenship (Cross 2009). The boundary between the zone and the surrounding informal economy was porous and, if anything, Cross (2010: 355) concludes, SEZs 'merely formalize conditions of precariousness and political subjectivity that already characterize working lives in much of South India'. As quintessentially neoliberal products, India's new economic zones are anything but exceptional—they merely legitimise the forms of labour control, informality and precariousness that have long underpinned capitalist production across the subcontinent (ibid.: 370).

In similar vein, studies of India's booming IT industry have indicated how recruitment and employment in the new 'knowledge' economy starkly reflect privilege—usually shaped by a combination of caste and educational background—and tap into the cultural capital of the existing middle classes (Fuller and Narasimhan 2007; Nisbett 2013; Upadhya 2011). While a discourse of 'merit' publicly represents this industry as an avenue for upward mobility, a growing body of evidence suggests that social capital remains key to access, that IT labour markets remain fragmented by gender, age and education, and that the sector itself thrives on and reproduces middle-class/upper-caste 'culture' (Fuller and Narasimhan 2014; Nisbett 2013). Moreover, rather than transforming gendered identities, the IT industry tends to reinforce notions of respectable femininity in the workplace, in which women's professionalism, career and ambition are tamed by a work culture that emphasises conservative values, 'Indian' culture, and women's domestic roles of wives and mothers (Fuller and Narasimhan 2008; Mukherjee 2008; Radhakrishnan 2011; Upadhya and Vasavi 2008).

Studies of the IT shop floor have also thrown light on shifting modes of labour control and novel labour processes. While work processes remain closely monitored, with surveillance now taking place through electronic devices, or the so-called 'information panopticon', Upadhya and Vasavi (2008: 24) also point to simultaneous processes of individualisation that turn software employees into 'entrepreneurial' workers who are forced to 'fashion their own careers through strategies such as job-hopping, self-improvement courses, and constant online and on-the-job learning'. IT workers end up in a double bind: they remain the subject of top–down surveillance through relentless online monitoring while at the same time being made personally responsible for their performance.

Emerging research on the rapidly expanding urban service economy has precisely honed in on the discursive practices through which an 'enterprise culture' is created and neoliberal subjectivities are instilled into a range of service sector workforces. In a number of fascinating studies on organised retail workers and private security guards, Gooptu has demonstrated how processes of liberalisation have promulgated a new enterprise culture rooted in ideas of self-management, self-governance and self-discipline, and driven by powerful aspirations for self-improvement and social mobility (Gooptu 2009, 2013a, 2013b). Labour processes and recruitment practices are increasingly geared towards generating a new, neoliberal subjectivity and transforming the individual into an enterprising self. Soft skills training and personality development courses increasingly contribute to the inculcation of neoliberal values of self-making and autonomy. Moreover, as much service sector work—from sales assistance to domestic and care work—involves intensive embodied and emotional engagement, scholars have rightly turned their attention to the affective dimensions of labour. In the service economy, employees' public appearance, body comportment and corporeal presentation become particularly important tools of the job and are, therefore, increasingly subjected to training, discipline and scrutiny (Gooptu 2013a; Upadhya 2016; Upadhya and Vasavi 2008). Indeed, service sector work has been shaped by what Gooptu (2013a: 9) aptly calls a regime of 'organized informality', in which 'recruitment and training... are systematically institutionalized and formalized by private agencies with the imprimatur of the state', while actual work conditions and employment relations remain informal, insecure and highly exploitative. Indeed, like most informal sector workers, disposability is service workers' main asset for employers. Moreover, the work environments themselves—such as homes and shopping malls—are permeated with a culture of subordination and servility that not only obstructs career development and upward mobility but is also emotionally draining, robbing low-end service workers from any sense of dignity at work (Gooptu 2009, 2013a).

Crucially, these new sectors not only promote novel labour processes, training strategies and subjectivities, but their particular employment relations and workplace cultures have also come to fragment the labour force and undermine collective action (Gooptu 2009: 46). For IT and service sector workers alike, risks and responsibilities have become privatised, while neoliberal discourses encourage 'individualised responses and personal strategies for coping with problems of work and employment' that are predominantly structural in nature (Gooptu 2009: 46). Soft management techniques that encourage team work and identification with the company divert attention away from the monotonous, regulated and stressful nature of work (Upadhya 2016; Upadhya and Vasavi 2008: 30). Failure is blamed on personal inadequacies or lack of ambition. The only remaining sense of agency, Gooptu asserts (2013a), lies in workers' ability to make choices and devise personal strategies rather than in their capacity to challenge the structural forces that shape their employment. This has significant implications for the deepening precariousness of service sector work as well as for the politics that workers engage in—or indeed fail to engage in. Political organisation and collective action have largely vanished as imagined possibilities from workers' minds, with dire consequences for the politics of labour in India's new economy.

The Road Ahead

The rise of new arenas of work in the post-liberalisation era has made it ever more challenging to draw a comprehensive map of Indian labour. What we do know, however, is that employment has enormously diversified at the bottom of the labour hierarchy; many employment relations have become indirect and mediated by recruiters and agencies; insecure, casual and irregular work is increasingly shrouded in a cloak of formality and regulation; and, yet, informality remains the root cause for the precarious livelihoods of the majority of labouring poor in India today. While increasing numbers of workers are migrating across regions and states in search of employment, and while ever larger numbers have joined a swelling urban workforce, the millions of workers who continue to labour in the agrarian and rural economy, often in the most humiliating, exploitative and unfree circumstances, continue to deserve scholarly attention too. And although we now know a good deal about the making of neoliberal subjectivities at work, there is plenty of scope for further explorations of how new identities are actually experienced and lived, as well as embodied and resisted at work, and how they intersect with 'older' identities and concepts of personhood that remain rooted in caste and community, thrive on patronage and dependency, and reproduce a more nodal or dividual understanding of the self.

Holmström (1976) made the point early on that factory work should not be studied as a closed system of relations, but that studies of industrial work need to look beyond the shop floor at the social organisation of neighbourhoods and communities where workers live and interact. Connections between workplace and the neighbourhood are vital not only to the recruitment and control of labour but 'also to the organisation and conduct of collective action' (Chandavarkar 1998: 8). Sociologists of labour would do well to heed this advice in future studies of work in India and to locate their informants within the wider social environments that sustain their livelihoods and shape their politics.

Finally, politics and power matter too. Little can be understood about labour outside the framework of how both state and capitalist production relations are being reconfigured in the post-liberalisation era. How do electoral democracy and fragmented party politics represent the rights of workers? Are new state social welfare policies able to alleviate the worst forms of deprivation among the labouring poor? Are labourers able to act as rights-bearing citizens in contemporary India? And how is capitalist production itself being transformed, fragmented and relocated in the era of late capitalism? While much work lies ahead, sociologists and anthropologists of Indian labour have in any case a wealth of insights to think with and build on.

References

Bhattacharyya, R. and K. Sanyal. 2011. 'Bypassing the Squalor: New Towns, Immaterial Labour and Exclusion in Post-colonial Urbanisation'. *Economic and Political Weekly* 46 (31): 41–48.
Brass, Tom. 1990. 'Class Struggle and the Deproletarianisation of Agricultural Labour in Haryana (India)'. *The Journal of Peasant Studies* 18 (1): 36–67.

Breman, Jan. 1985. *Of Peasants Migrants and Paupers: Rural Labour Circulation and Capitalist Production in West India*. New Delhi: Oxford University Press.

———. 1993. *Beyond Patronage and Exploitation: Changing Agrarian Relations in South Gujarat*. New Delhi: Oxford University Press.

———. 1994. *Wage Hunters and Gatherers: Search for Work in the Urban and Rural Economy of South Gujarat*. New Delhi: Oxford University Press.

———. 1996. *Footloose Labour: Working in India's Informal Economy*. Cambridge: Cambridge University Press.

Breman, Jan and I. Guérin. 2009. 'Introduction: On Bondage—Old and New'. In *India's Unfree Workforce: Of Bondage Old and New*, edited by J. Breman, I. Guérin and A. Prakash, 1–17. New Delhi: Oxford University Press.

Breman, Jan, I. Guérin and A. Prakash, eds. 2009. *India's Unfree Workforce: Of Bondage Old and New*. New Delhi: Oxford University Press.

Carswell, G. 2013. 'Dalits and Local Labour Markets in Rural India: Experiences from the Tiruppur Textile Region in Tamil Nadu'. *Transactions of the Institute of British Geographers* 38 (2): 325–38.

———. 2016. 'Struggles over Work Take Place at Home: Women's Decisions, Choices and Constraints in the Tiruppur Textile Industry, India'. *Geoforum* 77: 134–45.

Carswell, G. and G. De Neve. 2013a. 'From Field to Factory: Tracing Transformations in Bonded Labour in the Tiruppur Region, Tamil Nadu'. *Economy and Society* 42 (3): 430–54.

———. 2013b. 'Women at the Crossroads: Implementation of Employment Guarantee Scheme in Rural Tamil Nadu'. *Economic & Political Weekly* 48 (52): 82–93.

———. 2014. 'MGNREGA in Tamil Nadu: A Story of Success and Transformation?' *Journal of Agrarian Change* 14 (4): 564–85.

Chakrabarty, Dipesh. 1989. *Rethinking Working-class History: Bengal, 1890–1940*. Princeton, NJ: Princeton University Press.

Chandavarkar, Rajnarayan. 1994. *The Origins of Industrial Capitalism in India: Business Strategies and the Working Classes in Bombay, 1900–1940*. Cambridge: Cambridge University Press.

———. 1998. *Imperial Power and Popular Politics: Class, Resistance and the State in India, 1850–1950*. Cambridge: Cambridge University Press.

Corbridge, S., J. Harriss and C. Jeffrey. 2013. *India Today: Economy, Politics and Society*. Cambridge: Polity Press.

Cross, Jamie. 2009. 'From Dreams to Discontent: Educated Young Men and the Politics of Work at a Special Economic Zone in Andhra Pradesh'. *Contributions to Indian Sociology* 43 (3): 351–79.

———. 2010. 'Neoliberalism as Unexceptional: Economic Zones and the Everyday Precariousness of Working Life in South India'. *Critique of Anthropology* 30 (4): 355–73.

De Neve, Geert. 1999. 'Asking for and Giving Baki: Neo-bondage, or the Interplay of Bondage and Resistance in the Tamilnadu Power-loom Industry'. *Contributions to Indian Sociology* 33 (1–2): 379–406.

————. 2005. *The Everyday Politics of Labour: Working Lives in India's Informal Economy*. New Delhi: Social Science Press and Berghahn.

Dumont, Louis. 1970. *Homo Hierarchicus: The Caste System and Its Implications*. Chicago: University of Chicago Press.

Fernandes, Leela. 1997. *Producing Workers: The Politics of Gender, Class, and Culture in the Calcutta Jute Mills*. Philadelphia, PA: University of Pennsylvania Press.

Fuller, C.J. 1989. 'Misconceiving the Grain Heap: A Critique of the Concept of the Indian Jajmani System'. In *Money and the Morality of Exchange*, edited by J. Parry and M. Bloch, 33–63. Cambridge: Cambridge University Press.

Fuller, C.J. and H. Narasimhan. 2007. 'Information Technology Professionals and the New-rich Middle Class in Chennai (Madras)'. *Modern Asian Studies* 41 (1): 121–50.

————. 2008. 'Empowerment and Constraint: Women, Work and the Family in Chennai's Software Industry'. In *In an Outpost of the Global Economy: Work and Workers in India's Information Technology Industry*, edited by C. Upadhya and A.R. Vasavi, 190–210. New Delhi: Routledge.

————. 2014. *Tamil Brahmans: The Making of a Middle-class Caste*. Chicago, IL: University of Chicago Press.

Garikipati, S. 2008. 'Agricultural Wage Work, Seasonal Migration and the Widening Gender Gap: Evidence from a Semi-arid Region of Andhra Pradesh'. *European Journal of Development Research* 20 (4): 629–48.

Gooptu, Nandini. 2001. *The Politics of the Urban Poor in Early Twentieth-century India*. Cambridge: Cambridge University Press.

————. 2009. 'Neoliberal Subjectivity, Enterprise Culture and New Work-places: Organised Retail and Shopping Malls in India'. *Economic & Political Weekly* 44 (22): 45–54.

————. 2013a. 'Servile Sentinels of the City: Private Security Guards, Organized Informality, and Labour in Interactive Services in Globalized India'. *International Review of Social History* 58 (1): 9–38.

————. 2013b. 'Introduction'. In *Enterprise Culture in Neoliberal India: Studies in Youth, Class, Work and Media*, edited by N. Gooptu, 1–24. London: Routledge.

Guérin, Isabelle. 2013. 'Bonded Labour, Agrarian Changes and Capitalism: Emerging Patterns in South India'. *Journal of Agrarian Change* 13 (3): 405–23. Guérin, I., G. Venkatasubramanian and S. Michiels. 2014. 'Labour in Contemporary South India'. In *Capitalism in Development*, edited by J. Heyer and B. Harriss-White, 118–35. London: Routledge.

Harriss-White, Barbara. 2003. *India Working: Essays on Society and Economy*. Cambridge: Cambridge University Press.

Harriss-White, B. and N. Gooptu. 2001. 'Mapping India's World of Unorganized Labour'. In *Socialist Register 2001: Working Classes, Global Realities*, 89–118. London: Merlin.

Harriss-White, B. and S. Janakarajan, eds. 2004. *Rural India Facing the 21st Century*. London: Anthem Press.

Holmström, Mark. 1976. *South Indian Factory Workers: Their Life and Their World*. Cambridge: Cambridge University Press.

———. 1984. *Industry and Inequality: The Social Anthropology of Indian labour*. Cambridge: Cambridge University Press.

Kapadia, Karin. 1995a. 'The Profitability of Bonded Labour: The Gem-cutting Industry in Rural South India'. *The Journal of Peasant Studies* 22 (3): 446–83.

———. 1995b. *Siva and Her Sisters: Gender, Caste and Class in Rural South India*. Boulder, CO: Westview Press.

———. 1999. 'Gender Ideologies and the Formation of Rural Industrial Classes in South India Today'. *Contributions to Indian Sociology* 33 (1–2): 329–52.

Kolenda, Pauline. 1963. 'Toward a Model of the Hindu Jajmani System'. *Human Organization* 22 (1): 11–31.

Li, Tania Murray. 2010. 'To Make Live or Let Die? Rural Dispossession and the Protection of Surplus Populations'. *Antipode* 41 (s1): 66–93.

Mencher, Joan P. 1974. 'The Caste System Upside Down, or the Not-so-mysterious East'. *Current Anthropology* 15 (4): 469–93.

Mosse, D., S. Gupta, M. Mehta, V. Shah, J.F. Rees and KRIBP Project Team. 2002. 'Brokered Livelihoods: Debt, Labour Migration and Development in Tribal Western India'. *Journal of Development Studies* 38 (5): 59–88.

Mukherjee, Sanjukta. 2008. 'Producing the Knowledge Professional: Gendered Geographies of Alienation in India's New High-tech Workplace'. In *In an Outpost of the Global Economy: Work and Workers in India's Information Technology Industry*, edited by C. Upadhya and A.R. Vasavi, 50–75. New Delhi: Routledge.

Nisbett, N. 2013. 'Youth and the Practice of IT Enterprise: Narratives of the Knowledge Society and the Creation of New Subjectivities Amongst Bangalore's IT Aspirants'. In *Enterprise Culture in Neoliberal India: Studies in Youth, Class, Work and Media*, edited by N. Gooptu, 175–89. London: Routledge.

Pankaj, A. and R. Tankha, 2010. 'Empowerment Effects of the NREGS on Women Workers: A Study in Four States'. *Economic & Political Weekly* 45 (30): 45–55.

Parry, Jonathan. 2013a. 'Company and Contract Labour in a Central Indian Steel Plant'. *Economy and Society* 42 (3): 348–74.

———. 2013b. 'The "Embourgeoisement" of a "Proletarian Vanguard"?' In *Interrogating India's Modernity: Democracy, Identity, and Citizenship*, edited by S. Jodhka, 40–78. New Delhi: Oxford University Press.

Picherit, David. 2009. '"Workers, Trust Us!" Labour Middlemen and the Rise of the Lower Castes in Andhra Pradesh'. In *India's Unfree Workforce: Of Bondage Old and New*, edited by J. Breman, I. Guérin and A. Prakash, 259–83. New Delhi: Oxford University Press.

Radhakrishnan, Smitha. 2011. 'Gender, the IT Revolution and the Making of a Middle-class India'. In *Elite and Everyman: The Cultural Politics of the*

Indian Middle Classes, edited by A. Baviskar and R. Ray, 193–219. New Delhi: Routledge.

Raman, Bhuvaneswari. 2015. 'The Politics of Property in Land: New Planning Instruments, Law and Popular Groups in Delhi'. *Journal of South Asian Development* 10(3): 369–95.

Rogaly, Ben. 1996. 'Agricultural Growth and the Structure of "Casual" Labour-hiring in Rural West Bengal'. *The Journal of Peasant Studies* 23 (4): 141–65.

Rogaly, B. and A. Rafique. 2003. 'Struggling to Save Cash: Seasonal Migration and Vulnerability in West Bengal, India'. *Development and Change* 34 (4): 659–81.

RoyChowdhury, Supriya. 2003. 'Old Classes and New Spaces: Urban Poverty, Unorganised Labour and New Unions'. *Economic & Political Weekly* 38 (50): 5277–84.

Sanyal, K. and R. Bhattacharyya. 2009. 'Beyond the Factory: Globalisation, Informalisation of Production and the New Locations of Labour'. *Economic & Political Weekly* 44 (22): 35–44.

Sen, Samita. 1999. *Women and Labour in Late Colonial India: The Bengal Jute Industry*. Cambridge: Cambridge University Press.

Srivastava, Ravi. 2009. 'Conceptualising Continuity and Change in Emerging Forms of Labour Bondage in India'. In *India's Unfree Workforce: Of Bondage Old and New*, edited by J. Breman, I. Guérin and A. Prakash, 129–46. New Delhi: Oxford University Press.

Upadhya, Carol. 2011. 'Software and the "New" Middle Class in the "New India"'. In *Elite and Everyman: The Cultural Politics of the Indian Middle Classes*, edited by A. Baviskar and R. Ray, 167–92. New Delhi: Routledge.

———. 2016. *Reengineering India: Work, Capital and Class in an Offshore Economy*. New Delhi: Oxford University Press.

Upadhya, Carol and A.R. Vasavi. 2008. 'Outposts of the Global Information Economy: Work and Workers in India's Outsourcing Industry'. In *In an Outpost of the Global Economy: Work and Workers in India's Information Technology Industry*, edited by C. Upadhya and A.R. Vasavi, 9–49. New Delhi: Routledge.

Vera-Sanso, P. 2012. 'Gender, Poverty and Old-age Livelihoods in Urban South India in an Era of Globalisation'. *Oxford Development Studies* 40 (3): 324–40.

13

Hierarchy Without System? Why Civility Matters in the Study of Caste

Suryakant Waghmore

That caste has remained central to the study of social solidarity in India is no accident. In its dynamic form, caste mimics and adapts to the rapid political and economic changes to constitute a substantive part of public and private life. The critical role of caste in constructing particular and broader social solidarities continues to generate significant research interest among sociologists, political scientists and social anthropologists.

Scholarship on caste (or anti-caste) solidarity explores collectives that challenge caste hierarchies (Clark-Decès 2006; Gorringe 2005; Narayan 2006; Omvedt 1994; Waghmore 2013; Zelliot 1996) or collectives that construct the complex and layered inner worlds of caste (Bairy 2013; Fuller and Narasimhan 2008a). Besides challenging the caste system, caste solidarities could help consolidate cultural nationalism (Narayan 2009) or help marginal groups break away from totalising nature of class politics (Berg 2014). Sophisticated analyses on caste lie somewhere in the middle of these poles in exploring nuances of the changes in caste system. The rapid changes in economy and polity coupled with changes in form, content, ideology and social practice of caste have resulted in scholars announcing collapse of caste system in the village (Gupta 2005), and an obituary to caste as a system was written by Srinivas (2003). Caste was now seen more as about difference and identity and not hierarchy (Gupta 1984, 1991). In politics, we had democracy of castes (Kaviraj 1984), and caste was modernised and ethnicised (Jaffrelot 2000; Rudolph 1965). Ideology and the moral basis of caste was now seen as having less of a role to play in caste dominance. Prejudice and discrimination have turned significant and more active as castes compete for scarce resources in the domain of economics, politics and culture/social status (Jodhka 2015: 12). The end of the caste system and the making of discrete castes are followed by caste losing its tenacity (Béteille 2012). Exploring whether the caste system or caste hierarchy continues now may indeed seem like a futile exercise.

The hypothesis on the end of the caste system and hierarchy helps us raise newer questions about the persistence of caste and its significance in private and public spheres. Does the end of the caste system translate into the end of caste hierarchy? What happens to the values of caste? Does the new (public) ethics of equality (Béteille 1991) and justice erode hierarchical morals and practice of caste in private and public life? How does equality turn into social practice for those who face temporal impurity (women) and permanent impurity (the ex-untouchables)? More particularly, does the end of the caste system mean greater civility?

Hierarchy Without a System

From the utopia of a dying caste system and ending hierarchy, caste continues to construct economic inequalities and exclusion in newer forms (Thorat and Attewell 2007; Thorat and Newman 2010), and it generates violence against ex-untouchable castes (Carswell and De Neve 2015; Gorringe 2005; Waghmore 2013). Modern associations become modes of castes enunciating with the outside world (Bairy 2013). Caste in private life is not withering away and, if anything, it is consolidating in newer forms. While inter-caste marriages in rural spaces may generate violence and deep societal opposition (Chowdhry 2007), a new form of arranged endogamous companionate marriage is playing out and reproducing both caste and the middle class in contemporary India (Fuller and Narasimhan 2008b). The privilege of the (pure) cow continues in both public and private realms coupled with increased preference for vegetarianism in urban spaces. Caste purity is both masked and performed through politics of vegetarianism (Gorringe and Karthikeyan 2014). The values and morals of caste hierarchy indeed continue to affect and dominate public–private spheres, in newer forms. Women of privileged castes may continue to face temporal impurity and pollution attached to menstrual cycles (Narasimhan 2011) and even charity is affected by caste hierarchy, as impure castes are not the preferred recipient victims (Deshpande and Spears 2016). The various scholarship on changes in caste that emphasised the end of the caste system only confirm that obituaries to caste are premature and what we observe is rather flexibility and persistence of caste (Vaid 2014). The changes in material realm and the resulting social mobility continue to reflect persistence of caste hierarchy. Despite economic changes and the eroding of caste-based occupations, 'the lower castes are increasingly concentrated in the lowest-level occupations, including lower agriculture and manual work; the upper castes are better able to take advantage of the new opportunities' (Vaid 2014: 400). Caste, thus, has been both material and cultural and it persists, with changes (Natarajan 2005).

Broadly, caste hierarchy is a moral order of peace and, ideally, caste as a system can survive only on consensus, even of the untouchable (Deliege 1992). If one were to inversely use Kantian idea of perpetual peace (Kant et al. 2006), caste seems to be in search of perpetual peace based on the foundations of hierarchy and inequality however. Caste has, thus, long knitted diverse groups and individuals together in social, economic, cultural and political spheres to generate a localised civility of indifference (Bailey 1996). Such civility did not place equality of individuals at the centre and organised the opposites of pure and impure under a unifying ideology of homo hierarchicus (Dumont 1980). It is the complementarity of opposites—pure and impure—that holds the structure (Dumont 1971).

There has been disagreement among scholars over a neat ranking and well-founded structure of caste hierarchy that places Brahmins on the top. The ranking of priest over the king and the idea of encompassment—status encompassing power (Dumont 1980)—came under severe criticism (Quigley 1993; Raheja 1988). Both field view and book view of caste have in some form privileged the classical understanding of caste hierarchy that places Brahmin at the top. Quigley (1997) advances an alternative of seeing caste systems as relatively centralised forms of political organisation around local kings. Parvathamma (1978) too cautions against such simplicity. She suggests that Srinivas' field view and the resulting concept of Sanskritisation (1976) are a form of Brahmin odyssey which fails to note anti-Brahmin protest and reform. While placing of Brahmin above the ruler is contested, the centrality of hierarchy in persistence of caste seems to be the underlying current across scholars. Michaels (2004) suggests that the identificatory habitus of caste is largely Brahminic (or has its roots in Brahminic ideas), but, as a culturally dominant structure, it is not only Brahminic.

The flexibility of caste thus may seem paradoxical in present times, but it is the very dynamism of caste that survives hierarchical inequalities, consolidates democracy and simultaneously institutionalises violence and exclusion. Deeper sociological insights may be drawn from this paradox by problematising the nature of changes in caste instead of harping on the end of caste. Natarajan (2011) rightly cautions against forms of analyses that produce or celebrate 'culturalisation' of caste thesis which normalise a new form of casteism. Culturalisation, as counter-revolution, makes annihilation of caste appear like a quaint idea, and the silent revolution turns at best into democratisation of castes (Natarajan 2011). Caste may indeed affect the discipline of sociology as well as knowledge produced by sociologists (Kumar 2016).

We have good reasons, therefore, to look for newer and broader ways of theorising changes in caste so as to expose the endemic nature of hierarchy. Such an approach will need to locate the problem of justice at the heart of understanding flexibility and persistence of caste. It will also require bracketing the romance of syndicalism and the prescription that 'only' the class approach can unite the oppressed (Teltumbde 2007). The newness of caste offers considerable scope to understand the vernacular nature of subject formation, the endemic nature of hierarchy and exclusion in modern India, and also the localised struggles for greater civility. Caste may be changing but casteism continues to be an immanent part of the (new) caste (Natarajan 2011). Exploration of civil and uncivil forms of solidarity that caste constructs could help pose the problem of civility to changes accruing in caste.

Placing civility at the core of examining changes in caste could help us explore the possibilities of freedom for individuals in general and emancipation of marginal groups in particular. What changes in morals and ethics of caste groups? What persists? How is the change in caste affecting possibilities of citizenship, justice and equality? Are changes in caste sentiments voluntary or forced? Does the change in caste relations advance greater civility across castes and within families? How does caste sentiment get reorganised in private and public realms? What are the newer spaces of social solidarity beyond caste? Does the turning of caste into 'difference' encourage civility across castes? What are the newer incivilities? How are these cast in present times? It is questions of this nature that could unravel the limits of flexibility and the persistence of caste.

Civility is often understood as face-saving behaviour or as rule-patterned activity that does not mean much for individuals (Goffman 1990). Civility is thus paradoxical like caste—it could be about ideas and practices of dominance forced on/or imbibed at margins, or the very reversal of these by marginal groups seeking greater equality. Ethnography shows civility also as an activity through which people try to recognise what can be done and what has to be done, that is, customs *and* sense of justice (Gayet-Viaud 2009). Civility involves transforming social relations across sectors and groups, between men and women, between classes, between generations, between religious beliefs or sexual orientations (Gayet-Viaud 2009). The universality of civility not only applies to geographical dimensions but also to the different segments of a given society (Baumgarten et al. 2011). Locating civility as a critical concept while studying changes in caste could particularly help explore the persistent nature of unfreedom endemic to the dynamism of caste.

Caste Against Civility?

> The effect of caste on the ethics of the Hindus is simply deplorable. Caste has killed public spirit. Caste has destroyed the sense of public charity. Caste has made public opinion impossible. A Hindu's public is his caste. His responsibility is only to his caste [...] There is no sympathy for the deserving [...] Suffering as such calls for no response. There is charity, but it begins with the caste and ends with the caste. There is sympathy, but not for men of other castes. (Ambedkar 1936)

Ambedkar (1936) was foremost in posing the sociological problem of civility to caste *socius*. The spread of caste among non-Brahmins through imitation and excommunication exemplified the dynamic nature of caste (Ambedkar 1917). Ambedkar doubted possibilities of justice in or through caste; for him, Hindu civilisation based on graded inequality of caste amounted to felony. Ambedkar posed the opposition of reason and morals to caste solidarity, for justice or civility to prevail caste 'had' to be annihilated. As an emancipatory strategy, he did not evoke Western ideals for civility and instead revoked Buddhism as a civil religion to challenge the incivilities of caste (Fuchs 2001).

Caste thus may be losing its tenacity in present times but is getting normalised in cities and villages. Such normality tends to be a masculine process as women guard purity and embody honour, while men dominate the public and private spaces. Incipient individualism in cities along with persistence of caste solidarities, and the present moment of caste in the virtual world, furthers segmental loyalties of caste.

Caste is not in conflict against the procedures of democracy but may collide against the values and ideals of democracy. Due to the immanence of hierarchy—old and new—caste also tends to affect democratic civility. What we see in present times, therefore, is a sync between caste and democracy and increasing violence and exclusion facing marginal sections. Democratic procedures could well be used in advancing caste and hierarchic exclusion—democratically. Caste has indeed helped in consolidating democracy more than democratic deepening. Indian democracy is thus a peculiar case of high democracy and low civility (Waghmore 2013).

Studies on Dalits have helped explore the complexity of changes in caste. Caste may almost be invisible in the rural areas; Dalits, however, complain of oppressive caste sentiment persisting in the minds (Waghmore 2013) and the stomach of dominant groups (Still 2013). Such sentiments mostly generate disgust and anger against Dalits, particularly if Dalits are mobile and assertive. In my research on caste and Dalit politics in Marathwada, a Dalit respondent from the Mang caste shared the following:

> Shivaji: See things are changing; our women used to work at their place; we used to be totally dependent on them. Now things are changing; our boys dress better than them. In the panchayat, some posts get reserved for Dalits, which they do not like. They feel that the village belongs to them.
>
> Vishnu: No one is doing caste-based work now. Earlier, we used to wear their old clothes.
>
> Bandu: They do not like this. They cannot see this.
>
> Shivaji: Let the Marathas do it now (caste jobs). Now the Mahars and Mangs are doing well. Some have land and some have jobs. Let them come and drop *sarpan* (firewood) at ours. Why are they not doing it? Because they cannot do this *halkat* (lowly) work. Now our people are educated, we won't do it. So, they feel that we are transgressing (*maajalet*—one with excess body fat, turning deviant) and that is why conflicts have increased.
>
> Bandu: Because we do not do caste-based work, they think we are maajalet.
> Shivaji: Earlier, they used to say, 'Mang, Mahar please stay in your limits'. Now if they comment on caste, our people cannot

take it. They cannot tolerate it and become angry if you say anything on caste. (Group Interview: 9 March 2009)

That caste system is falling apart and consensus to hierarchy is difficult to find at the margins of caste is well established (Gorringe 2005). The incivilities of caste could be forced in present times through both dominance and hegemony. The rejection of hegemony could invite violence against marginal groups, especially Dalits. To counter dominance, at times subalterns may use morals and sacrificial ethics (of caste) and construct a vernacular democracy (Tanabe 2007). In their struggle for justice, they also use laws that force equality and ban caste discrimination (Carswell and De Neve 2015; Waghmore 2013). While the former may result in complementarity and consensus of sorts, the latter causes contradiction and ruptures in a caste habitus from below and above.

On the other hand, dominant kingly castes resort to newer discourses and tactics of domination. Kingship has a central role in the workings of caste hierarchy (Quigley 1993, 2002). Marathas in Maharashtra use the cultural resource of *rajeshahi* (kinghood) to consolidate their dominance in state and civil society (Waghmore 2013). While all Dalit castes are considered as lesser citizens, those untouchables who oppose caste hierarchy and dominance are excluded more. In rural Marathwada, there is a general proverb used among non-Dalits for choosing the right Dalit political representatives. A Maratha shared:

> *Mahara Peksha Mang Bara Ani Manga Peksha Chambar Bara*
> (A Mang is better than a Mahar and a Chambar better than Mang), the other one was more specific, '*Jai Bhim Peksha Ram Ram Bara*' (The one who greets as Ram-Ram is better than the one who greets as Jai Bhim). (Field notes: 22 April 2009)

While there is lesser clarity and agreement on the (higher) role and place of a Brahmin in the hierarchy, present-day hierarchy is more about identifying, segregating and excluding the lower and untouchable. Even ritual strategies of Sanskritisation cannot ensure social inclusion for permanently impure castes (Parvathamma 1978). Maharashtra has a history of violence against Brahmins by Marathas in the past (Patterson 1954) and increased violence against Dalits in democratic times (Waghmore 2013). While turning down the power of Brahmins, Marathas continue to follow the Brahminic notion of hierarchy in regulating Maratha women and untouchable castes. An extraordinary transgression of caste is seen as love relations between a Maratha woman and a Dalit man and most often invites violence.

Changing caste relations besides producing violence against Dalits or control of women also define the private sphere of connubial and commensal relations in contemporary times. Caste constructs new subjectivities that inhabit vernacular democracy. We see a new form of (Hindu) politeness[1] extended towards untouchable castes which is neither inclusive nor violent. Violence is, however, rendered banal through newer etiquettes of caste politeness.

Food transactions across caste relations have been changing in non-private spaces. However, food preferences continue to be influenced by notions of caste purity and pollution. For achieving purity of body and spirit, it is considered necessary to be both vegetarian and religious simultaneously (Mahar 1958). As the popular ideas of purity attached to vegetarianism and cow sacrality get increasingly institutionalised, meat has become a source of contention, violence and even governmental repression in parts of Northwest India. Such vegetarianism of purity and pollution could lead to disgust, social distance and occasional violence against non-vegetarians. The surge in power of purity associated with vegetarianism is aggravated through non-Brahmin imitation of vegetarianism. The practice of vegetarianism, however, among the subalterns is not always linked to Sanskritisation and may be part of subaltern sociality (Desai 2008). The power of vegetarianism has also normalised and institutionalised disgust against beef eaters, particularly against Dalits and Muslims. Ghassem-Fachandi's (2010) study of anti-Muslim violence in Gujarat points to the role of vegetarianism, sacrifice and bovine nationalism in propelling such violence.

The normalisation of caste also thrives through popular culture. Through popular culture, caste thrives as difference and simultaneously subsumes into the modern Hindu identity. There is limited scholarship

---

[1] Among the foremost philosophers to raise the cunning of politeness and lack of civility in civil society was Adam Ferguson (1767 [1966]). He framed politeness as a situation where great sentiments of heart are not awakened, arguing therefore for 'a need to look for what persuasion can turn the grimace of politeness into real sentiments of humanity and candour?' (ibid.: 39–40). Immanuel Kant foresees the problem that politeness poses for perpetual peace across nations: 'All that is good yet is not based on morally good convictions is nothing but pure outward show and shimmering misery' (Kant et al. 2006). Civility for Kant has thus both moral and behavioural dimensions and civility within nations is necessary for achieving civility across nations (ibid.).

on caste in popular culture, and much research remains to be done. Similarly, there is little focus on the study of humour which could provide insights into the new shape that caste relations take under vernacular democracy. Exploring caste and anti-caste dimensions of humour will help us decipher how caste sentiments are increasingly voiced in polite, non-violent and non-aggressive forms (Waghmore 2015). It could also provide insights into anti-Sanskritisation processes in subaltern movements, particularly the Dalit challenge to Hindu gods and customs and stigma of pollution surrounding untouchable worlds and bodies (Waghmore 2015). Caste thus constructs coopera-tion, competition and conflict, and caste power and dominance can be productively studied through its normalised and modernised form in present times, both in private and public spheres.

Withering Caste, Withering Incivilities?

Civility is indeed about power of the privileged to control and domi-nate. However, for those subjugated by caste, civility is also a process of causing radical changes in social relations towards substantive citizenship. Civility is gradual (Shils and Grosby 1997) and processual (Waghmore 2013), and a movement towards greater civility is perpet-ual. Due to the persistence of hierarchy, the discourse of civil rights and civility is still relevant in India. It was through the Constitution that ethics of citizenship and equality were forced upon Indian civilisation. Democracy thus preceded civility, and subaltern struggles for civility have produced new codes of politeness as a form of counter-revolution (Waghmore 2017).

Caste considerably affects the possibility of democratic civility. Using the concept of civility in the study of changes in caste could help us better comprehend the long and winding road of civil repair and intimate justice (Alexander 2001). A nuanced sociology of caste in public and private life could help excavate solidarities that produce cosmopolitan citizenship void of hierarchical morals and exclusions. The recognition and redistribution struggles of the marginalised could particularly unravel civility as a politics of dissent, voicing aspirations of dignity, freedom, equality and justice.

References

Alexander, J.C. 2001. 'The Long and Winding Road: Civil Repair of Intimate Injustice'. *Sociological Theory* 19 (3): 371–400.

Ambedkar, B.R. 1917. 'Castes in India: Their Mechanism, Genesis and Development'. *Indian Antiquary* 41: 81–95.

———. 1936. *Annihilation of Caste*. New Delhi: Shree Publishing House.

Bailey, F.G. 1996. *The Civility of Indifference: On Domesticating Ethnicity*. New Delhi: Oxford University Press.

Bairy, R. 2013. *Being Brahmin, Being Modern: Exploring the Lives of Caste Today*. New Delhi: Taylor & Francis.

Baumgarten, B., D. Gosewinkel and D. Rucht. 2011. 'Civility: Introductory Notes on the History and Systematic Analysis of a Concept'. *European Review of History: Revue européenne d'histoire* 18 (3): 289–312.

Berg, D.E. 2014. 'Karamchedu and the Dalit Subject in Andhra Pradesh'. *Contributions to Indian Sociology* 48 (3): 383–408.

Béteille, A. 1991. 'The Reproduction of Inequality: Occupation, Caste and Family'. *Contributions to Indian Sociology* 25 (1): 3–28.

———. 2012. 'The Peculiar Tenacity of Caste'. *Economic & Political Weekly* 47 (13): 41–50.

Carswell, G. and G. De Neve. 2015. 'Litigation Against Political Organization? The Politics of Dalit Mobilization in Tamil Nadu, India'. *Development and Change* 46 (5): 1106–32.

Chowdhry, P. 2007. *Contentious Marriages, Eloping Couples: Gender, Caste and Patriarchy in Northern India*. New Delhi: Oxford University Press.

Clark-Decès, I. 2006. 'How Dalits Have Changed the Mood at Hindu Funerals: A View from South India'. *International Journal of Hindu Studies* 10 (3): 257–69.

Deliege, R. (1992). 'Replication and Consensus: Untouchability, Caste and Ideology in India'. *Man* 27 (1): 155–73.

Desai, A. 2008. 'Subaltern Vegetarianism: Witchcraft, Embodiment and Sociality in Central India'. *South Asia: Journal of South Asian Studies* 31 (1): 96–117.

Deshpande, A. and D. Spears. 2016. 'Who Is the Identifiable Victim? Caste and Charitable Giving in Modern India'. *Economic Development and Cultural Change* 64 (2): 299–321.

Dumont, L. 1971. 'On Putative Hierarchy and Some Allergies to It'. *Contributions to Indian Sociology* 5 (1): 58–81.

———. *Homo Hierarchicus*. Chicago, IL: University of Chicago Press.

Ferguson, A. 1767 (1966). *An Essay on the History of Civil Society*. Edunburgh: Edunburgh University Press.

Fuchs, M. 2001. 'Religion for Civil Society? Ambedkar's Buddhism and the Imagination of Emergent Possibilities'. In *Charisma and Canon: Essays on the Religious History of the Indian Subcontinent*, edited by Vasudha Dalmia, Angelika Malinar and M. Christof, 250–73. Oxford: Oxford University Press.

Fuller, C.J. and H. Narasimhan. 2008a. *Tamil Brahmans: The Making of the Middle-class Caste*. Chicago, IL and London: University of Chicago.

Fuller, C.J. and H. Narasimhan. 2008b. 'Companionate Marriage in India: The Changing Marriage System in a Middle-class Brahman Subcaste'. *Journal of the Royal Anthropological Institute* 14 (4): 736–54.

Gayet-Viaud, C. 2009. 'Civility and Democracy'. *European Journal of Pragmatism and American Philosophy* 7 (1): 1–16.

Ghassem-Fachandi, P. 2010. 'Ahimsa, Identification and Sacrifice in the Gujarat Pogrom'. *Social Anthropology* 18 (2): 155–75.

Goffman, E. 1990. *The Presentation of Self in Everyday Life*. New York: Penguin Books.

Gorringe, H. 2005. *Untouchable Citizens: Dalit Movements and Democratisation in Tamil Nadu*, Vol. 4. New Delhi: SAGE.

Gorringe, H. and D. Karthikeyan. 2014. 'The Hidden Politics of Vegetarianism'. *Economic & Political Weekly* 49 (20): 21.

Gupta, D. 1984. 'Continuous Hierarchies and Discrete Castes'. *Economic & Political Weekly* 19 (48): 2049–53.

———. 1991. 'Hierarchy and Difference: An Introduction'. In *Social Stratification*, edited by D. Gupta, 1–24. New Delhi: Oxford University Press.

———. 2005. 'Whither the Indian Village: Culture and Agriculture in "Rural" India'. *Economic & Political Weekly* 40 (8): 751–58.

Jaffrelot, C. 2000. 'Sanskritization vs. Ethnicization in India: Changing Identities and Caste Politics Before Mandal'. *Asian Survey* 40 (5): 756–66.

Jodhka, S.S. 2015. 'Ascriptive Hierarchies: Caste and Its Reproduction in Contemporary India'. *Current Sociology*.

Kant, I., P. Kleingeld, J. Waldron, M.W. Doyle and A.W. Wood. 2006. *Toward Perpetual Peace and Other Writings on Politics, Peace, and History*. New Haven, CT: Yale University Press.

Kaviraj, S. 1984. 'On the Crisis of Political Institutions in India'. *Contributions to Indian Sociology* 18 (2): 223–43.

Kumar, V. 2016. 'How Egalitarian Is Indian Sociology?' *Economic & Political Weekly* 51 (25): 33–39.

Mahar, P.M. 1958. 'Changing Caste Ideology in a North Indian Village'. *Journal of Social Issues* 14: 51–65.

Michaels, A. 2004. *Hinduism: Past and Present*. Princeton, NJ: Princeton University Press.

Narasimhan, H. 2011. 'Adjusting Distances: Menstrual Pollution Among Tamil Brahmins'. *Contributions to Indian Sociology* 45 (2): 243–68.

Narayan, B. 2006. *Women Heroes and Dalit Assertion in North India: Culture, Identity and Politics*. New Delhi: SAGE.

———. 2009. *Fascinating Hindutva: Saffron Politics and Dalit Mobilisation*. New Delhi: SAGE.

Natarajan, B. 2005. 'Caste, Class and Community in India: An Ethnographic Approach'. *Ethnology* 44 (3): 227–41.

Natarajan, B. 2011. *The Culturalization of Caste in India: Identity and Inequality in a Multicultural Age*. New York, NY: Routledge.

Omvedt, G. 1994. *Dalits and Democratic Revolution*. New Delhi: SAGE.

Parvathamma, C. 1978. 'The Remembered Village: A Brahminical Odyssey'. *Contributions to Indian Sociology* 12 (1): 91–96.

Patterson, M. 1954. 'Caste and Political Leadership in Maharashtra: A Review and Current Appraisal'. *Economic & Political Weekly* 6 (39): 1065–68.

Quigley, D. 1993. *The Interpretation of Caste*. Oxford: Clarendon Press.

———. 1997. 'Kingship and "Contrapriests"'. *International Journal of Hindu Studies* 1 (3): 565–80.

———. 2002. 'Is a Theory of Caste Still Possible?' *Social Evolution and History* 1 (1): 140–70.

Raheja, G.G. 1988. 'India: Caste, Kingship, and Dominance Reconsidered'. *Annual Review of Anthropology* 17: 497–522.

Rudolph, L. 1965. 'The Modernity of Tradition: The Democratic Incarnation of Caste in India'. *The American Political Science Review* 59 (4): 975–89.

Shils, E. and S.E. Grosby. 1997. *The Virtue of Civility: Selected Essays on Liberalism, Tradition, and Civil Society*. Indianapolis: Liberty Fund.

Srinivas, M.N. 1976. *The Remembered Village*. New Delhi: Oxford University Press.

———. 2003. 'An Obituary on Caste as a System'. *Economic & Political Weekly* 38 (5): 455–59.

Still, C. 2013. 'They Have It in Their Stomachs but They Can't Vomit It Up: Dalits, Reservations, and Caste Feeling in rural Andhra Pradesh'. *Focaal: Journal of Global and Historical Anthropology* 2013 (65): 68–79.

Tanabe, A. 2007. 'Toward Vernacular Democracy: Moral Society and Post-postcolonial Transformation in Rural Orissa, India'. *American Ethnologist* 34 (3): 558–74.

Teltumbde, A. 2007. 'Khairlanji and Its Aftermath: Exploding Some Myths'. *Economic & Political Weekly* 42 (12): 1019–25.

Thorat, S. and K. Newman. 2010. *Blocked by Caste: Economic Discrimination in Modern India*. New Delhi: Oxford University Press.

Thorat, Sukhadeo and P. Attewell. 2007. 'The Legacy of Social Exclusion: A Correspondence Study of Job Discrimination in India'. *Economic & Political Weekly* 42 (41): 4141–45.

Vaid, D. 2014. 'Caste in Contemporary India: Flexibility and Persistence'. *Annual Review of Sociology* 40: 391–410.

Waghmore, S. 2013. *Civility Against Caste: Dalit Politics and Citizenship in Western India*. New Delhi: SAGE.

———. 2015. 'Challenging Normalised Exclusion: Humour and Hopeful Rationality in Dalit Politics'. In *From Margins to Mainstream: Institutionalising Minorities in South Asia*, edited by H. Gorringe, R. Jeffery and S. Waghmore, 169–93. New Delhi: SAGE.

Waghmore, S. 2017. 'From Hierarchy to Hindu Politeness?' In *Waning Hierarchies, Persisting Inequalities: Caste and Power in 21st Century India*, edited by S. Jodhka and J. Manor, 111–39. Delhi: Orient BlackSwan.

Zelliot, E. 1996. *From Untouchable to Dalit: Essays on Ambedkar Movement*. New Delhi: Manohar Publishers.

14

Caste and the Anthropology of Democracy

Lucia Michelutti

Introduction

One late afternoon in March 2014, I stopped to buy a sari at the local cloth shop in the central bazaar of a provincial town in western Uttar Pradesh (UP). It was a month before the general Lok Sabha elections. While I was looking at the different fabrics and sipping tea, the shop owner and four other clients started an animated debate about the current UP government and upcoming elections. The shop owner Manoj Yadav (65 years old) and the clients belong to the local Yadav community. I have known the three of them since 1998 when I started to conduct research in the area. In the preceding 10 years, I had regularly returned to this field site and spent 9 months there between 2012 and 2014.[1] The previous evening, Arvind Kejriwal (the leader of Aam Aadmi Party [AAP]) had held an improvised rally in town, and Manoj asked me if I had attended the meeting and if there had been a good turn-out. I said that the event had been quite a success. Arjun (in his 30s) interrupted and pointed out that AAP was a Delhi party, 'No chance

[1] My current research is funded by ERC-AIMSA/284080 and ESRC-ES/I036702/1.

of winning in this town.... AAP is against jatiwad (casteism)', he added laughing. 'This does not work in this town or in UP. Although', he added 'they are presenting the party as a "Bania party" locally. The Bania caste association has made Kejriwal into a new hero together with Gandhiji' (more laughter). Hari Singh commented, 'Banias will vote for Modi. Modi is a good leader. People will vote for development. He will change UP. You will see—give UP to Modi and it will be like Japan in few years' (more laughter). For about 20 minutes, they took turns criticising what they called the 'Yadav Raj' (the rule by Yadavs) in the state, the level of impunity that a number of local figures 'enjoyed' and the general chaos that *goondagardi* (criminal work) was creating in the area. Hari Singh again commented:

> We are tired of the Samajwadi Party government. It is 'Mulayam Singh's Parivar Raj'. It is not a caste party, it is a family racket. Everybody agrees with this.... Akhilesh Yadav took charge as Chief Minister on 15 March 2012 in the afternoon and local SP party workers were already grabbing land and properties by the evening.... The problem is that it is a badly organised racket. There is no strong leadership. We are governed by four and a half Chief Ministers: Mulayam Singh Yadav (Akhilesh's father), Ram Gopal Yadav and Shivpal Singh Yadav (Akhilesh's uncles) Azam Khan and Akhilesh is the half. We need someone like Modi to take charge. Democracy needs *danda* (force). Plus the SP is getting too cosy with the Muslims. Yadavs are getting upset about it....

After listening for a while, I entered the conversation and asked, 'So are you going to vote for BJP next elections?' They all looked at me in disbelief. 'Of course not, we will vote for Netaji' (aka Mulayam Singh Yadav). I was a bit puzzled. After about an hour of criticisms and malicious gossip about the 'Yadav *log*' (people) and simultaneous praising of Modi's strength and authority, I was expecting a different answer. 'Why?' I asked. The unanimous reply was, '*Mai Yadav hoon. Mulayam Singh Yadav hamari naak hai*', which literally means 'I am a Yadav. Our nose is Mulayam Singh Yadav'. This is a local Hindi expression. Nose symbolises status, prestige and power. 'Without Mulayam we are nothing—even if we appreciate Modi, we will vote for Mulayam.... We do not feel secure without caste, who will help us? Who will protect us?... No caste is for the people in Delhi'. As a way of further proving his statement, Manoj Singh called out to a young girl who was passing the shop and asked her who she would vote for (if she were old enough to vote). 'Mulayamji', she said without missing a beat. He then asked her, 'What is your caste?' She was a Yadav. He then called out to another little girl who was also passing by and asked the same questions; she answered that she would vote for Mayawati (the leader of BSP). She was a Jatav. Post-election results showed that despite the Modi wave and the increased role of class (rather than caste) in shaping Indian votes, Yadavs and Dalits largely remain loyal to their caste-based ('family'-based) parties: SP and BSP.[2]

A few days after the above conversation took place, I interviewed a local seasoned Jat Congress party leader. He explained, 'When it comes to the Lok Sabha elections there are three main vote blocs in the constituency: Jats, Brahmins and Rajput. Since Independence, political parties have never risked putting forward a Brahmin candidate'. He continued, 'Brahmins vote for Jats and Rajputs—but no Rajput or Jat will ever vote for a Brahmin ... this is a scientific fact'. Intrigued by this remark, I pressed him to explain the reasons behind such folk theory of voting behaviour and representation. He answered, 'Everybody knows that Brahmins need to be protected by Rajputs or Jats—they cannot protect us, they do not have the skills ... take for example the Banias ... they are useless ... they get easily scared'.

Caste and Politics

It is the analysis of this simple but at the same time complex vignette that frames this review essay on the ethnography of caste and politics and its contribution to the wider comparative anthropological study of democracy. Caste and politics has been a recurrent theme in the anthropology of India.[3] Indians have a unique passion for 'the political' and some of the highest rates of participation and contestation in the world. Politics shape everyday people's social lives, and it is generally something that people cannot (and/or do not want to) ignore (Michelutti 2008). Spending long hours at political party headquarters and pre-election campaigning times has taught me that politicians and campaign strategists are obsessed with 'caste' and 'numbers'. Every political party in the area has detailed caste data for each electoral booth. When choosing candidates, political parties pay a great deal of attention to his/her caste. However, this is not the most important criteria

[2] See recent analysis on caste and class by Jaffrelot (2015). Similar trends have been illustrated for the 2017 Vidhan Sabha elections. Yadavs and Jatav remained largely loyal to the SP and BSP, respectively.

[3] See Srinivas (1962) and Khotari (1970). Throughout the text, I will provide indicative references, as the list on the topic is extensive and impossible to cite in its full form in this short essay.

considered for success. 'Caste' needs to be combined with 'money' and/ or 'muscle', and a capacity to gain support across communities/class barriers.[4] Regardless of this, time and again informants refer to blood metaphors, kinship and notions of embodiment to render political strategies and decisions and their modes of governance 'natural'.[5] Why is this? In previous work, I suggested that the answer may be found by looking at how the centrepiece of 'democracy'—popular sovereignty— takes sociocultural roots in different societies and is actualised using locally available kinship ideals and practices (Michelutti 2008, 2013). As Spencer (2007: 137) pointed out two decades ago, one of the crucial aspirations of democracy is 'to make the bodies of all men and women the subjects, rather than the object of power'. It follows that contemporary political power and legitimacy derive largely from the ability to act in the name of 'the people' (Laclau 2005). However, constructions of this key element of the political imagination ('the people') and the ties that bind them to the government vary radically across the world (for a comparative analysis, see Forbess and Michelutti 2013).

A focus on the entanglements of statehood and kin provides insights into India's rich taxonomy of cultures of representation. On the one hand, we have 'electoral representation' conceptualised as a contract between the represented (the individual citizen) and the representative. In such contractual relationships, the representative is only temporarily mandated to put forward the views of those he/she represents, while those represented retain the right to recall if their views are misrepresented. On the other hand, we have 'embodiment-based representation' in which the representative encompasses the represented and identify with it (with or without electorate mandate). The expression *'Mai Yadav hoon. Mulayam Singh Yadav hamari naak hain'* hints at such common links of substance. When I returned to the neighbourhood in 2012 and asked who the new leaders were, the unanimous answer was, 'Everybody thinks they are Akhilesh', and 'Yadavs are all bosses'. The town is full of 'mini-Akhileshs' and 'mini-Mulayams' and even 'mini-Mayawatis'. The same is true of the Yadavs' Dalit competitors. Such attachment to 'caste' can be explained from the point of view of interest (such as material gains or improved livelihoods) as well as symbolic benefits (through the politics of dignity and recognition). However, affinities between political leaders and their voter communities go much deeper than the very idea of elections (and economic and security calculations) may assume, and reach far beyond the electoral

[4] See, for example, Verniers (2014).
[5] On blood, substance and relationality, see Carsten (2011).

context. Mulayam Singh, Akhilesh, Mayawati and many others are not simply elected to speak and act on behalf of their electorates (Michelutti 2004, 2014) by means of a 'contract', a flimsy connection compared to the substantive bonds of kinship they form; Yadav leaders are seen as embodying those they are said to represent. It could be said that 'Yadavs' have been encompassed by their leaders, to use Dumont's term. Or that they share 'a mutuality of being' and are 'members of one another' (Sahlins 2013: ix). Or that like in the old Rajas' days where 'everyone is united by his or her common relation to the king' (Quigley 2005: 5; see also Price 1989), they have come to internalise the potentialities of wealth, protection and power for the community as a whole. Crucially, such claims highlight that caste is not only an electoral cleavage and an instrument of mobilisation, but it also shapes how people rule. Anthropologists are uniquely equipped to explore such logics and conceptions of representation/sovereignty and how norms of personhood and relatedness, charismatic traditions, kinship tropes and ideals of descent shape them. However, this essay shows how South Asian anthropology, which was once the theoretical home of 'the dividual',[6] has paid very little attention to what is happening to 'caste and politics' in the normative spheres of kinship, kingship and 'the person' (rather than 'the people'). Equally, we know very little about how kinship (lineages, clans, biradaris) connects and combines with contemporary systems of governance by underpinning both 'caste sovereignties' and 'individual personal sovereignties'.[7]

Realignments?

'New' feelings of 'caste solidarity' and 'caste patriotism' were recorded by Ghurye as early as 1932. In many ways, through their enumeration practices, the institution of separate electorates for Hindus and Muslims, and reservation policies for marginalised sectors of society, the British Raj set up the conditions under which different groups of Indians could participate in the political process, and contribute to politicise and consolidate caste and community identities.[8] Postcolonial India has inherited this legacy and with it 'palimpsests of [caste] sovereignties' (Comaroff and Comaroff 2006: 9). Reservation

---

[6] For this point, see Kapila (2013). For a discussion of the work inspired by the ethnosociology school on personhood and relatedness and its critiques, see Parry (1989).

[7] On sovereignty, see Hansen and Steputtat (2005).

[8] See, for example, Appadurai (1993) and Bayly (1999: 97–144).

policies have further contributed to link rights to collectives rather than to individuals and render categories such as caste, tribe, religion and ethnicity open to endless political manipulation.[9] Such processes are also said to have shaped the horizontal consolidation of caste.[10] The caste system, defined by hierarchical relations, is said to have changed its nature. As a result, we are told that castes are increasingly becoming 'horizontal', disconnected groups with their own distinct culture and way of life (Searle-Chatterjee and Sharma 1994: 19–20). This shift is reflected by the substitution of the term *jati*, which refers to caste, with the term *samaj*, which refers to community (Mayer 1996: 59). Recent historical work by Guha (2013) shows that such processes were already active in pre-colonial times, that caste was not Hindu in essence and that 'purity' should be thus understood as one among several idioms through which groups' cultural distinctiveness was (and is) played out. For example, Yadavs have historically stressed the idiom of kinship and descent rather than the idiom of religious hierarchy. Equally among this community, 'substantialised' manifestations of caste are not a recent phenomenon (Michelutti 2008: Chapter 4).

From the 1950s to the early 1970s, anthropologists, together with political scientists and sociologists, produced a wealth of literature exploring how the new logics of democracy were shaping caste.[11] Concepts such as 'dominant caste' and 'vote bank' (Srinivas 1959) and 'vertical and horizontal mobilisation' (Rudolph and Rudolph 1967) were developed in this period. Such typologies suggested that Indians were not voting 'as individual(s)' and that by taking social roots in a 'caste society', Indian democracy was producing particularistic ideas of 'the people'. However, the specificities and the varieties of caste sovereignties and their fluidity and changes, and the role of the individual, remained largely ethnographically under-explored. As Jodhka (2006) pointed out, the literature on the subject was still deeply anchored in a macro-analysis of electoral politics or studies of caste associations, which talked about caste in general terms and failed to grasp the ways the interaction between caste and politics was experienced differently by different castes and in different localities. On the whole, there was a general reluctance to engage with different cultural understandings

[9] On the impact of affirmative action policies, see the special issue by Shah and Shneiderman (2013).

[10] The shift from 'caste' to 'caste as ethnic group' has been described as the 'substantialisation of caste' (Dumont 1980: 226–27) or as 'the ethnicisation of caste' (Barnett 1975: 158–59; see also Fuller 1996: 22–25).

[11] For a comprehensive review, see Jodhka (2006).

of power and their implications, particularly when these blurred the political/kin(g)ship/religious distinction in the realm of political modernity. In many ways, this trend reflected the acultural (and anti-cultural) political anthropology of the time (Spencer 2003: 48).

By the end of the 1990s, when I started my first fieldwork, there had been a general revitalisation of political anthropology, as anthropologists started to look at 'the state' and 'democracy' (Spencer 1997). In India, this corresponded to a revival in the study of local politics, as anthropologists intrigued by the phenomena of Hindu nationalism and the rise of lower castes had once again returned to studying this topic (see, e.g., Hansen 1999, 2001; Ruud 2003). By the 1990s, 'caste' had emerged as part of the 'politics of presence', and it had increasingly become 'respectable' to talk about it in the public-political domain (Yadav 1997). It is in this intellectual context that I explored how Indian democracy took sociocultural root among a community of Yadavs in UP and, in the process, informed changes in the morphology of their caste/community, affecting who they worship, who they marry, who they vote for, and how they perceive politics and political leaders.

Over the past decade, several studies have mapped out the social embeddedness of Indian democracy showing how it acquired different meanings and agendas according to the groups, castes, communities, movements, and political parties that deploy it (for a summary, see Ruud and Heirstad 2016). Folk understandings of democracy have become closely linked to caste-based ideas of justice and sovereignty (Michelutti and Heath 2013). These vary among different castes, drawing on the specificity of the particular histories, ritual status, kinship and religious practices of those groups. For example, Witsoe (2009) showed how Yadavs understand 'corruption as power' and celebrated it as a means to lower-caste empowerment in Bihar. Ciotti (2006) illustrated that members of the Chamar caste choose to repudiate their past and embrace democracy and modernity through the language of education and civilisation. Similarly, for the educated young people from the Chamar caste of the district of Bijnor (UP) studied by Jeffrey et al. (2008), the language of democracy was constructed through the discourses of 'genteel masculinity' and contrasted with the muscular strategies of the local Muslims and Jats. In Tamil Nadu, Gorringe (2006, 2010) highlighted the specificities of Dalit leadership and how the relation between leader and followers was shaped among this particular community, while Alpa Shah (2007), drawing on ethnographic material from Jharkhand, showed how the Munda, tribal peasants, saw the state as foreign and dangerous and thus participated in elections in order to keep the state away from themselves.

Conclusion

More recent studies are highlighting how new profitable economic opportunities are leading to a scramble for the available state resources and how 'caste and politics' are adapting to it. We learn that in the post-economic liberalisation era, 'dominant' castes are manipulating property markets for their own interest and accumulation projects (De Neve 2015). We also learn that businesses and politics (and hustling and muscle) are increasingly fusing in a mutual embrace (Berenschot 2011; Martin 2015a; Picherit 2015; Vaishnav 2011). Caste, kinship, dynastic politics and 'family parties/firms' are central to these political economies (Harriss-White 2003). Kinship ties, caste capital and the game of democracy are strategically deployed to mould the careers of ambitious entrepreneurial individuals. Becoming a politician entrepreneur has become a glamorous 'career path' for many young people (Michelutti et al. forthcoming.). Often individuals under the false impression of representing and settling scores of caste and faction are settling their personal scores (Kumar 2014: 10), and, in the process, some assemble personal fortunes and start building up their dynastic political turfs.

However, political economy is not the only engine behind new caste-family power configurations. Kinship inclusivity and simultaneous coercive power, both in their sacred and profane forms, are underpinning cultures of electoral representation and the ways castes (family/individual) rule de facto in their areas. The consecration of kin through *jatipuranas* (tales of caste origins) and the transformation of caste patron deities into political heroes have been singled out as an important aspect of the making of contemporary caste political order as well as legitimising powerful individuals.[12] Notions of divine kin(g)ship contribute to creating extraordinary 'politicians' and 'charismatic followers' by fashioning intimate links between them and their caste/community and kin. Ancestors, kings, gods, spirits and kin become part of a person's makeup (Michelutti 2014).

Over the past decades, such taxonomies of representation have also been in dialogue with the logics of Hindu nationalism, another by-product of democracy (Berti et al. 2011; Hansen 1999). Hindutva is promoting a form of Hinduism that aims to encompass castes as 'collective individuals'. Its ultimate goal is to create a homogeneous community of Hindus (and of Hindu gods) opposed to Muslims and other

---

[12] For Brahmins and Baniyas, see Babb (1999) and Gupta (2000); for Yadavs, see Michelutti (2008); for Marathas, see Hansen (2001).

religious communities (Fuller 1996: 24). The strengthening of Hindu communal identity—and the parallel substantialisation of Hinduism—can rightly be seen as part of the processes leading to the ethnicisation of caste.[13] Despite the fact that castes are becoming increasingly more internally differentiated in terms of class and status, and that religion-based politics is becoming stronger, caste (quasi-ethnic) boundaries are ultimately still maintained by endogamy. More specifically, the pollution barrier between 'clean-caste' communities and the former untouchables (generally called 'backward castes' or 'Scheduled Castes') is still strong.[14] Less clear is how processes of ethnicisation within 'clean' castes are intertwining with the making of a 'clean' category/community and how marriage alliances are contributing to it. Inter-caste marriages are often reported in urban contexts (Béteille 1996), but how frequent are such unions? As of today, there is no systematic study exploring such trends (Parry 2007). As a matter of fact, we know very little about processes of substantialisation of caste in the kinship domains as well as about the workings of kin(g)ship in its normative and sociological forms.[15] Most significantly, we have no systematic records of what is happening, for example, to hypergamy, to inheritance practices, to ideals of descent and how lineage and clan structures help to control territories and establish local 'territorial democracies' (Witsoe 2009). When they need information on the morphology of caste, contemporary scholars often have to look at the work of colonial ethnologists. This is quite remarkable, given the routinisation of dynastic politics in contemporary India democracy (see Chandra 2016). I suggest that it is precisely by studying how caste modes of relatedness are thinning or thickening and by mapping kinship (and personhood) normative foundations that we can understand what it means to say 'To rule people is in our blood'. Or to understand what the significance of wearing a Modi mask at a rally is. Or what the implications of saying 'My nose is Mulayam' are. A focus on how 'kinship is making politics' and 'how politics is making kinship' rather than on the technologies of

---

[13] Recently, the political scientist Chibber (2014) pointed out how close the relationship between religious practices and democracy is and how much 'caste religiosity' is indeed an integral part of this relationship.

[14] See Michelutti and Heath (2013); see also Bayly (1999), Osella and Osella (2000), Parry (2007) and Still (2014). Dalit studies have also become a field in itself.

[15] On the lack of interest in kinship studies in post-colonial India, see Kapila (2013). Noteworthy exceptions are Arumugam' (2015) work on Kallars' kinship polities, Piliavsky (2015) on Kanjars and Still (2014) on question of honour and patriarchy among Dalits.

democracy (see, e.g., Banerjee 2014; Pels 2007), or the gap between the promises and the on-the-ground achievements of democracy (cf. Paley 2002), has also the potential to advance a truly comparative anthropological study of democracy. Caste, ethnicity and indigeneity have become part of democratic experimentations which attempt to break vertical political pasts across the world. Much attention is devoted to how these groups are mobilised as electoral cleavages, but less is said about how their kin(g)ship polities shape the way they govern when they gain democratic sovereignty; how processes of 'vernacularisation of democracy' produce new hierarchies, inclusions and exclusions; and ultimately statements such as 'All of us are Presidents' in Bolivia or 'We are Chavez' in Venezuela' or 'I am Akhilesh' in UP.[16]

References

Appadurai, A. 1993. 'Numbers in the Colonial Imagination'. In *Orientalism and the Post-colonial Predicament*, edited by C.A. Breckenridge and P. van der Veer, 314–40. Philadelphia, PA: University of Pennsylvania Press.

Arumugam, I. 2015. '"The Old Gods Are Losing Power!" Theologies of Power and Rituals of Productivity in a Tamil Nadu Village'. *Modern Asian Studies* 49 (3): 753–86.

Babb, L.A. 1999. 'Mirrored Warriors: On the Cultural Identity of Rajasthan Traders'. *International Journal of Hindu Studies* 3 (1): 1–25.

Banerjee, M. 2014. *Why India Votes?* Delhi and London: Routledge.

Barnett, S.A. 1975. 'Approaches to Changes in Caste Ideology in South India'. In *Essays on South India*, edited by B. Stein, 149–80. Honolulu, HI: University Press of Hawaii.

Bayly, S. 1999. *Caste, Society and Politics in India: From the 18th Century to the Modern Age*. Cambridge: Cambridge University Press.

Berenschot, W. 2011. 'On the Usefulness of Goondas in Indian Politics: "Money Power" and "Muscle Power" in a Gujarati Locality'. *South Asia: Journal of South Asian Studies* 34 (2): 255–75.

Berti, D., N. Jaoul and P. Kanungo. 2011. *Cultural Entrenchment of Hindutva: Mediation and Resistance*. Delhi: Routledge.

Béteille, A. 1996. 'Caste in Contemporary India'. In *Caste Today*, edited by C.J. Fuller, 150–79. New Delhi: Oxford University Press.

Carsten, J. 2011. 'Substance and Relationality: Blood in Contexts'. *Annual Review of Anthropology* 40: 19–35.

---

[16] For Venezuela, see Michelutti (forthcoming); for Bolivia, see Grisaffi (2013); for Libya, see Cherstich (2014). Such a comparative approach will also help to break with a common Hindu-centric view of caste; on Pakistan, see Martin (2015b).

Chandra, K. 2016. *Democratic Dynasties: State, Party and Family in Contemporary Indian Politics*. New York: Cambridge University Press.

Cherstich, I. 2014. 'The Body of the Colonel: Caricature and Incarnation in the Libyan Revolution'. In *The Political Aesthetics of Global Protest: The Arab Spring and Beyond*, edited by P. Werbner, M. Webb and K. Spellman, 93–120. Edinburgh: University of Edinburgh Press.

Chibber, P. 2014. *Religious Practices and Democracy in India*. Delhi: Cambridge University Press.

Ciotti, M. 2006. 'In the Past We Were a Bit "Chamar": Education as a Self- and Community Engineering Process in Northern India'. *Journal of Royal Anthropological Institute* 12 (4): 899–916.

Comaroff, J. and J. Comaroff. 2006. *Law and Disorder in the Postcolony*. Chicago, IL: University of Chicago Press.

De Neve, G. 2015. 'Predatory Property: Urban Land Acquisition, Housing and Class Formation in Tiruppur, South India'. *Journal of South Asian Development* 10 (3): 345–68.

Dumont, Louis. 1980. *Homo Hierarchicus: The Caste System and Its Implications*. Chicago, IL: University of Chicago Press.

Forbess, A. and L. Michelutti. 2013. 'From the Mouth of God: Divine Kinship in Contemporary Popular Politics'. *Focaal—Journal of Historical and Global Anthropology* 67 (Winter): 3–18.

Fuller, C.J. 1996. 'Introduction'. In *Caste Today*, edited by C.J. Fuller, 1–30. New Delhi: Oxford University Press.

Ghurye, G.S. 1932. *Caste and Race in India*. London: Kegan Paul.

Gorringe, H. 2010. 'The New Caste Headmen? Dalit Movement Leadership in Tamil Nadu'. In *Power and Influence in India*, edited by P. Price and A.E. Ruud, 119–42. New Delhi: Routledge India.

Grisaffi, T. 2013. '"All of Us Are Presidents": Radical Democracy and Citizenship in the Chapare Province, Bolivia'. *Critique of Anthropology* 33 (1): 47–65.

Guha, S. 2013. *Beyond Caste: Identity and Power in South Asia, Past and Present*. Boston: Brill.

Gupta, D. 2000. *Interrogating Caste*. New Delhi: Penguin.

Hansen, T.B. 1999. *The Saffron Wave: Democracy and Hindu Nationalism in Modern India*. Princeton, NJ: Princeton University Press.

———. 2001. *Wages of Violence: Naming and Identity in Postcolonial Bombay*. Princeton, NJ and Oxford: Princeton University Press.

Hansen, T.B. and F. Stepputat, eds. 2005. *Sovereign Bodies: Citizens, Migrants, and States in the Postcolonial World*. Princeton, NJ: Princeton University Press.

Harriss-White, B. 2003. *India Working: Essays on Society and Economy*. Cambridge: Cambridge University Press.

Jaffrelot, C. 2015. 'The Class Element in the 2014 Indian Election and the BJP's Success with Special Reference to the Hindi Belt'. *Studies in Indian Politics* 3 (1): 19–38.

Jeffrey, C., P. Jeffery and R. Jeffery, eds. 2008. *Degrees Without Freedom? Education, Masculinities and Unemployment in North India.* Stanford, CA: Stanford University Press.

Jodhka, S. 2006. 'Caste and Democracy: Assertion and Identity Among the Dalits of Rural Punjab'. *Sociological Bulletin* 55 (1, January–April): 4–23.

Kapila, K. 2013. '...In South Asia: Comment on Sahlins, Marshall. 2013. What Kinship Is—and Is Not. Chicago: University of Chicago Press'. *HAU: Journal of Ethnographic Theory* 3 (2): 299–304.

Kothari, R. 1970. 'Introduction'. In *Caste in Indian Politics*, edited by R. Kothari, 3–28. New Delhi: Orient Longman.

Kumar, A. 2014. *Criminalisation of Politics.* Delhi: Rawat Publications.

Laclau, E. 2005. *On Populist Reason.* London: Verso Books.

Martin, N. 2015a. 'Rural Elites and the Limits of Scheduled Caste Assertiveness in Rural Malwa, Punjab'. *Economic & Political Weekly*, 50 (52): 37–52.

———. 2015b. *Politics, Landlords and Islam in Pakistan.* Delhi and London: Routledge.

Mayer, A.C. 1996. 'Caste in an Indian Village: Change and Continuity 1954–1992'. In *Caste Today*, edited by C.J. Fuller, 32–64. New Delhi: Oxford University Press.

Michelutti, L. 2004. '"We (Yadavs) Are a Caste of Politicians": Caste and Modern Politics in a North Indian Town'. *Contributions to Indian Sociology* 38 (1): 43–71.

———. 2008. *The Vernacularisation of Democracy.* Delhi and London: Routledge.

———. 2013. 'Sons of Krishna and Sons of Bolivar: Charismatic Kinship and Leadership Across India and Venezuela'. *Focaal: Journal of Global and Historical Anthropology* 2013 (67, Winter): 19–31.

———. 2014. 'Kingship Without Kings'. In *Patronage as Politics in South Asia*, edited by A. Piliavsky. Cambridge: Cambridge University Press.

———. Forthcoming. '"We Are All Chávez": Charisma as an Embodied Experience'. *Journal of Latin American Perspective* 44 (1): 232–50.

Michelutti, L., H. Ashraf, N. Martin, D. Picherit, P. Rollier, A. Ruud and C. Still. forthcoming. *Mafia Raj: The Rule of Bosses in South Asia* (unpublished manuscript). Standford: Standford University Press.

Michelutti, L. and O. Heath. 2013. 'The Politics of Entitlement: Affirmative Action and Strategic Voting in Uttar Pradesh, India'. *Focaal: Journal of Global and Historical Anthropology* 2013 (65): 56–67.

Osella, C. and F. Osella. 2000. *Social Mobility in Kerala: Modernity and Identity in Conflict.* London: Pluto Press.

Paley, J. 2002. 'Towards an Anthropology of Democracy'. *Annual Review of Anthropology* 31: 469–97.

Parry, J.P. 1989. 'The End of the Body'. In *Fragments of History of the Human Body*, edited by M. Feher, R. Naddaff and N. Tazi, 491–517. New York, NY: Urzone.

Parry, J.P. 2007. 'A Note on the "Substantialisation" of Caste and Its Hegemony'. In *Political and Social Transformations in North India and Nepal*, edited by I. Hiroshi and D. Gellner, 479–95. Delhi: Manohar Publishers.

Pels, Peter. 2007. 'Imagining Elections: Modernity, Mediation and the Secret Ballot in Late Colonial Tanganyika'. In *Cultures of Voting: The Hidden History of the Secret Ballot*, edited by Romain Bertrand, Peter Pels and Jean Louis Briquet, 100–13. London: Hurst; Bloomington, IN: Indiana University Press.

Picherit, D. 2015. 'Dalit Mobilisation and Faction Politics in Rural Andhra Pradesh: Everyday Life of a Dalit NGO and Agricultural Labour Union'. *Economic & Political Weekly* 50 (52): 74–82.

Piliavsky, A. 2015. 'Patronage and Community in a Society of Thieves'. *Contributions to Indian Sociology* 49 (2): 135–61.

Price, P.G. 1989. 'Kingly Models in Indian Political Behaviour: Culture as a Medium for History'. *Asian Survey* 29 (6): 559–72.

Quigley, D. 2005. *The Character of Kingship*. Oxford: Berg.

Rudolph L.I. and S.H. Rudolph. 1967. *The Modernity of Tradition*. New Delhi: Oxford University Press.

Ruud, A.E. 2003. *Poetics of Village Politics: The Making of West Bengal's Communism*. New Delhi: Oxford University Press.

Ruud, A.E. and G. Heirstad. 2016. *On the Diversity of India's Democracies*. Available at: https://www.idunn.no/file/pdf/66855034/1-on-the-diversity-of-indias-democracies.pdf (accessed on 1 May 2016).

Sahlins, M. 2013. What Kinship Is—and Is Not. Chicago, IL: University of Chicago Press.

Searle-Chatterjee, M. and U.M. Sharma. 1994. 'Introduction'. In *Contextualising Caste: Post-Dumontian Approaches*, edited by M. Searle-Chatterjee and U.M. Sharma, 1–24. Oxford: Blackwell Publishers.

Shah, A. 2007. '"Keeping the State Away": Democracy, Politics and the State in India's Jharkhand'. *Journal of the Royal Anthropological Institute*, n.s., 13 (1): 129–45.

Shah, A. and S. Shneiderman. 2013. 'Towards an Anthropology of Affirmative Action'. Special issue, *Focaal: Journal of Global and Historical Anthropology* 2013 (65, Spring).

Spencer, J. 1997. 'Post-Colonialism and the Political Imagination'. *The Journal of the Royal Anthropological Institute* 3 (1): 1–19.

———. 2003. 'Appalling Fascination: The Emerging Anthropology of "the Political" in Postcolonial South Asia'. *Journal des anthropologue* (92–93): 31–49.

———. 2007. *Anthropology, Politics and the State: Democracy and Violence in South Asia*. Cambridge: Cambridge University Press.

Srinivas, M.N. 1962. *Caste in Modern India and Other Essays*. London: JK Publishers.

Srinivas, M.S. 1959. 'The Dominant Caste in Rampura'. *American Anthropologist* 61 (1): 1–16.

Still, C. 2014. *Dalit Women: Honour and Patriarchy in South India*. Delhi: Social Science Press.

Vaishnav, M. 2017. *When Crime Pays: Money and Muscle in Indian Politics*. Yale: Yale University Press.

Verniers, G. 2013. 'The Root of the Goonda Raj: Why There Is So Much Violence in Uttar Pradesh'. *Daily Brief*, June 7. https://scroll.in/article/666450/the-roots-of-goonda-raj-why-theres-so-much-violence-in-uttar-pradesh (accessed on 24 August 2018).

Yadav, Y. 1997. 'Reconfiguration in Indian Politics: State Assembly Elections 1993–1995'. In *State and Politics in India*, edited by P. Chatterjee, 117–207. New Delhi: Oxford University Press.

15

'The Middle Class' and the Middle Classes

Raka Ray

Introduction

If there is a shared understanding among the many scholars and commentators who have written extensively about the middle class, it is that the middle class is a notoriously elusive concept. Yet its elusiveness has not prevented scholars from trying to pin it down. While there is a long history of attempts to analyse this class, it has been investigated and celebrated with particular interest in the last two decades by international development institutions. In these years, a new middle class is seen to have emerged, particularly in the Global South, and a plethora of studies illustrates how this 'new middle class' is understood, produced, and maintained. In India, the issue acquired a certain urgency after 1991, a year that was seen as marking 'an epochal shift' (Gooptu 2013) in the economy, after which the 'new middle class' was seen to have emerged. In this essay, I first present influential theories of the middle class that emerged in the West, then analyse scholarship about the old and new middle classes in India, and suggest that we consider this class which is seen as both elite and everyman (Baviskar and Ray 2011), in the singular as well as the plural. The singular refers to the idea of the middle class, which reflects thinking about the dominant fraction of this class; the plural refers to the emergent middle classes, which reflect a far wider range of practices than do the dominant ideas of the role of this class in Indian economic, civic, social and political life.

I begin with two strands of European thinking about the middle class because they have, in many ways, set the stage for subsequent thinking about this class, despite the varied conditions of its emergence. The first strand I consider is Marxist. In Marx's historical explanation for the development of capitalism in Europe, the bourgeoisie was a revolutionary class which transformed the economic processes and structure of society, and reshaped its politics and the structure of its values. But while the dominant section of the bourgeoisie would become the ruling class within capitalism, the lower strata of this group—the small tradespeople, shopkeepers and retired tradesmen generally—would sink gradually into the proletariat. He did not expect these segments to be revolutionary. The Marxist tradition was rich in debate, immersed as it was in the immediate experience of the growth of white-collar occupations in Europe. Thus, Karl Kautsky and Eduard Bernstein debated whether white-collar workers were objectively or (merely) subjectively separate from the working classes. Later, Harry Braverman and Nicos Poulantzas discussed the question of their possible proletarianisation. Adding the possession of authority and skills to possession of the means of production into the mix, Erik Olin Wright (1985) argued that the middle class must be thought to occupy a contradictory class position, while Alvin Gouldner saw in the technical intelligentsia and bureaucrats a future universal class, flawed in its politics—both potentially progressive and anti-democratic.

The second strand of European thought comes from French writer Alexis de Tocqueville, visiting America in the 19th century, who claimed that the strength of America's democracy lay in its middle class—the 'countless multitude of almost identical men, neither exactly rich nor poor, [who] own sufficient property to desire order but not enough to arouse the envy of others' (Tocqueville 2003 [1904]: 738). These men—and, for Tocqueville, they were specifically men of European ancestry—had a 'natural horror' of revolutions. The link between the middle class and democracy was re-asserted by Seymour Martin Lipset (1959), who believed that a middle class created both a more engaged citizenry and greater moderation (Baviskar and Ray 2011, 3). While these theories form the bedrock of our understanding about the middle class, it is important to consider that they emerged within certain material and cultural contexts in mid- to late 19th-century Europe, and subsequently in the political anxieties of mid-20th-century America. Underlying these debates lay two questions that have haunted our engagement with the middle class ever since: the first was the difference between the objective and subjective experience of middle class-ness, and the second, anxiety about the politics of the class.

While the middle class was, by and large, ignored in classical Indian Marxist traditions, historians such as Sumit Sarkar (1989) and Dipesh Chakrabarty (2000) and, more recently, Sanjay Joshi (2001), have described the Indian middle class as one that was brought into being by colonialism and by the anti-colonial struggle. The Bengali bhadralok came to stand in for that class, an administrative class, upper caste in origin, which understood itself as middle class and situated itself above those who worked with their hands and below the aristocracy of *dewans* and *banians* (Sarkar 1997). This was also a middle class with gendered concerns about respectability that lay at its nationalist core (Sangari 2002; Sarkar 2001). Jaffrelot and van der Veer (2008: 16) suggest that there were two wings to the early Indian middle class—a traditional petty bourgeoisie and a reformist intelligentsia, the latter a consequence of colonialism—but that they were both rooted in the upper castes.

While the traditional petty bourgeoisie has received less attention, what is now called the 'old middle class' in India is thought of as the nationalist vanguard, which William Mazzarella (2005) aptly describes as 'a Nehruvian civil service-oriented salariat, short on money but long on institutional perks'. It can be thought of as a public-sector middle class of the state managers and bureaucrats who had their origins in the colonial civil service. The state's investment in higher education and the massive expansion of the public sector in post-independence India served to consolidate its social base (Rudolph and Rudolph 1987). In contrast to this nationalist middle class, the 'new' middle class in the post-1991 liberalisation period—a class celebrated in the media and business as the newly aspirational middle class—forms the crux of scholarly attention and anxiety (Baviskar and Ray 2011). Members of this class are, according to Leela Fernandes (2006: 90), associated 'in structural terms with the expanded "new economy" service sectors and private sector professional workforces'. While the literature suggests that the new middle class derives its power not from the state but from the market, it is important to acknowledge the important role the state has played in enabling its creation, nurturing its existence, and promoting its agenda.

Debates about the size of the middle class formed the first focus of enquiry, perhaps because the initial interest in this class was market driven. The *India Market Demographics Report* by the National Council for Applied Economic Research (Rao 1994) sparked a fever of speculation, financial as well as intellectual, about the 'strength' of this class, as measured by its capacity to consume (Sridharan 2004). Combining a Tocquevillian faith in a middle class as important because it would lead by example, inculcate civic and democratic values, and create a new non-corrupt politics, with the economically freed entrepreneurial subject who would innovate and boost economic growth leading India closer to being a world power (Gooptu 2013), the first examinations of the post-1991 middle class were media driven and somewhat euphoric. For World Bank economist Martin Ravallion (2010: 445), the class was seen as 'important to economic development, such as through fostering entrepreneurship, shifting the composition of consumer demand, and making it more politically feasible to attain policy reforms and to implement institutional changes and public investments conducive to growth'. In India, commentator and political analyst Sanjaya Baru (2006) declared:

> From taking the lead in the national movement and heading powerful institutions of governance, to creating world-class higher education and research institutions and nurturing among the best and brightest in the corporate and financial sectors, the Indian middle class has been a powerhouse of talent and enterprise for the greater part of this century.

As the special issue of the RUPE (2014) sourly observes of, especially, the studies done by economists, '[w]ith very few exceptions, these studies find much to like about the middle class'.

At the same time, the consumption practices of this class made many nervous. Thus, scholars such as Pavan Varma (1998) and Dipankar Gupta (2000) condemned this class for its love of privilege and its weak commitment to democracy. This was swiftly followed by a scholarship that began to raise some fundamental questions about this new middle class: Who are they? What forms of labour do they do? What are their consumption patterns, their morality, familial relations, sociability and politics? What, ultimately, are the analytical and political consequences of the rise of the middle class in nations marked by such inequality as India?

The Objective and the Subjective Middle Class

Despite clear indications of the inadequacy, and contradictory nature, of most counts, the attempt to quantify this class has proven to be irresistible. Considering the Indian middle class in global terms, Ravallion (2010), and Banerjee and Duflo (2008), among others, suggest that the income range for the Indian middle class is about $2 (purchasing power parity or PPP) and above. By those estimates, the middle class is quite vast. Others put it at $10 PPP and higher, and by that estimate, the middle class is no more than 6 per cent of the population (RUPE 2014). The latest figures shift away from the early exaggerated expectations of booming numbers to a more sober understanding as reflected, for example, in the recent Pew Research Study (which uses the figure of $10–20 a day), which shows that China saw its middle-income proportion go up from 3 per cent in 2001 to 18 per cent in 2011. By that measure, India's middle-income population stands at 3 per cent today.[1] Other studies argue that assets, not income, are a better indicator of middle class-ness, since assets are not susceptible to seasonal fluctuation, and since so few in India actually receive monthly salaries. Anirudh Krishna and Devendra Bajpai (2015) use two-wheelers and cars as their markers and, by those parameters, the share of the middle class rose from 11 per cent of the Indian population in 1992–93 to 22 per cent in 2005–06. Despite the increase in numbers, the predictions that these numbers would increase exponentially, and the disappointments when those figures did not materialise, what must be understood is that the Indian middle class is not technically in the middle of the class spectrum, which stems, as Satish Deshpande (2003) has argued, from extreme income—and other—inequalities.

Setting aside the issue of actual numbers, Devesh Kapur and Milan Vaishnav (2015) show, through their multi-year panel survey by the Centre for Advanced Study of India, that about half the Indians in practically any bracket—urban, rural, lowest-income, highest-income—self-identify as middle class. Similarly, Dickey (2012: 573) found, over a decade and a half of working in Madurai, that a far wider range of people 'from autorickshaw drivers, masons, and occasionally cooks; to small business owners and merchants, office clerks, and teachers; to bureaucrats, doctors, lawyers, and academics from colleges or university faculties', all identified as middle class as opposed to as 'rich' or 'poor'. And yet, she noted, the precariousness of their class position also caused great anxieties. Much of the sociological and anthropological literature on the middle class has focused on the issue of identification, and on the practices that make the middle classes so. Many have come to believe that the idea of the middle class is more important than the actual parameters of the class itself. In Mazzarella's (2005) words, it

---

[1] The Pew Research Study uses the following system of classification: the poor (who live on $2 or less daily), low income ($2.01–10), middle income ($10.01–20), upper-middle income ($20.01–50) and high income (more than $50). Pew, thus, defines the middle class as ranging between $10 and $50 a day.

may be a 'questionable empirical entity', but it is most decidedly one to be reckoned with.

The Idea of the Middle Class Versus the Middle Classes

The importance of the idea of the middle class to the Indian nation is perhaps the one area of agreement in the scholarship on the middle class. Baviskar and Ray (2011: 5) cite Prime Minister Nehru's reference to himself as middle class, and argue that when he did so, 'he was being neither modest nor disingenuous' since he was invoking a certain mindset. For Nehru, and for many others of the class that followed him, middle class-ness implied a certain orientation towards modernity that involved being open-minded, embracing law and science, and setting aside the primordial loyalties of caste and kinship. If, as Sanjay Joshi (2012) argues, the creation of the middle class in India was a cultural project, then the culmination of this project is the idea of 'the Indian Middle Class' as a class destined to lift India to its rightful place in the world.[2] It is an idea that has required careful production, nurturing, protection and diffusion. The idea of the Middle Class is normative rather than representative, and claims to represent a populace far larger than it actually does.

In an essay of major importance, Satish Deshpande (2003: 139) divides the Indian middle classes into an elite fraction, which produces ideologies, and a mass fraction, which consumes them. He argues that the power of the Middle Class resides in its claim of representing all Indians—the *aam aadmi*—and that the category 'middle class' conjured up a universal, unifying identity that summoned legitimacy for projects that actually favoured elites in the nation. By claiming to speak for the nation, he argues, this category performs the cultural task of concealing inequality. The 'middle class is the class that articulates the hegemony of the ruling bloc' (Deshpande 2003: 139). In a democracy, the cultural reproduction of inequality requires a public discourse of equality. The task of maintaining this paradox is accomplished by the idea of the Middle Class—a class which speaks on behalf of all others. Political scientist Yogendra Yadav suggests that the Indian Middle Class is not to be thought of as a sociological category at all, but rather as a proper

---

[2] In the rest of the essay, when I capitalise the term middle class, I refer to the idea of the Middle Class to distinguish the term from the actual lives and practices of the middle classes.

noun. It is, he claimed, the term the Indian ruling class prefers to call itself. Salim Lakha (1999: 253) simply posits that 'the Middle Class' is the new rich who represent themselves as middle class.

This elite, masquerading as the Middle Class, then, demonstrates through its politics and its practices of consumption and work that it stands for the nation, or at least what the nation should be. Thus, essays in various anthologies on the middle classes (Baviskar and Ray 2011; Heimann et al. 2012; Jaffrelot and van der Veer 2008; Lobo and Shah 2015) refer to its practices of distinction and gate-keeping, and call attention to practices of consumption that mark its social identity as distinct from the middle class of the past and from the lower classes of the present (see Bourdieu 1987; Sheth 1999) while also signifying solidarity with 'people like us'. Work on consumption (Lakha 1999; Mankekar 1999; Rajagopal 1999), newly privatised spaces (Fernandes 2006; Srivastava 2012), spirituality (Gooptu 2013; Upadhya 2013), the home (Ray and Qayum 2009) and gender (Oza 2006), have critically evaluated and linked the practices of consumption and expression of this class with a complex, and contradictory, relationship to economic liberalisation, as well as to the nation.

Popular representations of new middle-class work also highlight the idea of the Middle Class, largely focusing on new forms of labour in IT and the knowledge economy as the emblematic representative of the new economy and the new middle class (Singh 2003). Carol Upadhya, a pioneer in this field, notes that while the industry is actually very small, its discursive and structural role is far larger. It represents not only a new industry but also the possibility of bringing into being a new India. To that effect, IT workplaces may feature new skills (soft skills) and new management practices (learned from the Art of Living), intent on creating a new working ethos (Upadhya 2011, 2013; Upadhya and Vasavi 2006). Scholarly work on the gendered nature of this class of IT workers highlights the ways in which upper-middle-class women manage conflicting calls to simultaneously represent the modern India of the future and be appropriately domestic. Fuller and Narasimhan's (2007) study of largely upper-caste 'new rich middle class' women in the IT industry finds women who are less ambitious than men because of their household responsibilities, but who insist that both genders are treated equally and perceived equally by management. Smitha Radhakrishnan's (2011) study of women in the IT industry in both Mumbai and Chennai reveals a group of women who see themselves as standard bearers of Indian womanhood, having succeeded in the world of work without sacrificing their families.

Beyond the world of work, given the centrality of gender to the nationalist Middle-class imaginary, how do we understand gender and the idea of the Middle Class today? Rupal Oza (2006) and Purnima Mankekar (1999) describe middle class women's consumption of representations of womanhood in the media in ways that, by and large, place the notion of women's education, upward mobility and independence within an overall narrative of familial and nationalist loyalties, while Jyoti Puri's (1999) study of urban middle-class sexuality also highlights the regulation of middle-class (and upper-class) women's bodies and desires in keeping with larger national narratives of Indian cultural identity. Bhatt, Murty and Ramamurthy (2010) find aggressive, confident, urban women who emerge as heroines in a range of television serials but who are eventually domesticated by social codes of heteronormative patriarchy and, in Purnima Mankekar's words, 'discourses of citizenship that enable "emancipated" Indian women to negotiate both "the home" and "the world"' (Mankekar 1999: 148, cited in Bhatt et al. 2010: 131).

The politics of this class is exclusionary. Recent elections, as well as survey data on middle-class voting preferences, reveal a picture not of a class that protects democracy but of a group zealous in protecting upper-caste privilege and more recently, in promoting Hindu nationalism, a politics that simultaneously embraces economic liberalisation and conservative values. This follows a long tradition of Indian politics, which, as historian Sanjay Joshi (2001), writing about the historical creation of the Indian middle class in UP, pointed out, has been able to simultaneously use reason *and* sentiment, call for radical change and the preservation of tradition, and advocate liberty *and* authoritarianism.

As the Mandal protests of 1990 revealed, this Middle Class came to see that its interests were being ill-served by increased democratisation. With the ascendancy of middle and backward castes in politics, politics came to be seen as a space of profanity (Hansen 1999). Fernandes and Heller (2006: 498) argue that Hindutva ideology's doctrines of nationalism and cultural essentialism provided an 'ideological frame for [new middle class] self-assertion as well as a political response to newly mobilized lower class constituencies and their varied claims for incorporation'. Amita Baviskar (2011) points to distinctive middle-class modes of mobilisation, showing how it prefers to channel causes through the courts and media, framing its causes as matters of 'public interest'. Sanjay Srivastava's work shows how, together with the new malls and highways, Delhi's Akshardham temple produces a space within contemporary modernity where the 'moral' middle class can display its mastery over consumption. In addition to controlling space, this class also reveals its politics through the control of culture (Srivastava 2012). William Mazzarella's (2013) work on censorship in Indian cinema reveals how the film censor board considers 'the masses' to be politically immature and sexually repressed and to require censorship to be protected from themselves.

Anna Hazare's cry against corruption at a moment when the government was mired in corruption scandals, and the brief (though heightened) moment of its popularity, emblematises the politics of this class. Khandekar and Reddy (2015) astutely suggest that this new middle class 'discursively constituted' and legitimised itself through this movement. In Vinay Sitapati's (2011) analysis, the new private sector-based, nationalist, post-1991 middle class believers in India Shining formed a core of the supporters of this movement. Indeed, the use of terms such as 'branding' and 'Team Anna' speaks to the elite nature of the class involved.

In sum, the scholarship on 'the Middle Class' critically evaluates this fraction, disputing its progressive role in political life and arguing that the cultural dominance of this group has resulted in the reproduction, not amelioration, of inequality (Deshpande 2003; Fernandes 2006). Yet the desire to be middle class, to belong properly to this superior social group, is also a powerful aspiration among excluded social groups. While the study of these groups was neglected in the past, recent scholarship has turned its attention to new and marginalised entrants to this class.

Conclusion: The Middle Classes

The newest and most promising work attends to sections of the emerging middle classes, those who fall outside of the 'idea of the middle class' but who increasingly claim ownership over the term. I refer to these groups as 'the middle classes' as opposed to 'the Middle class' or 'the idea of the Middle class' (Ray 2011). As skilled manual workers in public-sector firms begin to earn incomes that may put them in the middle class, and some Other Backward Caste (OBC) households and rural households experience an increase in their earnings, while subcontracted service sector workers may earn below the poverty line, the boundaries of middle class-ness are increasingly blurred. Despite a Centre for the Study of Developing Societies (CSDS) survey that indicated that while upper castes accounted for a quarter of the sample, they represented half of the 'new' middle class (Jaffrelot and van der Veer 2008: 22), it is clear that new groups are entering at least the lower sections of the middle class and that their voices are now being heard. In this final section, I discuss the work of scholars who explore these marginal middle classes. How, against the idea of the Middle Class, do the broader spectrum of the middle classes perceive themselves, and make decisions about themselves and their children? How do they labour? What are their anxieties as they aspire towards the idea of the Middle Class?

In general, scholars rely primarily on practices of consumption to elaborate the ways in which new, marginal or lower-middle-class actors aspire to hegemonic middle class-ness. The issue of the subjective versus objective middle class especially prevails in these studies. In her work on emerging middle classes in Madurai, Sara Dickey (2012) refers to them as 'people who call themselves "middle class"', and who differentiate themselves carefully from both wealth and subsistence, and insist on a certain morality—the ability to consume with moderation. These are clearly not the people Krishna and Bajpai (2015) envisioned in their analysis, for Dickey's subjects consider ownership of a car to be an upper-class phenomenon. This is a class which sees its middle class-ness as hard-won and tenuous, and whose anxieties about downward mobility are very high.

Ruchira Ganguly-Scrase and Timothy Scrase's (2009) work also showcases a small-town middle class (in Siliguri) which has far less faith in privatisation than 'the middle class' does, and which echoes the anxieties about decline that Dickey's respondents do. Nita Kumar (2011) and Sancho (2013) describe the anxious compulsions of the lower middle class to afford private tuitions and entrance-exam coaching classes for their children, since educational success is still seen as holding the key to upward mobility. Ritty Lukose (2009) looks at the complex paths woven by non-elite, college-attending youth in Kerala in whose future may lie in migration to the Gulf, but not to the West, and where failure is a more likely outcome than success. Work by Jeffery et al. (2011) highlights the problems faced by rural rich Jats who are trying to ease their way into the middle class, which in their imaginary can only be achieved through being urban. Craig Jeffrey's (2010) monograph, *Timepass*, showcases educated yet unemployed young Jat men who cannot be independent, or marry, lack the means to achieve the norms of acceptable masculinity in society, and are reduced, after deepening their efforts to educate themselves further and expand their social networks, to waiting. Important in this context is that for these young Jats, the globalised middle class was not their aspirational model. They distinguished themselves from the upper middle class and sought to build their strength locally. Van Wessel (2004: 110) too found a similar sentiment among the middle classes of

Baroda, who do not have a global or national imaginary in their minds (as other scholars may have predicted) but, rather, are focused on their families, on themselves, and on other people in their social strata. Minna Säävälä's (2001) work on upwardly mobile members of the Dalit Mala caste shows how they reinterpret Hinduism to focus on auspiciousness, rather than on purity and pollution, as they try to establish themselves as middle-class urban dwellers.

On the other end of the financial spectrum are the entrepreneurial Muslims of Kozhikode studied by Filippo Osella and Caroline Osella (2009, 2011). I include them in this section because even as they strive to recreate themselves as newly modern Muslims, shifting away from bazaar culture towards different forms of capital accumulation, to create a new moral self of 'individual responsibility, energetic activity, and self advancement' (Osella and Osella 2009: S215) through a combination of neoliberal and reformist Islamic orientations towards community and self-improvement, they cannot form part of the hegemonic fraction of the Middle Class which remains upper caste and Hindu in its ideological orientation.

Gendered analyses of these classes reveal a range of promises, continuities and contradictions in the gendered order. Ravinder Kaur (2014) suggests that the emerging (or lowest) end of this sector, which is potentially the largest segment of the middle class, limits its family size, has a preference for no daughters and avidly practices sex selection. Ganguly-Scrase (2003) shows a complex trade-off such that even as lower-middle-class women see liberalisation as affording more freedom in the form of employment and education opportunities, they also see that their household costs are rising and state support falling. Ritty Lukose (2009) finds that anxieties about globalisation in non-metropolitan Kerala are, in a manner consistent with the gaze on women's bodies through the nationalist and post-independence periods, once again expressed through anxieties about women's bodies, while Caroline Osella's (2012: 256) work on Muslim women in Kerala shows how young women borrow ideas about family and leisure from TV, films and the Gulf while carefully monitoring 'for excess'.

The idea of the Middle Class tries to bring the middle classes into its ambit in a controlled way. Young lower-middle-class people from small towns are thus represented as potential carriers of India's new entrepreneurial spirit, at least in films (see Mankekar's 2013 analysis of the film *Band Baaja Baaraat*). In terms of the labour market, as several essays in Nandini Gooptu's (2013) anthology show, the National Skill Development Corporation aims to harness that entrepreneurial spirit and to give these young people the skills the Indian economy needs. Aimed towards the lower end of the private sector, the scheme, financed by the government, has led to thousands of 'skill' development centres around the country which provide, at a cost, training programmes to youth. In addition to this training, personality development courses are taken by small-town youth who do not feel 'up to the mark' compared to their equivalents in the metros (McGuire 2013).

As against the civic orientation of the Middle Class, the political practices of the middle classes are wide-ranging. Kamath and Vijayabaskar (2009) turn their attention to Resident Welfare Associations (RWAs), which have traditionally been studied as an elite form of engagement. They find that upwardly mobile trader RWAs clash with the spatial demands of elite RWAs, and favour working with the local state far more than do elite RWAs. Wood's (2013) analysis of middle-class protest in Varanasi finds that traders are the group most likely to engage in disruptive contentious protest in the face of an unresponsive state. As opposed to the move away from politics, Christopher Jaffrelot (2008: 50–51) finds a Dalit middle class in which people do vote and deeply appreciate the empowering potential of democracy. At the moment of this writing, thousands of people were attending a protest rally in Gujarat in support of Hardik Patel's movement to recognise Patels as OBCs in order for the community to gain jobs and placement in government institutions and colleges. The aspirations of these new classes are, thus, strongly linked to the state.

While much more work needs to be done on these marginal and new entrants to the middle class who form, indeed, the bulk of the class, we do know that the entry of these groups has challenged and transformed, at least in part, the understanding of the middle classes in India. These studies make evident that some of the power of the idea of the Middle Class will crumble in the face of the many aspirational groups of OBC, BC, Muslim (and others) who now demand recognition for their middle class-ness. The world of the post-liberalisation, post-colonial, middle classes is infinitely more complex than the story of the Indian Middle Class, both in its subjective identifications and in its politics.

References

Banerjee, A.V. and E. Duflo. 2008. 'What Is Middle Class About the Middle Classes Around the World?' *Journal of Economic Perspectives* 22 (2): 3–28.
Baru, S. 2006. *Strategic Consequences of India's Economic Performance*. New Delhi: Academic Foundation Press.

Baviskar, A. 2011. 'Cows, Cars and Cycle-rickshaws: Bourgeois Environmentalism and the Battle for Delhi's Streets'. In *Elite and Everyman: The Cultural Politics of the Indian Middle Classes*, edited by Amita Baviskar and Raka Ray, 1–23. New Delhi: Routledge.

Baviskar, Amita and Raka Ray, eds. 2011. *Elite and Everyman: The Cultural Politics of the Indian Middle Classes*. New Delhi: Routledge.

Bhatt, A., Madhavi Murty and Priti Ramamurthy. 2010. 'Hegemonic Developments: The New Indian Middle Class, Gendered Subalterns, and Diasporic Returnees in the Event of Neoliberalism'. *Signs* 36 (1): 127–52.

Bourdieu, P. 1987. *Distinction: A Social Critique of the Judgement of Taste*. Boston, MA: Harvard University Press.

Chakrabarty, D. 2000. *Provincializing Europe: Postcolonial Thought and Historical Difference*. Princeton, NJ: Princeton University Press.

Deshpande, S. 2003. *Contemporary India: A Sociological View*. New Delhi: Penguin Books.

Dickey, S. 2012. 'The Pleasures and Anxieties of Being in the Middle: Emerging Middle-class Identities in Urban South India'. *Modern Asian Studies* 46 (3): 559–99.

Fernandes, L. 2006. *India's New Middle Class: Democratic Politics in an Era of Economic Reform*. Minneapolis, MN: University of Minnesota Press.

Fernandes, L. and Patrick Heller. 2006. 'Hegemonic Aspirations: New Middle Class Politics and India's Democracy in Comparative Perspective'. *Critical Asian Studies* 38 (4): 495–522.

Fuller, C.J. and Harapriya Narasimhan. 2007. 'Information Technology Professionals and the New-rich Middle Class in Chennai (Madras)'. *Modern Asian Studies* 41 (1): 121–50.

Ganguly-Scrase, R. 2003. 'Paradoxes of Globalization, Liberalization, and Gender Equality: The Worldviews of the Lower Middle Class in West Bengal, India'. *Gender and Society* 17 (4): 544–66.

Ganguly-Scrase, R. and Tim Scrase. 2009. *Globalisation and the Middle Classes in India*. New Delhi: Routledge.

Gooptu, N., ed. 2013. *Enterprise Culture in Neoliberal India: Studies in Youth, Class, Work and Media*. London and New York, NY: Routledge.

Gupta, D. 2000. *Mistaken Modernity: India Between Worlds*. New Delhi: HarperCollins Publishers.

Hansen, T.B. 1999. *The Saffron Wave: Democracy and Hindu Nationalism in Modern India*. Princeton, NJ: Princeton University Press.

Heiman, R., Carla Freeman and Mark Liechty, eds. 2012. *The Global Middle Classes: Theorizing Through Ethnography*, 57–84. Santa Fe, NM: School for Advanced Research Press.

Jaffrelot, C. 2008. 'Why Should We Vote?' The Indian Middle Class and the Functioning of the World's Largest Democracy'. In *Patterns of Middle Class Consumption in India and China*, edited by C. Jaffrelot and Peter van der Veer, 35–54. New Delhi: SAGE.

Jaffrelot, C. and Peter van der Veer, eds. 2008. *Patterns of Middle Class Consumption in India and China*. New Delhi: SAGE.

Jeffrey, C. 2010. *Timepass: Youth, Class and the Politics of Waiting in India.* Stanford, CA: Stanford University Press.

Jeffery, R., Patricia Jeffery and Craig Jeffrey. 2011. 'Are Rich Rural Jats Middle-class?' In *Elite and Everyman: The Cultural Politics of the Indian Middle Classes*, edited by A. Baviskar and R. Ray, 140–63. New Delhi: Routledge.

Joshi, S. 2001. *Fractured Modernity: Making of a Middle Class in Colonial North India.* New Delhi: Oxford University Press.

———. 2010. *The Middle Class in Colonial India.* New Delhi: Oxford University Press.

Kamath, L. and M. Vijayabaskar. 2009. 'Limits and Possibilities of Middle Class Associations as Urban Collective Actors'. *Economic & Political Weekly* 44 (26/27): 368–76.

Kapur, D. and Milan Vaishnav. 2015. 'Being Middle Class in India', *The Hindu*, 10 January.

Kaur, R. 2014. 'The "Emerging" Middle Class'. *Economic & Political Weekly* 49 (26/27): 15–19.

Khandekar, A. and Deepa Reddy. 2015. 'An Indian Summer: Corruption, Class, and the Lokpal Protests'. *Journal of Consumer Culture* 15 (2): 221–47.

Krishna, A. and Devendra Bajpai. 2015. 'Layers in Globalising Society and the New Middle Class in India'. *Economic & Political Weekly* 50 (5): 69–77.

Kumar, N. 2011. 'Social Production of the Middle Classes'. In *Both Elite and Everyman: The Cultural Politics of the Indian Middle Classes*, edited by A. Baviskar and R. Ray, 220–45. New Delhi: Routledge.

Lakha, S. 1999. 'The State, Globalization, and the Indian Middle-class Identity'. In *Culture and Privilege in Capitalist Asia*, edited by M. Pinches, 251–74. London: Routledge.

Lipset, S.M. 1959. 'Some Social Prerequisites for Democracy: Economic Development and Political Legitimacy'. *American Political Science Review* 53 (1): 69–105.

Lobo, L. and J. Shah. 2015. *The Trajectory of India's Middle Class: Economy, Ethics and Etiquette.* Newcastle Upon Tyne: Cambridge Scholars Publishing.

Lukose, R. 2009. *Liberalization's Children: Gender, Youth, and Consumer Citizenship in Globalizing India.* Durham, NC: Duke University Press.

Mankekar, P. 1999. *Screening Culture, Viewing Politics: An Ethnography of Television, Womanhood and Nation in Postcolonial India.* Durham, NC: Duke University Press.

———. 2013. '"We Are Like This Only": Aspiration, Jugaad, and Love in Enterprise Culture'. In *Enterprise Culture in Neoliberal India: Studies in Youth, Class, Work and Media*, edited by N. Gooptu, 27–42. London and New York: Routledge.

Mazzarella, W. 2005. 'Middle Class'. In *South Asia Keywords*, edited by Rachel Dwyer, 1. Available at: http://www.soas.ac.uk/csasfiles/key-words/Mazzarella-middleclass.pdf (accessed on 22 August 2015).

Mazzarella, W. 2013. *Censorium: Cinema and the Open Edge of Mass Publicity*. Durham, NC: Duke University Press.

McGuire, M.L. 2013. 'The Embodiment of Professionalism: Personality Development Programmes in New Delhi'. In *Enterprise Culture in Neoliberal India: Studies in Youth, Class, Work and Media*, edited by N. Gooptu, 109–23. London and New York: Routledge.

Osella, C. 2012. 'Desires Under Reform: Contemporary Reconfigurations of Family, Marriage, Love and Gendering in a Transnational South Indian Matrilineal Muslim Community'. *Culture and Religion* 13 (2): 241–64.

Osella, F. and Caroline Osella. 2009. 'Muslim Entrepreneurs in Public Life Between India and the Gulf: Making Good and Doing Good'. *Islam, Politics, Anthropology*, Special Issue, *The Journal of the Royal Anthropological Institute* 15 (S1): S202–21.

———. 2011. 'Migration, Neoliberal Capitalism, and Islamic Reform in Kozhikode (Calicut), South India'. *International Labour and Working-Class History* 79 (S1): 140–60.

Oza, R. 2006. *The Making of Neoliberal India: Nationalism, Gender, and the Paradoxes of Globalization*. New York and London: Routledge.

Puri, J. 1999. *Woman, Body, Desire in Postcolonial India: Narratives of Gender and Sexuality*. New York: Routledge.

Radhakrishnan, S. 2011. *Appropriately Indian: Gender and Culture in a New Transnational Class*. Durham, NC: Duke University Press.

Rajagopal, A. 1999. 'Hindu Nationalism in the U.S.: Changing Configurations of Political Practice'. *Ethnic and Racial Studies* 23 (3): 467–96.

Rao, S.L. 1994. *Consumer Market Demographics in India*. New Delhi: National Council for Applied Economic Research.

Ravallion, M. 2010. 'The Developing World's Bulging (but Vulnerable) Middle Class'. *World Development* 38 (4): 445–54.

Ray, R. 2011. '"The Middle Class": Sociological Category or Proper Noun?' *Political Power and Social Theory* 21: 313–22.

Ray, R. and Seemin Qayum. 2009. *Cultures of Servitude: Modernity, Domesticity and Class in India*. Stanford, CA: Stanford University Press.

Rudolph, L. and Susanne Rudolph. 1987. *In Pursuit of Lakshmi: The Political Economy of the Indian State*. Chicago, IL: University of Chicago Press.

RUPE. 2014. 'A Middle Class India?' *Aspects of India's Economy* 58 (September). Available at http://www.rupe-india.org/58/introduction.html (accessed on 24 August 2015).

Sancho, D. 2013. 'Aspirational Regimes: Parental Educational Strategies and the New Indian Youth Discourse'. In *Enterprise Culture in Neoliberal India: Studies in Youth, Class, Work and Media*, edited by N. Gooptu, 159–74. London: Routledge.

Sangari, K. 2002. *The Politics of the Possible: Essays on Gender, History, Narratives, Colonial English*. London: Anthem Press.

Sarkar, S. 1989. *Modern India 1885–1947*. Palgrave Macmillan.

———. 1997. *Writing Social History*. New Delhi: Oxford University Press.

Sarkar, T. 2001. *Hindu Wife, Hindu Nation: Community, Religion and Cultural Nationalism*. Delhi: Permanent Black.

Säävälä, M. 2001. 'Low Caste but Middle-class: Some Religious Strategies for Middle-class Identification in Hyderabad'. *Contributions to Indian Sociology* 35 (3): 293–318.

Sheth, D.L. 1999. 'Secularization of Caste and Making of New Middle Class'. *Economic and Political Weekly* 34 (34 and 35): 2502–10.

Singh, N. 2003. 'Information Technology as an Engine of Broad-based Growth in India'. In *The Knowledge Economy in India*, edited by F. Richter and P. Banerjee, 24–57. London: Palgrave Macmillan.

Sitapati, V. 2011. 'What Anna Hazare's Movement and India's New Middle Classes Say About Each Other'. *Economic & Political Weekly* 46 (30): 39–44.

Sridharan, E. 2004. 'The Growth and Sectoral Composition of India's Middle Class: Its Impact on the Politics of Economic Liberalization'. *India Review* 3 (4): 405–28.

Srivastava, S. 2012. 'National Identity, Bedrooms, and Kitchens: Gated Communities and New Narratives of Space in India'. In *The Global Middle Classes: Theorizing Through Ethnography*, edited by R. Heiman, C. Freeman and M. Liechty, 57–84. Santa Fe, NM: School for Advanced Research Press.

Tocqueville, A. 2003 (1904). *Democracy in America*. London: Penguin Classics.

Upadhya, C. 2011. 'Software and the "New" Middle Class in the "New India"'. In *Elite and Everyman: The Cultural Politics of the Indian Middle Classes*, edited by A. Baviskar and R. Ray, 167–92. New Delhi: Routledge.

———. 2013. 'Shrink-wrapped Souls: Managing the Self in India's New Economy'. In *Enterprise Culture in Neoliberal India: Studies in Youth, Class, Work and Media*, edited by N. Gooptu, 93–108. London and New York, NY: Routledge.

Upadhya, C. and A.R. Vasavi. 2006. 'Work, Culture and Sociality in the Indian Information Technology (IT) Industry: A Sociological Study'. Available at: http://eprints.nias.res.in/107/ (accessed on 28 May 2018).

Van Wessel, M. 2004. 'Talking About Consumption How an Indian Middle Class Dissociates from Middle-class Life'. *Cultural Dynamics* 16 (1): 93–116.

Varma, P.K. 1998. *The Great Indian Middle Class*. New Delhi: Penguin Books.

Wood, J. 2013. 'Protest, Politics, and the Middle Class in Varanasi'. *Economic & Political Weekly* 48 (13): 78–85.

Wright, E.O. 1985. *Classes*. London: Verso Books.

16

Tribe, Egalitarian Values, Autonomy and the State

Alpa Shah

One of the most significant human costs of the development trajectory of accumulation by dispossession (Harvey 2004) that India is currently pursuing for economic growth is that of the destruction of the liveli-hoods and lives of its forest-dwelling communities in central and east-ern India. The proposed corporate national and multinational mining projects to harvest the mineral reserves that lie under lands historically protected for Adivasis will not only alienate and pauperise them but also lead to the destruction of rich societies that have had relatively egalitarian values, in a country often seen as the land of quintessential hierarchy. In this essay, I analyse Adivasi egalitarian values, arguing that crucial to their persistence is Adivasi autonomy to access livelihoods (land and forests) for their social reproduction and for what is perhaps best described as a counter-politics. Also outlined are some of the pro-cesses that have been undermining Adivasi autonomy, in which the Indian state is shown to have played an increasingly destructive role.

Anyone who has spent any significant time living with Adivasi or tribal communities in the forests and hills across central and eastern India would have noted certain remarkable shared features of these communities.[1] Whether it is the Mundas of Jharkhand, the Konds of

[1] I focus here on the hills and forests of central and eastern India and not the northeastern states which have a substantial tribal population but with very different social histories and composition.

Odisha or the Koyas of Telangana, when one compares these forest-dwelling Adivasis to the caste-dominated communities of the agricultural plains, their relatively egalitarian values, and the dignity and pride with which they have held these values, stand out.

The difference between Adivasi society and much of the rest of Indian society has historically troubled many a scholar and administrator. A range of colonial administrators and anthropologists were keen to mark out the difference between tribes and castes (Hutton 1931; Risley 1891; Russell and Lal 1916; Thurston 1909) and went some way to ensuring special status for tribes in the making of the Indian nation state (Elwin 1943; Furer-Haimendorf 1994). In post-independence India, however, criticism arose that those who had highlighted the uniqueness of tribes were motivated by dubious theories of racial difference (Bates 1995) or romanticism (the accusations so often made of Elwin and Furer-Haimendorf—see, for instance, Prasad 2003). The overwhelming analytical push was to see the category of tribe in India as a colonial construction (Guha 1999),[2] to argue that tribes were simply 'backward Hindus' (Ghurye 1963 [1943]) to be absorbed into Hindu society (Bose 1941) to become peasants (Beteille 1974), or at best to see tribes in transition along a tribe-caste continuum in a process of absorption into the latter (Bailey 1960, 1961; Bose 1941; Kosambi 1965; Sinha 1965). The emphasis was to show tribes as some way along what we may call an 'assimilation model', the assumption being that loss of isolation and closer integration with wider society would make a tribe a caste, the impetus for this continuity undoubtedly underwritten by a desire that 'India is One' (indeed these were the concerns of the editors of *Contributions to Indian Sociology*, Dumont and Pocock, in 1961).

Yet, as Xaxa (1999) has pointed out, while tribes have continued to undergo changes of many kinds including Hinduisation, earning their livelihoods from a variety of occupations and often becoming peasants, these factors have not necessarily transformed them into castes nor taken away their distinctive identities. It is a shame that with the critique of the colonial production of knowledge and accusations of romanticism, and with the turn away from in-depth village studies, ethnographies of Adivasi society based on deep participant observation went out of fashion as did the ambition for a broad comparative anthropology which contrasted the similarities and differences between these communities across India. Moreover, Parry's (1974) complaint about the neglect of egalitarian values in the Indian sociological literature still

[2] A. Beteille, 'Construction of Tribe', *The Times of India*, 19 June 1995.

stands. Yet, as this essay will argue, though they are being increasingly undermined, contemporary India has seen the persistence of certain shared features of the forest-dwelling societies, the distinctive identities Xaxa (1999) alludes to.

Egalitarian Values and Social Organisation

To different degrees in different groups, across the forest-dwelling communities of India, there are a number of shared features of social organisation and values which mark out their relatively egalitarian character when compared with the caste-divided societies of the agricultural plains. It must be clarified at the outset, however, that to emphasise the egalitarian values of Adivasi society does not mean to argue that there is no hierarchy among Adivasis, or that Adivasi societies do not fluctuate seasonally between egalitarian and hierarchical structures (Wengrow and Graeber 2015), or that some Adivasi groups are not more like interdependent castes than tribes, or to suggest that all Adivasis groups are equally egalitarian and that processes such as Christianisation and affirmative action have not caused internal stratification. It is to argue that 'in relation to' the stark social hierarchies that mark caste society in the agricultural plains, Adivasi communities in the forests and hills have been notable for their *relatively* egalitarian values which leave them *comparably* free from unequal social divisions. Adivasi egalitarian characteristics have ranged across at least three different domains of life: kinship and political organisation, production and consumption ethic, and gender relations.

Kinship and Political Organisation

To take the first—kinship and political organisation—one of the crucial markers of tribal society all over the world (Sahlins 1968), which has been shared by many of the forest dwellers of India, is their 'segmental organization ... composed of a number of equivalent, unspecialized multi-family groups, each the structural duplicate of the other: a tribe is a congeries of equal kin blocs' (Sahlins 1968: 325). Indeed, this was Bailey's (1960) 'prima facie' distinction in separating the tribal Konds and their segmentary political system based on agnatic kinship, from the caste-divided Oriyas whose political system was marked by ordination and dependent relations with other hierarchically ordered groups. In the Indian case, Adivasi groups have lived in relative geographical isolation (notwithstanding trade links with other groups), allowing them to remain relatively self-contained and maintain a great deal of autonomy from the state. They have been fundamentally ordered by kinship principles implying an important degree of equality and have been essentially homogenous, undifferentiated and unstratified. Although tribal groups sometimes have untouchable communities attached to them, and with who they will have unequal relations marked by tribal superiority (Bailey 1961, for instance, noted that Konds have Pans who are landless low-caste people), these groups have not been essential to their social order and the kinship structure of tribal society has been conceptually self-sufficient. In contrast, caste society has been defined by a series of interdependent groups of people who cannot be kin, who are people of different kinds and who are needed to serve those above them in the hierarchy.

Endogenous forms of authority among Adivasi society have typically not encouraged internal stratification through attaining personal wealth and status. Although there were some Adivasi kingdoms in which the land of chiefs was turned into private property—like the Chero or the Nagabanshi Raj—they rarely had standing armies. Among many other Adivasi groups—for instance, the various Mundari tribes (Santhal, Ho, Munda)—land was collectively owned by the clan and though there were some dominant lineages, there was no kingdom. This is not to say that Adivasi societies had no authorities or leaders. But that their own systems represented a form of democracy that subverted the notion of leaders and authorities who were permanently invested with status and power, discouraging processes of stratification. Brian Morriss (2013) went as far as to suggest that India's forest-dwelling communities were marked by social systems of anarchy, that is, ordered societies without forms of rule which represent enduring structures of domination and exploitation.

Indeed, in the villages where I have lived in the Chotanagpur plateau, Mundas and Oraons have selected their own leaders (the *pahan* and the *paenbharra*) every three years by randomised selection through spiritual sortition (Shah 2010). These practices were so democratic that it was a lottery as to who will be chosen. Not everyone felt that they could hold such responsibility and some passed on the role to others they considered more appropriate. The authorities were to lead the resolution of disputes by being mere facilitators of discussion as decisions were ultimately to be made by consensus which could often take days to reach. These notions of democracy marked a sacral polity (Shah 2010) in which there was no division between the sacred and the secular. Spiritually endowed leaders got their powers by appeasing the spirits in the correct manner, allowing for an ideal of leadership that was not based on wealth, status, rank or charisma but on the values of society as a whole marked by egalitarianism. Even with the insertion of the electoral processes of the Indian state, these practices were still widespread across the Chotanagpur plateau. While the former were regarded as corrupt and associated with a negative concept of politics, the latter were perhaps a ritual reminder of the egalitarian values of Adivasi society.

Production and Consumption Ethic

A second feature of the relatively egalitarian values of forest-dwelling communities in comparison with the societies of the caste-divided plains was their production and consumption ethic. Adivasi societies have generally foraged and produced to meet not much more than their own subsistence needs, showing a greater propensity to live for the moment. The accumulation of wealth over time and the intergenerational transmission of property have not determined status and power within Adivasi society. Economic differences between households have been minimal and temporary (due to sickness or a life cycle ritual, for example) rather than permanent.

Eating, drinking and making merry were a central part of daily Adivasi sociality, but this consumption was first and foremost about sharing with others and not about showing your superiority, marking yourself apart from others. What Alfred Gell (1986) pointed out for the Muria Gonds of Bastar was widespread across Adivasi communities in the forests and hills—day-to-day expenditure was largely devoted to acquiring means, mainly in the form of liquor, to extend casual hospitality as freely as possible. Indeed, showing off one's wealth through conspicuous consumption was not something generally aspired to and risked social ostracisation. By the same token, if a wealthy person lost their wealth, they did not necessarily lose their status.

Production and reproduction within Adivasi societies have in general been non-commoditised. Mutual aid through systems of non-monetised labour exchange between households has been central to reproduction of households. The principle was that if you help me build my house, I will help you build yours. Or, if you help me sow my fields today, I will help you sow yours tomorrow. Emphasis was placed on valuing people as masters of their own production and consumption, producing without being forced to sell themselves or their products as a commodity.

Although direct access to sufficient resources for subsistence living is no longer possible for most Adivasi communities who have to engage in wage labour, as Bird-David (1983) has pointed out of the Naikens of Kerala, even with the entry of these hunter-gatherers into the wage economy, there was much greater continuity within Naiken society than change. This was because in the rubber plantations that developed at their doorstep, the Naikens found another source of gathering: 'wage gathering'. Seeing wages as just another form of gathering for subsistence enabled the Naiken to remain Woodburn's (1982) 'immediate return society' (Bird-David 1983: 60) and persist on Sahlin's (1972) 'zen route to affluence' (Bird-David 1983: 60). I would argue that much of the participation of Adivasis in the seasonal casual wage economy of contemporary India can be viewed in similar terms. Although they are undoubtedly super-exploited in the brick kilns or construction sector (see Shah et al. 2017), Adivasi ability to engage with this economy alongside their forest dwelling and land cultivation-based livelihoods enables their social reproduction in their own terms. Adivasi entry as labour into the markets of capital can also be seen as a form of wage gathering to meet immediate needs and rarely for accumulation or investing in personal wealth and status that would encourage internal differentiation of the community.

Gender Relations

Lastly, and perhaps most strikingly, across the forests of central and eastern India, what is remarkable is the relative gender equality and freedom that women have held in particular in comparison to the societies of the plains. Despite patrilineality, patriarchy was muted in the Adivasi hills and forests. It was not only the respect and autonomy in relation to decision-making power over their own lives and activities that women in Adivasi areas had that were telling but also what men did. In the hilly forests, it was common to find men cooking and doing other domestic work such as washing their own clothes, collecting water, sweeping and looking after children. The gender divide between production and reproduction was not as stark as it was in the plains.

Both sexes worked inside and outside the household and though there was often a sexual division of labour, it was neither very stark nor was it one of dominance and exploitation, asymmetry and hierarchy. Abuj Muria Gond women were noted to plough the land and the Bison Horned Maria women went on hunts. Among the Oraon, a mainly settled agricultural community, where the seasonal ritual hunting practised in the hot season has become the domain of men, every 12 years, the divisions are subverted and men give up hunting and women dress up as men and embark on a ritual hunt known as the *jani sirkar* (literally meaning women's hunt).

Tribal women work outside the household, a situation common among Dalit communities and among the elite in India, but much less so among other non-tribal counterparts (Singh 1994). Moreover, among the Oraon and Munda with whom I have lived, when Adivasi women participated in wage labour or sold things they produced, they controlled the money they brought in. Indeed, Singh noted that Ho and Kadar women, Tanakar Pardhi, Rajuar, Pallityan and Bondo women contributed to family income and controlled their family's expenditure. This intra-household autonomy between men and women gave power to women and helped limit their sexual exploitation.

Women have also had much greater sexual autonomy in Adivasi societies. Premarital sexual relations were not uncommon (see also Shah 2006). In some Oraon- and Munda-dominated villages, we still find the presence of the *dhumkuria*, and in Muria areas, the *ghotul*, a house or dormitory where youth—girls and boys—dance, drink, eat and sleep together in what may appear as hedonistic merriment and where, as Elwin (1947: 132) remarked, it was not uncommon to find women as the initiators of sex and courtship. In places where there were no physical dormitories, the institution of the ghotul or the dhumkuria carries on through Adivasi dancing at festivals. It is rare in other parts of India to find men and women holding each other, openly dancing closely and for sexual crossing on ritual occasions. Marriages by elopement were common (Singh 1994). It was not unusual for girls and boys to choose their co-habitation partners and for marriage rituals to take place (if they did at all) once the couple set up house and often after they had children. Joint-family households, often leading to the subordination of women, were rare. Divorce and remarriage were common—initiated by both women and men (see Shah 2006).

Drinking of alcohol, generally only the domain of men in the rest of India, was central to Adivasi sociality and religious life and openly shared between men and women (Shah 2011a). To drink in private circles, as in the rest of India, would be taken as an act of selfishness. The ancestors must regularly be given drink. Guests must be given alcohol as a sign of hospitality. And men and women must drink together in each other's company as much as possible and not just on ritual occasions.

To point out this relative gender equality does not mean to say that domestic violence against Adivasi women was absent, or that sexual exploitation of Adivasi women was non-existent, or that Adivasi women and men had the same role in societies. But it is to say that, historically, women were not the Second Sex in Adivasi society as much as they were in the rest of India.

Autonomy in Social Reproduction and Counter-politics

What, then, explains why, and the extent to which, Adivasi societies maintained their relatively egalitarian values in contrast to their neighbouring caste-divided communities? Autonomy in controlling direct access to their means of livelihood—especially land and forest resources—is clearly important as it limits the ability of structures of domination, stratification and exploitation in penetrating their societies, and allows for the social reproduction of Adivasi communities on their own terms. Bailey (1961: 14) marked the significance of this material independence through access to land,

> The larger the proportion of a given society which has direct access to the land, the closer is that society to the tribal end of the continuum. Conversely, the larger is the proportion of people whose right to land is achieved through a dependent relationship, the nearer does that society come to the caste pole.

Historically, a low population density was combined with an abundance of forests in which most Adivasis foraged and some cultivated using slash and burn techniques. With colonial rule came the deforestation and then reservation of the forests and the introduction of Hindu caste outsiders to extract revenue from the land and 'settle the population'. Many tribes moved further away into the hills and forests with the introduction of outsiders and a destruction of their livelihood base. Today, most Adivasi communities have to supplement their ability to live off the land and forests with wage labour through seasonal casual migrant work joining the mass of the Indian labour force working in the informal economy. However, unlike the Dalit lower-caste communities of the agricultural plains who are landless and do not have access to land and forest resources, Adivasis are not usually dependent on wage labour alone, and this is important for their ability to maintain their autonomy of social reproduction and their related egalitarian values.

Indeed, a comparison with Dalit communities is apt. At an all-India level, Dalits are usually thought to be better off than Adivasis and are, for instance, shown in the poverty statistics to be less poor. But income levels are not everything, and, in comparison with the forest-dwelling communities, Dalits suffer from greater domination, oppression and internal stratification. The crucial difference between Adivasis and Dalits, I suggest, is that the latter have no direct control over any part of the material basis of their social reproduction which is always mediated by other groups. This dependency means that there is a greater propensity to reproduce the hierarchical structures of caste against Dalits and within Dalit communities.

In contrast, for most Adivasis in the hills and forests of central and eastern India, wage gathering (locally or through seasonal migration) was just one of the ways in which they socially reproduce their households. The reliance on multiple sources of livelihoods, and in particular the direct control of some of the means of social reproduction, enabled Adivasis the autonomy to participate in the underbelly of capitalism in their own terms—for instance, as wage gatherers reproducing their own relatively egalitarian societies rather than as 'free' labour whose values fundamentally transform with capitalism.

The political implications are vast. Those who are waiting in the margins for societies like the Adivasis to enter full-scale proletarianisation for a working-class struggle have based their models on a particular European history of proletarianisation which does not exist in the rest of the world and is swiftly unfolding where it may have (Bernstein 2007; Breman and van der Linden 2014; Therborn 2012). In the Adivasi case, the fight for the protection of land rights and forest resources for Adivasis is more important than ever not just for the basic security of the protection of their livelihoods, as is commonly argued, but also because their control over some of the means of their social reproduction enables the persistence of the social values of egalitarianism in a society otherwise marked by hierarchy and inequality. Indeed, as argued by the recent High Level Committee, Government of India, report, 'beyond their marginality, the many positive features of tribal society must be appreciated and it must be recognized that non-tribal people have much to learn from the richness of tribal cultures and their systems of knowledge' (Government of India 2014: 25).

If autonomy to directly access some of the means of their social reproduction is one axis of the extent to which Adivasi communities are egalitarian, another is their counter-politics to the wider political–economic processes that they have been subjected to, drawing on and reinserting values that they have long held. Adivasis reacted against the colonial penetration of their areas and the erosion of their access to land and forests through a series of violent rebellions across the breadth of central and eastern India; the Kol insurrection, the Santhal Hul, the Sardar movement and the Birsa rebellion are just a few examples. While Kumar Suresh Singh (1982) and Ranajit Guha (1999 [1983]) have done much to draw our attention to these insurgencies, Adivasis have also responded to their oppressors by reinserting their own values, their own ideals, which, although are formed out of their contact with society around them, do not conform to those hierarchical societies. Adivasi egalitarian values and their ritual forms—the selection of leaders, the hunt led by women, for instance—were thus the idiom of their resistance. Indeed, one could argue that one of the results of the Adivasi rebellions of the past is that they were granted certain protections to access their land and forests (for instance, through the Chotanagpur Tenancy Acts, which were the result of the Birsa Munda Rebellion in the early 1900s) which have enabled them the autonomy for their counter-politics.

This counter-politics of Adivasi egalitarianism can be seen as a reaction to their class-based exploitation, a form of class struggle in E.P. Thompson's sense as 'class struggle without class' (Thompson 1978). This is a conception of class struggle that pays attention to the values of the working class as they actually exist in their day-to-day struggle against capitalism, and which moves beyond the 19th-century valourisation of the proletarian ideal of a class attack against capitalism. Whereas Thompson focused on ideals of fairness as central to this class struggle, in the Adivasi case it is perhaps the values of egalitarianism that are the idiom of class struggle against the exploitation of their own society expressed in their own terms.

Adivasi class struggle does not make them societies against the state, as Pierre Clastres (1987 [1974]) has argued of Amazonian Indians. Nor does it make them societies that are just running away from the state, as framed by James Scott (2009). They are societies that have developed right under the very systems of oppression that have been grinding against their doorstep—they have lived in its shadows (Shah 2010)—and developed a counter-politics in response to and negotiation with the state. Thus, to think of a counter-politics of Adivasi values and autonomy from their hierarchical neighbours as class struggle does not mean to say that Adivasis are in any way separated or isolated from the rest of India. For it is in negotiation with the processes of their integration into the state and the processes of capitalism that they have produced their own values. Moreover, to argue that Adivasis have developed a counter-politics is not to valourise them as museums from our past. They are our contemporaries. They are a constantly changing response to the circumstances they are in. They are what Levi-Strauss (1966) would call *bricoleurs*—constantly borrowing in order to create something different. It is the oppression of the politico-economic systems they have been subject to which has nurtured their counter-politics of autonomy.

Adivasis and the State

To conclude, I propose some brief reflections on the processes undermining Adivasi autonomy and related values. Fought for by the Adivasi insurgencies of the past, ironically, it is the Indian state that enabled Adivasis to maintain their counter-politics of egalitarianism, but it is also the Indian state that undermines these values. Although it is continuously shrinking, the reason why tribal communities in India still have access to some land and forests is because the state, in response to various Adivasi rebellions, was forced to introduce a series of land and forest right Acts—most notably in the Fifth and Sixth Schedules of the Indian Constitution—ensuring the protection of these spaces for Adivasis. Adivasi direct access to their livelihoods were thus, to a certain extent, protected, ensuring that they had continued material autonomy to reproduce their societies on their own terms, even if, as I will argue, that autonomy has continually been taken away from them.

However, while on the one hand the Indian state preserved the autonomy of Adivasis, on the other hand it also encouraged the greater integration of Adivasis through other processes. The first is the increasing infiltration of the state into Adivasi societies through developmental measures which cannot take due account of Adivasi cultural values. This includes forms of mainstream education as well as processes of affirmative action through reservations of seats in government for Scheduled Castes and Scheduled Tribes. These, I would argue, though instituted in the name of equality (equality before the law), were to be implemented by a state constituted of homo hierarchicus, of high-caste men who generally treated the Adivasis as *jungli*, as wild, savage and barbaric (Shah 2010). Although there are cases of tribal groups asserting their tribal identity, increasingly concerned to distinguish themselves from mainstream society to gain access to these seats, the overwhelming effect of reservations among the forest-dwelling Adivasis is that in the name of equality (as embodied in the Indian state), egalitarian societies are brought into the prevailing forces of hierarchy so that reservations become the force of internal stratification within those societies (Higham and Shah 2013).

Together these processes encourage Adivasis to develop ideals of individual accumulation of wealth, status, rank and commodification. They pull Adivasis more firmly into the forces of capitalism, and the processes of inequality within their own societies are brought therein. This increasing infiltration of the state and its related economic processes produces class stratification *within* Adivasi society and is likely to lead to the rise of patriarchy. It encourages some Adivasis to co-opt the values and aspirations for upward mobility held by the upper and middle classes, undermining their counter-politics of autonomy.

Moreover, while offering limited protection of Adivasi lands and forests, the Indian state has overwhelmingly promoted the interests of capital, eroding the autonomy that Adivasis have enjoyed in relation to their access to livelihoods in reproducing their societies. Mass dispossession due to mining, land grabbing for corporate interests, reform of the Land Acquisitions Act, all make it easier for capital to access land. These forms of primitive accumulation have a longer history—mining and industrialisation of these areas go back to the late 1800s—but the new waves of accumulation by dispossession in neoliberal India come with a brutal military face. Indeed, today the counter-insurgency forces of the Indian state in the forests and hills of India mark a social death of the Adivasis (Shah 2011b; Sundar 2016).

Resistance against this trajectory of development in the forests of central and eastern India has in recent years been headed by Maoist-inspired Naxalites who have been mobilising Adivasis. Despite their attention to 'from the masses to the masses', the Naxalite revolutionary class struggle, in its stagiest teleology of revolution strategy, has largely missed recognising Adivasi egalitarianism as a form of class struggle (Shah 2013), and has also brought the state and the values of capitalism closer to Adivasi lives (Shah 2014, 2018).

The overall effect of this development trajectory may be to turn Adivasis into pauperised tribal castes with nothing but their labour power to sell, stripped of their counter-politics of egalitarianism, and whose only capacity to aspire will be in the terms set by their oppressors. In India, in response to Adivasi resistance, the state has protected a degree of Adivasi autonomy by enabling Adivasis direct access to their livelihoods and to control the means of their social reproduction, but it is also the state which is eroding the possibility for this autonomy and thus Adivasi egalitarian values, and which is doing so through brutal repression.

What is perhaps most needed are in-depth studies which try to understand Adivasi social values in different parts of the country and a comparative theoretical framework which explains processes of change and continuity across the country. I have argued here that the degree of autonomy Adivasis have to directly access their livelihoods, that is, to socially reproduce, as well as their counter-politics of egalitarian values are key to both.

Acknowledgements

A version of the arguments presented here formed the Keynote Lecture at the Tribal Autonomy Conference in Hyderabad University in 2014, were presented at the 2015 Conference on 'Inequality, Scale and Civilisation' at the Max Planck Institute of Social Anthropology in Halle and were articulated as the Keynote Lecture at the Nirmala College, Ranchi University, Conference on 'Women in Colonial and Postcolonial History'. Thanks to Bhangya Bhukya for organising a conference on the theme of tribal autonomy, to Chris Hann and David Wengrow for the Halle conversations, and to the staff of Nirmala College for organising an inspiring session in Ranchi. I am also grateful to Gavin Smith and Winnie Lem for the enthusiasm they showed for some of the arguments made here and for their comments.

References

Bailey, F.G. 1960. *Tribe Caste and Nation: A Study of Political Activity and Political Change in Highland Orissa*. Manchester: University of Manchester Press.

———. 1961. '"Tribe" and "Caste" in India'. *Contributions to Indian Sociology* 5: 7–19.

Bates, C. 1995. 'Race, Caste, and Tribe in Central India: The Early Origins of Indian Anthropometry'. In *The Concept of Race in South Asia*, edited by P. Robb, 219–59. New Delhi: Oxford University Press.

Bernstein, H. 2007. 'Capital and Labour from Centre to Margins'. Paper presented at the Living on the Margins Conference, Stellenbosch on 26–28 March.

Beteille, A. 1974. 'Tribe and Peasantry'. In *Six Essays in Comparative Sociology*, edited by A. Beteille, 60–81. New Delhi: Oxford University Press.

Bird-David, N. 1983. 'Wage-Gatherings: Socio-economic Change and the Case of the Naiken of South India'. In *Rural South Asia*, edited by P. Robb, 57–86. Salem: Merrimark Publishing Circle.

Bose, N.K. 1941. 'Hindu Method of Tribal Absorption'. *Science and Culture* 7: 188–94.

Breman, J. and M. van der Linden. 2014. 'Informalising the Economy: The Return of the Social Question at a Global Level'. *Development and Change* 45 (5): 920–40.

Clastres, P. 1987 (1974). *Society Against the State: Essays in Political Anthropology*. New York, NY: Zone Books.

Dumont, L. and D. Pocock. 1961. *Contributions to Indian Sociology*. Vol. 5. Paris: Mouton and Co.

Elwin, V. 1943. *The Aboriginals*. Bombay: Oxford University Press.

———. 1947. *The Muria and Their Ghotul*. Bombay: Oxford University Press.

Furer-Haimendorf, C. 1994. *Tribes of India: The Struggle for Survival*. New Delhi: Oxford University Press.

Gell, Alfred. 1986. 'Newcomers to the World of Goods: Consumption Among the Muria Gonds'. In *The Social Life of Things: Commodities in Cultural Perspective*, edited by A. Appadurai, 110–38. Cambridge: Cambridge University Press.

Ghurye, G.S. 1963 (1943). *The Scheduled Tribes (The Aborigines So-called and Their Future)*. Bombay: Ramdas Bhatkal for Popular Prakashan.

Government of India. 2014. *Report of the High Level Committee on Socio-economic, Health and Educational Status of Tribal Communities of India*. New Delhi: Government of India.

Guha, R. 1999 (1983). *Elementary Aspects of Peasant Insurgency in Colonial India*. Durham, NC: Duke University Press.

Guha, S. 1999. *Environment and Ethnicity in India, 1200–1221*. Cambridge: Cambridge University Press.

Harvey, D. 2004. 'The "New" Imperialism: Accumulation by Dispossession'. *Socialist Register* 40: 63–87.

Higham, R. and A. Shah. (2013). *Secondary Education, Affirmative Action and the Post-liberalisation State: A Historical Analysis of Adivasis in Jharkhand, India*. (In Press).

Hutton, J.J. 1931. *Census of India*. New Delhi: Government of India.

Kosambi, D.D. 1965. *The Culture and Civilisation of Ancient India in Historical Outline*. London: Routledge and Kegan Paul.

Levi-Strauss, C. 1966. *The Savage Mind*. London: Weidenfeld and Nicolson.

Morriss, B. 2013. 'Anarchism, Individualism and South Indian Foragers: Memories and Reflections'. *Radical Anthropology* (November): 22–37.

Parry, J. 1974. 'Egalitarian Values in a Hierarchical Society'. *South Asian Review* 7 (2): 95–119.

Prasad, A. 2003. *Against Ecological Romanticism: Verrier Elwin and the Making of an Anti-modern Tribal Identity*. New Delhi: Oxford University Press.

Risley, H. 1891. *The Tribes and Castes of Bengal*. Harvard Library. Calcutta: Bengal Secretariat Press.

Russell, R.V. and H. Lal. 1916. *The Tribes and Castes of the Central Provinces of India*. London: Macmillan and Co.

Sahlins, M. 1968. *Tribesmen*. Englewood Cliffs, NJ: Prentice-Hall.

———. 1972. 'The Original Affluent Society'. In *Stone Age Economics*, edited by M. Sahlins, 1–40. New York, NY: Aldine de Gruyter.

Scott, J. 2009. *The Art of Not Being Governed: An Anarchist History of Upland Southeast Asia*. New Haven, CT: Yale University Press.

Shah, A. 2006. 'The Labour of Love: Seasonal Migration from Jharkhand to the Brick Kilns of Other States in India'. *Contributions to Indian Sociology*, n.s., 40 (1): 91–118.

———. 2010. *In the Shadows of the State: Indigenous Politics, Environmentalism and Insurgency in Jharkhand, India*. Durham, NC and London: Duke University Press.

Shah, A. 2011a. 'Alcoholics Anonymous: The Maoist Movement in Jharkhand, India'. *Modern Asian Studies* 45 (5): 1095–117.

———. 2011b. 'India Burning: The Maoist Revolution'. In *A Companion to the Anthropology of India*, edited by I. Clark-Deces 332–53. Chichester: Wiley-Blackwell.

———. 2013. 'The Tensions Over Liberal Citizenship in a Marxist Revolutionary Situation: The Maoists in India'. *Critique of Anthropology* 33 (1): 91–109.

———. 2014. 'The Muck of the Past: Revolution, Social Transformation and the Maoists in India (The Malinowski Memorial Lecture, 2012)'. *Journal of Royal Anthropological Institute*, n.s., 20 (2): 337–56.

———. 2018. *Nightmarch: A Journey into India's Naxal Heartlands*. New Delhi: HaperCollins India; London: Hurst, Chicago: University of Chicago Press.

Shah, A., J. Lerche, R. Axelby, D. Benbabaali, B. Donegan, J. Raj and V. Thakur. 2017. *Ground Down by Growth: Tribe, Caste, Class and Inequality in India*. New Delhi: Oxford University Press; London: Pluto Press.

Singh, K.S., ed. 1982. *Tribal Movements in India*. Vols 1 and 2. New Delhi: Manohar Publishers.

———. 1994. *The Scheduled Tribes*. New Delhi: Oxford University Press in Collaboration with the Anthropological Survey of India.

Sinha, S. 1965. 'Tribe-Caste and Tribe-Peasant Continua in Central India'. *Man in India* 45 (1): 57–83.

Sundar, N. 2016. *The Burning Forest: India's War in Bastar*. Delhi: Juggernaut.

Therborn, G. 2012. 'Class in the 21st Century'. *New Left Review* 78: 5–29.

Thompson, E.P. 1978. 'Eighteenth-century English Society: Class Struggle Without Class?' *Social History* 3 (2): 133–65.

Thurston, E. 1909. *The Tribes and Castes of South India*. Madras: Government Press.

Wengrow, D. and D. Graeber. 2015. 'Farewell to the "Childhood of Man": Ritual, Seasonality, and the Origins of Inequality'. *Journal of Royal Anthropological Institute* 21 (3): 597–619.

Woodburn, J. 1982. 'Egalitarian Societies'. *Man*, n.s., 17 (3): 431–51.

Xaxa, V. 1999. 'Transformation of Tribes in India: Terms of Discourse'. *Economic & Political Weekly* 34 (24): 1519–24.

17

Gendering Sociology, a Sociology of Gender or Studying Women? Some Reflections

Rajni Palriwala

Introduction

First, there was woman, then there was gender. And both came to be everywhere and nowhere. This epitaph could sum up conceptual and disciplinary trends in sociology and anthropology in India over the last four decades and the present state. This is a transformation from when informants were usually men and written of as if they made up the social world. In then prevalent structuralist frameworks, if and where sexual identity or difference was seen as a structural principle, the assumption was that we already know what sex and gender are and that the male voice spoke for all. From today's vantage point, it appears amazing that the analytic of women/men, even if not of gender, did not shape the scholarship in the themes that were the initial focus in the disciplines. Kinship studies were central in the development of social anthropology. Indeed, it was often seen as the arena in which an aspiring scholar had to show her competence (Dube 2000), the subject that would lay the claims of anthropology to theory and science, more so than the other themes that occupied the discipline, initial such as the elaboration of religion, 'primitive' thought and material cultures. The study of kinship had to note the differentiation of the sexes in genealogy and/or the exchange of women. The powers of gods and goddesses, the roles of specifically male priests and female shamans, and the sex of the officiant were also themes. That caste entailed, if not rested on, the control of women's sexuality was recognised early in the last century, by Ambedkar (1917), among others, and yet the studies that wove it into the conceptualisation of caste were rare (Yalman 1963). Social stratification was a theme with similar but not equivalent weight in sociology, linked to concerns of division of labour, communitas and modernity, but not gender. These were translated in the subcontinent within the twin frames of the disciplinary concerns in Europe and the link between orientalist thought and colonial interests. Indian society was constructed as an aggregate of the categories and institutions of religion, caste and tribe, family and kinship, and village community.

An occasional article focused on women, often when dealing with sexuality, marriage, the domestic or socialisation, arenas in which sexual difference could not but be noticed, but more commonly it was as a passing reference, if at all. This prehistory, though important in appreciating contemporary trends, is not the present focus, however. Much has been written on it (Ardener 1975a, 1975b; Millman and Kanter 1975; Moore 1988; Rege 2003a; Smith 1974), both in terms of the disciplines and on specific themes (Yanagisako and Collier 1987), more than can be listed here. At the same time, little of this has examined or drawn on the sociological and anthropological work in India and on India, other than Rege (2003a), while introducing an anthology of selected articles on women that appeared in the *Sociological Bulletin*, the journal of the Indian Sociological Society. This chapter is an attempt to trace some themes in which a focus on gender developed, including some early studies, and their effects for a gendered sociology. An important caveat is that these fields are wide-ranging, and all cannot be covered. In the brief mapping presented are also outlined some current concerns and issues in the sociology of gender that require more attention.

Framing a Gendered Sociology

Feminist and other critiques of the predominant currents of research and theoretical frameworks meant that much was questioned, even broken down. The knocking at sex as biological and pre-social was just one aspect. Self-critique led to a further move from a sociology of women to a sociology of gender that meant a new language in social life and in academia (Whitehead 1979). The categories of women and men can no longer be taken for granted; the divisions between and boundedness of social domains are to be explained rather than assumed; and the shaping of social relations through gender and power has almost become an academic truism. In the meantime, the sex–gender debate has continued, and it is argued that biology/nature is more than a social construction (Gatens 1983), that materialities entail a reality check (Hekman 2010). Analytically and cumulatively, there is a shift from sex identity and the position, status and role of women to gender relations as the central conceptual tool and problematic, a move that has not been ubiquitous or final.

It is important to recognise that intellectual developments have been deeply influenced by women's and other movements (Palriwala 2010; Rege 2003a).[1] These politics have demanded a rethinking of discriminations and oppressions in stratification and recognition that women and men are not internally homogeneous categories or identities, that women are not only women, and a breaking with the naturalisation of gendered binaries, heterosexuality and the privileging of heterosociality. Intersectionality has been argued as a productive idea in the context of the crossings of gender with race, caste, class, religious and ethnic community.[2] While analyses of multiple, context-specific identities are being pushed, that of their simultaneous dynamics remains the more difficult task. It demands a rethinking of feminist politics and scholarship in which recognition had become the dominant theme and a recouping of issues of redistribution and representation (Fraser 2013; Rege 1998). Critically, conceptual rethinking and ruptures are very unevenly present in ongoing work, reflected in the continuing presence of 'status/position of women' studies rather than processes and gendered relations.

The volume of sociological work in which gender is an analytic thread or the central problematic has grown exponentially, making any attempt to cover the field or listing references an encyclopaedic task.[3] Gendered experience and speaking voices are conceptual and methodological tools which much sociological research now pays attention to. Even where the research questions do not directly focus on

[1] The report of the Committee on the Status of Women in India (1974) had an effect in both scholarship and the women's movement.

[2] This has long been an element in scholarship on and politics of women/gender in India, even if not explicitly articulated (Crenshaw 1993), and hence also often forgotten.

[3] Thus, even as this chapter went through various drafts, much writing has been published, including a special issue of *CIS* (2016) that focuses on women and gender.

gender, both women and men are consciously selected as informants or, if that is not the case, it is made explicit; the literature referred to will include writings in which gender is a focus.[4] Much of this work, unfortunately, cannot be described as a gendered sociology, though some of it can be mined for gendered data.[5] It is in this light that one can see a simultaneous omnipresence and continuing marginality of women and gender in social science scholarship. Gendered and feminist sociologies have stimulated disciplinary questionings and new sociological questions, methodologies and areas of scholarship. These have grown as fields beyond gender (as reflected in this volume in the separate chapters on marriage, intimacies, masculinities and alternate sexualities), a development that can also have the impact of limiting gender to the 'remainder' or reinforcing what is more than a tendency to equate gender and women.

To examine disciplinary trends, one can look for research in which a women/gender focus is specified or such a concern is mentioned. In two different ways, however, such a tracing of the gendering of sociology is a much more complicated exercise. The sociological awareness of the sexing and gendering of the social (in its broadest sense) world may be present even without women/gender as a significant theme. Or it may be absent, even though women and gender find explicit mention; narratives of both female and male informants and tables of disaggregated data are presented or caveats given that a concern could not be followed up because of lack of data or other such reasons and gendered references are listed. In other words, gendered data and readings may be available and presented but not affect the thrust or details of the analysis. I point here to the distinctions between a recognition of sex difference and gender as significant issues, a sociology of gender and the gendering of sociology. These are undoubtedly linked and as we move from one to the next, we travel a path that pushes the theoretical premises and conceptual tools of sociology and social anthropology.

Comparing two social science journals in which work on gender appears—*Contributions to Indian Sociology* (*CIS*) and *Economic & Political Weekly* (*EPW*), particularly the *Review of Women's Studies* (*RWS*)[6]—

---

[4] A quick perusal of articles in *CIS* that are not explicitly about gender demonstrates this, both in their methodology descriptions and in the list of references.

[5] As Dube (2000: 4043) suggests was the case for the early dissertations on women that she was asked to examine.

[6] Articles focused on gender or on women in the *EPW* are by no means limited to the six-monthly *RWS*, though they may get overlooked in a reading for gender.

and one which is devoted to gender studies (*Indian Journal of Gender Studies* [*IJGS*]) is useful in mapping the sociology of gender, an exercise undertaken for *Sociological Bulletin* earlier (Rege 2003a). Given that *CIS* is a journal for sociological and social anthropological research on India and South Asia more broadly, it is to be expected that this defines the geographical locale of the research it carries. Articles on contexts other than South Asia, however, become fewer and rarer in *RWS-EPW* too, after the first issues and especially after the 1990s, unlike in the *IJGS*, particularly in its special issues. It may be that the exponential growth in work on women and on gender in India leaves little space for work on 'elsewhere'. The near absence of research on contexts other than India, however, is true of social science in India more generally. The lack of a comparative perspective in the social sciences in India couples with the hegemonic idea of nation-building to take the form that 'we have enough problems of our own' to be studied.[7] Yet, social anthropology and sociology emerged from a comparative interest, albeit often a non-self-reflexive approach. Comparative analyses were significant in producing a gender-sensitive sociology that denaturalised culture and social processes such as family, socialisation and the distinctions/unities between sex and gender (Mead 1935). The absence of a comparative sensibility, including between women and men, has also hindered the conceptual move from women as a category or the role and position of women to gender relations—male–female difference is either assumed or if not found, change is concluded. Recuperating comparative self-reflexivity continues to be important, for the study of 'other-than-ourselves' can provide important and needed sociological shock.

A second given difference is that the articles on women and gender in the *EPW* and in the *IJGS* fall in a wide and increasing range of social science disciplines and the liberal arts. In the *EPW*, they were rooted in the disciplines of economics and politics in earlier years, while in the *IJGS*—a much newer journal begun only in 1994—sociology was very present in the initial years. A number of scholars have argued that gendered and feminist research has to cut across various domains of social life compelling disciplinary exchanges. It is striking that in both the *EPW* and in *CIS*, it is articles that focus on gender and women that tend towards the interdisciplinary, cross-disciplinary, and transdisciplinary. In part, this is accomplished through papers from different disciplines that are not entirely serendipitous neighbours in special issues and are

---

[7] As I found in initial reactions to proposed research and a general lack of local interest subsequently to the study that colleagues and I undertook on gender and the welfare state in the Netherlands (Risseeuw et al. 2005).

thence read together. Thus, studies of gender, social reform and the state, published as a special issue of *CIS* in 1995, were from sociology, history, politics, law and economics. However, I would suggest that gendered social histories have drawn more from anthropology and sociology than the reverse. A greater historical sensibility is required in the sociology of gender if there is to be a careful analysis of continuity and change, a constant lay and disciplinary concern. At the same time, if the power of sociology and anthropology is to be brought into work on policy and state programmes, it has to take ethnographic tools and analysis more seriously (Ahmed 1994).

Disciplinary ruptures are critical in the gendering of sociology. Add women and stir has been a description of a first step in this direction, but at times women have been added with no stirring. This is so even in work on those domains that continue to be seen as eminently 'feminine' in everyday life in contemporary societies and cultures—the domestic, marriage, kinship, the personal, the private. This has to do with the questions asked and a research intention limited to 'filling in the data gaps'. We may be given some correlations, some narratives from both male and female informants, and little more. Not only does gender become just a 'new' way to write women, recognising gender in sociology (and in other disciplines) may be no more than the formal nod suggested earlier.

Critiques of development and development studies have been significant in the growth of a gendered sociology, linked to the idea of directed social change, empowerment and governance (Kabeer 1994). Policy and programme studies as well as 'evaluation' exercises were undertaken in or through funded research and institutions linked to government and non-government organisations. The aims of these studies and the depth of the research are very varied, depending on their stance as information gatherers or as critical and engaged scholars. I have seen two not-so-happy trends in many research proposals and papers I have had to read, even in the last decade. One is shaped by official language and governance and the other by the assumption that good politics is all that is required. Thus, in the first, empowerment of women will be stated as the aim and in the second, patriarchy is both the question and the conclusion. In neither are the terms made into researchable questions, the empirical may be thin and the analysis stops at either a summary of gender-disaggregated data, at what appear as just-so stories, or at a reiteration of conclusions made often enough already. This inadequacy is reflected in the contrast between studies in which there has been a terminological elision from position and status of women to integrating women in development to participation to empowerment of women and those in which there is a conceptual shift to a political and cultural economy of gender relations (Kabeer 2002; Palriwala and Uberoi 2008).

Despite what I have said above, only some of the political ferment and critique beyond academia entered into disciplinary questions and analyses, not least because of the spaces in which the former took place, the language used or the resistance of malestream academia, as Rege wrote when looking at the paucity of gendered research in the work on globalisation (2003b). A striking contrast between *RWS-EPW* and *IJGS* on the one hand and *CIS* on the other is that in the latter, little was said of gendered or caste oppression, patriarchy, the politics of gendering research, class exploitation or caste discrimination, even while the politics of culture and a Foucauldian bent towards the inherently political project of discourse was present. In *RWS*, as in its April 2016 issue, there is an explicit view of feminist and gendered research as a political project oriented to emancipation. The latter is perhaps more representative of gender studies in the Indian context but does not describe a large body of work on gender, sociological or otherwise. In the rest of this chapter, I will touch on a few specific areas of sociology, focusing largely though not exclusively on these three journals, to trace the directions taken or to be pursued.[8]

Gender in and out of Sociology

Dowry, marriage prestations and rules, aspects of family household, education and work were among the first substantive themes in Indian sociology in which the structural effects on and experience of women found a place.[9] Work such as Karve's (1968) magnum opus on kinship and Gough's (1956) paper on Tamil Brahmin kinship are classics in the study of kinship in India, among the few that carried insights on women and gender that were in more than passing. Not surprisingly, gendered divisions and segregation in space (Mandelbaum 1993/1988; Papanek and Minault 1982) were themes in which women/gender were the problematic and/or the theoretical frame early on. The multifarious nature of women's work, its links to class, property, domesticity and segregation, framed in concepts of production and reproduction

[8] Given the word limit, many significant sociological studies do not find mention here.

[9] Chapters in Rege (2003a) are in the areas of family, marriage and kinship, work, education and state.

came later, but relatively early in a gendered sociology (Palriwala 1993; Sharma 1980, 1986). Srinivas chose themes related to women for two memorial lectures, one on the 'changing position of women', elaborating on the withdrawal of women (or immurement) from the 'public' domain with upward social mobility (Srinivas 1978) and another on changing dowry practices (Srinivas 1984). In both, women were seen at the intersection of Sanskritisation and modernisation with education and employment as indices of the latter, themes which continue.

These two lectures were also responses to the publication of the 1974 Towards Equality report, the concern with civil rights after the Emergency of 1975–77 and the increasing visibility of 'bride-burnings'. There was an upsurge in the women's movement around issues of violence against women—rape, harassment and dowry related. Indian academia responded to the outcry on dowry violence, with many studies on dowry in different social, spatial and time contexts being undertaken and published (Basu 2005). Through specific incidents in rural and urban India, the women's movement highlighted that rape was a matter of the intersection of gender power with class and caste structures and their alignment with state institutions, but intensive, sociological work on rape, domestic violence or other gender-related violence remain few. Baxi (2014) ethnographically examines the law on rape, while Chowdhry's (2007) historical work looks at 'honour killings'. Not only is gender violence an issue that is extremely difficult to study ethnographically and ethically, but it is also related to violence being boxed as 'deviancy', with few studies of deviancy and violent crime in Indian sociology. Acknowledging the extent of gender-based violence can be threatening for even the more reflexive of scholars. In the obverse, gendered violence has become an overarching contemporary issue in international fora and in women's studies. This may have the political and policy effect of asserting the urgency of the concern, but it may obscure the everyday oppressions and discriminations and the social, economic, political and cultural processes that engender them.

Religion, ritual and rites of passage have been a continuing interest in Indian sociology and anthropology, the point at which Indology and sociology meet, even though all studies may not carry the twin disciplinary traditions. Male-centred religious concepts have been examined— such as the householder (Madan 1981) and Brahmacharya—and can feed into studies of masculinity but leave women in a limbo. Gendered perspectives have entered tangentially through research on goddess cults and spirit possession, more directly in studies of feminine religiosity in female sects and collective practices of prayers and teaching, or studies of auspiciousness and related concerns based on or including women informants. There is the danger of too easy an imputation of female agency as men acknowledge female power in rituals of goddess worship. The more complex assertion of ideologies of the danger of women's power and biology and the cultural contradictions (especially, but not only) between folk practices that belie common ideas and theological precepts have been studied (Hershman 1977; Ram 1992). The rituals that have most often been studied are marriage and funeral rites—rituals where men are the officiants. The Hindu ritual of *kanyadaan* has been interpreted as a reification of the daughter as property but also of the inseparability of (male) giver and (female) gift in a non-commodified culture. Here, one may also return to the analyses of marriage rituals in different parts of the subcontinent—Vergati (1982) in Kathmandu, Kolenda (1984) comparing south and north and Good (1991) in Tamil Nadu—as variously constructing the bride and groom as well as marriage itself and conjugal relations. A study of these domestic rituals also enables questioning of the private–public divide. Daily female rituals have received less attention, though it is in them that early gendered socialisation and the reiteration of gendered ideologies of the self may take place (Dube 1988). These studies open up the cultural diversity, contradictions, reificatory effects and disagreements, as well as agency and change in the notions and practice of gender.

Gender and feminist studies have questioned dichotomies of nature–culture, private–public, the affective and the rational (Palriwala 2015), the material and the cultural, the mind and the body along with disciplinary divisions. This has been significant in reframing and reviving marriage, kinship and family studies (Kaur and Palriwala 2013), in rethinking work and labour, and in making sexuality, embodiment, emotion and intimacy growing fields of analysis. Gender is a concern in new areas such as film, performance and the arts, visual cultures (Uberoi 2006), media, consumption and consumerism (Chowdhury 2001), displacement and refugees (Behera 2006), and environment. Questions pertaining to gender have also entered or been further pursued in scholarship on communitarian identity and ideologies, nationalism and the nation-state, migration and the diaspora, education and schooling, and state institutions, policy and law. The themes are more wide-ranging than this list.[10] The extent to which gender concerns have reframed the problematics, conceptual tools and analytical strategies in these areas is, however, moot.

[10] A number of these themes are discussed in other chapters in this volume.

The life cycle has also been of longstanding interest in anthropology and sociology in India. Hindu, upper-caste ideologies of Brahmacharya and householder (Madan 1981) gave us a world of men. Studies of the ideologies and practices of wifehood and motherhood give us a female perspective; together they can give us a gendered view of life course and of domestic life. The focus on rules and norms, however, not only placed widows, divorced, abandoned and single women as marginal categories but also reified wife and mother as women's destiny with fatherhood as being no more than the claim to a son and obscured the difficulties of the ageing. Furthermore, differentiation by class and caste of widowhood, marriage and mothering were flattened until later studies (Chen 1998; Lamb 1999), though non-Hindu groups still barely figure. Women's studies, demographic research and a concern with welfare and state policy renewed the interest in life course in sociology (including death), particularly bringing out how the life course and normative expectations regarding a later stage in life shape strategies, aspirations and practices in the present. This is evident in studies of the sex ratio, particularly of the declining juvenile sex ratio, a phenomenon that is both gendered and an expression of interweaving dynamics of reproduction and fertility, gender ideologies, class relations and social stratifications, livelihoods and aspirations (John et al. 2008).

Studies of sex ratio, violence and divisions of labour bring us to issues of political economy and the gendered access to livelihoods and employment, and economic dependence. Sociological and qualitative work on the practices and experiences of the gendered division of labour and of gendered patterns in paid employment have been intermittent and few (Sharma 1980, 1986), though there is a plethora of work in economics and using statistical analysis. An early concern in feminist sociology with the sexual division of labour and the invisibility and effects of women's domestic responsibilities in shaping gender relations has been reframed in the context of a neoliberal political economy wherein the divide between formal and informal work has become shaky even as women's access to paid work worsens. In particular, the gendered political economy of unpaid work, care labour and commodified labour (Palriwala and Neetha 2011) is a theme that sociology and anthropology in India can pay more attention to. It suggests simultaneously the continuing significance of a social category of women as well as the inequalities and relations of exploitation within the category and of gender relations in making political and economic structures. As Hekman (2010: 2) has argued, there is a need to 'bring the material back in' and to analyse the 'intra-action' of various levels of reality and discourse (ibid.: 125).

Conclusion: Moving Forward

To move on, we have to confront three ethnographic and analytic lacks, which have serious implications for the sociology of gender and the sociology of India more generally. A range of scholarship, including on gender, has brought them to the fore. The first, though indicated earlier, can do with further stress as the critique has not been taken on board sufficiently. It is the assumption of the ego as male and that male informants describe both male and female lives, even as masculinity studies have grown as a specific theme and fieldwork may be with both male and female informants. As early as in the 1975 *CIS* issue on kinship and marriage, Khare (1975) pointed to the multiplicity of lived perspectives in the gendered world of affinity in India, while Vatuk (1975) looked at marriage through the network of gifts beyond dowry that women were engaged in. The attempt to take this further to examine theories of kinship and kinship structures assuming a female ego came much later in Kapadia's (1993) significant paper or through an examination of post-marriage residential practices (Abraham 2013; Palriwala 1991).

The second aporia is a result of the hegemonic construct of India as upper caste and Hindu and thence the tendency to take Hindu texts and upper-caste practices as descriptions and explanations of the gendering of the social world across the subcontinent. This has been part of Orientalist and colonial reasonings that equate culture and religion and take the latter as determinant of women's lives and of gender relations. It has also framed discussions of gender relations and ideas among other groups that were studied, particularly tribes, which were presented as contrasts. Harlan and Courtright (1995) edited a fine volume, *From the Margins of Hindu Marriage*, that turned its eye away from 'Great Tradition' and rules. It brought to the fore that religious ideas, experience and practice may be varied, as well as the suggestion that the margins may be critical in the gendered operations of social institutions. Yet, much of the ethnographies included were of upper-caste groups. Ethnographic studies of Muslims (Jeffery 1979), Christians (Caplan 1984) and other religious minorities, Dalits (Kolenda 1992 [1982]) and regions such as the northeast (Nongbri 1988, 2003) that focused on women and gendered practices, concerns and relations were undertaken, but have been few and far between. Nor did they break the hold of a male, upper-caste, Hindu perspective in sociology more generally. Studies of non-Brahmin castes (Abraham 2013) and non-Hindu groups are emerging (Kumar 2006), but we are far from a critical accumulation of gendered work on the ethnographically unstudied.

Work on Adivasis and Dalits may assume difference from upper-caste Hindus rather than examine gender relations and processes through intensive study, particularly the gendering of ways of living, relating, thinking and meaning making.[11] To move beyond social categories and identities to a study of gender relations and a gendering of sociology, class and caste relations, inequalities and intersectionality, and not just difference, has to be part of our study of gender.

This points to a third concern—the assumption that rules and dominant viewpoints are the practice. This assumption has made many practices appear as deviance, obscured social change or presented variation as social change, though they may have long been strategies with which people worked through the contradictions of everyday life and culture. The latter has, of course, been argued not only by Bourdieu (1977) in his theory of practice and in Geertz's (1973) discussion of culture and meaning, but also through feminist assertions of everyday experience as a critical conceptual tool. This has analytical implications in a range of substantive fields that are significant in a sociology of gender. Thus, while sociologists have questioned the still widely held view that there is a decline in the extended family household with modernity (Shah 1998), it persists along with assumptions that a shift to nuclear/elementary forms would imply egalitarian and democratic relations. Domestic violence, the continuing exclusion of women from the public spheres of paid employment and politics and their overwhelming presence as unpaid workers question this idea. The complex shifts in the form and gendering of domestic organisation and relations have been highlighted in various studies that draw out bilateral practices, forms of domestic labour, the embedding of households in patrilineal kinship networks and the shaping of conjugal relations through gender ideologies. The last, both religiously and culturally made, asserts ideas and moralities of domesticity, chastity, sexual purity and wifehood for women and the dangers in public space, linking this to masculinity, men as livelihood providers and status honour (Abraham 2013; Chowdhry 2007).

My critique is not to suggest that the rules and viewpoints of the dominant are not of symbolic and material significance in a sociology of gender. These are reflected in the restrictions and absences of women from the public sphere and the social ignominy tied to women and men who cannot follow these norms. It is seen in the policing of the choices and sexualities of young women and men as well as those not so

[11] The debate in the pages of the *EPW* between Guru (1995) and Rege (1998) bring this issue out, as also Rao (2003).

young who may support them and which have been analysed in studies of 'love-marriage', 'honour killings' and the operations of law (Baxi 2014; Chowdhry 2007). A question which keeps emerging is whether the rules and practices of the dominant have changed? Have they, in their earlier or newer patterns, become more hegemonic in shaping the values and practices of subaltern communities and social categories? Or are other materialities leading to the spread of Hindu, upper-caste practices such as dowry and sex-selective abortion?

I come finally to that conceptual and theoretical question that perhaps is 'the' common concern in gender studies today—the question of agency. To put it simplistically, on the one hand, women's movements and their political actions point to collective agency. On the other, structuralist analyses as well as a tendency in Foucauldian discourse analysis deny women and men the agency to act to change. It appears as if men cannot help but be patriarchs and exploiters and women cannot but be dupes and victims! Or in reverse, all action, behaviours and choices could be taken to indicate free agency, such that women were their own exploiters or could immediately change their lives and society. Agency was everywhere or nowhere. People act and, undoubtedly, both men and women consciously flout social norms, find coping strategies, work towards pragmatic ends, resist and act for social change. These have been the problematics of study, even when dissolved into concepts of the integration of women, participation or empowerment, as have the themes of individual and collective resistance and struggle, self, the subject and personhood. A gendered sociology will have to push much further not only in analysing the intermeshing of structure, discourse and agency, the dynamics of power and agency, or choice and agency but also the cultural and social contradictions and processes that shape, limit, enhance and engender agency.

References

Abraham, Janaki. 2013. '"Why Did You Send Me Like This?" Marriage, Matriliny and the "Providing Husband" in North Kerala, India'. In *Marrying in South Asia: Shifting Concepts, Changing Practices in a Globalised World*, edited by Ravinder Kaur and Rajni Palriwala, 293–310. Delhi: Orient BlackSwan.

Ahmed, Sara. 1994. 'The Rhetorics of Participation Re-examined: The State, NGOs and Water Users at Varanasi, Uttar Pradesh'. *The Environmentalist* 14 (1): 3–16.

Ambedkar, Bhim Rao. 1917. 'Castes in India: Their Mechanism, Genesis and Development'. *Indian Antiquary* 41: 81–95.

Ardener, Edwin. 1975a. 'Belief and the Problem of Women'. In *Perceiving Women*, edited by Shirley Ardener, 1–17. London: Malaby Press.

———. 1975b. 'The Problem Revisited'. In *Perceiving Women*, edited by Shirley Ardener, 19–27. London: Malaby Press.

Basu, Srimati, ed. 2005. *Dowry and Inheritance: Issues in Contemporary Indian Feminism*. New Delhi: Women Unlimited.

Baxi, Pratiksha. 2014. *Public Secrets of Law: Rape Trials in India*. New Delhi: Oxford University Press.

Behera, Navnita Chadha. 2006. *Gender, Conflict and Migration: Women and Migration in Asia*. New Delhi: SAGE.

Bourdieu, Pierre. 1977. *Outline of a Theory of Practice*. Translated by Richard Nice. Cambridge: Cambridge University Press.

Caplan, Lionel. 1984. 'Bridegroom Price in Urban India: Class, Caste and *"Dowry* Evil*" Among Christians* in Madras'. *Man*, n.s., 19 (2): 216–33.

Chaudhuri, Maitrayee. 2001. 'Gender and Advertisements: The Rhetoric of Globalisation'. *Women's Studies International Forum* 24 (3/4): 373–85.

Chen, Marty, ed. 1998. *Widows in India: Social Neglect and Public Action*. New Delhi and Thousand Oaks, CA: SAGE.

Chowdhry, Prem. 2007. *Contentious Marriages, Eloping Couples: Gender, Caste and Patriarchy in Northern India*. New Delhi: Oxford University Press.

Committee on the Status of Women in India. 1974. *Towards Equality*. Delhi: Government of India.

Crenshaw, Kimberle. 1993. 'Mapping the Margins: Intersectionality, Identity Politics and Violence Against Women of Colour'. *Stanford Law Review* 43 (6): 1241–299.

Dube, Leela. 1988 'On the Construction of Gender: Socialization of Hindu Girls in Patrilineal India'. *Economic & Political Weekly* 23 (18): WS11–19.

———. 2000. 'Doing Kinship and Gender'. *Economic & Political Weekly* 35 (46): 4037–47.

Fraser, Nancy. 2013. *Fortunes of Feminism: From State Managed Capitalism to Neo-liberal Crisis*. New York, NY: Verso Books.

Gatens, Moira. 1983. 'A Critique of the Sex/Gender Distinction'. In *Beyond Marxism? Interventions After Marx*, edited by J. Allen and P. Petton, 142–61. Sydney: Interventions Publications.

Geertz, Clifford. 1973. *The Interpretation of Cultures*. New York, NY: Basic Books.

Good, Anthony. 1991. *The Female Bridegroom: A Comparative Study of Life-crisis Rituals in South India and Sri Lanka*. Oxford: Clarendon.

Gough, Kathleen. 1956. 'Brahman Kinship in a Tamil Village'. *American Anthropologist* 58 (5): 826–53.

Guru, Gopal. 1995. 'Dalit Women Talk Differently'. *Economic & Political Weekly* 30 (42): 2548–50.

Harlan, Leslie and Paul B. Courtright, eds. 1995. *From the Margins of Hindu Marriage: Essays on Gender, Religion, and Culture*. Oxford: Oxford University Press.

Hekman, Susan. 2010. *The Material of Knowledge: Feminist Disclosures*. Bloomington and Indianapolis, IN: Indiana University Press.

Hershman, Paul. 1977. 'Virgin and Mother'. In *Symbols and Sentiments: Cross-culture Studies in Symbolism*, edited by I.M. Lewis, 269–92. London: Academic Press.

Jeffery, Patricia. 1979. *Frogs in a Well: Indian Women in Purdah*. London: Zed Books.

John, Mary E., Ravinder Kaur, Rajni Palriwala, Saraswati Raju and Alpana Sagar. 2008. *Planning Families, Planning Gender: The Adverse Child Sex Ratio in Selected Districts of Madhya Pradesh, Rajasthan, Himachal Pradesh, Haryana and Punjab*. Bengaluru: Books for Change.

Kabeer, Naila. 1994. *Reversed Realities: Gender Hierarchies in Development Thought*. London: Verso Books.

———. 2002. *The Power to Choose: Bangladeshi Women and Labour Market Decisions in London and Dhaka*. London: Verso Books.

Kapadia, Karen. 1993 'Marrying Money: Changing Preference and Practice in Tamil Marriage'. *Contributions to Indian Sociology* 27 (1): 25–51.

Karve, Irawati. 1968. *Kinship Organization in India*. Bombay: Asia Publishing House.

Kaur, Ravinder and Rajni Palriwala, eds. 2013. *Marrying in South Asia: Shifting Concepts, Changing Practices in a Globalised World*. Delhi: Orient BlackSwan.

Khare, R.S. 1975. '"Embedded" Affinity and Consanguineal "Ethos": Two Properties of the Northern Kinship System'. *Contributions to Indian Sociology* 9 (2): 245–61.

Kolenda, Pauline. 1984. 'Woman as Tribute, Woman as Flower: Images of "Woman" in Weddings in North and South India'. *American Ethnologist* 11 (1): 98–117.

———. 1992 (1982). 'Widowhood Among "Untouchable" Chuhras'. In *Concepts of Person: Kinship, Caste, and Marriage in India*, edited by A. Ostor, Lina M. Fruzetti and Steve Barnett, 172–220. New Delhi: Oxford University Press.

Kumar, Pushpesh. 2006. 'Gender and Procreative Ideologies Among the Kolams of Maharashtra'. *Contributions to Indian Sociology* 40 (3): 279–310.

Lamb, Sarah. 1999. 'Aging, Gender and Widowhood: Perspectives from Rural West Bengal'. *Contributions to Indian Sociology*, n.s., 33 (3): 541–70.

Madan, Triloki Nath. 1981. 'The Ideology of the Householder Among the Kashmiri Pandits'. *Contributions to Indian Sociology* 15 (1–2): 223–49.

Mandelbaum, David G. 1993/1988. *Women's Seclusion and Men's Honor: Sex Roles in North India, Bangladesh, and Pakistan*. Tucson, AZ: Arizona University Press.

Mead, Margaret. 1935. *Sex and Temperament in Three Primitive Societies*. New York, NY: William Morrow.

Millman, Marcia and Rosabeth M. Kanter, eds. 1975. *Another Voice: Feminist Perspectives on Social Life and Social Science*. Garden City, NY: Anchor Press/Doubleday.

Moore, Henrietta. 1988. *Feminism and Anthropology*. Cambridge: Polity Press.
Nongbri, Tiplut. 1988. 'Gender and the Khasi Family Structure: Some Implications of the Meghalaya Succession to Self-Acquired Property Act, 1984'. *Sociological Bulletin* 37 (1/2): 71–82.
Nongbri, Tiplut. 2003. *Development, Ethnicity and Gender: Select Essays on Tribes in India*. Jaipur: Rawat Publications.
Palriwala, Rajni. 1991. 'Transitory Residence and Invisible Work: A Case Study of a Rajasthan Village'. *Economic & Political Weekly* 26 (48): 2763–77.
———. 1993. 'Economics and Patriliny: Consumption and Authority in the Household—A Rajasthan Case-study'. *Social Scientist* 21 (9–11): 47–73.
———. 2010. 'Gendering Sociological Practice: A Case Study of Teaching in the University'. In *Understanding Indian Society—Past and Present: Essays in Honour of A.M. Shah*, edited by Baburao S. Baviskar and Tulsi Patel, 308–30. New Delhi: Orient BlackSwan.
———. 2015. 'Rationality, Instrumentality, and the Affective: Crossings and Blurrings in Relations of Care and Intimacy'. *Korean Journal of Sociology* 49 (3): 21–37.
Palriwala, Rajni and N. Neetha. 2011. 'Stratified Familialism: The Care Regime in India through the Lens of Childcare'. *Development and Change* 42 (4): 1049–78.
Palriwala, Rajni and Patricia Uberoi, eds. 2008. *Marriage, Migration and Gender*. New Delhi: SAGE.
Papanek, Hanna and Gail Minault, eds. 1982. *Separate World: Studies of Purdah in South Asia*. Delhi: Chanakya.
Ram, Kalpana. 1992. *Mukkuvar Women: Gender, Hegemony, and Capitalist Transformation in a South Indian Fishing Community*. New Delhi: Kali for Women.
Rao, Anupama. 2003. *Gender and Caste: Issues in Contemporary Indian Feminism*. New Delhi: Kali for Women.
Rege, Sharmila. 1998. 'Dalit Women Talk Differently: "Difference" and Towards a Dalit Feminist Standpoint Position'. *Economic & Political Weekly* 33 (44): WS39–46.
———, ed. 2003a. *Sociology of Gender: The Challenge of Feminist Sociological Knowledge*. New Delhi: SAGE.
———. 2003b. 'More than Just Tacking Women on to the "Macropicture": Feminist Contributions to Globalisation Discourses'. *Review of Women's Studies, Economic & Political Weekly* 38 (43): 4555–63.
Risseeuw, Carla, Kamala Ganesh and Rajni Palriwala. 2005. *Care, Culture and Citizenship: Revisiting the Politics of Welfare in the Netherlands*. Amsterdam: Spinhuis.
Shah, Arvind M. 1998. *The Family in India: Critical Essays*. New Delhi: Orient Longman.
Sharma, Ursula. 1980. *Women, Work and Property in North West India*. London: Tavistock.

Sharma, Ursula. 1986. *Women's Work, Class, and the Urban Household: A Study of Shimla, North India*. London: Tavistock.

Smith, Dorothy. 1974. 'Women's Perspective as a Radical Critique of Sociology'. *Sociological Inquiry* 44 (1): 7–13.

Srinivas, M.N. 1978. *The Changing Position of Indian Women* (Huxley Memorial Lecture). New Delhi: Oxford University Press.

———. 1984. *Some Reflections on Dowry* (J.P. Naik Memorial Lecture). New Delhi: Oxford University Press.

Uberoi, Patricia. 2006. *Freedom and Destiny: Gender, Family, and Popular Culture in India*. New Delhi: Oxford University Press.

Vatuk, Sylvia. 1975. 'Gifts and Affines in North India'. *Contributions to Indian Sociology* 9 (2): 155–96.

Vergati, Anne. 1982. 'Social Consequences of Marrying Visnu Nārāyana: Primary Marriage Among the Newars of Kathmandu Valley'. *Contributions to Indian Sociology* 16 (2): 271–87.

Whitehead, Anne. 1979. 'Some Preliminary Notes on the Subordination of Women'. *IDS Bulletin* 37 (4): 10–13.

Yalman, Nur. 1963. 'On the Purity of Women in the Castes of Ceylon and Malabar'. *The Journal of the Royal Anthropological Institute of Great Britain and Ireland* 93 (1): 25–58.

Yanagisako, Syliva J. and Jane F. Collier, eds. 1987. *Gender and Kinship: Essays Toward a Unified Analysis*. Stanford, CA: Stanford University Press.

18

Contemporary Intimacies

Perveez Mody

Intimacy is what the best ethnography was about.

—Arjun Appadurai (1997)

Introduction

In 2008, a leading Indian English language magazine conducted an 11-metro-wide survey on the sexual secrets of Indians. In popular parlance in South Asia, the English word 'intimacy' and the terms 'being intimate' or 'having intimate relations' are often used as pejorative euphemisms for inappropriate sexual relationships that dare not speak their name, and the survey was clearly designed to titillate and unearth the unspeakable. Interestingly, the survey made no mention of caste or religious identity, as though intimate relations are the only ones with the potential to jettison all cultural and ethno-religious constraints, the implication being that respondents act and behave as denizens of cities or as genders rather than as members of any other socially significant grouping. The survey focused on urban distinctions that apparently made themselves manifest through the study. So, for example, here is one initial observation provided by the agency commissioned to analyse the survey results for female respondents:

Celebrity porn (32%) and Indian porn (31%) are the most common types of pornography watched. The highest incidence of bisexual porn viewing is in Chennai (20%) and Ahmedabad (20%). At 42 percent, rape is, far and away, the most preferred porn theme in Lucknow.[1]

Issues of globalisation, consumption, gender and sexuality collide with no context in the survey to produce such observations about a league table of preferences for 'rape' porn. In thinking critically about intimacy and its place in understanding our societies, what are we to make of such blunt assertions of people's viewing habits? How are we as social scientists to study and describe the massive changes convulsing our societies on every level, but particularly at the level of that which is most intimate when intimacy is reduced to all things sexual? In this chapter, I will identify why we might look to the study of intimacy to provide new questions and better answers to the changes we can discern around us. What follows is a description of what intimacy is, why it might be anthropologically interesting and how it can be an important lens through which to better understand contemporary change in South Asia.

What Is Intimacy?

In addition to the morally loaded connotation of intimacy as sexual intercourse, the word also brings to mind a whole range of affective states. So, for instance, the *Oxford English Dictionary* characterises intimacy as '(a) (i) a quality or condition of being intimate, (ii) a euphemism for sexual intercourse, (iii) closeness of observation, knowledge or the like; (b) intimate or close connection or union; (c) inner or inmost nature, an inward quality or feature'.

Intimacy is a latecomer to the anthropological scene, so we would do well to begin by understanding its close conceptual relatives. After all, why bother with intimacy, if other analytics (for instance, 'kinship', 'relatedness', 'love') can do the same work using different categories. The answer to this must lie in the way in which intimacy describes the quality of relationships as open-ended and almost nebulous in nature. Intimacy connotes both 'something' and 'nothing'—being simultaneously a quality of closeness and the 'process' for generating closeness that is in the making. It is a productive space in which possibility is

[1] I provide the quote in full, but it will be obvious to the reader that the data presented here is almost meaningless without further qualification (e.g., the sample size, the number of respondents to a particular question and so on). The point here is to illustrate the uncritical way in which the data was both collected and offered in order to illustrate apparent sexual secrets.

maximised and social recognition of it is not a prerequisite; indeed, very often, intimacy is an internal relation between people that is not public or even necessarily acknowledged, so unlike marriage, for example, it does not require social recognition to exist. Intimacy is inter-subjectively experienced, and it is often unclear how and to what effect a third party may begin to comprehend the quality and nature of the relationship. At the same time, and paradoxically, intimacy is a highly stylised cultural trope.

Lynn Jamieson provides an insightful definition categorising intimacy as a term that 'complements rather than supplants' other terms of sociological interest:

> Although there may be no universal definition, intimate relationships are a type of personal relationships that are subjectively experienced and may also be socially recognised as close. The quality of 'closeness' that is indicated by intimacy can be emotional and cognitive, with subjective experiences including a feeling of mutual love, being 'of like mind' and special to each other. Closeness may also be physical, bodily intimacy, although an intimate relationship need not be sexual and both bodily and sexual contact can occur without intimacy. (Jamieson 2011: 1)

Jamieson's observation illustrates that intimacy ranges over multidimensional aspects of sociality, in the manner of an adjective. In my analysis, anthropologically speaking, intimacy is adverbial—both conceptually as an inter-subjective experience and methodologically, as the means by which participant observation becomes meaningful ethnography.

Intimacy serves as a placeholder for the quality of inter-subjective closeness in relationships as well as the process of generating such mutual familiarity. This process is as much in evidence in the bazaar as it is in the bedroom—as Zelizer (2005: 5) warns, intimacy is not a 'fragile flower that withers on contact with money and economic self interest'. Critiquing the 'hostile worlds thesis' that perpetuates the boundary between the market and the intimate, Zelizer shows how systematically we veil the financial aspects of all manner of intimacies, not least in the shape of highly gendered marital contributions of labour, finance and care that are culturally elided in Euro-American kinship until they are rudely brought to the fore in the event of divorce. Similarly, Faier's work on the commodification of intimacy among Filipino bar girls falling in love with and marrying Japanese farmers seeking wives looks at the ways in which marriage and love come to be treated as intimate relations that are 'being made meaningful through global processes' (Faier 2007). In this vein, Constable argues against studies of intimacy that seek to morally authenticate relationships, and instead urges us to focus on the ways in which intimate relations are commodified, that is, 'bought or sold; packaged and advertised; fetishized, commercialised, or objectified' and furthermore, the ways in which those involved in such relationships and processes understand and experience these processes (Constable 2009: 50–54). The salience of these studies has been to systematically demonstrate that intimacy is, in fact, a commodity (Bernstein 2007; Heywood 2009). The anthropological task remains one of synthesising the emotional and economic values and constraints of these exchanges as we find them.

Others have defined intimacy in a more active sense as a self-conscious and well-defined process. The sociologist Anthony Giddens' work *The Transformation of Intimacy* (1992) set out a thesis that intimacy is a particularly contemporary sense of individual identity that grows out of the surge of global capitalism, the democratisation of society, an increasing stress on gender equality and is driven by practices of intimate self-disclosure and the need for personal fulfilment in marriage. For Giddens, intimacy is a 'pure relationship' based on the equality of the genders, entered into for its own sake, and terminated by either partner when their needs are no longer satisfied. Giddens' thesis has attracted much attention, particularly from detractors who have found it unreasonably narrow and unable to explain the intimate relationships they encounter on the ground. The argument was particularly disputed by those who found that intimacy continued to be sustained *despite* gender inequality and other forms of hierarchy (see also Jamieson 1999; Parry 2001; Srivastava 2007).

Love-Marriage

My own work on love-marriage in Delhi (Mody 2002, 2006, 2008) has sought to synthesise the place of intimacy with respect of the law. Through an ethnographic study of the debates and processes through which marriages for Indians came to be legitimated by the state, I was able to identify the ways in which love-marriages have always occupied a liminal social and legal space in which love continued to be regarded over a long period of time as an unacceptable basis for marriage. For instance, the mere presence of a heterosexual pair entering the Tis Hazari court premises where I conducted my fieldwork triggered the suspicion among touts and marriage room lawyers that 'the couple' were there to have a love-marriage. Over 125 years after India obtained a law that allowed the state to legitimate intimacies through court marriage, couples attending the court were marked out as doing something visibly transgressive that made them vulnerable both to society and to the law as practised in the court.

Conducting fieldwork with love-marriage couples revealed the striking observation that the intimacy that society was so quick to identify was very far from the reality experienced by most couples. For many couples, the intimacy they experienced was both alarming and surprising—and the mixed emotions generated by the process of sharing communications frequently meant that such intimacies were often unacknowledged and unnamed, holding in abeyance the troubling social ramifications that could follow acts of publicity. The tension between declaring even to each other that the relationship meant 'something' or was really 'nothing' was notable. Love and intimacy were frequently foisted upon them by third parties who sought to uncover the intimacies they feared, and name and shame the couple through such publicity. This reveals once again the extent to which the nebulous and adverbial nature of intimacy is a productive space that can be shaped to suit the purposes at hand. For much the same reason, I discovered that even after legally legitimate marriages, women who had had a love-marriage were at pains to conceal their love-marriages and to act the 'traditional' wife in order not to be seen as 'bad' women for having exercised spousal choice.

The anthropologist Jonathan Parry (2001: 783–88), working in Bhilai, Chhattisgarh, has shown how conjugal intimacy (as he defines it, 'familiar and affectionate companionship and the sharing of inner thoughts and feelings') among his Satnami informants does not necessarily engender equality nor that people come to see their relationships as essentially dissoluble. Parry's work successfully deconstructs Giddens' version of the global transformation of intimacy. Parry assembles his ethnographic evidence; the older generation of Satnamis had very high rates of marriage and divorce (Parry [2001: 786] only half-jokes when he says that this pocket of India has divorce rates higher than contemporary California), whereas their children appear to be adopting a more companionate model of conjugality in which love and marriage are definitively for keeps. The anthropological fieldwork revealed that the older generation are cold-brained (*thanda dimag*) when it comes to marrying, whereas the younger generation, eager to leave the uncivilised ways of their parents behind, seek companionate (and lifelong) love-marriages, and these carry a heavy moral freight. In the process of this surprising 'transformation of intimacy', younger women give up their earning capacity and the world of labour and work (with all its sexual temptations) that their mothers enjoyed and sequester themselves into domesticity and the home. Parry provides a fascinating anthropological parable for the study of conjugal intimacy in South Asia, ending with the sage advice—do not believe the man on the train who wants to tell you that Indians do not go in for divorce or extra-marital sex.

Intimacy has many obvious overlaps with other anthropologically salient terms such as kinship, relatedness, subjectivity and sexuality—all of which constitute sufficient conditions for intimacy but do not necessarily engender it. For example, Veena Das (1976) has shown how Punjabi joint-family kinship demands that some categories of kin maintain 'masks' and do not publicly display familiarity between spouses because conjugal intimacy is known to be threatening to the cohesiveness and collective values of the household; for example, the newly married son publicly avoids any intimacy with his wife. Intimacy can develop through cohabitation, or through friendship, with knowledge, trust and care—but its social configuration can be more convoluted (including by way of an apparent denial or repression), which brings to mind Srivastava's (2007: 275) description of intimacy as 'competing senses of the self in relation to others'. This understanding of intimacy as a convoluted state is explored by Lawrence Cohen (2007) in his study of the way pornographic political satire manifests an outlet through which men attending Holi festivities in Varanasi can find ways of expressing themselves both socially and sexually.

The almost total effacement of the self is brought home by Chopra (2007) in her work on migrant male domestic workers in middle-class Indian homes. Chopra has argued that in order to survive and be permitted as a 'safe' presence within the home, these male domestic employees must carefully manage any intimacies that may be generated by their presence within small and cramped households in which they find employment. Chopra argues that male workers can only be considered 'a part of the family' if they fully enact the rules of 'exclusion, permission and prohibition' through emasculating actions such as maintaining a servile style of bodily comportment likened to veiling and through a subservient demeanour. This performatively asserts that the male domestic worker is a 'safe' male stranger within the home. These men are expected to be continually managing their masculinity so as to ensure that they are non-threatening to the women of the household who are their employers (Chopra 2007: 191). Such male veiling and self-effacement draw attention to the potential for everyday intimacies to challenge values of social and economic hierarchy. In both Das and Chopra, the absence of intimacy comes to define the intimate space.

Intimacy will always have relevance and meaning in our domestic lives, due to the fundamental potential for sociality generated within shared space. The age of the Internet has expanded that space beyond measure, and so has expanded the potential for intimacy. Appadurai (1997: 116) presciently observed the way in which globalisation (and nascent social networks) produced and reproduced intimacy:

> However far people may travel, however porous the boundaries between cultures, however mobile the values and meanings of the world in which we live, human life still proceeds through the practices of intimacy—the work of sexuality and reproduction, the webs of nurture and of friendship, the heat of anger and violence, the nuance of gesture and tone. The world of globalisation may have generated some cyborg forms of sociality, but the routine work of social reproduction still usually involves the boundless mysteries of intimacy as an everyday social practice.

Intimacy may be most obviously quantifiable in kinship and social reproduction, but it is also able to be powerfully present in all forms of sociality, whether they are Facebook friendships, love affairs, political alliances or Twitter storms.

Due to globalisation and mass communication, the experience of intimacy risks ballooning to the point of omnipresence. This has been poignantly captured by the term 'ambient intimacy', coined in 2007 by a technology critic Leisa Reichelt, describing the way fragments of information communicated via various social platforms allow people to follow and experience the rhythms of each other's lives:[2]

> I've been using a term to describe my experience of Twitter [...]. I call it Ambient Intimacy. Ambient intimacy is about being able to keep in touch with people with a level of regularity and intimacy that you wouldn't usually have access to, because time and space conspire to make it impossible.

Ambient intimacy describes the co-presence generated by digital media, and the task for social scientists is to understand what kind of

---

[2] http://www.disambiguity.com/ambient-intimacy/ (accessed on 17 July 2016).

intimates people become when they share such space.[3] Kyle Chayka[4] argues that the intimate ambience is now a loud noise because too many 'entities', from friends to corporate advertising, are trying to be intimate with us at once, usually on the same platform. Intimacy as inter-subjective, digitised ambience that is unobtrusive and meaningful has expanded to such an extent as to be experienced by some users as becoming 'mundane' or stressful, and effectively objective. It is too hard to keep up with the proliferation of online intimacies such that intimate opportunities become increasingly superficial experiences, and the world of online communication is filled with users who seek to filter out undesirables or who simply turn off. As Alfred Gell (2011 [1996]) has argued, intimacy is as much about secrecy and trust as it is about knowledge and communication.

Conclusion

Anthropologists are extremely well-placed to understand these everyday intimacies and the culturally salient ways in which they are expressed. The quote by Arjun Appadurai with which I began this article—that intimacy is what the best ethnography has always been about—reminds us of the adverbial nature of the term. Intimacy adds meaning to relationships; it is also a way of being in relationships.

The ethnographic understanding of intimacy is delicately poised. Generated in ethnography, it is balanced between trust and the risk of destroying trust that comes from sharing knowledge and experience. Anthropology has been internally enlivened to the intersubjectivity of anthropologists and informants even if our representations of these are always partial (e.g., see Trawick 1992). It is precisely the intimacy generated out of long-term relationships typical of anthropological fieldwork that stand to distinguish anthropological studies of intimacy

---

[3] It is certainly clear that the nature of the different platforms facilitates intimacies in different ways—take Boellstorff's observation that online social world Second Life users protested greatly when the facility for voice communication was offered—the complaint that caused it to be removed was that the anonymity afforded to one's avatar would be spoilt by the intrusion of voice-based (as opposed to online text-based) communication (Boellstorff 2008).

[4] Kyle Chayka, 'How Ambient Intimacy Became So Overwhelming', *Pacific Standard*, 2 January 2015. Available at: https://psmag.com/how-ambient-intimacy-became-so-overwhelming-3a9e9190af14#.dre014tn2 (accessed on 17 July 2016).

from those proliferating qualitative methods that eagerly assert academic legitimacy with the claim of providing an 'ethnography' or using 'ethnographic method'.

References

Appadurai, Arjun. 1997. 'Fieldwork in the Era of Globalisation'. *Anthropology and Humanism* 22 (1): 115–18.

Bernstein, Elizabeth. 2007. *Temporarily Yours: Intimacy, Authenticity, and the Commerce of Sex*. Chicago, IL: University of Chicago.

Boellstorff, Tom. 2008. *Coming of Age in Second Life: An Anthropologist Explores the Virtually Human*. Princeton, NJ: Princeton University Press.

Chopra, Radhika. 2007. 'Invisible Men: Masculinity, Sexuality and Male Domestic Labour'. In *Sexualities*, edited by Nivedita Menon, 177–96. Delhi: Women Unlimited.

Cohen, Lawrence. 2007. 'Holi in Banaras and the Mahaland of Modernity'. In *Sexualities*, edited by Nivedita Menon, 197–223. Delhi: Women Unlimited.

Constable, Nicole 2009. 'The Commodification of Intimacy: Marriage, Sex, and Reproductive Labor'. *Annual Review of Anthropology* 38: 49–64.

Das, Veena. 1976, January. 'Masks and Faces: An Essay on Punjabi Kinship'. *Contributions to Indian Sociology* 10 (1): 1–30.

Faier, Lieba. 2007. 'Filipina Migrants in Rural Japan and Their Professions of Love'. *American Ethnologist* 34 (1): 148–62.

Gell, Alfred. 2011 [1996]. 'On Love' in *Anthropology of this Century*, Issue 2, October 2011, London (available at http://aotcpress.com/articles/love/, last accessed 2 August 2018). Published in French as 'Armour, Connaissance et Dissimulation' in *Terrain: Revue d'ethnologie de l'Europe*, No. 27, September 1996 (Translated by Catherine Rouslin).

Heywood, Paolo. 2009. 'Topographies of Love: Two Discourses on the Russian Mail-order Bride Industry'. *Cambridge Anthropology* 29 (2): 26–45.

Jamieson, Lynn. 1999, August. 'Intimacy Transformed? A Critical Look at the "Pure Relationship"'. *Sociology* 33 (3): 477–94.

———. 2011. 'Intimacy as a Concept: Explaining Social Change in the Context of Globalisation or Another Form of Ethnocentrism?' *Sociological Research Online* 16 (4): 15.

Mody, Perveez. 2002. 'Love and the Law: Love-Marriage in Delhi'. *Modern Asian Studies* 36 (1): 223–56.

———. 2006. 'Kidnapping, Elopement and Abduction: An Ethnography of Love-Marriage in Delhi'. In *Love in South Asia: A Cultural History*, edited by F. Orsini, 331–44. Cambridge: Cambridge University Press.

———. 2008. *The Intimate State: Love-Marriage and the Law in Delhi*. Delhi and London: Routledge.

Parry, Jonathan. 2001, October. 'Ankalu's Errant Wife: Sex, Marriage & Industry in Contemporary Chhattisgarh'. *Modern Asian Studies* 35 (4): 783–820. Cambridge: Cambridge University Press.

Srivastava, Sanjay. 2007. *Passionate Modernity: Sexuality, Class, and Consumption in India*. Delhi: Routledge.

Trawick, Margaret. 1992. *Notes on Love in a Tamil Family*. Berkeley, CA: University of California Press.

Zelizer, Viviana 2005. *The Purchase of Intimacy*. Princeton, NJ: Princeton University Press.

19

Conjugality and Marital Dissolution in Historical Perspective

Shalini Grover

Introduction

The rapid social change in the Indian society that has accompanied transmutations in the economic sphere has led to a spate of enquiries about the manner in which marriage and intimacies are being transformed (Chowdhury 2014; Grover 2011a, 2017; Kaur and Palriwala 2014; Osella 2012; Srivastava 2007). An increasing number of scholars are embracing these topics as core research areas. Previously, anthropology and sociology employed a functionalist approach, neglecting the fluidity, dynamism and diversity of arrangements inherent in everyday marital relations (Grover 2009: 2). Prominent monographs of the 1970s (see, e.g., Parry 1979) would magisterially impart the norms, structures and rules of kinship systems. In contrast to this exclusive focus method, South Asia research now examines conjugality as a 'lived experience' (Basu 2015; Basu and Ramberg 2014; Holden 2008; Lemons 2016; Mody 2008; Parry 2001; Vatuk 2017). Apart from adding deeper insights, these redefined explorations have also opened imperative heterodox debates around non-marriage, same-sex unions and homosociability. The growing visibility of movements like the LGBT (lesbian, gay, bisexual and transgender) exemplifies the exciting fusion of activism and research.

The association of globalisation with new social and economic subjectivities has led scholars to closely review marriage systems. Key questions probed include moves from 'collective' family-arranged alliance to 'self-initiated' love-marriages, as well as the advent of formal divorce. Of continued relevance here is Goode's (1963) influential modernisation paradigm and Giddens' (1999) insistence of the 'pure relationship' as a global phenomenon.[1] Fine-grained ethnographies have countered popular predictions emanating from the modernisation paradigm. These contributions, as I shall recount, establish how the arranged marriage system remains resilient, while caste endogamy is being modified only to certain degrees (Fuller and Narasimhan 2008; Parry 2001). As a consequence, even new forms of Internet spouse selection that are replacing traditional matchmaking often seem to be reinforcing caste-community hierarchies (Agrawal 2015; Chakraborty 2012). In parallel, in areas of North India with the most skewed sex ratios, marriage has not lost its function. The 'solution', in these pockets of local shortage, has been to 'import' cross-regional brides (Kaur 2004).

Furthermore, marital practices that entail courtship and premarital intimacy are increasingly conspicuous in India's globalised cities. In certain middle-class milieus, the flexibility of the 'arranged–love' dichotomy and their new accretions are emerging (Donner 2002; Fuller and Narasimhan 2008; Mody 2008). Paradoxically, in other urban settings, where young people have assimilated modern ideas, marriage has led to a reinforcement of gender inequality (Parry 2001). This is chiefly because marriage is also becoming an expression of class status and adopting middle-class mores has led to a lessening of women's autonomy (ibid.). Thus, there are no easy answers as to the direction in which marriage is evolving. Emerging subject areas such as masculinities and transnational marriages are being appraised in texturing intimacies with new cultural understandings (Charsley 2013; Qureshi 2016).

For the purposes of this article, the study of divorce brings into sharp focus a set of emotional dynamics extending well beyond the wedding phase of rituals. If nuptials constitute one spectrum of the adult life cycle, the media's voyeuristic fascination with marriages that end

---

[1] Goode (1963) suggests that developing nations and emerging economies will replicate the Western nuclear family as the norm. A nuclear unit as Goode envisages is emotionally autonomous or disconnected from wider kin. In a similar vein, Giddens' (1999: 58) 'pure relationship' is one where 'relations are entered into for its own sake'. The 'pure relation' is built upon ideals of spousal equality and voluntary choice in initiating and ending relationships.

finds its way in captions such as 'Rising Divorce Rates: India Joins the Western Bandwagon', 'In Tradition-bound India, Female, Divorced and Happy' and 'What Makes Delhi the Divorce Capital' (*Times of India* 2007).[2] Such commentaries suggest that Indian marriage is in the middle of a major overhaul. Rising divorce is attributed to 'ego clashes', intolerance, incompatible lifestyles, individual prosperity and neoliberal aspirations. As Qureshi (2016: 25) perceptively argues, 'A rise in marital breakdown is often conflated with the wider societal trends towards modern individualism'. My research brings into discussion new questions whereby marital dissolution is being ascribed to gender, class and modernisation. This discussion gestures at the methodological problems of the modernisation claim with respect to the subject of marriage and divorce.

For deciphering India's divorce phenomenon,[3] I draw upon ethnographic observations from New Delhi's family courts and Crime Against Women (CAW) cells.[4] During 2010–12, I collected and interpreted divorce statistics, observed matrimonial disputes and court judgments, and conducted interviews with the legal fraternity. This research brought me in contact with a diverse spectrum of middle-class families. My respondents included professionals, entrepreneurs and those from business industrial families. They were from an economically protected echelon. While I conducted participant observation in courts and mediation cells, I established other independent networks with families and individual women through the snowballing method.

To gain a recent historical perspective, I draw extensively on Rama Mehta's (1975) remarkable study on urban Hindu divorced women, which has largely gone unnoticed. Her insights allow for a valuable 50-year perspective for sociological comparisons. In-depth case material from her book enabled me to foreground incisive inferences from

[2] Biju Qadir, 'Rising Divorce Rates: India Joins the Western Bandwagon', *Young Muslim Digest*, April 2011; Pallavi Pasricha, 'What Makes Delhi the Divorce Capital?' *The Times of India*, 4 August 2007, 8; Emily Wax, 'In Tradition-bound India, Female, Divorced and Happy', *Worldview*, September 2008.

[3] To reiterate, my enquiry is aimed at the specificities of formal or legal divorce. Formal divorce entails a process of dissolution in a court of law under the Hindu Marriage Act, 1955. The literature for India indicates an undeniable presence of informal separation and divorce which offers a more complex story of marital practices (Grover 2011b, 2014; Holden 2008; Lemons 2016; Parry 2001; Vatuk 2017).

[4] In New Delhi, four Family Courts were set up during 2008–12. The new courts operate in Dwarka, Rohini, Saket and Patiala House. In the same period, 12 CAW cells were also established across the city.

the 1970s in the context of modernity ideologies and divorce stories of Hindu couples. The ensuing section turns to this analysis.

The Past and the Present: Tracing Divorce from the 1970s

In India, today, the prospect of mutual-consent divorce is located within discourses of modernity. Although this may not be apparent to the layperson, every generation seems inclined to believe that they are more progressive than the previous. This is presented through juxtapositions on how they imagined the past and how they envisage the contemporary (e.g., 'it used to be like that but no longer is'). Societal trends within a nation state are often justified through 'teleological explanations' or 'timeframes of development' (Hart 2007). This is nowhere more evident than the assumption of an increasing number of fragile marriages in the current post-market reform era, that is, from 1980s–1990s onwards. In her study of divorce, Aura (2008: 28) observes: 'All professionals—the judges, the lawyers, the family counsellors, the workers and activists of women's organizations—I came across during my fieldwork convinced me that divorce is becoming more common in Bangalore, particularly among the urban educated middle and upper class people'. I found Delhi's legal fraternity to be stating similar views, talking with fervour about the modern-day conundrum of 'petty ego clashes'. In the family courts, lawyers, litigants and my respondents remarked on a portrait (Photo 19.1) that showcases the nuclear family. The 'exit' in the portrait's mid-point seemed to command considerable discussion on how marriage and family life are in disarray.

Even so, as anthropologists and sociologists, we need to methodologically probe how it is viable to measure an increase or decline in formal divorce, given sparse inventories of marital break-up and lack of statistical information from previous epochs. For example, my endeavours to interpret the 'divorce rate' for New Delhi were challenged, when despite possessing the necessary permission letters, the district courts (Tis Hazari, Karkardooma and Vishwas Nagar) refused to assemble and share divorce statistics. Only after citing the 'Right to Information Act' (RTI Act, 2005), did officials cooperate. Then again, while in the family courts it was easier to access divorce statistics, their computerised data systems generated tabulations that were difficult to discern. Aura (2008: 26) confirms how 'other than a gap of ethnographic knowledge there is a gap of reliable statistical knowledge on divorce and separation in India'.

PHOTO 19.1 *Saket Family Courts (Room No. 1)*

Source: Author.

In the early 1970s, the influence of modern forces was seen as linked to a rising divorce rate. Mehta's (1975: 5) study of 50 middle-class[5] Hindu separated and divorced women from Delhi, Bangalore and Udaipur forms the backdrop to this assertion: 'However, the divorce rate is on the increase, marital difficulties being more evident now than before'. Mehta describes conflict scenarios that escalated into separation and divorce: extreme dominance by affines, dowry demands, male infidelity, domestic violence, physical blemishes on a woman's face and a husband's inability to treat wives equally. She clarifies differences in attitudes of the 25 'upper'- and 25 'lower'-middle-class cohort cases she studied with regard to upbringing, conjugal expectations, marital dissolution and support of natal kin. Lower-middle-class women grew up in a conservative joint-family milieu where family honour was the norm (p. 8): 'Their parental environment emphasised the fact that a woman, in order to receive respect from others, must be pliable, self-sacrificing,

[5] As I will go on to explain, there is a split between 25 'upper'- and 25 'lower'-middle-class women.

and at all times, obedient to her husband and his parents'. Education enhanced the prospect of family-arranged marriage, while post marriage, women were expected to lead a secluded life, with employment being discouraged. Crucially, despite legal reforms, marriage was viewed as a sacred and indissoluble union.[6] This ideal fostered acute stigma around divorce. Out of 25 lower-middle-class women who had arranged marriages, the majority were not the initiators of divorce; that is, they did not take any form of legal action. Their decision to cooperate in terminating a marriage did not coincide with the desire for a better life after divorce. While 18 women did separate without legal protection, of the remaining 7, 4 were divorced and 3 had legal protection. Many women were 'discarded' by their husbands, who did not consider them as 'worthy' companions. To circumvent shame, most women eschewed the courts. As divorced daughters, they were tolerated by their parents, but not always welcomed. The support they received was varied and temporary.

On the other hand, upper-middle-class women were raised in a 'free atmosphere where only parents exercised control over them'. In these nuclearised families that comprised the professional elite, daughters were made to pursue a Western-oriented education that would match employment prospects (Mehta 1975: 93): 'Whereas parents did regard marriage as the most important goal in life, they did not exclude the possibility of a career for their female children'. Then again, in spite of the greater freedom accorded to these women, with careers being accentuated, marriage was still regarded as an indissoluble union. Yet the motivations for marital break-up appear to be somewhat dissimilar from those in the lower middle classes. From 25 women, 12 separated without legal protection, and of the remaining 13, 9 divorced and 4 had judicial separation. These women's expectations of marital equality were higher, and they were better informed about their rights. Consequently, they were a more confident group than their lower middle counterparts. They were unfettered in making their domestic angst public. Post divorce, many abstained from residing for a long term with their natal kin, and sought economic autonomy instead. They faced a drastic fall in their standard of living and a reduced level of social status.

[6] The Hindu marriage was 'indissoluble sacrament' until the Hindu Marriage Act of 1954–55. Still, there were provisions even before 1954–55 for a marriage to be dissolved.

In foregrounding the 'divorce rate' and gender ideologies of the 1970s, it suffices to say that the practice of legal divorce was highly stigmatised. This is supported by earlier sociological reflections on 'marital adjustment' on the part of women (Kapur 1970; Singh and Uberoi 1994a, 1994b). Activist writings also stressed upon the attributes of honour and shame that middle-class women were expected to embody (Gandhi and Shah 1992; Kishwar 1989). In parallel, popular Hindi cinema cogently projected conservative family values (Vasudevan 1995), while this continued well into the 1990s (Uberoi 1998). Therefore, it is not surprising that most permanent separations among couples as reported by Mehta were informally negotiated within the family. In Mehta's upper-middle-class sample, judicial separation is more apparent. Keeping in mind our time-frame perspective, how does the information we have from the 1970s from three cities compare with today's elusive 'divorce rate'?

Let us start with the statistics from the family courts. For May 2009–June 2012, my data denotes a total of 13,000 divorce-related cases filed in the family courts.[7] During the same period, 3,528 divorces were granted by 'mutual consent'. No information is available about the background of the petitioners. The courts also acknowledge a backlog of matrimonial disputes that remain under consideration. Moreover, prior to the establishment of family courts, divorce cases were adjudicated in the district courts. The number of registered cases in the district courts were as follows: 8,543 in 2005, rising to 10,022 in 2006, to 10,441 in 2007, to 11,047 in 2008, to 11,109 in 2009 and dropping to 6,388 in 2010. While we can detect a steady increase in registered cases per annum, the noticeable post-2009 decline relates to the transfer of cases to the new family courts. With the functioning of the latter from 2009–12, litigants from the district courts were told to transfer their disputes to the family court nearest in distance to their residential neighbourhood. To reiterate, data from the family courts shows 13,000 filed cases. Here, the administrative readjustment period of transfer cases, combined with the lack of forthcoming statistical information, denotes the difficulties of contextualising the status quo of registered cases.

More so, these statistics from 2005–12 should not be conceptualised entirely as the 'divorce rate'. The above data also cover divorce-related disputes. Saliently, the existing figures hardly point to radical transitions or a dramatic escalation in divorce over the last 50 years, as has

[7] For an in-depth understanding of these divorce-related statistics and further information, see Grover (2016).

been apparent in several Euro-American nations. In the United States and Britain, social policy debates are largely concentrated around single mothers, welfare and 'unstable families', prompting Giddens' (1999: 61) description of 'separating and divorcing societies'. For India, while my data set intimates the increased deployment of divorce laws, the narrative of dramatic rise in marital dissolution is nonetheless hyperbolic. My research turns this sociological debate on marriage and family to the more significant metropolitan trend of changing legal behaviour. From previous eras, consider the enhanced availability of mediation services and other quasi-legal forms of assistance related to family conflict such as domestic violence and property disputes (Grover 2016). The Delhi High Court, National Commission for Women (NCW), CAW cells, Government of Delhi and a host of private firms, all offer mediation services. The latter are being widely advertised in public spaces such as metro stations and road junctions (see Photos 19.2 and 19.3).

In actuality, these mediating institutions are largely assisting litigants with manoeuvring bureaucratic legal systems and complex laws. Besides mutual-consent divorce, other forms of marital dissolution, such as

PHOTO 19.2   *Dwarka Metro Station*

Source: Author.

PHOTO 19.3 *CAW Cells, Special Police Unit*

Source: Author.

'unilateral or one-party divorce', can be easily contested by one spouse, resulting in lengthy and costly procedures and processes. The irony is that while there is much hype about escalating divorce in India, it is by no means easy to procure a formal divorce.

Statistics and figures often form the mainstay for substantiating country-specific marriage patterns. From our collated statistics for Delhi, demographers and economists may form the impression about marriage and family life as static and unchanging. Alternatively, ethnographic renderings may reveal different subjectivities. My investigations elucidate specific yet prominent ideological shifts that can be historically traced. In the 1970s, indissolubility was a powerful ideal even among the upper middle classes who endorsed liberal values. Today, marriage evokes gendered and class-specific caveats. Accordingly, the significance of lifelong stability is in question. In the context of divorce and other rights, my male respondents accent how the state is unfairly regulating family life by favouring women (see Chowdhury 2014 for pro-women laws). My female respondents express how martial instability needs to be viewed through the lens of gender parity; unequivocally as marital partners, women desire more egalitarian relationships. As with Charsley's (2013) ruminations, the threat of divorce is now emphasised by men and women as a major part of the changing landscape of family life.

For other allied gendered transformations pertaining to the family unit, it is instructive to compare marital strife from the 1970s. At this juncture, a legal anthropology of court disputes will illustrate how the conflicts of previous decades are equally conspicuous today. Akin to Mehta's data is the recurring tenor of 'affinal interference' (perceived domination on the part of the husband's family) as intensely rupturing the conjugal bond. Across the social divide, I found affinal interference to be a standard complaint, signalling persistent patriarchy and striking continuities. This grievance formed a sizeable category in quotidian mediation sessions and with respect to divorce petitions and legal remedies. Let us juxtapose how affinal interference unfolded in the 1970s, followed by its articulation in today's matrimonial disputes. For the lower and upper middle classes respectively, Mehta states that

> The dominance of the in-laws over the respondents and the desire on the part of the older generation to still view a daughter-in-law as wholly subordinate to their wishes—thus resulting in extreme resentment on the part of women that led to domestic tensions which were later aggravated by other circumstances. (1975: 44)

> There was very little evidence to show that the marriage contract had broken because of the tyranny of the in-laws though the unsatisfactory relationship between the respondents and their in-laws contributed to irreconcilable differences between the respondents and their husbands. (1975: 107)

The subsequent examples of matrimonial disputes related to affinal interference are drawn from my fieldwork (28 March 2012).

Sudha vs Vinod in the Family Courts

> Along with her parents and brothers, Sudha is waiting for her hearing. Her husband, Vinod, has filed for restitution of conjugal rights, while she has petitioned for spousal maintenance and for a separate residence.

> Sudha: I want to live separately.... I have asked for INR 20,000 per month in maintenance. Last year I left Vinod to live with my parents. For 15 long years, I have put up with

my mother-in-law. There was never a moment of peace in our house. Whenever she got an opportunity, she would instigate fights. Vinod would mostly listen to his mother. This meant that we could not work on our marriage.

I meet Vinod separately. His accusations are bitterly framed around Sudha not being a good wife and daughter-in-law. After all, his elderly mother deserves respect, while Sudha has just walked out on them.

Two other stories resonate with Sudha's rebellion. First, a litigant's wife had left the matrimonial home because she did not want to live with his mother.

Author (Grover): Is that the main reason she has left you?

Litigant: Yes, Alka says she is fed up of my mother.
Second, a young man narrates how his wife, Shruti, has filed three court cases against him and has left the matrimonial home because she wants to live separately.

Mehta underscores how the older generation viewed daughters-in-law as 'wholly subordinate', and these peremptory norms led to irreconcilable differences between spouses. From the above court scenes, it suffices to say that in the metamorphosis today lies in how middle-class women are acting upon affinal dominance. As indicated by Mehta, most women, at least from the lower middle classes, circumvented the courts, seeking instead 'traditional' interventions that eclipsed any sign of familial severance (e.g., elderly kin and caste–community mediation). The unremitting stories of Sudha and others wanting to break away from affines find their way to courtrooms, police stations and CAW cells. Women do not just file singular cases, but multiple ones. Legal aid and free mediation may be on offer (Photo 19.2), and women are encouraged by their natal kin and counsellors to avail these services. This is suggestive of greater gendered agency. It points towards the acceptance of involving the legal system and the declining stigma attached to divorce. It confirms the altering nature of conventional gender norms and overt state intervention as part of contemporary family life. Hitherto for India's middle classes, intergenerational bonds between extended kin and the conjugal couple continue to be intensely negotiated and guarded, rather than the prediction of 'individualized emotions taking precedence over all other social and family relationships' (Giddens 1999. 58) coming to fruition. This is also the opposite of the media's projection of 'individualism' as part of societal trends. As Qureshi (2016: 7, 300) reminds us, women's recourse to state laws relates to 'hard-hitting gender inequalities' and 'very different underly-ing processes and moral compulsions', rather than a 'fallout of tradi-tion'. Her attempt to refashion the debate from individualism to gender inequality is apt here for the cosmopolitism middle classes. Superficial assumptions that women like Sudha, Alka and Shruti are 'walking out' of the affinal home as 'liberated modern subjects' need to be dispelled. It is precisely this sort of reproach that women face, as facile beliefs about 'ego clashes' and 'selfish wives' dominate legal verdicts.

Conclusion: From Indissolubility to Precariousness

Popular discourse and sociological texts often validate the modernisa-tion claim for explicating rising divorce. Mehta (1975: 159 and Preface) used expressions along similar lines of reasoning such as 'divorce is a totally new concept in the traditional Hindu family system'. Qureshi (2016) stresses how the notion of 'modern forces' is deeply entrenched in Euro-American sociology. She cites Richard Berthoud (2000: 24) who simplistically claims that the direction of change among the white British majority lies 'from old-fashioned values to modern individualism'. Hart (2007: 351–53) offers this nuanced corrective: 'It is more accurate to say that individuals and societies are in flux'. For India, moral panics and debates around gender and marriage rekindle themselves intermittently. Our case material validates the persistence of affinal interference over decades and its newly instituted character in legal discourse and behaviour. Identifying features which are 'novel' and those that represent structural continuity is paramount. From Mehta's text, I was struck how her vivid descriptions of gendering and family conflict in the 1970s resonate so effectively with the contempo-rary moment. So much for what is deemed to be modernisation! This interrogation of the recent history of the modernisation–divorce dyad is acutely imperative in an epoch (post market reform) that is being singled out as embracing social reconfigurations and gender equality like never before.

Consecutively, as I have argued in this article, in a certain echelon, there is an ideological loosening of the 'indissolubility' axiom. In her seminal work on marriage, family and kinship, Uberoi (1993) identifies marriage as a 'critical institution'. While marriage has not lost its moral valiance, this critical institution is being viewed with much trepida-tion. Women equate the marital bond less and less with the ideal of lifelong stability, linking divorce with persistent gender inequality. Affines are singled out for still not accepting a 'modern' woman and her choices. Opting out of marriage altogether or the desire to remain single or embrace live-in relationships were also opined by a range of female respondents as pivotal choices being negotiated. Men voice a loss of power and discomfort through the metaphor of state intervention. As sociologists, we need to complicate these gendered perspectives that invoke conjugal precariousness. Euro-American nations have amassed large data sets on divorce and concomitant transitions, that is, permutations in gender roles, the ramifications of divorce on children, evidence from divorce-prevention programmes and post-divorce trajectories. It is time for sociology departments in India to commence rigorous methodological training(s) that encourage longitudinal studies and multi-layered ethnographic approaches for further developing this subject area.

Acknowledgements and Tribute

I thank the *CIS* team for this generous opportunity and interpretative space. I am particularly appreciative of Janaki Abraham and Sanjay Srivastava's thoughtful suggestions. I am grateful to Ajay Mehta for handing me Rama Mehta's elided work. This chapter is a tribute to a feminist sociologist who died after the publication of her book. For scholarly input, I have drawn generously from Kaveri Qureshi's excellent work. This chapter and additional divorce ethnography have benefited from comments I received in May 2016, at the Centre for Development and the Environment (SUM), University of Oslo. In September 2016, I was part of a Swedish South Asian Studies Network (SASNET) panel in Lund, Sweden, on 'Staging Marriage and Modernity Amongst the Middle-Classes in South Asia'. I would like to thank Ajay Bailey and Anindita Datta for their encouragement. Finally, as for long-term institutional support and award fellowships, I am indebted to the Institute of Economic Growth (IEG), the Indian Council of Social Science Research (ICSSR) and University of Edinburgh.

References

Agrawal, Anuja. 2015. 'Cyber-matchmaking Among Indians: Re-arranging Marriage and Doing "Kin-Work"'. *South Asian Popular Culture* 13 (1): 15–30.

Aura, Siri. 2008. 'Women and Marital Status Breakdown in South India'. Doctoral Dissertation, Research Series in Anthropology. University of Helsinki.

Basu, Srimati. 2015. *The Trouble with Marriage: Feminists Confront Law and Violence in India*. Berkeley, CA: University of California Press.

Basu, Srimati and Lucinda Ramberg, eds. 2014. *Conjugality Unbound: Sexual Economies, State Regulation and the Marital Form in India*. New Delhi: Women Unlimited.

Berthoud, Richard. 2000. 'Family Formation in Multi-Cultural Britain: Three Patterns of Diversity', ISER Working Paper Series, No. 2000-34, ISER, Colchester.

Chakraborty, Kabita. 2012. 'Virtual Mate-seeking in the Urban Slums of Kolkata, India'. *South Asian Popular Culture* 10 (2): 197–216.

Charsley, Katharine. 2013. *Transnational Pakistani Connections: Marrying 'Back Home'*. Oxfordshire: Routledge.

Chowdhury, Romit. 2014. 'Family, Femininity, Feminism: "Structures of Feeling" in the Articulation of Men's Rights'. In *Women, Gender, and Everyday Social Transformations in India*, edited by Kenneth Bo Nielsen and Anne Waldrop, 189–202. London: Anthem Press.

Donner, Henrike F. 2002. '"One's Own Marriage": Love-Marriages in a Calcutta Neighbourhood'. *South Asia Research* 22 (1): 79–94.

Fuller, C.J. and Haripriya Narasimhan. 2008. 'Companionate Marriage in India: The Changing Marriage System in a Middle-class Brahman Sub Caste'. *Journal of the Royal Anthropological Institute* 14 (4): 736–54.

Gandhi, Nandita and Nandita Shah. 1992. The *Issues at Stake: Theory and Political Practice in the Contemporary Women's Movement in India*. New Delhi: Kali for Women.

Giddens, Anthony. 1999. *Runaway World: How Globalization Is Reshaping Our Lives*. London: Profile Books.

Goode, William J. 1963. *World Revolution and Family Patterns*. New York, NY: Free Press of Glencoe.

Grover, Shalini. 2009. 'Lived Experiences: Marriage, Notions of Love and Kinship Support Amongst Poor Women in Delhi'. *Contributions to Indian Sociology* 43 (1): 1–33.

———. 2011a. *Marriage, Love, Caste, and Kinship Support: Lived Experiences of the Urban Poor in India*. New Delhi: Social Science Press.

———. 2011b. '"Purani Aur Nai Shaadi": Separation, Divorce, and Remarriage in the Lives of the Urban Poor in New Delhi'. *Asian Journal of Women's Studies* 17 (1): 67–99.

———. 2014. '"Purani Aur Nai Shaadi": Separation, Divorce, and Remarriage in the Lives of the Urban Poor in New Delhi'. In *Marrying in South Asia: Shifting Concepts, Changing Practices in a Globalising World*, edited by Ravinder Kaur and Rajni Palriwala, 311–33. New Delhi: Orient BlackSwan.

———. 2016. 'Jural Relations of Middle-class Marriage and Women as Legal Subjects in the Imaginary of "New India"'. *The Australian Journal of Anthropology (TAJA)*. doi.10.1111/taja.12188.

———. 2017. *Marriage, Love, Caste, and Kinship Support: Lived Experiences of the Urban Poor in India*. Revised new International Edition: United Kingdom and New York: Routledge.

Hart, Kimberly. 2007. 'Love by Arrangement: The Ambiguity of "Spousal Choice" in a Turkish Village'. *Journal of the Royal Anthropological Institute* 13 (2): 345–62.

Holden, Livia. 2008. *Hindu Divorce: A Legal Anthropology*. Aldershot: Ashgate.

Kapur, Promilla. 1970. *Marriage and the Working Women in India*. New Delhi: Vikas Publishing House.

Kaur, Ravinder. 2004. 'Across-region Marriages: Poverty, Female Migration and the Sex Ratio'. *Economic & Political Weekly* 39 (25): 2595–603.

Kaur, Ravinder and Rajni Palriwala, eds. 2014. *Marrying in South Asia: Shifting Concepts, Changing Practices in a Globalising World*. New Delhi: Orient BlackSwan.

Kishwar, Madhu. 1989. 'Towards More Just Norms for Marriage: Continuing the Dowry Debate'. *Manushi* 53 (July–August): 2–9.

Lemons, Katherine. 2016. 'The Politics of Livability: Tutoring "Kinwork" in a New Delhi Women's Arbitration Center'. *POLAR (Political and Legal Anthropological Review)* 39 (2): 244–60.

Mehta, Rama. 1975. *Divorced Hindu Woman*. Delhi: Vikas Publishing House.

Mody, Perveez. 2008. *The Intimate State: Love-Marriage and the Law in Delhi*. Delhi: Routledge.

Osella, Caroline. 2012. 'Desires Under Reform: Contemporary Reconfigurations of Family, Marriage, Love, and Gendering in a Transnational South Indian Matrilineal Muslim Community'. *Culture and Religion* 13 (2): 241–64.

Parry, Jonathan P. 1979. *Caste and Kinship in Kangra*. London: Routledge and Kegan Paul.

———. 2001. 'Ankalu's Errant Wife: Sex, Marriage and Industry in Contemporary Chhattisgarh'. *Modern Asian Studies* 35 (4): 783–820.

Qureshi, Kaveri. 2016. *Marital Breakdown Among British Asians: Conjugality, Legal Pluralism and New Kinship*. London: Palgrave.

Singh, Amita Tyagi and Patricia Uberoi. 1994a. 'Adjustment Is the Key: Post-marital Romance in Indian Popular Fiction'. *Manushi* 61 (November–December): 15–21.

———. 1994b. 'Learning to Adjust: Conjugal Relations in Indian Popular Fiction'. *Indian Journal of Gender Studies* 1 (1): 93–120.

Srivastava, Sanjay. 2007. *Passionate Modernity: Sexuality, Class and Consumption in India*. New Delhi: Routledge.

Uberoi, Patricia, ed. 1993. *Introduction: Family, Marriage and Kinship in India*. New Delhi: Oxford University Press.

———. 1998. 'The Diaspora Comes Home: Disciplining Desire in *DDLJ*'. *Contributions to Indian Sociology* 32 (2): 305–36.

Vasudevan, Ravi S. 1995. '"You Cannot Live in Society—and Ignore It": Nationhood and Female Modernity in *Andaz*'. *Contributions to Indian Sociology* 29 (1–2): 83–108.

Vatuk, Sylvia. 2017. *Marriage and Its Discontents: Women, Islam and the Law in India*. New Delhi: Kali for Women.

20

Gender and Law

Srimati Basu

An incantation of all-too-familiar women's names tells the history of gender and law in India: Rukhmabai, Mathura, Shah Bano, Bhanwari Devi, Soni Sori, Jyoti Singh. The litany reminds us that public memory around gender and law is strung along such crises, and feminist interventions in law and policy mobilised around such episodes of torture, death and dismemberment. (We could, unfortunately, produce many such lists. But doing so would nonetheless leave out anonymous victims of crimes of gender-based violence, and the quotidian nature of many legal encounters which do not draw public scrutiny.) These cases are instructive not only because they generated public debate and roused social movements but because they also bear the scars of unhappy outcomes (these legal icons having died or persistently failed to get justice) and of the unpredictable effects of the reforms produced in their names.

We could examine the trajectory of gender and law in many different permutations and intersections, including labour, reproductive justice, the structural violence of caste and religion, heteronormativity in law or forms of citizenship. This essay follows the threads of law woven between family, kinship and gender-based violence, which necessarily intersect with the above topics, to demonstrate the resilience of power and the circuits of violence in governing class, religion and sexuality.

Lawyers, including feminist lawyers, look to the legal realm in the most concrete of ways, whether in drafting laws or working with clients on strategy. Those (like me) studying gender and law through the lens of social science are wont to dwell more on the dysfunctional co-dependency of the two terms, 'the intimate and mutually defining' relationship between the categories women and state (Rajan 2003: 24): on the one hand, the promise of law to bring about gender justice, and this promise as an alibi for law's benevolent power; on the other, the limitations of law as a vehicle of justice. Demanding legislative change has thus been a cornerstone of feminist campaigns because we need the imprimatur of formal law in order to indicate the weightiness of certain issues: 'to couch a claim in terms of rights is a major step towards a recognition of a social wrong', making the claim 'popular' and 'accessible' (Smart 1989: 143). But rights claims are also a dilemma, in that 'legal rights do not resolve problems. Rather they transpose the problem into one that is seen as having a legal solution' (ibid.: 144). Following Foucault and Derrida (through very different approaches), the notion that law is a disciplining force that creates epistemological categories, and modifies habits and practices because of the shadow of its implicit sanctions, has proved immensely popular.[1]

Wendy Brown reminds us that using the force of law for gender justice is an inherently fraught prospect because 'freedom' and 'protection' can only proliferate through existent forms of power:

If the institutions, practices and discourses of the State are as inextricably, however differently, bound up with the prerogatives of manhood in a male-dominated society, as they are with capital and class in a capitalist society and white supremacy in a racist society, what are the implications for feminist politics? (Brown 1992 [1995]: 8)

Feminist jurisprudence (in contrast to descriptive accounts of 'gender and law') has been a critical intervention in tracking such ambivalent mechanisms of institutionalised power and cultural negotiation, 'shifting the focus on law-as-rule to law-as-process, written law to spoken law and law as a site where meaning is produced, interpreted and conveyed as a field of force' (Baxi 2008: 80). Drawing on perspectives central to law and society studies, that laws are subverted, transformed and applied in context (as Foucault also suggested), and that power is negotiated in overt and subtle ways (Ewick and Silbey 1998; Greenhouse

---

[1] Derrida (1992: 281) speaks of violence as foundational to law: 'in its origin and its end, in its foundation and its preservation, law is inseparable from violence'. Foucault's discussion of 'juridical' power is part of a schematic of forms of power that lie between 'discipline and governance' of the state (Foucault 1991; Wickham 2006).

et al. 1994; Merry 1999 are some classic examples), it draws out pluralities of institutions, actions and methods (Baxi 2008). In similar vein, this essay tracks the multiple forms of power that are made explicit through law, as well as the worlds precipitated by the establishment of new laws, noting how laws may fall short of producing the social justice envisaged in them.

Historians of colonial India have established that the ostensible rationale of 'helping women' was the ground for justifying many legal interventions, contrary to the colonial state's claims to let colonised populations follow their customary rules of kinship. Widow immolation, widow remarriage and age at marriage stand out as the most incendiary examples of using women's issues as the conduit for political negotiations (Mani 1990). Historians have contended that such interventions were instrumental in establishing discourses of civilisational superiority for purposes of governance while also serving as a mobilising cry for imperial feminists (e.g., Sinha 1995). The hypocrisy of colonial solicitude is plainly revealed by the focus on the domestic realm, notably on when to marry and whom to marry, with scarce attention to women's conditions of labour or property inheritance (Nair 1996). Moreover, the codification of laws relied on select native experts who proffered a model based on upper-caste North Indian patrilineal Hindu practices, closing off the diversity of customary law in a process that Spivak (1988) memorably terms 'epistemic violence'. This resulted in a narrowing of women's entitlements, including their access to natal property, and their possibilities of remarriage or forms of sexual life outside of marriage (Arunima 2003; Chowdhry 1994; Sreenivas 2011).

But there is ample evidence that colonial power was neither all-encompassing nor uncontested. Tanika Sarkar (2008: 261) castigates scholarship in which 'the colonised subject is absolved of all complicity and culpability', establishing that 'colonial structures of power compromised with—and indeed learnt much from—indigenous patriarchy and upper-caste norms and practices which, in certain areas of life, retained considerable hegemony'. Core 'ideas about Hindu conjugality at the heart of militant nationalism' continued to erupt through post-colonial attempts at liberal reform of gender as marks of native distinction (ibid.: 259). Historians have also documented that women engaged with new laws rather than being passive subjects of reform, whether by availing of formal laws which gave them an advantage over custom (Anagol 2008; Kozlowski 2008) or by strenuously resisting the narrowing of their rights, narrating their sexual and social lives in courts and hearings in order to argue for economic resources (Arunima 2003; Chowdhry 1994; Sreenivas 2011).

Gender inequalities were not, of course, eliminated in post-colonial India, both because colonial categories had come to be constitutive of many ways of imagining gender, caste and religion and because many groups asserted privileges of gender, caste and religion in the name of return to native values and as opposition to colonial modernity. The new Constitution guaranteed equal rights by gender, caste and religion, and new laws enumerated grounds of divorce for Muslims and Hindus, ushered in Hindu monogamy, created a non-religious option for marriage, developed adoption and custody, and specified women's partial rights to family property. But each of these provisions was whittled down in legislative debates, many legislators equating new rights for women as a form of Western modernity, in conflict with a vision of the 'traditional' woman at the heart of the new state (Basu 2015a; Parashar 1992; Williams 2006). Flavia Agnes (2005: 115) argues that the consolidation of hegemonic high-caste Hindu male power continued, with 'vested, patriarchal and community interests of the influential sections supersed[ing] the rights of women and children'. An apt example is the Special Marriage Act, 1954, which made marriage into a secular and civil contract and could have been the basis for 'a comprehensive code of marriage and divorce', but was structured in terms of Hindu upper-caste marriage rules, and protected Hindu joint-family property for men (ibid.: 117).

No doubt these new laws created innovative social practices: some norms shifted ever so slightly (such as Hindu monogamy becoming seemingly common), but there was continued resistance to the whittling away of privileges through legal change. When beginning my fieldwork on family inheritance more than 30 years after the Hindu Succession Act of 1956 had passed, I found that few women (in my class-stratified sample in Delhi) had inherited any natal property. The conditions under which they could be equal inheritors were already limited at the time—pertaining only to intestate cases and self-acquired property—but they were still persuaded or coerced to sign away their shares, the common logic being that to act otherwise would bring disharmony to the family (Basu 1999). These were not empty threats: the rare inheritance disputes pursued by women were met by forceful family wrath even in litigation-averse families. Property was often represented as sons' compensation for eldercare and ritual responsibilities, and as a parallel to daughters' dowry being pre-mortem inheritance, despite the evidence that daughters did not get property whether or not they were given dowry, and that sons got it whether or not they undertook eldercare. Significantly, while women acceded to the logic of family disharmony in surrendering their shares, across classes they spoke of inheritance being a form of affective connection they might like to pass on if they could, and of the importance of women having access to economic resources such as cash or immovable property, not just dowry goods or jewellery or the promise of elder support (see also Datta 2006).

Bina Agarwal's (1994) magnum opus, *A Field of One's Own*, documented women's exclusion from property resources across South Asia, compellingly establishing the social and economic harms of such exclusion. Agarwal went on to coordinate efforts at legislative change to bring about gender equality in the Hindu Succession Act (amended in 2005).[2] However, women continue to be disenfranchised from natal property despite such provisions, as Fazalbhoy's (2012) study of Muslim women illustrates. Discourses of disenfranchising women from natal property through the language of family loyalty inscribe marriage as the primary conduit of socio-economic well-being. Notably, this spectre of the rights-bearing modern woman as a threat to 'Indian' family cohesion echoes anxieties about trouble and 'misuse' when women turn to law, as described later in this essay.

During my fieldwork on gender and inheritance, I often wondered whether thinking about property was a Virginia Woolf-style elite claim with no resonance for most women's concerns. My worries were only compounded by sitting in on legal advice sessions of women's NGOs in a number of cities, where women who came in with questions about property disputes were not usually accepted as clients and were sent off to fee-based lawyers, understandable strategies given the limited time and resources of the organisations and the deluge of violence-related cases that faced them. In the decades since, I have become convinced that questions of property are not elite issues—they are fundamental to women's material and social well-being, including protection against violence (see also Baruah 2007; Panda and Agarwal 2005).

The focus of feminist legal action has justifiably been on having women be free from violence within homes (and other settings), and

[2] The two most significant changes were as follows: including women as coparceners of joint family property and removing the equal inheritance exceptions to agricultural land. Bina Agarwal's interview with Sonu Jain, 'Women Didn't Receive Rights Without Struggle', *The Indian Express*, 13 September 2005. Available at: http://www.binaagarwal.com/popular%20writings/hsaa_interview%20_indianexpress_13sep05.pdf (accessed on 31 May 2018).

on making sure that they are not arbitrarily divorced and that they have recourse to alimony and/or child support if they are separated or divorced. However, these efforts rely on women's economic dependence within marriage. Dowry and alimony, the only two resources women are imagined to have access to, encapsulate a profoundly gendered logic of patriarchal property ownership. Marriage payments, whether dowry or bridewealth, index performances of status for families and do little to build up a property fund for women (Basu 2005: v–xxi). The families I interviewed typically represented dowry as 'custom' rather than 'demand', but their practices affirmed Tambiah's (1989) theory of dowry as affinal property and the centrality Srinivas assigned to patrilineal hypergamy (Srinivas 1984):

> Both families' (wedding) expenses seem to be directed toward increasing the assets (through gifts) and status (through hospitality) of the groom's family, which is supposed to be the 'joint family' into which the bride merges, and whose continued prosperity makes it less likely that the daughter will turn to the natal family for help or property shares later. (Basu 1999: 96)

Alimony, in parallel vein, implies support for a dependant family member, underemphasising women's entitlement based on their contributions to their households through labour and capital, or housewives' depletion of their labour market value in withdrawing from paid labour. Women's organisations, including those working on land rights, have long advocated matrimonial shares and joint title, with minimal effect (Basu 2005: xlvi–xlviii). In a recent measure with more traction, some feminist lawyers proposed implementing matrimonial property division upon divorce in response to a legislative move to add 'irretrievable breakdown of marriage' as a ground of divorce, hoping to prevent husbands leaving marriages without economic settlement (Marriage Laws [Amendment] Bill, 2010). The resulting furore over the mathematics of calculating shares and the confusion between conjugal and joint property demonstrated the sacrosanct status of patriarchal property ownership; the proposition has not re-emerged in a Parliamentary session across successive governments (Basu 2017).

The focus on alimony or dowry also centres on the married (or incipiently married) woman, revealing the heteronormativity, and associated sexual respectability, at the heart of these (Brahminical) patriarchal discourses. The spoils of marital assets, such as they might be, have gone to favour the (first) wife among Hindu women, implicitly deeming parallel forms of sexual and social labour unworthy. The

Supreme Court judgment *D. Velusamy* v. *D. Patchaiammal* (2010, 10 SCC 469) illustrates this morality well: in extending the economic reliefs of the Domestic Violence Act, 2005, to a long-term relationship as a 'relationship in the nature of marriage', the judges purported to have upgraded to norms of other 'modern' nations. But their articulation of the category of 'keep' and its differentiation from 'live-in relationships' and 'meretricious contract[s] exclusively for sexual service' signalled the moral superiority assigned to formal marriage. A variety of sexual and labour arrangements may constitute such 'relationships in the nature of marriage'—same-sex relationships, transgender marriages, short-term cohabitation contracts like *maitri karar*, visiting husbands in *sambandham*,[3] customary remarriage like *nata* or long-term extra-marital households (Partners for Law in Development 2010)—but recognising them in terms of forms of compensation or shared property is seen to destabilise the fragile entitlements of heteronormative marriage.

Feminist support for economic rights in marriage has also been premised on the normatively upper-caste, upper-middle-class, heterosexual woman as the standard of 'women's rights', ignoring such women's roles in upholding privileges of caste and sexuality through discourses of merit and just remuneration, or proper marriage and sexuality (Rege 1998). Rege critiques feminist approaches that incorporate caste and religion as diversity, arguing for an analysis of rights that centres forms of 'material' privilege by placing Dalit women's labour and sexual exploitation at the heart of theorising gender relations. LGBTQIA (lesbian, gay, bisexual, transgender, queer, intersex, asexual) identities are also invoked only in discussions of public sex, criminal persecution or health, not in conceptualising Personal Law and economic entitlements of family. There is little recognition of alternate distributive norms within particular queer communities (Manayath 2015). Ashley Tellis' (2014: 346) accusation that the Indian feminist movement is complicit in the failure to imagine 'spaces outside marriage within which same-sex subjects can breathe and imagine their lives the way they want' underlines that (feminist) encounters with law have worked with scripts of respectable gender and sexuality.

Marriage rights have also become fertile ground for public debates about the religious autonomy of communities. The Shah Bano case is the iconic post-colonial example: the Indian Supreme Court decreed that Muslim women could avail of maintenance under Section 125 of

---

[3] *Sambandham* is a form of marriage within the sex-gender system of Kerala, involving matrilineal households and visiting 'husbands' (see Gough 1959).

the Criminal Procedure Code (an anti-penury measure) irrespective of Personal Law provisions, only to be followed by a law which overturned the verdict to restrict Muslim women's post-divorce maintenance far more narrowly than that of other Indian women. Shah Bano's situation highlighted the contradiction between 'protective' discourses of nation, religion and gender and the erasure of her subjectivity (Pathak and Rajan 1989).

The Shah Bano case typified Muslim women's rights as the rationale of state legal intervention in the name of the Uniform Civil Code, often an unsubtle extension of Hindu nationalist agendas. Judicial determinations have reshaped the spirit of laws in line with this agenda as well. Despite the Muslim Women's Act's (1986) seeming constriction of Muslim women's entitlement to the length and amount of post-divorce maintenance as compared to other Indian women, judges routinely interpreted the phrase 'fair and reasonable provision' expansively to include very large payments beyond the *iddat*[4] period, for example, *Danial Latifi* v. *Union of India* (Basu 2008). The original ruling against triple *talaq* came from a judge with strong affiliations to Hindutva ideology (Basu 2003). Special Marriage Act (1954) judges, Perveez Mody (2008) shows, encourage conversion to Hinduism over secular/multi-religious marriages. Muslim polygyny (low though its numbers are) elicits cries for urgent reform, a discourse that asserts Hindu masculinity as modern and nationalist, and Muslim masculinity as excessive and temporally backward, while conveniently veiling the structural gendered problems of marriage dissolution across communities (Basu 2016).

Women have not been mere conduits of the lucrative political rationale of highlighting their interests. As with colonial-era law, they have sought out courts and alternate dispute resolution reforms as active negotiators and narrators, availing of multiple civil and criminal fora across classes, castes and religions to settle questions of maintenance, property, custody and freedom from violence (Lemons 2010; Solanki 2011; Vatuk 2001). Remedies have been uneven, in part due to the structural constraints and unevenness of multiple venues, and in part due to the gendered dependence inscribed in marriage law (Basu 2015a).

Women's groups are active negotiators of these debates. Post Shah Bano, Muslim women's groups, and many Indian women's movement groups following their lead, refused to be drawn into championing

---

[4] In Islamic jurisprudence, the period during which wives are proscribed from marrying, following widowhood or divorce.

the politicised Uniform Civil Code and proposed various alternative models of gender equity across Personal Laws (Basu 2008). Yet the recent call to have triple talaq be reviewed by the Supreme Court and the Law Commission, while clearly part of the Hindutva politicisation of Personal Law (Basu 2016), has seen the All India Muslim Women's Personal Law Board critique the All India Muslim Personal Law Board for its campaign of 'misleading' women and seek a robust conversation.[5] This explicit divergence may be connected to the burgeoning of Muslim women's political and civil groups, who have developed autonomous spaces alongside feminist and Muslim rights focused groups (Vatuk 2008).

Since the 1980s (arguably in the wake of feminist organising during the UN Decade for Women), the women's movement has been most memorably associated in the public imaginary with protests against gender-based violence, particularly so-called 'dowry deaths' and stranger rape cases: the figure of the burning bride ablaze from an exploding kerosene stove and the figure of the aspiring young student who is fatally gang-raped. The affective optics of these violent incidents have spurred public outrage, generating feminist legal intervention and resulting in stern carceral remedies, even as other forms of sexual assault and domestic violence elicit more ambiguous responses. Globally, these episodes iterated the figure of the Indian woman as victim of an overweening patriarchal culture, without noticing its continuity with forms of gender-based violence elsewhere in the world (Narayan 1997; the film *India's Daughter* by Leslee Udwin is an exemplar).

Jyoti Singh Pandey's rape in December 2012 brought out agitated crowds of women who narrated many daily forms of violence and harassment; the mass turnout may also be tied to her representation in terms of discourses of aspirational modernity, class and religion (Roychowdhury 2013; Shandilya 2015). It led to immediate prosecution, capital punishment sentences and broad changes in the Criminal Law Amendment Act, 2013.[6] A 2016 case of rape where the judge unambiguously relied on a violation of consent (rather than honour or shame) standard has been hailed as a landmark even as it generates

---

[5] *The Hindu*, 'Muslim Women Slam AIMPLB on Triple Talaq', *The Hindu* (National), 2 December 2016. Available at: http://www.thehindu.com/news/national/Muslim-women-slam-AIMPLB-on-triple-talaq/article16438510.ece (accessed on 31 May 2018).

[6] While these changes were less broad than recommended by the Verma Commission, they extended to a range of issues pertaining to categories of assault and forms of custodial rape.

new controversies (Baxi 2016). But before being assured that these responses reflect overdue attention to the crime of rape, we might recall the unhappy trajectory of legal responses to sexual assault. Perhaps the two most foundational cases inspiring feminist legal reform in India—Mathura's 1972 rape leading to the 1979 Open Letter from Delhi law professors and the subsequent Criminal Law Amendment Act, 1983, and Bhanwari Devi's gang rape as retaliation by influential men in her village which generated the entire apparatus of sexual harassment law—involved Dalit women who lost their cases and encountered multiple compounded (sexual and governmental) violence from various arms of the state. Other forms of retaliatory sexual assault from the state—in Kashmir or Chhattisgarh or Manipur—merit little response, while the prosecution of prominent personages results in much anxiety around parsing definitions of consent and assault. The illusion of state vigilance is exemplified in the Prevention of Atrocities Act, 1989, which aims to apply strict punishment to hate crimes towards Scheduled Caste and Schedule Tribe groups, but has failed to secure convictions. Intent of caste-based animus proves difficult to establish judicially even where a person may have been criminally convicted on the related charges, or people are coerced to 'compromise' by powerful local groups, such that the ubiquity of caste violence becomes invisible in the legal record, and sexual assault is imagined by default to occur on the body of the afore-mentioned hegemonic woman (Baxi 2014; Gowda 2011; Rege 1998).

Rape prosecutions, typically, end without conviction; rape 'charges', on the other hand, may be filed to sediment patriarchal norms of kin-ship and control (further explaining poor conviction rates). Pratiksha Baxi's moving ethnography identifies the ways in which temporality, social location and forms of bureaucratic knowledge—such as eviden-tiary 'proof' of body or memory, or 'compromise' between parties in which the victim turns 'hostile witness' to her own crime—ensure that most rape trials end without criminal sanctions (Baxi 2014). But rape charges are ever popular to kin and community, with many rape cases filed by parents of daughters who have eloped, in order to control mar-riage choice (Chowdhry 2007). Another set of charges involves false 'promise to marry', where the failure of an ongoing sexual relationship to result in marriage is deemed to be rape, as a violation of meaningful consent under case law.[7] Both these categories interpret rape law very

---

[7] Aarefa Johari, 'Can Sex After a False Promise Be Called Rape?' Scroll.in, 18 April 2014. Available at: https://scroll.in/article/661695/can-sex-after-a-false-promise-of-marriage-be-called-rape (accessed on 31 May 2018); S. Rukmini, 'The Many Shades of Rape Cases in Delhi', *The Hindu*, 29 July 2014. Available

differently from feminist understandings: they negate autonomy over one's sexuality, locate sexual activity solely within heteronormative caste-and-religion-appropriate marriage and dismantle the very notion of consent (Basu 2011).

Meanwhile, public sensitivity to rape as typified by the Jyoti Singh Pandey case may create awareness and anger, but it also translates into greater surveillance of women's mobility, communication, education and sexual and romantic choices. Religious nationalism furthers familial control, such as in Hindutva-fuelled threats to launch 'love jihad' against relationships of Hindu women and Muslim men, or to establish an 'anti-Romeo squad' to 'protect' women's education.[8] Caste panchayats and 'fatwas' from clerics imposing violent corporeal punishment become arbiters of behaviour, sex and education, with authority and impunity beyond formal laws.

'Dowry violence' is also foundational to the Indian women's movement's interventions in legal reform. The movement highlighted young brides' murders and encouragement to suicides by affines in the 1980s, emphasising the extreme vulnerabilities of the daughter-in-law in the extended household. It spurred a slew of legal changes, from laws prohibiting dowry to ensuring return of dowry goods, to strict criminal scrutiny of suicides in new marriages and prosecution of husbands and affines for domestic violence (Basu 2005). Ironically, the eponymity of 'dowry' makes it synonymous with domestic violence, pushing the many other physical and psychological components of such violence out of scrutiny (Kumari 1989; Umar 1998).[9] It takes over legal action: even though the Dowry Prohibition (Amendment) Act, 1986, has been largely unenforceable and marriage payment practices have evolved

---

at: http://www.thehindu.com/data/the-many-shades-of-rape-cases-in-delhi/article6261042.ece (accessed on 31 May 2018). A provisional revision of the 'promise to marry' norm appears in a recent Mumbai High Court case. Shibu Thomas, 'Educated Girl Can't Cry Rape if Ditched by Boyfriend, Says Court', *The Times of India*, Mumbai, 21 January 2017. Available at: http://timesofindia.indiatimes.com/city/mumbai/educated-girl-cant-cry-rape-if-ditched-by-boy-friend-says-hc/articleshow/56696363.cms (accessed on 31 May 2018).

[8] 'BJP Will Form an Anti-Romeo Squad to Protect Girls in Uttar Pradesh: Amit Shah', *Scroll.in*, 29 January 2017. Available at: https://scroll.in/latest/828024/bjp-will-form-an-anti-romeo-squad-to-protect-girls-in-uttar-pradesh-amit-shah (accessed on 31 May 2018).

[9] See also Avani Chokshi and Mansi Binjrajka, 'Conversation with Flavia Agnes', *Journal of Indian Law and Society Blog*, 6 August 2015. Available at: https://jilsblognujs.wordpress.com/2015/08/06/conversation-with-flavia-agnes-director-majlis-legal-centre/ (accessed on 31 May 2018).

around the law (Basu 2010), the range of legal remedies around dowry recovery and domestic violence have proved very popular.

Cases filed under Section 498A of the Indian Penal Code ('Cruelty'[to married women]) regularly constitute almost half of all cases filed under the 'Crimes against Women' category documented by the Indian National Crimes Record Bureau; in the wake of 'dowry deaths', the law was written to allow for immediate arrest without investigation, to recognise multiple modes of violence and recognise a broad category of affines as perpetrators (Basu 2015a). The troubling question has been whether its popularity means that people want more stringent prosecution of domestic violence through criminal law, or whether, like rape charges, prosecutions end in compromise and negotiation, focused on economic settlement. In studying the simultaneity of divorce cases and domestic violence prosecutions, I found that people navigate between family courts, police stations, mediation cells or other local forms of mediation. Such legal pluralism is often praised as useful by feminist scholars who find that it allows for customised solutions to mitigate violence and secure economic support (Nagaraj 2010; Solanki 2011); I found that these venues often have mutually contradictory demands and require impossible balance. Section 498A has been a prime target of backlash by men's rights activists who find its criminal reach corrupt and arbitrary, their claims buoyed by legal judgments such as the Supreme Court verdict anointing the provision 'legal terrorism' (Basu 2015b). The Domestic Violence Act, 2005, purported to offer a civil remedy to mitigate these unpopular criminal sanctions (Rajan 2003) but appears to be similarly burdened by lack of resources to sustain the imagined logistical structures as well as residual attitudinal problems (Roychowdhury 2015).[10] These measures have indeed produced greater sensitisation and more options—my concern, however, is that violence is too often only significant as a ground of mediation, raised in order to shake loose intransigent financial settlements of marriage. Domestic violence thereby becomes a subsidiary concern to the (justifiable) crises of gendered economic entitlements within families.

The legal pursuit of gender justice is so palpably Sisyphean that we are inevitably left frustrated. But by following the approach that law is a critical site at which culture is shaped, whether to secure structural

[10] Prita Jha, 'Is the Indian Law on Domestic Violence Fit for Purpose?' *OpenDemocracy*, 13 January 2017. Available at: https://www.opendemocracy.net/5050/prita-jha/is-indian-law-on-domestic-violence-fit-for-purpose (accessed on 31 May 2018).

power or to push against its logic (however uncertain the results), we better understand that there are no ideal applications of a given provision: laws work as a political tool; the notion of 'compromise' is used to deflect criminal prosecution into social or economic compensation; gender and caste and religious protection are evoked to signal a progressive state only to be unrecognizable in legal application. Gender justice is best thought of as indexing the effects of feminist discourse within the power of state, kin and community, rather than as a forward march towards a goal.

References

Agarwal, B. 1994. *A Field of One's Own: Gender and Land Rights in South Asia.* Cambridge and New York, NY: Cambridge University Press.

Agnes, F. 2005. 'Law and Gender Inequality: The Politics of Women's Rights in India'. In *Writing the Women's Movement: A Reader*, edited by M. Khullar, 113–30. New Delhi: Zubaan.

Anagol, P. 2008. 'Rebellious Wives and Dysfunctional Marriages'. In *Women and Social Reform in Modern India: A Reader*, edited by S. Sarkar and T. Sarkar, 282–313. Bloomington, IN: Indiana University Press.

Arunima, G. 2003. *There Comes Papa: Colonialism and the Transformation of Matriliny in Kerala, Malabar, c. 1850–1940.* New Delhi: Orient Longman.

Baruah, B. 2007. 'Gendered Realities: Exploring Property Ownership and Tenancy Relationships in Urban India'. *World Development* 35 (12): 2096–109.

Basu, S. 1999. *She Comes to Take Her Rights: Indian Women, Property and Propriety.* Albany, NY: State University of New York Press.

———. 2003. 'Shading the Secular: Law at Work in the Indian Higher Courts'. *Cultural Dynamics* 15 (2): 131–52.

———. ed. 2005. *Dowry and Inheritance.* New Delhi: Women Unlimited.

———. 2008. 'Separate and Unequal: Muslim Women and Un-uniform Family Law in India'. *International Feminist Journal of Politics* 10 (4): 495–517.

———. 2010. 'Legacies of the Dowry Prohibition Act in India: Marriage Practices and Feminist Discourses'. In *Dowry: Bridging the Gap Between Theory and Practice*, edited by T. Bradley, E. Tomalin and M. Subramanian, 177–96. London: Zed Books.

———. 2011. 'Sexual Property: Staging Rape and Marriage in Indian Law and Feminist Theory'. *Feminist Studies* 37 (1): 185–211.

———. 2015a. *The Trouble with Marriage: Feminists Confront Law and Violence in India.* Oakland, CA: University of California Press.

———. 2015b. 'Gathering Steam: Organizing Strategies of the Indian Men's Movement'. *Economic & Political Weekly* 50 (44): 67–75.

Basu, S. 2016. 'Unfair Advantage? Polygyny and Adultery in Indian Personal Law'. In *Filing Religion: State, Hinduism, and Courts of Law*, edited by D. Berti, G. Tarrabout and R. Voix, 301–24. New Delhi: Oxford University Press.

———. 2017. 'The Spoils of Marriage: Irretrievable Breakdown and Matrimonial Property in the Law Commission of India Reports'. *Journal of Indian Law and Society* (2015 monsoon): 22–43. http://jils.ac.in/archives/volume-6-monsoon/!

Baxi, P. 2008. 'Feminist Contributions to Sociology of Law: A Review'. *Economic & Political Weekly* 43 (43): 79–85.

———. 2014. *Public Secrets of Law: Rape Law in India*. New Delhi: Oxford University Press.

———. 2016. '"Carceral Feminism" as Judicial Bias: The Discontents Around State v. Mahmood Farooqui'. *Interdisciplinary Law* 3 (October): 1–30.

Brown, W. 1992 (1995). 'Finding the Man in the State'. *Feminist Studies* 18 (1): 7–34.

Chowdhry, P. 1994. *The Veiled Women: Shifting Gender Equations in Rural Haryana, 1880–1990*. Delhi and New York, NY: Oxford University Press.

———. 2007. *Contentious Marriages, Eloping Couples: Gender, Caste, and Patriarchy in Northern India*. New Delhi and New York, NY: Oxford University Press.

Datta, N. 2006. 'Joint Titling: A Win-Win Policy? Gender and Property Rights in Urban Informal Settlements in Chandigarh, India'. *Feminist Economics* 12 (1–2): 271–98.

Derrida, J. 1992. 'Force of Law: The "Mystical Foundation of Authority"'. In *Acts of Religion*, edited by G. Anidjar, 230–98. New York, NY: Routledge.

Ewick, P. and S.S. Silbey. 1998. *The Common Place of Law: Stories from Everyday Life*. Chicago, IL: University of Chicago Press.

Fazalbhoy, N. 2012. 'Negotiating Rights and Relationships: Muslim Women and Inheritance'. In *Negotiating Spaces: Legal Domains, Gender Concerns, and Community Constructs*, edited by F. Agnes, S.V. Ghosh and Majlis, 311–34. New Delhi: Oxford University Press.

Foucault, M. 1991. 'Governmentality'. Translated by R. Braidotti. In *The Foucault Effect: Studies in Governmentality*, edited by G. Burchell, C. Gordon and P. Miller, 87–104. Chicago, IL: University of Chicago Press.

Gough, Kathleen E. 1959. 'The Nayars and the Definition of Marriage'. *JRAI* 89 (1): 23–34.

Gowda, C. 2011. 'Adjudicating Atrocity'. Paper presented at the Law and Social Exclusion in India Conference, Yale University, New Haven, CT, 13 May.

Greenhouse, C.J., B. Yngvesson and D.M. Engel. 1994. *Law and Community in Three American Towns*. Ithaca, NY: Cornell University Press.

Kozlowski, G. 2008. 'Muslim Women and the Control of Property in North India'. In *Women and Social Reform in Modern India: A Reader*, edited by S. Sarkar and T. Sarkar, 326–41. Bloomington, IN: Indiana University Press.

Kumari, R. 1989. *Brides Are Not for Burning*. New Delhi: Stosius Inc.

Lemons, K. 2010. 'At the Margins of Law: Adjudicating Muslim Families in Contemporary Delhi'. PhD Dissertation. University of California, Berkeley, CA.

Manayath, N. 2015. 'The Shameless Marriage: Thinking Through Same-sex Erotics and the Question of "Gay Marriage" in India'. In *Conjugality Unbound: Sexual Economies, State Regulation and the Marital Form in India*, edited by S. Basu and L. Ramberg, 251–80). New Delhi: Women Unlimited.

Mani, L. 1990. 'Contentious Traditions: The Debate on Sati in Colonial India'. In *Recasting Women: Essays in Indian Colonial History*, edited by K. Sangari and S. Vaid, 88–126. New Brunswick, NJ: Rutgers University Press.

Merry, S.E. 1999. *Colonizing Hawai'i: The Cultural Power of Law*. Princeton, NJ: Princeton University Press.

Mody, P. 2008. *The Intimate State: Love-Marriage and the Law in Delhi*. New Delhi: Routledge India.

Nagaraj, V. 2010. 'Local and Customary Forums: Adapting and Innovating Rules of Formal Law'. *Indian Journal of Gender Studies* 17 (3): 429–50.

Nair, J. 1996. *Women and Law in Colonial India*. New Delhi: Kali for Women.

Narayan, U. 1997. 'Cross-cultural Connections, Border-crossings and "Death by Culture": Thinking About Dowry-murders in India and Domestic-violence Murders in the United States'. In *Dislocating Cultures: Identities, Traditions and Third-World Feminism*, edited by U. Narayan, 81–118. New York, NY: Routledge.

Panda, P. and B. Agarwal. 2005. 'Marital Violence, Human Development and Women's Property Status in India'. *World Development* 33 (5): 823–50.

Parashar, A. 1992. *Women and Family Law Reform in India: Uniform Civil Code and Gender Equality*. New Delhi: SAGE.

Partners for Law in Development. 2010. *Rights in Intimate Relationships: Towards an Inclusive and Just Framework of Women's Rights and the Family*. New Delhi: Partners for Law in Development.

Pathak, Z. and R.S. Rajan. 1989. 'Shahbano'. *Signs* 14 (3): 558–82.

Rajan, R.S. 2003. *The Scandal of the State: Women, Law and Citizenship in Postcolonial India*. Durham, NC: Duke University Press.

Rege, S. 1998. 'Dalit Women Talk Differently: A Critique of "Difference" and Toward a Dalit Feminist Standpoint Position'. *Economic & Political Weekly* 33 (44): WS39–46.

Roychowdhury, P. 2013. '"The Delhi Gang Rape": The Making of International Causes'. *Feminist Studies* 39 (1): 282–92.

———. 2015. 'Victims to Saviors: Governmentality and the Regendering of Citizenship in India'. *Gender & Society* 29 (6): 792–816.

Sarkar, T. 2008. 'Conjugality and Hindu Nationalism: Resisting Colonial Reason and the Death of a Child Wife'. In *Women and Social Reform* in *Modern India: A Reader*, edited by S. Sarkar and T. Sarkar, 259–81. Bloomington, IN: Indiana University Press.

Shandilya, K. 2015. 'Nirbhaya's Body: The Politics of Protest in the Aftermath of the 2012 Delhi Gang Rape'. *Gender & Society* 27 (2): 465–86.

Sinha, M. 1995. *Colonial Masculinity: The 'Manly Englishman' and the 'Effeminate Bengali' in the Late Nineteenth Century*. Manchester: Manchester University Press.

Smart, C. 1989. *Feminism and the Power of Law*. London: Taylor & Francis.

Solanki, G. 2011. *Adjudication in Religious Family Laws: Cultural Accommodation, Legal Pluralism, and Gender Equality in India*. Cambridge: Cambridge University Press.

Spivak, G.C. 1988. 'Can the Subaltern Speak?' In *Marxism and the Interpretation of Culture*, edited by C. Nelson and L. Grossberg, 271–313. Urbana, IL: University of Illinois Press.

Sreenivas, M. 2011. 'Creating Conjugal Subjects: Devadasis and the Politics of Marriage in Colonial Madras Presidency'. *Feminist Studies* 37 (1): 63–92.

Srinivas, M.N. 1984. *Some Reflections on Dowry*. New Delhi: Oxford University Press.

Tambiah, S.J. 1989. 'Bridewealth and Dowry Revisited: The Position of Women in Sub-Saharan Africa and North India'. *Current Anthropology* 30 (4): 413–35.

Tellis, A. 2014. 'Multiple Ironies: Notes on Same Sex Marriage for South Asians at Home and Abroad'. In *Marrying in South Asia: Shifting Concepts—Changing Practices in a Globalising World*, edited by R. Kaur and R. Palriwala, 333–35. New Delhi: Orient BlackSwan.

Umar, M. 1998. *Bride Burning in India: A Socio-legal Study*. New Delhi: APH Publication.

Vatuk, S. 2001. '"Where Will She Go? What Will She Do?": Paternalism Toward Women in the Administration of Muslim Personal Law in Contemporary India'. In *Religion and Personal Law in Secular India*, edited by G.J. Larsen, 226–48. Bloomington, IN: Indiana University Press.

———. 2008. 'Islamic Feminism in India: Indian Muslim Women Activists and the Reform of Muslim Personal Law'. *Modern Asian Studies* 42 (2–3): 489–518.

Wickham, G. 2006. 'Foucault, Law and Power: A Reassessment'. *Journal of Law and Society* 33 (4): 596–614.

Williams, R.V. 2006. *Postcolonial Politics and Personal Laws: Colonial Legal Legacies and the Indian State*. New Delhi: Oxford University Press.

21

Masculinities and Culture

Joseph S. Alter

Introduction

If masculinity has lost its centre of gravity—and the gravity of being normatively centred—that is a good thing, not only politically and morally, with respect to the realisation of greater equity and justice, but also analytically.

With the essentialism of gender categories fully in question, we are now able to better appreciate, and more clearly understand, the broader implications of masculinity relative to class, caste, ethnicity and region, as well as in relation to a spectrum of embodied experiences (Baas 2016; Staples 2005, 2011) and sexualities (Boyce 2007; Reddy 2005). What this does, apart from liberating a critique of normative categories from the hegemony of normative conceptualisation itself, is to refine our understanding of gendered power, as well as sharpen our sensitivity to the way in which structures of inequality—keyed to education, employment, age, and rural–urban/margin–centre geography—are linked to the experience and expression of masculinities in specific contexts (Ahmed 2006; Banerjee 2005; Chattopadhyay 2011; Chowdhry 2013; Doron and Broom 2014; Majumdar 2006; Nakassis 2013).

The past 20 years or so have seen a shift from masculinity being a topic of ethnographic or sociological study to it being an analytic of power and a framework for articulating critiques of culture (Chopra 2002, 2007; Chopra et al. 2004; C. Osella and F. Osella 1998; F. Osella and C. Osella 2000, 2003; Srivastava 2004, 2010). This corresponds to the realisation that there is nuance, ambiguity and complexity even in the most bombastic manifestations of essentialised masculinity (Baas 2016; Srivastava 2015), and that only some forms of it are essentially congruent with chauvinism and patriarchy. In other words, although the world is certainly populated by people who think they are morally upright men, there is no coherent framework that defines their collective experience as 'masculinity'; and although men are most certainly capable of distinctive forms of violence and domination, as well as more particular vices and virtues, this is increasingly being analysed and understood in terms of iterated social, political and economic dynamics (Qayum and Ray 2010; Srivastava 2004), rather than in terms of identity, psychology and local articulations of cultural holism.

It is also important to note that masculinity is increasingly disembodied, or finds expression in powerfully disembodied forms. Real 'flesh and blood' men are only 'masculine' in ways that are partial, problematic and paradoxical (Dasgupta and Gokulsing 2014; Gupta 2011; Srivastava 2010); and masculinity finds clearest—if by no means coherent—expression in social, political and economic forms, rather than as a delimited cultural construct. The disarticulation of meaning from the body is, in part, a function of analyses that show how historical narratives, and the circulation of ideas through time, transubstantiate cultural categories such as celibacy, semen anxiety and various aspects of kinetic sex and physiological sexuality (Alter 2011; Haynes 2012). Perhaps this is how it has always been. But contemporary masculinity as a discursively mediated social fact seems to be increasingly independent of anything that bears on the truth of concrete experience. Even when processed through the mill of phenomenology, masculinity's meaning is much more dependent on a mythos of disarticulated and fragmented significance than on ethnographic fictions of descriptive realism or the telos of a seamless ethos.

Revolutionary changes in the form and flow of information and in the production, consumption and performance of heavily mediated idea-things have transformed the nature of cultural reality over the past 15 or 20 years, making it virtually impossible to exist unselfconsciously, and quite impossible to do so virtually. This is, in many ways, the logical extension of late capitalism, and what might now be called late nationalism, in the sense that both of these distinctive articulations of modernity essentialise and fetishise individuality in relation to larger ideals. Whatever problems attend to hyper-mediated culture—and there are many—a virtue, expressed particularly in the disarticulation of masculinity, is a general trend away from individuality towards what might be characterised as virtual sociality. Mediated forms of sociality cut across and through the located and embodied 'idealism' of commodity-based consciousness and imagined communities. Needless to say, pathologies of distorted individuality persist and are sometimes amplified by new media, but the structure of virtual communication, extending from relatively simple, beautiful 20th century forms (Rajan 2006) to what we have today, gives radically new potential to the presciently revolutionary and transgendering notion that no man is an island. This is certainly an area for creative future research examining the way in which mobile phones and social media articulate new configurations of meaning, new forms of sociality and new dimensions of cohesion and fragmentation (Doron 2011, 2012; Doron and Jeffrey 2013).

Congruent with the magnified and increasingly matrixed mediation of masculinity in modernity are three increasingly important trends in current research.

The first trend—not entirely new but certainly a feature of contemporaneity—reflects a shift in the locus and significance of masculinity, relative to the transformation of embodied patriarchy, into forms that articulate governmentality. In other words, globalised, transnational procedures and systems of disembodied regulation and codification instantiate gender more definitively than do individuals, social collectives or constellations of cultural meaning. Public health, for example, and family planning projects—among other forms of medical regulation and development work—articulate gender in terms of ingrained bio-politics (van Hollen 2013). Linked to this is the way in which globalisation and governmentality disambiguate politics and patriarchy, both one in relation to the other and relative to the state. I see this reflected in recent work by Boyce (2007, 2014) and Hinchy (2013) on sexuality and Verniers (2013) and Jeffrey (2010) on education and its discontents.

A second trend is manifest in the development of more complex and nuanced analyses of violence and domination. In many ways, physical violence is intimately but subtly linked to mediated forms of gendered representation, as well as to forms of mediated sociality (McDuie-Ra 2012). To better understand virulent articulations of masculinity, including aspects of it in nationalism and fundamentalism, it will become increasingly important to understand changing technologies, the interface between technologies and bodies, and the question of how users engage technology in new ways (Gupta 2015). I see this anticipated in recent work by Mehta (2006).

A third trend is linked to the political economy of social distinctions, and the way in which ambition and alienation, on the one hand, and new forms of exploitation, on the other, reflect a harmonics of multidimensional hierarchy, shifting the parameters of visible and invisible exploitation (Chopra 2000), re-coordinating conceptions of 'centralised' and 'marginalised' forms of power (Qayum and Ray 2010) and also twisting the apparent hegemony of elite, corporate fashion into a conflicted articulation of 'ishtylish' subalternity (Cohen 2012; Srivastava 2007). Structured systems of ranked inequality, defined either by caste or class, are no longer so clearly structured. The rapid growth of the so-called 'new' middle class—whose emergence is fragmenting established categories of clear-cut distinction—demands new ways of understanding heavily mediated relationships that are at once virtual and intimate (Baas 2016; Gupta 2010; Jeffrey 2010; Ray 2008).

But the decentring of masculinity—which is not simply an academic affair—produces strong and dangerous reactions in the public sphere. Nostalgia for the lost centre finds easy purchase in the minds of men who are concerned about the 'changing structure' of family roles, relationships and values; nervous and frustrated by limited job opportunities that do not match up with educational expectations and qualifications; and disillusioned by the burden of real constraints on the imagined possibility of alternative futures. Dislocation, transience and mobility of one kind or another enable forms of transcendent sociality, to be sure; but these decentring processes can also generate virtual fundamentalisms that shapeshift in very real and very menacing ways.

More generally, freedom, manifest in the decentring of masculinity, including the embodiment of alternative sexualities, produces performances of cultural retrenchment and a kind of defensive conservatism bent on relocating masculinity as a central axis in—if not the axis mundi of—the cultural politics of fundamentalism. In many ways, therefore, the decentring of masculinity can produce the illusion of its opposite, and, more problematically, criticism of this illusion can easily lose sight of its hyper-performative character. If it did not have such serious, often violent consequences, this kind of bombastic, derivative 'masculinism' would appear to be a tragic farce, a production scripted in the language of realism that inevitably succumbs to burlesque self-parody when performed—as always it must be—on the stage of public culture.

As the articulation of a shifting, performed set of relations that structure gender, and the discursive manifestation of power that animates the experience of men and women in relation to themselves and to each other, decentred masculinity turns real men into caricatures of an essentialist, embodied, anachronistic ideology. Quite apart from the sense of subjective nervousness that this might provoke among some, analytical work that deconstructs the normative centre of masculine power has made the problem of masculinity—and the erasure of essentialised men—more directly relevant to understanding many aspects of society and culture that were previously thought to not be gendered in any significant way. Once real men have 'disappeared', it is much easier to see masculinity for what it was and what it is becoming.

For these reasons, decentring gender has also resulted in a productive blurring of boundaries, an erosion of the 'retaining walls' designed to delimit and support the edifices of embodied, experiential masculinity. All of this is to say that literature on the localised 're-centring' of masculinity—as it is embodied, as it is represented, as it is materialised, as it is contested—no longer turns inwards to psychology, culture and the structure of myths and symbols for sense making, but opens outwards to a critical analytic of power in the history of the present.

Baba Ramdev: Virtually Masculine

For a number of interrelated reasons, Baba Ramdev—popular yoga guru, charismatic media sensation, ayurvedic medical entrepreneur and advocate for Hindu revitalisation (see Alter 2008; Ramdev 2015d: 3; Sarbacker 2014)[1]—embodies many aspects of contemporary de-centred masculinity. However, what makes him interesting and important as a subject of critical analysis is the fact that his persona as a guru is so closely linked to central themes in the history and cultural analysis of gender, sexuality and power in South Asia (see Copeman and Ikegame 2012; Singleton and Goldberg 2014). As a *sannyasi* who claims to embody the ideals of yoga, and as a person whose rhetoric is suffused with mythological references, Ramdev is a religious figure who both consciously and unconsciously invokes a kind of resurgent, centred virtual masculinity, albeit one that is no less ambiguous than the masculinity of historic figures such as Vivekananda, Dayananda and Samarth Ramdas or mythologised ones such as the Buddha (Powers 2009).

Because of the way in which his persona invokes world renunciation and the mythos of *sannyas*, Ramdev could be understood as a kind of postmodern counterpoint to Gandhi's very modern embodiment of

[1] http://www.swamibabaramdevmedicines.com/ (accessed on 13 January 2016).

androgyny. Although Gandhi's experimentation with celibacy was on the order of his transcendent political philosophy, on a pragmatic and programmatic plane, he purposefully subverted masculinity in relation to colonialism, fundamentalism and sexuality. The history of Gandhi's experimentation with sex makes sense in terms of Foucault's history of sexuality, and clearly reflects colonial cosmopolitanism. His biomoral politics instantiate more complex forms of contradictory masculinity. And there is, certainly, an important aspect of Ramdev's gendered identity that similarly finds expression in and through the interplay of sexuality, sensuality and asceticism. However, unlike Gandhi, who was caught in a matrix of gendered dualities and binary oppositions—mediated through a problematic discourse of androgynous self-overcoming—Ramdev engages a more complex, global figuration of gendered meanings. And this engagement produces more robust forms of displaced and disarticulated masculinity.

Baba Ramdev is a controversial figure, at once enormously popular among a significant number of the new Indian middle class, and yet also reviled by a bracket of the same middle class who see him as a fraud, a cheat and a con artist. Regardless, he is tremendously successful as an entrepreneur. In collaboration with Acharya Balkrishna, a close associate, he has established a number of institutions over the past 15 years, including Divya Pharmacy, Patanjali Ayurved, Patanjali Yogpeeth and Yog Gram, all near Haridwar.[2] These institutions are closely intermeshed with one another and are collectively based on a nationalist philosophy promoting the development of pure, indigenous, scientific yoga and ayurveda (Khalikova forthcoming).

In conjunction with these enterprises, Ramdev has developed his own persona as a brand unto itself, with his distinctive image as the brand icon. This brand supports his commercial interests and various subsidiary market brands such as a line of pharmaceuticals, tonics and health foods produced under the label Patanjali Ayurved. Taught and practised under the rubric of Patanjali Yogpeeth at Yog Gram—a health retreat in the Shivalik foothills near Haridwar—postural yoga is closely linked to Ramdev's persona brand. As will be discussed in more detail below, as a brand—with all that signifies in terms of fetishism, the commodification of self, the marketing of a healthy lifestyle and the

---

[2] *India Today*, 'Ramdev: Putrajeevak Beej Has Nothing to Do with Child's Gender', *India* Today, 1 May 2015. Available at: http://indiatoday.intoday.in/story/ramdev-putrajeevak-beej-patanjali-products/1/433164.html (accessed on 13 January 2016).

subtle engendering of these processes (Mazzarella 2003)—Baba Ramdev entered the national stage by way of television in the 1990s. His morning television broadcasts guide viewers through postural practice and breathing exercises to the embodiment of a nationalist discourse on health and well-being. More recently, social media and YouTube serve to enable new forms of mediation encompassing masculinity among many other idea-things: Baba as a wrestler engaged in *pahalwani*;[3] Baba as a kisan giving a guided tour of his *gaushala* (2015c);[4] Baba as an alternative biotech businessman explaining the production of *amla* juice tonic (2015d).[5]

Precisely because he does not 'fit the mould' of centred, normative masculinity, but because he embodies a certain kind of charismatic entrepreneurial spirit of fundamentalism, it is important to understand how gender factors into Ramdev's public persona, and into the discourse that his activities have generated.

One factor which seems to be unambiguously clear is that Baba Ramdev's persona is deeply intertwined with the growth and development of India's new middle class, and particularly with the consumer culture of this class. Along with his distinctively national and diasporic appeal, this class dynamic is what distinguishes Ramdev from the global 'god men' of an earlier era such as Swami Sivananda, Swami Rama, Maharishi Mahesh Yogi and Rajneesh. Not to say that Ramdev himself embodies the attributes of the new middle class in any straightforward way. Quite the contrary. He is, I would argue, a contrapuntal figure, a person who embodies a set of complex gendered displacements and fragmented masculinities. And it is precisely his embodiment of these characteristics that render powerful what might otherwise be simply marginal, fractured, contradictory elements of culture in a rapidly changing environment.

Although there are many aspects of Ramdev's life story that seem to be strategically censored or kept secret—such as his initiation into the

---

[3] Bharat Swabhiman, 'Swami Ramdev Shows His Power of Yoga in the Wrestling | Must Watch', YouTube video, televised on 4 January 2015. Available at: https://www.youtube.com/watch?v=yRghVMT97Yc (accessed on 13 January 2016).

[4] Bharat Swabhiman, 'Glorious 18 Years of Divya Yoga Mandir and Patanjali Yogpeeth', YouTube video, televised on 24 January 2013. Available at: https://www.youtube.com/watch?v=Z5TuBu3KMbU (accessed on 13 January 2016).

[5] 'The Manufacturing of Patanjali Amla Juice', YouTube video, televised in 2015. Available at: https://www.youtube.com/watch?v=ChEyBsoFEVw (accessed on 13 January 2016).

practice of yoga and various elements of his education and training—his rural Haryana ancestry has become an important part of his public persona, as when he talks authoritatively about tending to the needs of cows in his gaushala. So has his education at Gurukul Kangri in Haridwar, a distinctively modern institution of 'traditional' Sanskrit learning. Closely linked to this is a remarkable facility with language and public speaking. Ramdev artfully combines styles of speech that cross the register from that of an erudite pundit, on the one hand, to a folksy, down-to-earth peasant 'boy', on the other. Somewhere in the middle is a man who 'speaks the language' of a large number of middle-class men and women in contemporary India. Ramdev's appeal is precisely that he is able to articulate very clearly, and seemingly without manifest contradiction, an alternative model of modernity, one in which antithetical dualities—English vs Sanskrit, ascetic renouncer vs capitalist entrepreneur, rural vs urban, biomedical public health vs yoga and 'traditional' ayurvedic medicine, scientific objectivity vs subjective knowledge, self-interest vs public service—are apparently synthesised and transcended. No small part of this has to do with the way in which gender is performed, thus depersonalising, disembodying and deracinating masculinity.

˙ What happens, however, is that the performance of decentring opens up spaces—consciously and unconsciously, purposefully and by chance—for the articulation of 'bad' old-fashioned aggressive, heteronormative, patriarchal masculanism. This comes out when Ramdev's supporters defend him for dressing up in a sari to escape detection—full-flowing beard notwithstanding—during police action in Delhi (Sarbacker 2014: 366). Smug accusations of effitism reify the heteronormative prejudices of those intent on besmirchment, just as they insight chest thumping on the part of Baba's supporters. Derivative masculanism also finds expression in Ramdev's virulent criticism of homosexuality and his condemnation of so-called 'unnatural' sex. As discussed in more detail below, it finds expression in his advocacy for heteronormative family values while defending the terms under which Patanjali Ayurved markets a tonic that strongly suggests—through nominal Sanskrit denotation—that women who drink it will surely give birth to sons. In each case, however, these articulations of centred masculinity reflect a kind of grossly conservative retrenchment into spaces that are inherently defined by the disarticulation of gender and gendered experience in the public sphere. Controversially, Baba Ramdev consistently embodies this virtual indeterminacy.

Yoga lessons—as broadcast on TV and as staged and performed at public events—epitomise the embodied performance of decentred gender. To a large extent, this simply has to do with the cultural history of postural yoga and breathing exercises in the popular imagination. Certainly, there are forms of practice that have come to reflect aspects of masculinity. This is especially true for certain schools of 20th-century derivation, where the emphasis is on physicality; and there is also the important, but somewhat unremarkable, fact that some teachers are more assertively and affectedly masculine than others. But *asana* and *pranayama*, despite modern interpretation and reinterpretation, bend the body into configurations that are gender neutral, albeit animated, at least in the experience of some adepts, with the power of contained sexuality.

There are so many forms of practice around the world that postural yoga should be interpreted as a grammar for endless elaboration rather than a scripted text with definitive cultural meaning. Ramdev's lessons, workshops and demonstrations—often on a massive scale—make use of this grammar to produce something unique. He makes the performance of yoga seem effortless and easily accessible. He is playful, casual and funny, but also intense and very serious. On the one hand, he turns yoga into a form of exercise for healthy living. On the other hand, as an adept performer of asana and pranayama, whose running Hindi commentary is suffused with references to the vedas and Sanskrit texts, his practice is taken to be authentic, transcendent and, in some sense, concretely mystical. Unlike many less sagely, secular teachers of postural yoga, Baba Ramdev is able to convincingly—and concurrently—reveal and make public, control and keep secret the mystery of yoga. There are very interesting and important ways in which this correlates with the twisted practices of branding, marketing and advertising (Mazzarella 2003).

Although his physical presence on stage, as a youthful energetic sadhu, entails what might be called unremarkable mundane masculinity, his yoga performances, as they are mediated through television, and as they involve the collective, choreographed participation of hundreds, and sometimes thousands, of men, women and children, are inherently disembodied. That is, these staged performances depersonalise yoga, producing a space where men and women are not their gendered selves.

And there is something about the experience of anonymous, displaced, virtual sociality in these spaces that helps to account for Ramdev's popularity. He is certainly charismatic. But what is generated in and through mass drill yoga routines is a kind of displaced collective effervescence that prevents masculinity from eloping with charisma to produce, and then go on reproducing, heirs to the throne of patriarchal authority. Mass drill yoga, which is a spectacle designed for media consumption, produces a modern, relatively unmarked space—comfortably virtual, comfortably anonymous and seductively intimate—where men and women come together in ways that are, if not totally unique, at least noteworthy with respect to the destabilisation of embodied, binary gendered categories.

There is, of course, a very different way in which the practice of yoga has involved the displacement of masculinity and femininity. Tantric iconography highlights the most explicit articulation of this in various forms, especially the cosmic embrace of Shiv/Shakti in eternal *maithuna* (sexual intercourse). But whereas other godmen have 'experimented' with the real-world application of tantra, their all-too-human masculinity almost always gets in the way of their transcendental sexuality, and vice versa. Whatever his faults and flaws may be, Baba Ramdev does not aspire to embody one half the aspect of erotic asceticism. His creative, very virtual masculine energy is directed elsewhere.

Just as the mediated performance of yoga literally decentres and disembodies some aspect of masculinity, other aspects are re-centred and re-animated in terms of nationalist discourse and practice. Moreover, the fetishisation of commodities serves to materialise masculinity in ways that not only displace but also re-centre sex and power (Islam and Kuah-Pearce 2013).

Patanjali Ayurved and Divya Pharmacy are tremendously successful commercial enterprises based on the simple—and by no means unique—idea that pure, authentic herbal decoctions can be transformed into modern tonics and pharmaceuticals by means of science and technology. The power and authority of classical, intuitive wisdom is combined with data from 'research and development' to produce commodities that do, in effect, precisely what Ramdev does to himself via the technology of television and YouTube.

While there are many important and interesting features to this process of commodity fetishisation, only one specific issue concerns us here: the way in which ancient wisdom materialises anachronistic masculinity, the fetishisation of patriarchy in relation to materialisation and the way in which the logic of the market is comparable to the 'twisted' logic of yoga, wherein truth is purportedly revealed but always kept secret. As we shall see, everything is in the problematic propriety of names and denotation (Mazzarella 2015).

Baba Ramdev has recently been embroiled in a controversy concerning a product his company has developed called putrajeevakbeej.[6] Marketed by Divya Pharmacy to 'enhance' fertility, the product name is coded in the pure language of ayurveda, but translates, very problematically, into crude English, as 'son-breeding seed', or, more simply, 'son seed'. The controversy revolves around the way putrajeevakbeej is bought and sold as a form of pre-conception sex selection. Whether or not it works, the very idea—materialised and fetishised in medicinal form—serves to reinforce conservative sexism that is out of step with government policies and non-governmental programmes designed to protect, empower and support girls and women. In other words, putrajeevakbeej can easily be seen as an insidious marketing ploy that takes advantage of incipient sexist prejudices, and the legacy of a preference for sons (see Purewal 2010). Son seed's popularity casts a dark shadow on the real achievements of feminism in contemporary India.

Consequently, it is not at all surprising that politicians and activists—particularly Kishan Chand Tyagi, Janata Dal member of the Rajya Sabha—have demanded that Divya Pharmacy pull the product and stop production. *Nirod*, plain and simple. Some have demanded that the government pull out and revoke the company's licence.

However legitimate Tyagi's argument may be, what is important to recognise is the way in which patriarchal masculinity is deployed both as a marketing strategy by Divya Pharmacy and as a political and legal attack against Baba Ramdev. Beyond this, it is equally important to recognise the extent to which the 'controversy' is largely a mediated controversy in the sense that the issue lends itself to television talk shows rather than street protests. Tyagi's charges against Ramdev, made on the floor of the Rajya Sabha, are passionately pure political theatrics, levelled directly against the 'brand ambassador of Haryana'[7,8]

[6] ABP News, 'Ramdev Selling Medicine That Guarantees a Male Child: KC Tyagi', YouTube video, televised on 30 April 2015. Available at: https://www.youtube.com/watch?v=XtE_E8r8f24 (accessed on 31 May 2018).

[7] Ibid.

[8] Zee News, 'KC Tyagi Can Try "Putrajeevak Beej", He Will Surely Have a Girl', 2015. Available at: http://zeenews.india.com/news/india/kc-tyagi-can-try-putrajeevak-beej-hell-surely-have-a-girl-baba-ramdev_1597289.html (accessed on 13 January 2016).

But in defending himself and his product,[9] Ramdev invokes the ambiguity of mediated language, both in and out of translation, the essential, unchangeable nature of ayurvedic knowledge, and 'traditional' heteronormative family values defined in such a way as to place equal responsibility on husband and wife and equal value on boys and girls.[10] At a time when truth is what you make of it—and what you know will be made of it in the media—Ramdev argues, very assertively, that the word *putra* is gender neutral.

In other words, the case of putrajeevakbeej provides a striking example of the way in which a virtual discourse on incipient masculinity, as distinct from securely centred masculinity in the form of culture—Jat culture, for example, if not the whole male aspect of what used to be called 'Hindu identity'—structures questions of legitimacy, market transparency, fairness in advertising, gender equality, the politics of language and the integrity of claims to intellectual property rights, among any number of other things. The challenge, of course, is to not let the specific gravity of this brave new decentred world lead anyone to believe that they cannot construct—by virtually planting the seed, if you will—an alternative moral, ethical and analytical reality within this field of power relations.

References

Ahmed, S.M.F. 2006. 'Making Beautiful: Male Workers in Beauty Parlors'. *Men and Masculinities* 9 (2): 168–85.
Alter, J.S. 2008. 'Yoga *Shivir*: Performativity and the Study of Modern Yoga'. In *Yoga in the Modern World: Contemporary Perspectives*, edited by M. Singleton and J. Byrne, 36–48. London: Routledge.
———. 2011. *Moral Materialism: Sex and Masculinity in Modern India*. New Delhi: Penguin.
Baas, M. 2016. 'The New Indian Male: Muscles, Masculinity and Middle Classness'. In *Routledge Handbook of Contemporary India*, edited by Knut A. Jacobsen, 444–56. London: Routledge.
Banerjee, S. 2005. *Make Me a Man: Masculinity, Hinduism, and Nationalism in India*. Albany, NY: State University of New York Press.

[9] ABP News, 'Baba Ramdev Responds to KC Tyagi; Says Drugs Do Not Guarantee Baby Boy', YouTube video, televised on 1 May 2015. Available at: https://www.youtube.com/watch?v=jL3Mw0m-dRM (accessed on 13 January 2016).
[10] http://www.swamibabaramdevmedicines.com/ (accessed on 13 January 2016).

Chattopadhyay, S. 2011. 'Bengali Masculinity and the National-Masculine: Some Conjectures for Interpretation'. *South Asia Research* 31 (3): 265–79.

Chopra, R. 2002. *From Violence to Supportive Practice: Family, Gender, and Masculinities in India*. New Delhi: United Nations Development Fund for Women, South Asia Regional Office.

———. 2007. *Reframing Masculinities: Narrating the Supportive Practices of Men*. Hyderabad: Orient Longman.

Chopra, R., C. Osella and F. Osella. 2004. *South Asian Masculinities: Context of Change, Sites of Continuity*. New Delhi: Women Unlimited.

Chowdhry, P. 2013. 'Militarized Masculinities: Shaped and Reshaped in Colonial South-east Punjab'. *Modern Asian Studies* 47 (3): 713–50.

Cohen, L. 2012. 'Style'. In *Handbook of Gender*, edited by R. Ray, 249–68. New Delhi: Oxford University Press.

Copeman, J. and a. Ikegame. 2012. *The Guru in South Asia*. London: Routledge.

Dasgupta, R.K. and M.K. Gokulsing, eds. 2014. *Masculinity and Its Challenges in India: Essays on Changing Perceptions*. Jefferson, NC: McFarland and Company.

Doron, A. 2011. 'Youth, Society and Mobile Media in Asia'. *Asian Studies Review* 35 (3): 405–07.

———. 2012. 'Mobile Persons: Cell Phones, Gender and the Self in North India'. *Asia Pacific Journal of Anthropology* 13 (5): 414–33.

Doron, A. and A. Broom. 2014. *Gender and Masculinities: Histories, Texts and Practices in India and Sri Lanka*. New Delhi: Routledge.

Doron, A. and R. Jeffrey. 2013. *The Great Indian Phone Book: How the Cheap Cell Phone Changes Business, Politics, and Daily Life*. Cambridge: Harvard University Press.

Gupta, C. 2010. 'Feminine, Criminal or Manly? Imagining Dali Masculinities in Colonial North India'. *The Indian Economic and Social History Review* 47 (3): 309–42.

———. 2011. 'Anxious Hindu Masculinities in Colonial North India: *Shuddhi* and *Sangathan* Movements'. *Crosscurrents* 61 (4): 441–54.

Gupta, N. 2015. 'Rethinking the Relationship Between Gender and Technology: A Study of the Indian Example'. *Work Employment and Society* 29 (4): 661–72.

Haynes, D.E. 2012. 'Selling Masculinity: Advertisements for Sex Tonics and the Making of Modern Conjugality in Western India, 1900–1945'. *South Asia: Journal of South Asian Studies* 35 (4): 787–831.

Hinchy, J. 2013. 'Obscenity, Moral Contagion and Masculinity: *Hijras* in Public Space in Colonial North India'. *Asian Studies Review* 38 (2): 274–94.

Islam, M.N. and K.E. Kuah-Pearce. 2013. 'The Promotion of Masculinity and Femininity Through *Ayurveda* in Modern India'. *Indian Journal of Gender Studies* 20 (3): 415–34.

Jeffrey, C. 2010. 'Timepass: Youth, Class, and Time Among Unemployed Young Men in India'. *American Ethnologist* 37 (3): 465–81.

Khalikova, V. Forthcoming. 'Medicine for the Nation: The Biopolitics of Plural Medicine and Discourses of National Belonging in India'. PhD Dissertation. Department of Anthropology, University of Pittsburgh.

Majumdar, B. 2006. 'Tom Brown Goes Global: The "Brown" Ethic in Colonial and Post-colonial India'. *The International Journal of the History of Sport* 23 (5): 805–20.

Mazzarella, W. 2003. *Shovelling Smoke: Advertising and Globalization in Contemporary India*. Durham, NC: Duke University Press.

———. 2015. 'On the Im/Propriety of Brand Names'. *South Asia Multi-disciplinary Academic Journal* (12): 1–17.

McDuie-Ra, D. 2012. 'Leaving the Militarized Frontier: Migration and Tribal Masculinity in Delhi'. *Men and Masculinities* 15 (2): 112–31.

Mehta, D. 2006. 'Collective Violence, Public Spaces, and the Unmaking of Men'. *Men and Masculinities* 9 (2): 204–25.

Nakassis, C.V. 2013. 'Youth Masculinity, "Style" and the Peer Group in Tamil Nadu, India'. *Contributions to Indian Sociology* 47 (2): 245–69.

Osella, C. and F. Osella. 1998. 'Friendship and Flirting: Micro-politics in Kerala, South India'. *The Journal of the Royal Anthropological Institute* 4 (2): 189–206.

Osella, F. and C. Osella. 2000. 'Migration, Money and Masculinity in Kerala'. *The Journal of the Royal Anthropological Institute* 6 (1): 117–33.

———. 2003. 'Ayyappan Saranam: Masculinity and the Sabarimala Pilgrimage in Kerala'. *The Journal of the Royal Anthropological Institute* 9 (4): 729–54.

Powers, J. 2009. *A Bull of a Man: Images of Masculinity, Sex and the Body in Indian Buddhism*. Cambridge: Harvard University Press.

Purewal, N.K. 2010. *Son Preference: Sex Selection, Gender and Culture in South Asia*. Oxford: Berg Publishers.

Qayum, S. and R. Ray. 2010 'Male Servants and the Failure of Patriarchy in Kolkata (Calcutta)'. *Men and Masculinities* 13 (1): 111–25.

Rajan, G. 2006. 'Constructing–Contesting Masculinities: Trends in South Asian Cinema'. *Signs* 31 (4): 1099–124.

Ray, R. 2008. 'India's New Middle Class: Democratic Politics in an Era of Economic Reform'. *Contemporary Sociology: A Journal of Reviews* 37 (2): 128–29.

Reddy, G. 2005. *With Respect to Sex: Negotiating Hijra Identity in South India*. Chicago, IL: University of Chicago Press.

Sarbacker, S. 2014. 'Swami Ramdev: Modern Yoga Revolutionary'. In *Gurus of Modern Yoga*, edited by M. Singleton and E. Goldberg, 351–72. Oxford: Oxford University Press.

Singleton, M. and E. Goldberg. 2014. *Gurus of Modern Yoga*. Oxford: Oxford University Press.

Srivastava, S. 2004. *Sexual Sites, Seminal Attitudes: Sexualities, Masculinities and Culture in South Asia*. New Delhi: SAGE.

———. 2007. *Passionate Modernity: Sexuality, Class, and Consumption in India*. New Delhi: Routledge.

Srivastava, S. 2010. 'Fragmentary Pleasures: Masculinity, Urban Spaces, and Commodity Politics in Delhi'. *Journal of the Royal Anthropological Institute* 16 (4): 835–52.

———. 2015. 'Modi-masculinity: Media, Manhood, and "Traditions" in a Time of Consumerism'. *Television & New Media* 16 (4): 331–38.

Staples, J. 2005. 'Becoming a Man: Personhood and Masculinity in a South Indian Leprosy Colony'. *Contributions to Indian Sociology* 39 (2): 281–305.

———. 2011. 'At the Intersection of Disability and Masculinity: Exploring Gender and Bodily Difference in India'. *Journal of the Royal Anthropological Institute* 17 (3): 545–62.

Van Hollen, C. 2013. *Birth in the Age of AIDS: Women, Reproduction, and HIV/AIDS in India*. Stanford, CA: Stanford University Press.

Verniers, G. 2013. 'Degrees Without Freedom? Education, Masculinities and Unemployment in North India'. *Contributions to Indian Sociology* 47 (3): 461–64.

22

The Sociology of Disability

Conceptual Ethnography of an Analytical Category in India

Renu Addlakha

Is there a sociology of disability[1] in India? Until a decade ago, the answer would have been an unequivocal no; today, it is a qualified yes. I feel privileged to have both witnessed, participated in and contributed to this ongoing process. Although still a niche area of scholarship within the larger sociological–anthropological domain in the country, the research output is steadily increasing, particularly from the emerging domain of disability studies that straddles academic and activist concerns of knowledge production and social transformation. In this chapter, I will try to capture the contemporary status of the disability category within the larger disciplinary frameworks of sociology and anthropology with a particular focus on India.

Like any embodied category, disability has two interconnected components, namely medical limitation(s) and social prejudice, which often

[1] For purposes of this chapter, disability is being simply defined as any physical or psychological impairment that has material, social, cultural, economic and political consequences for a person having the impairment. It is an analytical determinant in the same manner as socio-economic status, caste, class or gender.

get translated into discriminatory behaviour towards the person with a disability and even her family. Being a heterogeneous concept, its causes, forms and manifestations are highly variable: most intellectual disabilities and autism are congenital; childhood disabilities like polio may be attributed to malnutrition, micronutrient deficiencies and infections; disabilities may be acquired later in life due to accidents, injuries or advancing age, significantly affecting people's lives. Many disabilities such as schizophrenia and bipolar disorder are characterised by episodic upsurge of symptoms and/or progressive degeneration. A disability may be static such as the loss of a limb due to an amputation or spinal cord injury due to an accident. Diabetes and epilepsy are hidden disabilities, while leprosy and blindness are visible conditions. Although a universal characteristic of the human condition in the course of the life cycle, disabilities may be temporary or permanent; a fracture may result in temporary disablement, while quadriplegia sustained in an automobile accident would lead to permanent disability. Besides cause, time of onset, body parts affected, there are many gradations of disability ranging from mild to severe. While the location of a disability is an individual body or psyche, macro-level factors such as natural disasters, conflict and wars, environmental degradation and climate change are increasing the burden of disabilities worldwide.

Medical and legal definitions of disability show isomorphism but have distinctive epistemic and practical connotations. In the latter context, disability is defined in terms of what qualifies for public assistance. For instance, in India, having 40 per cent is the minimum threshold for eligibility for public assistance. In light of the sheer diversity of this overarching category, the United Nations Convention on the Rights of Persons with Disabilities (UNCRPD) defines 'persons with disability' in Article 1 as those

> Who have long-term physical, mental, intellectual or sensory impairments which, in interaction with physical, social and attitudinal barriers, may hinder their full and effective participation in society on an equal basis with others.[2]

In order to configure the biological and social dimensions of this particular form of difference, concepts of impairment and disability need to be understood. While impairment remains close to the medical model referring to 'lacking all or part of a limb, or having a defective limb,

[2] http://www.un.org/disabilities/convention/conventionfull.shtml (accessed on 19 April 2017).

organism or mechanism of the body', disability is 'the disadvantage or restriction of activity caused by a contemporary social organisation which takes no or little account of people who have physical impairments and thus excludes them from the mainstream of social activities' (UPIAS 1976: 3–4).

Towards a Sociology/Anthropology of Impairment and Disability

Notwithstanding its apparent marginal presence in university courses in the Indian academy, disability has always been a part of the sociological canon right from Durkheim's *Suicide*, published in 1897, and Parsons' (1951) concept of the 'sick role' in his *The Social System*. The configuration of difference as deviance by Lemert (1962) in connection with social problems and social control and by Goffman (1963) in the context of stigma are other highly regarded pioneering sociological analyses of disability. Other seminal works that have driven the sociological discourse on disability include Bury's (1982, 1991, 1992) and Gerhardt's (1989) analyses of the disabling consequences of chronic illness, Mechanic's concept of illness behaviour (Mechanic and Volkart 1961), Gordon's (1966) analysis of illness in terms of role theory and Jenkin's work (1991) on disability as social stratification. These works have influenced many empirical studies, creating the sub-discipline of medical sociology.

Wading into the choppy waters of medical sociology and chronic illness, leading disability scholars (many of whom were not only themselves disabled persons but also trained social scientists and passionate activists) like Colin Barnes and Mike Oliver have argued that 'sociological analyses of disability have been theoretically and methodologically inadequate' (Barnes 1998: 75) along the same lines that feminist scholars contended that gender has been marginalised. In the case of disability, abilism (dominance of the able-bodied perspective) replaces patriarchy, and emancipatory research undertaken by disabled scholars is the counterpoint to feminist research. According to these pioneering disability scholars who laid the foundation of disability studies as a distinctive academic domain (Barnes 1991, 1998; Barnes and Mercer 1996; Barnes et al. 2002; Campbell and Oliver 1996; Finkelstein 1980, 1998; Oliver 1990, 1996), the standard sociological interpretations are deterministic, ignoring the social, economic and political factors configuring disability; they mirror the values of the able-bodied (for instance, disability is a devalued experience that needs to be prevented at all costs) filtered through the lens of medical experts; they deny subjectivity of the actual persons with disabilities who are unambiguously depicted as unfortunate, tragic and undesirable. Even Goffman's very influential concept of stigma reflects the perspective of the oppressor/labeller than that of the labelled. Symbolic interactionism's focus on meaning-making, interaction and identity is a fertile area for sociological investigation on disability, only if it is possible to denude it of its abilist underpinnings.

Pushing for the reconfiguration of disability from an individual medical problem with social consequences affecting a small segment of the population to an identity politics and civil rights issue, disability studies scholars have ensured that it becomes an analytical category along the lines of class, gender and ethnicity that has relevance to the population as a whole. Given that accounts of disability have been largely generated by 'experts' within applied disciplines such as special education, social work and the paramedical fields, the need of the hour is to develop a database of the experiences by and of disabled persons which is summed up in the famous slogan 'nothing about us without us' (Charlton 1998).

So while one can say that disability has not been overlooked in sociological analysis, the individual-based medical-centric approach has generated research output which contemporary disability studies scholars would regard as problematic because it does not question the underlying assumptions and preconceptions of 'abilism of society' in general and the conceptions of normality of medicine in particular.

A similar critique with some qualification can also be made of the standard anthropological studies on disability. Corresponding with Durkheim's foundational concepts of normal and abnormal social facts in terms of statistical variations is Ruth Benedict's (1934) famous essay that dwells on the issue from a cross-cultural relativistic perspective. The norm as average and as culturally specific opened the window for some of the earliest socio-anthropological accounts of disability. One of the earliest anthropological monographs is Edgerton's (1967) study of the impact of de-institutionalisation on American public life captured through the experiences of intellectually disabled persons. Other pioneering works in this genre include Groce (1985) and Gwaltney (1970) on hearing and visual impairments, respectively. Joan Ablon's (1984, 1988) work on dwarfism in American culture is another noteworthy contribution to the anthropology of impairment and disability. Following in the tradition of Goffman's (1961) *Asylums* is Angrosino's (1997) ethnographic study of Opportunity House, a facility for the intellectually challenged. Initiating the cross-cultural trend of the study of institutionalised life was Nakamura's (2013) study of Bethel House, a community of persons with psychiatric disabilities in Japan. Lawrence Cohen's (1998) work is a path-breaking study on the intersection of ageing and disability in Banaras, India. If lived experience, cultural meaningfulness and diversity are the hallmark of the anthropological perspective, then the study of disability might be most at home within this discipline. However, as Ginsberg and Rapp (201) point out in their review, disability has found a limited space in anthropology and that too largely only within the narrow confines of medical anthropology, a situation not very different from the study of disability within medical sociology.

Anthropology's engagement with disability can be classified into three main trends, namely the critique of medicalisation from a cultural perspective such as Rouse's (2009) study of sickle cell anaemia in the lives of African Americans; ethnographic studies of conceptions and experiences of impairment in non-Western contexts across space and time such as Ingstadt and Whyte's (1995, 2007) path-breaking volumes that capture the diversity of the disability category cross-culturally to the extent of contesting its very existence in certain places where varieties of impairments may exist but there is no recognised category of disability per se. For instance, epilepsy may be conceptualised as a divine gift or ancestral curse instead of a neurological impairment accompanied by discrimination and stigma. Third, not only ethnography but also auto-ethnography has emerged as a distinct anthropological genre to capture the experiences of disablement of individual anthropologists as sufferers (Greenhalgh 2001; Martin 2007; Murphy 2001; Zola 1982), and as parents of children with disabilities (Berube 1996; Grinker 2007; Kittay 1999; Landsman 2009) who highlight, in a very poignant fashion, the personal, interpersonal and cultural dynamics of disablement. Kohrman's (2005) study of the emergence of disability as a state-recognised category through a strategic linking of statistics, ideology and social changes in China incorporates these multiple perspectives.

One of the most intellectually stimulating developments in the study of deafness is its configuration not as a medical problem or even as a disability but as a distinctive linguistic minority culture and community united by sign language. Nora Groce's (1985) study of Martha's Vineyard shows how sign language becomes the lingua franca, wherein hearing-persons also adopted it as a means of communication in a society where hereditary deafness was the norm. In the community of residents of Martha's Vineyard between the 17th century and early decades of the 20th century, being deaf was so statistically prevalent that having normal hearing became an aberration. Deaf (with a capital D connoting deafness as constituting a distinctive cultural or linguistic community) studies (Blume 2010; Ladd 2003; Lane et al. 1996; Nakamura 2006) has emerged as a distinct academic speciality which shares an ambivalent relationship with disability studies, because deafness is not regarded as a hearing impairment or disability per se. Autism is another condition that is generating anthropological interest by virtue of its non-normative manifestations in terms of key categories of communication, sociality and relationality (Bumiller 2008; Ochs and Solomon 2010; Ochs et al. 2004).

Disability, Sociology and Anthropology in India: The Present Scenario and Future Directions

While using standard disciplinary concepts such as the sick role, impaired role, rehabilitation role, disabled identity, adaptation, lived experience and cultural diversity is a possible pathway into a sociology and anthropology of disability in India, such a research pathway at the current conjuncture in thinking about disability would be regarded as epistemically and ethically questionable given the emergence of disability studies that the Society for Disability Studies describes as follows:

> Using interdisciplinary and multidisciplinary approaches, Disability Studies sits at the intersection of many overlapping disciplines in the humanities, sciences, and social sciences. Programs in Disability Studies should encourage a curriculum that allows students, activists, teachers, artists, practitioners, and researchers to engage the subject matter from various disciplinary perspectives.[3]

The main ideological and theoretical underpinning of disability thinking today is the social model of disability which reconfigures the phenomenon not as an individualistic biomedical fact but as a multifaceted bio-psychosocial reality, created, sustained and marginalised by social, economic, cultural, historical and political forces in every epoch and culture with few exceptions. Theoretically, the principal marker of disability studies is that it conceptualises the phenomenon as a sociopolitical reality, a form of oppression and not a personal tragedy

[3] https://disstudies.org/index.php/about-sds/what-is-disability-studies/ (accessed on 1 June 2018).

or misfortune. The social model questions both the medicalisation and stigmatisation of difference. Pioneering disability studies scholars such as Sally Tomlinson (1982), Mike Oliver (1996), Tom Shakespeare (2006), Tanya Titchkosky (2000) and Simi Linton (1998), among others, hold that the ubiquity and universality of the disability experience throughout history is a sufficient reason for its study within the social sciences. Disability may be investigated from a variety of interlinked topics such as care, social movements, eugenics, social policy, human rights and citizenship across a range of disciplines (economics, history, sociology, psychology) using a range of methodologies, namely statistical, activist, reflexive, experiential, narrative and phenomenological in understanding what it is like living with particular impairments at macro and micro levels.

Disability has emerged as a legislative and policy issue on the Indian scene since the 1970s with a particular focus in the areas of health, education, employment-accessible environments and social security. The Indian Parliament enacted the historic Persons with Disabilities (Equal Opportunities, Protection of Rights and Full Participation) Act in 1995. In 2007, India signed and later ratified UNCRPD. In 2016, new disability laws such as the Rights of Persons with Disabilities Act and the Mental Health Care Act had been enacted by the Parliament in order to make the legal regime compliant with the Convention. While state and civil society discourses on disability in India have largely shifted from charity and welfare to human rights, disability studies, as an interdisciplinary academic terrain that focuses on the contributions, experiences, history and culture of persons with disabilities, has not yet taken root. Even though a number of scholars, activists and policy-makers (Addlakha 2008, 2013; Das and Addlakha 2001; Davar 1999; Dhanda 2000; Ghai 2003, 2015; Hans 2015; Hans and Patri 2003) have produced path-breaking work on disability, it still remains marginalised within the wider research and advocacy communities, although the situation is rapidly changing.

Although the fields of history of medicine and sociological/ anthropological studies of health and illness have emerged in the Indian academy, they have either not dealt with the phenomenon of disability at all or largely focused on its disease/illness dimensions in the tradition of medical sociology and anthropology. The medical model has dominated the traditional approach to disability. In reviewing how scholarship in India has engaged with the issue of disability, the distinction between disability as a medical issue largely focusing on provision of clinical and rehabilitation services and disability studies as a scholarly approach to examining various dimensions of disability as a form of difference along the lines of race, class, caste and gender has to be borne in mind.

In the absence of reliable clinical, empirical and demographic data for the country as a whole, a large number of empirical studies on impairment and handicap have been generated by professionals in the helping professions such as special education, rehabilitation, clinical psychology and other paramedical specialities. Although since 2001 the Census and the National Sample Survey Organisation (2002) have produced some baseline data on the issue, it is largely regarded as under-representative of the actual prevalence of the issue. Concern with prevalence, incidence, management and prevention of disabilities is still a stark reality in the government and NGO sectors (Bacquer and Sharma 1997; Narasimhan and Mukherjee 1986). This situation is further complicated by India's official commitment to UNCRPD that seeks to operationalise many of the basic tenets of the social model. The absence of a valid empirical database on disability is a serious limitation implying that the meaning of disability and its social ramifications largely remain invisible in academic discourse, public understanding and policy formulations.

If one examines the social science literature on disability, excluding the empirical studies from the applied professions referred to above, one finds some work addressing the sociocultural reality of disability (Bhatt 1963; Dalal 2002; Miles 1995, 2001). Following the trend of feminist disability studies in the West seen in the works of Michelle Fine and Adrienne Asch (1988), Rosemarie Garland-Thomson (2009), Marian Corker (Corker and French 1999) and Susan Wendell (1996), among many others, a number of books focusing on mental—or what is now referred to as psychosocial—disability (Addlakha 2008; Davar 1999, 2001, 2008) engage with this theme from the perspectives of the women's movement, the law and the psychiatric profession, respectively. Hariss-White and Erb's (2002) and Klasing's (2007) studies examine the social exclusion of disabled persons in rural India falling in the category of area-specific empirical studies. More specifically addressing the issue of women with disabilities are Anita Ghai's (2003) account of the emergence of disability feminism within Western feminism vis-à-vis the marginalisation of the issue within the Indian women's movement, and Asha Hans and Annie Patri's (2003) edited collection of the proceedings of an international seminar on women with disabilities. Two of the above authors have come out more recently with publications that revisit some of the issues raised in their earlier works (Ghai

2015; Hans 2015). The intellectual alliance between women's studies and disability studies has been and continues to be a productive area of research and advocacy. Further, the work of Rukmini Sekhar (2005), Malini Chib (2011) and Preeti Monga (2013) make a beginning in the area of autobiography and disability.

The socio-anthropological studies such as Das and Addlakha (2001) and Addlakha (2008) and research by women with disabilities has helped bring attention to a hitherto much neglected terrain of research both within the social sciences and the women's and disability rights movements in India, namely sexuality. Following Addlakha's (2007) work on disability, youth and sexuality are detailed accounts of lives of women with disabilities in India (Ghosh 2015, 2016). The social model's focus on built environments and accessibility issues is increasingly being found to be inadequate to address the multi-layered dimensions of disability opening new areas of investigation by young scholars in the social sciences and humanities.

Many disability scholars and activists are attempting to unquestioningly take a Western agenda on disability to a reality which has different epistemological and ontological moorings. Hence, the need for a perspective that not only critically assesses the relevance of concepts and theories on disability developed in the West but also engages in uncovering meaningful discourses and developing strategies that address the local realities of disability in the Indian context. Nilika Mehrotra (2013) combines an anthropological perspective on the study of autism and intellectual disabilities to highlight the existential reality of individuals and families, on the one hand, and the macro-level forces of neoliberalisation, identity politics and social movements, on the other. Shubhangi Vaidya (2010, 2011, 2015) dwells on similar issues but from the perspective of a parent of a child with autism.

While the study of mental illness and psychosocial disability is well established in disability studies in India as seen from the works of Addlakha, Davar and Dhanda, deaf studies has not taken root in the Indian context. Recent pioneering works by Sandhya Limaye (2010) and Michel Friedner (2015) from the perspective of deafness as hearing impairment and as a minority culture, respectively, offer a productive direction for future research.

Law has been a pillar of social transformation in India since the colonial era. It continues to exercise a salient influence in areas that involve both intellectual endeavour and social change such as caste, gender and disability. Enactment of disability legislation and India's signing of UNCRPD are embedded in a burgeoning scholarship on law and disability (Addlakha and Mandal 2009; Dhanda and Raturi 2010; Kothari 2012).

Discussion and Conclusion

Countering the common-sense perspective that disability is an individual medical problem, the social model of disability asserts that physical or mental pathology are not the defining characteristics of disability: material barriers, social prejudice and exclusion define who is disabled. While some people have physical, intellectual or emotional differences from a statistical norm, these impairments do not have to lead to disability unless society fails to accommodate and include them in the way it would those who are 'normal'. This is a paradigmatic shift in envisioning disability. While the social model does not reject medical knowledge and technology in dealing with the problem of bodily impairments, it shifts the focus of research and advocacy to analysing how a given society disables its impaired members. Consequently, the spotlight of enquiry and intervention shifts to how physical, social, economic, political, communication and attitudinal barriers create disabling environments that lead to the marginalisation, oppression and invisibilisation of disabled persons. In the light of this radical change of perspective on the meaning of disability and in the absence of full-fledged degree programmes on disability studies in Indian universities, it is imperative that it is introduced in sociology and anthropology programmes at undergraduate and postgraduate levels.

Although early disability studies scholars linked the systematic oppression of disabled people to the rise of industrial capitalism, which created a market where those who could not sell their labour power were devalued and stigmatised, materialist interpretations focusing on socio-structural determinants is not the only approach to the study of disability. Linguistic, discursive and cultural practices are fertile areas of research which disability scholars may engage in. From the available literature on disability in India, scholars seem to be adopting a combination of methodologies, perspectives and data sources, depending on their individual training and competencies. For example, Davar judiciously combines her training in philosophy and experience of psychiatric illness in her family and in her own life with a textual analysis of Indian psychiatric literature, feminist psychology and her own experiences of participation in the Indian women's movement.

In the United States, minority group politics deriving from the prevailing black civil rights and women's movements influenced the development of disability activism and disability studies with the resulting emphasis on tackling social subordination, exclusion and developing strategies for empowerment. Although minority religious and caste identities have been a central feature of the Indian landscape, disability has not until recently been acknowledged as a valid axis of oppression which needs redressal through affirmative action.[4] A variety of reasons such as heterogeneity of the disability category, geographical dispersal of the disabled population, devaluation of personhood and not constituting an obvious vote bank have ensured the invisibility of disability. Not only is there a need to mainstream disability in academia, the economy and the polity per se, but intersectional analysis highlighting how it interacts with other socio-demographic variables such as caste, class, gender and ethnicity is also an area sociology is ideally equipped to research. In the context of marginalisation, the category of social exclusion may be fruitfully deployed to capture and ameliorate the experiences of disability at individual and group levels. Indeed, disability studies is the logical outcome of a trajectory pioneered by the interdisciplinary domains of caste and tribal studies, women's studies and queer studies, which have also entered the academy after hectic activist politics and social mobilisation.

In keeping with its critical epistemology and radical politics, disability studies has also reconfigured research paradigms. Mike Oliver (1997) proposed the notion of emancipatory disability research, which transforms the material and social relations of research production. Essentially, this is a form of participatory action research that questions the notions of objectivity and value neutrality in which research has traditionally been determined by non-disabled professionals and academics. Persons with disabilities have been 'cases', and the results of the research have been used largely to serve the interests of doctors and policy-makers. Indeed, the rationale for emancipatory research is to displace control from non-disabled to disabled individual. Emancipatory

---

[4] There are a number of policy measures instituted to ameliorate the plight of disabled persons such as assistance in acquiring assistive aids such as artificial limbs and wheelchairs free of cost or at subsidised rates, 3 per cent reservation in education and public employment, scholarships, pension schemes, 3 per cent allotment of resources in poverty-alleviation programmes, among other measures. The central government schemes are supplemented by state-level programmes such as financial incentives in marriage when one of the partners is disabled being implemented in states like Haryana, Chhattisgarh and Andhra Pradesh.

disability research attempts to ensure both academic authenticity and social accountability of knowledge production and its application. Can emancipatory disability research become a part of the academic enterprise? Is research by non-disabled researchers necessarily abilist? Such questions on authenticity and objectivity of research on disability are linked to sociological and anthropological concerns with interpretations and representations of experience.

In the light of the above, the moot questions are as follows: What kind of sociology or anthropology of disability can be configured from the perspective of disability studies, a perspective that strongly contests the conception of disability generated by the fields of medical sociology and medical anthropology? Is there a possibility of some rapprochement between the two divergent, if not opposing, perspectives on disability? Does bringing in the analytical lens of sociology of and sociology in medicine and anthropology respectively create an opening for such a rapprochement? Or is disability studies the only location or standpoint for a sociology of disability? And, with the gap between the academy and activism narrowing in the context of new social movements, disability studies, sociology and anthropology are coming together intellectually. This is something which is very evident in the way the study of disability is emerging in India. As elsewhere, disability studies researchers in India have multiple identities, namely scholars, activists and self-advocates. This also challenges the traditional conception of the sociologist/anthropologist as an outsider, a value-neutral observer solely engaged in the pursuit of knowledge production.

References

Ablon, J. 1984. *Little People in America: The Social Dimensions of Dwarfism.* New York, NY: Praeger.
———. 1988. *Living with Difference: Families with Dwarf Children.* New York, NY: Praeger.
Addlakha, R. 2007. 'How Young People with Disabilities Conceptualise the Body, Sex and Marriage in Urban India: Four case studies'. *Sexuality and Disability* 25(3): 100-13.
———. *Deconstructing Mental Illness: An Ethnography of Psychiatry, Women and the Family.* New Delhi: Zubaan Books.
———. 2013. *Disability Studies in India: Global Discourses, Local Realities.* New Delhi: Routledge.
Addlakha, R. and S. Mandai. 2009. 'Disability Law in India: Paradigm Shift or Evolving Discourse?' *Economic & Political Weekly* 44 (41 and 42): 62–68.

Angrosino, M. 1997. *Opportunity House: Ethnographic Stories of Mental Retardation*. Walnut Creek, CA: Alta Mira.

Bacquer, A. and A. Sharma. 1997. *Disability: Challenges vs. Responses*. New Delhi: Concerned Action Now.

Barnes, C. 1991. *Disabled People in Britain and Discrimination*. London: C. Hurst and Co. Publishers.

———. 1998. 'The Social Model of Disability: A Sociological Phenomenon Ignored by Sociologists'. In *The Disability Reader: Social Science Perspectives*, edited by Tom Shakespeare, 65–78. London: Cassell.

Barnes, C. and G. Mercer, eds. 1996. *Exploring the Divide: Illness and Disability*. Leeds: The Disability Press.

Barnes, C., M. Oliver and L. Barton, eds. 2002. *Disability Studies Today*. Cambridge: Polity Press.

Benedict, R. 1934. 'Anthropology and the Abnormal'. *The Journal of General Psychology* 10 (1): 59–80.

Berube, M. 1996. *Life as We Know It: A Father, a Family and an Exceptional Child*. New York, NY: Pantheon.

Bhatt, U. 1963. *The Physically Handicapped in India: A Growing National Problem*. Mumbai: Popular Book Depot.

Blume, S. 2010. *The Artificial Ear: Cochlear Implants and the Culture of Deafness*. New Brunswick, NJ: Rutgers University Press.

Bumiller, K. 2008. 'Quirky Citizens: Autism, Gender, and Reimagining Disability'. *Signs* 33 (4): 967–91.

Bury, M.B. 1982. 'Chronic Illness as Biological Disruption'. *Sociology of Health and Illness* 4 (1): 167–87.

———. 1991. 'The Sociology of Chronic Illness: A Review of Research and Prospects'. *Sociology of Health and Illness* 13 (4): 451–68.

———. 1992. 'Medical Sociology and Chronic Illness: A Comment on the Panel Discussion'. *Medical Sociology News* 18 (1): 29–33.

Campbell, J. and M. Oliver, eds. 1996. *Disability Politics: Understanding Our Past, Changing Our Future*. London: Routledge.

Charlton, J.I. 1998. *Nothing About Us Without Us: Disability Oppression and Empowerment*. Berkeley, CA: University of California Press.

Chib, M. 2011. *One Little Finger*. New Delhi: SAGE.

Cohen, L. 1998. *No Aging in India: Alzheimer, the Bad Family, and Other Modern Things*. Berkeley, CA: University of California Press.

Corker, M. and S. French. 1999. *Disability Discourse*. Buckingham: Open University Press.

Dalal, A.K. 2002. 'Disability Rehabilitation in a Traditional Indian Society'. In *Disability and Rehabilitation Issues in South Asia*, edited by M. Thomas and M.J. Thomas, 17–24. Bangalore: National Printing Press.

Das, V. and R. Addlakha. 2001. 'Disability and Domestic Citizenship: Voice, Gender, and the Making of the Subject'. *Public Culture* 13 (3): 511–31.

Davar, B.V. 1999. *Mental Health of Indian Women: A Feminist Agenda*. New Delhi: SAGE.

Davar, B.V., ed. 2001. *Mental Health from a Gender Perspective*. New Delhi: SAGE.

———. 2008. 'From Mental Illness to Disability: Choices for Women Users/ Survivors of Psychiatry in Self and Identity Constructions'. *Indian Journal of Gender Studies* 15 (2): 261–90.

Dhanda, A. 2000. *Legal Order and Mental Disorder*. New Delhi: SAGE.

Dhanda, A. and R. Raturi, eds. 2010. *Harmonizing Laws with the UNCRPD*. New Delhi: Human Rights Law Network.

Durkheim, E. 1970. *Suicide: A Study in Sociology* (trans. J.A. Spauding and G. Simpson). London: Routledge and Kegan Paul.

Edgerton, R.B. 1967. *The Cloak of Competence: Stigma in the Lives of the Mentally Retarded*. Berkeley, CA: University of California Press.

Fine, M. and A. Asch, eds. 1988. *Women with Disabilities: Essays in Psychology, Culture and Politics*, 1–37. Philadelphia, PA: Temple University Press.

Finkelstein, V. 1980. *Attitudes and Disabled People: Issues for Discussion*. New York, NY: World Rehabilitation Fund.

———. 1998. 'Emancipating Disability Studies'. In *The Disability Reader: Social Science Perspectives*, edited by Tom Shakespeare, 28–49. London: Cassell.

Friedner, M. 2015. *Valuing Deaf Worlds in India*. New Brunswick, NJ: Rutgers University Press.

Garland-Thomson, R. 2009. *Staring: How We Look*. Oxford and New York, NY: Oxford University Press.

Gerhardt, U. 1989. *Ideas About Illness: An Intellectual and Political History of Medical Sociology*. London: Macmilian.

Ghai, A. 2003. *(Dis)Embodied Form: Issues of Disabled Women*. New Delhi: Shakti Books and Har-Anand Publications.

———. 2015. *Re-thinking Disability in India*. New Delhi: Routledge.

Ghosh, N. 2015. *Pratyaha: Everyday Lifeworlds Dilemmas, Contestations and Negotiations*. New Delhi: Primus Books.

———. 2016. *Interrogating Disability: Theory and Practice (Dynamics of Asian Development)*. New Delhi: Springer.

Ginsberg, F. and R. Rapp. 2013. Disability Worlds. *Annual Review of Anthropology* 42: 53–68.

Goffman, E. 1961. *Asylums: Essays on the Social Situation of Mental Patients and Other Inmates*. Harmondsworth: Penguin Books.

———. 1963. *Stigma: Notes on the Management of a Spoiled Identity*. Harmondsworth: Penguin Books.

Gordon, G. 1966. *Role Theory and Illness: A Sociological Perspective*. New Haven, CT: Connecticut College and University Press.

Government of India. 2002. *Disabled Persons in India*. National Sample Survey Organisation 58th round Report No. 485.

Greenhalgh, S. 2001. *Under the Medical Gaze: Facts and Fictions of Chronic Pain*. Berkeley, CA: University of California Press.

Grinker, R.R. 2007. *Unstrange Minds: Remapping the World of Autism*. New York, NY: Basic Books.

Groce, N.E. 1985. *Everyone Here Spoke Sign Language: Hereditary Deafness on Martha's Vineyard*. Cambridge, MA: Harvard University Press.

Gwaltney, J.L. 1970. *Thrice Shy: Cultural Accommodation to Blindness and Other Disasters in a Mexican Community*. New York, NY: Columbia University Press.

Hans, A., ed. 2015. *Disability, Gender and the Trajectories of Power*. New Delhi: SAGE.

Hans, A. and A. Patri, eds. 2003. *Women, Disability and Identity*. New Delhi: SAGE.

Harriss-White, B. and S. Erb. 2002. *Outcast from Social Welfare: Disability in Rural India*. Bangalore: Books for Change.

Ingstad, B. and S.R. Whyte, eds. 1995. *Disability and Culture*. Berkeley, CA: University of California Press.

———. 2007. *Disability in Local and Global Worlds*. Berkeley, CA: University of California Press.

Jenkins, R. 1991. 'Disability and Social Stratification'. *British Journal of Sociology* 42 (4): 557–80.

Kittay, E.F. 1999. *Loves Labor: Essays on Women, Equality and Dependency*. New York, NY: Routledge.

Klasing, I. 2007. *Disability and Social Exclusion in Rural India*. Jaipur: Rawat Publications.

Kohrman, M. 2005. *Bodies of Difference: Experiences of Disability and Institutional Advocacy in the Making of Modern China*. Berkeley, CA: University of California Press.

Kothari, J. 2012. *The Future of Disability Law in India: A Critical Analysis of the Persons with Disabilities (Equal Opportunities, Protection of Rights and Full Participation) Act 1995*. New Delhi: Oxford University Press.

Ladd, P. 2003. *Understanding Deaf Culture: In Search of Deafhood*. Clevedon: Multilingual Matters.

Landsman, G.H. 2009. *Reconstructing Motherhood and Disability in the Age of 'Perfect' Babies*. New York, NY: Routledge.

Lane, H., R. Hoffmeister and B. Bahan. 1996. *A Journey into the Deaf-world*. San Diego, CA: Dawn Sign Press.

Lemert, E. 1962. *Human Deviance: Social Problems and Social Control*. Englewood Cliffs, NJ: Prentice-Hall.

Limaye, S. 2010. *Developmental Task of Adolescents with Hearing Impaired: In Indian Context*. Saarbrucken (Germany): Lambert Academic Publishing.

Linton, Simi. 1998. *Claiming Disability: Knowledge and Identity*. New York, NY: New York University Press.

Martin, E. 2007. *Bipolar Expeditions: Mania and Depression in American Culture*. Princeton, NJ: Princeton University Press.

Mechanic, D. and E.H. Volkart. 1961. 'Stress, Illness Behavior and the Sick Role'. *American Sociological Review* 26 (1): 51–58.

Mehrotra, Nilika. 2013. *Disability, Gender and State Policy: Exploring Margins*. Jaipur and New Delhi: Rawat Publications.

Miles, M. 1995. 'Disability in an Eastern Religious Context: Historical Perspectives'. *Disability and Society* 10 (1): 49–69.

———. 2001. 'Studying Responses to Disability in South Asian Histories: Approaches Personal, Prakrital and Pragmatical'. *Disability and Society* 16 (1): 43–60.

Monga, P. 2013. *The Other Senses: Story of a Visually Impaired Woman and Her Road to Success*. New Delhi: Roli Books.

Murphy, R. 2001. *The Body Silent*. New York, NY: W.W. Norton.

Nakamura, K. 2006. *Deaf in Japan: Signing and the Politics of Identity*. Ithaca, NY: Cornell University Press.

———. 2013. *A Disability of the Soul: An Ethnography of Schizophrenia and Mental Illness in Contemporary Japan*. Ithaca, NY: Cornell University Press.

Narasimhan, M.C. and A.K. Mukherjee. 1986. *Disability: A Continuing Challenge*. New Delhi: Wiley Eastern.

Ochs, E. and O. Solomon. 2010. 'Autistic Sociality'. *Ethos* 38 (1): 69–92.

Ochs, E., T. Kremer-Sadlik, K.G. Sirota and O. Solomon. 2004. 'Autism and the Social World: An Anthropological Perspective'. *Discourse Studies* 6 (2): 147–83.

Oliver, M. 1990. *The Social Politics of Disablement*. Basingstoke: Macmillan Palgrave.

———. 1996. *Understanding Disability: From Theory to Practice*. New York, NY: St Martin's Press.

———. 1997. 'Emancipatory Research: Realistic Goal or Impossible Dream? In *Doing Disability Research*, edited by C. Barnes and G. Mercer, 15–31. Leeds: The Disability Press.

Parsons, T. 1951. *The Social System*. London: Routledge and Kegan Paul.

Rouse, C. 2009. *Uncertain Suffering: Racial Health Care Disparities and Sickle Cell Disease*. Berkeley, CA: University of California Press.

Sekhar, R. 2005. *Naseema: The Incredible Story*. Translated by A. Deodhar. New Delhi: Viveka Foundation.

Shakespeare, T. 2006. *Disability Rights and Wrongs*. London: Routledge.

Titchkosky, T. 2000. 'Disability Studies: The Old and the New'. *The Canadian Journal of Sociology* 25 (2): 197–224.

Tomlinson, S. 1982. *A Sociology of Special Education*. London: Routledge and Kegan Paul.

UPIAS (Union of the Physically Impaired Against Segregation). 1976. *Fundamental Principles of Disability*. London: UPIAS. Available at: https://disability-studies.leeds.ac.uk/files/library/UPIAS-fundamental-principles.pdf (accessed on 19 April 2017).

Vaidya, S. 2010. 'Researcher as Insider: Opportunities and Challenges'. *Indian Anthropologist* 40 (2): 25–36.

———. 2011. 'Mothering as Ideology and Practice: The Experiences of Mothers of Children with Atism Spectrum Disorder'. In *The Anthropology of Mothering*, edited by N. Watts and M. MacPherson, 326–39. Toronto: Demeter Press.

Vaidya, S. 2015. 'Developmental Disability and the Family: Autism Spectrum Disorder in Urban India'. In *Disability, Gender and the Trajectories of Power*, edited by Asha Hans, 155–77. New Delhi: SAGE.

Wendell, S. 1996. *The Rejected Body: Feminist Reflections on Disability*. New York, NY: Routledge.

Zola, I. 1982. *Missing Pieces: A Chronicle of Living with a Disability*. Philadelphia, PA: Temple University Press.

23

Alternating Sexualities
Sociology and Queer Critiques in India

Paul Boyce and Rohit K. Dasgupta

Introduction: Alternations

Questions of alternation might be read as intrinsic to sociological approaches to sexual difference and diversity. By this, we mean ways in which the sexual as a social scientific subject/object has often been conceived of against the background of fluctuating conceptual and contextual registers. Terms for the empirical description, recognition and analysis of sexual life-worlds have most often been contested and queried. This might be especially so with regard to 'sexually dissident' subjects—those for whom terms of depiction in research and polity might be complicated given it runs counter to claims to normative modes of sanitised representation. Such processes, in turn, might be seen to respond to the alternating experiential and political framings of contemporary and historical sexual life-worlds. This has been evident in India in recent times, for instance, as non-cisgendered and non-heteronormative subjects have found themselves on the cusp of legislative and social changes.

In April 2014, in the case of *National Legal Services Authority* v. *the Union of India*, the Supreme Court of India passed legislation recognising the rights to gendered self-determination for people of transgender experience—as male, female or 'third gender'. Seemingly running counter to such an erstwhile progressive measure, the Supreme Court's 2013 overturning the Section 377 of the Indian Penal Code (IPC 377) has been widely interpreted as a regressive re-criminalisation of homosexuality. In each of these legislative scenarios, judicial subtleties and effects are especially multifaceted; linear interpretations of the relation between sex and gender in respect of law, governmentality and subjectivity are particularly unsustainable in these terms. Rather, the present situation in India might be read as characterised by ongoing alternations in respect of the potentialities for queer (mis)recognitions (Khanna 2016). The practical enactment of frameworks for the official recognition of transgender subjects in varied regional contexts in India, for example (after the 2014 Supreme Court judgment), have been criticised by trans* activists for passing the verification of 'authentic' trans-identities over to external authorities, writing over varied trans-experiential possibilities that might not be readily rendered via such external registers. In West Bengal, for instance, transgender activists and community engagement officers have found that within boards entrusted with the formal registration of transgender subjects, power and decision-making are largely centred on government and state actors for determining 'who counts' as authentically transgender in biologically determinist terms—processes that are external to actual trans* social actors' self-understandings. As Aniruddha Dutta (2014) has pointed out, this exemplifies ways in which the interpretation of the judgment has been varied across and within regions, restricting and excluding certain gender-variant people over others. The nature of such contradictory tendencies, which Dutta calls 'oscillating', resonates with our 'alternating' framework as proposed in this chapter.

Problems with registration and alternation reverberate with attendant issues involved in bringing sexed and gendered subjects into view within social analysis. Critical concerns arise out of the potential misrepresentation of ambiguity and indeterminacy. In citing sexual and gendered life-worlds as sites of social scientific enquiry (as with their being named objects of governance), intrinsic traces of alternative possible terms of depiction remain. This may especially pertain to sexual or gendered subjects who fall outside of prevailing frames of representation at any given sociopolitical moment, or in any given locale. But such is also germane to the alternating possibilities 'within' a sense of the subjective. Sexed and gendered subjects are not whole or singular but internally differentiated, such that any singular term of identification inevitably resides in relation to a sense of self as incomplete or partial (Khanna 2016; Moore 2007). Consequently, the naming of sexuality as an object attribute of experience strips away the more indeterminate affective attributes of sexuality in the social context (Boyce 2012, 2013; Moore 2012).

The effects of naming may be especially pronounced in contexts wherein sexual connections and experiences might be particularly characterised by secrecy or obfuscation—this being an attribute often attributed to both queer life-worlds and sexualities more generally in India (John and Nair 1998). In such circumstances, the relation between sexual and gendered life projects and their designation in respect of terms of identity might be felt by social actors to be especially fissured. Accordingly, spaces between representation, secrecy and senses of selfhood might transect in a particularly countervailing manner. Such observations, in turn, engender questions about whether sexual secrecy can be imagined as a specific cultural or contextual attribute (e.g., pertaining to sexualities in India especially) or a ubiquitous condition, running alongside ways in which sexualities might be otherwise openly proclaimed—either as normative or as anti-normative possibilities.

With these perspectives in mind, in this chapter, we want to build on a new conceptual framework of 'alternating sexualities' to offer some reflections on ways in which non-heteronormative sexualities have been conceived of in the sociology of India, an assemblage that for us encompasses work that might also be labelled anthropology, cultural or media studies. We are especially interested in how non-heteronormative sexual and gendered experience has been imagined in social sciences, activism and everyday practices. In pursuing this interest, we seek to query ways in which sexualities—and especially gender and sexual differences—have been located as analytical and ethical objects within social scientific and political paradigms, often in respect of contested tropes pertaining to expression and concealment, transgression and transformation. We seek to bring some regional standpoints on such issues into dialogue with wider sociological analyses—drawing on research carried out over time in India and elsewhere. In doing so, we propose synergies across sites and temporalities that, taken together, might provide insights into the current state of play vis-à-vis the sociology of sexuality in contemporary India.

Transgressions: Sexualities in the Moment

In seeking a starting point for our reflections, we have found it helpful to return to foundational viewpoints on the sexual contemporary. In a recent review of sociological work conducted over several decades,

Ken Plummer (2015: 1) has reminded us that sexualities and intimacies might be imagined as endlessly multiple, across time and space and in respect of different religions, states and economies; a 'vast labyrinth of desire, gender and reproduction'. Given the evocation of such complexity, questions arise pertaining to how, and in what terms, sexualities might be conceived and portrayed. This pertains, for example, to how the sexual might be imagined in relation to ongoing social transformations—for example, with respect to socio-economic flows associated with what is often called modernity, globalisation and/or neoliberalism (Altman 2001; Giddens 1992). Changes in attitudes towards sexuality have become one of the markers around which alterations to prevailing or 'traditional' values have been witnessed, as the sexual has been imagined as a political object on a global scale. Progressive attitudes towards gender and sexual non-normative subjects have been seen to perform as a marker of how a given state might signify (aspiring) inclusion within global, neoliberal political–economic systems, or conversely might be marked as regressive in these terms (for not bearing such values). This has been a concern in the present political moment in India, where the reinstating of IPC 377 by the Indian Supreme Court has compelled a range of responses associated with the seeming 're-criminalisation of homosexuality' and the significance of this as transgressing an image of India as an otherwise modern and progressive state (Boyce and Dutta 2013; Dasgupta 2014; Rao 2014). Questions of queer citizenship—the positive inclusion of sexual and gender 'non-normative subjects' within state legislative actions—have accordingly emerged as a central theme around which the politics of sexual difference are being enacted in India in the present (also see Dutta 2012c; Plummer 2003; Richardson 2000).

Transgression, and its relationship to forms of inclusion and exclusion, has a rich genealogy within sociology, anthropology and cultural studies. Chris Jenks (2003: 2) has defined transgression as follows: 'To go beyond the bounds or limits set by commandment or law or convention, it is to violate or infringe ... [a] reflexive act of denial and affirmation'. Following Jenks' transgressive standpoint, current queer citizenship activism in India might be interpreted as a mobilisation for the reintegration of the potential for militant and protest politics. One of the rallying cries of activists post the reinstatement of IPC 377 has been 'No going back'. This evocation of past, pre- and post-colonial alternatives (referencing the colonial origins of IPC 377) also brings up the issue of sexual subjects being constructed through externality, where their very existence invokes transgression of the implicit and explicit rule of the heteronormative patriarchal construction of the (post-colonial) nation state (also see Anderson 1991). In a society where transgression threatens the social order, advocating for the recognition of 'alternative sexualities' and alternate sexual futures is a way of reimagining and conceiving of a new sociality. Foucault (1986: 33) argues that '[transgression is] regulated by a simple obstinacy: transgression incessantly crosses and re-crosses a line'. In other words, transgressive identities open up the possibility of the shifting and the slippery subject, one that is completely impossible to control or even comprehend.

Terms of transgression, and their relation to politics of sexual alternatives, can be especially complex. This can be mapped across the politics of remembrance: what we remember and what we deny in any given political movement—and what kind of alternative realities we may construct in the process, in relation to who is included in a movement and in what frame of reference. Queer politics in India has been criticised by several people for its lack of intersectionality in such terms—for example, in respect of issues pertaining to caste-, class- and gender-based exclusions (Banerjea and Dasgupta 2013; Dasgupta 2014; Dutta 2012a). Activists in India have argued that cosmopolitan queer politics end up denying sexual and gender-dissident subjects whose appearance and social status might mark them as unsuitably modern. This has been seen as so in respect of those of lower caste or class, those from rural contexts and/or those whose performance of gender might evoke overly effeminate forms of otherwise 'male' embodiment, which may not readily reconcile with a 'gay' cosmopolitan subjectivity (Boyce and Dasgupta 2017; Dutta 2012a, 2012b). As queer theorist Jack Halberstam (2011) has argued that the ethics of complicity and the ways in which a 'politically pure history' (p. 171) may be written might cast away the classed, racist (and cast-ed in the case of India) nature of some queer formations. Claims made for the necessary recognition of queer citizen subjects might thus be taken as a signifier for a progressive Indian polity, yet the integration of such politics with the politics of caste-, class- and gender-based exclusion remains unresolved in many instances.

To take an instructive comparative example, Gloria Wekker's work on homonostalgia (cited in Haritaworn 2016) explores ways in which the Netherlands is imagined as progressive in the context of proactive legislation for queer rights and 'gay marriage'. Against this background, racial and racist anxieties in the Netherlands are often conceived around the figure of the Muslim (migrant), who is typically constructed as a figure whose social integration might drag these rights back. A similar sentiment is also being expressed by some in queer movements in India where Muslims and migrants are being constructed as the new 'degenerative other', threatening 'our' mode of being (Haritaworn 2016).[1] A sociology of sexualities, then, requires paying attention to these fissures, taking sexuality as point of intersectionality and bridging our tent with other minorities across ongoing diversities and contestations.

Failure—and After

Taking the theme of connections and alternatives further, Halberstam (2011) has described 'the alternative' as a political project, and a way by which radical utopians continue to search for new ways of being in the world (also see Boyce and Dasgupta 2017). Halberstam particularly frames this idea through the concept of 'in-between spaces' as a way of projecting a different being outside the expected realms of hegemony and respectability. Queer spaces in India, as Dasgupta (2014) has described, are transitory contexts that are vulnerable and under constant threat of erasure. The disappearance of cruising grounds in the contexts of new forms of surveillance and lack of places to socialise outside straight normative or 'NGO-ised' spaces beyond all but a few urban contexts might be seen to have thrown queer existence and being in India into a chaotic realm. By chaotic, we mean the multiple interactions of sexual identities with nationality, class, caste and ethnicity which form critical levels of solidarity as well as mistrust and fracture. The idea of a homogenous queer community remains flawed (Dasgupta 2015; Halberstam 2011; Haritaworn 2016).

Gordon Ingram, Anne-Marie Bouthillette and Yolanda Retter (1997: 449) have defined a queer community as a 'full collection or select subset of queer networks for a particular territory, with relatively stable relationships that enhance interdependence, mutual support and protection'. These interdependence and support are predicated upon the interaction, solidarity and affirmation of queer subjects who position themselves and their ongoing presence within an allied commonality. Queer spaces in this case can be read as locales of alternative politics which are invested within the discourse of inclusion and exclusion and a recognition that queer contexts are alternative and temporal modes of being, proffering heterogeneity.

[1] R.K. Dasgupta, 'Why Queer Folk Must Vote Against Brexit', *The Huffington Post*, 15 July 2016. Available at: http://www.huffingtonpost.in/dr-rohit-k-dasgupta/why-queer-folk-must-vote-_b_10349774.html (accessed on 1 June 2018).

Against this background, Halberstam has described contemporary queer modes of being as constructed through neoliberal discourses of success and freedom. Whilst success in a heteronormative capitalist society might be thought of as reproductive ability, wealth accumulation and freedom of movement, queer people might, in some cases, be seen to have taken on and subverted these very static models of achievement. Halberstam criticises the pressures of success and rather offers failure, 'unaming' and unbecoming as more creative and surprising ways of imagining (queer) being in the world. Failure stands as an alternative to the grimness of neoliberal discourses of conformity. Halberstam (2012: 133) expands on this in more detail in the book *Gaga Feminism*, arguing that 'in an economy that engineers success for an elite few at the expense of the failure of the many, failure becomes a location for resisting, blocking, slowing, jamming the economy and the social stability that depends upon it'.

These thoughts particularly resonate with the contemporary moment in queer politics of India, where the perceived failure of the campaign against IPC 377 has extended important figurative questions about the locus of sexually dissident politics, and why they might be so oriented towards achieving recognition from orthodox state formations—such as legal systems—or in respect of normative aspirations for recognition, for example, through social respectable monogamy (Boyce and Khanna 2011; Narrain 2007; Narrain and Gupta 2011). Might queer citizenship work in other directions, against state and other orthodox formations and their linkages to forms of normative socio-economic status? Such a rethinking involves taking seriously a perspective on sexual lives as not readily definable within categorical frames of identity or as imagined entities with linear narratives. Rather it is important to open up the domain term, sexuality, and especially sexual dissidence, as a terrain of contextual and conceptual movement—a field of alternating possibilities.

Such reflections, in turn, engender the question of locating non-normative gender and sexualities in India, as elsewhere, within fields of extending and multiple points of reference. One regional response in these terms has been to imagine India as offering specific potentialities for conceiving sexuality as multiple. Yet how do we reconcile a sense of regional- or cultural-specific sexual and gender diversity with a sociological standpoint from which, in any case, sexualities might be imagined as ubiquitously experientially multiple? (Khanna 2013, 2016). And how does such a question relate to the ambiguous and indirect ways in which sexuality has been conceived in South Asian sociology, against the background of more direct forms of social action?

Silence, Object, Subject

India has been particularly significant as a geopolitical domain within which the conceptualisation of sexuality as a multiple intersecting, analytical and political object has been contested—for instance, in respect of caste, class and gender as noted. Yet intriguingly, one of the ways in which this has occurred, historically, has been with respect to the seeming disavowal of the sexual also. Sexuality has emerged as a site of study in Indian sociology against the background of the complex deferral of sexuality as a social scientific object in the region. This has been so, for example, where sexuality has been conceived of as some-how silenced or absent within Indian public culture. In these terms, sexuality has often been approached as an indirect object—present but conceived of as socially askance (John and Nair 1998; Lambert 2001). At the same time, (male) homosociality has been conceived of as an (implicit) counterpoint to the heteronormative orientations of the contemporary Indian (Osella 2012).

This silencing and indirection can be connected to preoccupations with celibacy, this being an example of a way in which the sexual, as a regional object, has been both claimed and disavowed in social stud-ies. Joseph Alter's ethnographic work on wrestlers in North India, for example, has recounted forms of seeming erotic exercise and activity between men in North Indian *akhara*, focusing on how this produces forms of 'sexual' arousal that are sublimated through semen retention (Alter 1992). Akhil Katyal (2013) explores similar work on homosocial bonding where he describes *laundebaazi* (or a habitual orientation for boys to 'play' with other boys) as a social framing characterised through a show of excess. He argues that same-sex desire in the colo-nial archive is framed as an object of one's habits or interests, similar to other vices like alcohol, prostitution or playing cards. Through an exploration of advertisements, pamphlets and indigenous literary texts from 20th-century India, Katyal has worked to establish laundebaazi as a political metaphor to describe alternative registers of male–male eroticism in South Asia. This echoes a trope that has been an especially significant preoccupation within regional studies of (male) sexual embodiment linked to post-colonial preoccupations. This may have been especially so whereby celibacy and/or asexuality was produced with forms of colonial resistance—as a discourse that challenged otherwise colonial fantasies of the (excessively) erotic colonised sub-ject (Srivastava 2004). It might also be followed as a metaphor for the sublimation of the sexual subject within Indian sociological and anthropological traditions.

Such discourses have contributed to a chaste self-image within India's public culture—one that has endured in multifaceted ways. It may be claimed, for example, that sexualities in the subcontinent have not been so much conceived of with respect to hetero- and homosexual bifurcations, but instead with regard to an asexuality versus celibacy contrast (Srivastava 2004). To take a practical example, early days of HIV prevention in India were accompanied by claims that the epidemic would not take hold, due to the sexually virtuous nature of society and culture (Lambert 2001). Yet it was this same problematic claim that helped to galvanise new social scientific responses to sexuality in India and South Asia more widely. In the early to mid-1990s, it became apparent that HIV would not pass India by. New forms of knowledge emerged as an urgent requirement, as these might enable effective, contextually relevant health promotion responses. This circumstance was not unique to India as the development of international responses to HIV and AIDS helped to propel social scientific study into new directions, often in critical dialogue with biomedical and epidemiological studies. Resources directed into HIV-prevention research offered new opportunities for social studies of the sexual, as it became apparent that, on a global scale, there was insufficient knowledge available to construct culturally sensitive and effective forms of intervention— these being typically oriented around safer sex promotion with often so-called marginal sexual populations imagined to be most at risk of HIV infection.

India became an important context within which such forms of knowledge were developed and taken forward—as national and international investments helped to propel new studies of same-sex practices, risks and contexts. These not only supplied new information bases but also went on to stimulate queer and other critiques. Knowledge of same-sex practices and subjects produced in HIV prevention typically galvanised around seemingly empirically verifiable (and often quantifiable) subjects—in contexts of funding for HIV-prevention community work (Boyce 2007; Khanna 2011). However, the production of certain kinds of sexual subjects and subjectivities within the registers of HIV-prevention work has also been located as another instance of silencing, as alternative sexually dissident lives and life-worlds most often fell off the epidemiological map. This might be read as a 'pre-echo' of queer critiques of sexual rights movements in India, which have arguably tended to focus on the most legible, often cosmopolitan and 'suitably modern' sexual and gender subjects (as noted above). Against this background, the reclaiming of queer subjects has performed as an especially important political and sociological strategy in India, often involving an examination of histories of both repression and sexual expression in order to better comprehend the present.

Past and Present: Public and Private

Anjali Arondekar (2009) has examined the colonial archive in India (legal documents and narrative outputs) as having suppressed homo-erotic texts, recovering these from a state of loss and obfuscation. In describing *Queen Empress* v. *Khairati* (1884), one of the earliest sodomy cases in the subcontinent, Arondekar treats homosexuality in the colonial archive as both 'obvious and elusive'. In this case, Khairati was framed as a 'habitual sodomite' whose unnatural sexual practices needed to be checked. He was initially arrested for dressing up in women's clothing and subjected to physical examination by the civil surgeon. On examination, it was found that he had 'the characteristic mark of a habitual catamite' (Arondekar 2009: 68). Despite no records of the crimes, testimony or victims of the crime ever being located, Judge Denniston rendered a guilty verdict. When the case came up again at the Allahabad High Court, Judge Straight overturned the previous judgment due to lack of evidence. However, he noted that the plaintiff was 'clearly a habitual sodomite' and he appreciated the desire of the authorities to 'check such disgusting practices' (ibid.: 69). Surprisingly, this instance set a precedent for further cases where Section 377 was enforced, and has been cited numerously in legal commentaries on unnatural offences as a cautionary tale. Despite being a 'failed' case, it thus nonetheless became a precedent that the colonial authorities used to control 'sexual irregularities', providing a display of the anxiety of administrators towards non-normative, non-reproductive sexualities. The elusiveness and ubiquity of queerness being played out rearticulates Macaulay's claim when he passed the law:

> I believe that no country ever stood so much in need of a code of law as India and I believe also that there never was a country in which the want might be so easily supplied. (cited in Bhaskaran 2002: 20)

The anxiety over non-normative sexualities espoused through colo-nial puritanism had a major influence on the development of Indian national identity (Aldrich 2002; Ballhatchet 1980; Dasgupta 2017; Vanita and Kidwai 2000). As Bose and Bhattacharya (2007: x) critically note, 'questions of identity are complex to begin with, and they become even more so when one has to relate questions of sexual identities or preferences with questions of national specificity'. The major factors that are commonly seen to contribute to the particularity of the Indian experience are the legacy of long-term colonialism, uneven economic development and the complex socio-ethnic diversity of Indian society. Chatterjee (2004) emphasises that the heightened division between private and public life in Indian society, despite being a normative proposition of modernity, was greatly exacerbated by the colonial presence. The private realm within which sexuality is firmly placed is most assiduously maintained as a domain of traditional and indigenous social practices. The persistence in post-colonial India of the tradition and modernity binary, with a significantly gendered dimension, remains a very distinctive feature of social life. It is, therefore, no surprise that the homophobia that was introduced through colonialism was also internalised by modern India.

However, against this background, we are also aware of the various ways through which new and alternative forms of queer kinships have emerged in post-colonial India. Debolina's ethnographic film *Ebang Bewarish* (And the Unclaimed) recently showed how married trans*[2] men are forging bonds with their wives, and Dasgupta's (2013) work on *launda* dancers (trans* and kothi dancers performing in rural belts of India) in West Bengal and Uttar Pradesh presented the close friendship that exists between the dancers and their lovers' wives. These alternative forms of family and kinship networks demonstrate a revision and reworking of the social organisation of friendship and community to form non-state-centred (alternative) forms of support and alliance.

Dave (2012), in her recent work on the ethics of queer activism, focuses on the formation of lesbian communities in India from the 1980s to the early 2000s, questioning whether it was ethical or crucial to practise a Western lesbian identity politics or provide a more 'authentic' framework for same-sex desire. This is also an instance of where the politics of funding comes in, and Dave (2012: 29) argues that the authenticity produced by certain identity terminologies were directly produced by foreign donor agencies who 'encouraged a diversity of fundable niches across the world' (also see Cohen 2005 who also discusses the production of terminologies through NGO discourses). Dave describes the founding of PRISM (an organisation providing a space for sexual and gender diversity in Delhi) and its members' 'insistences

---

[2] When the asterisk is put on the end of trans*, it expands the boundaries of the category to be radically inclusive. It can be understood as the most inclusive umbrella term to describe various communities and individuals with non-conforming gender identities and/or expressions. Also see Tompkins (2014).

on a freedom from subjection to identity ... enable[ing] new ethical possibilities' (2012: 96).

Dave is critical of the fraught yet crucial relationship between the lesbian movement and the larger mainstream women's movement in India. The dependence that lesbian activists might have on the larger women's movement both financially and symbolically makes it a critical factor in the politics of queer activism. Dave makes a strong case for an investigation of the relationship between the ethics of activism and the social norms and conditions from which queer activism emerges. This provides for a new potential for social arrangements and also questions the ways in which goals are being achieved.

To Conclude

In this chapter, we have attempted to introduce and explore the domain term 'alternating sexualities'. In doing so, we have also presented various contemporary critiques of queer studies within sociology, anthropology and related disciplines in India and elsewhere. Since de Lauretis' (1991) first use of the term queer theory, queer studies has embarked on a journey that now includes post-colonial and queer-of-colour critiques. This encompasses an intersectional lens directed at studying queer experiences in the Global South, particularly paying attention to inflections of caste, class and religion. In a place like India, especially these various categories of identity can be difficult to reconcile yet they also converge in complex ways. There have been longstanding tensions between different sexual identities and/or ways of being within the queer spectrum in India, some of which are also related to the fight for resources and sexual health funding. Yet there has also been a renewed sense of radicalising queer politics that resists categorical imperatives (e.g., Dave 2012; Dutta 2014; Khanna 2016). Such a perspective offers a critical counterpoint to shifts in queer political movements globally towards what has been described as assimilationist politics. Lisa Duggan (2003) has defined such trends as homonormativity—'a politics that does not contest dominant heteronormative assumptions and institutions but upholds and sustains them'. In some contexts, among some constituencies, this has signalled a retreat from the radicalism espoused by early queer movements. Petrus Liu suggests that many 'gay men and women' now believe that the best strategy for mainstream inclusion and rights is to 'show society they are morally upstanding citizens who are no different from anyone else' (Liu 2015: 2).

Against this background, experiences of sexual and gender difference have appeared to us as fields of ongoing alternation as opposed to sites of singular normative or non-normative inclusion, exclusion or resistance. In such terms, queer identifications in India—for instance before the law or in activism—can be seen to engender new possibilities for both recognition and misrecognition 'together'. This has been so wherein queer movements might be effecting promises for new kinds of futurity for sexually dissident peoples but might also complicit in the erasure of queer subjects. These might perhaps most often be those subjects not readily received as signifying cosmopolitan progressive modernities or those not included with bio-essentialist measures of gender and sexual difference and diversity (Dutta 2014).

As an instance of an obligation to alternating queer discursive possibilities, this chapter has sought to develop a commitment to the continued perusal of the sexual as a sociological object—as a subject always out of reach, never total nor consolidated. In these terms, we have found looking back, for example, to questions of silence, transgression and subjectivity in both queer and South Asian studies of sexuality to be especially instructive, for conceiving of the sexual subject in terms of traces and affects, over time, as much explicit forms of knowledge or contextualisation. Such reflections, we proffer, can help to prefigure new questions and analytical directions for queer regional engagements within the politics of indeterminate sexual futures in India and beyond.

References

Aldrich, R. 2002. *Colonialism and Homosexuality*. London: Routledge.

Alter, J.S. 1992. *Wrestler's Body: Identity and Ideology in North India*. Berkeley, CA: University of California Press.

Altman, D. 2001. *Global Sex*. Chicago, IL: University of Chicago Press.

Anderson, B. 1991. *Imagined Communities: Reflections on the Origin and Spread of Nationalism*. London: Verso Books.

Arondekar, A. 2009. *For the Record: On Sexuality and the Colonial Archive in India*. Durham, NC: Duke University Press.

Ballhatchet, K. 1980. *Race, Sex and Class Under the Raj: Imperial Attitudes and Policies and Their Critics, 1793–1905*. London: Weidenfeld and Nicholson.

Banerjea, N. and D. Dasgupta. 2013. 'States of Desire: Niharika Banerjea & Debanuj Dasgupta on Homonationalism and LGBT Activism in India'. Available at: http://sanhati.com/articles/7185/#sthash.HHFJElzW.dpuf (accessed on 1 June 2018).

Bhaskaran, S. 2002. 'The Politics of Penetration: Section 377 and the Indian Penal Code'. In *Queering India: Same Sex Love and Eroticism in Indian Culture and Society*, edited by R. Vanita, 15–29. London: Routledge.

Bose, B. and S. Bhattacharya, eds. 2007. *The Phobic and the Erotic: The Politics of Sexualities in Contemporary India*. Kolkata: Seagull Books.

Boyce, P. 2007. '"Conceiving Kothis": Men Who Have Sex with Men in India and the Cultural Subject of HIV Prevention'. *Medical Anthropology* 26 (2): 175–203.

———. 2012. 'The Ambivalent Sexual Subject: HIV Prevention and Male-to-Male Intimacy in India'. In *Understanding Global Sexualities: New Frontiers*, edited by P. Aggleton, P. Boyce, H. Moore and R. Parker, 75–88. Abingdon: Routledge.

———. 2013. 'The Object of Attention: Same-sex Sexualities in Small-town India and the Contemporary Sexual Subject'. In *Sexuality Studies*, edited by S. Srivastava, 183–202. New Delhi: Oxford University Press.

Boyce, P. and A. Dutta. 2013. 'Vulnerability of Gay and Transgender Indians Goes Way Beyond Section 377'. *The Conversation*. Available at http://theconversation.com/vulnerability-of-gay-and-transgender-indians-goes-way-beyond-section-377-21392 (accessed on 1 June 2018).

Boyce, P. and A. Khanna. 2011. 'Rights and Representations: Querying the Male-to-Male Sexual Subject in India'. *Culture, Health & Sexuality* 13 (1): 89–100.

Boyce, P. and R.K. Dasgupta. 2017. 'Utopia or Elsewhere: Queer Modernities in Small Town West Bengal'. In *Urban Utopias: Excess and Expulsion in Neoliberal South Asia*, edited by T. Kuldova and M. Varghese, 209–25. London: Palgrave.

Chatterjee, P. 2004. *The Politics of the Governed: Reflection of Popular Politics in Most of the World*. New Delhi: Permanent Black.

Cohen, L. 2005. 'The Kothi Wars: AIDS Cosmopolitanism & the Morality of Classification'. In *Sex in Development*, edited by V. Adams and S. Pigg, 269–303. Durham, NC: Duke University Press.

Dasgupta, R.K. 2013. 'Launda Dancers: The Dancing Boys of India'. *Asian Affairs: Journal of the Royal Society for Asian Affairs* 44 (3): 442–48.

———. 2014. 'Parties, Advocacy and Activism: Interrogating Community and Class in Digital Queer India'. In *Queer Youth and Media*, edited by C. Pullen, 265–77. Basingstoke: Palgrave Macmillan.

———. 2015. 'Dissident Citizenship: Articulating Belonging, Dissidence and Queerness on Cyberspace'. *South Asian Review* 35 (3): 203–23.

———. 2017. *Digital Queer Cultures in India: Politics, Intimacies and Belonging*. London: Routledge.

Dave, N. 2012. *Queer Activism in India: An Anthropology in Ethics*. Durham, NC: Duke University Press.

De Lauretis, T. 1991. 'Queer Theory. Lesbian and Gay Sexualities: An Introduction'. *Differences: A Journal of Feminist Cultural Studies* 3 (2): iii–xviii.

Duggan, L. 2003. *The Twilight of Equality? Neoliberalism, Cultural Politics, and the Attack on Democracy*. Boston, MA: Beacon Press.

Dutta, A. 2012a. *'Kon Rooper Ontor: "Transgender" o "Rupantarkami" Poirchoy borgo o kichhu Lingo-prantik Manusher Atmoprokasher Bhasha'* [Which Gender? 'Transgender' and 'Rupantarkami' Identity Categories and the Self-narratives of a few Gender-marginalized Persons]. *Swikriti Patrika* (10): 1–9 Bengali.

———. 2012b. 'An Epistemology of Collusion: Hijra, Kothi and the Historical (Dis)continuity of Gender/Sexual Identities in Eastern India'. *Gender & History* 24 (3): 825–49.

———. 2012c. 'Claiming Citizenship, Contesting Civility: The Institutional LGBT Movement and the Regulation of Gender/Sexual Dissidence in West Bengal, India'. *Jindal Global Law Review* 4 (1): 110–41.

———. 2014. 'Contradictory Tendencies: The Supreme Court's NALSA Judgment on Transgender Recognition and Rights'. *Journal of Indian Law and Society* 5 (Monsoon): 225–36.

Foucault, M. 1986. 'Of Other Spaces'. *Diacritics* 16 (1): 22–27.

Giddens, A. 1992. *The Transformation of Intimacy: Sexuality, Love & Eroticism in Modern Societies*. Stanford, CA: Stanford University Press.

Halberstam, J. 2011. *The Queer Art of Failure*. Durham, NC: Duke University Press.

———. 2012. *Gaga Feminism*. Boston, MA: Beacon Press.

Haritaworn, J. 2016. *Queer Lovers and Hateful Others*. London: Pluto Press.

Ingram, G.B., A. Bouthilette and Y. Retter, eds. 1997. *Queers in Space*, 447–58. Lacey, WA: Bay Press.

Jenks, C. 2003. *Transgression*. New York, NY: Routledge.

John, M.E. and J. Nair, eds. 1998. *A Question of Silence: The Sexual Economies of Modern India*. London: Zed Press.

Katyal, A. 2013. 'Laundebaazi: Habits and Politics in North India'. *Interventions: International Journal of Postcolonial Studies* 15 (4): 474–93.

Khanna, A. 2011. '*Meyeli Chhele* Becomes MSM: Transformation of Idioms of Sexualness into Epidemiological Forms in India'. In *Politicising Masculinity*, edited by A. Cornwall, Jerker Edstrom and Alan Greig. London: Zed Books.

———. 2013. 'Three Hundred and Seventy Seven Ways of Being: Sexualness of the Citizen in India'. *Journal of Historical Sociology* 26 (1): 120–42.

———. 2016. *Sexualness*. New Delhi: New Text.

Lambert, H. 2001. 'Not Talking About Sex in India: Indirection and the Communication of Bodily Intention'. In *An Anthropology of Indirect Communication*, ASA Monographs 37, edited by Joy Hendry and C.W. Watson, 51–67. London and New York, NY: Routledge.

Liu, P. 2015. *Queer Marxism in Two Chinas*. Durham, NC: Duke University Press.

Moore, H. 2007. *The Subject of Anthropology: Gender, Symbolism and Psychoanalysis*. Cambridge: Polity Press.

Moore, H. 2012. 'Sexuality Encore'. In *Understanding Global Sexualities*, edited by P. Aggleton, P. Boyce, H. Moore and R. Parker, 1–18. Abingdon: Routledge.

Narrain, A. 2007. 'Rethinking Citizenship: A Queer Journey'. *Indian Journal of Gender Studies* 14 (1): 61–71.

Narrain, A. and A. Gupta, eds. 2011. *Law Like Love: Queer Perspectives on Law*. Delhi. Yoda Press.

Osella, F. 2012. 'Malabar Secrets: South Asian Muslim Men's (Homo)sociality Across the Indian Ocean'. Asian Studies Review, special edition *Queer Asian Subjects* 35 (4): 531–49.

Plummer, K. 2003. *Intimate Citizenship: Private Decisions and Public Dialogues*. Seattle, WA: University of Washington Press.

———. 2015. *Cosmopolitan Sexualities*. Cambridge. Polity Press.

Rao, R. 2014. 'Queer Questions'. *International Feminist Journal of Politics* 16 (2): 199–217.

Richardson, D. 2000. *Rethinking Sexuality*. London: SAGE.

Srivastava, S. 2004. 'Introduction: Semen, History, Desire and Theory'. In *Sexual Sites, Seminal Attitudes: Sexualities, Masculinities and Culture in South Asia*, edited by Sanjay Srivastava, 11–48. New Delhi: SAGE.

Tompkins, A. 2014. 'Asterisk'. *TSQ: Transgender Studies Quarterly* 1 (1–2): 26–27.

Vanita, R. and S. Kidwai. 2000. *Same Sex Love in India: Readings from Literature and History*. New York, NY: St Martins Press.

24

Ageing, Ambivalent Modernities and the Pursuit of Value in India

Sarah Lamb

Introduction

The ethnographic record suggests that ageing figures centrally in people's understandings of the contemporary. This piece examines how it is that old age, as a socially constructed phase of the life course, has become part of new national imaginaries of subjectivity and value in India, and tied to larger debates about self, family, gender, society, nation and modernity.

Two meanings of old overlap in public conceptualisations: old as tied to the individual body and person experiencing the passage of time and accumulation of years over the life course and old in terms of a nation's or society's past—the way things 'used to be' 'before' in an older or more 'traditional' era. In India, elders are associated with both senses of the term—as those who are advanced in years and have accumulated life experiences, as well as those who are emblematic of a more traditional national-social past. A paradigmatic feature of such a past is the multigenerational joint family, in which the figure of the elder plays a central role (Cohen 1998; Lamb 2009). In addition, the joint family as emblem of the traditional past carries qualities such as plentiful time, spirituality, the intimacy of kinship, respect for elders, home-cooked meals, material frugality and more conventionally 'Indian' values, in contrast to the multiple social changes of the current era of global modernity.

At the same time, anthropological and sociological research on ageing in India has revealed how many elders and their families are finding themselves—by choice and necessity—engaging in novel forms of living. Especially among the urban middle classes, older Indians are practising activities such as moving into elder residences, sending aspiring cosmopolitan children abroad for higher education and work, using new information and communications technologies, and pursuing globally circulating ideologies of 'active' and 'healthy' ageing—participating in new kinds of urban-middle-class society conducive to novel ways of organising ageing (e.g., Ahlin 2018; Lamb 2009, 2014: 50). Such changes evoke considerable public anxiety, even as some are embraced.

Perhaps because older people are taken to be so quintessentially representative of the traditional, debates over the place of elders in contemporary society become especially revealing of tensions, cultural flux and the recalibration of difficult life choices. People across India are asking, how will they work out ageing, and with it a valued society, in a terrain where family members are dispersed across the country and world, and values such as individualism and materialism seem to have taken centre stage? Television serials, newspaper stories, films and everyday conversations abound with this question, many of them concerned with the proliferation of old-age homes in India, a new and exceptional phenomenon in the nation; with the scattering of families around the globe in response to labour markets; and with new imaginaries of egalitarian ideals at the heart of modern subjectivities. Emerging novel modes of ageing are taken by many Indians, at home and abroad, to represent a profound transformation, involving not only ageing per se but also principles underlying the foundation of society and the very identity of India as a nation and culture (Cohen 1998: xvii; Lamb 2009: 3).

These tensions, debates and competing aspirations are fruitful to look at, for scholars interested in understanding the present. Paul Rabinow writes of how older and newer elements of moral landscapes making up a contemporary ethos are not opposed but paired and work together. He reflects:

If one no longer assumes that the new is what is dominant ... and that the old is somehow essentially residual, then the question of how older and newer elements are given form and worked together, either well or poorly, becomes a significant site of inquiry. I call that site the contemporary. (Rabinow 2008: 2–3)

Arjun Appadurai (1990: 17) sees family life and generational relations as a key site where much of today's complicated task of cultural reproduction transpires—out of older and newer, more local and more far-flung elements—as we can no longer assume 'the sort of trans-generational stability of knowledge' that was presupposed in earlier theories of enculturation and socialisation. Appadurai (1990: 17–18) reflects:

> As families move to new locations, or as children move before older generations, or as grown sons and daughters return from time spent in strange parts of the world, family relationships can become volatile, as new commodity patterns are negotiated; debts and obligations are recalibrated; and rumors and fantasies about the new setting are manoeuvred into existing repertoires of knowledge and practice.... Family members pool and negotiate their mutual understandings and aspirations in sometimes fractured spatial arrangements.

This chapter uses ageing as 'good to think with' regarding the fashioning of social, ethical and political worlds in India today. It examines how ageing has become a provocative medium via which people are envisioning moral landscapes, pursuing forms of social value and engaging in debates about self, family, gender, society and nation. Exploring some key themes in these debates, I draw heavily from my own fieldwork in West Bengal spread out over the past 25 years, as well as other important research on the sociology and anthropology of ageing in India.

Local and Transnational Families, Intimacy and Dispersal

The majority, or more than three-quarters, of elders in India reside with their kin in multigenerational households,[1] at the same time that public discourse emphasises the ways Indian joint-family living, and all it entails, is waning. Technically, a patrilineal joint family refers to a

---

[1] Sathyanarayana et al. (2012: 13, Table 6) present data from the National Family Health Survey (NFHS) of 2005–06 finding that 77.5 per cent of women and 79.3 per cent of men aged 60 and over reside in multigenerational households with married children (predominantly sons) and (usually) grandchildren. See also Lamb (2009: 174).

household composed of related married couples linked either through patrilineal descent or collaterally as brothers, although in popular usage any household containing a grandparent or grandparents and married child/ren—usually a son or sons—is commonly referred to as 'joint'. Everyday discourse widely describes the joint family as the most natural and appropriate way of managing ageing—a way of living that not only provides material and emotional care for elders but also fosters family intimacy, practical frugality, as members pool resources, and the cultural reproduction of newer generations (Brijnath 2014: 5–6; Lamb 2000, 2009, 2013; van Willigen and Chadha 1999; Vatuk 1990; Wadley 2010). Although joint families are sometimes labelled Hindu, the notion that adult children are naturally obligated to care for and live with their elder parents is spoken of regularly by Hindus and Muslims alike.

The workings of a joint-family system rest on a notion of the value and appropriateness, even naturalness, of relations of long-term intergenerational reciprocity, as well as an acceptance of interdependence as a normal part of the human condition. Just as parents naturally care for their children when they are young and need help, so naturally do adult children for their parents in their older years. Bengalis in both rural and urban settings speak of lifelong bonds of reciprocal indebtedness and love: Adult children—especially sons and daughters-in-law—live with and care for their ageing parents, out of love, a deep respect for elders, and a profound sense of moral, even spiritual, duty to attempt to repay the inerasable debts they owe their parents for all the effort, expense and affection the parents expended to produce and raise them (Lamb 2000, 2009). Indians often refer to acts of caring for elders as *seva*—emotional and physical care and service—which can be likened to serving a deity (Brijnath 2014: 5–6; Lamb 2000: 59–62). Narayan Sarkar, a retired engineer who lived with his wife in their South Kolkata home, their only two children settled abroad in the United States, reflected:

> In our families, we raised our children—why? Our idea, our dream, was that when we grew *old*, our sons and daughters-in-law would serve us (*seva korbe*). And it is our dream, and a natural thing, to hope for this, to want this. We did this for our parents, and they for theirs.[2]

Others speak of the value of multigenerational family living in terms of its sociality. Although single-person and married-couple households are highly common, quite the norm, in Western nations such as the United

[2] Unless otherwise noted, all quotes are drawn from the author's own fieldwork materials.

States, where 81 per cent of women and 91 per cent of men who are 65 years of age and above live either alone or as a married couple, in India, among the over 60 years of age, only 4.8 per cent live alone and 9.8 as a couple only.[3] Yet even these relatively small figures of elders living without junior kin are higher than in the past (Sathyanarayana et al. 2012). Some older Bengalis finding themselves in such situations reflect on the strangeness of solitary living, as did this retired math professor who lived entirely alone after her husband had died and children moved abroad: 'Human beings have always lived together; it's not part of human nature to live alone', and, 'We couldn't have even dreamed earlier that people would be living like this!... We had no concept at all even that a person could live alone'.

Not only older persons but also many adult children express the naturalness and value of joint-family living. Benu, an IT manager working in the Kolkata office of a major transnational corporation, while residing with his parents, wife, son and married brother in the family flat in which he grew up, said:

Many people don't want to care for their parents any more. They think, 'I'll just put them in an old age home, or live separately'. Perhaps they might get offered an apartment as a perk through their job, and they want to accept it so they can move ahead. But perhaps their parents aren't allowed in the apartment, or there's no space for them there.

Benu went on to tell of how he himself was totally against abandoning his parents in this way, and plans to live permanently in a joint family. He spoke with emotion, 'Could a tree live without its roots? No, it would die. My parents are my roots! They are the ones who raised me and nourished me and still sustain me. If they were gone, I couldn't exist—right?' Some younger women, who do not have the luxury of living with their own roots given the patrilocal patrilineal family system, express a wish to marry into joint-family households where they envision feeling less lonely than they would in a nuclear-style household, and where they imagine valuing the protective support of many kin.

At the same time, widespread is the sense that myriad changes are under way in India and the wider world, profoundly impacting the

[3] These figures are from the 2011 Census of India. Available at: http://timesofindia.indiatimes.com/india/15-million-elderly-Indians-live-all-alone-Census/articleshow/43948392.cms (accessed on 22 April 2017).

joint-family way of life. What this means for older people—and how the society and nation will envision the appropriate way to live across the later phases of the life course—is at the heart of contemporary concerns and debates.

One salient change here is the transnational and transregional dispersal of junior kin. Among the cosmopolitan urban middle classes in particular, common appraisals are that 'most' families now have adult children living abroad, where the younger generation has streamed to pursue higher education and professional opportunities. Dipesh-da of Kolkata told of how he and his wife had at first been so very proud of their children and delighted by their opportunities—'The chance to go to the U.S.! It's like El Dorado!'—an ultimate prize that one might spend one's life seeking. 'We all think this at first', he went on, 'But then, as the years go by—now we are starting to feel lonely. There is some regret. It would be so nice if we could live closer together, so we could share our joys and sorrows'. Later, he sent me an email with further reflections: 'Socially in our country, it is a matter of pride to be NRI [Non-Resident Indian] parents, but the euphoria is lost with the passage of time when both age and loneliness catch up'. Village families, who still make up the majority of India's residents, are also witnessing a widespread dispersal of junior kin for work, sometimes abroad to the oil-rich countries of the Middle East, and often to India's major cities such as Mumbai, Delhi, Kolkata and smaller regional hubs. Older parents remaining in the villages both want their children to go—the alternative is a sense of failure and lack if their sons hang on in the village underemployed—and wish that they could want them to come back. Some older village parents now live in big fancy brick homes that they never could have afforded to build if not for the money their employed sons and daughters[4] send. The homes signify material success yet feel empty of family intimacy, as the top-floor rooms remain unfurnished and dusty, shown off to the rare visitor but otherwise vacant.

Such changes and movements arouse mixed interpretations; there is no single dominant narrative at play. Viraj Ghosh, who resides with his wife in an upscale Kolkata flat purchased by their US-settled son, commented: 'At this age, it's better to live separate.... If an old man

[4] In most areas of India, as in West Bengal, it is generally not considered standard or appropriate for a married daughter to support her parents financially; however, increasingly, women who are employed, and especially if unmarried, are providing financial support to their own parents. Employment opportunities for women are changing the familial intergenerational landscape in significant ways.

says that he needs to have his son live with him, then the son won't advance, and the country won't advance'. The fact that more women are working out of the home than in earlier generations also gives younger wives some agency to assert their desire to live separately from in-laws (for those who wish such separations); and some older women support such changes for their daughters and daughters-in-law. In fact, at the same time that nuclear-style families are often referred to critically as 'Western', they have become wrapped up with Indian middle-class aspirations. Billboards for flats within the modern apartment complexes springing up across India's cities feature images of nuclear-style families—a father, mother, son and daughter—smiling, fair-skinned and well-dressed in cosmopolitan attire, with captions such as '450 Lucky Families Are Living an Active Life. When Are You Joining?'[5] As Indrajit Roy (2016: 82) examines, 'Egalitarian ideals constitute an important ingredient of modernity' across most scholarly and popular conceptualisations, and nuclear-family-style living fosters the kind of gendered and aged egalitarianism that many value as modern. Yet, even among geographically dispersed families, the norm is for younger generations to continue to offer various kinds of material and social–emotional support, through sending money, phone and video calls, visits and the like.

Amidst such real and perceived social changes to the Indian family, and debates over the proper site of elder care, the Government of India, in 2007, passed a Maintenance and Welfare of Parents and Senior Citizens Act, making adult children—and anyone standing to inherit property from a senior citizen—not only morally but also now legally obligated to provide care (Brijnath 2012; Lamb 2013: 74–76). Under this law, implemented as of October 2009, children may be fined ₹5,000 and jailed for up to three months if found guilty of neglecting parents. Under 'Need for the Legislation', the Bill's preface declares: 'It is an established fact that the family is the most desired environment for senior citizens/parents to lead a life of security, care and dignity'.[6] Local courts and police stations also take on cases in which elders complain of neglect, while judges and police tend overwhelmingly to side with the elders (Lamb 2009: 242–49), bringing junior kin in to chastise

---

[5] Billboard advertisement for Active Acres Kolkata by Ruchi Realty, displayed on the EM Bypass in the winter of 2016.

[6] The text of the 2007 Bill is available at: http://www.prsindia.org/uploads/media/1182337322/scr1193026940_Senior_Citizen.pdf (accessed on 9 May 2016).

them for their moral and legal failings, as in this case reported by the *Anandabazar Patrika* newspaper:

Today, right at the beginning of the case, the judge asked [the son], 'What is this? You don't take care of your mother, give her food? This old woman had to come to the court—aren't you ashamed?' With folded hands, [the son] replied, 'Sir, I have committed a wrong, my Lord. I apologize. From now onwards, I shall take care of my mother'.[7]

At the same time, some judges, policy-makers, social workers and those among the public argue that practically—coming to terms with the realities of contemporary living—and perhaps ethically, it is better to foster generational independence and individual self-sufficiency. India's 1999 OASIS (Old Age Social and Income Security) report, for instance, opens by declaring that both family and state support are inadequate in India. About the family, the report's opening lines declare: 'In a world where the joint family is breaking down, and children are unable to take care of their parents, millions of elderly face destitution'. The answer is that the nation must work to develop modes of individual self-reliance:

The problem [of old age security] will have to be addressed through thrift and self-help, where people prepare for old age by savings accumulating through their decades in the labour force.... We must educate people that old age is inescapable and that saving for old age could be a painless process if started early in life.... The government should encourage fully funded old age income security systems that emphasise the values of thrift and self-help.[8]

The blockbuster Bollywood film *Baghban*, one of India's biggest cinematic hits, elucidates these kinds of competing perspectives—the assemblage of disjunct newer and older values, aspirations and lifeways that make up Indian ageing and family systems today. Produced in 2003, the film is still shown by parents to children to teach them Indian family values. On the surface, *Baghban* is a classic story of the morality and rightness of caring for and respecting one's elders. The 'bad' sons, daughters-in-law and grandchildren in the film are those who live in

---

[7] *Anandabazar Patrika*, '*Māke dekhen nā, lajjā kare nā! Mucalekā nila court*' [You Don't Take Care of Your Mother—Don't You Feel Ashamed?! Court Requires Son to Post Bond], *Anandabazar Patrika*, 19 March 2008, 1.

[8] 'OASIS (Old Age Social and Income Security): A Report', 1 February 1999. Available at: http://www.seniorindian.com/oasis__.htm (accessed on 22 April 2017).

modern nuclear-style apartments, are self-centred and materialistic, do not appropriately care for and adore their parents and fail to appreciate how their own very lives and livelihoods are the result of the devotion, guidance and material support their parents extended to them in their youth. During the film's closing climactic moments, as the elder father and film's hero gives a speech to an enthralled audience at an awards ceremony for his bestselling book, titled *Baghban* like the film itself, the father exposes the mistreatment he has received from his four sons:

> That is why, today, I ask ... that the children for whose joy a father happily spends every penny he has earned, why do these children hesitate to shine a little light for the parents when their eyes become weak? If a father can help his son to take the first step in his life, then why can't that son help his father take the last step of his life? Why are the parents, who spend their entire lives bestowing pleasures on their children, punished with tears and loneliness?[9]

But in the end, the (very modern, it turns out) parent heroes reject their one 'good' adopted son's plea to live with him and his wife, while choosing instead to reside independently as a dyadic couple, supported by the earnings from the hero's self-authored book.

Old-age Homes as Alien and Indian

In the working together of older and newer lifeways and aspirations of ageing in India, the family is not the only institution at play. Quite dramatic has been the rise of what are commonly termed in English 'old-age homes'. Still used by only a small fraction of the population, elder residences are springing up across India's urban centres[10] and figure prominently in the public imagination—in news media, films, television serials, blogs—and in everyday talk about the contemporary (Lamb 2009). Old-age homes represent the conjuncture of elements old and new, modern and traditional, good and bad, alien and Indian—with no isomorphism among these elements in a tidy structural alignment. That is, the traditional can be read and experienced as both bad

---

[9] Translated from Hindi by my research assistant Rachana Agarwal (Chopra 2003).

[10] To date, old-age homes in India are primarily for the middle classes and largely a Hindu and Christian phenomenon; researchers have yet to encounter Muslim-specific homes (Lamb 2009: 58–59; Liebig 2003: 166), although a few Muslim residents reside in Kolkata's oldest Christian-sponsored charity home run by the Little Sisters of the Poor.

and good, as can the old-age home, just as the old-age home can be regarded as both Western and familiarly Indian.

One of India's most prominent discourses of the elder home is that of Western-style alienation. Dr. Ranjan Banerjee, a retired psychiatrist living in an exclusive old-age home in the Kolkata suburbs, proclaimed:

Old age homes are not a concept of our country. These days, we are throwing away our culture. The U.S. is the richest nation in the world and therefore has won us over. Now we, too, are only after material wealth as a nation and have become very unhappy. Some are here because their families dumped them here, and there are others whose children are living abroad and can easily afford the money [to pay the old-age-home bills]. But old age homes are not our way of life. My parents died right with us.

Kalyani Chatterjee had been 'thrown away', as she put it, into an old-age home by her son shortly after her retirement as a secretary, following 16 years of co-residence with her son, daughter-in-law and grandchildren in a conventional multigenerational household. Several years later, she still felt shocked to be there, reflecting:

If we had grown up with the idea that we might live separately from our children, then it might not be so hard to get used to now. But with our own eyes we had never seen or known anything like this. We never could have even dreamed that a *briddhabas* [elder abode] existed, that we would be here, in a place like this!

Newspaper coverage commonly portrays the old-age home as a site of eroding Indian values and moral devastation, as in the *Hindu*'s 'Homes of the Future?' exposé: 'Shunned by those whom they breastfed, ... the ignored aged have no choice but to exist in the cages of old age homes'.[11]

However, other more complex narratives of familiarity and value can be found. Two lady friends in their 50s who established a lovely old-age home on the outskirts of Kolkata, on land one had inherited within an old mango orchard, reflected on their motivations: 'We are trying to start to wipe out the stigma of living in an old age home.... "Come and happily stay with us!" is our motto'. One of their first residents was a Harvard professor who had returned to his native West Bengal after

[11] Goutam Ghosh, 'Homes of the Future?' Special issue on 'Ageing' with the Sunday Magazine, *The Hindu*, 18 October 1998.

retiring and appreciated finding a place offering convenience, safety, good home-style food and tea faithfully prepared and served, supportive care, and the sociality of conversing with like-minded peers. The new elder residences also open up options for living for those without conventional families or sons. I found quite a few never-married women, for instance, in the Kolkata old-age homes I studied from 2003 to 2007. Some of these women's life stories reveal actively resisting marriage and pursuing a vision of gendered egalitarianism and individual freedom, as they followed the path of education and cultivated careers as schoolteachers and nurses. To be able to pay for one's care with a pension in an old-age home rather than depend as a peripheral spinster aunt on remote kin was a great relief for several unmarried lady residents I grew to know.

Further, some argue that old-age homes are perhaps not so radically 'new' or fundamentally 'Western' after all. For example, some compare old-age homes to the 'forest-dwelling' or *vanaprastha* life phase presented in Hindu texts as appropriate for older age, where one purposefully loosens ties to family and the world while pursuing spiritual realisation. In addition, old-age-home residents receive quite a bit of sustained seva or respectful service, a key component of conventional Indian ways of ageing. Although offered by hired staff and proprietors rather than kin—a not insignificant distinction—many residents praise the seva they receive, including the arrival of 5 AM bed tea, meals served, oil massaged into hair, and bath water warmed and delivered. Some also compare old-age-home living to the crowded, intimate joint families of yore, where all eat meals from the same hearth, chat in shared rooms as they fall asleep at night and no one is ever alone (Cohen 1998: 115; Lamb 2009: 133–71).

The Census of India 2011 documentary film includes a segment on old-age-home residents, portraying these elders as both abandoned yet incorporated as part of 'the Great Indian Family', displaying the ambivalence at the heart of this new mode of living and ageing: 'These are the eyes whose tears have run dry. They are abandoned and forgotten by their children, relatives, and friends. They live in old age homes. Through the Census, these lonely people became a part of the Great Indian Family'.[12] Amidst these varied narratives, we see no simple story

---

[12] 2011censusindia, 'Census of India 2011' (shorter version), YouTube video, televised on 22 January 2012, produced by National Film Development Corporation Limited (NFDC) in 2011 on behalf of the Office of the Registrar General & Census Commissioner, Government of India. Available at: https://www.youtube.com/watch?v=he0DTmbzluQ (accessed on 22 April 2017).

of good or bad, progress or decline, but instead complicated conjunctures of disjunct elements.

Medicine, *Maya* and the Body: Health and Decay, Transience and Attachment

Imaginaries and aspirations of ageing in contemporary India also concern existential questions regarding the permanence or transience of the self and body in this world. Here also, we see older and newer, more local and global values configured together in multifaceted ways.

According to the classical vision of the four stages of life or *asramas* known to most Hindus, two life stages emphasise older age as a period of cultivating spirituality and embracing the transience of the human condition. As a disengaged forest dweller (vanaprastha) and finally a wandering renouncer (*sannyasi*), an older person strives to loosen ties to family, household, material possessions and one's own body, in preparation for the myriad leave-takings and transitions of dying (Doniger and Smith 1991: 117–27). Although few Hindus literally move to a forest or take up the sannyasi lifestyle, much everyday talk in India among elders highlights resonant themes—of late life as a valuable time for focusing increasingly on spiritual awareness, and for cultivating an attitude of readiness for death. Purnima-di spoke to me about being ready to die almost every time I saw her over a period of several years while she remained in quite vigorous good health as a retired English professor in her 60s and then 70s, remarking: 'I am not afraid of death, because it is inevitable. Because I am born, I know I have to die. No one born can escape death'. And: 'We have to accept decay. I have accepted'. And: 'God is a giver and a taker. Today is mine; tomorrow I will go and the day will be someone else's. I should not be sorry for that'. And: 'A machine also has retirement. When clothes are worn out, you just take them off and wear new ones. The body is also like that'. Another retired man, Arjun DasGupta, had been speaking of his recent bodily ailments, when I commented casually, 'I guess these things happen with age'. He replied cheerfully, 'Of course! Naturally! And we wouldn't want it any other way. Imagine what would happen to the earth if none of us got sick and died!' In fact, it seems that expected cultural discourse among older Bengalis emphasises accepting one's own bodily impermanence.

For many Bengalis, especially in rural areas, much of this talk of later-life transience revolves around the concept of *maya* (Lamb 2000). Maya—meaning most readily love, affection and attachment—is conceived as both an emotional and a bodily phenomenon. A person's bodily emotional ties of maya grow in intensity and number over the life course, and yet it is in late life when people poignantly realise that they must cut their maya through dying. Competing aspirations are the norm, however; when it comes right down to it, it is hard to pull away. Some older persons purposefully practise loosening ties—such as through going to temples, praying, eating a vegetarian diet, sleeping apart from other kin—while also still seeking intimacy and engagement, enjoying being surrounded by the bustle of family, hoping to see another grandchild's wedding or anticipating another May of delicious, tree-ripened mangoes. One older gentleman from Delhi wrote to me by email about the virtues of the Hindu philosophy of *iccha mrtyu* or self-willed death. He felt that he was approaching his own death and wanted to be ready. But then he added:

> I feel that people are attached to physical objects, to their memories, to their children and loved ones. This feeling of attachment has been well discussed in Indian philosophy…. In this sense we are also attached to our physical being-self and fear that this will end in death. I feel that we are deeply attached to our life.

Interpenetrating with such visions of a natural human transience are globally circulating discourses of 'healthy' and 'active' ageing. The World Health Organization, the European Union, and medical and academic centres across the United States are promoting a 21st-century vision of individual responsibility for maintaining one's own independence, health and a kind of agelessness in later life (Lamb 2014). Healthy Aging India is one Delhi-based organisation founded in 2013 that has picked up this global discourse. Among its vision statements is this bold, very Western-sounding aspiration: 'We are striving to create a unique self-sustaining model for the elder generation so that they don't need to ever depend upon others for their survival'.[13] The organisation's strategies include health education and promoting physical exercise through activities such as walk-a-thons. Lots of older Indians are also taking up healthy-active ageing projects in their daily lives, as they can be seen increasingly in urban parks enjoying vigorous morning walks in their sneakers while socialising with peers. Others seek out advanced medical care abroad, sometimes taking up permanent residence with children in places like the United States in order to partake in the elaborate medical technologies offered there to sustain the older body.

[13] http://www.healthyagingindia.in/ and http://www.healthyagingindia.in/?page_id=1576 (accessed on 9 May 2016).

We see, then, that in some narratives, pursuing health through medicine and exercise constitutes progress and modern success. Not all agree, however, in any simple way, at least. One gentleman had come to the United States from India many years earlier and enjoyed many facets of life in America with his married daughter and her family, but he shunned the idea of being hooked up to medical machines at the end of life: 'I have visited the nursing home. I have visited, yes, and I have seen people suffering. I tell you, such a bad situation has come over here [in the US]—that because of medical facilities, we are living too long'. Still others, like many elders I have grown to know in Kolkata, express with seeming genuine happiness that they are pleased to sit inside, surrounded by junior kin, barely leaving the house, with no felt need to cultivate an individual self's bodily health through exercise, projects and activities. We see a complex assemblage of competing ideologies of the body and self, health as an individual project and acceptance of decline, transience and attachment, as older persons seek disparate yet intersecting forms of value in later life.

Conclusion

Through this chapter, I have wished to explore how—for scholars interested in understanding the present in India—tensions, debates and competing aspirations surrounding ageing are fruitful to examine. As people fashion how best to live and age in the contemporary era, they configure assemblages of disjunct newer and older, more local and global values and lifeways in complicated and ambivalent ways. How best to age is at once an existential tale, an ethical tale, a political–economic tale, a tale of family aspirations and intimacies, a tale of love and loss, a tale of India and globalisation and a tale of pursuing heterogeneous kinds of value (Nakassis and Searle 2016) in the daily practice of social–cultural life in India today.

References

Administration on Aging, US Department of Health and Human Services. 2014. *A Profile of Older Americans: 2014*, 5, Figure 3. Available at: http://www.aoa.acl.gov/aging_statistics/profile/2014/docs/2014-profile.pdf (accessed on 9 May 2016).

Ahlin, Tanja. 2018. 'Only Near Is Dear? Doing Elder Care with Everyday ICTs in Indian Transnational Families'. *Medical Anthropology Quarterly* 32 (1): 85–102.Appadurai, Arjun. 1990. 'Disjuncture and Difference in the Global Cultural Economy'. *Public Culture* 2 (2): 1–24.

Brijnath, Bianca. 2012. 'Why Does Institutionalised Care Not Appeal to Indian Families? Legislative and Social Answers'. *Ageing and Society* 32 (4): 697–717.

———. 2014. *Unforgotten: Love and the Culture of Dementia Care in India.* New York, NY: Berghahn.

Chopra, Ravi, director. 2003. *Baghban.* India/UK: B.R. Films.

Cohen, Lawrence. 1998. *No Aging in India: Alzheimer's, the Bad Family, and Other Modern Things.* Berkeley, CA: University of California Press.

Doniger, Wendy and Brian K. Smith, trans. 1991. *The Laws of Manu.* New York, NY: Penguin.

Lamb, Sarah. 2000. *White Saris and Sweet Mangoes: Aging, Gender and Body in North India.* Berkeley, CA: University of California Press.

———. 2009. *Aging and the Indian Diaspora: Cosmopolitan Families in India and Abroad.* Bloomington, IN: Indiana University Press.

———. 2013. 'In/dependence, Intergenerational Uncertainty, and the Ambivalent State: Perceptions of Old Age Security in India'. *South Asia: Journal of South Asian Studies*, n.s., 36 (1): 65–78.

———. 2014. 'Permanent Personhood or Meaningful Decline? Toward a Critical Anthropology of Successful Aging'. *Journal of Aging Studies* 29: 41–52.

Liebig, Phoebe S. 2003. 'Old-age Homes and Services: Old and New Approaches to Aged Care'. In *An Aging India: Perspectives, Prospects and Policies*, edited by Phoebe S. Liebig and S. Irudaya Rajan, 159–78. New York, NY: Haworth.

Nakassis, Constantine V. and Llerena Guiu Searle. 2016. 'Introduction: Social Value Projects in Post-liberalisation India'. *Contributions to Indian Sociology* 47 (2): 169–83.

Rabinow, Paul. 2008. *Marking Time: On the Anthropology of the Contemporary.* Princeton, NJ: Princeton University Press.

Roy, Indrajit. 2016. 'Equality Against Hierarchy: Imagining Modernity in Subaltern India'. *Contributions to Indian Sociology* 50 (1): 80–107.

Sathyanarayana, K.M., Sanjay Kumar and K.S. James. 2012. 'Living Arrangements of Elderly in India: Policy and Programmatic Implications'. BKPAI Working Paper No. 7. United Nations Population Fund (UNFPA), New Delhi. doi:10.1017/CCO9781139683456.005.

Van Willigen, John and Narender K. Chadha. 1999. *Social Aging in a Delhi Neighborhood.* Westport, CT: Bergin and Harvey.

Vatuk, Sylvia. 1990. '"To Be a Burden on Others": Dependency Anxiety Among the Elderly in India'. In *Divine Passions: The Social Construction of Emotion in India*, edited by Owen Lynch, 64–88. Berkeley, CA: University of California Press.

Wadley, Susan S. 2010. '"One Straw from a Broom Cannot Sweep": The Ideology and Practice of the Joint Family in Rural North India'. In *Everyday Life in South Asia.* 2nd ed., edited by Diane Mines and Sarah Lamb, 11–22. Bloomington, IN: Indiana University Press.

25

New Cultures of Food Studies

Amita Baviskar

Introduction

During his travels in South Asia in the 1940s, Claude Lévi-Strauss visited a young teacher's flat in Dhaka (then Dacca) and shared a meal with his family. As he recounted in *Tristes Tropiques*:

> Squatting on the concrete floor, in the dim light of a single bulb hanging by its flex from the ceiling, I once—oh, Arabian nights!—ate a dinner full of succulent ancestral savours, picking up the food with my fingers: first, *Khichuri*, rice and the small lentils.... Then *nimkorma*, broiled chicken; *chingri cari*, an oily fruity stew of giant shrimps, and another stew with hard-boiled eggs called *dimer tak*, accompanied by cucumber sauce, *shosha*; finally the dessert, *firni*, made of rice and milk. (Lévi-Strauss 1973 [1955]: 129, quoted in Khare 2012: 240)

Later, Lévi-Strauss (1983 [1964]) would go on to write *The Raw and the Cooked*, analysing how oppositional pairs permeated and organised the structure of meals and myths. The piling up of oppositions that repeat themselves could, he argued, be boiled down to a logic or 'mental pattern' that persists across cultures and times. However, his grand theory unifying categories of thought and action was dismissed by Mary Douglas (1972: 62) who complained that

[H]e takes leave of the small-scale social relations that generate the codification and are sustained by it. Here and there his feet touch solid ground, but mostly he is orbiting in rarefied space where he expects to find universal food meanings common to all mankind.

Douglas also criticised Lévi-Strauss' exclusive reliance on binary analysis: 'Worse than clumsy, his technical apparatus produces meanings which cannot be validated' (ibid.).[1]

Ironically, it is Lévi-Strauss' passing description of his meal in Dhaka that, in many ways, captured the culturally specific meanings that Douglas demanded. His brief sketch highlighted elements which were to become key in contemporary analyses of food. First, there is the attention to social relations and the sociality around food: the passage describes the teacher's household, including a 'brother-in-law, who acted as a butler, a maid, a baby, and lastly my host's wife who was in the process of being emancipated from purdah. She was like a silent, frightened doe...' (Lévi-Strauss 1973 [1955]: 129). Notably, there is no structural analysis of kinship here. Instead, there is sensitivity to the atmosphere between the couple and to the subtle play of tension during the meal. Second, the embodied act of eating—squatting on the floor, mixing morsels of food with one's fingers—is acknowledged here. Bodily dispositions unfamiliar to the foreign visitor are noted. Third, there is palpable pleasure in the food itself (Sutton 2010). The recital of the sequence and the sensuous description of taste, texture and ingredients highlight an essential element that is altogether missing in the anthropologist's formal writings: food is not only good to think, but it is also good to eat.

Caste and Cosmology:
Early Studies of Food in India

These aspects of food were to remain muted in sociological and anthropological studies on India during the 1960s and 1970s. While early village studies (cf. Mayer 1960) did focus on social relations around food, they were interpreted primarily as reflections of an all-encompassing caste hierarchy, the grand unified theory for the subcontinent at that time. Thus, McKim Marriott constructed a matrix that meticulously

---

[1] Douglas does not refer to Lévi-Strauss' rare departure from binary codes in his elaboration of the 'culinary triangle' which classified cooking techniques along the three poles of 'raw, cooked and rotten' (Lévi-Strauss 1966 [1965]), but her critique remains pertinent for this theory as well.

recorded exchanges of *sidha* (raw), *pakka* (superior), *kachcha* (inferior) and *jhootha* (leftover) food between 24 Hindu and Muslim castes in a village in Aligarh district, Uttar Pradesh, in order to arrive at how villagers ranked each other in the caste hierarchy and, sometimes, competed for upward mobility (Marriott 1968). Marriott's preoccupation with caste as it shaped everyday life was mirrored and magnified in Louis Dumont's (1970) *Homo Hierarchicus*, which folded food (and pretty much all else) into a larger fabric of transactions organised around the central principle of purity and pollution. Marriott's minutiae and Dumont's grand design, both assumed that the substance of food was to signify the caste order. Other social meanings inherent in the acts of cooking, feeding and eating—or for that matter, in how food was produced and procured—went unnoticed. Equally ignored was the increasing presence of 'neutral foods' (Baviskar 2018; Gillette 2000) or industrially manufactured edible commodities within Indian diets, items that had spread across the world since the late 19th century (Goody 1982: 154–74). Also missing from the analysis were practices of eating outside the home in teashops and 'hotels', places that served an increasingly mobile population.

A wider field of meaning and action was accorded to food by R.S. Khare, who proposed the idea of 'gastrosemantics' to encompass 'a culture's distinct capacity to signify, experience, systematize, philosophize, and communicate with food' (Khare 1992: 44; also see Khare and Rao 1986). Moving beyond Indian anthropology's singular preoccupation with caste, Khare pointed to the depth and density of the cosmological, ritual, social, economic and nutritional meanings of food, dimensions that could not be disentangled from each other. 'Good and proper food not only creates a good body (medicine) but also a good mind (yoga). What you eat both reflects who you are and determines what you will be…. What one eats both demarcates one's social boundaries and demonstrates one's spiritual aspirations' (Olivelle 1995: 370). Far from being confined to members of the village community, food is offered to the gods and the divine leftovers distributed as *prasad* (Breckenridge 1986; Toomey 1994). Food is bestowed on casteless renunciants as alms and presented to ancestors as *pinda daan*, forging relationships that link this world to others. Food also connects ecological landscapes to the human body (Zimmerman 1987). The changing of seasons—of climate as well as the stages of life—is marked by changes in diet. Everyday eating is interrupted by fasting and feasting, occasioned by concerns that range from the ritual and the spiritual to the medical and the moral (Alter 2000; P. Roy 2010).

While the notion of 'gastrosemantics' opened up the subject of food to a fuller appreciation of its meanings, in practice, Khare's analysis equated 'Indian' with 'Hindu' and culled textual and ethnographic data from widely varying regions and historical periods to construct a reified, unchanging Hindu identity in his later work. This was especially disappointing since his 1976 book *The Hindu Hearth and Home* was an exceptionally nuanced, closely observed ethnography that was fully alive to the differences between orthodox and secular practices, to urban and rural variations, and to differences in gendered roles within caste-specific households in the Kanpur–Lucknow region of Uttar Pradesh (Khare 1976).[2] And, though Khare mentioned the economic and nutritional aspects of food in passing, the secular political economy of food production, distribution and consumption—exemplified in Sidney Mintz's (1986) *Sweetness and Power*, for instance—was marked by its absence in his work. Food-related practices were interpreted in terms of Advaita philosophy, vedic rituals and ayurvedic elements, but their changing ecological and economic materiality remained indeterminate.

The intellectual weight of this body of work has left its impress upon more recent scholarship. For instance, a special issue of the journal *South Asia* discusses the persistence of vegetarianism in contemporary India, examining its changing contours in the light of caste politics, gendered norms within the family and concerns about health (Osella 2008; also see Donner 2008). An earlier study by Appadurai (1981) focused on 'gastropolitics' and how caste-specific practices were calibrated to account for conflicting roles within the hierarchy of the household and its wider kin, injecting more agency into Khare's 1976 account of domestic dynamics. Manpreet Janeja (2010) extended this approach by considering Muslim as well as Hindu Bengali households, by analysing the place of domestic workers in the production of food demarcated as properly *bhadralok* (upper-class) and by including food transactions outside the home in restaurants and coffee houses.[3] These studies broaden and deepen the field of transactions that Marriott and Khare explored, fruitfully bringing together the home and the world.

[2] Khare's focus on the household also provided a different vantage point from which to understand Indian society, in relation to, but distinct from, the caste- and village-based perspectives that prevailed at the time.

[3] Janeja's work stands out for showing how physical spaces and kitchen appliances mediate the work of storing and cooking food, thereby affirming or altering gender and class identities and notions of purity and pollution. However, her aim of treating food itself as an actor (Latour 2005) is not achieved since her analysis does not systematically address how the specific characteristics of particular foods affect the processes she describes.

From Caste to Cosmopolitanism

In the 1990s, new forms of globalisation of the world economy, such as the time–space compression induced by information and travel technologies that in turn enabled the accelerated movement of capital and labour, led social scientists to look critically at how they constituted their subjects (Appadurai 1996). The hitherto taken-for-granted boundaries of India were first breached by historians who traced the transnational provenance of ingredients that had come to be regarded as intrinsic elements of Indian diets (Achaya 1994, 1998). Chillies, maize, potatoes and tomatoes were among the diverse items incorporated into cooking on the subcontinent. Further research delineated not only the spread of new foods and drinks (such as tea) but also the adoption of cooking techniques and recipes, including biryani and Bengali cheese-based sweets (Collingham 2006). These studies emphasised that Indian food was a hybrid creation, with native elements cross-fertilised by Mughal, Portuguese and British influences, themselves the product of intercontinental lineages.

While acknowledging hybridity, other scholars focused on its denial by sections of Indian society who sought to carve out an autonomous and authentic domain of Indian culture (Chatterjee 1993). Asserting an Indian identity as part of an anti-colonial nationalist discourse entailed new modes of gendered domesticity that centred on food (Ray 2015; also see Banerjee-Dube 2016; Sengupta 2012).[4] Cookbooks and other manuals instructed the housewife about the ideals of economic management and scientific nutrition, to be combined with older values of spiritual and moral sustenance. Such texts and popular journal articles from 19th- and early-20th-century Bengal have been extensively analysed to show how the making of nationalist subjects was inflected by concerns about caste, class, religion and sexuality. In particular, (Hindu) bhadralok food practices have been the locus of academic attention for their tense tango with colonial meals and manners as well as their anxieties about maintaining a proper distance from Muslims and lower castes. Agonising over bread and biscuits, which meats to eat, the warring virtues of milled and hand-pounded rice, and whether and when

---

[4] Utsa Ray's (2015) comprehensive analysis is noteworthy for linking what people ate to changing agricultural practices such as the introduction of new crops by missionaries and the colonial government. In addition, she places dietary changes in the context of wider social processes, such as urbanisation and industrialisation, providing a fuller framework for understanding the production and consumption of food.

to use onion and garlic was part of adjudicating and policing social boundaries. At the same time, cooking was extolled as a fine art that could only be practised by the housewife, and not by domestic servants, a strategy that aestheticised middle-class female labour to set it apart from working-class toil and strip it of economic value (Ray 2015: 123ff.). This debate on the ideal *grihani* (housewife) and other discussions also indicate that the principle of purity and pollution remained central to the cultural compass orienting food practices even as diets became more diverse.

A considerable literature details the nationalist Hindu bhadralok preoccupation with the invention of culinary traditions that reflected their distinctive social location (Bourdieu 1984 [1979]) at the cusp of colonial modernity. However, there is far less discussion of the counter-trend towards embracing cosmopolitanism. While there is mention of elite Bengali households (and royalty in other parts of the subcontinent) cooking Western food for male members and their White guests by maintaining separate kitchens, information about how the rest of society encountered and incorporated alien foods in their diets remains scant. Frank Conlon's (1996) pioneering essay on public dining in Bombay states that migrants from the hinterland who migrated to the colonial city to work in the textile mills ate in caste-specific *khanaval* (eating houses), but suggests that the freedom and desire to taste other cuisines remained confined to white-collar workers and well-off people who could patronise Irani cafés and other restaurants. Writing about the post-Independence period, Arjun Appadurai (1988) noted the rising numbers of such urbanised professionals, especially that segment which moved from one city or town to another because of transferable jobs in the civil services and armed forces. Cultural exposure to different parts of the country, albeit from the standardised and contained setting of staff quarters and cantonments, made middle-class women curious about the dishes they encountered in other people's homes. Cookbooks catered to them by cobbling together a 'national cuisine' by compiling recipes from different regions (ibid.). The workplace as a site that brings together heterogeneous social groups, fostering camaraderie and conviviality across caste boundaries, was the subject of Strümpell's (2008) study among Rourkela's public-sector steel mill workers.[5] He showed how men who followed caste norms about commensality when visiting their native village regarded the industrial township as a 'modern' place where it was incumbent upon them to

---

[5] Parry (1999) also shows that the ethic of equality that prevailed among work teams at the Bhilai steel plant extended to sharing meals across caste lines.

shed their parochial baggage. Such modes of inter-dining indicate that cosmopolitanism is not simply the unwitting outcome of commodity flows and labour mobility, but it is a value that is actively pursued and embraced. For the accomplished cook, cultivating cosmopolitanism by learning to prepare new recipes is as much a goal today as mastering the traditional repertoire of one's community that was once the sole definition of culinary virtuosity (Baviskar 2012).[6]

Frank Conlon's essay on Bombay traced the rise of the 'discretionary' diner, who ate out from choice and not necessity. His observations about cosmopolitan restaurant-goers who seek food that is different from what they eat at home, but which has been domesticated to suit their tastes, remain insightful (Conlon 1996: 103–14). Thus, the hugely popular 'Chinese food' served across India in restaurants and street stalls bears little resemblance to its putative parent. One would expect that sociological studies of restaurants would reveal that patrons who venture to eat novel cuisines are also open to eating food whose social provenance is not known. However, in the case of Udupi restaurants that serve South Indian vegetarian tiffin and meals, studies show that the management is careful to assuage the caste-related anxieties of their patrons by employing Brahmin cooks and servers who wear caste-marks on their foreheads so as to appear upper-caste (Iverson and Raghavendra 2006; also see Madsen and Gardella 2012). This suggests that, for many patrons, the purity–pollution matrix not only endures within the home but is also extended to cover new sites and forms of food, often under the euphemistic guise of 'hygiene'. Cosmopolitanism is thus cultivated, but in measured, even mincing, modes. However, when cosmopolitanism is perceived not as a civic virtue to be cautiously embraced but as a threat to the body politic, hybrid foods may be caught in the crossfire. Solomon (2015) describes the career of the *vada pao* in Mumbai, where the nativist Shiv Sena party has attempted to brand this street food as quintessentially Maharashtrian, erasing its patently multicultural origins. The desire to invent tradition and claim cultural authenticity is also noted in Shaffer's (2012) lively essay on *dum pukht* cuisine in Lucknow. Taken together, these studies show that the meanings and practices that accrue around 'outside' food, or food prepared beyond

---

[6] Staples (2014) describes how, for young people in Guntur, Andhra Pradesh, eating out in restaurants is part of the process of performing the middle-class identity they aspire towards, transcending caste by appearing educated and modern. Also see Caplan (2002) on the gradual globalisation of domestic food in Madras from the 1970s onwards.

the more manageable boundaries of the home, are much more volatile than the conventional containers of caste–village–family can hold.

At first glance, the mobile meanings of food are, paradoxically, the least evident among the Indian diaspora. Nostalgia seems to be the chief motif in Indian migrants' stories about food, harmonising with the sense of exile that many experience in their transplanted home. The work of memory is focused on fixing 'how we ate back home' and either mourning its loss or seeking to resurrect its spirit by sticking to signature practices such as vegetarianism (Saunders 2007).[7] Preserving foodways, thus, serves as a key expression of ethnic identity in the face of a foreign culture (Mankekar 2002). Krishnendu Ray's (2004) study among Bengalis settled in the United States complicates this narrative by showing how migrants negotiate between nostalgic notions of food and the lure of novel modes of consumption, especially those that promise freedom from domestic drudgery and gastronomic monotony. However, it is in studies analysing how Indian food is adapted and incorporated into the diets of a non-Indian population that the full flavour of globalisation is realised (Narayan 1995; Ray and Srinivas 2012). Buettner's (2012) essay on the cuisine epitomised by *chicken tikka masala*, the food brought to Britain by working-class South Asian migrants which has now become its de facto national cuisine, carefully charts how the changing contours of race and class have shaped this process of culinary inclusion from the margins to the middle of a multicultural stage. The focus shifts from the cosmopolitanism of Indian consumers to that of those who encounter Indian food in colonial and post-colonial settings (M. Roy 2010; also see P. Roy 2010).

Dearth, Deprivation and Discrimination

A major area where the sociology and anthropology of food have been seriously remiss is in studying the 'lack' of food. India is home to the world's largest undernourished and food-deprived population. Hunger is an existential crisis, quite literally, experienced every day or for long periods by almost 200 million people in India or 15.2 per cent of the total population (FAO, IFAD and WFP 2015: 46).[8] Yet its presence in

---

[7] Diasporic popular writers on food (see, e.g., Banerji 2006) bring a refined elegiac aesthetic to their work.

[8] These statistics are about 'undernourished' populations and are being used here as rough approximations to account for hunger, a more subjective category than nutrition. The very fact that there is a large literature on undernutrition and malnutrition, but not on hunger, shows the absence of research

the Indian sociological literature is non-existent. There is no study that comes close to *Death Without Weeping*, the compelling delineation of hunger, violence and emotions in a Brazilian favela by Nancy Scheper-Hughes (1993).[9] Nor is there any work that equals the incisive political and economic analysis in Michael Watts' (1983) account of food, famine and agrarian change in northern Nigeria.[10] That sociologists and anthropologists of India have failed to engage with a social phenomenon of such scale and significance is not only staggering but also scandalous.

In their stead, we are compelled to turn to writers of fiction and autobiography, especially of Dalit lives (Anand 2014; Valmiki 2003).[11] The accounts of particular Dalit castes, especially those traditionally assigned to deal with household waste, show that hunger has been inseparable from humiliation. Compelled by poverty to eat *jhoothan* (leftover food considered ritually polluted by contact with saliva) or cheaper meats such as beef and pork (that are proscribed for upper-caste Hindus) and then castigated for it, this vicious circle of logic continues to bind Dalits in contemporary India. Indeed, beef is the centre of controversy today in a way that demands sociological engagement. The recent violence against Dalits and Muslims in the name of cow protection, and Dalit assertions about eating beef on university campuses, are only two threads in a taut social fabric being unravelled and rewoven. That a hitherto stigmatised practice—eating beef—has been revalorised and publicly asserted shows the distance that Indians have travelled from the shackles of purity–pollution (Staples 2008). At the same time, the upper-caste backlash against this indicates that dominant culture will not cede ground easily.

that treats this widespread and acute social phenomenon as a social fact and anthropological field.

[9] Human rights activist Harsh Mander (2012) has tried to redress this gap by writing empathetic and detailed accounts of how poor, old and infirm people cope with hunger. Literary critic Parama Roy (2010) also focuses on representations of hunger and famine in her insightful assemblage of food writings. However, most of the extant information about the incidence of hunger, and especially on state practices to address it, is to be found in the literature around the Right to Food (Drèze 2004; Shukla 2014), a field where economic policy and public administration concerns predominate and where sociological and anthropological concerns with meanings and actions do not figure.

[10] For more recent, global surveys of the political economy of hunger and food, see Patel (2007) and Drèze et al. (1998).

[11] Also see excerpts in anthologies on food by Roy (2004) and Thieme and Raja (2007).

While beef constitutes a dense node of meanings that demands sociological analysis, it would be misleading to concentrate solely on this for understanding deprivation, discrimination and collective assertion. In common with other poor people, Dalits rarely get to eat meat. Their everyday diets are meagre, gleaned from minimum wages in cash and kind (Rege et al. 2009). In addition, the experience of hunger incorporates emotional states other than humiliation and social relations other than oppression. How people collaborate and conspire to cope with hunger, how they act individually and collectively to deal with state agencies, with landlords and bosses who employ them, with the varying needs and capabilities of different household members, remains to be studied. Above all, we await an account of poor people not as organic machines processing nutrients for bare survival but as cultural beings—people who inhabit a complex, changing world, who bring to it tongues that taste and minds that aspire, embodied skills and the power of abstraction, for whom food is not merely biological sustenance but is the stuff of cultural life.[12] Among the many lines of enquiry that the sociology of food might pursue in the future, this is surely the most urgent.[13]

References

Achaya, K.T. 1994. *Indian Food: A Historical Companion*. New Delhi: Oxford University Press.

———. 1998. *A Historical Dictionary of Indian Food*. New Delhi: Oxford University Press.

Alter, Joseph S. 2000. *Gandhi's Body: Sex, Diet, and the Politics of Nationalism*. Philadelphia, PA: University of Pennsylvania Press.

Anand, Mulk Raj. 2014 (1935). *Untouchable*. New Delhi: Penguin Classics.

Appadurai, Arjun. 1981. 'Gastro-politics in Hindu South Asia'. *American Ethnologist* 8 (3): 494–511.

———. 1988. 'How to Make a National Cuisine: Cookbooks in Contemporary India'. *Comparative Studies in Society and History* 30 (1): 3–24.

[12] Bhrigupati Singh's (2015) writing on the place of millets in the diet of villagers in Rajasthan reflects such an understanding of food. On the changing meanings of millets and their incorporation into affluent, metropolitan diets, see Finnis (2012).

[13] Other important and understudied areas of research include the study of gendered practices around food; the increasing presence of industrial foods; food practices among non-Hindus; and food, health and ecology. Also, since food studies have so far focused mostly on well-to-do, urban social groups, it is important that less well-off, rural or migrant people be brought into the picture.

Appadurai, Arjun. 1996. *Modernity at Large: Cultural Dimensions of Globalization*. Minneapolis, MN: University of Minnesota Press.

Banerjee-Dube, Ishita. 2016. 'Modern Menus: Food, Family, Health and Gender in Colonial Bengal'. In *Cooking Cultures: Convergent Histories of Food and Feeling*, edited by Ishita Banerjee-Dube, 100–21. Delhi: Cambridge University Press.

Banerji, Chitrita. 2006. *Feeding the Gods: Memories of Food and Culture in Bengal*. Kolkata: Seagull Books.

Baviskar, Amita. 2012. 'Food and Agriculture'. In *Cambridge Companion to Contemporary Indian Culture*, edited by Vasudha Dalmia and Rashmi Sadana, 49–66. Cambridge: Cambridge University Press.

———. 2018. 'Consumer Citizenship: Instant Noodles in India'. *Gastronomica* 18 (2, May): 1–10.

Bourdieu, Pierre. 1984 (1979). *Distinction: A Social Critique of the Judgement of Taste*. Translated from French by Richard Nice. Cambridge, MA: Harvard University Press.

Breckenridge, Carol A. 1986. 'Food, Politics and Pilgrimage in South India, 1350–1650 A.D'. In *Food, Society and Culture: Aspects of South Asian Food Systems*, edited by R.S. Khare and M.S.A. Rao, 21–53. Durham, NC: Carolina Academic Press.

Buettner, Elizabeth. 2012. '"Going for an Indian": South Asian Restaurants and the Limits of Multiculturalism in Britain'. In *Curried Cultures: Globalization, Food, and South Asia*, edited by Krishnendu Ray and Tulasi Srinivas, 143–74. Berkeley, CA: University of California Press.

Caplan, Pat. 2002. 'Food in Middle-class Madras Households from the 1970s to 1990s'. In *Asian Food: The Global and the Local*, edited by Kataryzna Cwiertka and Boudewijn C.A. Walraven, 46–62. Richmond, VA: Curzon.

Chatterjee, Partha. 1993. *The Nation and Its Fragments: Colonial and Postcolonial Histories*. Princeton, NJ: Princeton University Press.

Collingham, Elizabeth. 2006. *Curry: A Tale of Cooks and Conquerors*. New York, NY: Oxford University Press.

Conlon, Frank F. 1996. 'Dining Out in Bombay'. In *Consuming Modernity: Public Culture in Contemporary India*, edited by Carol A. Breckenridge, 90–127. New Delhi: Oxford University Press.

Donner, Henrike. 2008. 'New Vegetarianism: Food, Gender and Neo-liberal Regimes in Bengali Middle-class Families'. *South Asia: Journal of South Asian Studies*, n.s., 31 (1): 143–69.

Douglas, Mary. 1972. 'Deciphering a Meal'. *Daedalus* 101 (1): 61–81.

Drèze, Jean. 2004. 'Democracy and Right to Food'. *Economic & Political Weekly* 39 (17): 1723–31.

Drèze, Jean, Amartya Sen and Athar Hussain, eds. 1998. *The Political Economy of Hunger: Selected Essays*. Oxford: Clarendon Press.

Dumont, Louis. 1970. *Homo Hierarchicus: An Essay on the Caste System*. Chicago, IL: Chicago University Press.

FAO, IFAD and WFP (Food and Agriculture Organization of the United Nations, International Fund for Agricultural Development and World

Food Programme). 2015. *The State of Food Insecurity in the World 2015: Meeting the 2015 International Hunger Targets: Taking Stock of Uneven Progress*. Rome: FAO.

Finnis, Elizabeth. 2012. 'Redefining and Representing Minor Millets in South India'. In *Reimaging Marginalized Foods: Global Processes, Local Places*, edited by Elizabeth Finnis, 109–32. Tucson, AZ: University of Arizona Press.

Gillette, Maris Boyd. 2000. 'Children's Food and Islamic Dietary Restrictions in Xi'an'. In *Feeding China's Little Emperors: Food, Children and Social Change*, edited by Jun Jing, 71–93. Stanford, CA: Stanford University Press.

Goody, Jack. 1982. *Cooking, Cuisine and Class: A Study in Comparative Sociology*. Cambridge: Cambridge University Press.

Iverson, Vegard and P.S. Raghavendra. 2006. 'What the Signboard Hides: Food, Caste and Employability in Small South Indian Eating Places'. *Contributions to Indian Sociology* 40 (3): 311–41.

Janeja, Manpreet K. 2010. *Transactions in Taste: The Collaborative Lives of Everyday Bengali Food*. New Delhi: Routledge.

Khare, R.S. 1976. *The Hindu Hearth and Home*. New Delhi: Vikas Publishing House.

———, ed. 1992. *The Eternal Food: Gastronomic Ideas and Experiences of Hindus and Buddhists*. Albany, NY: State University of New York Press.

———. 2012. 'Globalizing South Asian Food Cultures: Earlier Stops to New Horizons'. In *Curried Cultures: Globalization, Food, and South Asia*, edited by Krishnendu Ray and Tulasi Srinivas, 237–54. Berkeley, CA: University of California Press.

Khare, R.S. and M.S.A. Rao, eds. 1986. *Food, Society and Culture: Aspects of South Asian Food Systems*. Durham, NC: Carolina Academic Press.

Latour, Bruno. 2005. *Reassembling the Social: An Introduction to Actor-Network-Theory*. Oxford: Oxford University Press.

Lévi-Strauss, Claude. 1966 (1965). 'The Culinary Triangle'. *Partisan Review* 33 (4): 586–96.

———. 1973 (1955). *Tristes Tropiques*. Translated from French by John and Doreen Weightman. New York, NY: Atheneum.

———. 1983 (1964). *The Raw and the Cooked. Mythologiques*. Vol. 1. Translated from French by John and Doreen Weightman. Chicago, IL: University of Chicago Press.

Madsen, Stig Toft and Geoffrey Gardella. 2012. 'Udupi Hotels: Entrepreneurship, Reform, and Revival'. In *Curried Cultures: Globalization, Food, and South Asia*, edited by Krishnendu Ray and Tulasi Srinivas, 91–109. Berkeley, CA: University of California Press.

Mander, Harsh. 2012. *Ash in the Belly: India's Unfinished Battle Against Hunger*. New Delhi: Penguin Books.

Mankekar, Purnima. 2002. '"India Shopping": Indian Grocery Stores and Transnational Configurations of Belonging'. *Ethnos* 67 (1): 75–97.

Marriott, McKim. 1968. 'Caste Ranking and Food Transactions: A Matrix Analysis'. In *Structure and Change in Indian Society*, edited by Milton Singer and Bernard S. Cohn, 133–71. New York, NY: Wenner-Gren Foundation.

Mayer, Adrian. 1960. *Caste and Kinship in Central India: A Village and Its Region*. London: Routledge.

Mintz, Sidney W. 1986. *Sweetness and Power: The Place of Sugar in Modern History*. New York, NY: Penguin Books.

Narayan, Uma. 1995. 'Eating Cultures: Incorporation, Identity, and Indian Food'. *Social Identities* 1 (1): 63–86.

Olivelle, Patrick. 1995. 'Food in India: A Review Essay'. *Journal of Indian Philosophy* 23 (3): 367–80.

Osella, Caroline. 2008. 'Introduction'. Special issue on *Food: Memory, Pleasure and Politics, South Asia: Journal of South Asian Studies*, n.s., 31 (1): 1–9.

Parry, Jonathan. 1999. 'Two Cheers for Reservations: The Satnamis and the Steel Plant'. In *Institutions and Inequalities: Essays in Honour of André Béteille*, edited by Ramachandra Guha and Jonathan Parry, 128–69. New Delhi: Oxford University Press.

Patel, Raj. 2007. *Stuffed and Starved: What Lies Behind the World Food Crisis*. London: Portobello Books.

Ray, Krishnendu. 2004. *The Migrant's Table: Meals and Memories in Bengali–American Households*. Philadelphia, PA: Temple University Press.

Ray, Krishnendu and Tulasi Srinivas. 2012. 'Introduction'. In *Curried Cultures: Globalization, Food, and South Asia*, edited by Krishnendu Ray and Tulasi Srinivas, 3–28. Berkeley, CA: University of California Press.

Ray, Utsa. 2015. *Culinary Culture in Colonial India: A Cosmopolitan Platter and the Middle-Class*. Delhi: Cambridge University Press.

Rege, Sharmila, Deepa Tak, Sangita Thosar and Tina Aranha, eds. 2009. *Isn't This Plate Indian? Dalit Histories and Memories of Food*. Pune: Krantijyoti Savitribai Phule Women's Studies Centre, University of Pune.

Roy, Modhumita. 2010. 'Some Like It Hot: Class, Gender and Empire in the Making of Mulligatawny Soup'. *Economic & Political Weekly* 45 (32): 66–75.

Roy, Nilanjana S. 2004. *A Matter of Taste: The Penguin Book of Indian Writings on Food*. New Delhi: Penguin Books.

Roy, Parama. 2010. *Alimentary Tracts: Appetites, Aversions, and the Postcolonial*. Durham, NC: Duke University Press.

Saunders, Jennifer B. 2007. '"I Don't Eat Meat": Discourse on Food among Transnational Hindus'. *Contributions to Indian Sociology* 41 (2): 203–33.

Scheper-Hughes, Nancy. 1993. *Death Without Weeping: The Violence of Everyday Life in Brazil*. Berkeley, CA: University of California Press.

Sengupta, Jayanta. 2012. 'Nation on a Platter: The Culture and Politics of Food and Cuisine in Colonial Bengal'. In *Curried Cultures: Globalization, Food, and South Asia*, edited by Krishnendu Ray and Tulasi Srinivas, 73–87. Berkeley, CA: University of California Press.

Shaffer, Holly. 2012. 'Dum Pukht: A Pseudo-historical Cuisine'. In *Curried Cultures: Globalization, Food, and South Asia*, edited by Krishnendu Ray and Tulasi Srinivas, 110–25. Berkeley, CA: University of California Press.

Shukla, Siddheshwar. 2014. 'Mid-day Meal'. *Economic & Political Weekly* 49 (7): 51–57.

Singh, Bhrigupati. 2015. *Poverty and the Quest for Life: Spiritual and Material Striving in Rural India*. New Delhi: Oxford University Press.

Solomon, Harris. 2015. '"The Taste No Chef Can Give": Processing Street Food in Mumbai'. *Cultural Anthropology* 30 (1): 65–90.

Staples, James. 2008. '"Go on, Just Try Some!" Meat and Meaning-making Among South Indian Christians'. *South Asia: Journal of South Asian Studies* 31 (1): 36–55.

———. 2014. 'Civilising Tastes: From Caste to Class in South Indian Foodways'. In *Food Consumption in Global Perspective: Essays in the Anthropology of Food in Honour of Jack Goody*, edited by Jakob A. Klein and Anne Murcott, 65–86. New York, NY: Palgrave Macmillan.

Strümpell, Christian. 2008. '"We Work Together, We Eat Together": Conviviality and Modernity in a Company Settlement in South Orissa'. *Contributions to Indian Sociology* 42 (3): 351–81.

Sutton, David. 2010. 'Food and the Senses'. *Annual Review of Anthropology* 39: 209–23.

Thieme, John and Ira Raja, eds. 2007. *The Table Is Laid: The Oxford Anthology of South Asian Food Writing*. New Delhi: Oxford University Press.

Toomey, Paul M. 1994. *Food from the Mouth of Krishna: Feasts and Festivities in a North Indian Pilgrimage Centre*. Delhi: Hindustan Publishing Corporation.

Valmiki, Omprakash. 2003. *Jhoothan: A Dalit's Life*. Translated by Arun Prabha Mukherjee. New York, NY: Columbia University Press.

Watts, Michael. 1983. *Silent Violence: Food, Famine, and Peasantry in Northern Nigeria*. Berkeley, CA: University of California Press.

Zimmerman, Francis. 1987. *The Jungle and the Aroma of Meats: An Ecological Theme in Hindu Medicine*. Berkeley, CA: University of California Press.

26

Cinematic Cultures

Sara Dickey

Introduction

In 1985, when I began anthropological research on Tamil film-watching and film-making, I knew of only one English-language ethnographic study of Indian cinema (Pfleiderer and Lutze 1985).[1] Several others followed in the early and mid-1990s, focusing primarily on film consumption and meaning-making (Dickey 1993a; Thiruchandran 1993); fans, actors and politics (Dickey 1993b; Pandian 1992); emerging technologies of film music (Manuel 1993); and the production, reception and political uses of film posters and hoardings (Jacob 1997, 1998). In the 20-plus years that have followed this early work, the scholarly landscape has been radically altered. As the field has burgeoned, audiences in particular have received increasing attention from sociologists and anthropologists (and from others using similar methods), as the purview of cinema-related practices and technologies has meanwhile continued to broaden. Until very recently, however, the geographic area(s) of this research remained limited, with the great preponderance focusing on North Indian middle-class audiences and South Asian diasporic viewers, with Tamil and Bengali cinema also figuring with some frequency. By 2010, however, the scope had begun to widen to

[1] Robert L. Hardgrave, Jr. (1973, 1975) had also carried out research on Tamil films and their roles in the making of politicians that was, if not exactly ethnographic, qualitative and interview-based.

other industries and to take up the complicated notion of 'Bollywood film' itself (see Dickey and Dudrah 2010).

Since then, the landscape has altered again. In this chapter, I examine research that has pushed new boundaries over the past several years. I move broadly from audiences to producers, and from cinema-centric to extra-cinematic activities. As the research itself compels us to recognise, however, neither of these distinctions can be sustained. Audiences perform and produce, producers consume, and cinematic 'culture' is vivified with a life of its own.

Audiences and Genres, Diversified

Still, I begin this review with audiences, where my own interests in cinema studies originated in a time when audiences seemed clearly demarcated from producers. Within the literature about spectators of Indian films that has appeared over the past two decades, a high proportion has focused on diasporic South Asian audiences. It has been argued that much of this work has depicted diasporic viewers either as nostalgic consumers 'now "hooked" on the supposed "traditions" of the mother country' or as successful professional migrants 'using "Bollywood" as a source of pride' (Banaji 2013: 394). Recent studies, however, have complicated such approaches, demonstrating the heterogeneity of and boundary maintenance within audiences; the multiplicity of viewing practices and responses to films; and consumers' uses of cinematic texts, activities and imaginations in everyday life (see, e.g., Banaji 2012, 2013; Dudrah 2012; Lallmahomed-Aumeerally 2014; Vandevelde 2013; Vandevelde et al. 2015).

Newer trends in audience analyses expand our knowledge of Indian cinema viewers and industries even further. Shakuntala Rao's (2007) research with 'non-elite' Punjabi audiences not only forcefully revealed those viewers' rejection of mainstream Bollywood as irrelevant to their lives and tastes, it also interrogated the invisibility of such audiences in Indian cinema scholarship. Similarly, Kalpana Ram (2008) took to task middle-class viewers and critics alike for hypocritically denigrating South Indian goddess films and their viewers. Such genres and audiences have slowly begun to appear in recent scholarship (Dickey and Dudrah 2010: 207–08), featuring primarily in studies of 'regional' industries and non-mainstream genres.

Two prime examples regard the Santali and Bhojpuri film industries, both of which rely heavily on a VCD technology that makes the films relatively inexpensive to produce, purchase and rent (Manuel 2012; Schleiter 2014). Markus Schleiter (2014) examines Santal communities' divergent responses to Santali films, which are typically set in rural backdrops in the Santali 'homeland' in Odisha. Focusing his investigation on three groups that vary by rurality/urbanity, class and region, Schleiter (2014: 193) argues that 'imagining a Santal community in connection with Santali movies mainly derives from regionally specific ways of mediating a Santal belonging and does not follow a unified pattern throughout the regions'. Thus, while villagers in Odisha incorporate video showings into 'pre-existing cultural practices' such as 'traditional dance' performances, middle-class Santal families residing in Kolkata—who, unlike Odisha villagers, have adopted Bengali *bhadralok* ideals—have 'felt an urge to put Santal tradition into writing and to institutionalize their culture associations' (Schleiter 2014: 193). These Kolkata viewers self-consciously position their class tastes and practices by rejecting the films' depictions as too 'modern' and therefore culturally inauthentic. Santal migrants in a hostile Assam, on the other hand, use the videos to envision connections with a large, imagined Santal community elsewhere, despite perceiving the ethnic practices in these films as diverging from their own (ibid.). Schleiter's work addresses the diversity of ways in which an industry associated with ethnic 'traditions' and 'homeland' can be adopted in the service of producing and performing (disparate) identities.

It also raises the question of what a cinema's region *is*. This question arises even more forcefully in key studies of the much larger Bhojpuri industry, whose viewers are precisely the subaltern whom Rao and Ram evoke. The problematic of location begins with the contention that a Bhojpuri 'region' does not in fact exist (Hardy 2015; Manuel 2012: 228). Bhojpuri, which is stereotyped as a 'rustic' language, is spoken in eastern Uttar Pradesh, western Bihar and nearby areas in surrounding states. It is 'highly regionalized, with speech patterns changing, as the saying goes, every nine *kos* (about every 18 miles)' (Hardy 2010: 232). For these reasons, Kathryn Hardy (2015) in particular argues that the Bhojpuri region is a fictive one—that is, a 'location' that has neither clear territorial boundaries (and no coincidence with official state borders) nor a clearly circumscribed dialect community. Moreover, Bhojpuriya is a 'community' that defines itself in part through male urban migration circuits, thus extending beyond (or exceeding) the putative region, and Bhojpuri films often trace 'the physical circuits between rural, urban, and back again' in both narrative and production, representing a 'new

Bhojpuri identity that spans migrants and farmers' (Hardy 2010: 241; Srivastava 2015). Finally, and most intriguingly, many of the working-class urban men who perforce perform membership in the community by virtue of regularly constituting the films' audiences are not, in a linguistic or geographical origin sense, Bhojpuri (Hardy 2015; also see Srivastava 2011: 124). In troubling and teasing the assumed equivalence and containment of geography, language and identity, Hardy throws open the entire notion of a region and its role as affective signifier. For whom, we might ask, does Bhojpuriya comprise a nostalgic and aspirational address, and why?

Cinematic genres that might themselves be considered 'subaltern' have also received more scholarly attention of late. One example is soft porn. Bhrigupati Singh (2008: 250, 257) calls the 'C-circuit "morning show"' in a Delhi theatre 'the experience of modernity in its most distinctly urban form', with many of these films as transnational in their creation and circulation as any Bollywood A-list film. William Mazzarella (2013: 164–65) discusses the post-liberalisation production of *desi* porn, while Navaneetha Mokkil Maruthur (2011) scrutinises the history of public and critical reaction to the widely circulated Malayalam film *Avalude Ravukal* (*Her Nights*, 1978) that is commonly seen as initiating the genre. Maruthur traces hegemonic attitudes towards *Avalude Ravukal* from early castigation as pornography to the later recuperation of the film as 'art' cinema. Her innovative analysis looks broadly at the 'different modes of circulation' of the film, including criticism, screenplay, posters and music. Singh, Mazzarella and Maruthur force us to question our understandings of the conception and criticism of 'soft porn' films in India.[2]

Fan club members are often imagined as the most visibly (male) subaltern of viewers. Some of the earliest social science research on cinema focused on fans, fan clubs and politics, and 'rowdy' fan associations have featured centrally in both public and scholarly discussions. Recent research on fans undermines assumptions, however, that fans are motivated by absolute devotion and political fervour, and pushes us to focus on fans' own potency and performativity. Roos Gerritsen, who has worked with both film star fans and party workers in Tamil Nadu, argues that supporters who produce banners and other visual images of these figures act as 'kingmakers' not just for the star/politician but also

[2] Also see Hoek (2013) for Bangladesh.

for themselves, 'as they transpose the power of their leader onto them-selves via these images' (Gerritsen 2014: 552; see also Srinivas 2016: 194–98). Similar processes are seen in Andhra Pradesh in S.V. Srinivas' (2009) *Megastar*, which offers by far the most thorough and chrono-logically deep research among fans associations to date. Re-examining his own earlier work on Telugu fandom, Srinivas provides a nuanced understanding of fans' relationships to the star, foregrounding their organisational independence as well as the 'conditional nature of the fan's loyalty' centred on 'their well defined set of entitlements related to [the star] and his films' (ibid.: xxviii).

Srinivas goes further, however. He argues that fans' activities are not simply bids for resources. We must also recognise them, he contends, as acts rooted in cinema itself. In exploring this 'cinematic' nature of fan activity, Srinivas proffers an especially fascinating discussion of the 'meaninglessness and "pure surfaces" of "fan productions"'—meaningless, that is, 'in that [such production] gestures towards an obsessive engagement with the cinema and not some hidden cultural or political foundation of the actions performed' (ibid.: 46). This 'pure performance' (ibid.: 45) is particularly visible during celebrations at first-day showings, where 'what really matters during these shows is not so much the spectacle on screen but the one before it, in which the viewer/fan is also the performer' (ibid.: 37).[3]

Lakshmi Srinivas recounts strikingly similar performances in Bangalore. For new releases in the city, 'fans territorialize the theater and in large numbers even take over the streets' (Srinivas 2016: 195). While S.V. Srinivas refers to an 'inversion' in which 'the presence of fans... seems to make the film happen' (Srinivas 2009: 7), Lakshmi Srinivas identifies another intriguing inversion in which youth who are typically 'marginalized in society' gain 'visibility and influence' during new release festivities (Srinivas 2016: 195). She too sees fans acting in their own interests as well as the star's: the demands they make on exhibitors and distributors for a proper new release celebration, for example, are intended to give 'face' to both the star and the fan (ibid.: 197). Going beyond her earlier analysis of 'active audiences', Srinivas argues that these performative fans 'produce entertainment spectacle while routinely overturning the order that separates film space from

---

[3] For another approach to the fan as performer, see Kakar (2010).

theater or audience space'. Indeed, she notes, 'reception is performance using the film as backdrop' (ibid.: 217–18). The line between fan/star and audience/actor blurs.[4]

Cinematic Spaces

Cinema halls and theatres have themselves received a burst of scholarly attention, examined both as sites on which elites project class anxieties and as spaces that yield particular types of audiences. From their inception, it seems, Indian cinema halls have reflected and invigorated social divisions (Hughes 2000; Kumar 2016; Mazzarella 2013: 200–01; Srinivas 2000). A new 20th-century public space, one that soon proved worrisome for the dominant elite (Hughes 2000), emerged with the cinema hall and has since formed a key part of cinematic cultures. Not only do cinema halls accommodate the cultural production of spectacle and ritual, but they are also themselves, it might be said, creators of culture. Multiplex theatres have recently received extended analysis in this vein. While 'upper class' cinema halls pre-existed multiplexes (see, e.g., Singh 2008: 254; Srinivas 2016), multiplexes are credited with crafting a new kind of middle- and upper-class audience. These spectators—most of whom, Adrian Athique (2013: 407) argues, are actually middle-class 'aspirants', not the truly wealthy—have (again) taken up public film-viewing, ironically, in order to consume the multiplex's private, controlled, individualised space from which the masses are barred. But spectators themselves are molded by this space, as 'the carefully considered architecture of the multiplex transforms the cinema crowd, long associated with mob behavior, into a marketable commodity for retailers and advertisers' (ibid.: 413). Thus, such theatres produce an audience that is both 'proper'—that is, a 'decent' rather than

---

[4] Other recent work explores different forms of fandom. Aswin Punathambekar (2013: 187) fruitfully directs us beyond 'the cinema hall and the political party' to new sites, in this case to online fans of music director A.R. Rahman. Such fan groups are quite different from those usually studied: Punathambekar notes that the 'Rahman fan community is an elite space and one that is defined explicitly in opposition to "rowdy" fan associations... [they] are not dominated by men... [nor] mobilizing around caste or linguistic identity' (ibid.: 185). (Also see C.S. Venkiteswaran [2009] on members of art cinema film societies.) Online fans have received surprisingly little attention from social scientists (cf. Maruthur 2011: 283, n. 7), though see Hassam (2012) and also Baker (2013) and Dudrah (2012: 3, 100–03) on *actors* uses of social media to connect with fans.

a 'cheap' crowd—and primed to consume in this aspirational space (see also Athique and Hill 2010; Ganti 2012; Vandevelde et al. 2015).[5]

Theatres may influence audiences' decision-making even more broadly. The halls' attributes, along with other elements that viewers take into account when choosing films, emerge most clearly in Lakshmi Srinivas' (2016) ethnography. Srinivas argues cogently that audiences are not simply consuming a *film*; rather, a great deal more is at play—and at stake—in what they experience, enjoy, imbibe and consume. Her research reveals that Bangalore viewers pay less attention to the content or cast of a film than to numerous other features: the location of the theatre in which it plays; the availability of tickets in specific sections; the confluence of the film's language with other potential audience members' class, 'ethnicity' and gender; and the availability of friends and family to attend a movie on a specific day or at a specific time. Srinivas expands the activity of 'viewing' to include a lengthy process that begins with deliberations about which film to attend (a large part of which apparently centres on cinema space and locality), and continues on to acquiring the tickets, 'watching' and 'reworking' a film collaboratively with other audience members, and enjoying intermission activities, and finally extends to the discussions that ensue once the film has ended (see also Vandevelde et al. 2015). Srinivas (2016: 98) provides an especially provocative discussion of 'the public and social life... played out in queues', underscoring the role class plays in this social phenomenon: how people in the line are read by staff, which people choose to stand in the queue and which avoid it, who gets tickets using 'pull' rather than by waiting in line, who uses scalpers and how scalpers apply class assumptions in order to sell their tickets (ibid.: 95–115).

Crafting Film, Crafting Ethnography

Perhaps it is only my predilection for the subject, but to my mind, much contemporary Indian cinema analysis continues the literature's longstanding exploration of class issues—much more so than, say, caste, religion, gender or ethnicity, though most of these appear occasionally

---

[5] Cinema halls have become animated in other ways as well. Singh (2008) narrates what is essentially a life history of a Delhi cinema hall, following its trajectory from A- to B- to C-circuit showings, and Srinivas (2016: Chapter 3) portrays Bengaluru theatres as spaces with characters, personalities, histories and nostalgic 'folklore'.

as analytical themes.[6] ('Race', on the other hand, does form a frequent theme in research on the diaspora, a point to which I return below.) This is true in different ways of two recent ethnographies of film production personnel—Tejaswini Ganti's (2012) *Producing Bollywood* and Clare M. Wilkinson-Weber's (2014) *Fashioning Bollywood*—though a third ethnography, Anand Pandian's (2015) *Reel World*, is less focused on class. These three texts are, as far as I am aware, the first full-length ethnographies of film production personnel written in English[7] (appearing, for reasons worth considering, a full 20 years after the first ethnographic monographs on Indian cinema audiences were published). A side-by-side reading of these three studies reveals a number of consonant findings, as well as key points on which the authors differ.

Ganti's intricately and compellingly argued study explores Hindi film-makers' distinction-creating practices. While she interviewed and observed 'producers, directors, actors and actresses, writers, distributors, exhibitors... [and] journalists' (Ganti 2012: 25), Ganti builds from the premise that 'the *figure of the audience* is central to understanding the nature of Hindi film production' (ibid.: 23, emphasis added). Film-makers struggle to gentrify and rationalise their work in order to 'resolve the dilemmas posed by the central features of the production culture... of the Hindi film industry: the immense disdain that filmmakers express for both the industry and their audiences, as well as the tremendous uncertainty that characterizes the filmmaking process' (ibid.: 6). Thus, their drive for distinction derives from both class insecurity and financial insecurity, with the audience (whether the derided audience of the mass or the 'valourised' elite audience conjured in current audience imaginaries—see Ganti 2012: 36 and Chapter 8) serving as cipher for film-makers' own class boundary maintenance. Ganti documents a continuing process to create respectability in an industry that until very recently has been morally suspect on a variety of grounds. These film-makers' discursive strategies echo the sentiments I heard from Tamil and Telugu film-makers in Madras in the mid-1980s, and are echoed in return in Srinivas' (2016: 51) discussion of the drive for 'decency' among stars and film-makers, which demands disdain for mass audiences. But while the performance of such disdain may be widespread,

[6] See, for example, Srinivas (2009) on caste, Derné (2000) and Nakassis (2016) (as well as most studies of fans associations, at least implicitly) on masculinity, and ethnographies of regional audiences (including those reviewed above) that address ethnicity.

[7] These were preceded by Emmanuel Grimaud's (2004) *Bombay Film Studio: ou comment les films se font à Bombay*.

if not universal (see Pandian 2015: 290, n. 19 for a counter-example), Ganti, more than any of the rest of us, demonstrates the imbrication of the audience in the production of producers.

Clare Wilkinson-Weber's perspicacious *Fashioning Bollywood* explores another set of personnel—most of whom rarely feature in cinema studies—and highlights distinct class features of the industry. Wilkinson-Weber describes an array of socio-economic processes in the creation of film costume, arguing that 'costume is never simply about "fashion" or about a form of signaling behavior, but about labor, commodity consumption, enactment, and audience appropriation' (ibid.: 2). The political economy of costume involves designers, tailors, dressmen, retailers, stars, viewers and wearers, among many others. Wilkinson-Weber charts shifting class schisms among these personnel from the 1940s onward. Like Ganti, she highlights the struggles to maintain (or dissolve) group boundaries, to claim modernity, and to assert cultural capital. Ideologies of caste, gender and the body also shape the many processes of costuming as well as claims to distinction (or attempts to counter them). Here again, we see an intertwining of producers and consumers. Wilkinson-Weber's work underscores Srinivas' contention that all of cinema is a 'collective' endeavour and experience (Srinivas 2016: 33). She argues that 'there are no singular geniuses presiding over the look or the meaning of a film' (Wilkinson-Weber 2014: 1), in addition to highlighting the dialectical meaning-making between those who create costumes/fashions and those who don them.

Anand Pandian offers a different sort of ethnography. Like almost all the other authors discussed here, he rejects the model of passive reception and active production; but his stylistically innovative writing demonstrates the illusory nature of this divide most thoroughly of all. Rollicking and contemplative in equal measure, *Reel World* is organised around concepts/features/compulsions of cinema—with chapters, for example, on 'Sound', 'Time', 'Imagination' and 'Fate'. Pandian too attends to a vast array of personnel: editors, directors, producers, theatre owners, distributors, art directors, cameramen, a vinyl poster maker, actors, choreographers, composers and music directors, sound studios, dubbing artistes—and the managers of many of these people. The narrative draws from fieldwork on 17 different Tamil film projects to move chronologically, though not linearly, through the processes of making a film. Rather than documenting 'cinematic cultures', however, Pandian explores the extent to which culture *is* cinematic—'life when everything begins to look and feel like film' (Pandian 2015: 2)—and compares the crafting of cinema with the crafting of ethnography. It would be hard to choose a favourite chapter, but at this moment, I find myself taken with 'Pleasure', in which he muses and twirls through the pleasures (and some agonies) of making and watching a dance scene. Unlike most critics and even scholars of Indian cinema (see Dickey 2009), Pandian neither distrusts nor disdains pleasure (or dreams, or fantasy), instead exploring its construction and sensual experience as a crucial affect in cinema and cinematic life.[8] He calls his work 'an anthropology of creation'.

Extra-cinematic Performances, Identities, Hegemonies

Finally, a burgeoning segment of Indian media scholarship explores extra-cinematic aspects of 'cinematic culture', particularly those enactments that have aptly been termed 'reanimations' (Nakassis 2016). Amanda Weidman (2012: 308) describes such reanimations as processes in which filmic elements are 'appropriated and performed—in everyday interactions and in performance contexts, to accomplish specific kinds of social and cultural work'. 'Consumers' become producers yet again, (re)corporealising filmic elements in service of a self.[9]

The diverse literature on Indian films' song and dance elements serves especially well to illustrate the process of 'self-fashioning' within the many examples of such reanimations.[10] Weidman, for example, analyses amateur 'culture shows and singing contests' in which girls enact song and dance scenes from Tamil films—wearing clothing and performing movements that are much more sexually conservative than

---

[8] Other studies of film personnel include Srinivas (2009) on the actor Chiranjeevi (see also Srinivas 2013), Weidman (2012, 2014) on playback singers, Singh (2008) on theatre owners and managers, and Mazzarella (2013) on censors.

[9] Note that cinema personnel themselves may reanimate filmic performances, as when playback singers perform in concerts (Weidman 2012); when actors, dancers and singers enact a live preview on stage at a film showing (Singh 2008); and when artistes present Bollywood roadshows (Dudrah 2012).

[10] Two fertile areas that I must largely neglect for reasons of space are popular music and still images. For several examples of current work on popular music in relation to Bollywood, see Gregory D. Booth and Bradley Shope's (2014) wide-ranging collection *More than Bollywood: Studies in Indian Popular Music*. For recent ethnographic studies of cinematic visual culture, see in particular Roos Gerritsen's (2009) photo essay on posters, as well as the many evocative essays that appear in *Tasveer Ghar*. Available at: http://www.tasveergharindia.net/frmessaylisting.aspx (accessed on 5 June 2018).

in the originals (ibid.: 313–14). These shows, which circulate widely on YouTube, 'derive their meaning from their similarity or difference from the film version of the song sequence' (ibid.: 307), and therein 'figure in complex projects of self-fashioning by young women negotiating the boundaries of acceptable female public performance' (ibid.: 314). It is fascinating to compare these carefully circumscribed performances with Nakassis' spectacular discussion of the intricate, precisely modulated and highly quotidian ways in which male college youth in Chennai and Madurai constantly produce 'style' through the reanimations of cinema 'fractions' (Nakassis 2016: 159–87). These youths do *not* take part in song-and-dance shows, having the gendered privilege to exceed patriarchally scripted and staged performances.

Elsewhere, dance as a productive practice is somewhat less gendered. In Mumbai and other locales, 'Bollywood dance' schools are finding success (Morcom 2015; Shresthova 2011). Anna Morcom (2015: 291) depicts the Bollywood 'dance craze' as 'a model case of a neoliberal cultural formation, foregrounding ideas, aesthetics and socio-economic realities of work, entrepreneurship, mobility, success, and individualism'. Sangita Shresthova's (2011) groundbreaking work employs Bollywood dance as a lens on diaspora and identity in Los Angeles, negotiations of gender ideologies in Kathmandu, and (like Morcom) bodies in Mumbai. Class, gender and their intersections with modernity are lucidly foregrounded in these analysts' explorations of the discipline of dance.

Race too figures prominently in studies of 'Bollywood' dance performances in the diaspora. Several authors examine the articulation of dance with diasporic negotiations of race, asking how identity is enmeshed in and determined by local structures of and discourses about inequality. Meena Khandelwal and Chitra Akkoor (2014: 279) write about college dance competitions as platforms for South Asian-American students to 'work out the tensions and contradictions of ethnic identity'. As an expression of ethnicity, they argue, Bollywood dance provides several advantages for these youth: it is secular and thus cuts across religious identities; it can appear suitably modest in the eyes of a parental generation while still being 'cool' in the eyes of white peers; and, compared to classical music and dance, it is easy to learn. Khandelwal and Akkoor argue that dance as an emblem of 'culture' 'exemplifies the dynamic by which US multiculturalism depoliticizes racial conflict by focusing on the celebration of culture' (ibid.: 291).

Omme-Salma Rahemtullah (2012) extends this criticism further in her analysis of a Bollywood dance club in Toronto. Like earlier writers on diasporic film consumption, she sees Bollywood as critical to the construction of a shared diasporic 'South Asian' identity. Yet in a cultural context in which non-dominant identities must respond to a racism cloaked in multiculturalism, she contends that the alleged South Asian identity must 'be knowable: straight, Indian, Hindu, and middle class' (ibid.: 244). The function of Bollywood dance reanimations, she argues, is less to emblematise a nostalgic identity than to 're-center the white Canadian as the subject of national formation' (ibid.: 250). Just as Bhojpuri and Santali film viewers in India have discursively constructed unequal communities parsed by class, region, dialect and ethnicity, so the South Asian tag in this diaspora is shaped to some extent by hegemonic forces outside its bearing.

Conclusion

To return to the landscape metaphor I briefly cultivated at the opening, Rajinder Dudrah (2012: 8) reminds us that 'we might also ask about routes and circuits that are not easily familiar, or tracks that are not yet fully known to us in and through the films and therefore unworn academically'. My aim in this chapter has been to identify some of those paths now being revealed and explored in the most fruitful ways. Cinema is a collective creation. Many elements and constructions exceed their bounds: regions, participants and cinema itself, as its 'fractions' (Nakassis 2016) enter and inform everyday cultural processes. Subnational or transnational identities may unwittingly serve local, national and international ideologies of class, race and gender. The questions become: Who performs? Who produces? Who consumes? Given such processes, which communities are created through cinema, and who rightly belongs? Most importantly, what *exactly* is performatively brought into being through the medium/media of cinema, and to what ends?

References

Athique, Adrian. 2013. 'Cinema as Social Space: The Case of the Multiplex'. In *Routledge Handbook of Indian Cinema*, edited by K. Moti Gokulsing and Wimal Dissanayake, 402–14. New York, NY: Routledge.

Athique, Adrian and Douglas Hill. 2010. *The Multiplex in India: A Cultural Economy of Urban Leisure*. London: Routledge.

Baker, Steven. 2013. 'Virtual *Darshan*: Social Networking and Virtual Communities in the Hindi Film Context'. In *Routledge Handbook of Indian Cinema*, edited by K. Moti Gokulsing and Wimal Dissanayake, 415–26. New York, NY: Routledge.

Banaji, Shakuntala. 2012. '"Bollywood" Adolescents: Young Viewers Discuss Childhood, Class and Hindi Films'. In *Postcolonial Audiences: Readers, Viewers and Reception*, edited by Bethan Benwell, James Procter and Gemma Robinson, 57–72. London: Routledge.

———. 2013. 'Hindi Film Audiences Outside South Asia'. In *Routledge Handbook of Indian Cinema*, edited by K. Moti Gokulsing and Wimal Dissanayake, 391–401. New York, NY: Routledge.

Booth, Gregory and Bradley Shope, eds. 2014. *More than Bollywood: Studies in Indian Popular Music*. Oxford: Oxford University Press.

Derné, Steve. 2000. *Movies, Masculinity, and Modernity: An Ethnography of Men's Filmgoing in India*. Westport, CT: Greenwood Press.

Dickey, Sara. 1993a. *Cinema and the Urban Poor in South India*. Cambridge: Cambridge University Press.

———. 1993b. 'The Politics of Adulation: Cinema and the Production of Politicians in South India'. *The Journal of Asian Studies* 52 (2): 340–72.

———. 2009. 'Fantasy, Escape, and Other Mixed Delights: What Have Film Analysts Seen in Popular Indian Cinema?' *Projections: Journal of Movies and Mind* 3 (2): 1–19.

Dickey, Sara and Rajinder Dudrah. 2010. 'South Asian Cinemas: Widening the Lens'. *South Asian Popular Culture* 8 (3): 207–12.

Dudrah, Rajinder. 2012. *Bollywood Travels: Culture, Diaspora and Border Crossings in Popular Hindi Cinema*. London: Routledge.

Ganti, Tejaswini. 2012. *Producing Bollywood: Inside the Contemporary Hindi Film Industry*. Durham, NC: Duke University Press.

Gerritsen, Roos. 2009. 'Cine-addictions: Image Trails Running from the Intimate Sphere to the Public Eye'. South Asian Visual Culture Series, no. 2. Edited by Christiane Brosius. Available at: http://crossasia-repository. ub.uni-heidelberg.de/219/1/Roos_Gerritsen_2009._Cine_Addictions.pdf (accessed on 1 May 2016).

———. 2014. 'Canvases of Political Competition: Image Production as Politics in Tamil Nadu, India'. *Ethnos* 79 (4): 551–76.

Grimaud, Emmanuel. 2004. *Bombay Film Studio: ou comment les films se font à Bombay* [Bombay Film Studio: Or how films are made in Bombay]. Paris: CNRS Éditions.

Hardgrave, Robert L., Jr. 1973. 'Politics and the Film in Tamilnadu: The Stars and the DMK'. *Asian Survey* 13 (3): 288–305.

———. 1975. 'When Stars Displace the Gods: The Folk Culture of Cinema in Tamil Nadu'. Occasional Paper Series, no. 3. Center for Asian Studies, the University of Texas, Arlington, TX.

Hardy, Kathryn C. 2010. 'Mediating Bhojpuriya: Migration, Circulation, and Bhojpuri Cinema'. *South Asian Popular Culture* 8 (3): 231–44.

———. 2015. 'Constituting a Diffuse Region: Cartographies of Mass-mediated Bhojpuri Belonging'. *BioScope* 6 (2): 145–64.

Hassam, Andrew. 2012. 'Bollywood Internet Forums and Australian Cultural Diplomacy'. In *The Magic of Bollywood*, edited by Anjali Gera Roy, 254–76. New Delhi: SAGE.

Hoek, Lotte. 2013. *Cut-pieces: Celluloid Obscenity and Popular Cinema in Bangladesh*. New York, NY: Columbia University Press.

Hughes, Stephen P. 2000. 'Policing Silent Film Exhibition in Colonial South India'. In *Making Meaning in Indian Cinema*, edited by Ravi S. Vasudevan, 39–64. New Delhi: Oxford University Press.

Jacob, Preminda. 1997. 'From Co-star to Deity: Popular Representations of Jayalalitha Jayaram'. *Woman: A Cultural Review* 8 (3): 327–37.

———. 1998. 'Media Spectacles: The Production and Reception of Tamil Cinema Advertisements'. *Visual Anthropology* 11 (4): 287–322.

Kakar, Shalini. 2010. '"Starring" Madhuri as Durga: The Madhuri Dixit Temple and Performative Fan-Bhakti of Pappu Sardar'. *International Journal of Hindu Studies* 13 (3): 391–416.

Khandelwal, Meena and Chitra Akkoor. 2014. 'Dance On! Inter-collegiate Indian Dance Competitions as a New Cultural Form'. *Cultural Dynamics* 26 (2): 277–98.

Kumar, Akshaya. 2016. 'Bhojpuri Cinema and the "Rearguard": Gendered Leisure, Gendered Promises'. *Quarterly Review of Film and Video* 33 (2): 151–75.

Lallmahomed-Aumeerally, Naseem. 2014. 'A Reading of Bollywood Cinema as a Site of Melancholia for Indo-Mauritian Muslim Female Youth'. *South Asian Popular Culture* 12 (3): 149–62.

Manuel, Peter. 1993. *Cassette Culture: Popular Music and Technology in North India*. Chicago, IL: University of Chicago Press.

———. 2012. 'Popular Music as Popular Expression in North India and the Bhojpuri Region, from Cassette Culture to VCD Culture'. *South Asian Popular Culture* 10 (3): 223–36.

Maruthur, Navaneetha Mokkil. 2011. 'Re-viewing *Her Nights*: Modes of Excess in Indian Cinema'. *South Asian Popular Culture* 9 (3): 273–85.

Mazzarella, William. 2013. *Censorium*. Durham, NC: Duke University Press.

Morcom, Anna. 2015. 'Terrains of Bollywood Dance: (Neoliberal) Capitalism and the Transformation of Cultural Economies'. *Ethnomusicology* 59 (2): 288–314.

Nakassis, Constantine V. 2016. *Doing* Style*: Youth and Mass Mediation in South India*. Chicago, IL: University of Chicago Press.

Pandian, Anand. 2015. *Reel World: An Anthropology of Creation*. Durham, NC: Duke University Press.

Pandian, M.S.S. 1992. *The Image Trap*. New Delhi: SAGE.

Pfleiderer, Beatrix and Lothar Lutze, eds. 1985. *The Hindi Film: Agent and Re-agent of Cultural Change*. New Delhi: Manohar Publishers.

Punathambekar, Aswin. 2013. *From Bombay to Bollywood: The Making of a Global Media Industry*. New York, NY: New York University Press.

Rahemtullah, Omme-Salma. 2012. 'Bollywood in da Club: Social Space in Toronto's "South Asian" Community'. In *The Magic of Bollywood*, edited by Anjali Gera Roy, 234–53. New Delhi: SAGE.

Ram, Kalpana. 2008. 'Bringing the Amman into Presence in Tamil Cinema: Cinema Spectatorship as Sensuous Apprehension'. In *Tamil Cinema*, edited by Selvaraj Velayutham, 44–58. London: Routledge.

Rao, Shakuntala. 2007. 'The Globalization of Bollywood: An Ethnography of Non-elite Audiences in India'. *The Communication Review* 10 (1): 57–76.

Schleiter, Markus. 2014. 'VCD Crossovers: Cultural Practice, Ideas of Belonging, and Santali Popular Movies'. *Asian Ethnology* 73 (1–2): 181–200.

Shresthova, Sangita. 2011. *Is It All About Hips?* New Delhi: SAGE.

Singh, Bhrigupati. 2008. '*Aadamkhor Haseena* (The Man-eating Beauty) and the Anthropology of a Moment'. *Contributions to Indian Sociology*, n.s., 42 (2): 249–79.

Srinivas, Lakshmi. 2016. *House Full: Indian Cinema and the Active Audience*. Chicago, IL: University of Chicago Press.

Srinivas, S.V. 2000. 'Is There a Public in the Cinema Hall?' *Framework* 42. Available at: http://media.wix.com/ugd/32cb69_95584ff57df547febaf04c3e0bafa3fc.pdf (accessed on 1 May 2016).

———. 2009. *Megastar: Chiranjeevi and Telugu Cinema After N.T. Rama Rao*. New Delhi: Oxford University Press.

———. 2013. *Politics as Performance: A Social History of the Telugu Cinema*. Ranikhet: Permanent Black.

Srivastava, Madhusri. 2011. 'Bhojpuri Cinema: Reasserting the "Bhojpuria" Roots of Migrants in Mumbai'. *Journal of Creative Communications* 6 (1 and 2): 123–39.

———. 2015. 'The "Bhojpuriya" Mumbaikar: Straddling Two Worlds'. *Contributions to Indian Sociology*, n.s., 49 (1): 77–101.

Thiruchandran, Selvy. 1993. 'The Ideological Factor in the Subordination of Women'. PhD Dissertation. University of Vrije.

Vandevelde, Iris. 2013. 'Revisiting the NRI "Genre": Indian Diasporic Engagements with NRI and Multiplex Films'. *South Asian Popular Culture* 11 (1): 47–60.

Vandevelde, Iris, Philippe Meers, Sofie Van Bauwel and Roel Vande Winkel. 2015. 'Sharing the Silver Screen: The Social Experience of Cinemagoing in the Indian Diaspora'. *BioScope* 6 (1): 88–106.

Venkiteswaran, C.S. 2009. 'Reflections on Film Society Movement in Keralam'. *South Asian Popular Culture* 7 (1): 65–71.

Weidman, Amanda. 2012. 'Voices of Meenakumari: Sound, Meaning, and Self-fashioning in Performances of an Item Number'. *South Asian Popular Culture* 10 (3): 307–18.

———. 2014. 'Neoliberal Logics of Voice: Playback Singing and Public Femaleness in South India'. *Culture, Theory and Critique* 55 (2): 175–93.

Wilkinson-Weber, Clare M. 2014. *Fashioning Bollywood: The Making and Meaning of Hindi Film Costume*. London: Bloomsbury Publishing.

27

The Sociology of Consumption in India

Towards a New Agenda

Margit van Wessel

Consumption and Culture

Sociological research of consumption in India so far has largely centred on the (mostly urban) middle class. Authors have predominantly situated the study of middle-class consumption in the context of the globalisation, economic liberalisation and economic growth. Thirty years have passed since liberalisation policies opened up the Indian economy, making ever more consumer goods available to those increasing numbers of Indians who could afford them. However, publications on consumptions have kept on framing the middle class and the Indian economy as 'emergent', as part of a wider advent of 'emergent economies' that through their growth were able to involve more consumption, of new goods and services, by more people (Eckhardt and Mahi 2012; Myers and Kent 2003).

Consumption in India has received considerable sociological and anthropological interest. Scholarship has focused on contextual and qualitative empirical study, zooming in on diverse practices of consumption, ranging from fashion to gold, household appliances, cell phones and cars, to less material practices such as yoga and wellness. The consumers authors focus on are mostly categorised as 'middle class' with some exceptions looking into consumption by lower classes (Nakassis 2012; Osella and Osella 1999).

The study of the 'new' consumption, mostly by the 'new' middle class which has come about over the past few decades, has by and large been done with an interest in the contribution of consumption to social identity. People's understandings and behaviours around consumption have consistently been studied as forms of self-actualising practices of people as member of social groupings. More specifically, consumption has also consistently been approached in terms of socially defined status aspirations, with consumption practices geared to meeting expectations deciding class belonging and distinction. Research from this stance has centred on consumers' strategies towards achievement of identity and status. It has brought forth detailed and insightful analyses of consumers as agents acting on these fronts (see, e.g., Askegaard and Eckhardt 2012; Dickey 2013; Nakassis 2012; Nisbett 2007; Osella and Osella 1999), as also more broad-ranging analyses (Brosius 2012; Mathur 2010). At the same time, consistently similar problematisations have been leading: ambivalence around meaning, cultural and moral dilemmas emerging from these, and consumers' navigation of these.

Research then typically revolves around tensions between meanings associated with the national, vernacular, traditional or moral, on the one hand, and meanings associated with the global or modern on the other (see, e.g., Harindranath 2013; Mathur 2010; van Wessel 2004). Scholars typically zoom in on one particular area of tension, often involving specific consumer practices, such as Gilbertson (2014) on fashion and respectability and Dean (2013) on prestige and the evil eye. Mostly, research thereby focuses on implications of specific consumption practices for consumer identity and status (Dean 2013; Gilbertson 2014; Mathur 2010; Nakassis 2012; van Wessel 2004). But creation and negotiation of the meaning of the consumed things themselves have also been addressed, as with the research of Nielsen and Wilhite (2015) on the Nano car, Nakassis' (2012) exploration of the meaning of counterfeits, Askegaard and Eckhardt's (2012) work on yoga and Annavarapu's (2016) on wellness.

The orientation of the research, focusing on creativity, appropriation, and interplay between meanings and reinterpretation for identity and status purposes by consumers as agents, has meant that consumption has primarily been explored as a new world of possibility for consumers themselves, in a private sense, within their social and cultural contexts. For sociologists and anthropologists, it appears that consumption has similarly offered a world of possibility—to look closely how consumption reshapes Indian society, be it with this constricted focus. Interestingly, little attention has been paid to wider implications of ever-growing consumption for Indian society and the world at large, especially considering how questions of sustainability and consumption have risen to the forefront in other parts of the world, for social science scholars and consumers alike.

Questions of Sustainability

It is time for a new research agenda regarding the study of consumption in India. This is not because culture is not of great importance when it comes to understanding present-day Indian society, or that consumption has waned, or that status aspirations have shifted or diminished. Beyond the 'newness' having worn off, other questions rooted in the same rise of consumption need researchers' attention. Beyond understanding what drives consumption behaviour and its significance for understanding Indian society in terms of identity and status, it is time for students of India to concentrate more on the wider implications of the same ever-growing consumption that scholars do not get tired of pointing out. This consumption has consequences beyond the identity and status that consumers seek to build through consumption. Furthermore, a concern for the societal relevance of sociological research will be productive: how to adjust and 'limit' consumption in order to address urgent sustainability concerns connected with the expansion of consumption. This is important considering major societal challenges India is faced with, including the threat and the already-felt implications of climate change in terms of drought, flooding and food security; ever-increasing waste; and serious air pollution. This is a matter of importance to Indian society at large, including middle-class consumers themselves. It is also a question of social justice, with the poor often likely to be more at risk and suffering relatively more of the adverse consequences of the expansion of consumption. It is also a question of taking a broader outlook, considering consumption as more than an Indian question, taking into account the limits of the earth's capacity to sustain consumption. While middle-class consumption in India so far has been studied through focusing upon what the global has meant for the local, it is now time to take a more cosmopolitan approach to the matter, zooming in on what local consumption means for our one planet (Beck 2006).

The 'emergent' economies have raised serious interest as developments that are 'transforming' patterns of economic wealth and consumption around the world. The UNDP's (2013) *Human Development Report*, for example, states, 'By 2030, more than 80% of the world's middle class is projected to be residing in the South and to account for 70% of total consumption expenditure', with the Asia-Pacific region hosting about two-thirds of the world's middle class by that time (ibid.: 14). Scholars of consumption who study the phenomenon from an interest in sustainability frame the rise and spread of consumption as problematic. Consumer choices are widely understood to be contributing to serious environmental problems (see, e.g., Dauvergne 2010; Hansen 2016; Shwom and Lorenzen 2012). The growth of consumption and the choices consumers make raise a range of questions about its wider implications: What are its environmental consequences? Who gets to be faced with these consequences? How can questions of responsibility and sustainability be addressed to deal with the consequences of consumption? (Dauvergne 2008, 2010). For Hansen et al. (2016: 6), the growth of consumption in the 'emergent' economies makes the study of changing consumption practices in the South indeed a critical area of academic enquiry from a sustainability perspective. They call for a deeper understanding of the social, economic and cultural processes implied in these changes. Going beyond this, others argue that it is high time to address the systemic backgrounds of consumption (see, e.g., Dauvergne 2010; Fernandes 2009).

Attention towards sustainability in the study of consumption in India is notably limited. 'There is no body of literature that links the study of India's middle classes with the question of sustainability', Fernandes wrote in 2009 (ibid.: 233). Five years later, Knorringa and Guarín (2014) still note that the attention to sustainability is scant. Some research that has been done broadly sketches the issue at hand, as with Knorringa and Guarín (2014), who delineate the growth of consumption in India, in a discussion from a sustainability perspective. Otherwise, existing research tends to be critical, again offering mainly broad sketches of an apparent problem. Taking a political economy perspective, some scholars argue that India is faced with the environmentally negative consequences of the middle class's dominance of politics, resulting in environmental exploitation, social injustice and disregard for the common good (Gadgil and Guha 1995; Lange et al. 2009; Varma 1998). Fernandes (2009) argues that consumption is ideologically integrated into visions of national development, with promotion of middle-class lifestyle as the central component of the development model advanced by the Indian state. Beyond such broad arguments, there is little research looking to specific consumer practices from a sustainability perspective. A few publications do focus on such practices in order to present them as problematic from a sustainability perspective, discussing, for example, the growth of meat consumption (Eckhardt and Mahi 2012), cars (Hansen et al. 2016), expansion of (largely fossil-fuel-based) electricity consumption going into household appliances and air conditioning, and the growth of relatively unsustainable forms of building construction (Hansen et al. 2012; Myers and Kent 2003). Mawdsley (2004) and Anantharaman (2014) discuss the problem of waste from what they understand to be a broader apparent problem of lack of concern for the public good among the middle class. In addition, Anantharaman (2014) looks at how the middle class tends to distance itself from problems of waste and displaces responsibility for dirty living environments to the poor. He also points to the decline in sustainable habits such as repair and reuse.

While there is thus some attention to sustainability issues around consumption that problematises and criticises consumption practices, there is little in-depth research on key issues beyond this. Many issues remain under-researched or are not even articulated. For example, the key question of how to adjust or limit consumption, now central to considerable consumption research in the West, is hardly addressed beyond some instances of marketing research (Ishaswini and Datta 2011; Tait et al. 2016). This is not only noteworthy but also interesting as a missed opportunity because of the available entry point for research that many scholars are in fact aware of. Consumption has been shown to be morally problematic for at least some middle-class consumers (Anantharaman 2017; van Wessel 2004; for a discussion of a similar ambivalence around consumption in Western societies, see Warde 2015). Frugality appears still to carry virtue at least to a degree for some, as 'simple living' detached from materialistic desires (Ekhardt and Mahi 2012; Mawdsley 2004; van Wessel 2004). Some researchers do suggest apparent (Elgin 2013; Lange et al. 2009) or growing environmental activism and concern (Anantharaman 2014). However, these arguments are as yet supported with only limited substantiation. When relatively more evidence is offered, it is largely in the form of the results of survey research that may reflect actual behaviour to a minimal degree. This is much in line with what has been found in other contexts where researchers commonly find a 'citizen–consumer paradox' or an 'attitude–behaviour gap' (Aerts 2013; Knorringa and Guarín 2014), with attitudes or expressed opinions finding little reflection in the choices consumers make. Clearly more in-depth research is due.

Sustainable Consumption

But how to move forward? For understanding and addressing consumption from a sustainability perspective, the cultural perspective dominating the research of middle-class consumption in India seems rather unhelpful. Indeed, the field of consumer culture studies as such seems to offer little guidance. Consumer culture theory has neglected questions of sustainability (Joy and Li 2012: 159). A recent review of the sociology of consumption notes the turning away from culture as a theme that used to dominate this field (Warde 2015). For the study of consumption from a sustainability perspective, other upcoming approaches appear more helpful. Increasingly, research of consumption focuses on the political and ethical dimensions of consumption, often from a sustainability perspective (Warde 2015). However, while this shifts questions of culture as such to the background as primary research questions, this does not mean culture has become irrelevant.

Working on consumption in India, some researchers seek to confront the sustainability approach to consumer behaviour as a result of the interplay of social, economic and cultural factors (Knorringa and Guarín 2014: 31; see also Banbury et al. 2012). From a similar approach, Hansen et al. (2012) call for a deeper understanding of the social, economic and cultural processes implied in the growth of consumption in India (ibid.: 6). However, these publications, while offering meaningful glimpses into the said complexities and interrelations, do not as yet dive deeply into these. The tradition of high-quality qualitative and interpretive sociological study of consumption in India discussed in the introduction to this chapter could well form part of the foundation for the further development of the research of consumption from a sustainability perspective. Reasons for this lie not only in the linkages between culture, economy, politics and social context but also in the complexities around the meanings of consumption that this tradition has brought forth, excellently.

'Sustainable consumption', a much touted concept, is key to the problem at hand. What sustainable consumption means differs widely across consumers as much as the scholars, activists, policy-makers and producers involved with the idea. Markkula and Moisander (2012: 105) chart what they call 'the discursive confusion that arises from a simultaneous existence of multiple, continuously changing and partly clashing discourses of sustainable consumption'. For them, '"sustainable consumption" is socio-culturally constructed, premised upon and supported by particular discourses of sustainable development, which have both material and linguistic, interconnected dimensions (Hall [1997] 2009; Potter and Wetherell 2007) and have different effects' (ibid.: 106–07).

Different meanings of sustainable consumption may link up more or less successfully with Indian understandings and value constructs around consumption and its effects beyond the satisfaction of, for example, attainment of social status among one's class peers. The development of different approaches to consumption in Indian society may give rise to different understandings of the role consumption can play in people's lives, and this may well form part of consumers' own reflections and shifts in thought and behaviour when it comes to consumption.

For example, sustainable consumption has been understood as 'buying green', much in line with the perspective and discourse of ecological modernisation that holds that economic growth and sustainability can be made compatible through the greening of production and consumption. For the Indian context, such understandings of sustainable consumption could be translated, for example, into adjustment of forms of transport, recycling, reuse and repair (something long part of Indian tradition, see, e.g., Anantharaman 2014; Vyas 2012), or selection of less resource-intensive products.

For others, sustainable consumption is rooted in a perspective that problematises growth as such, and revolves around buying less, from an understanding that the ideals of economic growth and consumption themselves must be problematised as foundations for a sustainable way of living. For example, 'voluntary simplicity', a transnational movement advancing shifts in lifestyle away from consumption on the basis of sustainability ideals (Elgin 2013), may link up and revive, in a new garb, Indian cultural ideals of austerity, frugality or (relative) dissociation from consumerism.

Soper (2007) argues for the need to recognise the extent to which moral concerns may now coincide with more self-interested forms of disaffection with 'consumerist' consumption. The benefits of this consumption may be compromised by its negative effects (including congestion, pollution, overwork, stress) and pre-emptive of other possible pleasures and satisfactions. Such concerns can indeed contribute to revisions on the part of consumers themselves about the 'good life' and what is conducive to human flourishing and personal fulfilment. This may well be already a reality for some among middle-class

Indians who are experiencing environmental problems closely related to consumption practice. While poor Indians often suffer more gravely from environmental problems than richer Indians (because of the lack of clean water and greater exposure to waste dumps), richer Indians cannot escape air pollution, poor management of ever-increasing waste and climate change effects of different kinds.

I propose that for the study of consumption in India, a new key question can be: How to advance sustainable consumption? Finding answer to this question demands research sensitive to the interplay of social, economic and cultural factors while engaging with the complexities of meaning around sustainable consumption itself. I here wish to highlight one rare study that I think can stand as exemplary to illustrate the aptness and possibilities of such research.

Anantharaman (2014) researched citizens' initiatives to develop waste management in Bengaluru. New recycling and composting initiatives seek to help managing waste generated in middle-class homes. The middle-class actors involved in these initiatives invoke environmental discourses and create new social norms to encourage the adoption of recycling and composting activities in their communities in the city. In their efforts to mobilise people for more sustainable consumer behaviour, leaders 'repackage and re-envision' old practices using new labels and, through this repackaging, help validate and legitimise these activities again (e.g., changing the meaning of recycling from a thrifty practice to a green practice). The initiatives are run by residents while involving mobilisation and incorporation of various actors from domestic workers to vendors and city government. Change is thereby enacted collectively.

Anantharaman interprets these new middle-class initiatives as collectively engendering behavioural, cultural and institutional changes. She starts out from ecological citizenship, which she approaches as enacted through collective and socially embedded efforts, speaking of 'networked ecological citizenships' that are culturally situated. Anantharaman asserts that 'the collective dimensions of these processes are essential to its private expression' (ibid.: 181) and that the individuals and communities involved actively leverage their class-derived cultural, social and economic capital to effect changes to their structural and social contexts (ibid.). She also points out that such initiatives are able to draw on the power of the middle class in terms of access to and grasp of technology, contact, access to media and government, and capacity to use the courts (cf. Mawdsley 2004).

A key lesson to learn is that actions sensitive to cultural, social and political context may enable the advancement of sustainable consumption behaviours among Indian consumers. While the study centres on localised activity, such new practices can become movements. They can come to offer examples for organisational form and alternative lifestyle that may well speak to middle-class aspirations for identity, meaning, life in a 'clean and green' urban habitat, and beyond. In India's digitally hyper-connected middle-class society, initiatives can spread and grow through peer-to-peer mobilisation, as has been found with other sustainability-oriented movements worldwide such as Transition Network (Feola and Him 2016). The middle class could therein, as Anantharaman suggests, harness its power over Indian society for the advancement of sustainability.

Anantharaman (2014: 182) calls for 'critical ethnographic studies that look at the social, cultural and political processes that produce behaviours that are recognizable as pro-environmental or constituting ecological citizenships'. I hope her research and her call for more research from these starting points will find resonance. Such research, especially when developed in cooperation with involved citizens, policy-makers, environmental groups and movements, and private sector actors with an interest in the advancement of sustainable consumption, could contribute to addressing our common issues of climate change, pollution and sustainable resource use. It would also turn the sociological study of consumption in India into a research domain of prime societal relevance.

References

Aerts, S. 2013. 'The Consumer Does Not Exist: Overcoming the Citizen/Consumer Paradox by Shifting Focus'. In *The Ethics of Consumption*, edited by Helena Röcklinsberg and Per Sandin, 172–76. Wageningen: Wageningen Academic Publishers.

Anantharaman, M. 2014. 'Networked Ecological Citizenship, the New Middle Classes and the Provisioning of Sustainable Waste Management in Bangalore, India'. *Journal of Cleaner Production* 63: 173–83.

———. 2017. 'Elite and Ethical: The Defensive Distinctions of Middle-class Bicycling in Bangalore, India'. *Journal of Consumer Culture* 17 (3): 864–86.

Annavarapu, S. 2016. 'Consuming Wellness, Producing Difference: The Case of a Wellness Center in India'. *Journal of Consumer Culture*. Advance Access. http://journals.sagepub.com/doi/10.1177/1469540516682583

Askegaard, S. and G.M. Eckhardt. 2012. 'Glocal Yoga: Re-appropriation in the Indian Consumptionscape'. *Marketing Theory* 12 (1): 45–60.

Banbury, C., R. Stinerock and S. Subrahmanyan. 2012. 'Sustainable Consumption: Introspecting Across Multiple Lived Cultures'. *Journal of Business Research* 65 (4): 497–503.

Beck, U. 2006. *The Cosmopolitan Vision*. Cambridge: Polity Press.

Brosius, C. 2012. *India's Middle Class: New Forms of Urban Leisure, Consumption and Prosperity*. London: Routledge.

Dauvergne, P. 2008. *The Shadows of Consumption: Consequences for the Global Environment*. Cambridge: MIT Press.

———. 2010. 'The Problem of Consumption'. *Global Environmental Politics* 10 (2): 1–10.

Dean, M. 2013. 'From "Evil Eye" Anxiety to the Desirability of Envy: Status, Consumption and the Politics of Visibility in Urban South India'. *Contributions to Indian Sociology* 47 (2): 185–216.

Dickey, S. 2013. 'Apprehensions: On Gaining Recognition as Middle Class in Madurai'. *Contributions to Indian Sociology* 47 (2): 217–43.

Eckhardt, G.M. and H. Mahi. 2012. 'Globalization, Consumer Tensions, and the Shaping of Consumer Culture in India'. *Journal of Macromarketing* 32 (3): 280–94.

Elgin, D. 2013. 'Voluntary Simplicity–A Path to Sustainable Prosperity'. *Social Change Review* 11 (1): 69–84.

Feola, G. and M.R. Him. 2016. 'The Diffusion of the Transition Network in Four European Countries'. *Environment and Planning A* 48 (11): 2112–15.

Fernandes, L. 2009. 'The Political Economy of Lifestyle: Consumption, India's New Middle Class and State-led Development'. In *The New Middle Classes: Globalizing Lifestyles, Consumerism and Environmental Concern*, edited by Hellmuth Lange and Lars Meier, 219–36. Dordrecht: Springer Netherlands.

Gadgil, M. and R. Guha. 1995. *Ecology and Equity: The Use and Abuse of Nature in Contemporary India*. London and New York, NY: Routledge.

Gilbertson, A. 2014. 'A Fine Balance: Negotiating Fashion and Respectable Femininity in Middle-class Hyderabad, India'. *Modern Asian Studies* 48 (1): 120–58.

Hansen, A., K.B. Nielsen and H. Wilhite. 2016. 'Staying Cool, Looking Good, Moving Around: Consumption, Sustainability and the "Rise of the South"'. *Forum for Development Studies*. Advance Access. https://www.tandfonline.com/doi/abs/10.1080/08039410.2015.1134640

Harindranath, R. 2013. 'The Cultural Politics of Metropolitan and Vernacular Lifestyles in India'. *Media International Australia* 147 (1): 147–56.

Ishaswini, N. and S.K. Datta. 2011. 'Pro-environmental Concern Influencing Green Buying: A Study on Indian Consumers'. *International Journal of Business and Management* 6 (6): 124–33.

Joy, A. and E.P.H. Li. 2012. 'Studying Consumption Behaviour Through Multiple Lenses: An Overview of Consumer Culture Theory'. *Journal of Business Anthropology* 1 (1): 141–73.

Knorringa, P. and A. Guarín. 2014. 'Standards and Consumer Behaviour of the Rising Middle Class in India'. In *Globalization and Standards: Issues and Challenges in Indian Business*, edited by Keshab Das, 23–40. New Delhi: Springer India.

Lange, H., L. Meier and N.S. Anuradha. 2009. 'Highly Qualified Employees in Bangalore, India: Consumerist Predators?' In *The New Middle Classes: Globalizing Lifestyles, Consumerism and Environmental Concern*, edited by Hellmuth Lange and Lars Meier, 281–98. Dordrecht: Springer Netherlands.

Markkula, A. and J. Moisander. 2012. 'Discursive Confusion over Sustainable Consumption: A Discursive Perspective on the Perplexity of Marketplace Knowledge'. *Journal of Consumer Policy* 35 (1): 105–25.

Mathur, N. 2010. 'Shopping Malls, Credit Cards and Global Brands: Consumer Culture and Lifestyle of India's New Middle Class'. *South Asia Research* 30 (3): 211–31.

Mawdsley, E. 2004. 'India's Middle Classes and the Environment'. *Development and Change* 35 (1): 79–103.

Myers, N. and J. Kent. 2003. 'New Consumers: The Influence of Affluence on the Environment'. *Proceedings of the National Academy of Sciences* 100 (8): 4963–68.

Nakassis, C.V. 2012. 'Counterfeiting What? Aesthetics of Brandedness and BRAND in Tamil Nadu, India'. *Anthropological Quarterly* 85 (3): 701–21.

Nielsen, K.B. and H. Wilhite. 2015. 'The Rise and Fall of the "People's Car": Middle-class Aspirations, Status and Mobile Symbolism in "New India"'. *Contemporary South Asia* 23 (4): 371–87.

Nisbett, N. 2007. 'Friendship, Consumption, Morality: Practising Identity, Negotiating Hierarchy in Middle-class Bangalore'. *Journal of the Royal Anthropological Institute* 13 (4): 935–50.

Osella, F. and C. Osella. 1999. 'From Transience to Immanence: Consumption, Life-Cycle and Social Mobility in Kerala, South India'. *Modern Asian Studies* 33 (4): 989–1020.

Shwom, R. and J.A. Lorenzen. 2012. 'Changing Household Consumption to Address Climate Change: Social Scientific Insights and Challenges'. *Wiley Interdisciplinary Reviews: Climate Change* 3 (5): 379–95.

Soper, K. 2007. 'Re-thinking the Good Life: The Citizenship Dimension of Consumer Disaffection with Consumerism'. *Journal of Consumer Culture* 7 (2): 205–29.

Tait, P., C. Saunders, M. Guenther and P. Rutherford. 2016. 'Emerging Versus Developed Economy Consumer Willingness to Pay for Environmentally Sustainable Food Production: A Choice Experiment Approach Comparing Indian, Chinese and United Kingdom Lamb Consumers'. *Journal of Cleaner Production* 124: 65–72.

Van Wessel, M. 2004. 'Talking About Consumption: How an Indian Middle Class Dissociates from Middle-class life'. *Cultural Dynamics* 16 (1): 93–116.

Varma, P.K. 1998. *The Great Indian Middle Class*. New Delhi: Penguin Books.

Vyas, D.M. 2012. *More than Simple Living: A Cultural Perspective on Sustainable Living*. Enschede: University of Twente.

Warde, A. 2015. 'The Sociology of Consumption: Its Recent Development'. *Annual Review of Sociology* 41: 117–34.

UNDP (United Nations Development Programme). 2013. *Human Development Report—The Rise of the South: Human Progress in a Diverse World*. New York, NY: UNDP.

28

The Challenge of Urban Space

Smriti Srinivas

Urban India and Patrick Geddes

The Scottish polymath Patrick Geddes (1854–1932) is legitimately recognised as one of the founders of Indian sociology and anthropology (Uberoi et al. 2007). Geddes, who spent a decade in the subcontinent involved with urban issues and plans (many of them now relegated to historical amnesia), should really be recognised as the 'first sociologist of urban India' or 'the first urban sociologist of India'. While his contribution to urban planning is difficult to evaluate and there have been some critical readings of his work, Geddes was one of the few comparative urbanists of his time and deeply interested in cities, history and urban form in Europe as well as Asia. From 1914 to 1924, working in India and Palestine, his thought and designs were enriched by non-European contexts becoming a significant contribution to the internationalisation of the town planning movement (Meller 1990: 201–03).[1]

---

[1] Geddes' European work has been discussed by several scholars and the centrality of his influence in America has been competently evaluated (see, e.g., Boardman 1978; Mairet 1957; Meller 1990; Welter 2002). However, his South Asian urban designs and reports—comprising his largest body of mature work— have not received comprehensive treatment. For a discussion of Geddes' Indian contribution and legacy and a more complete bibliography, see Srinivas (2015).

The Indian urban situation during his time was changing: although the percentage of urban to rural populations was small at the turn of the century, the scale of urbanisation was such that the proportion living in cities was three-fourths of the entire population of Britain in 1901. While some Indian cities were quite large in the early 19th century (e.g., in 1823, Calcutta had 900,000 people and Banaras had 580,000), large cities were getting larger. New industrial cities like Jamshedpur were coming up and cities with about 100,000 people or so were also becoming important for Indian urbanisation. The Indian sociologist G.S. Ghurye (initially a student of Geddes in Bombay) suggested that one of the most important trends in Indian urbanisation was the development between 1881 and 1941 of large cities in every region of the country and smaller but still significant a group of cities alongside. Local self-government became a venue for political action for Indian nationalists while plague, famine and huge rural to urban migrations were important concerns. Cities were beginning to set up improvement trusts: Bombay in 1889 was the first (Heitzman 2008a; Meller 1990: 205–08). Geddes travelled extensively in India, covering large cities like Delhi in the north, princely cities like Indore, provincial ones like Bellary and temple towns like Kanchipuram in the south. His India years are marked by a large number of city reports (perhaps 50 or so is the received common sense) solicited by British administrators, Indian rulers and citizens. I have discussed elsewhere (Srinivas 2015) the implications of these plans for a philosophy of the urban and the practice of citizenship.

Indian social science was also emerging during this time: Geddes was appointed to a new chair of sociology at Bombay University and occupied it between 1919 and 1924. He had come to hold the perspective that sociology as 'civics' and as a science of cities could reunite all the social sciences. This transdisciplinary project allows us to construct both a genealogy for urban sociology in India *and* its potential futures. Geddes took the approach that the student of cities was primarily a pedestrian and his/her walking and moving body was a methodological tool for the study of cities. Not only in Edinburgh but also in Indian cities, Geddes demonstrated again and again that this technique of the body—what he described separately as his 'sentinel's walk' on the walls of Ahmedabad city or the diagnostic survey conducted by walking through Indore's streets and alleys—was the initial pathway for (social) science. In *Cities in Evolution*, Geddes (1949 [1915]) also asserted that travel/pilgrimage and the experience of past and present cities are critical for the renewal of cities and citizenship. Adapting his method to this essay, I take us on a mobile survey, including my own journey into the field of urban studies, several educational institutions and cities, as well as some modes of thought about the urban. I do not separate sociology from anthropology and history for philosophical and conceptual reasons, shared also with Geddes and *Contributions to Indian Sociology* (*CIS*).

Models of the Indian City and Urbanism

I encountered *CIS* for the first time when I came from Bangalore and Madras after an undergraduate education to study in Delhi University in 1986. Delhi then was a city recovering from several wounds, including the assassination of Prime Minister Indira Gandhi in 1984, the spiral of violence that resulted in the pogrom against Sikhs and months of terror. Rajiv Gandhi, the pilot turned politician, succeeded his mother in office and in the years to come ushered in India's economic liber-alisation. A few years earlier, in 1982, by hosting the ninth Asiad and athletes from 33 countries, Delhi's claim to be a 'world city' seemed to be on sure ground. Although the decision for Delhi to be the host had been made several years earlier, the mid-1970s Emergency had delayed the process. By the early 1980s, however, Delhi's infrastructure had been indisputably altered by flyovers and new roads, thousands of telephone cables, the Indira Gandhi Indoor Stadium, the Jawaharlal Nehru Stadium, the Games Village, the Siri Fort auditorium and other large-scale modifications. Jantar Mantar, an early-18th-century obser-vatory, was appropriated into the cultural repertoire of the Games as its logo while existing communities of the urban poor and informal settlements were displaced from various parts of the city. Contrast this massive infrastructural transformation with the first Games also held in Delhi in 1951 when 11 newly independent Asian countries participated: all events were held in the National Stadium (the renamed 1933 Irwin Amphitheater) and adjoining pool. Delhi's experience was by no means unique: life-worlds in several Asian and African cities were also being culturally and spatially transformed through transport networks, urban restructuring and suburbanisation processes in the 1980s and 1990s (see, e.g., Ali and Rieker 2009; Ghannam 2002; Goh 2002; Kusno 2000).

The palpable signs of changed times at the Delhi University campus were the proliferation of police booths in and around it, Delhi now an increasingly securitised city, and the fast-moving public transport on wide roads and flyovers. I was a graduate student at the Delhi School of Economics' Department of Sociology that became functional in 1949 soon after Indian independence. Associated with the august economist V.K.R.V. Rao, 'D-School' was located near the colonial Civil

Lines outside the ramparts of the Red Fort and the Old City of Delhi. On the south side of Delhi were the Jawaharlal Nehru University, grid-patterned housing colonies, national bureaucratic classes, medical and scientific institutes, and corporate headquarters. In the interests of decolonisation, my department refused to make the choice between anthropology and sociology, in part because the classificatory apparatus of colonial knowledge girded the distinction. In any case, if the social complexity of India ranged from tribal groups to industrial strata and large urban populations that sometimes included both, what intellectual sense did the separation make? J.P.S. Uberoi (1974: 149) described this context in a reflection on the sociology of India as 'the unity of man as well as the complexity of India as a civilization'—a reflection that Geddes would surely have shared.

The ambidextrous training that we received was liberating, although physical anthropology was never a part of the curriculum, quantitative techniques were better taught in the Department of Economics and, as a whole, it seems as if my peers were more historically and philosophically inclined in their investigations than many sociology departments worldwide. *CIS* was a close partner in these enquiries emerging from the neighbouring multidisciplinary locale of the Institute of Economic Growth also founded by V.K.R.V. Rao in 1958. My teachers in sociology at D-School such as Andre Beteille, Veena Das and J.P.S. Uberoi, scholars at the nearby Centre for the Study of Developing Societies, and at Jawaharlal Nehru University in South Delhi, contributed to its vigorous debates that also involved scholars worldwide.

While we had one course on urban sociology at D-School, in spite of altered times in Delhi and other cities, the study of the urban was still not an active field of study. If cities were studied, most of them were simply a stage where other social issues were played out—much like the ninth Asiad in Delhi—a descriptive category rather than a conceptual one. *CIS'* new series is a good barometer of the state of the field: it commenced in 1967 under T.N. Madan, and in 1969 came the first 'urban' article—a review essay by B. Abbi (1969: 116–27) on the urban family in India. Another by Agehananda Bharati (1970: 36–49) on superstition in urban Hinduism followed a year later. It was not until 1975, when it became a biannual publication, that *CIS* featured more essays: one on caste and religion in urban India by P.D. Weibe and G.N. Ramu (1975: 1–17) and another on voluntary associations in a West Bengal city by Raymond Owens and Ashis Nandy (1975: 19–53). Two years later came the first reflection on 'Indian urbanism: A sociohistorical perspective' by Satish Saberwal (1977:

1–19), beginning with a brief invocation of Patrick Geddes and G.S. Ghurye. Saberwal's essay was largely a consideration of stratification in colonial and post-colonial India alongside a complete *CIS* issue featuring urban themes such as industrial entrepreneurs in Faridabad (M.N. Panini), great and little traditions in a Bengal town (Lauren Conwin), an urban social movement (Dipankar Gupta), Christians in Madras (Lionel Caplan), students in Bangalore (N. Jayaram), urbanism and Scheduled Castes (Victor D'Souza) and scientific laboratories (Shiv Visvanathan and Robert Anderson). It is difficult to know what to attribute this spike to—coinciding with the Emergency—because two years go by before another urban article appeared in the journal: Jim Masselos (1979: 145–67) on social stratification in 19th-century Bombay. For the decades of the 1980s and 1990s, the number of articles on urban South Asia and its cities (merely judging by titles that mention 'urban', 'city', 'urbanisation', or name a city) in *CIS* was negligible (number of essays per year are indicated in parentheses): 1980 (1), 1981 (0), 1982 (2), 1983 (0), 1984 (1), 1985 (1), 1986 (1), 1987 (2), 1988 (0), 1989 (0), 1990–96 (0), 1997 (1), 1998 (0). In 1999 (*CIS* 33 [1 and 2]), when CIS became a triannual issue, came a joint issue devoted to the industrial sector and labour, and thus numerous cities were featured from Bombay and Surat to Bhilai, Kanpur, Agra and others. From 2000 to 2016, *CIS* featured between one and six articles every year. This analysis is not meant to devalue the significance of the journal and its undoubted strengths: *CIS* was, and is, a world-class Indian journal in the anthropology and sociology of South Asia with scholarly contributions from around the globe featuring high-quality essays and debates from several theoretical perspectives.

The analytical and empirical lacunae in the urban sociology of India up until the late 1990s can probably be linked to the dominance of three models of the city. First, temple cities, pilgrimage centres or the city as sacred or cosmological space (e.g., Eck 1982; Kalia 1994; Smith and Reynolds 1987); second, the colonial city (usually Bombay, Calcutta or Delhi) or urban sites under colonialism (see, e.g., Bayly 1998 [1983]; Chaudhuri 1990; Dobbin 1972; Haynes 1991; Kosambi 1986; Llewellyn-Jones 1985; Patel and Thorner 1995a, 1995b); third, the city as the site of development and modernisation accompanied by concerns of poverty, stratification, industrialisation or caste (e.g., Bapat 1981; D'Souza 1968; Fox 1969; Harris 1978; Holmstrom 1994; Joshi and Joshi 1976; Lynch 1969). Given the paucity of other models for the study of the urban, it was not surprising that I chose dissertation work in the Himalayan region of Ladakh. Having spent my childhood in Assam,

Malaysia and China, I felt at home in this border zone between South Asia and East Asia. Although Ladakh's primary city, Leh, had been a entrepot in Himalayan and Central Asian exchanges for several centuries, I instead conducted fieldwork with Buddhists and Muslims in villages located near the ceasefire line between India and Pakistan and the Karakoram mountains.

Urban sociology in (and of) India is a field that is still defining and constituting itself. The first reason for this is that much of the early energies in Indian sociology had been directed to rural India, especially in the years after independence when concerns about the economic and cultural transformation of the rural and tribal landscape permeated social science research. The second reason is a definitional one that has haunted many scholars: D.F. Pocock (1960) alluded to this in an early paper in *CIS*' initial incarnation where he claimed that the distinction between urban and rural sociologies was superfluous, since the city and the village in South Asia demonstrated a continuity of form. Others, such as Singer (1972), whose enquiry was based in Madras city, nevertheless de-territorialised the urban by emphasising civilisational processes in South Asia. The third is a chronological one: the preoccupation with the colonial city and its physical and imaginative presence in the post-colonial period made it difficult to move beyond the four Presidency cities, key sites of the British Raj. The fourth reason is that even when the post-colonial city appeared as an object of study, most urban research until the latter half of the 1990s proceeded in the shadow of the developmental state and the three 'Ps'—planning, political change and poverty. Fifth, although there has been an output of writing over many decades on ancient, medieval and pre-colonial cities or cities in Indian history (e.g., Banga 1991; Blake 1991; Broeze 1989, 1997; Chakrabarti 1995; Champakalakshmi 1996; Fritz et al. 1984; Michell and Eaton 1992), these have been inadequately integrated into the urban sociology of India.

Constructing Urban Worlds

In 1993, while completing my doctoral thesis at D-School, I returned to Bangalore, a city in which I had spent a few years in the late 1970s and early 1980s. I began work at the Institute for Social and Economic Change, the third social science research centre founded by V.K.R.V. Rao in 1972: there were few sociologists there, most economists did serious quantitative and demographic work, and those concerned with the city tended mostly to study urban poverty, planning or rural–urban migration. This was also the moment when concerns about the impact of the structural adjustment policy—the comprehensive economic reform package supported by the World Bank—preoccupied many social scientists. The research institute was set up on land on the western periphery of the city. Urban sprawl had overtaken this region by the mid-1990s: houses and apartment buildings, many of them unauthorised, stood crowded on various hillocks encircling older villages in that area and were characterised by poor road, water and sewage connections. Travelling to the institute on a somewhat infrequent bus, besides houses, I would pass an entire dental college crowded into two floors of a rather small building, a busy local market, and several village temples and newer shrines. This kind of patchwork suburban growth was characteristic of other parts of the city as well.

Between 1994 and 1995, pondering on this kind of urban form, its relationship to core city areas, and the similarities and differences between Bangalore and Delhi, I began fieldwork in the city on three popular religious centres: an Infant Jesus church in a marginal and largely Tamil neighbourhood of the city, a Kutchi Memon-patronised *dargah* in the Cantonment and a Shirdi Sai Baba temple in a middle and upper-class suburb of the expanding metropolis. This was my first 'urban' engagement. In mid-April 1995, in another project, I stood outside the Dharmaraja temple in the Old City in the early hours of the morning surrounded by thousands of people to get a view of the Karaga procession as it emerged from the temple. Suddenly, gunshots were fired and the temple doors opened to let the sword-bearing 'hero–sons' (*virakumaras*) rush through the spectators. In their midst, barely visible to those sitting or standing at street level, was a male priest dressed in a turmeric-coloured sari, bearing a huge floral arrangement made of jasmine on his head under which sat the 'Karaga', the symbol of the goddess' power. Within moments, the procession of the priest and his protectors had moved down the temple road on its tour of the Old City, visiting houses, shrines and stores, the priest-as-goddess granting benediction in his/her wake and the hero-sons creating a powerful, mobile ring of protection around him/her.

Bangalore, the capital of Karnataka state with a population of about 10 million today, has been cast as a centre for high technology research and production, the 'Silicon Valley of India', since the 1990s. The Karaga performance continues to occur annually over nine days in Bangalore in the months of March or April in the Old City, its suburbs, and surrounding towns of the metropolis attracting about 200,000 people on the final day in the Old City alone. The ritual players are an old community of Tamil migrants to Bangalore, traditionally gardeners by occupation and a Backward Class, who now occupy other occupational niches in the city. Although considered a sacred event because of the long-awaited appearance of the goddess, the festival also displays a carnivalesque spirit such that a bustling industrial and software metropolis becomes a fairground under a night canvas of sparkling lights with chariots bearing deities from different shrines moving through the streets.

With these ethnographic immersions, I was forced to critically engage with Bangalore's spatial, religious and historical complexity, and reevaluate the urban scholarship I had encountered. Some of Bangalore's historical connections stretch backwards into the last great empire in South India in the 16th century, while others intersect more contemporaneously with British colonial rule, migrations from neighbouring regions and the city's place within a transnational economy. Religious events, performances and practices of the body related to them weave in and out of these numerous histories. Memories of place, like my own about the city, also follow these cultural pathways. These recollections of place, which I termed 'landscapes of urban memory', are not static even if they are locally marked and are modes of cultural self-invention intimately tied to historical, spatial, somatic and ritual practices. They are registers of the many mobilities and migrations that traverse and constitute the Indian city. I became an urban scholar, tying sociology to history, as a result of my Bangalore research (Srinivas 2001), examining the entangled pathways that religion, memory and the body take in a city inserted anew within global processes. This attention to the acts of habitation, agency and improvisation that make places viable in a vital sense, that seek to create communities and selves in fraught times, reaching beyond cultural amnesia and normal/metric constructs of what it means to live spatially, has been registered in recent years by some other scholars working globally (see, e.g., de Boeck and Plissart 2004; Huyssen 2008; Joseph 2013; Kusno 2013; Simone 2010). The persistence of what we may call the ethical, religious or spiritual within urban landscapes and the complex ways in which they intersect with other aspects of culture, the market or land use have also been recognised by several collaborative and global projects.[2]

---

[2] See Hancock and Srinivas (2008); Waghorne (2016); 'Global Prayers' from Berlin. Available at: http://globalprayers.info (accessed on 12 November 2012); the multi-city 'Urbanizing Faith' project. Available at: www.abdoumaliqsimone.com/current-projects.html (accessed on 5 June 2014); the University of California Multi-campus Research Group 'Urban Place-making and Religiosity'. Available at: http://urbanreligions.net (accessed on 2 January 2014).

Although cities like Bangalore or Hyderabad have become sites for global flows of capital and labour in recent years, these were, for many decades and centuries before that, embedded in several transnational circuits. The roles that London or New York play on the world stage and the sometimes-economistic arguments about the globalisation process obscure the several temporal layers of regional and global circuits that occupy many urban spaces. Further, apart from the special role accorded to 'first world' or 'global' cities, culture is sometimes seen in these urban perspectives as functionally serving the processes of capital accumulation. Post-colonial and postmodern theoretical perspectives, by contrast, employ spatialised languages which are deeply sensitive to heterogeneity but tend not to focus on 'lived' spaces concentrating on texts, colonial discourses, master narratives and their imaginaries (for critiques, see, e.g., Bishop et al. 2003; Mayaram 2008; Roy and Ong 2011). Constructions of space, urban, global or otherwise, however, can emerge from both existing cultural milieus and older histories, demonstrate the continuing agency of communities, and the cultural aesthetics and ethics of movements, migrations, memories and other protocols.

The spatial considerations emerging from my Bangalore research seemed to demand comparative urban projects that take into account our immersion within forms of intellectual, historical and social contemporaneity. They required a transdisciplinary approach linking the body with the social, several spatial scales and temporalities, or biography and history (Srinivas 2008, 2015).[3] In my case, it was also the outcome of movement institutionally and spatially in the last two decades: I moved from a position in sociology in Bangalore to a position in anthropology at the University of California via stopovers in

---

[3] From Bangalore, I turned to the study of a global religious movement centred on the Indian guru Sathya Sai Baba (1926–2011), where I traversed the terrain between social theories for the study religion or cities—themselves a product of modernity and a largely liberal discourse—and the modernity of many contemporary religious movements that reject the terms of secularism, fundamentalist violence or nationalism to seek out other futures. *In the Presence of Sai Baba* (Srinivas 2008) examines the movement in three large cities—Bangalore, Nairobi and Atlanta—linking regimes of spatial, somatic and symbolic production. *A Place for Utopia* (Srinivas 2015) examines the valency of the idea of 'utopia' for designs for occluded, vernacular or counter-urbanisms from princely Indore to colonial/post-colonial Madras and global Bangalore and Los Angeles, by religious movements such as Theosophy and American Vedanta, urban planners like Patrick Geddes, pilgrims, migrants and ordinary city-dwellers.

New York City, Washington, DC, Atlanta, and Columbus as an urban scholar and a scholar of comparative religion. These types of urban, comparative, mobile, transdisciplinary engagements on my part and others (see, e.g., Arif 2016; Bayat 2010; Simone 2004) at the level of theory and ethnography are a response to a kind of global, transnational or contemporaneous imagination and practice that Arjun Appadurai, Marc Augé and George Marcus (among others) separately urged about 20 years ago; D-School is, in my imagination, its Indian analogue. It is also a response to recent calls for urban theories and understandings of space (e.g., Massey 2005; Robinson 2006) that are as cosmopolitan as the diverse cities and spaces that urbanists and geographers inhabit or study.

Towards Urban Futures

There is cause to take Indian/South Asian urban sociology forward for two basic reasons. First, the sheer significance of urban centres in India and South Asia today: in 1950, the urban population of South Asia was about 71 million persons out of a total population of about 454 million. In 1950, only two places in South Asia stood on the list of the world's 20 largest cities—Calcutta and Bombay. In 2007, the urban population in South Asia reached approximately 477 million and accounted for one-third of the macro-region's total population. There were 56 cities with at least 1 million inhabitants (including 46 with between 1 and 5 million), and 10 'mega-cities' had populations greater than 5 million including older centres such as Bombay/Mumbai and newer ones such as Dhaka (Heitzman 2008a). The urban population of South Asia in 2014, according to World Bank figures, was approximately 33 per cent of the total population. Between 2000 and 2011, the number of people officially living in South Asia's towns and cities swelled by slightly more than 130 million—equivalent to more than the entire population of the world's 10th most populous country, Japan—from 382 million to 511 million. An increase of almost 302 million people living in recognised urban settlements in South Asia between 2011 and 2030—almost equivalent to the entire population of the United States—is the forecast.[4]

Second, writings by historians or those with historical lenses have steadily uncovered thriving urban cultures and a diversity of urban

[4] See https://openknowledge.worldbank.org/bitstream/handle/10986/2254 9/9781464806629.pdf (accessed on 5 December 2016).

forms in the pre-colonial and colonial period. They serve to remind us that the peasantisation of the social science imagination in South Asia may be a colonial and early national product. The historical record shows that cities in South Asia were part of a world system in the past in different ways and emphasises why we need to theorise cities of the South more completely both in time and in space.

Alongside publications in *CIS*, and my own urban turn, the significance of cities, urbanism and the urban in South Asia and India is visible in the growing number of book series and publications since 2000. Routledge India, for example, now features a book series edited by Sujata Patel on 'Cities and the Urban Imperative'; Oxford University Press India's Sociology list has a 'urban studies and urbanization' section; and Orient BlackSwan, in steady and consistent ways, has published a very large number of urban sociology and history titles. Recent published works include a wide variety of themes; for the remainder of this essay, I shall gesture to some key bodies of literature that have emerged in the field of urban sociology/history and point to the lacunae in the study of urban sites in India and South Asia.

First, there has been a significant growth of city writings that expand our understanding of South Asian urbanism. Even if we look only at the major presses just mentioned (and include Permanent Black) and do not examine popular writings, recent titles range from comprehensive studies of the city in South Asia (e.g., Heitzman 2008b) and anthologies of city life (e.g., Lal 2013) to studies of single cities pursuing several foci (e.g., Dossal 2010; Ghertner 2015; Heitzman 2004; Nair 2005; Shah 2014; Spodek 2012).

Second, there is now a large body of work on religion in urban locales that includes research on religious nationalism, communal violence and secularism, as well as the ways in which the urban is produced by agents and communities who bring a range of other religious imaginations and practices to the city (e.g., Chatterjee 2016; Chatterjee and Mehta 2007; Hansen 2001; Henn 2014; Iqtidar 2011; Srinivas 2001, 2008; Waghorne 2004). From the late 1990s onwards—in part a response to the communalisation of urban life—scholars from several theoretical orientations have demonstrated that cityscapes are sites not only for liberal acts of citizenship, nor mainly secularised domains, but also for multiple enactments of urban and religious contemporaneity.

Third, studies of urban infrastructure, in some ways linked to the older model of the developmental city, form another key realm of urban enquiry (e.g., Kumar 2014; Sharan 2014; Sreedhar 2010). Privatisation of urban services, public service delivery, participatory governance, social justice, urban poverty and labour, or the quality of life in Indian cities, are some of the concerns of this literature located at the interface of economics, planning, sociology, development studies and ecology.

Fourth, the interlinked domains of architecture, urban design and geography provide insights into the making of global/world cities and contestations over space (e.g., Dey et al. 2013; Ghertner 2015; Stallmeyer 2011), medieval and modern architecture (e.g., Juneja 2008; Lang 2010), exclusion, enclosure and the neoliberalisation of space (for instance, Anjaria and McFarlane 2016; Brosius 2014; Srivastava 2014) and urban informality and work (e.g., Gill 2009).

Metro cities, that is, cities with a population of over 1 million, and especially the megalopolises among them (i.e., with over 5 million and sometimes over 10 million persons) such as Karachi or Mumbai, have dominated urban studies of South Asia in the last 2 decades, a period when the field has also become a somewhat self-conscious project. However, a fuller treatment of the urban cannot merely rest on such large cities but must encompass a range of smaller cities and towns within the urban settlement hierarchy. Geddes made an early case for small cities, for example, in his 1918 Indore report where he argues that small cities and city states were the historical heritage of India and Europe; his was, however, also a futurological argument based on the merits of decentralisation and the promise of Indian society. These 'middle towns', 'middle cities' or 'secondary cities' of South Asia (Heitzman 2008a, 2008c) continue to be demographically significant for Indian and South Asian urbanisation, but we have a poor understanding of the histories of, and contemporary urban processes in, these sites.

The other area of research that has received little attention is the 'city-nature dialectic' (Davis 2002: 363) that necessarily involves a consideration of urban sustainability and ecology. Geddes' writings are an early example of a 'biocentric' urban philosophy that takes into account waste, gardens, children, zoos, trees, schooling, public health, work and a range of other matters (Srinivas 2015). In the South Asian urban present, we have to acknowledge that cities are faced with enormous demographic shifts; populations, the poor and environmental concerns seem expendable in the large-scale urbanisation taking place; urban disasters seem to abound; and there is a drive towards standardisation in the forms of city life. While there are a few recent examples of such work (Alley 2002; Nagendra 2016; Rademacher 2011; Rademacher and Sivaramakrishnan 2013), for a South Asian urban sociology of the future, we need to think about ways in which to reconcile 'nature', sustainable practices and city life; examine issues of urban power and exclusion within their environmental habitat; look for post-industrial urban futures; and connect urban nature, pedagogy and performances of citizenship.

References

Abbi, B. 1969. 'Urban Family in India: A Review Article'. *Contributions to Indian Sociology* 3: 116–27.

Ali, Kamran and Martina Rieker, eds. 2009. *Comparing Cities: The Middle East and South Asia*. Oxford: Oxford University Press.

Alley, Kelly D. 2002. *On the Banks of the Ganga: When Wastewater Meets a Sacred River*. Ann Arbor, MI: University of Michigan Press.

Anjaria, Jonathan S. and Colin McFarlane, eds. 2016. *Urban Navigations: Politics, Space and the City in South Asia*. New Delhi: Routledge.

Arif, Yasmeen. 2016. *Life, Emergent: The Social in the Afterlives of Violence*. Minneapolis, MN: University of Minnesota Press.

Banga, Indu, ed. 1991. *The City in Indian History: Urban Demography, Society and Politics*. Delhi: Manohar Publishers.

Bapat, Meera. 1981. *Shanty Town and City: The Case of Poona*. Oxford and Elmsford, NY: Pergamon Press.

Bayat, Asef. 2010. *Life as Politics: How Ordinary People Change the Middle East*. Stanford, CA: Stanford University Press.

Bayly, C.A. 1988 (1983). *Rulers, Townsmen, and Bazaars: North Indian Society in the Age of British Expansion, 1770–1870*. Cambridge and New York, NY: Cambridge University Press.

Bharati, Agehananda. 1970. 'The Use of "Superstition" as an Anti-Traditional Device in Urban Hinduism'. *Contributions to Indian Sociology* 4: 36–49.

Bishop, Ryan, John Phillips and Wei Wei Yeo, eds. 2003. *Postcolonial Urbanism: Southeast Asian Cities and Global Processes*. New York, NY: Routledge.

Blake, Stephen P. 1991. *Shahjahanabad: The Sovereign City of Mughal India, 1639–1739*. New York, NY: Cambridge University Press.

Boardman, Phillip. 1978. *The Worlds of Patrick Geddes: Biologist, Town Planner, Re-educator, Peace-warrior*. London: Routledge and Kegan Paul.

Broeze, Frank, ed. 1989. *Brides of the Sea: Port Cities of Asia from the 16th–20th Centuries*. Honolulu, HI: University of Hawaii Press.

———, ed. 1997. *Gateways of Asia: Port Cities of Asia in the 13th–20th Centuries*. London and New York, NY: Kegan Paul International.

Brosius, Christiane. 2014. *India's Middle Class: New Forms of Urban Leisure, Consumption and Prosperity*. Delhi: Routledge India.

Chakrabarti, Dilip K. 1995. *The Archaeology of Ancient Indian Cities*. New Delhi: Oxford University Press.

Champakalakshmi, R. 1996. *Trade, Ideology and Urbanization: South India 300 BC to AD 1300*. New Delhi: Oxford University Press.

Chatterjee, Ipsita. 2016. *Spectacular Cities: Religion, Landscape, and the Dialectics of Globalization*. New Delhi: Oxford University Press.

Chatterjee, Roma and Deepak Mehta. 2007. *Living with Violence: An Anthropology of Events and Everyday Life*. New Delhi: Routledge India.

Chaudhuri, Sukanta, ed. 1990. *Calcutta: The Living City*. 2 vols. Calcutta: Oxford University Press.

Davis, Mike. 2002. *Dead Cities*. New York, NY: The New Press.

De Boeck, Filip and Marie-Francoise Plissart. 2004. *Kinshasa: Tales of the Invisible City*. Ghent: Ludion; Tervuren: Royal Museum for Central Africa; Antwerp: Vlaams Architectuurinstituut.

Dey, Ishita, Ranabir Samaddar and Suhit K. Sen. 2013. *Beyond Kolkata: Rajarhat and the Dystopia of Urban Imagination*. Delhi: Routledge India.

Dobbin, Christine E. 1972. *Urban Leadership in Western India: Politics and Communities in Bombay City, 1840–1885*. London: Oxford University Press.

Dossal, Mariam. 2010. *Theatre of Conflict, City of Hope*. New Delhi: Oxford University Press.

D'Souza, Victor S. 1968. *Social Structure of a Planned City, Chandigarh*. Bombay: Orient Longman.

Eck, Diana L. 1982. *Banaras, City of Light*. New York, NY: Alfred A. Knopf.

Fox, R.G. 1969. *From Zamindar to Ballot Box: Community Change in a North Indian Market Town*. Ithaca, NY: Cornell University Press.

Fritz, John M., George Michell and M.S. Nagaraja Rao. 1984. *Where Kings and Gods Meet: The Royal Centre at Vijayanagara, India*. Tucson, AZ: University of Arizona Press.

Geddes, Patrick. 1949 (1915). *Cities in Evolution*. New and rev. ed. London: Williams and Norgate.

Ghannam, Farha. 2002. *Remaking the Modern: Space, Relocation and the Politics of Identity in a Global Cairo*. Berkeley, CA: University of California Press.

Ghertner, Asher. 2015. *Rule by Aesthetics: World-class City Making in Delhi*. New Delhi: Oxford University Press.

Gill, Kaveri. 2009. *Of Poverty and Plastic: Scavenging and Scrap Trading Entrepreneurs in India's Urban Informal Economy*. New Delhi: Oxford University Press.

Goh, Beng-Lan. 2002. *Modern Dreams: An Inquiry into Power, Cultural Production, and the Cityscape in Contemporary Urban Penang, Malaysia*. Ithaca, NY: Cornell University Press.

Hancock, Mary and Smriti Srinivas, ed. 2008. 'Symposium on Religion and the Formation of Modern Urban Space in Asia and Africa'. *International Journal of Urban and Regional Research* 32 (3): 617–709.

Hansen, Thomas B. 2001. *Wages of Violence: Naming and Identity in Postcolonial Bombay*. Princeton: Princeton University Press.

Harris, Nigel. 1978. *Economic Development, Cities and Planning: The Case of Bombay*. Bombay: Oxford University Press.

Haynes, Douglas E. 1991. *Rhetoric and Ritual in Colonial India: The Shaping of a Public Culture in Surat City, 1852–1928*. Berkeley, CA: University of California Press.

Heitzman, James. 2004. *Network City: Planning the Information Society in Bangalore*. New Delhi: Oxford University Press.

———. 2008a. 'Secondary Cities and Spatial Templates in South India, 1300–1800'. In *Secondary Cities and Urban Networking in the Indian Ocean Realm, c. 1000–1800*, edited by Kenneth R. Hall, 303–34. Lanham, MD: Lexington Books.

———. 2008b. *The City in South Asia*. New York, NY and London: Routledge.

———. 2008c. 'Middle Towns to Middle Cities in South Asia, 1800–2007'. *Journal of Urban History* 35 (1): 15–38.

Henn, Alexander. 2014. *Hindu-Catholic Engagements in Goa: Religion, Colonialism, and Modernity*. Hyderabad: Orient BlackSwan.

Holmstrom, Mark. 1994. *Bangalore as an Industrial District: Flexible Specialisation in a Labour-surplus Economy?* Pondicherry: Institut Francais de Pondicherry.

Huyssen, Andreas, ed. 2008. *Other Cities, Other Worlds: Urban Imaginaries in a Globalizing Age*. Durham, NC: Duke University Press.

Iqtidar, Humeira. 2011. *Secularizing Islamists? Jama'at-e-Islami and Jama'at-ud-da'wa in Urban Pakistan*. Hyderabad: Orient BlackSwan.

Joseph, May. 2013. *Fluid New York: Cosmopolitan Urbanism and the Green Imagination*. Durham, NC: Duke University Press.

Joshi, Heather and Vijay Joshi. 1976. *Surplus Labour and the City: A Study of Bombay*. New Delhi: Oxford University Press.

Juneja, Monica, ed. 2008. *Architecture in Medieval India: Forms, Contexts, Histories*. Hyderabad: Orient BlackSwan.

Kalia, Ravi. 1994. *Bhubaneswar: From Temple Town to a Capital City*. Carbondale, IL: Southern Illinois University Press.

Kosambi, Meera. 1986. *Bombay in Transition: The Growth and Social Ecology of a Colonial City, 1880–1980*. Stockholm: Almqvist and Wiksell International.

Kumar, M. Dinesh. 2014. *Thirsty Cities*. New Delhi: Oxford University Press.

Kusno, Abidin. 2000. *Behind the Postcolonial: Architecture, Urban Space and Political Cultures in Indonesia*. London: Routledge.

———. 2013. *After the New Order: Space, Politics and Jakarta*. Honolulu, HI: Hawaii University Press.

Lal, Vinay, ed. 2013. *The Oxford Anthology of the Indian City*. Vols. I and II. New Delhi: Oxford University Press.

Lang, Jon. 2010. *A Concise History of Modern Architecture in India*. Hyderabad: Orient BlackSwan.

Llewellyn-Jones, Rosie. 1985. *A Fatal Friendship: The Nawabs, the British, and the City of Lucknow*. Delhi and New York, NY: Oxford University Press.

Lynch, Owen. 1969. *The Politics of Untouchability: Social Mobility and Social Change in a City of India*. New York, NY: Columbia University Press.

Mairet, Phillip. 1957. *Pioneer of Sociology: The Life and Letters of Patrick Geddes*. London: Lund Humphries.

Masselos, Jim. 1979. 'Social Segregation and Crowd Cohesion: Reflections Around Some Preliminary Data from 19th Century Bombay City'. *Contributions to Indian Sociology* 13: 145–67.

Massey, Doreen. 2005. *For Space*. London: SAGE.

Mayaram, Shail, ed. 2008. *The Other Global City*. New York, NY: Routledge.

Meller, Helen. 1990. *Patrick Geddes: Social Evolutionist and City Planner*. London: Routledge.

Michell, George and Richard Eaton. 1992. *Firuzabad: A Palace City of the Deccan*. London and New York, NY: Oxford University Press.

Nagendra, Harini. 2016. *Nature in the City: Bengaluru in the Past, Present and Future*. New Delhi: Oxford University Press.

Nair, Janaki. 2005. *The Promise of the Metropolis: Bangalore's Twentieth Century*. New Delhi: Oxford University Press.

Owens, Raymond and Ashis Nandy. 1975. 'Organizational Growth and Organizational Participation: Voluntary Associations in a West Bengal City'. *Contributions to Indian Sociology* 9 (1): 19–53.

Patel, Sujatha and Alice Thorner, eds. 1995a. *Bombay: Metaphor for Modern India*. Bombay: Oxford University Press.

———, eds. 1995b. *Bombay: Mosaic of Modern Culture*. Bombay: Oxford University Press.

Pocock, D.F. 1960. *Contributions to Indian Sociology* 4.

Rademacher, Anne. 2011. *Reigning the River: Urban Ecologies and Political Transformations in Kathmandu*. Durham, NC: Duke University Press.

Rademacher, Anne and K. Sivaramakrishnan, eds. 2013. *Ecologies of Urbanism in India: Metropolitan Civility and Sustainability*. Hong Kong: Hong Kong University Press.

Robinson, Jennifer. 2006. *Ordinary Cities: Between Modernity and Development*. London and New York, NY: Routledge.

Roy, Ananya and Aihwa Ong, eds. 2011. *Worlding Cities: Asian Experiments and the Art of Being Global*. Oxford: Blackwell Publishers.

Saberwal, Satish. 1977. 'Indian Urbanism: A Sociohistorical Perspective'. *Contributions to Indian Sociology* 11 (January): 1–19.

Shah, Svati P. 2014. *Street Corner Secrets: Sex, Work, and Migration in the City of Bombay*. Hyderabad: Orient BlackSwan.

Sharan, Awadhendra. 2014. *In the City, Out of Place*. New Delhi: Oxford University Press.

Simone, Abdou Maliq. 2004. *For the City Yet to Come: Changing African Life in Four Cities*. Durham, NC: Duke University Press.

———. 2010. *City Life from Jakarta to Dakar: Movements at the Crossroads*. New York, NY: Routledge.

Singer, Milton. 1972. *When a Great Tradition Modernizes*. Chicago, IL: Chicago University Press.

Smith, Bardwell and Holly Baker Reynolds, ed. 1987. *The City as a Sacred Center: Essays on Six South Asian Contexts*. Leiden: E.J. Brill.

Spodek, Howard. 2012. *Ahmedabad: Shock City of Twentieth-century India*. Hyderabad: Orient BlackSwan.

Sreedhar, K.S. 2010. *State of Urban Services in India's Cities*. New Delhi: Oxford University Press.

Srinivas, Smriti. 2001. *Landscapes of Urban Memory: The Sacred and the Civic in India's High-tech City*. Minneapolis, MN: University of Minnesota Press.

———. 2008. *In the Presence of Sai Baba: Body, City, and Memory in a Global Religious Movement*. Leiden and Boston: Brill; Hyderabad: Orient Longman.

———. 2015. *A Place for Utopia: Urban Designs from South Asia*. Seattle, WA and London: University of Washington Press; Hyderabad: Orient BlackSwan.

Srivastava, Sanjay. 2014. *Entangled Urbanism: Slum, Gated Community and Shopping Mall in Delhi and Gurgaon*. New Delhi: Oxford University Press.

Stallmeyer, John C. 2011. *Building Bangalore: Architecture and Urban Transformation in India's Silicon Valley*. London: Routledge.

Uberoi, J.P.S. 1974. For a Sociology of India: New Outlines of Structural Sociology, 1945–1970'. *Contributions to Indian Sociology* 8 (1): 149.

Uberoi, Patricia, Nandini Sundar and Satish Deshpande, eds. 2007. *Anthropology in the East: Founders of Indian Sociology and Anthropology*. New Delhi: Permanent Black.

Waghorne, Joanne Punzo. 2004. *Diaspora of the Gods: Modern Hindu Temples in an Urban Middle-class World*. New York, NY: Oxford University Press.

———, ed. 2016. *Place/No Place in Urban Asian Religiosity*. Singapore: Springer.

Weibe, P.D. and G.N. Ramu. 1975. 'Caste and Religion in Urban India: A Case Study'. *Contributions to Indian Sociology* 9 (1): 1–17.

Welter, Volker. 2002. *Biopolis: Patrick Geddes and the City of Life*. Cambridge, MA: MIT Press.

29

Feet on the Ground, Eyes on the Horizon

The Anthropology of Environment and Climate Change

Rita Brara

I make, remake and unmake my concepts along a moving horizon, from an always decentered centre, from an always displaced periphery which repeats and differentiates them.

–Gilles Deleuze (1994: xxi)

We were, perhaps, never in doubt about the ups and downs of terrains covered by environmental anthropology and sociology. The spread and diversity of forests, pastures, rivers and mountains were grist to the mill as the disciplines' practitioners went about exploring how common folks represented and eked their subsistence from nature alongside the escalating conflicts over land and water, trees and animals. But this sweep was apparently not wide, tall or deep enough for the new climate in environmental studies.

The amplitude of the environmental did not collapse under the weight of the new, as the earth sciences stretched out farther to probe planetary climate change. And while we do not still have a term as encompassing as the environment to capture the canvas of changes across atmospheres, land, flora, fauna, water and climate, these were increasingly affecting peoples, places and perceptions. Everything from the colour of clouds and the melt of glaciers to the depths and girth of the earth was investigated now by scientists with more sophisticated instruments, computer modelling and innovative knowhow—and questioned or affirmed by close-to-the-ground analyses in labs and outside.

Gradually, a 'horizoning' vocabulary emerged from what Petryna (2012) refers to as an 'intellectual labour', underscored by the data and analysis of the earth sciences. It introduced terms such as the anthropocene, planetary boundaries, tipping points, black carbon, global warming and geoengineering, permeated with risk and uncertainty that travelled to the social sciences (Schuler 2015). Apart from this recent lexicon generated by climate science, a set of terms with a longer genealogy, such as adaptation, vulnerability, risk and resilience, environmental impacts and mitigation featured within this subfield.

The encounter of the social sciences, environmental activism and the environmental humanities with the natural and earth system sciences reconstituted and produced its 'own' vocabulary. We had new terms for the anthropocene, evolving conceptualisations of environmental justice and fleshed out posthuman/multispecies ecologies, for example—a third realm, as it were, to contest the scientisation of this discourse and come to terms with environmental and climate change that is both ontologised and embodied in down-to-earth experience. Here Latour (2015: 6) reminded us that 'both science and politics are… pedestrian activities open to doubt, revision and prone to mistakes'.

The extraordinary changes in the climate and environment field present new horizons. Anthropology engages with these changes as these affect ordinary people on the ground. Oriented to imaginings, anticipations and intentions, horizons can appear nebulous juxtaposed against the situatedness and the immanence of the here-and-now. The horizon distinguishes a distant vision from what is close at hand. Horizons can advance or recede and contrast with knowing what is what, keeping feet on the ground. Yet horizons develop in relation to a ground and practices draw on both the lofty of the horizon and the material of the down-to-earth. The two terms, horizon and ground, seem to provide a useful analytic for this sub-discipline in its current phase, and I will draw on these notions to engage with the varied positionings of earth scientists, social scientists and peoples.

Forecasting forms a fair part of 'horizoning' in the ecological sciences, and its predictive statements on global warming or glacier melting, for instance, now pervade the popular consciousness. Social scientists, too, keep these horizons in view as ecological forecasts or benchmarks in their field studies. And local actors devise their own (and often hybrid) knowledge practices to ground the short-run (the weather or the everyday) and generate long-run (the climate or intergenerational) horizons.

The horizons of scientists, too, evolve in local milieus and social institutions including professional, scientific institutions as well. Their forecasts may draw upon field or ground surveys, but the views of people on the ground cannot establish the truth-claims of their science or validate those horizons. Nevertheless, Husserl (1954 [1970]) suggests that scientific practices fall within the curve of human experience and fold back into the life-world. It is this renewed encounter with the life-world that offers the possibilities of rendering the practices of the ecological sciences variable and multiple. In this position-taking, the environmental anthropologist assumes the ground view as her locus, even as she becomes an interlocutor whose horizon partly overlaps with the peoples/non-humans of her enquiry and is partly congruent with the horizons of academia.

Horizon...ing the Ground: Ecological Ideas and the Social Sciences

In this section, I will discuss a handful of contemporary concepts that horizon the ground of ecological studies. I shall first take up the currently influential conception of the anthropocene and illustrate its anthropological avatars. Next, I will briefly sketch out a few ecological concepts such as vulnerability, adaptation and risk that are sought to be applied in the field and are often reconfigured in the process.

The Anthropocene

The term anthropocene, to take up a contemporary coinage from the natural sciences, has been popularised by the Nobel Prize-winning atmospheric chemist Paul Crutzen and E. Stoermer (2000). It marks the time of a great acceleration in the scale, speed and complexity of the human impact on earth in the period following the Holocene. The prefix 'anthro' in the anthropocene has come to stand for the overwhelming changes in the planet's parameters wrought by the dominance of the human species, while the suffix or 'cene' of the anthropocene signifies the time of this epoch in conformity with the series Holocene, Pleistocene and so on. The precise beginnings of the Anthropocene, whether these date back to agriculture, the use of fossil fuels, the steam engine or the atom bomb, are still to be confirmed by the International Commission on Stratigraphy, but the term anthropocene has already arrived in the social sciences and the popular imagination.

The anthropocene now horizons the 'human' impact on the planet brought about by increased carbon, sulphur and nitrogen emissions, global warming, biodiversity loss and sea-level rise, to mention just some significant parameters. Cast in this mode, the epoch of the anthropocene in Chakrabarty's (2009) view has the scope to unite the history of the human species and capital. Others are still mulling the substantive differences between the generic human of the Anthropocene and the situated humans who may have adversely impacted the planet or will be among those who most feel its deleterious effects. The concept's planetary scale, too, diverges from ordinary human reckonings that simultaneously rescale horizons and bring them down to earth. From an anthropological perspective, notwithstanding the marking of geological periods, humans differ further in that many still practise livelihoods, such as primitive pastoralism and hunting–gathering, which geologists may associate with times past.

A veritable explosion in renaming the anthropocene surfaced soon after the inauguration of the term. For instance, the 'chthulucene' is proposed as an alternative because it connotes multispecies assemblages (Haraway 2015), the plantationocene considers the havoc wreaked by plantation economies (Tsing 2015) and the anglocene (Fressoz 2015) marks the ecological devastation said to have been set in motion by the privileged North. Each term horizons a different perspective on who is responsible, but the signposting of a crisis is more readily accepted.

Does the anthropocene resonate in the environmental discourses prevalent in India? The Eurocentrism of the anthropocene, from a postcolonial standpoint, makes it inapplicable in the Indian context and so it should be decolonised or 'provincialised' from Morrison's (2015) perspective. While Moore (2015) proposes the capitalocene as *the* term for the anthropocene, Baskin (2015: 15) wonders why 'not think of it as the Shiva-cene, after the Indian deity's characterisations as destroyer and transformer'?

Certainly, Hindu India's cultural periodisation of epochs (*yugs*) runs alongside the geological classifications of the anthropocene. The dark epoch (*kaliyug*) of the present is characterised in doggerel 'as a time when swans will eat rats and crows will feed on pearls'. Vernacular notions of the apocalyptic Great Flood (*pralay*) that portends the end of the world, ominously as sea levels rise it would seem, are alive in the cultural imaginary. From this cosmogonic horizon, however, the cycle of the world starts anew without the linear cast of the anthropocene.

Keeping an ear to the ground in the present, Hull notes: 'Hardly a day goes by that choke points of the Anthropocene are not discussed in major media: water, energy, climate, population, poverty, urbanization, green economy, globalization, health and human rights'.[1] The capitalocene (Moore 2015) reverberates in the unabated effects on the health of Bhopal's residents who suffered the chemical disaster at the Union Carbide factory or still live in its vicinity. Maurya (2014) highlights the risks from the 'indiscriminate' use of antibacterial consumer products that enter the water stream. Diseases stemming from the sourcing of radioactive minerals in Kerala en route to the country's atomic energy plant, an unspeakable signature of the anthropocene in India are, however treated as classified, sensitive information (Abraham 2012).

While the anthropocene as a concept is capacious in its horizoning of the contemporary planetary crisis, enquiries into 'the multiplicity and unequal social values, relations and practices of power that accompany actual humans', as Baskin (2015: 16) puts it, warrant social analysis. We shall return to this subject in the latter part of the chapter after considering other ecological concepts in what follows.

Harnessing Ecological Concepts

One of the consequences of the interdisciplinary study of ecology has been the movement of concepts from the natural sciences to the social sciences and vice versa. Such borrowings, as with the anthropocene, have increased over the last few decades in the wake of widespread environmental degradation and climate change as well as the Intergovernmental Panel on Climate Change's (IPCC 2014) calls for adaptation and mitigation in the new context.

The endeavour of social scientists is often to embed ecological concepts in peopled milieus to gauge how these offer insights or are out of sync with the social situation. What we have here is a triangulated process. First, the concepts of ecology provide a lens through which environmental phenomena may be viewed by the social scientist. The extent of partial consonance or complete dissonance is investigated empirically by delineating vernacular or emic categories and contexts

[1] Bruce Hull, 'India as Anthropocene'. Available at: http://cligs.vt.edu/india-as-anthropocene/ (accessed on 22 April 2016).

that may resonate, modify or interrogate these notions. What it often leads to is alternative concepts or the prefixing of the ecological concept with the term 'social' such that, in this mode, the field is replete with depictions of social adaptation, social resilience, social impacts and tipping points, which seek to impart a flesh-and-blood quality to what is apparently biophysical.

I will illustrate the use of a battery of ecological terms—such as vulnerability, adaptation, resilience, risk and tipping points—with examples drawn from studies of the conjoined natural and cultural milieu of farming. Farmers and agriculture afford a good arena for studying vulnerability. The practice of agriculture is vulnerable to weather conditions and market prices that are exacerbated by soil degradation, groundwater exhaustion, salinity, pests and now global warming.

So the first question from the horizon of adapting to climate change is to figure out who is at risk. In an account from Ladakh, it is the women who are more risk-prone since the men have migrated or taken to other activities such as tourism (Barrett 2014). Current adaptations often take the shape of crop shifts and shifts in the sowing season. For instance, with a warmer climate in the cold desert of Ladakh in the Himalayan region, farmers in some stretches have taken to growing wheat, apples and potatoes at higher altitudes where earlier only millets and oil seeds could be raised (ibid.). Another striking adaptation in this region is the channelling and freezing of the glacial run-off of water in the shade for subsequent use in what is the new agricultural season. This pioneering technique was conceived by Chewang Norphel who is locally known as the Glacier Man.[2] These innovations are regarded as boons by the farmers and envisaged as practices of resilience from a researcher's standpoint.

However, water-guzzling by the wheat crop is not perceived as a problem by the farmers as long as their profit margins improve. Global warming is viewed as less of a concern by the locals who consider the provisioning of education, coping with unemployment and the political problems at the border as bigger worries and orient their current practices to horizons that grow out of this ground (Barrett, 2014). And so what constitutes a social adaptation for a Ladakhi farmer is, perhaps, a failure to adapt to the need to reduce water for agriculture, viewed from a planetary vantage point. The socially critical threshold or tipping

[2] Dinakar Peri, 'Climate Change Is Changing Landscape of Ladakh', *The Hindu*, 29 November 2015.

point for the Ladakhi farmer, however, emerges from her different relationship to ground realities and emergent horizons.

Or again, regulatory norms, based on the ecological sciences, may specify the desirable carrying capacity of pastures or the ratio of aged trees to young trees that should be maintained while harvesting timber. As technoscientific inputs into health issues, scientists also draw up what are considered to be appropriate parameters for drinking water. The potability of drinking water, in this apparently benign horizoning, is fixed by the WHO at international norms that limit it to 1,500 parts per million (ppm) of total dissolved solids, apart from the norms for specific salts.

These seemingly apolitical parameters, however, become the objects of alarm and political action, since the mandated norms for drinking water can restrict its use for reasons that prove to be insufficient on the ground. The parameters for water quality, for instance, were lowered in the state of Rajasthan, but the state government could still not meet the need for potable water, which was the biophysical tipping point, in 34 of the worst-affected villages in the Lacchmangarh *tehsil* (sub-district) of Sikar district. However, the social tipping point in these villages was reached only when the government could not ensure an improved drinking water supply but would no longer defray the costs of pumping water from these wells, its former practice, since this water had officially been declared 'not potable' (Brara 2007).

The unsettling of norms and metrics, cast by scientists and mandated by states, is a way of recasting benchmarks and horizons that may not accord with the social time of practices on the ground and the risk thresholds of locals. Political doings then develop in the midst of cracks between technoscientific and local norms, apart from the overtly political which is explored in the next section.

Political Ecology: Ground…ing the Horizons

The 'ecological is political' could well be the mantra of political ecology. The horizons of its practitioners envisage environmental justice on the ground and link it to human rights, beyond narrow and seemingly apolitical ecological impact studies. Below I outline what I consider to be its major strands. I begin with the ground of environmental activism, traverse the territory of multispecies/posthuman anthropology and urban ecologies, before turning to environmental justice viewed from the vantage point of the juridical.

ENGOs and Environmental Movements

Activists have been the prime movers in the arena of environmental politics and justice, though occasionally anthropologists have joined their efforts and fashioned standpoint anthropology in this domain (Padel 2010). Just as the political can reside in the benchmarking practices of science, indigenous knowledge, alternative science and science, too, find a place in politics as practised.

Environmental non-governmental organisations (ENGOs) run the length and breadth of the country. Most of these citizen groups articulate local micro-environmental concerns dealing with water, land and air; engage with vernacular and scientific knowledge; or mobilise on local problems. Ideal volunteering is oriented towards the common good (*lok kalyan*) in idioms that vary from the contemporary ENGO mode to the Gandhian, the Marxian or other alternative and environmentally friendly lifestyles.

Some ENGOs are well-known national think tanks and publish extensively, such as the Centre for Science and Environment (CSE), Navdanya and Gene Campaign. Researches carried out by these organisations are appraised by academia, political representatives and global corporations (Bose and Lyons 2010). The leaders of these ENGOs are often charismatic public intellectuals who create new knowledge horizons on environmental matters, ground up and define or redefine national policy as well. The CSE, for instance, drew attention to the unequal use of non-expandable carbon space by developed and developing countries, distinguished 'luxury emissions' from the 'survival emissions' of the poor and laid the groundwork for India's climate agenda globally (Agarwal and Narain 1991). Navdanya and Gene Campaign have worked against the patenting of indigenous flora and genetically modified seeds, to cite two other well-known examples. However, the political horizons of the state and ENGO often diverge as well.

ENGOs spearhead movements that make demands on the state on issues such as environmental degradation, construction of big dams, privatisation of forests and other commons, land acquisition for dubious public purposes or inactions against big corporations or mining interests, to highlight just some causes that are regularly protested. The choreography of protests often draws on methods enunciated and practised against the colonial state. Slogans such as 'Monsanto Quit India' and flags made from indigenous strains of cotton, for instance, were deployed at demonstrations against genetically modified organisms.

National and international ENGOs also band together for common causes. The current Campaign for Survival and Dignity, for example, is a coalition of national ENGOs from 11 states trying to secure the rights of forest dwellers. It opposes the dilatory tactics and deliberate acts of non-recordation of the Forest Department, which is read as a reminder of the doings of the colonial state in this sector (Sivaramakrishnan 1995). A combine of national and international ENGOs successfully organised the resistance against a bauxite mining lease to a private firm in the Niyamgiri hills, sacred to the Kondh tribals.

The issues considered above largely fall within the domain of 'human' rights, politics and justice. We will turn to environmental interests beyond the human next.

Environmental Ethics, Posthuman and Multispecies Anthropology

At one level, multispecies ontologies and environmentally ethical practices find a comfortable niche on Indian soil as these resonate with strains of Indic beliefs and practices. The cosmic horizon of rebirth connects the existence of plants, peoples and animals in common lore (Dalal and Taylor 2014). Sacred groves are anthropological favourites, and the study of tree animism has revived (Haberman 2013). The feeding of birds (and other animals) as part of an everyday ethic, vegetarianism as a principle emanating from *ahimsa* or non-violence, the sacredness of the monkey and the care of the cow and pariah dogs are part of pious practices pursued vis-à-vis fauna in the country.

In the popular mind, J.C. Bose and Mahatma Gandhi afford two examples of distinguished Indians who were sensitive to the notion of interspecies associations. Bose was drawn to showing empirical connections between the human, animate and inanimate worlds from his grounding in a milieu that fostered the oneness of life (Anon 2016). In a similar spirit, Mahatma Gandhi (1929 [2005]: 114) declared: 'I want to realize brotherhood or identity not merely with the beings called human but... with all life, even with such things as crawl upon earth'. Moreover, livelihoods still bring people and animals together—through pastoralism, minor hunting and the use of animal draft power, for example—such that the human–animal interspecies communication is intimate. Contemporary multispecies writing (Fuentes and Kohn 2012) in India has focussed on monkeys, elephants and cranes (Rangarajan 2013). These animals are envisaged as thinking and feeling 'non-human' persons (Locke 2013; Munster 2014).

At a cross-cutting plane, however, propounding vegetarianism or underscoring the upper-caste taboo on consuming the flesh of animals and especially beef in the public sphere has become an escalating political phenomenon that disallows the interests of citizens of other faiths and castes (Ghassem-Fachandi 2012). Local-level politics also penetrate disputes over whether marauding animals should be saved when farmers, for example, are being subjected to the rigours of protecting wild life and the impositions of 'environmentality' (Agrawal 2005). Further, there is urban concern over monkeys that are increasingly moving into spaces inhabited by humans (Gandhi 2012). Both the ensuing friction and the mutual ties lead us to look at the horizon of the posthuman in the density of urban ecologies as well.

Urban Political Ecologies

With the striking growth of cities, the study of the urban has gained ground. Recent environmental writing is concerned with a plethora of issues about land, water and atmosphere that comprise a city's 'second nature' (Lefebvre 1976). Peri-urban ecologies focus on the acquisition of common lands by the state, the resettlement of the poor away from urban heartlands and construction on ecologically unsuitable tracts. The gamut of issues on water run a long course including concerns with the privatisation of groundwater, time budgets of women, saving rivers and urban water supply. Air pollution, too, is now on the radar and is being pursued on multiple counts ranging from boards displaying real-time air quality in public spaces to health impacts.

Class divisions are easily superimposed on urban issues, evident in the positing of familiar binaries—slums and gated communities, cars and bicycles, open drains vs underground sewage. On the one hand, a series of city processes such as greening, the displacement of slums and the ban on informal, industrial workshops are aptly subsumed under the ideology of what Baviskar (2002) terms 'bourgeois environmentalism'. Here, political ecology overlaps with the political economy.

On the other hand, Eckersley (1988: 147) notes that Marxist critiques of 'bourgeois environmentalists' in the 1970s were superseded by attempts to synthesise 'red and green imaginations' by post-Marxists. The flows of the political economy catch up with the affluent in gated colonies and the labour resident in adjoining slums to make for a 'mutual ecology' between these classes (Fuentes 2010; Srivastava 2015). From another perspective, Das (2012) argues that the poor should not be homogenised as a category that thinks only about survival when, in fact, their lives reveal rich horizons. On the environment as ground, what we have then are multiple ways through which citizens are activating their citizenship and contesting the sole right of the state (and the upper classes) to claim the political (cf. Anand 2011).

Environmental Justice… or Does Justice Know No Adjective[3]

If courts of law must feature in the space of political ecology, it is because the judiciary has played a remarkable role in the legal 'horizoning' of environmental rights and issues in India. It has been christened an environmental activist[4] in a context where the executive and representative wings of the state have been unable to ensure human rights vis-à-vis the environment (Sahu 2014). The right to a safe and wholesome environment, built into the law as part of the right to life in 1991 and guaranteed under Article 21 of the Constitution, was an outcome of such jurisprudence.

The shaping of public interest litigation (PIL) from 1979 onwards, path-breaking judgements, the nudge towards new legislation and the setting up of a Green Tribunal, with scientists and judges on board, have been some of the judiciary's initiatives. Environment-minded lawyers and citizens have made use of its potential in rural as well as urban areas (Brara 2007; Padhy 2008; Rajamani 2007), but the sociological appreciation of court judgments is often enriched when these are situated in their social contexts.

Parmar (2015) shows how the protest against a Coca-Cola facility in Kerala buttressed the legal case against groundwater extraction but lost the plot that spoke of the dispossession of local Adivasis from their resources. Brara (2006) brings out how the legal battle against the privatisation of a pasture was simultaneously an ongoing political battle between the well-off Scheduled Castes and the dominant Jats in the village. By adjudging that polluting industries have to shift out of the city (Baviskar 2012), the courts overlooked the impact on workers who lost their livelihoods. And on the issue of CNG in Delhi, Kalra (2015) finds

[3] I borrow this phrase from Chris Hammons. Available at: https://reflectionandchoice.org/2012/10/25/justice-knows-no-adjective/ (accessed on 4 May 2016).

[4] Romi Jain, 'The Supreme Court as Environmental Activist', *The Diplomat*, 24 January 2014. Available at: http://thediplomat.com/2014/01/the-indian-supreme-court-as-environmental-activist/ (accessed on 7 June 2018).

that the recommended shift to alternative fuels by the court can work only if it is supported by automobile manufacturers and fuel suppliers.

From the perspective of affected groups, the judicial was just the justiciable tip of the iceberg.

Concluding Remarks

The conceptual practices of environmental anthropology and sociology draw upon the practices of the people being considered to understand what lies betwixt and between the visions of a horizon and the materiality of the ground, proffering vistas of the middle distance. I have tried to sketch the inter-discipline, first, as it reshapes ecological concepts and horizons in the field, in one of its modes. As political ecology with heels dug in, in the other mode, it sees its beacon in justice without an adjective. In an overarching sense, these two horizons intersect, overlap and collide in the ecological ground of life but without merging, giving rise to new practices that affirm the power of decentring and diversity.

References

Abraham, I. 2012. 'Geopolitics and Biopolitics in India's High Natural Background Radiation Zone'. *Science, Technology & Society* 17 (1): 105–22.

Agarwal, Anil and S. Narain. 1991. *Global Warming in an Unequal World.* New Delhi: Centre for Science and Environment.

Agrawal, Arun. 2005. *Environmentality: Technologies of Government and the Making of Subjects.* Durham, NC: Duke University Press.

Anand, N. 2011. Pressure: The PoliTechnics of Water Supply in Mumbai. *Cultural Anthropology* 26 (4): 542–64.

Anon. 2016. 'Sir Jagadis Chandra Bose'. *Encyclopedia of World Biography. Encyclopedia.com*, 3. Available at: http://www.encyclopedia.com (accessed on 2 April 2016).

Barrett, K.Y. 2014. 'Assessing the Determinants Facilitating Local Vulnerabilities and Adaptive Capacities to Climate Change Impacts in High Mountain Areas: A Case Study of Northern Ladakh India'. PhD Dissertation, Paper 4395. University of Montana, Dilon, MT.

Baskin, Jeremy. 2015. 'Paradigm Dressed as Epoch: The Ideology of the Anthropocene'. *Environmental Values* 24 (1): 9–29.

Baviskar, Amita. 2002. 'The Politics of the City'. *Seminar* 516: 40–42.

———. 2012. 'Public Interest and Private Compromises: The Politics of Environmental Negotiation in India'. In *Law Against the State Ethnographic Forays into Law's Transformations*, edited Julia Eckert, Brian Donahoe, Christian Strümpell and Zerrin Özlem Biner, 171–201. Cambridge: Cambridge University Press.

Bose, Purnima and L.E. Lyons. 2010. *Cultural Critique and the Global Corporation*. Bloomington, IN: Indiana University Press.

Brara, Rita. 2006. *Shifting Landscapes: The Making and Remaking of Village Commons in India*. New Delhi: Oxford University Press.

———. 2007. 'The Public Sphere and Water Provisioning: Discontinuities in the Present'. In *Waterscapes: The Cultural Politics of a Natural Resource*, edited by Amita Baviskar, 117–38. Delhi: Permanent Black.

Chakrabarty, Dipesh. 2009. 'The Climate of History: Four Theses'. *Critical Inquiry* 35 (2): 197–222.

Crutzen, P.J. and E.F. Stoermer. 2000. 'The Anthropocene'. *Global Change Newsletter* 41: 17–18.

Dalal, Neil and Chloe Taylor. 2014. *Asian Perspectives on Anomal Ethics: Rethinking the Non-human*. New York, NY: Routledge.

Das, Veena. 2012. 'Poverty and the Imagination of a Future: The Story of Urban Slums in Delhi, India'. *Asia Colloquia Papers* 1 (4): 1–33.

Deleuze, G. 1994. *Difference and Repetition*, trans. Paul Patton. London: The Athlone Press.

Eckersley, Robyn. 1988. 'The Road to Ecotopia: Socialism Versus Environmentalism'. *The Ecologist* 18 (4 and 5, April–May): 142–47.

Fressoz, J.P. 2015. 'Losing the Earth Knowingly: Six Environmental Grammars around 1800'. In *The Anthropocene and the Global Environmental Crisis: Rethinking Modernity in a New Epoch*, edited by C. Hamilton, F. Gemenne and C. Bonnueil, 70–83. London: Routledge.

Fuentes, Agustín. 2010. 'Naturalcultural Encounters in Bali: Monkeys, Temples, Tourists, and Ethnoprimatology'. *Cultural Anthropology* 25 (4): 600–24.

Fuentes, Agustín and Eduardo Kohn. 2012. 'Two Proposals'. *Cambridge Anthropology* 30 (2): 136–46.

Gandhi, Ajay. 2012. 'Catch Me if You Can: Monkey Capture in Delhi'. *Ethnography* 13 (1): 43–56.

Gandhi, M.K. 1929 (2005). *All Men Are My Brothers*. London: A & C Black.

Ghassem-Fachandi, Parvis. 2012. *Pogrom in Gujarat: Hindu Nationalism and Anti-Muslim Violence*. Princeton, NJ: Princeton University Press.

Haberman, D.L. 2013. *People Trees: Worship of Trees in Northern India*. New York, NY: Oxford University Press.

Haraway, Donna. 2015. 'Anthropocene, Capitalocene, Plantationocene, Chthulucene: Making Kin'. *Environmental Humanities* 6 (1): 159–65.

Husserl, E. 1954 (1970). *The Crisis of European Sciences and Transcendental Phenomenology*. Translated by D. Carr. Evanston, IL: Northwestern University Press.

IPCC (Intergovernmental Panel on Climate Change). 2014. 'Summary for Policymakers'. In *Climate Change 2014: Impacts, Adaptation, and Vulnerability*. Part A: Global and Sectoral Aspects. Working Group II Contribution to the Fifth Assessment Report of the Intergovernmental Panel on Climate Change, 1–32. Cambridge: Cambridge University Press.

Kalra, Harsimran. 2015. 'The Case of CNG Fuel'. *SOAS Law Journal* 2 (1): 110–75.

Latour, Bruno. 2015. 'Telling Friends from Foes in the Time of the Anthropocene'. In *The Anthropocene and the Global Environmental Crisis: Rethinking Modernity in a New Epoch*, edited by C. Hamilton, F. Gemenne and C. Bonnuei, 145–55. New York, NY: Routledge.

Lefebvre, H. 1976. *The Survival of Capitalism: Reproduction of the Relations of Power*. London: Allison and Busby.

Locke, Piers. 2013. 'Explorations in Ethnoelephantology: Social, Historical, and Ecological Intersections Between Asian Elephants and Humans'. *Environment and Society: Advances in Research* 4 (1): 79–97.

Maurya. 2014. 'Science, Society and Risk in the Anthropocene'. *Economic & Political Weekly* 49 (41): 20–23.

Moore, Jason. 2015. *Capitalism in the Web of Life*. New York, NY: Verso Books.

Morrison, Kathleen D. 2015. 'Provincializing the Anthropocene'. *Seminar* 673: 75–80.

Munster, Ursula. 2014. 'Working for the Forest: The Ambivalent Intimacies of Human–Elephant Collaboration in South Indian Wildlife Conservation'. *Ethnos: Journal of Anthropology* 81 (3): 425–47.

Padhy, Sanghamitra. 2008. 'Greening Law: A Socio-legal Analysis of Environmental Human Rights in India'. PhD Dissertation. University of Southern California, Los Angeles, CA.

Parmar, Pooja. 2015. *Indigeneity, and Legal Pluralism in India: Claims, Histories, Meanings*. New York, NY: Cambridge University Press.

Petryna, Adriana. 2012. 'What Is a Horizon?' American Anthropological Association Meetings, San Francisco, CA, 14 November.

Rajamani, Lavanya. 2007. 'Public Interest Environmental Litigation in India: Exploring Issues of Access Participation, Equity, Effectiveness and Sustainability'. *Journal of Environmental Law* 19 (3): 293–321.

Rangarajan, M. 2013. 'Animals with Rich Histories: The Case of the Gir Lions, Gujarat, India'. *History and Theory* 52 (4): 109–27.

Sahu, Geetanjoy. 2014. *Environmental Jurisprudence and the Supreme Court*. New Delhi: Orient BlackSwan.

Schuler, Barbara, ed. 2015. *Environmental and Climate Change in South and Southeast Asia: How Are Cultures Coping*. Leiden: Brill.

Sivaramakrishnan, K. 1995. 'Colonialism and Forestry in India: Imagining the Past in Present Politics'. *Comparative Studies in Society and History* 37 (1): 3–40.

Srivastava, Sanjay. 2015. *Entangled Urbanism: Slum, Gated Community, and Shopping Mall in Delhi and Gurgaon*. New Delhi: Oxford University Press.

Tsing, A. 2015. 'Feral Biologies'. Paper presented at Anthropological Visions of Sustainable Futures, University College London, 12–14 February 2015.

30

Beyond Medical Pluralism

Medicine, Power and Social Legitimacy in India

V. Sujatha

The term 'medical pluralism' was used in the 1980s by medical anthropologists to denote the prevalence of multiple systems of medicine in South Asia due to non-availability of biomedical facilities. Pluralistic health behaviour and the resort to traditional and irrational therapies found in the less developed world were points of discussion in development discourse in the 1950s. Lately, however, medical pluralism appears in sociological literature as a sign of the postmodern condition. It has come to denote the freedom of choice and self-assertion of post-industrial populations in the Global North (Scambler 2002). The trajectory of this term in the social sciences itself is quite interesting, indicating, as it were, the profound changes in medicine and health throughout the world in the past decades.

The coexistence of multiple systems of medicines in the public domain could be understood at three levels: first at the level of institutions (state interventions, market initiatives, educational and research institutions), second at the level of physicians (physician families, professional associations) and third at the level of the people (choice and patterns of resort of the general public—known as health behaviour). This chapter will outline key concerns with regard to medical pluralism in the Indian context at all the three levels. Towards the end, we would see how the emergence of a new discipline called 'integrative medicine' (IM), following the globalisation of Asian medicines, has made issues around pluralism more complicated.

The emergence of state regulation in medical practice in the colonial period is a crucial breaking point for our understanding of medical pluralism, to which we turn.

I

State and 'the' Official Medicine

The history of medicine in colonial India presents a rich account of the interplay of political power, medical knowledge and health status. Any understanding of medical pluralism will have to begin with the arrival and encounter between medical systems, their authorisation and legitimisation by the colonial state, and the interests of various strata of medical professionals (Sujatha and Abraham 2012).

Medical practices from Europe interacted and coexisted with prevailing practices in the subcontinent well into the 20th century until the establishment of an official system of medicine. There are some interesting works on the initiatives of the first Indian doctors of Western medicine. They started an Urdu medical journal in 1875 and discussed the induction of *vaids* and *hakims* (practitioners of ayurveda and unani) to the government medical services (Sivaramakrishnan 2006), were interested in including Indian remedies for venomous bites, leprosy and skin diseases into allopathic treatments (Ramanna 2000) and attempted to translate biomedical texts to Indian languages (Kumar 1997). In ayurvedic medical education, on the other hand, heterodox Hindu and Sikh sects in Punjab were organising the translation of Sanskrit medical texts to Punjabi around 1878 and facilitating the entry of middling and lower classes into ayurveda (Sivaramakrishnan 2006). In the 1890s, the onset of printing gave access to both unani texts and college education in traditional medicine to many aspirant Muslims without family legacy of medical practice (Attewell 2007). The state unani service in Hyderabad attracted several college-educated unani physicians from the North who saw robust employment potential in traditional medicine; they combined the advantages of free learning in the modern institutions with personal apprenticeship under prominent physicians (ibid.).

Homeopathy also made its entry in India through a direct disciple of Samuel Hahnemann who won the trust of Raja Ranjit Singh in the 1840s. Although the British government opposed it, there was popular support for homeopathy among the public, and from 1890 onwards, homeopathic medical schools grew in India through private funding (Kumar 1998). It seems that the holistic and natural therapies, banished from Europe under the hegemony positivist biomedicine, found refuge in the Indian subcontinent (Nandy and Viswanathan 1990).

Indian allopathic doctors did have a flourishing practice since the 1880s and about one-tenth of the population went to them; the rest went to the vaids and hakims because their charges were less or none (corporate village grants to vaids made individual payments unnecessary). So they took to allopathy only when it was offered free of cost (Ramanna 2004).

Vaid *sammelans* (gathering or convention) demanded drug research laboratory for the Indian systems and regulatory measures for clinical practice on par with allopathy to weed out quackery (ibid.). The Madras Medical Registration Act passed in 1914 assigned the right to certify before law and the right to hold positions in the government department of health only to registered practitioners of allopathy. Representatives of siddha, ayurveda and unani fought against the Act and argued that such an Act may be justified in countries where there is only one system of medicine (Muraleedharan 1992).

An overview of the process by which state control over medical care shaped up during the colonial regime in the 20th century, the responses of physicians from diverse persuasions and the health issues that were emerging at that time is presented by Sujatha (2014). As we can see, the question of establishing an official health care system in India was not one of mere transplant under colonial rule, but a question of political struggle between systems of medicine for state patronage and a process of internal reform. Practitioners of traditional medicine pioneered critical changes to their systems that would help them enter the 20th century along with allopathy, including starting new enterprises for the manufacture of ayurveda and unani medicines in the 1890s. This sets the ground for an understanding of medical pluralism not so much as the sheer coexistence of systems of medicine, but as an ongoing negotiation between state authority and social legitimacy with regard to medical practices.

In independent India, public health care delivery was designed around biomedicine and the government was ambivalent towards non-biomedical practitioners. In the 1950s, there was serious concern that the low health status of the rural poor ravaged by epidemics and famines was compounded by their faith in archaic and ritual practices.

Government-run facilities were inadequate and a variety of practitioners—vaids, hakims, shamans, healers, folk practitioners and mystics—were providing health care.

Under Development and Pluralistic Health Behaviour

Medical anthropology in India was fostered by biomedical physicians from the United States who came to India in the 1950s as part of funded development programmes such as those of Rockefeller Foundation, with a keen interest in studying the health behaviour of the village communities. They tried to find out why people held on to traditional practitioners when the more efficacious modern medicine was available and whether they were resisting biomedicine because of the tenacity of superstition. The folk practitioners, however, had already introduced injections, tablets and stethoscope in their kit. McKim Marriott (1955) suggested that modern medicine will have to present itself in the 'homespun of the Indian village' in order to be accepted.

Many studies found a pattern in people's resort to different therapies—they opted for 'modern medicine' for acute ailments and other systems for chronic ailments. So it seemed that there was some strategy in people's health behaviour, not just tenacity.

Physicians in Plural Settings

By the 1970s, anthropologists shifted their focus from health behaviour to the knowledge and practices of physicians of traditional medicine—the vaids and hakims. Leslie (1976) adopted the term 'cosmopolitan' medicine for ayurveda, biomedicine and unani in terms of their spread and brought them into the discussion on models of health care. He also introduced the concept of medical pluralism to denote the Asian model of health care based on multiple systems as opposed to the hierarchical American model based on a single system. In Leslie's formulation, medical pluralism became a desirable phenomenon to be adopted by the Anglo-Saxon world. A number of ethnographic studies on ayurvedic vaids and hakims followed Leslie's work in the next three decades. Based on his study of the clinical encounter in biomedical, ayurvedic and unani clinics in Lucknow, Khare (1996) argued that at the level of practice, the impregnable walls between religion, science and culture do not seem to matter; qualified physicians of any system in the Indian setting creatively employed communicational messages towards curative functions.

Sociologists at home, however, were sceptical about 'traditional' medicines and argued that their romanticisation could promote quackery and other dubious practices (Minocha 1980). Public health researchers found that the people did prefer the curative services of biomedicine when they were available and accessible (Banerji 1986). In the meanwhile, sociologists were looking at issues of professionalisation in bureaucracies. Oommen (1978) examined how professionals like doctors and semi-professionals like nurses in public hospitals in Delhi perceived and performed their roles. Venkataratnam (1979) compared two hospitals to see how far the professional performance of doctors departed from the normative role expectation. Writing in the late 1970s, Jeffery pointed out that though the physician was respected in Indian society, the modern medical profession was not politically dominant as their counterparts in the United States, for instance. There were several reasons for the weak professional power of the Indian bio-medical community, foremost being the wider Indian understanding of medicine as a social profession rather than a commercial one and the socialisation of doctors into vague social ideals like 'service to humanity'. The Indian Medical Association had low membership, unlike its counterparts in the United States and Europe (Starr 1982). Although there was large segment of private medical practice in India, this did not augment the allopath's professional authority because of stringent state regulations and competition with non-biomedical practitioners that required them to adopt populist measures to satisfy clients for survival (Jeffery 1978). Madan (1980) enquired into the relation that doctors in developing countries had with the larger society and found that doctors came mostly from urban background and the class difference between them and their patients was huge. He thought that under such a social hiatus, the medical profession in India may not contribute to modernisation. Tracing the growth of private medical care in India, Baru (1998) explained how the members of the landowning Reddy community in Andhra entered the medical profession after the Green Revolution, ushering the corporatisation phase in medical care with the inauguration of Apollo hospitals in the 1980s.

Neo-traditionalism

While there was unanimity that education in traditional medicine should be institutionalised and professionalised, there has been profound conflict over the content, curriculum and inclusion of bio-medical subjects which often went up to 70 per cent in some states. There were about 55 strikes by students of indigenous medicine between 1958 and 1964, demanding equal status and pay with biomedical doctors and change of the name of their degree from *ayurvedacharya* to those bearing English titles like MBBS (Brass 1972).

There are several ways in which physicians straddle the world of ancient medicine and the demands of the world they now live in. Rather than viewing contemporary ayurvedic discourses as cultural exclusives, sociological approaches view culture and medical knowledge as deeply connected to the changing social coordinates of the subjects of knowledge who are graduating from modern colleges of traditional medicine. As shown by historical studies on college-educated physicians of traditional medicine for more than a century, historical and epistemic disparities in medical knowledge and practices tend to converge in the contemporary life-world of the practitioner and reflect the exigencies of the times. A college-educated botanist from a family of siddha vaidyas, for instance, by virtue of his existential situation of living in a small town, having modern school and college education, access to computers and the internet, will naturally integrate knowledge from modern botany and biochemistry in making sense of siddha medicines; he may also draw upon his cultural capital in siddha cosmology to create vernacular environmentalism through his NGO and find some solace in Tamil nationalism (Sujatha 2011a).

Similarly, a study of ayurvedic education in Kerala (Abraham 2013) shows how the students in the ayurveda degree course managed to cope with the gap between their school training in the modern biological sciences and the theories in ancient Sanskrit and Malayalam texts of ayurveda. Ayurveda is part of the larger culture of Kerala and primary socialisation in the family. This cultural background and familiarity with ayurveda at home serves as an epistemological bridge between the worlds of biological science and ayurveda.

Johannessen and Lazar (2006) borrow Bryan Turner's concept of 'elective affinity' to understand the relation between praxis, knowledge and power at different levels, in a situation of medical pluralism, namely how and when a particular cultural code and praxis come together. When there is no tension between two factors in terms of interests and principles, an elective affinity is formed.

Another phase in the trajectory of medical systems was ushered due to the globalisation of Asian medicine, and in the following section, we examine the dynamics at all the three levels—institutions, physicians and the people.

II

Institutionalisation and Mainstreaming of Traditional Medicine

In the 1990s, New Age health movements ended centuries of standalone biomedicine in the West and demanded that complementary and alternative medicine (CAM) be accepted as part of public health care in Europe and North America, despite the fact that CAM was delegitimised by scientific lobbies. It is remarkable that social movements demanding more therapeutic options for the numerous and chronic ailments of modernity could win over the authority of hard core science and the power of pharmaceutical industry to persuade their governments in favour of a pluralist policy like the Asian societies. Thus, plural health behaviour in the 1990s acquired a postmodern character, and the demand for herbal and lifestyle remedies brought ayurveda and yoga into the global health market (Cant and Sharma 1999).

The Indian government created a separate department for all non-biomedical systems under the acronym AYUSH (ayurveda, unani, siddha, yoga and homeopathy) in 2002, making medical pluralism and export of raw herbs an explicit policy of the state. The acronym AYUSH systems clubs together quite diverse therapies, but it has for the moment resolved the confusion about which generic term is to be used to refer to the non-biomedical systems—traditional, alternative or indigenous. Biomedicine in India is also in the global health map because it has expanded significantly and achieved excellence in super specialties as to attract clients from other countries. Medical consultants point out that India is a favoured location for medical tourism, not only because of the cost advantage but also because of the high success rate in surgical treatments in Indian hospitals at par with international standards. It is said that the success rate of cardiac bypass in India is 98.7 per cent against 97.5 per cent in the Unites States.[1] But there is not much of sociological or anthropological engagement with biomedicine as an object of study in India at the moment.

[1] http://www.surgeryinindia.in/cardiac-surgery-in-india.php (accessed on 1 May 2016).

The health care delivery mechanism in India today has AYUSH systems co-located with biomedicine in the National Rural Health Mission (NRHM), and ayurveda and yoga have also been introduced in corporate biomedical establishments, but the budgetary allocations for AYUSH are 10 times less than biomedicine. This has set up new questions: What kind of a relation inheres between biomedicine and other medicines when they are co-located in public institutions? What are the effects of mainstreaming some non-biomedical systems of medicine? What are the exclusions that the privileging of textual systems of medicine creates?

Sadgopal (2012) presents the case of *dai*, or the indigenous midwife, who is often outside the pale of traditional textual medicine and at the lower end of the caste hierarchy. She may not be considered on par with vaids and hakims of respectable status as she performs the polluting tasks associated with childbirth. The dai is often blamed for the high rates of maternal mortality in developing countries, but as she is the grass-roots-level service provider, the policy of training her and involving her in the maternity services as the traditional birth attendant (TBA) for the poorer sections was adopted. Sadgopal shows how this was a piecemeal intervention that used the dai at the lowest end of the health care delivery mechanism with little infrastructure, rather than incorporating her skill and knowledge constructively. Sadgopal points out that several long-held obstetrical practices such as lithotomy position and episiotomy have been found to be unsound. Similarly, practices such as squatting, caregiver support, perineal massage and delayed cord-cutting followed by the dai, or the indigenous midwife, have found to be efficacious and life-saving, and Sadgopal argues that it is high time that we view traditional midwifery not just as a cultural legacy but also in terms of efficacy.

Another key institutional player in the field of medicine in India has been the flourishing pharmaceutical industry both for traditional and modern medicine, whose development has been parallel. The shift from household to bulk production of ayurvedic and unani drugs in India started early, and Kottakkal in Kerala and Hamdard in Delhi were already into mass production of medicines by the first decade of the 20th century.

While the development of ayurvedic formulations in the model of biomedical tablets and syrups was initially seen as a market strategy that hampers the integrity of traditional principles of pharmacology, a careful study of recent developments, however, reveals that there is much innovation not just in products of ayurveda but also in the process of drug action when cutting-edge techniques of biochemical analysis are applied to classical ayurvedic formulations (Banerjee 2014). Pordie and Gaudilliere (2014) regard the innovative pharmacological practices that go into the making of new ayurvedic proprietary drugs as a constructive 'reformulation' of ayurveda in the direction of an alternative pharmacology that combines the best of laboratory techniques, on the one hand, and tested ancient herbal sources, on the other. In any case, these authors highlight that the 'pharmaceuticalisation' and 'reformulation' processes in ayurveda have made possible its entry into the global health market.

But globalisation does not seem to have affected unani and siddha as much. Quaiser's (2012) enquiry into the emergence of medical communism in independent India points out that unani physicians do sense institutional discrimination in the provisioning for unani medicine within the AYUSH ministry. The internal differences between ayurveda, unani and siddha, the varied institutional support they receive and the social constituency they cater to, however, have been relatively less explored.

Mainstreaming AYUSH and the Epistemo-politics of Pluralism: The Physicians

The core concern in the politics of pluralism under AYUSH is how non-biomedical systems cope in an asymmetrical relationship where biomedicine sets the gold standard for scientific medicine. In the process of mainstreaming AYUSH systems and bringing them under NRHM, non-biomedical practitioners are called upon to deliver allopathic services and vertical health campaigns for polio and TB and fill the shortage of allopathic staff. Mainstreaming AYUSH has led to the creation of a cadre of ad hoc physicians of AYUSH systems who could substitute the allopath in remote areas (Priya 2012).

Researches on the AYUSH systems in the Council of Scientific & Industrial Research (CSIR) labs invariably involve validation of classical pharmacological formulations through laboratory trials and animal experiments (Sujatha 2011a). Adams and Fei-Fei Li (2008) argue that laboratory-based, randomised, controlled trials suited to the mono-modal therapies of biomedicine are not appropriate for testing the validity of systems like Tibetan medicine which are multi-modal; that is, they have multiple components in therapy—drug, external applications, change in diet and lifestyle and so on. The authors cite the case of a clinical trial on hepatitis in which the Tibetan doctors treated eight significant symptoms such as abdominal pain, abdominal distension, rumbling stomach ache, diarrhoea, acid regurgitation, vomit, dyspepsia and constipation. The follow-up after five months found improvement in all the eight symptoms in 83.3 per cent–100 per cent of the patients and did not show any symptom recurrence after one year. Yet the biomedical doctors concluded that the treatment was unsuccessful because it did not eradicate the bacteria. The Tibetan doctors argued that in their system, the disease is understood not as the presence of bacteria but as symptoms reported by patients which are indicative of the physiological functions. Adams' study shows that systems of medicine could have different parameters of the same disease, in this case hepatitis, and that biomedical doctors, by insisting on germ theory of disease, delegitimised the treatment, though the patients found it to be effective.

The compromises in the core theories of non-biomedical systems in the process of mainstreaming them is an important concern and has been variously described as syncretism, epistemological violence, hybridisation and creolisation, drawing attention to the asymmetrical relationship between the reductionist laboratory methods of modern biology and biotechnology that overshadow the functional and multi-modal approach of the traditional systems of medicine. However, the acceptance of medical pluralism as an official state policy across the world is significant as it draws attention to the crucial fact that efficacy of medical treatments could be understood in more than one way, something that challenges the hegemony of laboratory sciences over the life-world of the people.

Medical Marginalities and Health-seeking Behaviour

What about the host of practices outside the AYUSH frame? Just as the colonial government in the early 20th century rendered ayurveda and unani as unofficial systems to fend for themselves through social support, the AYUSH regime in the 21st century creates its own fragments. Invoking the Deleuze and Guattarian notion of molecular micro-politics that elude a central molar power, Hardiman and Mukharji (2012) suggest that a whole range of secular therapeutics such as bone setting and piles surgery survive at the margins without state patronage or regulation. These are subaltern therapeutics that thrive vibrantly among the weaker sections. Mukharji describes 'Chandshir chikitsa', a therapy attributed to a Namasudra family in the 18th century and survived as a popular stream of medicine into the next century. Two medicines were revealed in his dream to Bishnuhori Daktar of Chandshir, and in the course of two centuries, the methods of Chandshir chikitsa changed from a form of surgery to non-surgical therapy. A whole range of ailments came to be included under this treatment and newer ingredients were introduced by the subsequent generations as to make it difficult to say what defines the therapy. The absence of affordable and reliable health care for the lower sections has, in their view, led to the proliferation of medical marginalities.

Presently, the *jhola chap* doctors or unqualified medical practitioners dispensing allopathic drugs are said to provide something like 40 per cent of the medical care in the country, and their booming practice even in the vicinity of government health centres is attributed to accessibility and instant personalised caregiving.

Health seeking in the context of medical pluralism, in Kalpana Ram's (2011) view, is seen as pragmatic behaviour by a layperson which assumes that the laywoman has all the range of therapies before her. Rarely has pluralist health behaviour seen from the prism of class background of the layperson and the limits it sets. In her essay on class and the clinic, Ram draws upon her ethnography among fishing communities in Tamil Nadu to show that therapeutic choices made by women are actually a settlement between pre-familiarity with the cultural universe of the medical system whether it is biomedicine or traditional medicine (habitus) and class position (habit) of the subject. The point is that social inequality is played out in the clinic when the layperson encounters the doctor. The habitus of the elite patient is appreciated as heritage when it is traditional, whereas the traditional practices invoked by the Dalit women tend to be ostracised.

Naraindas' (2006) study among middle-class urban patients suggests that they have internalised the language of biomedical disease names and diagnostic tests and approach AYUSH physicians with allopathic diagnosis. AYUSH physicians are bilingual in that they have to reckon with the theories, language and nosologies of biomedicine as they are often approached as the second option. However, AYUSH doctors handle these cases, as their medical education consists of 50 per cent or more of biomedical subjects. Even among the working population in a Delhi neighbourhood, Das (2015) finds that the symptoms are described as 'little bit of TB' and 'low-BP'. She argues that these articulations should not be viewed in terms of 'culturally standardized practices of classification' of medical systems, rather from the 'regimes of labour through which both body and temporality were produced and consumed in these local settings' (ibid.: 45).

The role of shrines and religious healers in addressing psychosocial distress is another area of marginality in the light of the Mental Health Act, 1987, that recommends coercive rehabilitation of persons found in *dargahs*, temples and churches in mental hospitals (Davar 2013). Noting that a significant proportion of the population do access local healing shrines, Davar shows how psychosocial distress cannot be reduced to psychiatric definitions as it is embedded in a social context. Dargahs allow for the acting out of emotions which is seen as cathartic and the person-centric relationship invoking some notion of the transcendental becomes critical to healing. Davar advocates a community-centred approach to mental health that is pluralistic. Addlakha's (2008) research in the psychiatric ward of a Delhi public hospital shows that psychiatrists are also aware of the significance of other healing forms, or at least do not stop patients from visiting them.

Beyond Pluralism: Physicians of 'Integrative' Medicine

The globalisation of Asian medicines has opened up the market for a commoditised version of traditional medicines, but the process has also thrown some new social and epistemic formations.

The new epistemic development is the emergence of the concept of 'evidence-based medicine'[2] (EBM) which suggests that non-biomedical treatments, for which there is strong and reliable evidence in clinical trials, may be selectively adopted. A large machinery for identifying active ingredients in ayurvedic formulae under controlled laboratory conditions is at work, and there are many studies to correlate ayurvedic remedies for biomedical nosological categories. This new kind of research involving a team of ayurvedic/unani/siddha physicians with biotechnologists has given rise to a nascent field called IM which also has journals of its own. A search of medical databases shows that from 46 articles published in 1970, the number of clinical-trial-based articles in CAM had crossed 687 publications by 2009 (Keshet 2009). What constitutes scientific evidence of efficacy of drugs, how it is to

[2] The concept of EBM is attributed to works by Dr Archibald Cochrane (1972) to stress the importance of having reliable evidence from well-designed research for the biomedical treatments protocols mechanically adopted in health care delivery.

be recorded for CAM and how to separate the placebo effect in holistic therapies are questions that the international community of CAM doctors is negotiating with their opponents in scientific lobbies and mainstream biomedical journals like the *Lancet*.

In the Indian context, AYUSH, especially the ayurveda physicians, have been quite prolific in the field of IM. About 30 refereed online journals from the AYUSH sector, mostly ayurveda, have been started since 2011–13 when the boom in publications on AYUSH/IM occurred, and they are of uneven quality. These journals have research articles and also report case studies, which attract the attention of patients seeking information. AYUSH doctors from government medical colleges get calls seeking consultation and appointment from international and national clientele who have read their case studies.[3] The scientific journal intended for peer review and communication has, in the case of the nascent discipline of IM, connected the physician directly to the user through the internet, blurring the boundary between publication and social marketing.

Although there has been much criticism of IM as a challenge to the integrity of traditional medicines (Sujatha 2011b), the field of IM is growing rapidly and there are exclusive institutions and courses on IM. Drawing upon the approach of science and technology studies, Ganguly (2014) examines the research work at an institute for IM in South India. She explains how the institute is engaged with developing independent protocols for probing and verifying ayurvedic concepts in their own terms, without fitting them into clinical trials, an approach called by the research team as 'open-minded' science. The task of setting up research methodology according to the ayurvedic epistemology, utilising available digital and lab technologies, is indeed a novel one and calls for a multidisciplinary team. It involves the creation of reliable tools and sensory experiments to document secondary qualities of substances such as taste and colour that vary with human subjects, and it seeks to grasp both somatic and psychic responses of the subjects and standardise them.

The case studies presented by Banerjee (2014) of individual researchers engaged in fundamental research on the pharmacological action of ayurvedic drugs also point to a shift from a situation of compromise with the hegemony of biomedical criterion to an active reshaping of the parameters and structure of clinical trials to suit ayurvedic principles.

---

[3] Author's ongoing fieldwork in government AYUSH institutions at Delhi as part of UPE project, JNU.

As for health behaviour, it remains to be seen whether the postmodern condition, of which the herbal products from the Asian territories are becoming part, will lead to the erosion of botanical resources at home and raise the threshold of natural substances that were regular food and medicine of the ordinary people to make them available for the elite (global) seeker of health. This will leave the food and medicines produced with chemicals for the consumption of the poor (Sujatha 2017).

The realities of Asian medicines are thus far more nuanced than can be accounted for by terms such as 'mimicry', 'hybrid' and 'creole' that frame them only as text/discourse. As we just saw, integration of medical knowledge is happening at various domains—institution building and policy, clinical practice and research engagements of the physicians, the shifting priorities of health seekers and their health status, and individual bodily experience, not all of which can be understood as a discourse, or could be subject to the same logic. This will explain why medical pluralism will continue to occupy the imagination of the social sciences in the years to come.

References

Abraham, Leena. 2013. 'Reproduction of Indigenous Knowledge in Plural Cultures: Ayurveda Education in Contemporary India'. In *Sociology of Education in India: Disciplinary Perspectives and Contemporary Concerns*, edited by Geetha B. Nambissan and S. Srinivasa Rao, 245–72. New Delhi: Oxford University Press.

Adams, Vincanne and Fei-Fei Li. 2008. 'Integration or Erasure? Modernizing Medicine at Lhasa's Mentsikhang'. In *Tibetan Medicine in the Contemporary World: Global Politics of Medical Knowledge and Practice*, edited by Laurent Pordie, 105–31. London: Routledge.

Addlakha, Renu. 2008. *Deconstructing Mental Illness. An Ethnography of Women, Illness and the Family*. New Delhi: Zubaan Books.

Attewell, Guy. 2007. *Refiguring Unani Tibb: Plural Healing in Late Colonial India*. New Delhi: Orient Longman.

Banerjee, Madhulika. 2014. 'Contemporary Conversations Between Ayurveda and Biomedicine: From Reformulating Drugs to Reformulating Parameters'. *Asian Medicine* 9 (1–2): 141–70.

Banerji, Debabar. 1986. *Social Science and Health Services Development in India: Sociology of Formation of an Alternative Paradigm*. New Delhi: Lok Paksh.

Baru, Rama. 1998. *Private Health Care in India: Social Characteristics and Trends*. New Delhi: SAGE.

Brass, Paul. 1972. 'The Politics of Ayurvedic Education: A Case Study of Revivalism and Modernization in India'. In *Education and Politics in India: Studies in Organization, Society and Policy*, edited by Susanne Rudolph and Lloyd Rudolph, 342–71. New Delhi: Oxford University Press.

Cant, Sarah and Ursula Sharma. 1999. *A New Medical Pluralism: Alternative Medicine, Doctors, Patients and the State*. London: UCL Press.

Cochrane, A.L. 1972. *Effectiveness and Efficiency. Random Reflections on Health Services*. London: Nuffield Provincial Hospitals Trust.

Das, Veena. 2015. *Affliction: Health Disease and Poverty*. Hyderabad: Orient BlackSwan.

Davar, Bhargavi. 2013. 'Recovering from Psychosocial Traumas: The Place of Dargahs in Maharashtra'. In *Medical Pluralism in Contemporary India*, edited by V. Sujatha and Leena Abraham, 255–76. New Delhi: Orient BlackSwan.

Ganguly, Ritika. 2014. 'Sense and Evidence: Ayurvedic Experiments and the Politics of an "Open-minded" Science'. *Asian Medicine* 9 (1–2): 102–40.

Hardiman, David and Projit Bihari Mukharji, eds. 2012. *Medical Marginality in South Asia*. London: Routledge.

Jeffery, Roger. 1978. 'Allopathic Medicine in India: A Case of De-professionalisation?' *Economic & Political Weekly* 11 (3): 101–13.

Johannessen, Helle and Imre Lazar. 2006. *Multiple Medical Realities: Patients and Healers in Biomedical, Alternative and Traditional Medicine*. New York, NY: Berghahn Press.

Keshet, Yael. 2009. 'The Untenable Boundaries of Biomedical Knowledge: Epistemologies and Rhetoric Strategies in the Debate over Evaluating Complementary and Alternative Medicine'. *Health: An Interdisciplinary Journal for the Social Study of Health Illness and Medicine* 13 (2): 131–55.

Khare, R.S. 1996. 'Dava, Daktar and Dua: Anthropology of Practiced Medicine in India'. *Social Science Medicine* 43 (5): 837–48.

Kumar, Anil. 1998. *Medicine and the Raj: British Medical Policy in India, 1835–1911*. New Delhi: SAGE.

Kumar, Deepak. 1997. 'Unequal Contenders, Uneven Ground: Medical Encounters in British India, 1820–1920'. In *Western Medicine as Contested Knowledge*, edited by Andrew Cunningham and Bridie Andrews, 172–90. Manchester and New York, NY: Manchester University Press.

Leslie, Charles. 1976. *Asian Medical Systems: A Comparative Study*. Berkeley, CA: University of California Press.

Madan, T.N. 1980. *Doctors and Society: Three Asian Case Studies—India, Malaysia and Sri Lanka*. Delhi: Vikas Publishing House.

Marriott, Mckim. 1955. 'Western Medicine in a Village in North India'. In *Health, Culture and Community*, edited by B.D. Paul, 239–68. New York, NY: Russell Sage Foundation.

Minocha, Aneeta. 1980. 'Medical Pluralism and Health Services in India'. *Social Science and Medicine* 14 (4): 217–23.

Muraleedharan, V.R. 1992. 'Professionalising Medical Practice in Colonial South-India'. *Economic & Political Weekly* 27 (4): 27–37.

Nandy, Ashis and Shiv Visvanathan. 1990. 'Modern Medicine and Its Non-modern Critique: A Study in Discourse'. In *Dominating Knowledge: Development, Culture and Resistance*, edited by Frederique Apffel Marglin and Stephen Marglin, 145–84. New Delhi: Oxford University Press.

Naraindas, Harish. 2006. 'Of Spineless Babies and Folic Acid: Evidence and Efficacy in Biomedicine and Ayurvedic Medicine'. *Social Science and Medicine* 62 (11): 2658–69.

Oommen, T.K. 1978. *Doctors and Nurses: A Study in Occupational Role Structure*. New Delhi: Macmillan.

Pordie, Laurent and Jean-Paul Gaudilliere. 2014. 'The Reformulation Regime in Drug Discovery: Revisiting Polyherbals and Property Rights in the Ayurvedic Industry'. *East Asian Science, Technology and Society* 8 (1): 57–79.

Priya, Ritu. 2012. 'AYUSH and Public Health: Democratic Pluralism and the Quality of Health Services'. In *Medical Pluralism in Contemporary India*, edited by V. Sujatha and Leena Abraham, 103–29. New Delhi: Orient BlackSwan.

Quaiser, Neshat. 2012. 'Tension, Placation and Complaint: Unani and Post-colonial Medical Communism'. In *Medical Pluralism in Contemporary India*, edited by V. Sujatha and Leena Abraham, 130–62. New Delhi: Orient BlackSwan.

Ram, Kalpana. 2011. 'Class and the Clinic: The Subject of Pluralism and the Transmission of Inequality'. In *Health, Culture and Religion in South Asia*, edited by Doron Assa and Broom Alex, 7–20. London: Routledge.

Ramanna, Mridula. 2000. 'Indian Attitudes Towards Western Medicine: Bombay, a Case Study'. *Indian Historical Review* 27 (1): 44–55.

———. 2004. 'Local Initiatives in Health Care: Bombay Presidency, 1900–1920'. *Economic & Political Weekly* 39 (41): 4560–67.

Sadgopal, Mira. 2012. 'Strengthening Childbirth Care: Can the Maternity Services Open Up to Indigenous Traditions of Midwifery?' In *Medical Pluralism in Contemporary India*, edited by V. Sujatha and Leena Abraham, 211–31. New Delhi: Orient BlackSwan.

Scambler, Graham. 2002. *Health and Social Change: A Critical Theory*. Buckingham: Open University Press.

Sivaramakrishnan, Kavita. 2006. *Old Potions, New Bottles: Recasting Indigenous Medicine in Colonial Punjab (1850–1945)*. New Delhi: Orient Longman.

Starr, Paul. 1982. *The Social Transformation of American Medicine*. New York, NY: Basic Books.

Sujatha, V. 2011a. 'Innovation Within and Between Traditions: Dilemma of Traditional Medicine in Contemporary India'. *Science, Technology & Society* 16 (2): 191–213.

Sujatha, V. 2011b. 'What Could "Integrative" Medicine Mean? Social Science Perspectives on Contemporary Ayurveda'. *Journal of Ayurveda and Integrative Medicine* 2 (3): 115–23.

———. 2014. *Sociology of Health and Medicine: New Perspectives*. New Delhi: Oxford University Press.

———. 2017. 'Economic and Existential Understanding of Food: Analysing Economic Growth and Nutritional Status in South India'. *Indian Journal of Human Development* 11 (3): 1–16.

Sujatha, V. and Leena Abraham, eds. 2012. *Medical Pluralism in Contemporary India*. New Delhi: Orient BlackSwan.

Venkataratnam, R. 1979. *Medical Sociology in an Indian Setting*. New Delhi: Macmillan.

About the Editors and Contributors

Editors

Sanjay Srivastava is Professor of Sociology at the Institute of Economic Growth, Delhi University (North Campus), Delhi. His publications include *Constructing Post-colonial India: National Character and the Doon School* (1998), *Asia: Cultural Politics in the Global Age* (2001, co-authored), *Sexual Sites, Seminal Attitudes: Sexualities, Masculinities and Culture in South Asia* (2004, contributing editor), *Passionate Modernity, Sexuality, Class and Consumption in India* (2007), *Sexuality Studies* (2013, contributing editor) and *Entangled Urbanism: Slum, Gated Community and Shopping Mall in Delhi and Gurgaon* (2015). From 2012 to 2016, he was co-editor of *Contributions to Indian Sociology* (*CIS*).

Yasmeen Arif is Associate Professor of Sociology, Delhi School of Economics, University of Delhi, Delhi. Her book *Life, Emergent: The Social in the Afterlives of Violence* (2016) explores a politics of life across multiple global conditions of mass violence. Her forthcoming book *The Unusual Urban: Cities in Conversation* compiles her work on cities. She has held positions at the University of Minnesota (Twin Cities), Minneapolis; the Graduate Institute, Geneva; Centre for the Study of Developing Societies (CSDS), Delhi; and the American University of Beirut, Lebanon. Her work has been supported by the Mellon Foundation, the Ford Foundation and the Fulbright–Nehru Scholarship, among others. From 2012 to 2016, she was co-editor of the Book Reviews section in *CIS*.

Janaki Abraham is Associate Professor of Sociology, Delhi School of Economics, University of Delhi, Delhi. Her research interests include the study of kinship, gender and caste, visual anthropology, and gender and space, particularly the study of towns. She is currently finalising her manuscript entitled *Gender, Caste and Matrilineal Kinship: Shifting Boundaries in Twentieth-century Kerala*. Outcomes of a project on visual culture were presented at an exhibition entitled 'Exploring the Visual Cultures of North Kerala: Photographs, Albums and Videos in Everyday Life' at the Jawaharlal Nehru University, New Delhi in 2008, and was based on her postdoctoral research. From 2012 to 2016, she was co-editor of the Book Reviews section in *CIS*.

Contributors

Renu Addlakha is currently Professor at the Centre for Women's Development Studies, New Delhi. She is presently engaged in research on health, disability, gender and development. She did her masters in social work from Delhi University, Delhi, followed by an MPhil and PhD in sociology from the same university. Her doctoral work focused on the psychiatric profession in India, with a particular focus on gender issues. She has published widely in national and international peer-reviewed journals. Her most important publications are *Deconstructing Mental Illness: An Ethnography of Psychiatry, Women and the Family* (2008), *Disability and Society: A Reader* (2009, co-edited with Stuart Blume, Patrick J. Devlieger, Osamu Nagase and Myriam Winance), *Contemporary Perspectives on Disability in India: Exploring the Linkages Between Law, Gender and Experience* (2011) and *Disability Studies in India: Global Discourse, Local Realities* (2013).

Joseph S. Alter teaches anthropology at the University of Pittsburgh, Pittsburgh, and has published a number of books, including *The Wrestler's Body, Knowing Dil Das, Gandhi's Body, Asian Medicine and Globalization, Yoga in Modern India* and *Moral Materialism*. His research is based in South Asia and is currently focused on the cultural history of nature cure as a globalised system of medicine, biosemiotics and social theory, and the natural history of animals in the human imagination. With a focus on ecology and natural history, he runs a semester-long study-abroad programme *Pitt in the Himalayas*.

Srimati Basu is Professor of Gender and Women's Studies at the University of Kentucky, Lexington. She is the author of the monographs *The Trouble with Marriage: Feminists Confront Law and Violence in India*

(2015) and *She Comes to Take Her Rights: Indian Women, Property and Propriety* (1999), editor of *Dowry & Inheritance* (2005) and co-editor of *Conjugality Unbound: Sexual Economy and the Marital Form in India* (2014, with Lucinda Ramberg).

Amita Baviskar is Professor of Sociology at the Institute of Economic Growth, Delhi University (North Campus), Delhi. Her research focuses on the cultural politics of environment and development in rural and urban India. Her book *In the Belly of the River: Tribal Conflicts over Development in the Narmada Valley* and subsequent publications explore the themes of resource rights, subaltern resistance and discourses of environmentalism. Her current work examines food practices and agrarian environments in western India. Her recent publications include *Elite and Everyman: The Cultural Politics of the Indian Middle Classes* (with Raka Ray) and *First Garden of the Republic: Nature on the President's Estate.*

Aditi Bhonagiri works as a development researcher and digital media producer. Her projects focus on issues of gender, environment, agriculture, social and political movements. She holds an MA in development studies (IDS, University of Sussex, Brighton), a graduate diploma in international relations (London School of Economics and Political Science, London) and a BA in public communications and the media arts (University of Technology, Sydney). Her recent work includes co-producing an online learning module on 'Health, Environment, and Development' to strengthen health research across Africa and Asia, and authoring a topic guide on *Social Movements*, aimed at UK's Department for International Development (DFID) officials.

Paul Boyce is Senior Lecturer in Anthropology and International Development in the School of Global Studies at the University of Sussex, Brighton. Boyce's work traverses applied and theoretical anthropological imaginaries.

Rita Brara is a Senior Fellow at the Department of Sociology, University of Delhi, Delhi. She is the author of *Shifting Landscapes: The Making and Remaking of Village Commons in India.* Her research interests include the study of climate change, development studies and popular culture. She is presently the co-editor of *CIS.*

Roma Chatterji is Professor at the Department of Sociology, Delhi School of Economics, Delhi University, Delhi. Apart from an abiding interest in folk art and culture, she has also worked on social gerontology and collective violence. She is the author of *Speaking with Pictures:*

Folk Art and the Narrative Tradition in India (2012, 2016), *Writing Identities: Folklore and Performing Arts in Purulia, West Bengal* (2009) and *Living with Violence: An Anthropology of Events and Everyday Life* (2007, with Deepak Mehta). She has edited *Wording the World: Veena Das and Scenes of Instruction* (2014) and co-edited *Riot Discourses* (2007, with Deepak Mehta).

Lawrence Cohen is Sarah Kailath Professor of India Studies and Professor of Anthropology and of South and Southeast Asian Studies at the University of California, Berkeley. He is, also at Berkeley, Director of the Institute for South Asia Studies and former Director of the Medical Anthropology Program and of the Center for the Study of Sexual Culture. His research has engaged the ways the body is entangled in local familial and political worlds, with a focus on age and ageing, on sexuality, on organ transplantation and on the presumptions of biometric governance. He is the author of *No Aging in India: Modernity, Senility and the Family* (1999) and co-editor of *Thinking about Dementia: Culture, Loss and the Anthropology of Senility* (2006). His many essays include 'The Pleasures of Castration' (1995), 'Where It Hurts' (1999), 'The Kothi Wars' (2005), 'Song for Pushkin' (2007) and 'The Gay Guru' (2012). His research has been supported by grants from the Fulbright–Hays Program, the American Institute of Indian Studies, the Fulbright Program, the Mellon Foundation, the MacArthur Foundation, the Open Society Institute, the Arcus Foundation, the University of California, Harvard University, the MOVE Consortium and the United States Department of Education National Resource Centers Program.

Jacob Copeman is Senior Lecturer in Social Anthropology at the University of Edinburgh, Edinburgh. He is the author of *Veins of Devotion: Blood Donation and Religious Experience in North India* (2009) and editor or co-editor of *Blood Donation, Bioeconomy, Culture* (2009), *South Asian Tissue Economies* (2013), *The Guru in South Asia: New Interdisciplinary Perspectives* (2012), *Social Theory After Strathern* (2014) and *On Names in South Asia: Iteration, (Im)propriety and Dissimulation* (2015).

Rohit K. Dasgupta is Lecturer at the Institute for Media and Creative Industries, Loughborough University, Loughborough, where he teaches across a range of modules on media and cultural studies. As an ethnographer, his work cuts across several disciplines with particular interests in digital media, Indian cinema, protest culture, queer politics and South Asia. Prior to his current position, he held the position of lecturer in Global Media at the University of Southampton, Southampton; an associate lecturer at University of the Arts London, London; and has also held teaching and research posts at University of Sussex, Brighton; University of West London, London; and University of Westminster, London. He has co-edited *Masculinity and Its Challenges in India: Essays on Changing Perceptions* and *Rituparno Ghosh: Cinema, Gender and Art*.

Geert De Neve is Professor of Social Anthropology and South Asian Studies at the University of Sussex, Brighton. He is the author of *The Everyday Politics of Labour: Working Lives in India's Informal Economy* (2005) and has published multiple articles on labour and ethical governance in India's garment sector in *Economy and Society*, *Modern Asian Studies* and *Ethnography*, among other publications. He is also a co-editor of *Hidden Hands in the Market: Ethnographies of Fair Trade, Ethical Consumption, and Corporate Social Responsibility* (2008) and of *Unmaking the Global Sweatshop: Health and Safety of the World's Garment Workers* (2017).

Sara Dickey is Professor of Anthropology at Bowdoin College, Brunswick, in the United States. She has studied the production, consumption and circulation of Tamil cinema, and the roles of cinema and fan clubs in state politics; she also carries out research on class identities and relations in urban South India. Her books include *Cinema and the Urban Poor in South India* and *Living Class in Urban India*.

Shalini Grover is currently Associate Professor in Social Anthropology and Gender Studies at O. P. Jindal Global University, Department of Liberal Arts and Humanities. She has published widely on marriage, kinship, divorce, legal pluralism and labour relations. Through the lens of 'lived experience', her ethnographic data engages with sections of India's urban poor and middle classes. Grover's articles have appeared in the *Australian Journal of Anthropology* (*TAJA*), *CIS*, *Asian Journal of Women's Studies* (*AJWS*) and an edited volume on *Marrying in South Asia*. Her 2011 monograph is now available as a new revised international edition (2017). Her publications and affiliation with the Institute of Economic Growth since 2007 can be viewed on http://www.drshalinigrover.com/

Thomas Blom Hansen is the Reliance–Dhirubhai Ambani Professor of Anthropology and the Director of Stanford University's Center for South Asia, Stanford. He has broad interests spanning South Asia and Southern Africa, theoretical and disciplinary interests spanning political theory, continental philosophy, psychoanalysis, comparative religion and contemporary urbanism.

He is the author of *The Saffron Wave: Democracy and Hindu Nationalism in Modern India* (1999), *Wages of Violence: Naming and Identity in Postcolonial Bombay* (2001) and *Melancholia of Freedom: Social Life in an Indian Township in South Africa* (2012), as well as many articles, book chapters and edited volumes.

Surinder S. Jodhka is Professor of Sociology at JNU, New Delhi. His research interests include the study of rural society and dynamics of agrarian change; social inequalities—old and new—and their reproduction; the dynamics of caste and the varied modes of its articulation with the nature of social and economic change in contemporary India; and the political sociology community identities. His research publications include *Caste in Contemporary India* (2015), *Interrogating India's Modernity* (2013, edited), *Caste: Oxford India Short Introductions* (2012), *Village Society* (2012, edited) and *Community and Identities: Contemporary Discourses on Culture and Politics in India* (2001, edited, SAGE). He is among the first recipients of the ICSSR–Amartya Sen Award for Distinguished Social Scientists, for the year 2012.

Mekhala Krishnamurthy is Associate Professor in the Department of Sociology and Social Anthropology at Ashoka University. As a social anthropologist, Mekhala is interested in the ethnographic study of the state and market, particularly the political economy, regional histories, everyday lives, knowledge resources, and institutional practices of public systems and programmes in contemporary India. Over the last decade, her research, policy and professional engagements have involved work across a number of field sites and subjects, including women's courts and dispute resolution, community health workers and public health systems, agricultural commodity markets and regulation, and rural development, livelihoods and land acquisition.

Sarah Lamb is Professor of Anthropology at Brandeis University, Waltham. Her research focuses on ageing, gender, families, and understandings of personhood and modernity in India and the United States. Her books include *White Saris and Sweet Mangoes: Aging, Gender and Body in North India* and *Aging and the Indian Diaspora: Cosmopolitan Families in India and Abroad*. With Diane Mines, she co-edited *Everyday Life in South Asia*. Her newest book is an edited volume, *Successful Aging as a Contemporary Obsession: Global Perspectives*.

Lucia Michelutti is Associate Professor (Reader) in the Department of Anthropology at the University College London, London. Her major research interest is the study of popular politics, religion, law and order, and violence across South Asia (India) and Latin America (Venezuela). She is the author of *The Vernacularisation of Democracy* (2008) and has published articles on caste/race, leadership, muscular politics, crime and mafias, and political experimentations. She is currently the convenor of an international research programme 'Democratic Cultures' (http://www.ucl.ac.uk/democratic-cultures).

Perveez Mody is a Social Anthropologist and Lecturer at the Division of Social Anthropology at the University of Cambridge, Cambridge. She is a Fellow and Senior Tutor of King's College, Cambridge. She is interested in transformations in South Asian kinship, intimacy, marriage, gender, sexuality and care. She has written a monograph about the practice of love-marriage in urban India and the history of civil marriage legislation and practice from the colonial period into the present (*The Intimate State: Love-Marriage and the Law in Delhi* 2008). More recently, her work concerns the legal protections against the phenomenon known as 'forced marriage' in the United Kingdom.

Nicholas Nisbett is currently Research Fellow, Institute of Development Studies, University of Sussex, Brighton, where he works on politics and interventions to do with child malnutrition in India, Bangladesh and elsewhere. His research on Internet cultures was carried out in Bengaluru's Internet cafes and IT institutes and considered the role of gender, class and capital in shaping friendship, courtship and strategies for social mobility within the Indian IT economy. His monograph *Growing Up in the Knowledge Society* was published in 2009. He has worked for the British government on food, agricultural and trade policy.

Rajni Palriwala, MA (JNU), MPhil, PhD (Delhi) is Professor at Department of Sociology at Delhi University, Delhi. Her research interests include gender, kinship and marriage, care, citizenship, the state, feminist theory and politics, agrarian and development studies and comparative sociology. She has authored *Changing Kinship, Family and Gender Relations in South Asia: Processes, Trends and Issues* (1994) and co-authored *Care, Culture and Citizenship: Revisiting the Politics of the Dutch Welfare State* (2005, with C.I. Risseeuw and K. Ganesh). She has co-edited *Marriage, Migration, and Gender* (2008, with P. Uberoi), *Shifting Circles of Support: Contextualising Kinship and Gender Relations in South Asia and Sub-Saharan Africa* (1996, with C.I. Risseeuw) and *Structures and Strategies: Women, Work and Family in Asia* (1990, with L. Dube).

Ronie Parciack is a faculty member at the Department of East Asian Studies of Tel Aviv University, Israel. Her research interests include the vernacular planes of political theology in India, political and aesthetic aspects in South Asian mass media and popular culture, and Indo-Islamic visual culture. She has published in refereed journals and anthologies, and co-edited a special issue of the *Journal of South Asian Popular Culture* on terror and media. Her book *Popular Hindi Cinema: Aesthetic Formations of the Seen and Unseen* (2016) is an analysis of core aesthetic and philosophical premises embedded in the visual language in Hindi cinema, as well as the recent transformations to local and digitalised VCD (video compact disc) industries in the Hindi and Urdu belt.

Johannes Quack is Assistant Professor of Social Anthropology at the University of Zurich, Switzerland. His (ethnographic) research interests include popular Hinduism; religion, secularism and non-religion; medicine and therapeutic pluralism; and ethics and knowledge (trans)formations. He is the author of *Disenchanting India: Organized Rationalism and Criticism of Religion in India* (2012). He co-edited the volumes *The Problem of Ritual Efficacy* (2010), *Asymmetrical Conversations: Contestations, Circumventions and the Blurring of Therapeutic Boundaries* (2014) and *Religious Indifferences: New Perspectives from Studies on Secularization and Nonreligion* (2017).

Raka Ray (AB, Bryn Mawr College, Bryn Mawr, 1985; PhD, University of Wisconsin-Madison, Madison, 1993) is Professor of Sociology and South and Southeast Asia Studies at the University of California, Berkeley. She is the former Chair of the Institute of South Asia Studies and the Department of Sociology. Her areas of specialisation are gender and feminist theory, inequality, emerging middle classes, cultures of servitude, social movements and post-colonial sociology. Her publications include *Fields of Protest: Women's Movements in India* (1999, 2000), *Social Movements in India: Poverty, Power, and Politics* (2005, co-edited with Mary Katzenstein), *Cultures of Servitude: Modernity, Domesticity and Class in India* (2009, co-edited with Seemin Qayum), *Both Elite and Everyman: The Cultural Politics of the Indian Middle Classes* (2011, co-edited with Amita Baviskar), *The Handbook of Gender* (2011) and many articles.

Alpa Shah is Associate Professor (Reader) in Anthropology at the London School of Economics (LSE). She is the author of *Ground Down by Growth* (2017) and *In the Shadows of the State: Indigenous Politics,*

Environmentalism and Insurgency in Jharkhand, India (2010). She has also written about affirmative action, labour migration, agrarian change and India's and Nepal's Maoist-inspired revolutionary struggles.

Smriti Srinivas is Professor of Anthropology and Director of the Middle East/South Asia Studies Program at the University of California, Davis. She is also Co-Director of the Mellon Research Initiative in 'Reimagining Indian Ocean Worlds'. Her research over the last two decades has focused on the relationship between cities, religion, cultural memory and the body. She is the author of *The Mouths of People, The Voice of God* (1998), *Landscapes of Urban Memory* (2001), *In the Presence of Sai Baba* (2008) and *A Place for Utopia: Urban Designs from South Asia* (2015). Her research has been supported over the years by a Mellon Fellowship, a Rockefeller Humanities Fellowship, a National Endowment for the Humanities Fellowship, UC Humanities Network Multi-Campus Working Group and Multi-Campus Research Group Awards, the American Academy of Religion, the Davis Humanities Institute, the Indian Foundation for the Arts and CSDS, among others. She currently serves on the advisory board of the *International Journal of Urban and Regional Studies* and the editorial board of *Contemporary South Asia*.

Tulasi Srinivas is Professor of Anthropology and Religion at Emerson College, Boston, and a fellow Luce-American Council of Learned Societies for 2018–19. Srinivas is the author of several books including *Winged Faith Rethinking Globalization and Religious Pluralism* (2010) and the co-editor of *Curried Cultures: Food, Globalization and South Asia* (2012, with Krishnendu Ray). Her new work *The Cow in the Elevator: Explorations in an Anthropology of Wonder* was published in Spring 2018. She has held several prestigious fellowships: at the Center for the Study of World Religions at Harvard University, the Berkley Center for Religion, Peace and World Affairs at Georgetown University and at the Kate Hamburger Kolleg, Bochum, Germany. Her research has been supported by the National Endowment of the Humanities, the Pew Foundation, and the Rockefeller Foundation. Srinivas is a primary advisor to the World Economic Forum, Davos, on the Global Agenda Council on the Crisis of Global Inequality.

V. Sujatha is Professor at the Centre for the Study of Social Systems, JNU, New Delhi, and she specialises in sociology of knowledge and sociology of medicine. Her research and publications have focused on the politics of lay, folk, expert and non-expert knowledge, and changes in systems of knowledge under new institutions and structures, with special reference to medical knowledge. Her publications include, among other things, two monographs, *Health by the People* (2003) and *Sociology of Health and Medicine: New Perspectives* (2014), and an edited volume, *Medical Pluralism in Contemporary India* (2013, co-edited by Leena Abraham).

Meenakshi Thapan is Professor of Sociology at the Delhi School of Economics, University of Delhi Delhi, and Coordinator of the D.S. Kothari Centre for Science, Ethics and Education, University of Delhi, Delhi. She has been Coordinator of the European Studies Programme (funded by the European Union, 2010–11), University of Delhi, Delhi. She is also a Trustee of the Krishnamurti Foundation (India) since 2012. Meenakshi's work in the field of education has focused on schools and schooling processes in India and in Vancouver and Paris. Her first book was *Life at School: An Ethnographic Study* (1991, 2006) and the most recent are *Education and Society: Themes, Perspectives, Practices* (2015, edited), *Ethnographies of Schooling in Contemporary India* (2014, edited, SAGE), *Living the Body: Embodiment, Womanhood and Identity in Contemporary India* (2009, SAGE) and *Contested Spaces: Citizenship and Belonging in Contemporary Times* (2010, edited). She is also Series Editor of a Series on the Sociology and Social Anthropology of Education in South Asia (2015–17, SAGE) and of a five-volume series on Women and Migration in Asia (2005–08, SAGE). A new series on Education and Society is underway (2018–22).

Carol Upadhya, a social anthropologist, is Professor in the School of Social Sciences at the National Institute of Advanced Studies (NIAS), Bengaluru, where she directs the Urban and Mobilities Studies research programme. Upadhya has been researching and writing on changing alignments of class, caste and capital in contemporary India for over three decades, including agricultural development and class formation in Coastal Andhra, software capital and labour and 'new' middle class, and transnational migration and regional diasporas. Upadhya's current projects focus on the urbanisation of rural landscapes in Andhra Pradesh and the restructuring of land, labour and livelihoods in Bengaluru. She is the author of *Reengineering India: Work, Capital, and Class in an Offshore Economy* (2016).

Margit van Wessel completed her PhD in 2001 at the Amsterdam Institute for Social Science Research, Amsterdam. The topic of her (ethnographic) thesis was the way members of the newly emerging urban middle class in India confront globalisation and, with that, the diversity of cultural phenomena that are part of their daily lives. Her interest in interactions and in questions of meaning, developed in these years, continues to inspire and inform present research projects and teaching. Presently, Margit is Assistant Professor at the Department of Communication, Technology and Philosophy of Wageningen University & Research, the Netherlands. She researches present-day manifestations of citizenship and civil society and its interactions with politics and policy-making.

Suryakant Waghmore is Associate Professor of Sociology at the Department of Humanities and Social Sciences, Indian Institute of Technology Bombay, Mumbai. He is the author of *Civility Against Caste* (2013).

Index

Baba Ramdev, 63, 67, 69, 302–309
Babri Masjid demolition in 1992, 36
Basic National Education scheme (1937) in India, 145
Batla House encounter (2008), 36
Baviskar, Amita, 152, 209, 211, 212, 214, 215, 216, 363, 428, 429
Bengali
    bhadralok, 211, 377
    folklore, 24
bhakti, 7
biomedicine, 436–437, 439
biomoral politics, 303
BJP, 13, 196
bonded labour, 165
bourgeois
    environmentalism, 428
Brass, Paul, 8, 9, 165, 438
bribes, 10
bride-burnings, 247, 290
bridewealth, 287
BSP, 197
Buddha, 302
business process outsourcing (BPO), 153

caste/caste system, 3
    against civility, 186–190
    and politics, 197–199
    panchayats, 292
Chakrabarty, Dipesh, 8, 45, 170, 211, 422
cinema
    and class, 381–384
        audiences in, 376–377
        Bollywood, 353, 376, 378, 382–383, 385
        regional, 377–378
        subaltern, 378–380
cinematic spaces, 380–381
city-nature dialectic, 413
class, 169, 170, 172
    divisions on urban issues, 428
        city and class, 428
    struggle, 165

cohabitation
    short term contracts, 288
Cohen, Lawrence, 262, 301, 317, 340, 347, 356
Cohn, Bernard, 6–7, 80
commodity markets, 96
communal harmony, 77
communal violence, 36–37, 412
communalisation, of urban life, 412
community development programmes (CDP), 82
complementary and alternative medicine (CAM), 439
conjugality, as lived experience, 267
consumer culture theory, 395
consumption, in India
    a new agenda for research, 392–395
    sustainability and cultural perspective of, 395–398
contemporary religiosities, 4, 15
cookbooks, 366
Coomaraswamy, Ananda, 22, 25–26, 29
corruption, 8, 9, 11
Criminal Law Amendment Act, 2013, 290
cultural
    reproduction, 348
    training of IT workers, 156

Dalits, 139, 197, 250
    activism, 133
    studies on, 187
dance culture, in Indian films, 384–386
Das, Veena, xiv, xxiv, 10, 48, 49, 51, 123, 262, 263, 319, 428, 443
death
    iccha mrtyu (or self-willed death), 358
democratic politics, 12
demonetisation of currency in 2016, 109